MW01517069

Weavers of the Tapestry

Weavers *of the* Tapestry

Kathrine E. Bellamy, RSM

FLANKER PRESS LTD.
ST. JOHN'S, NL
2006

Library and Archives Canada Cataloguing in Publication

Bellamy, Kathrine E., 1923–
  Weavers of the tapestry / Kathrine E. Bellamy.

Includes bibliographical references and index.
ISBN 1-894463-84-6

  1. Sisters of Mercy of Newfoundland--History. I. Title.

BX4483.6.N4B44 2006   271'.920718   C2006-901830-8

PRINTED IN CANADA

FLANKER PRESS
PO BOX 2522, STATION C
ST. JOHN'S, NL, CANADA   A1C 6K1
TOLL-FREE: 1-866-739-4420
WWW.FLANKERPRESS.COM

COVER ART: ADAM FREAKE

First Canadian edition printed April 2006

10 9 8 7 6 5 4 3 2 1

Canada   Canada Council   Conseil des Arts
          for the Arts   du Canada

We acknowledge the financial support of: the Government of Canada through the Book
Publishing Industry Development Program (BPIDP); the Canada Council for the Arts which
last year invested $20.3 million in writing and publishing throughout Canada; the
Government of Newfoundland and Labrador, Department of Tourism, Culture and Recreation.

This book is dedicated to the memory of Sister M. Francis Creedon, Sister M. Francis Xavier Bernard, and their companions, who established the Congregation of the Sisters of Mercy in Newfoundland.

CONTENTS

AUTHOR'S NOTE

IN THE SPRING OF 1998, I was invited to meet two members of the Leadership Team of the Sisters of Mercy, Helen Harding and Nellie Pomroy, to discuss the possibility of publishing a new version of the history of our congregation, the Sisters of Mercy of Newfoundland. It had been suggested on various occasions that I might be interested in trying my hand at writing the story of the sisters. Now, the Leadership Team made a formal request that I gather up the threads of the story and weave them together in a book. It was a difficult decision and one that I pondered for several weeks before deciding to accept the invitation.

In September 1998, I resigned from my former ministries and began the long journey into the past. Now that the work is finished, I look back with gratitude to the many people who provided advice and assistance as I went about my task. First of all, I thank Marie Michael Power, RSM, archivist of the Sisters of Mercy of Newfoundland, for her uncomplaining and inexhaustible patience with my many requests and for the countless hours she spent in looking up information. I express my gratitude to the members of the Leadership Team of the Newfoundland Sisters of Mercy for their encouragement and support, financial and otherwise; to Madonna Gatherall, RSM, and Anne Beresford for their painstaking and meticulous editing of the book; to Charlotte Fitzpatrick, RSM, for reading the manuscript and for many helpful suggestions; to Diane Smyth, RSM, for providing many of the pictures contained in this volume; and to Nelson White for supplying sketches and maps. I acknowledge with admiration the splendid contribution of M. Basil McCormack, RSM, in her master's thesis, "The Educational Work of the Sisters of Mercy of Newfoundland," and the work of M. Williamina Hogan, RSM, in

her book, *Pathways of Mercy*. I appreciate sincerely the assistance of the follow-
ing: Marion McCarthy, RSM, archivist of the Institute of Our Lady of Mercy,
England, for access to Bermondsey Archives and for providing information and
encouragement; Barbara Jeffery, RSM, archivist of the Sisters of Mercy of the
Union of England, Scotland & Wales, for information on the life of M. Rose
Lynch; M. Ursula Gilbert, RSM, of Tasmania, for information on M. Rose
Lynch during her years in Australia; Rose Marie Rocha, RSM, archivist of the
Sisters of Mercy Regional Community of Providence, R.I., and also Veronica
Lima, archivist for the Diocese of Providence, for information on the four
Sisters of Mercy who founded the congregation at Sandy Point, St. George's;
Patricia March, RSM, Agnes Gleason, RSM, and Margaret McGarrity, RSM,
for checking documents in the archives at Mercy International Centre;
Marianne Cosgrave, archivist of the Congregation of the Sisters of Mercy of
Ireland; Michael O'Connell of the Genealogical Society of Cork, Ireland, for
valuable information on the family of M. Francis Creedon; Dr. John E.
FitzGerald for his invaluable help and advice; Brother Joseph B. Darcy for pro-
viding access to the Mount St. Francis Monastery Library and for information
on the chronology of Bishop Fleming; Larry Dohey, archivist of the
Archdiocese of St. John's; Rev. John Halleran and Mr. Edward Halleran for
providing copies of letters written by M. Teresa O'Halleran; M. Perpetua
Kennedy, PBVM, archivist of the Presentation Sisters, Newfoundland; Shane
O'Dea, Paul O'Neill, and Frank Galgay for their advice and assistance; Mary
and Aiden Craig for their research in the Registry of Deeds; Gregory Doyle for
his help in solving computer problems; Patricia White, Karl Wells, and the
Canadian Broadcasting Corporation for providing a copy of a drawing by Wally
Brandt; the staff in the Newfoundland Section of the A. C. Hunter Library, St.
John's, and also the staff of the Provincial Archives; Helen Miller, archivist for
the City of St. John's; and Mrs. Julia Baker of Marystown, Mrs. Marion
Manning of Burin, Mr. Herb Slaney of St. Lawrence, Mrs. Mary Hawco of
Conception, and Mrs. Angela Burke of Brigus for providing valuable informa-
tion on the life and work of the Sisters of Mercy in the 1920s and '30s. I thank
the members of my community of St. Joseph's Convent for listening with
patience as I prattled on endlessly about things that happened a hundred years

ago and for tolerating my frequent lapses into silence as I struggled to make sense out of small, incomplete scraps of information.

When referring to members of religious congregations, our own and others, I encountered a problem. Up until the 1970s, each member of a congregation was given a religious name at the time of her reception into the novitiate. As a rule, each new name was preceded by the name "Mary." I decided to omit titles as far as possible and refer to each sister by her religious name, e.g. "M. [Mary] Francis." However, when the decision was made to return to the use of baptismal names, I was faced with a dilemma. To distinguish between religious and other women who are part of our story, I decided to use the title "Sister" (abbreviated Sr.) when referring to a member of the Mercy congregation. I realize that this makes for a certain inconsistency between the earlier and later chapters.

This book has been a long time in the making due to frequent and unavoidable interruptions. However, the task of delving into the past has been a valuable experience. It has provided me with many salutary lessons as I pondered the dedication, commitment, and total self-sacrifice of those women who gave their lives in service to the people of our land.

Because there are few contemporary documents dealing with the early days of the Mercy congregation in Newfoundland, I have used the scanty sources available and presented a possible scenario of the events as they unfolded. I take full responsibility for any errors or mistakes that may have crept into the manuscript in spite of the vigilance of Madonna Gatherall, RSM. My hope and prayer is that those who read this book may share my admiration for and gratitude to those women who, in the face of almost insuperable obstacles, succeeded in bringing the blessings of education and health care to the people of Newfoundland and Labrador. Through their genuine concern for all humankind, these Sisters of Mercy were living witnesses to the enduring compassion and healing presence of the Christ to whom they had given their lives.

INTRODUCTION

THE STORY OF THE SISTERS OF MERCY OF NEWFOUNDLAND

> Let us make haste to write down the stories and traditions of
> the people before they are forgotten.
> Heni-Raymond Casgrain, *Les Soirées Canadiennes 1861–65*

ach religious institute over the years of its life weaves a story that is uniquely its own. The story of the Congregation of the Sisters of Mercy of Newfoundland was begun before the first Sisters of Mercy ever set foot on the island of Newfoundland. The circumstances of the founding; the character, example, and teachings of the foundress; the sufferings, hardships, joys, and triumphs of the members; the accounts of new missions undertaken; and the tales of saintly and not-so-saintly individuals are all elements in a congregational history that has been passed down through the years and is still unfolding.

But the story of a religious congregation is not and cannot be a straightforward narrative that moves coherently and logically to a preordained and predictable conclusion. The traditions of the congregation, the charism, the spirit, or whatever it is that makes us Sisters of Mercy, were informed, molded, and shaped by all the hundreds of women who devoted themselves to the mission of Jesus through a variety of ministries.

During the past years, as I became more familiar with the lives of those Sisters of Mercy who lived and struggled to establish the congregation in this

1

land, I discovered that, since 1842, a wonderful, beautiful tapestry of Mercy had been woven by these women. The person and ministry of each Sister of Mercy represents a thread in the tapestry. Each sister is at the same time a weaver and a strand woven into the fabric of this work. The colours are varied and distinct. There are the darker threads of human weakness, bewildering pain, and failure that make the bright shades of selfless, compassionate service all the more resplendent. As I gathered up the years, I found lovely patterns where, in the living, we saw only chaos, for the weavers themselves were too close to the material to appreciate the astonishing beauty of the work they were creating.

While the tapestry is indeed woven from all the individual strands of the congregation members, there are some who, through their wisdom, initiative, and courage, were the artists who gave the principal outline and shape to the tapestry. I have attempted to tell the story from the perspective of those who have woven the threads that form the fabric of our history. Except in a few cases, there was nothing extraordinary in the lives of these women unless, in a world where fidelity is so rare, faithfulness itself is extraordinary.

The first chapter of this book tells the story of the foundress of the Sisters of Mercy, Catherine McAuley. It was important to start with Catherine for it all began with this dynamic, generous-hearted, and courageous woman. Catherine's commonsensical approach to life, her determination to assist women, her passion for justice—all of this is what fired the first Mercy Sisters to come to Newfoundland and remains our inspiration and our goal.

Subsequent chapters address the establishment of separate convents in a broad chronological fashion without too much attention to the details of the development of the ministries in each locality. Rather, the focus is on the women who developed these ministries. Since some of the foundations lasted only a short time, it is possible to tell their story in its entirety. In the case of communities whose history spanned over a hundred years, it is necessary to revisit them periodically in order to trace the careers of those women who were the most visible agents of change and development. This is not to denigrate the persons or the service of other Sisters of Mercy who toiled faithfully day in and day out to feed the hungry, clothe the naked, instruct the ignorant, visit the sick and imprisoned, and bury the dead—in short, those who gave their lives in the corporal and spiritual works of Mercy.

Perhaps a professional historian would present in separate chapters an account of each convent from its foundation to the present day. This was the approach taken by M. Williamina Hogan, RSM, who wrote the definitive history of the Newfoundland Sisters of Mercy in her book, *Pathways of Mercy*, published in 1986. This present work is not a history per se. I anticipate that whatever emerges will be in the form of a narrative with no pretensions to great history or literature. My hope is that it will present in truth and simplicity the story of a group of ordinary women who did ordinary things but who did them extraordinarily well. It is an attempt to capture the spirit that called young women to give up home, with all that this implies, in an attempt to bring a little more equality and justice to the world. They did this by educating the young, caring for the poor and the sick, and empowering people to take control of their own lives and destinies so that all people might live in dignity and peace.

CHAPTER ONE

A WOMAN NAMED CATHERINE

> What does the Lord ask of you? Only this—to act justly, to
> love tenderly, and to walk humbly with your God.
>
> Micah 6:8

It began with a woman named Catherine. Catherine Elizabeth McAuley
was born in Dublin, Ireland, on September 29, 1778,[1] one of three children of James and Elinor McGauley.[2] James McGauley, a prosperous
Catholic gentleman, was more than fifty years of age when he married Elinor, the
daughter of a former business associate, John Conway. At the time of the marriage,
Elinor was in her early twenties, a good-looking, charming young lady, whose outlook on life was in striking contrast to that of her more serious, devout husband.
A deeply religious man, possessed of a social conscience, James McGauley delighted in offering material support and religious instruction to the poor of the neighbourhood. Elinor was more interested in the social life of fashionable Dublin.

---

1. There is some confusion as to the exact date of Catherine McAuley's birth. For a discussion of the problem see Mary C. Sullivan, *Catherine McAuley and the Tradition of
Mercy* (Dublin: Four Courts Press, 1995), p. 344 n. 4.

2. There are several variations in the spelling of the name, McAuley. Catherine's parents
inserted the letter G (McGauley), while Catherine herself omitted it. Her sister Mary married William Macauley. M. Bertrand Degnan, *Mercy Unto Thousands: The Life of Mother
Mary Catherine McAuley, Foundress of the Sisters of Mercy* (Westminister, Md.: Newman
Press, 1957), p. xi.

Nevertheless, James was devoted to his young wife and their children, and for her part, Elinor loved and respected her elderly husband. Thus, in a happy, stable home environment, young Catherine McAuley passed her early years.

Then, in the summer of 1783, James McGauley died, and Elinor was left with the responsibility of raising three young children all under the age of six years: Mary, Catherine, and James. Even though Elinor continued her round of social activities, she was careful to ensure a good education for the children and saw to it that they made their First Communion and received the sacrament of confirmation.[3] James provided well for his family, but Elinor was young, extravagant, and totally incapable of managing the family finances. After the death of her husband, Elinor moved from Stormanstown House where she and James had lived, to a house in Glasnevin, Dublin.[4] In 1787, she sold this property and leased part of a house at 52 Queen Street, Dublin,[5] to be close to her friend Mrs. St. George, who lived in the other part of the same house.[6] Mrs. St. George, was a gifted, well-educated lady and a Protestant. The fact that Elinor was a Catholic was regrettable but something that Mrs. St. George was prepared to overlook. Elinor was readily influenced by the opinions of Mrs. St. George and her circle of friends. She began to neglect the practice of her religion and spent her time in an endless round of social activities. When money ran out, she sold one piece of property and then another, until finally, in 1796, she and her children moved to the home of her brother, Dr. Owen Conway.[7] It is probable that by the time she moved to her brother's home, Elinor was already a very sick woman. It is not known exactly when she became ill, only that the illness was of long duration, culminating in a difficult and painful death on October 21, 1798.[8] Her final days were filled with remorse because

3. Annals, Convent of Our Lady of Mercy, Bermondsey Anno MDCCCXLI, cited in Sullivan, Catherine McAuley, p. 99.

4. Sullivan, Catherine McAuley, p. 10.

5. Ibid.

6. Roland Burke Savage, Catherine McAuley: The First Sister of Mercy (Dublin: M. H. Gill & Son, 1950), p. 19. Savage notes that he was unable to trace any information about this lady. Biographies of Catherine McAuley refer to her as "Mrs. St. George."

7. Ibid.

8. Sullivan, Catherine McAuley, p. 10.

of her failure to practice her religion and to instruct her children adequately in the teachings of the Catholic faith. The memory of her mother's tortured last days haunted Catherine to the end of her life, so much so, that later on she impressed upon her Sisters of Mercy the importance of visiting the sick and assisting them at the hour of death.

After Elinor's death, Catherine and her siblings were left with very little money or property. What was left was invested in a company directed by William Armstrong,[9] a relative of the Conways who assumed responsibility for the McAuley children. Mary and James became part of the Armstrong household and adopted the Protestant religion. Catherine, however, continued to live with her uncle, Dr. Owen Conway. She was about the same age as her cousin Ann, the doctor's only child, with whom she had formed a close friendship. Like his sister, Owen Conway was both generous and extravagant. Within a year or so after Elinor's death, Dr. Conway faced financial ruin. Almost overnight, the family was reduced to poverty. Catherine, feeling that she was an additional burden, accepted William Armstrong's invitation to make her home with him. And so began a difficult period in her life.

William Armstrong, a staunch Protestant, was a generous, sympathetic individual and a man of deep and strong religious convictions. Religious matters were often the topic of discussion and debate in the Armstrong household, and the supposed teachings of the Catholic Church were treated with polite disdain. All of this was very painful for Catherine.

Although she had learned something of her faith from the instructions of Father Andrew Lube, whom she met while staying with the Conways, she was in no position to respond to questions and comments on religious matters. Tormented by her inability to find satisfactory answers to some of the questions posed, Catherine turned to Father Thomas Betagh, a learned priest of Dublin. He was quick to appreciate her problem and provided her with sound advice and plenty of material to supply what had been lacking in her religious education. Catherine read, studied, pondered, and prayed. During this period,

---

9. Sister M. Ignatia Neumann, ed., *Letters of Catherine McAuley, 1821–1841* (Baltimore: Helicon Press, 1969), p. 4.

the seed of faith planted by God was nurtured in what might be termed her "dark night of the soul."[10]

Among the visitors to the Armstrong home were William and Catherine Callaghan, newly returned from India. The Callaghans were immediately attracted to Catherine. Mrs. Callaghan, in particular, enjoyed her conversation and her companionship. Because they had no children of their own, they urged Catherine to make her home with them. She accepted the invitation and, around the year 1801, she moved to the Callaghan's residence, an estate called Coolock on the outskirts of Dublin.[11]

For almost twenty years, Catherine lived with the Callaghans at Coolock as a cherished and beloved daughter. With their approval, she cared for the poor of the village, distributing gifts of food and money provided by Mrs. Callaghan. The only wrinkle in the smooth unfolding of Catherine's relationship with the Callaghans was, again, the matter of religion, for the Callaghans were devout Quakers. Although they disapproved of Catholicism, their genuine fondness for Catherine made them hesitant to interfere with her practice of her faith. Provided she refrained from any overt display of "popery" in their home, she was free to attend mass and other religious activities when the opportunity offered. And so the years passed—tranquil, happy years, during which the prayers and quiet example of the young woman they had befriended were slowly but surely obliterating the ingrained prejudices against Catholicism the Callaghans had held throughout their lives.

By the year 1817, Catherine Callaghan's health had deteriorated so that she was confined to her room. For two long years, Catherine cared for her every need. Always a deeply religious woman, Mrs. Callaghan began to ask questions about Catherine's beliefs. She agreed to see a priest and received instructions in the Catholic faith. Whether Mrs. Callaghan was actually baptized before she died in

10. A term coined by St. John of the Cross to describe one of the stages in the soul's advance to union with God. The stage known as "the Dark Night of the Soul" is characterized by periods of darkness and doubt that sometimes beset the human person.
11. Sullivan, *Catherine McAuley*, p. 10.

1819 is uncertain.[12] After his wife's death, William Callaghan found consolation in Catherine's thoughtfulness and care. He had always admired her management of the household and the good judgment she showed in financial matters. When the time came for him to conclude his affairs, he considered carefully how to dispose of his large holdings in a manner consistent with his practice of Christian charity. Realizing that his time on earth was almost over, he sent for a clergyman to ask advice on how best to prepare for death.[13] Dissatisfied with the gentleman's response, he turned to Catherine. She never spoke of what passed between them, but in the last months of his life, William Callaghan was instructed in the Catholic faith by a Dublin priest and was received into the Church on November 9, 1822.[14] He died the following day, leaving the bulk of his estate to Catherine McAuley.

William Callaghan, well aware of Catherine's concern for the poor, supported her efforts to assist those in need. A year before his death, Catherine had provided a home at Coolock for two orphans, Mary Anne Kirwan and Ellen Corrigan.[15] Then, in 1821, she adopted her godchild, Teresa Byrn, the youngest child of her cousin Ann Conway Byrn. Ann died a year later, leaving three other children, whereupon Catherine adopted her namesake, the ten-year-old Catherine Byrn.[16]

By this time, Catherine McAuley was in her mid-forties. She was familiar with and attracted to the work of the Irish Sisters of Charity, and, although she greatly admired their efforts to help the poor, she was uneasy about some

---

12. Savage claimed she was baptized by Rev. Michael Keogh. Savage, *McAuley*, p. 38. The writer of the "Bermondsey Manuscript" stated that she died without baptism. Sullivan, *Catherine McAuley*, p. 100.

13. Sullivan, *Catherine McAuley*, p. 38.

14. Ibid., p. 10.

15. Mary Ann Kirwan married Richard Malone on December 26, 1825. Catherine and her brother James McAuley witnessed the marriage ceremony. Ellen Corrigan was professed as a Sister of Mercy on January 25, 1837, and died of malignant typhus two weeks later, on February 9. See Sullivan, *Catherine McAuley*, p. 16.

16. Teresa Byrn became a Sister of Mercy with the religious name, Mary Camillus. Later she served in New York and Baltimore. Catherine Byrn received the habit of the Sisters of Mercy on January 23, 1832, but left to enter the Dominican Sisters on December 1, 1832, where she was known as Mary Raymond. See Sullivan, *Catherine McAuley*, pp. 13,14.

details of the organization, principally the interference of a non-resident committee. There was also the matter of prejudice. In general, Irish Protestants of the nineteenth century regarded all Roman Catholic religious orders with deep suspicion. Catherine could not avoid being influenced by these opinions and wanted nothing to do with nuns.[17] Her design was to gather around her a group of women who, without adopting the canonical structure of religious life, were prepared to devote themselves to works of charity, specifically the education of poor girls, the care of young women, and the visitation and relief of the sick poor. Pondering how best to put into action her plans to help the poor, she sought advice from Father Edward Armstrong and his friend Dr. Michael Blake. Her idea was to build a house that would be large enough to incorporate a school for poor children and a shelter for homeless women, where they could be trained to become self-supporting. She intended to make her own home there and invite young women who had leisure time to join her in teaching poor children and providing care and profitable occupation for the homeless.

On June 22, 1824,[18] Catherine purchased land on the corner of Baggot Street and Herbert Street on which to erect a building that would serve as a centre for religious, educational, and charitable activities. To provide adequate financing for the project, Catherine sold the Coolock property in mid-1828.[19] By divesting herself of all her property, Catherine took literally the words of Jesus to the rich young man, "Go sell what you have, give the money to the poor, and come, follow Me."[20] She realized, however, that it would take more than goodwill and the provision of a building to effect real change in the lives of the poor—they needed a sound education. And so, while awaiting the completion of the house on Baggot Street, she prepared herself for her future ministry by investigating the educational methods that were being developed in the

---

17. Savage, *McAuley*, p. 46.
18. Sullivan, *Catherine McAuley*, p. 10.
19. Ibid., p. 12.
20. Mark 10:21.

best schools of the city. Not completely satisfied, she visited France to observe other methods used on the continent.[21]

Meantime, the house on Baggot Street was beginning to take shape. Passersby wondered about the purpose of such an edifice in the heart of fashionable Dublin. One of these was a young woman, Anna Maria Doyle.[22] On learning that this new building on Baggot Street was to be used to provide education and shelter for the poor, Miss Doyle found an opportunity to meet Catherine McAuley and, after hearing the details of her plans, expressed a desire to join her in the work. Years later, when asked for an account of the rapidly growing institute, Catherine wrote, "It commenced with 2, Sister Doyle & I. The plan from the beginning was such as in now in practice."[23]

Toward the end of the summer of 1827, the house on Baggot Street was completed and ready for occupancy. This posed a problem for Catherine. Her sister, Mary, was critically ill, and Catherine was obliged to devote much of her time to caring for the patient and her family. When Mary died on August 11, 1827, Catherine's brother-in-law, William Macauley, begged her to remain with them for a few months so that the children would have her love and support at this critical time in their lives.[24]

For her part, Anna Maria Doyle was anxious to begin work immediately. Catherine agreed that Anna Maria should move into the new centre with young Catherine Byrn as her assistant. These two permanent residents, with a number of young ladies who were eager to volunteer their time, comprised the first staff of the new centre. Catherine McAuley, with her eldest niece, Mary Teresa Macauley, went daily to help with the work. Anna Maria settled

21. Degnan, *Mercy Unto Thousands*, p. 45.
22. M. Bonaventure Brennan, *"It Commenced with Two . . ." The Story of Mary Ann Doyle* (Northern Province, Ireland: Sisters of Mercy, 2001), pp. 4, 16. One of Anna Maria's brothers, John Doyle, moved to England and became one of the greatest political sketchers of the day. John's grandson was Sir Arthur Conan Doyle of Sherlock Holmes fame.
23. M. Catherine McAuley to Sister M. Elizabeth Moore, January 13, 1839. May C. Sullivan, ed., *The Correspondence of Catherine McAuley, 1818–1841* (Baltimore: Catholic University of America Press, 2004), p. 179. See also, M. Austin Carroll, *Leaves from the Annals of the Sisters of Mercy*, vol. 1, *Ireland* (New York: Catholic Publication Society, 1881), p. 13.
24. Mary Macauley married William Macauley, an apothecary by profession, in 1804. They had five children: Mary, James, Robert, Catherine, and William.

on the date for the opening, September 24. A short time later, learning that the date coincided with the feast of Our Lady of Mercy, she suggested that the building be named, "House of Mercy." And so, on September 24, 1827, the House of Mercy opened, classes began in the school, and a number of young women found shelter in the house. Little did Catherine and her companions realize that this was the first step in the establishment of a worldwide institute of women religious, the Sisters of Mercy.

From the beginning, the House of Mercy on Baggot Street was a success. The building consisted of classrooms dedicated to the education of poor girls, a dormitory to house unemployed young women, a chapel, and rooms to accommodate a volunteer staff. Years later, Catherine wrote, "In a year and a half we were joined—so fast that it became a matter of general wonder."[26]

One of Catherine's clear objectives was to train young girls to be self-supporting. Sewing and other housekeeping skills were taught. But before recommending a young woman for employment, Catherine and her associates made sure that she was well-versed in correct speech, good manners, and proper behaviour. Education, however, was always a priority, and the classrooms at Baggot Street were operated according to the best educational principles of the time. At the House of Mercy, the school day began with a short period of religious instruction. In the general education courses that followed, Catherine and her companions tried to link each subject with the religious topic of the day so that children would not regard religion as something apart from the ordinary concerns of life.[27]

In June 1828, Catherine took up permanent residence in the House of Mercy. Within six months, William Macauley was dead, leaving his children free to choose as their guardian either Catherine or her brother, Dr. James Macauley.[28] The three boys, James, Robert, and William, and their two sisters,

25. Savage, *McAuley*, p. 62.

26. M. Catherine McAuley to Sister M. Elizabeth Moore, January 13, 1839. Sullivan, *Correspondence*, p. 179.

27. Savage, *McAuley*, p. 76.

28. Ibid., p. 68. Catherine's brother, James, adopted the Protestant spelling of his name, Macauley.

Mary and Catherine, all chose their Aunt Catherine. Catherine decided to keep the girls with her at Baggot Street and hired a governess to attend to their education.[29] During the school year, the boys attended boarding school at Carlow College. At holiday time, Catherine arranged for them to stay with friends of hers who lived near Baggot Street so that brothers and sisters could spend as much time together as possible.

As time passed, life for the volunteers at the House of Mercy took on a regularity that was almost conventual in nature. The ladies prayed together, some rising very early in the morning to recite the entire Psalter. They adopted a special dress that they wore when visiting the sick poor in the neighbouring courts and lanes. One of the early companions of Catherine McAuley described the outdoor costume as follows, "For winter a coarse grey Cloak with a hood, black silk bonnet and muslin veil; in summer the Cloak was replaced by a black rock-spun shawl."[30]

When she built the House of Mercy, Catherine had no intention of founding another religious congregation of women, but gradually she became convinced that if their work were to endure, a more permanent foundation would have to be laid. After months of prayer and discussion among themselves, Catherine and her companions agreed to seek canonical status as a religious institute within the Roman Catholic Church. After reviewing the rules of several religious congregations, they chose the Presentation Rule as that most suitable to their plans. And so, on September 8, 1830, Catherine McAuley, Anna Maria Doyle, and Elizabeth Harley[31] left Baggot Street for the convent of the Presentation Sisters at George's Hill, Dublin, to begin a three-month postulancy in preparation for their novitiate. Fifteen months later, the three novices made their profession as Sisters of Mercy. The vow formula pronounced by Catherine and her companions states very clearly the purposes for

---

29. When Catherine moved into the House of Mercy she brought with her Ellen Corrigan and Teresa Byrn, her two wards. Her third ward, Catherine Byrn was already there.

30. Sullivan, *Catherine McAuley*, p. 49. Sullivan cited "The Derry Large Manuscript, Notes on the Life of Mother Catherine McAuley by One of the First Sisters of Mercy," in which the outdoor costume was described.

31. Elizabeth Harley joined the community at Baggot Street on November 30, 1829. See Sullivan, *Catherine McAuley*, p. 12.

which the Institute of Sisters of Mercy had been established: "I, Sister Catherine McAuley, called in religion Mary Catherine, do vow and promise to God perpetual poverty, chastity and obedience, and to persevere until the end of my life in the Congregation called of the Sisters of Mercy established for the visitation of the sick poor and the instruction of poor females."[32]

Once the ceremony of profession had been concluded, Catherine and her companions lost no time returning to the House of Mercy on Baggot Street, where their return was eagerly awaited by the little group of associates who had faithfully carried on the works of Mercy during their absence. Since many of them were scarcely out of their teens, they needed the support and prudent leadership that had been so sadly lacking during the past fifteen months. Now that the three newly professed Sisters of Mercy had returned, plans were made for these associates to begin their novitiate training. On the day after Catherine's return, Archbishop Murray formally opened the first convent of Mercy and appointed Catherine as superior.

Other matters that required immediate attention were the *Horarium*, or daily schedule of prayers and other duties, and the adaptation of the Presentation Rule to the needs and objectives of the Sisters of Mercy. One very obvious change that distinguished members of the new congregation from the Presentation Sisters was the absence of the rule of enclosure and the emphasis on the ministry of visitation of the sick poor in their homes. The Sisters of Mercy were free to go wherever there was need. Catherine also eliminated the clause in the Presentation Rule that required the sisters to dedicate their efforts solely to the education of the poor. Catherine, perhaps because of the inadequacies of her own upbringing, recognized the value of solid Catholic education at every level of society:

> Though the Order was founded especially for the poor, Mother McAuley was desirous that her children should aid and serve every class as circumstances might allow. And she frequently explained that the three objects peculiarly characteristic of her Institute . . . were not intended to exclude other good works, but only to have

32. Ibid., p. 60.

the preference and precedence. She particularly desired that the Sisters should train and educate women, young and mature, and to this end she inserted a remarkable passage in the Rule: "The Sisters shall feel convinced that no work of charity can be more productive of good to society … than the careful instruction of women … since whatever be the station they are destined to fill their example and advice will always possess influence."[33]

Other modifications to the Presentation Rule were the elimination of lengthy prayers and emphasis on the liturgy and common litanies.[34]

Early in the year 1832, Archbishop Murray received seven candidates as novices in the Congregation of the Sisters of Mercy. One of them, Mary Frances Warde, was to establish the Sisters of Mercy in the United States, and another, Mary de Pazzi (Mary Ann) Delany, played a part in the mystery of the Newfoundland foundation. The steady flow of postulants into the Baggot Street community ensured the future of the new congregation. Among those who entered in 1834 was Clara Frayne, later Mary Ursula, a member of the first community of Sisters of Mercy to come to Newfoundland. Up to this time, the foundress herself performed the duties of novice mistress, but in December 1835, she appointed M. de Pazzi Delany to this duty. In her book *Mercy unto Thousands*, M. Bertrand Degnan wrote, "Fortunately for the novices, several months passed before Mother Catherine began foundations. She therefore remained in a supervisory position. To use an expression of those first Sisters, Mother de Pazzi was 'a little on the severe side.'"[35]

The growth of the new congregation was phenomenal. In January 1839, just seven years after the first novices received the Mercy habit in Baggot Street, Catherine wrote, "We have now gone beyond 100 in number—and the desire to join seems rather to encrease [sic]. Though it was thought foundations would retard it—it seems to be quite otherwise."[36] In March 1835, Catherine

---

33. Carroll, *Leaves*, vol. 1, p. 98.

34. Degnan, *Mercy Unto Thousands*, p. 136.

35. Ibid., p. 174.

36. M. Catherine McAuley to Sister M. Elizabeth Moore, January 13, 1839. Sullivan, *Correspondence*, p. 179.

purchased a house in Kingstown, about six miles southeast of Dublin. She planned to use this house, which she named St. Patrick Convent, as a branch house of the Baggot Street convent, where sick and overworked sisters might go for a period of rest. She limited their charitable work to visitation of the sick poor of the neighbourhood. However, as she walked though the streets on her visits to the sick, Catherine found it impossible to ignore the poor, especially the young girls, who wandered through the streets of this seaport town. Her own resources being insufficient, she determined to seek help to provide a school where they could receive the education and skills necessary to be self-supporting. When the school was built, it met with immediate success, having an enrolment of over two hundred students. It was, however, to be a source of considerable anxiety and trouble for Catherine because of a dispute with the parish priest over the financing of the school buildings.[37] One of the most memorable maxims of the foundress dates from this troublesome period, "God . . . knows I would rather be cold and hungry than that the poor in Kingstown or elsewhere should be deprived of any consolation in our power to afford."[38]

In spite of all the trouble in Kingstown that eventually led to the withdrawal of the sisters,[39] Catherine never lost her sense of humour. In the midst of the difficulties she wrote to M. Frances Warde:

> There also [in Kingstown] we find a nice little cross. Law proceedings for building the school—though we expressly said that we could not contribute more than the ground, coach-house & fifty pounds from the Bazaar . . . I am hiding from some law-person who wants to serve a paper on me personally. . . . This has caused more laughing than crying, you may be sure, for every man is suspected of being the process man, and kept at an awful distance by dear Teresa Carton.[40]

---

37. An account of the troubles at Kingstown may be found in Carroll, *Leaves*, vol. 1, pp. 65–70, and in a letter from M. Catherine McAuley to Sister M. Frances Warde, January 17, 1838. Sullivan, *Correspondence*, pp. 119–120.

38. M. Catherine McAuley to Sister M. Teresa White, November 1, 1838. Sullivan, *Correspondence*, p. 164.

39. The convent in Kingstown reopened in 1840 but was closed again after Catherine's death.

Nevertheless, Catherine and her community had much to celebrate. In March 1835, after examining two chapters of the Rule of the Sisters of Mercy, the Holy See sent a letter of praise to Archbishop Murray stating that Pope Gregory XVI approved the establishment of the Sisters of Mercy and declared it "worthy of his paternal benevolence and Apostolic Benediction."[41] One aspect of the Mercy Rule that distinguished it from most congregations of women at that time was, as previously noted, freedom from the rule of enclosure. The Mercy Sisters went to the homes of the poor and the sick, or wherever people needed care. This new form of apostolate was quite a change from the style of religious living recognized by the people of Dublin, and so the Sisters of Mercy were called "the walking nuns."

Catherine's work spread quickly beyond the Dublin diocese. On April 21, 1836, the first foundation outside of Dublin was made in Tullamore in the diocese of Meath. The community consisted of Catherine's first co-worker and novitiate companion, Anna Maria Doyle, now Mary Ann, whom she named superior, and M. Teresa Purcell, a novice who was about to be professed. Until other novices joined them, two sisters were sent from the Baggot Street convent to complete the community and help with the work.[42] Catherine herself went with them on the foundation and remained for about six weeks. The house that had been prepared for them was very old, and its architecture was peculiar, to say the least. "There were crooked corridors with unexpected steps here and there, dead-walls, narrow windows . . . and good light nowhere."[43] The austerity of the structure, however, was quite attractive to the new superior, Mary Ann Doyle. Catherine, who used to tease Mary Ann for her serious approach to life, wrote as follows: "Sister Mary Ann

---

40. M. Catherine McAuley to Sister M. Frances Warde, January 17, 1838. Sullivan, *Correspondence*, pp. 119–120.

41. Sullivan, *Catherine McAuley*, p. 15. Sullivan noted (pp. 21–22) that Pope Gregory XVI gave final approval to the "Rule and Constitutions of the Sisters of Mercy" on June 6, 1841. Catherine received notice of the papal decree of approval and confirmation of the Rule sometime after August 19, 1841.

42. Savage, *McAuley*, p. 182.

43. Carroll, *Leaves*, vol. 1, pp. 95–96.

has met her *beau ideal* of a conventual building at last, for our rooms are so small that two cats could scarcely dance in them."[44] Within a short time of their arrival, seven young women joined them, and the community continued to grow and prosper. It was in Tullamore that the practice of establishing "pension schools" was initiated in 1836 and approved by Catherine McAuley.[45] The pastor was so delighted with the progress of the sisters' schools that he thought it a pity that any of his parishioners should be deprived of the superior education and training offered by the sisters.

It was, perhaps, inevitable that Catherine would have had a special interest in the education of girls from the middle or upper classes, for a majority of the members of her new congregation came from such families and had benefited from better than average educational opportunities. Furthermore, Catherine realized that if the congregation were to grow and if the sisters were to minister effectively in the fields of health care and education, future novices would, of necessity, be drawn from the ranks of the more highly educated young women. This is illustrated in a remark made by Catherine to M. Frances Warde in Carlow when, resting her hand on the shoulders of two young girls from the pension school, she said, "It is from schools like these we get our best novices."[46]

Requests for foundations in other dioceses multiplied. Before her death in 1841, Catherine saw the establishment of fourteen convents, two of them in England, and a third planned for Newfoundland. In the case of each new foundation, one or two experienced sisters from Baggot Street were sent to remain with the new community for a few months until the mission was established on a firm footing. This practice is an example of Catherine's wisdom and foresight, for it must be remembered that the congregation itself was still in its infancy and most of the sisters were young. The presence of a more experienced religious person during the first few months of a founda-

---

44. Savage, *McAuley*, p. 185.

45. Carroll, *Leaves*, vol. 1, p. 98. Students in pension schools were charged a fee for instruction. The income from these schools helped support the sisters' schools for the poor.

46. Neumann, *Letters*, p. 86.

tion ensured that the spirit of the institute and the principles underlying each Mercy ministry were clearly understood and firmly established in each local community.

Within a year of the foundation in Tullamore, Catherine established two more convents: one in Charleville and another in Carlow (1837). Other foundations followed in quick succession. In 1838, Catherine founded a branch convent and school in Booterstown. Near the sea and a short distance by rail from Baggot Street, Booterstown offered advantages similar to those that governed Catherine's decision to open a convent in Kingstown. This time, however, she had the support of a number of businessmen anxious to have the Sisters of Mercy established in the town.[47] Of the six members of the founding community, four became superiors of important foundations: M. Ursula Frayne, whom Catherine named superior, accompanied the first group of sisters to Newfoundland and founded the congregation in Perth, Australia; M. Teresa White was the foundress of the convent in Galway; M. Aloysius Scott was first superior of the convent in Birr; and M. Cecilia Marmion succeeded M. de Pazzi Delany as superior of Baggot Street. This led to the legend that Catherine intended Booterstown to be a training ground for future superiors.[48]

The year 1839 saw the first foundation of the Sisters of Mercy in England. The chosen site was Bermondsey, a section of London on the south side of the Thames just below Tower Bridge. It was one of the poorest and most crowded quarters of London. The parish priest, Father Peter Butler, had organized a group of ladies to operate a school for the poor children of the area. Before long, the young priest realized that, if the work was to have any permanence, his group of dedicated women needed the stability afforded by a religious congregation. He began negotiations with the Sisters of Mercy. Catherine McAuley agreed and sent two ladies of Father Butler's group to pass their novitiate in Cork where M. Clare Moore was superior. This decision had far-reaching effects. M. Clare went to Bermondsey with the founding group

---

47. Catherine Kovesi Killerby, *Ursula Frayne: A Biography* (Freemantle, Australia: University of Notre Dame, 1996), p. 36.

48. Ibid. I have found no other source for this statement.

and, except for a brief return to Cork, remained there until her death in 1874. She was one of the Sisters of Mercy who volunteered to care for the sick and wounded during the Crimean War, where she and Florence Nightingale formed a friendship that was to endure for the rest of their lives. The Convent of Mercy in Bermondsey had the distinction of being the first Catholic convent erected in London since the Reformation. The foundation in London was followed two years later, in August 1841, by St. Ethelreda's (now St. Mary's) in Birmingham.

Catherine McAuley accompanied the founding sisters on each of these journeys to England, although her failing health was a source of anxiety to all her sisters. Perhaps Catherine was the only one to realize the seriousness of her condition. She wrote from Birmingham to Teresa Carton at Baggot Street directing her to have a very low bedstead made and placed in the infirmary, to which she planned to retire on her return to Dublin.[49] She ended the letter with this sentence that reveals so much of Catherine's character: "It is strange to me, my Dear Sr. Teresa, to write so much about myself—and to give such trouble."[50]

Catherine arrived back in Dublin on September 21, 1841, suffering from fatigue and extreme weakness. Although she remained in her room, she was not preoccupied with her own condition. In fact, she wrote to her friend Mary Ann Doyle in Tullamore asking for hospitality for M. Justina Fleming, who was suffering from tuberculosis. Catherine wrote: "I need not recommend her to your tenderness, I know she will receive every mark of affection, tho' a stranger. All expenses, of course, will be defrayed."[51] These words reflect Catherine's concern for the sick sister and also her thoughtfulness in relieving Mary Ann of any financial burden that might result from caring for one so seriously ill. In the thirteen letters that survive, written between September 24 and October 26, Catherine rarely referred to her own illness. On October 4, she wrote to M. Aloysius Scott, "Pray who gave you such a false account of me, I am just as you saw me. Pray fervently that God may grant me the grace of a

---

49. M. Catherine McAuley to Sister Teresa Carton, September 6, 1841. Sullivan, *Correspondence,* p. 436.

50. Ibid.

51. M. Catherine McAuley to Sister Mary Ann Doyle, September 24, 1841. Ibid., p. 439.

happy death. God bless you all."[52] Then, on October 15, she wrote to M. and
M. Dowling of Dublin, "I would have replied immediately to your communication but have not been well for some days."[53] With the foresight that was so
characteristic of this remarkable woman, Catherine put her affairs in order and
began to prepare for death.

When she lay dying, Catherine must have wondered what the future
would hold for her Sisters of Mercy. She had agreed to send the sisters to the
"fog-draped isle" of Newfoundland[54] but she could not have known that, within two years, her dearest friend M. Frances Warde would leave Ireland and
establish the Sisters of Mercy in the United States. Still less could she have
foreseen that, within the decade, M. Ursula Frayne and her companions would
sail off to the other side of the world to bring her spirit of mercy and compassion to Australia. As she felt her life slipping away, it is not too much to imagine that the words of her own prayer, known as her *Suscipe*, were often on her
lips: "Take from my heart all painful anxiety."

M. Vincent Whitty recorded Catherine's last days in letters to M. Cecilia
Marmion, the mistress of novices, who was "on loan" at the newly established
Birmingham community. The reluctance of the community to accept the fact
that Catherine was really dying is evident. M. Vincent wrote, "Revd. Mother
is more restless and feverish last night & today than she was yesterday or the
day before . . . Sr. Xavier sends you her affectionate love. . . . She defers hers
[i.e. her letter] until Tuesday when she hopes to have better news—indeed I
at least have great hopes—God is too good to take Revd. Mother from us
yet."[55]

As the fateful day drew near, Catherine had some unfinished private
business to be concluded—something no one, not even her closest friends

---

52. M. Catherine McAuley to Sister Mary Aloysius Scott, October 4, 1841. Ibid., p. 447.
53. M. Catherine McAuley to M. and M. Dowling, October 15, 1841. Ibid., p. 451.
54. Mary Austin Carroll, *Leaves From the Annals of the Sisters of Mercy*, vol. 3,
Newfoundland and the United States (New York: Catholic Publication Society, 1883), p. 22.
M. Austin seemed to be fascinated by Newfoundland fog, for she mentioned it several
times when writing of the foundation in St. John's.
55. M. Vincent Whitty to M. Cecilia Marmion, November 7, 1841, cited in Sullivan,
Catherine McAuley, p. 241.

suspected. During the latter years of her life, there seems to have been a curious discrepancy between the advice Catherine gave to her sisters and her own
personal penitential practices. Years before, when she was in the novitiate at
the Presentation Convent, some of her associates at Baggot Street assumed
the direction of their own spiritual life. "One took to fasting, another took the
discipline, another slept in haircloth, while a fourth and fifth thought proper
to remain up half the night at their prayers."[56] Such unwise practices took a
dreadful toll on the health of some of these young women, and throughout
her life, Catherine insisted that the practical difficulties arising from the
labour of teaching and caring for the sick were more than sufficient penance
for the Sisters of Mercy. Nevertheless, she adopted penitential practices not
in accordance with her advice to others. Years later M. Clare Augustine Moore
wrote of Catherine's last illness, "Besides the internal abscess she had a
hideous ulcer on her back brought about by the use of haircloth and a large
chain."[57] In the context of the time, Catherine's use of external instruments
of penance is not unusual. Popular writings on the lives of medieval saints
described how men and women of bygone ages punished their bodies in an
attempt to atone for their own sins and the sins of the world. Even so, one
wonders why the level-headed Catherine McAuley felt it necessary to engage
in such painful mortification. She was careful to conceal these practices from
the sisters, and her use of such cruel instruments of penance was discovered
only after her death.

     Shortly after midnight on November 11, Catherine sent Sr. Teresa
Carton for a large quantity of heavy brown paper and some cord. Teresa was
instructed to draw the curtains around the invalid's bed, and soon the nervous
little attendant heard the familiar sounds of a package being wrapped. After a
few minutes had passed, Catherine called Teresa and told her to go to the
kitchen, put the package in the fire and remain in the kitchen until the package
was utterly destroyed. Then came the stern order, "I forbid you under obedi-

---

56. M. Clare Augustine Moore, "A Memoir of the Foundress of the Sisters of Mercy in
Ireland, The Dublin Manuscript," cited in Sullivan, *Catherine McAuley*, pp. 205, 375
n.1.

57. Ibid., p. 215.

ence to open it or look at it while it is burning."[58] Teresa, disturbed and alarmed by this time, stood motionless. Sensing her fear, Catherine asked gently, "Would you be afraid, dear?" The frightened little sister burst out, "Oh, Reverend Mother, I would be afraid I might look."[59] The foundress did not insist. Instead, she sent for M. Vincent Whitty to whom she gave the same directions. M. Vincent did as she was told but later hinted to M. Clare Augustine Moore that the package contained a haircloth. M. Bertrand Degnan posed the question, "Did Sister M. Vincent smell the haircloth burning, or see charred evidences as she banked the fire again?"[60] Years later, M. Vincent's confessor released her from the obligation to preserve the secret of these penitential practices.

Before mass on November 11, 1841, Catherine sent for all the sisters and spoke to each one, giving her some special word of encouragement or advice. Catherine's enduring love and affection for her sisters remained a preoccupation for her right to the end. Realizing that her death was imminent, she reminded Teresa Carton, "Will you tell the Srs. to get a good cup of tea—I think the community room would be a good place—when I am gone & to comfort one another—but God will comfort them."[61] During this, her last day on earth, her brother James with his wife and daughters visited, as well as some members of the clergy. M. Vincent Whitty, who recorded faithfully Catherine's final moments, wrote as follows:

> When her doctor arrived she greeted him with the words, "Well, Doctor, the scene is drawing to a close." About five in the evening she asked for the Candle to be placed in her hand. We commenced the last prayers; when I repeated one or two she herself had taught me, she said with energy, "God may bless you." When we thought the senses must be going and that it might be well to rouse attention by praying a little louder, she said: "No occasion,

---

58. Ibid., p. 216.

59. Ibid.

60. Degnan, *Mercy Unto Thousands*, p. 342.

61. M. Vincent Whitty to M. Cecilia Marmion, November 11, 1841. Sullivan, *Catherine McAuley*, p. 242. Mary C. Sullivan noted that this is the source of the "good cup of tea" tradition among Sisters of Mercy all over the world. She identified also the source of the term "comfortable cup of tea" as M. Austin Carroll, *Life of Catherine McAuley* (St. Lewis, Mo.: Vincentian Press, 1887), p. 436.

my darling, to speak so loud, I hear distinctly." In this way she continued till 10 minutes before 8 when she calmly breathed her last sigh.[62]

Who was Catherine McAuley? She was foundress, educator, social activist, compassionate nurse, friend of the poor and the disenfranchised—she was all of these but so much more. She was passionately committed to the struggle for justice. She was particularly sensitive to the wrongs that the social structures of the time inflicted on women and on the children of the poor, and she tried to do something about it. A woman of action, she was not satisfied with just discussing what might be done, she went ahead and did it. Always gentle and considerate, she took into account the feelings and sensibilities of others. When offering advice or correction to her sisters, it was done with love, kindness, and humour. Forty years after the death of Catherine McAuley, M. Teresa White wrote of her:

> I was deeply attached to our cherished mother. She was a perfect nun and a perfect lady—one to whom you could open your whole heart. . . . She made the interests of every convent her own, and gave each Sister a place in her heart. . . . If you came to speak to her on the most trifling matter, although occupied with the most important affairs, she would instantly lay all aside and give you any satisfaction in her power. She was rather tall, about five feet five inches, and had a queenly air. [63]

Although declared venerable by the Church, a step on the way to canonization, Catherine was no plaster saint, gliding serenely above the woes that afflict ordinary mortals. She felt the cold and experienced hunger and the helplessness of being dependent on others. Later, enjoying comparative wealth, she gave it all away so that the poor could receive the shelter, education, and training that would lift them from the depths of poverty to a state of self-reliance and independence. She was wonderfully, beautifully human. She could be

62. Sullivan, *Catherine McAuley*, p. 179. The sentence, "God may bless you," is quoted as it appeared in M. Vincent Whitty's letter.
63. Degnan, *Mercy Unto Thousands*, p. 346.

impulsive, impatient, funny, witty, serious, but always self-forgetful and kind. She took time for others, writing comic little verses to chide a sister who took herself a little too seriously, or to liven up a feast day celebration. She had a practical, commonsensical approach to life—especially to religious life. She warned a superior who was inclined to be over-vigilant, "Be careful not to make too many laws, for if you draw the string too tight, it will break."[64] It is not just because it all began with Catherine McAuley that the Sisters of Mercy love and revere her. It is because she was, above all, a woman of mercy who knew how to translate into the small change of everyday human experience the astonishing event of salvation.

---

64. M. Clare Moore, "A Life of Catherine McAuley" in the "Bermondsey Manuscript," cited in Sullivan, *Catherine McAuley*, p. 115.

CHAPTER TWO

THE NEWFOUNDLAND FOUNDATION

Majestic cliffs, pounded by the ever-restless sea,
Fragile homesteads clinging to the rocks,
The ever-circling gulls uttering shrill cries . . .
While spruce and pine stand silently on guard.

Kathrine E. Bellamy, RSM

n the days following Catherine McAuley's death, the sisters at Baggot Street seem to have been reluctant to take steps to fill the office of superior. It was not in the nature of the self-effacing Catherine McAuley to express any preference in the matter. "On her death bed, on the last day of her life, being asked to name the Sister whom she would like to succeed her, she answered, 'The Constitutions give the sisters the liberty of choosing for themselves and I will not interfere.'"[1]

The initiative for the election of a new superior came from Archbishop Murray. This information is contained in a letter to Sr. Mary Anne Doyle on November 21, 1841. M. Elizabeth Moore wrote, "A letter from Baggot Street: His Grace desires them prepare for an Election."[2] Possibly it was still

---

1. Mercy International Centre, Dublin. The quotation is found in a framed inscription that hangs on the wall of the room in which Catherine McAuley died. The source is not identified.

2. M. Elizabeth Moore to Mary Ann Doyle, November 12, 1841, cited in Sullivan, *Catherine McAuley*, p. 256.

too soon for the sisters to contemplate filling Catherine's position. Nevertheless, a chapter was held on December 2, 1841, just three weeks after Catherine's death, resulting in the election of M. de Pazzi Delany as superior. The fact that M. de Pazzi suffered from frequent and severe epileptic seizures and was ill-suited by temperament for responsibility[3] may have been a cause of concern to the sisters, but obviously Archbishop Murray was satisfied with the choice, for there is no evidence of any expression of disapproval on his part.

There were many reasons for the election of M. de Pazzi as superior. She had held the office of assistant since March 6, 1840. She was one of the early volunteers at the House of Mercy,[4] and before leaving to enter the Presentation novitiate, Catherine appointed her to be in charge of the house. M. de Pazzi was the only one left at Baggot Street of the first group of sisters to be professed at Baggot Street. She had both seniority and experience.

Furthermore, the regular exodus of competent sisters to new foundations placed a heavy demand on the community. Catherine herself remarked "feet and hands are numerous enough, but the heads are nearly gone."[5] Thus, the sisters who remained at Baggot Street were left with very little choice in the naming of a superior. No doubt they crossed their fingers and hoped for the best.

The immediate task facing M. de Pazzi was to plan for the foundation in St. John's, Newfoundland. From what we know of M. de Pazzi, this was not something she approached with much enthusiasm. M. Austin Carroll wrote: "It was well-known that Mother de Pazzi did not love foundations; she was the only one of the early members who had but little of the missionary spirit."[6] In

3. Savage, *McAuley*, p. 393. See also Sullivan, *Catherine McAuley*, p. 214.

4. Mary Ann Delany joined the ladies of the Baggot Street community on July 1830. When she was received as a Sister of Mercy on January 23, 1832, she was given the religious name, Mary de Pazzi. Sullivan, *Catherine McAuley*, p. 13.

5. M. Catherine McAuley to Sister M. Frances Warde, August 23, 1839. Sullivan, *Correspondence*, p. 151.

6. Carroll, *Leaves*, vol. 3, p. 11.

spite of the fact that M. de Pazzi and, for that matter, most of the community acted on Catherine's facetious remark, "Whoever could take tea without milk would go [to Newfoundland] as superior,"[7] it is doubtful that anyone took the gesture seriously. We are not told how long M. de Pazzi persevered in taking her tea without milk, but what is known is that she constantly deplored the "depopulation" of Baggot Street for the sake of foundations. Nevertheless, she was scrupulous in carrying out, in every detail, the wishes of the foundress. And so, within a comparatively short time, she set in motion preparations for the overseas foundation.

Neither Catherine McAuley nor M. de Pazzi Delany would have had a clear idea of conditions in Newfoundland or of the different classes of people among whom the sisters would live and work. The history of Newfoundland and the socio-economic climate of the place were the stuff of fairy tales to most of the sisters in Dublin in 1842—as they are to some mainland Canadians today.

Just as St. John's is a modern, thriving city according to today's standards, so it was a busy commercial centre in 1842. As a matter of fact, since the early sixteenth century, St. John's has been a haven and a supply base for European fishermen. By the end of the eighteenth century (1780) it was, according to Governor Erasmus Gower, ". . . a port of extensive Commerce . . . importing nearly two-thirds of the supplies for the whole Island, and furnished with extensive Store-Houses and Wharfs for trade."[8] There was a sizeable and lucrative commerce with merchants from England, Ireland, and Scotland, who came to Newfoundland to take the products of the fishery to international markets. The Newfoundland-based traders were, in the main, immigrants from the British Isles, the majority of Irish origin:

> While the merchant class was mainly from England or Scotland, the Irish dominated trades and crafts, such as tailoring, coopering and shoemaking, and made up the majority of publicans and shop-

---

7. Ibid., p. 15.

8. Erasmus Gower, Governor of Newfoundland, cited in *Encyclopedia of Newfoundland and Labrador* (henceforth *ENL*), 5 vols. (St. John's, NL: Newfoundland Book Publishers and Harry Cuff Publications, 1981–94), s.v. "St. John's."

keepers . . . the Irish outnumbering the English by nearly two to one.[9]

In his doctoral thesis, "Conflict and Culture in Irish-Newfoundland Roman Catholicism, 1829–1850," historian John E. FitzGerald identifies two principal waves of Irish migrations, the first of which was a general but sporadic seasonal migration throughout the eighteenth and early nineteenth centuries. A second, much larger migration occurred between 1811 and 1816.[10] Many of these were "economic migrants attracted by the tremendous expansion of Newfoundland's land-based sedentary fisheries during the French wars."[11] FitzGerald continues:

> Newfoundland was settled and remained so because of the prospects of accumulating wealth. Reliable returns for population date only for 1827, 1830, and 1836. In 1827 the Newfoundland population was about 59,900; . . . and by 1836, the first Newfoundland census found that out of a total Newfoundland population of 75,000 there were 38,000 Irish with 14,000–15,000 Irish in St. John's.[12]

FitzGerald claims that the Irish in Newfoundland "were already a well-established, cohesive cultural group long before the potato famine of the 1840s."[13] In 1845, three years after the arrival of the Sisters of Mercy, the population of Newfoundland had reached a total of 96,506, with St. John's numbering 18,986 residents, 12,776 of whom were Irish Roman Catholics.[14]

---

9. Ibid.

10. John Edward FitzGerald, "Conflict and Culture in Irish-Newfoundland Roman Catholicism, 1829–1850" (Ph.D. diss., University of Ottawa, 1997), p. 30.

11. Ibid.

12. Ibid., p. 33. FitzGerald cited John Mannion, "Tracing the Irish: A Geographical Guide," *Newfoundland Ancestor* 9, no. 1 (May 1993): p. 13.

13. FitzGerald, "Conflict and Culture," p. 29. FitzGerald quoted as his source, John Mannion, "Tracing the Irish," pp. 6–7.

14. Ibid.

By the mid-nineteenth century, Newfoundland was maturing economically and politically. The Supreme Court of Newfoundland was established in St. John's in 1824, and in 1832 the struggle to achieve representative government was successful.[15] The new government recognized the need to provide some assistance for the community-supported schools then in existence, and in 1836 the House of Assembly passed Newfoundland's first Act for the Encouragement of Education.[16] This act offered assistance to existing schools in the form of grants made to school boards in the nine electoral districts of the colony.

It is not known when the first attempts at formal education began in Newfoundland. The Society for the Propagation of the Gospel (SPG), founded in London in 1701, sent Church of England (C of E) missionaries to parts of the British Empire where the colonists could not afford to support their own clergy. Among the duties of the SPG missionary was the organization of churches and schools. Throughout the eighteenth century and half of the nineteenth century, the SPG was active in various places in Newfoundland. As early as 1726, the C of E clergyman at Bonavista received help from the SPG to support a school.[17] The first school in St. John's of which there is a record was opened in 1744 by Reverend William Peaseley with the aid of the SPG. He added ammunition to his request for funding by warning that ". . . without his proposed school the residents might have their children educated by 'Papists.'"[18] There is no doubt that throughout Newfoundland, even in the smallest places, attempts were made to see that people could at least read and write and do simple arithmetic. For instance, in Swain's Island, Bonavista Bay,

---

15. Representative government was granted to Newfoundland after many years of active campaigning by the residents of the colony. The system that was put into place was one that divided the Island of Newfoundland into nine electoral districts that returned a total of fifteen members to the Legislative Assembly. The governor, appointed by the British Parliament, remained relatively autonomous, but final authority rested with the British House of Commons that had the power to approve or reject all bills passed by the Newfoundland Legislature. See *ENL*, s.v. "Government."

16. *Journal of the House of Assembly* (henceforth *JHA*), 1836, p. 85, Provincial Archives of Newfoundland.

17. *ENL*, s.v. "Schools."

18. Ibid.

the chief planter is said to have requested a literate fishing servant to "stop ashore and teach the children, and I'll pay thee the wages as though thee went in the boat."[19] In 1802, at the instigation of Governor Erasmus Gower, the St. John's Charity School was founded. It was an inter-denominational school, although its teachers were all Protestant. The education it offered was entirely secular, but students could leave the regular class to receive religious instruction if their parents so desired. The Roman Catholic bishop and his priests in St. John's sat on the Charity School's board of directors, and leading Catholics in St. John's contributed to its support.[20] In 1823, the Newfoundland School Society for Educating the Poor (NSS) was founded by a group interested specifically in promoting the Church of England. Historian John Greene described the reaction of Roman Catholics to the schools established by the NSS:

> One of the most immediate and more pronounced effects of the NSS in St. John's was to excite the alarm and jealousy of the Roman Catholics. Their children had long been attending the St. John's Charity School. . . . The presence of the new school after 1824 caused serious anxiety in some Catholic quarters, especially since the Charity School began to lose ground and some Catholic parents enrolled their children in the rival institution. . . . Patrick Morris [Future president of the Benevolent Irish Society (BIS)] . . . felt there were not enough schools to meet the increasing needs of the expanding population of St. John's.[21]

A couple of years later, in 1826, the Benevolent Irish Society (BIS)[22] founded in St. John's a charity school, which came to be known as the

---

19. Ibid.

20. John P. Greene, *Between Damnation and Starvation: Priests and Merchants in Newfoundland Politics, 1745–1855* (Montreal and Kingston: McGill-Queen's University Press, 1999), p. 42.

21. Ibid.

22. The Benevolent Irish Society was started in 1806 by a number of Irish residents of St. John's who were concerned with finding a way to alleviate the large number of poor. Funds for carrying out this objective were provided through donations and membership fees. The members of the Society were to be Irish or of Irish descent, but the Society was to be non-sectarian and charity was to be dispensed to all in need regardless of country of origin or of religion.

Orphan Asylum School (OAS). This school was officially non-denominational and expressly forbade religious education during school hours. However,
after a while the OAS was attended almost exclusively by Roman Catholics
and quickly became the largest school in the colony. It was the cause of some
resentment among the Catholic population that schools operated by the NSS
and the SPG were to some extent encouraged by the government while the
OAS was refused support.[23]

   In light of all this, the state of religious education and practice was a
matter of grave concern to the dynamic missionary, Michael Anthony
Fleming. Within three years after his appointment in 1830 as vicar apostolic
of Newfoundland, Fleming had more than doubled the number of priests on
the island.[24] Although the supply was still far from adequate, Catholics in
almost every settlement on the island could avail of the services of a priest,
at least once a year.[25] Having thus attended, insofar as possible, to the sacramental needs of the people, Fleming was determined to address the lack of
educational opportunities for girls. In language typical of the time he
wrote:

> Viewing the great influence that females exercise over the
> moral character of society—the great and useful and necessary
> influence that the example and the conversation of the mother
> has in the formation of the character of her children, as well
> male as female—I judged it of essential importance to fix the
> character of the female portion of our community in virtue and
> innocence, by training them in particular in the ways of integri-
> ty and morality; . . . These feelings and opinions were the
> motives that led me to consider the establishment of a

---

23. *ENL*, s.v. "Schools."

24. In 1829, Michael Anthony Fleming was consecrated coadjutor vicar apostolic of
Newfoundland and bishop of Carpasia in *partibus*. A year later, in 1830, he succeeded
Bishop Scallan as vicar apostolic. Seventeen years later, in 1847, Newfoundland was
elevated to the status of a diocese and Bishop Fleming became the first bishop of
Newfoundland.

25. The Very Reverend M. F. Howley, *Ecclesiastical History of Newfoundland* (Boston:
Doyle and Whittle, 1888), p. 275. According to a list of clergy given by FitzGerald,
"Conflict and Culture," p. 466, there were at least twenty-three priests in Newfoundland
in 1842.

Presentation Convent essential to the permanent success of the Mission.[26]

In this statement of Bishop Fleming we find an echo of Catherine McAuley's words: "The Sisters shall feel convinced that no work of charity can be more productive of good to society, . . . than the careful instruction of women, since whatever be the station they are destined to fill, their example and advice will always possess influence."[27]

Having decided on a course of action, the bishop put the wheels in motion. He sailed to Ireland and, on the morning of June 29, 1833, carrying his belongings in a carpet bag, he presented himself at the door of the Presentation Convent in Galway and asked permission to celebrate mass. After mass, he was shown around the school by young Sr. M. Magdalen O'Shaugnessy.[28] Fleming was delighted with his tour guide and lost no time in describing to her the desolation of his country and the great need there was of generous, dedicated young Presentation Sisters to educate the daughters of the poor Irish settlers of St. John's. By the time the tour was concluded and he was escorted back to the community room, M. Magdalen was converted—lock, stock, and barrel—to his cause.[29] The bishop's enthusiasm was so contagious that he convinced three more sisters to volunteer for the Newfoundland mission. Before giving her consent, however, the cautious superior, M. John Power, insisted that Bishop Fleming sign the following agreement:

---

26. Bishop Michael Anthony Fleming to the Very Rev. Dr. O'Connell, January 11, 1844, "Letters on the State of Religion in Newfoundland," Archives of the Archdiocese of St. John's (henceforth AASJ), 103/2/27. See also *The Newfoundland Indicator,* March 16, 1844, p. 2.

27. "Rule and Constitutions of the Sisters of Mercy," chapter 2, article 5, cited in Sullivan, *Catherine McAuley,* p. 297. On p. 297 n. 8, Sullivan suggested that article 5 is entirely Catherine's own composition.

28. Sister M. Magdalen O'Shaughnessy, quoted in M. Raphael Consedine, *A Listening Journey* (Victoria, Australia: Congregation of the Presentation of the Blessed Virgin Mary, 1983), pp. 261–62.

29. Howley, *Ecclesiastical History,* p. 280.

> It is that this community shall have it in their power to recall our
> Sisters at any time after six years, should the Convent at
> Newfoundland be then sufficiently established; or should the
> present flattering prospect of promoting the great end of our
> holy institute, by co-operating in the instruction of the poor
> female children of St. John's, *not succeed* to their satisfaction, or
> should they wish to return for any other particular cause, which
> they may *deem necessary*, that in that case your Lordship would
> have them safely conducted back to their own convent in
> Galway.[30]

With the approval and blessing of the bishop of Galway, arrangements were made for the departure of the missionaries. After a long and very stormy passage across the Atlantic, the four Presentation Sisters arrived in St. John's on September 21, 1833.[31]

From the beginning, the ministry of the Presentation Sisters was a success. Within a remarkably short time, their schools acquired a reputation for solid instruction and excellent training in the skills necessary for young women to become successful wives and mothers. Above all, the sisters provided their pupils with a thorough grounding in knowledge of Catholic faith and doctrine. Students flocked to their schools, and, after a few years, more than 850 girls were enrolled in their classes.[32] Bishop Fleming was elated and spared no efforts to provide the sisters with a succession of better accommodations and adequate classroom space. For their part, the sisters appreciated the bishop's care, "Nothing can equal the kind attentions of the bishop," wrote M. Xaverius Lynch.[33] It is obvious that the bishop was keenly aware of the debt of gratitude he owed these brave young women and of the responsibilities he had assumed in their regard. In a letter to the superior of the Presentation

---

30. Consedine, *A Listening Journey*, pp. 275–276.

31. Paul O'Neill, *A Seaport Legacy: The Story of St. John's, Newfoundland*, vol. 2 (Erin, ON: Press Porcepic, 1976), p. 788.

32. Fleming to O'Connell, June 11, 1844, "Letters on the State of Religion in Newfoundland," AASJ, 103/2/27.

33. M. Xaverius Lynch to Reverend Mother, Galway, 1833. "Sesquicentenary Souvenir" (Presentation Convent, Galway), 1965, p. 16, Archives of the Presentation Sisters, Galway (henceforth APSG).

Convent in Galway just prior to the departure of the sisters from Ireland, he wrote: "I feel a load of care and trouble fall from my shoulders, and inspired by the most lively confidence that God will grant me now that favour which I humbly and fervently pray for, *every opportunity of contributing to the spiritual and temporal happiness of these my dear Sisters, for His greater honor and glory.*"[34]

Bishop Fleming had great confidence in the ability and dedication of the Presentation Sisters. That he took seriously his position as the ecclesiastical superior of the community is evident. M. Xavcrius Lynch wrote, "The bishop expects a great deal from us, he never lets us forget that we are nuns and he our Superior."[35] In light of some unfavourable comments concerning Fleming's dealings with, among others, the Sisters of Mercy,[36] it is interesting to note how the Presentation Sisters regarded him. The bishop's concept of his responsibilities toward the religious in his jurisdiction did not upset these kind-hearted and level-headed women to any perceptible degree. Apparently, they were prepared to put up with a certain degree of episcopal pomposity. In fact, they seem to have had no problems maintaining cordial relations with the hotheaded and impetuous prelate. Letters written by the sisters spoke of their respect and affection for their frequently beleaguered bishop and evidence a tender concern and solicitude for him in his ceaseless efforts to secure the rights of Catholic citizens. In a letter of January 1834, M. Xaverius Lynch wrote:

> His only breathing seems to be for the good of Religion and the salvation of souls. He stayed up all night with two men who were to be executed. . . . We sometimes think he will be famished with the cold for in the most severe weather and the snow coming down in flakes, he will be with the workmen in the open air and perhaps will not eat a bit until 5 or 6 o'clock and sometimes not then itself. We wonder how he lives for he takes no care of himself, his whole heart being on the good of Religion.[37]

34. Fleming to Rev. Mother Superior, August 5, 1833, cited in Howley, *Ecclesiastical History*, p. 286.
35. M. Xaverius Lynch to Reverend Mother, Galway, 1833, "Sesquicentenary Souvenir," p. 18, APSG.
36. Killerby, *Frayne*, pp. 68–77.
37. M. Xaverius Lynch to Ann, January 26, 1834, "Sesquicentenary Souvenir," p. 18, APSG.

Well-pleased with the success of his venture in establishing the Presentation Order in Newfoundland, Bishop Fleming turned his attention to another problem that had exercised his patience and troubled his conscience for many years. He expressed this concern in a letter to Archdeacon O'Connell of Dublin. The bishop wrote, "I saw that so far I had only provided for the religious instruction of a portion of my people, and I sighed over the wants of the more respectable, the more wealthy, and comfortable classes, because the want of good female schools even for these was deplorable."[38] Fleming went on to describe what he called "the laxity" that prevailed amongst middle-class Catholics who, to curry favour with members of the professional classes, most of whom were Protestants, made a practice of attending religious services of other denominations. This was something that was strictly forbidden to Roman Catholics in those days. The bishop complained:

> Yet from the aping after gentility, particularly amongst those who wish to be considered as respectable Catholic young ladies, you would be astonished to behold their eagerness to show themselves off at a Protestant ceremony, or to any little Protestant that may present himself.
>
> Thus it was incumbent upon me, by every exertion in my power, to apply a remedy to this evil, to raise the character of Catholicity, to give it a position in public estimation that it had not before; and therefore, as no school had ever been established in Newfoundland where respectable young Catholic ladies could receive a good and religious education, I determined, as the means best calculated to accomplish this end, to introduce a community of nuns of the Order of Mercy, whose rule would permit them to keep a pension school.[39]

Lack of educational opportunities for the more affluent members of his flock was not the only motive that inspired Fleming to turn to Catherine McAuley in search of the Sisters of Mercy for his diocese. The compassionate

---

38. Fleming to O'Connell, February 19, 1844, "Letters on the State of Religion in Newfoundland," AASJ, 103/2/27.

39. Ibid.

bishop felt keenly the sufferings of the sick poor among his flock who were so vulnerable to the various epidemics of typhus and other contagious diseases that frequently afflicted the people of St. John's.[40] Thus, the advantage of introducing into his diocese a community of religious not bound by enclosure and whose Rule identified the visitation of the sick as one of their main duties was not lost on Bishop Fleming.[41]

Having resolved to establish a convent of Sisters of Mercy in his diocese, the bishop presented his plans to Catherine McAuley. Apparently, he was acquainted with the foundress, for an early Mercy historian referred to him as her "warm friend,"[42] and Catherine, in a letter to M. Teresa White, identified him as "my Bishop."[43] How close the friendship was between Catherine and Fleming, or of what duration, is not known. Fleming's brother John was a member of St. Andrew's Parish where two of Catherine's friends and advisors, Father Edward Armstrong and Dr. Michael Blake, had been pastors.[44]

It is conceivable that when he was in Dublin during this period, Bishop Fleming would have visited his brother and heard of the Sisters of Mercy;[45] for a few years later, John Fleming's daughter Anne joined the community at

---

40. Paul O'Neill, *The Oldest City: The Story of St. John's, Newfoundland*, vol. 1 (Erin, ON: Press Porcepic, 1974), pp. 293–94.

41. Fleming to Msgr. De Luca, April 2, 1842. AASJ, 103/3/28.

42. M. Austin Carroll wrote "Bishop Fleming was a warm friend of Mother McAuley, and thought of her as one who could give him efficient aid herself or through her daughters." Carroll, *Leaves*, vol. 3, p. 4.

43. M. Catherine McAuley to M. Teresa White, July 27, 1840, Sullivan, *Correspondence*, p. 281.

44. Sullivan, *Catherine McAuley*, pp. 12, 13. Savage, *McAuley*, pp. 48–49. I have been unable to discover primary evidence that John Fleming of St. Andrew's Parish, Dublin, father of M. Justina Fleming, was a brother of Bishop Fleming. Both M. Angela Bolster, ed., The *Correspondence of Catherine McAuley 1827–1841* (Cork and Ross: Sisters of Mercy, 1989), p. 140 and M. Ignatia Neumann, *Letters*, p. 314 claimed that M. Justina Fleming was the niece of Bishop Fleming. The tradition handed down by Sisters of Mercy in Dublin and Newfoundland supports the theory that John Fleming and the bishop of Newfoundland were brothers. Barring definitive evidence to the contrary, I have accepted the authenticity of this tradition.

45. In an email letter to the author on January 11, 2001, John FitzGerald pointed out that Fleming would likely have known of the Sisters of Mercy through his correspondence with More O'Ferrall, Archbishop Murray, the Franciscans, Carmelites, and other clergy in Dublin with whom he corresponded frequently.

WEAVERS OF THE TAPESTRY

Baggot Street.[46] Recent studies suggest that Bishop Fleming encouraged his niece to become a Sister of Mercy so that she would come to Newfoundland with the founding group.[47] Whether or not Fleming entertained such hopes for his niece, he had great confidence in his young protege, Marianne Creedon, a young Irish woman who had lived in St. John's since 1833.[48] He mentioned this young lady in a letter to Dr. O'Connell:

> . . . in compliance with this determination [i.e. to establish a Convent of Sisters of Mercy in Newfoundland] I sent to their parent institution, at Baggot Street, under the care of the sainted Foundress, the late Mrs. M'Cauley [sic], a young lady [i.e. Marianne Creedon] who had resided several years in Newfoundland, and who was intimately acquainted with the circumstances of the country, and the peculiar wants that I particularly needed to supply, to pass there her profession, together with such other ladies as should be inspired to accompany her, in order to found a Convent of Mercy at St. John's and open a school—a day school for such as could pay for their education—a school where children may be taught the elegant and fashionable accomplishments of the day, and at the same time may have their young minds properly imbued with the principles of religion.[49]

The question remains, however, when was the subject of a Newfoundland foundation first broached to Catherine McAuley? Before sending Marianne Creedon from Newfoundland to Dublin, the bishop must have had some assurance from Catherine that Marianne would be admitted as a postulant. He needed, also, Catherine's commitment to a foundation in his diocese and an agreement on the amount to be paid for Marianne's support dur-

---

46. Anne Fleming entered the Sisters of Mercy on February 5, 1839, received the habit on July 23, 1839, and was professed on August 19, 1841. She died December 12, 1841. Archives, Mercy International Centre, Dublin (henceforth AMIC).

47. Brother J. B. Darcy, *Fire upon the Earth: The Life and Times of Bishop Michael Anthony Fleming, O.S.F.* (St. John's, NL: Creative Book Publishing, 2003), p. 82.

48. Marianne Creedon came to Newfoundland in 1833 with her sister and brother-in-law, John Valentine Nugent. Nugent, originally from Waterford, was a personal friend of Fleming.

49. Fleming to O'Connell, February 19, 1844, AASJ, 103/2/27.

ing the novitiate. That such an arrangement was in place is clearly stated in a letter of the bishop to Cardinal Fransoni: "I have paid to the Sisters of Charity [*sic*][50] in Dublin the sum of £60 Sterling which is the stipend agreed on with them for the Novices whom I maintain in their convent, to come from there to Newfoundland."[51] Burke Savage noted:

> Two visits from the Right Reverend Michael Anthony Fleming, Vicar-Apostolic of Newfoundland, turned Catherine's eyes once more westward, this time across the Atlantic. Dr. Fleming cele-brated Mass for the Sisters in Baggot Street on 12th July [1840] and later earnestly begged Catherine to send a foundation to St. John's. With Birmingham already promised she could do nothing immediately, but agreed to prepare for it, and May or June of the following year was fixed provisionally."[52]

But by the time of this visit, Marianne Creedon, now Sister Mary Francis, had already begun her novitiate, having entered the Baggot Street convent on July 4, 1839, and been received as a novice on February 27, 1840. Therefore, one would assume that tentative arrangements for the Newfoundland foundation had been made some time prior to July 1839.[53]

---

50. On at least two occasions Bishop Fleming referred to the Sisters of Mercy as "Sisters of Charity."

51. Fleming to Cardinal Fransoni, August 28, 1840, AASJ, 103/1/18.

52. Savage, *McAuley*, p. 362. There is some doubt about the accuracy of the date, July 12, 1840. In a letter to Fransoni, August 28, 1840 (AASJ, 103/1/18), Fleming wrote that he "decided to embark this time for Ireland" and arrived in Cork on July 16. If this is so, then he could not have been in Dublin on July 12. It is clear that he visited Catherine McAuley sometime in July 1840, for in a letter to M. Teresa White, dated July 27, 1840, Catherine wrote, "Doctor Fleming (my Bishop) is quite pleased with his child." (Sullivan, *Correspondence*, p. 281). However, it appears that Fleming made a second visit to Baggot Street during the summer of 1840. The date of this second visit is more easily established, for Savage noted (*McAuley*, p. 317) that Bishop Fleming assisted Archbishop Murray at the ceremony of reception for the Birmingham novices on August 10, 1840.

53. Bishop Fleming visited Dublin in the summer of 1838. This was around the time that his niece, Anne Fleming, was making arrangements to enter the Baggot Street convent early the following year. It is interesting to speculate whether Bishop Fleming visited Catherine McAuley with his niece at this time. I am indebted to Brother J. B. Darcy for Bishop Fleming's chronology.

In the extract from Fleming's letter to Cardinal Fransoni, quoted above, it is interesting to note his use of the plural, "Novices." This raises the question of the identity of these novices. One was, of course, Marianne Creedon. It has been suggested that the other was Anne (M. Justina) Fleming.[54] Although these are reasonable inferences, so far no supportive primary evidence has been discovered. Whatever the bishop's hopes and plans were for his niece—if, indeed, she was his niece—they were doomed to disappointment, for less than four months after her profession on August 19, 1841, M. Justina Fleming died.[55]

In the absence of any contemporary documentation, many of these questions will remain unanswered. The student of Mercy history is forced to take the scanty evidence available and present a possible sequence of the events that occurred before the first contingent of Mercy Sisters departed from Ireland to brave the stormy Atlantic and the mists of "the fog-draped isle" of Newfoundland.[56]

Although Catherine McAuley left nothing in writing to show that she intended to go herself to St. John's, there is a strong oral tradition to that effect. This tradition is reinforced by the Mercy historian M. Austin Carroll ". . . the colony destined for St. John's did not set out this year (1841), and another had the honour of sending it, though the Foundress would gladly have been the first Sister of Mercy to set foot on American soil. Her arrangements, however, were made."[57] Bishop Fleming revealed these arrangements in his relatio to Propaganda Fide: "To obtain the Ladies of Mercy I visited the Parent House of Baggot St., Dublin, where I professed the Newfoundland Lady, and through the recommendation of the gifted Superior and Foundress of the Order in Ireland, Mrs. McAuley, I took the other three from amongst a number of volunteers in the House."[58] Fleming's assertion, "I professed the Newfoundland Lady" is open to question. He could not have been present at the actual ceremony of profession for, when M. Francis Creedon was pro-

54. Darcy, *Fire upon the Earth*, p. 210.

55. Sullivan, *Catherine McAuley*, p. 18.

56. A term used by M. Austin Carroll to describe Newfoundland. Carroll, *Leaves*, vol. 3, p. 22.

57. Carroll, *Leaves*, vol. 3, p. 15.

58. Fleming, Relatio to Propaganda Fide, November 26, 1844, AASJ, 103/2/27.

fessed in Dublin on August 19, 1841, Fleming was in Newfoundland. An explanation of the bishop's statement might be found in an article of the Mercy Rule
that stated: "When the Bishop is not at leisure to attend in person, the Superior
appointed by him shall officiate at the Reception of Sisters to the Habit and at
their Profession. . . . He shall sign the Acts of Profession."[59] There is no doubt
that M. Francis Creedon was professed for the Diocese of Newfoundland and
not for the Archdiocese of Dublin. It is possible that Fleming, who frequently
used Archbishop Murray as his agent,[60] would have regarded Murray as his
representative at the ceremony of profession and have seen no inconsistency in
claiming that he, Fleming, professed "the Newfoundland Lady." There was
plenty of opportunity for him to have signed the Acts of Profession when he
returned to Dublin in November 1841. Whether or not he did so is another
part of the story that has been lost forever.

   The most interesting statement in the bishop's report to Rome is found
in the following sentence, ". . . *through the recommendation of the gifted Superior and
Foundress* . . . I took the other three from amongst a number of volunteers in the
House."[61] Thus, it appears that Catherine McAuley had a direct hand in the
selection of Newfoundland's founding community. The sisters chosen for this,
the first overseas mission, were, in addition to M. Francis Creedon, M. Ursula
Frayne, M. Rose Lynch, and a postulant, Maria Supple from Dublin. The choice
of Miss Supple was in line with Catherine's custom of sending a postulant along
with a founding community so that, within a few months of the establishment
of the convent, a ceremony of reception would take place. In this way she hoped
to attract other young women to join the community. It is doubtful that
Catherine McAuley would have agreed to the Newfoundland foundation if she
had known of Fleming's refusal to admit native Newfoundlanders to the religious life or to the priesthood.[62] However, it is easy to understand why

59. Sullivan, *Catherine McAuley*, p. 317.
60. John FitzGerald, conversation with author, June 9, 2002.
61. See n. 60 above. (Italics mine.)
62. FitzGerald, "Conflict and Culture," p. 100. FitzGerald stated, "Fleming's refusal of Newfoundland-born clergy and religious placed an Irish stamp on Newfoundland Roman Catholicism which survived well into the twentieth century."

Catherine recommended Ursula Frayne and Rose Lynch, for both sisters had the experience of going on foundations, and Catherine seemed to have had a high regard for each of them. Thus, it might be helpful to include a brief account of their careers up to May 2, 1842.

Clara Mary Frayne, the youngest of several children of Robert and Bridget Frayne, was born in Dublin in October 1816 or 1817.[63] Her father was a prosperous businessman, and Clara grew up in very comfortable circumstances. She was well-educated and was "a proficient embroiderer and pianist."[64] On July 1, 1834, at the age of sixteen, she entered the Mercy community at Baggot Street. Six months later, she was received as a novice and given the name, Mary Ursula.[65] On January 25, 1837, she made her profession as a Sister of Mercy. In her biography of M. Ursula Frayne, Catherine Killerby mentioned that the newly professed religious chose as her motto, "But Jesus was silent,"[66] a maxim that Ursula seemingly had great difficulty in observing in her future dealings with the clergy.

We are told by those who knew her later in life that Ursula Frayne was rather tall and well-built, with fair complexion and blue eyes. In her dealings with others, she was a very practical woman, and later memories recall her as charming, gracious, and unfailingly gentle. This gentleness must have been learned over the years, for in some of her letters she displays very human touches of impatience and intolerance. Her letters reveal also a sense of humour and an eye for the ridiculous, along with common sense and a pulsing energy. This energy found expression in her willingness to venture into unknown territory and to explore new ideas.

While still a very junior sister, Ursula participated in the challenge and excitement of new foundations. In 1837, the year of her profession, she was a

---

63. Killerby, *Frayne*, p. 16. Killerby pointed out that Ursula herself gave two different possibilities for the year of her birth. In 1846, she declared she was nineteen years old at the time of her profession, and in 1857, she wrote that she was twenty at the time.

64. Ibid., p. 17. On p. 283, n. 10, Killerby referred to an anonymous typescript in the Archives at Booterstown that states that Clara was educated by governesses and in a private lay school.

65. January 20, 1835, AMIC.

66. Killerby, *Frayne*, p. 22.

member of the Mercy foundation in Carlow with M. Frances Warde. The foundress hinted that she was not altogether satisfied with M. Ursula at that point and wanted her to receive further training from the wise and talented M. Frances Warde. In a letter to Frances, Catherine wrote, "I expect to find Sister Ursula very improved from what I see of the effects of Carlow. Sister Mary Teresa would never tire of speaking of the instruction and advantages she received there."[67] However, after five months in Carlow, Ursula became ill, and in August of the same year, she was sent to Kingstown to recover. Even when she returned to Carlow, her health was a cause of concern. In a letter to M. Frances Warde, Catherine wrote, "Please God Sister M. Ursula will be soon quite restored."[68] It may have been because of Ursula's fragile health that in June 1838, Catherine assigned her to the new foundation in Booterstown by the sea and named her superior. The convent in Booterstown, established as a branch house of Baggot Street, remained under Catherine McAuley's direction. As local superior, Ursula was responsible for the everyday matters of community living but exercised her authority under Catherine's supervision. It appears that from the beginning, the foundress recognized Ursula's potential as an administrator. On a more personal and informal level, the busy foundress and the twenty-two-year-old superior delighted in exchanging humorous little verses dealing with everyday events.

M. Ursula Frayne remained at Booterstown until October 1841 when she returned to Baggot Street. Ursula's former novice mistress, M. de Pazzi Delany, now the assistant and acting superior during Catherine's illness, commissioned Ursula to notify the superiors of the other Mercy convents that Catherine was seriously ill, and it was Ursula who wrote to inform them of Catherine's death.

It was not quite six months after the death of the foundress that Ursula set sail from Ireland bound for Newfoundland. Accompanying her were Maria Supple, M. Francis Creedon, and M. Rose Lynch.

---

67. M. Catherine McAuley to Sister M. Frances Warde, March 24, 1838. Sullivan, *Correspondence*, p. 129.
68. M. Catherine McAuley to Sister M. Frances Warde, November 22, 1837. Ibid., p. 104. Killerby mentioned that throughout her life M. Ursula was frequently unwell, but the nature of her illness has never been identified.

Catherine Lynch was born in the parish of St. Paul's, Dublin, daughter of Richard and Margaret Lynch. Little is known of her childhood, but the fact that she was recommended for the Newfoundland foundation to teach in a pension school suggests that she had received a very good education. She entered the Baggot Street convent on July 3, 1838, was received the following January and given the name, Mary Rose. Catherine wrote of this ceremony of reception as follows: "Dr. Blake is to perform the ceremonies here on the 21st. . . . Mr. Lynch is to Preach."[69] This Mr. Lynch, chaplain to the Baggot Street convent, is mentioned in several of Catherine's letters. Apparently, he was a close relative of M. Rose, either her brother or her uncle.[70] In one letter, Catherine mentioned that M. Rose met a priest who was curate to her uncle, but on another occasion, she wrote, "Mr. Lynch called late this day and said he would leave town for Carlow at one tomorrow, but finding from his sister that he may go at eight, I am come back to my corner after all are gone to Bed—to write a few lines to my poor old child."[71]

During the first fourteen months of M. Rose's novitiate, M. de Pazzi Delany was the novice mistress. However, in March 1840, fearing that M. de Pazzi was inclined to be too strict, Catherine appointed M. Cecilia Marmion to this position, and Rose remained under her direction until her profession on December 15, 1840. Twelve days later, on December 27, 1840, Catherine McAuley whisked her off to the new foundation at Birr and named her assistant to the superior, M. Aloysius Scott.[72] It was in Birr that Rose Lynch, through her quick wit and sense of humour, endeared herself to the foundress, who mentioned her in several letters written from Birr. Shortly after their arrival in Birr, Catherine took M. Rose on a visit to a family that had suffered a recent bereavement: "Sister Mary Rose & I walked one mile and half yester-

69. M. Catherine McAuley to Sister M. Elizabeth Moore, January 13, 1839. Sullivan, *Corresondence*, p. 180. On p. 176, n. 7, Sullivan suggested that this Mr. Lynch might be a brother of M. Rose Lynch.

70. M. Catherine McAuley to Sister M. Cecilia Marmion, January 15, 1841. Ibid., p. 346.

71. M. Catherine McAuley to Sister M. Frances Warde, January 6, 1839. Ibid., p. 176. See n. 70 above.

72. M. Catherine McAuley to Sister M. deSales White, December 7, 1840. Ibid., p. 326.

day in all the snow, to visit an unfortunate family."[73] In another letter, Catherine referred to Rose's small stature and fair complexion. Catherine mentioned, too, the difficulty Rose had in controlling her tendency to burst out laughing when faced with some of the idiosyncrasies of the people she visited.[74] In her last letter to Birr, October 4, 1841, Catherine referred to Rose as "my own old child," and chided M. Rose and some of the other sisters for not writing to her.[75] A little over a month later, the foundress was dead. M. Rose was still in Birr, but she returned to Baggot Street in February 1842 to prepare for the first big adventure of her life, the Newfoundland foundation.[76]

This picture of M. Rose Lynch gives a clue to Catherine's reason for recommending her for the Newfoundland mission—she had a sense of humour, had no fear of new foundations, and apparently got on well with the sisters at Birr. There is nothing in this picture to indicate the bleak and tragic future that awaited this light-hearted young woman.

Marianne Creedon, the younger daughter of John and Ellen Creedon of Coolowen, County Cork,[77] was baptized on December 5, 1811.[78] Nothing is known of her early childhood except that her father died in the summer of 1817 when she was not yet six years of age.[79] Five years later, on May 12, 1822, her older sister, Ellen, married John Valentine Nugent of King Street,

73. M. Catherine McAuley to Sister M. Cecilia Marmion, January 4, 1841. Ibid., p. 341.
74. M. Catherine McAuley to Sister Teresa Carton, January 19, 1841. Ibid., p. 349.
75. M. Catherine McAuley to Sister Mary Aloysius Scott, October 4, 1841. Ibid., p. 447.
76. Carroll, *Leaves*, vol. 1, p. 439.
77. The Register at Mercy International Centre (MIC) Baggot Street incorrectly spells the name, "Colowen."
78. The Register at MIC spells the baptismal name of M. Francis Creedon, "Marianne." The Baptismal Register of St. Mary's Parish, Cork, records the birth of Mary Ann Creedon, daughter of John Creedon and Mary Foley. This is the only baptismal record discovered so far that corresponds to what is known of the origins of M. Francis Creedon. The discrepancy in the mother's name can be explained by the custom of the time of attaching the name "Mary" to female children.
79. *The Limerick Chronicle*, August 13, 1817, "Died in York Street, Cork, Mr. John Creedon." York Street, which is mentioned in the 1817 directory, is still in existence and was off King Street, renamed McCurtain Street. The same 1817 Cork City directory has the following entry, "Creedon, John, gent., York Street." I am indebted to Michael O'Connell of the Cork Genealogical Society for this information.

Waterford.[80] There are several reasons for concluding that after Ellen Creedon married John V. Nugent, she brought her little sister to live with her in Waterford.

The first hint that Marianne Creedon may have resided with the Nugents in Waterford is found in the baptismal records of St. Patrick's Parish and of the Cathedral Parish, Waterford. These records identify Mary Ann Creedon as a sponsor to three of the Nugent children: John, baptized January 5, 1825; Ellen, baptized September 14, 1826; and Agnes, baptized January 17, 1830.[81] A further hint that Marianne Creedon resided in Waterford is found in an item in a St. John's newspaper that was reprinted from the *Waterford Mirror*: "We have advices from Newfoundland to the 7th inst. A private letter of that date states that 'Dr. Fleming arrived in St. John's . . . with . . . five ladies of the Sisters of Charity [*sic*]. It is expected that the Right Reverend Prelate intends to found a house of that order in St. John's, and that Miss Creeden [*sic*], *late of your city* is to be the Superioress. . . . Your old friend, Father Troy, *also of Waterford*, lives on an island in this bay, called Merasheen.'"[82]

Although no record of the death of Marianne's mother, Ellen Creedon, has been found, it would seem unlikely that a widow residing in Cork would have been able to provide her daughter with the superior educational opportunities that we know Marianne enjoyed. The Nugents, on the other hand, were all highly educated, and John V. Nugent was an educator by profession.[83] Growing up in such a family would account for Marianne's well-rounded educational development. Finally, when John V. Nugent and his family moved to St. John's, Newfoundland, in 1833, Marianne Creedon came with them, for her name appeared in an advertisement placed by John V. Nugent in a local newspaper:

---

80. In a letter to the author, March 15, 2000, Michael O'Connell, Cork Genealogical Society, wrote, "Some further information relates to the marriage of the eldest daughter Ellen, of the late John Creedon on the 12th May, 1822 to Mr. Nugent, King St., Waterford."

81. Baptismal Register 1817, St. Patrick's Parish, Waterford, pp. 83, 112. Baptismal Register, Cathedral Parish, Waterford, Register B/1819–38, p. 113.

82. *The Patriot and Terra Nova Herald*, July 13, 1842, p. 3. (Italics mine.)

83. John V. Nugent was president of the Waterford Literary Society for several years. He claimed, also, to have had legal training.

MR. NUGENT

Takes leave to acquaint his friends and the public generally, that he has, for the summer season, taken the House of Mr. Houlton (opposite the Ordnance Yard), where he will open his ACADEMY for Young Gentlemen on MONDAY, the 10th inst. . . .

On the same day, Mrs. and Miss NUGENT will be ready to receive young Ladies at their School at Mrs. LITTLE'S, Water-street, where they will be instructed in the Italian, French and English Languages, Writing and Arithmetic, Geography, History, etc., Needle and Fancy Work, Mezzo-Tinto Drawing, Oriental Tinting, Mother of Pearl and Setim-wood Inlaying, Wax-Works, etc., etc.

Miss NUGENT and Miss CREEDON will give lessons in Music to a few young Ladies.

No Summer Vacation.[84]

It was by Bishop Fleming's invitation that John V. Nugent came to St. John's,[85] and the friendship that had existed between the two since 1827[86] became even closer. John V. Nugent was not only an educator. After his arrival in St. John's, he made a name for himself as a writer, newspaper editor and proprietor, politician, and finally High Sheriff of Newfoundland.

Living as a member of John V. Nugent's family, Marianne Creedon was aware of the burning desire of Bishop Fleming to extend the benefits of Catholic education to the more affluent members of his flock. For his part, the bishop saw in this talented young woman the means of achieving his aim of securing a group of women religious whose rules allowed them to teach the daughters of the more well-to-do citizens and, at the same time, care for the needs of the sick poor.

Whatever conversations took place between Bishop Fleming and Marianne Creedon, the end result was that between them they convinced

84. *The Public Ledger*, June 14, 1833, p. 3.

85. *Waterford Mirror*, April 6, 1833, p. 4. During a speech given at a dinner held in Nugent's honour, the speaker mentioned that Nugent is going to Newfoundland on the express invitation of the bishop of Newfoundland.

86. FitzGerald, "Conflict and Culture," p. 142.

Catherine McAuley that Marianne was indeed being called by God to become a Sister of Mercy. It was understood from the beginning that after her profession, Marianne Creedon would return to St. John's and establish a convent of the Sisters of Mercy in Newfoundland.[87] With this in mind, Marianne Creedon sailed back to Ireland and entered the Baggot Street community on July 4, 1839. Seven months later, on February 27, 1840, she received the habit of a Sister of Mercy and the name, Mary Francis. It is interesting to note that from February to December 1840, M. Francis Creedon and M. Rose Lynch were in the novitiate together.

Little is known of M. Francis's early life, but thanks to the efforts of M. Austin Carroll,[88] a picture of her emerges through the recollections of the women with whom she lived in Baggot Street. Carroll quoted "the late superior of the Belfast convent" who wrote of M. Francis: "When I entered the novitiate in 1841 I found there Sister M. Frances [sic] Creedon, who had been sent there some years before to prepare for the Newfoundland mission. She was a most exemplary religious, a great lover of poverty, full of zeal and piety, which made me very glad to be appointed to visit the sick and perform other duties with her."[89] In contrast to this very "edifying" description, M. Austin Carroll, paraphrasing what she was told by other sisters who knew Francis, portrayed a very human and attractive woman. She wrote, ". . . her (i.e. Francis's) large-hearted friendship, which was a blessing and a support to those who enjoyed it, her beautiful simplicity and thorough unselfishness, caused her to be loved and revered."[90] M. Austin went on to describe M. Francis as a gift-

---

87. The same procedure had been followed by Bishop Griffeths of London who, in 1838, requested Catherine McAuley to accept two young ladies as novices so that they would return and establish the Order in Bermondsey. Similarly, in 1840, Bishop Walsh of Birmingham sent two young ladies to Baggot Street so that they would return and establish a convent of Mercy in that city.

88. In preparation for writing her series, *Leaves from the Annals of the Sisters of Mercy*, M. Austin Carroll visited all the convents of Mercy in Ireland and wrote to other convents around the world, gathering information for her books. I am indebted to M. Hermenia Muldrey, the biographer of M. Austin Carroll, for this information.

89. Carroll, *Leaves*, vol. 3, p. 21.

90. Ibid.

ed and beloved teacher, a person of culture and sensitivity, and a woman who gave unreservedly of herself in service to poor and suffering humanity.

These were the three young women charged with the task of establishing the first community of Sisters of Mercy in the New World: the determined, dedicated, and talented Ursula Frayne; the light-hearted and fun-loving Rose Lynch; and the gentle, kindly, and courageous Francis Creedon. Only one remained to be named of those who were to sail on the first overseas mission, a postulant. This decision was left to Catherine's successor, M. de Pazzi Delany.

The career of Miss Supple in the Mercy community was very brief, indeed. She was recommended for the Newfoundland mission by an unidentified clergyman in Ireland. In a letter from Fleming beginning with the salutation, "Very Rev. & Dear Sir," the bishop wrote:

> My principal object in thus troubling you with a line is to convey to you my thanks for your goodness in recommending Miss Supple to this mission. She seems to me to possess all the requisites to enable her to fulfill the duties of the Order. Her mildness and engaging demeanour will prove a great recommendation to the confidence of the poor creatures whom her duty calls upon her to visit, while her musical talent and other educational endowments will greatly enhance the value of their school. [91]

The bishop's reference to the duty of visiting the poor makes it clear that Maria Supple arrived in St. John's as a member of the Mercy and not the Presentation community. At that time, the Presentation Sisters were bound by the rule of enclosure and exercised their ministry within the confines of the school and convent. Perhaps some inherent instability or something that happened on the voyage caused Maria to change her mind about entering the Mercy novitiate. Immediately on her arrival in St. John's, she left the Mercy Sisters and was accepted as a postulant by the Presentation Sisters. The Annals of the

---

91. Fleming to Very Rev. and Dear Sir, Feast of St. John the Baptist [June 24], 1842, AASJ 103/1/8. Although the recipient of the letter is not identified, the greeting is standard for a bishop in the 1800s.

Presentation Convent in St. John's note that after a few months' trial, Maria Supple was dismissed as being unsuited to religious life.[92] Another source indicates that Miss Supple became mentally ill and was obliged to return to Ireland.[93] In a letter to Bishop Fleming early in 1843, M. de Pazzi Delany told him that she had cautioned the Sisters of Mercy in St. John's not to allow any letters to leave the convent without the usual inspection of the superior. She stated as her reason for this, "observations we heard on letters coming from Miss Supple."[94] Nothing further is known of this enigmatic young lady. One hopes that she recovered from whatever illness she suffered and that she settled down to enjoy a full and satisfying life at home in Ireland.

Bishop Fleming was in Ireland from December 1841 until April 1842. While he was there, plans for the Newfoundland mission were finalized and arrangements made for the sisters to travel to St. John's. In a letter to Monsignor De Luca in Rome, the bishop wrote, "I have booked passage on a vessel to bring to Newfoundland a community of Nuns of the Order of Mercy . . . for the education of the rich and for the assistance of the sick and the indigent."[95]

The days between the announcement that arrangements for the mission had been completed and the actual day of their departure for St. John's must have passed quickly for the four young missionaries. For three of them, there was the pain of parting from family and friends coupled with the excitement of sailing off into the unknown. For Francis Creedon, however, there was the anticipated joy of being reunited with her beloved sister, Ellen, with the Nugent children, and even with her irascible brother-in-law, John V. Nugent.[96]

92. Annals, Presentation Convent, St. John's, 1833, Archives of the Presentation Sisters, St. John's (henceforth APSSJ).

93. Unsigned note in the Archives of the Sisters of Mercy, St. John's (henceforth ASMSJ).

94. M. de Pazzi Delany to Bishop Fleming, Dublin Diocesan Archives (henceforth DDA), Murray Papers, AB 3/32/1, (1843–44) Addenda.

95. Fleming to De Luca, April 2, 1842, AASJ, 103/3/38. Because the Mercy Sisters were not an enclosed Order, the bishop did not feel it necessary to provide a separate ship for them as he had done for the Presentation Sisters.

96. The fiery temperament of John V. Nugent is revealed in his frequent letters to newspapers both in Waterford, Ireland, and in St. John's.

She was already familiar with the narrow, almost perpendicular streets of St. John's and the picturesque harbour held in the secure embrace of surrounding hills that lean against the sky. Did she describe, over and over again, that harbour with its flotilla of boats whose white sails made a counterpoint in colour with the stern, forbidding cliffs that guard the entrance and the dark green of the hills a mile or so inshore? Did she mark off the days on a calendar against the day of her return?

In the days leading up to May 2, 1842,[97] the date set for the departure of the missionaries, Baggot Street was a beehive of activity as friends and relatives flocked to the convent for a final visit. The departure itself was noted in *Weekly Orthodox Journal*:

> Wednesday the following clergymen and religious ladies sailed in the *Sir Walter Scott*, from Kingstown Harbour, for their mission in Newfoundland: Rev. John Regan, of the Newfoundland mission (formerly of Ireland); Rev. Jas. Gleeson, Waterford; Rev. Matthew Scanlan, Cashel; Rev. John O'Neill, ditto; Rev. John Cullen, Wexford; Sister Mary Teresa [sic] of the House of Mercy, Baggot Street; Sister Mary Rose, ditto; Sister Mary Ursula, ditto;
> Miss Maria Supple, Dublin, Miss Catherine Waters, ditto; and Miss Catherine Phelan, ditto. Previous to their departure they were visited by several of their friends and relatives. This ship carries out nearly one thousand tons of finely cut stone for the splendid new cathedral of St. John [sic], Newfoundland.[98]

As the sisters strained for a last glimpse of their beloved Ireland, the first qualms of seasickness turned their thoughts to more urgent matters.

97. The Register held in the Archives at Mercy International Centre in Dublin noted the date of the departure of the Newfoundland community, "II May, 1842." The person who made the entry was accustomed to using Roman numerals when writing dates. In later years this was interpreted as indicating the 11th of May, rather than the actual date, which was May 2nd, a fact confirmed in another section of the Register that recorded the information on M. Francis Creedon. See chapter two, n. 5.

98. *Weekly Orthodox Journal* 14. (London and Dublin), May 14, 1842, p. 315. The writer incorrectly identified the first sister named as Sister Mary Teresa. It was, of course, Sister M. Francis Creedon. The two young ladies, Catherine Phelan and Catherine Waters, were on their way to join the Presentation Convent in St. John's.

Nevertheless, we are told that once they became accustomed to the ship's motion, the travellers enjoyed the experience of the sea voyage across the Atlantic.[99] As the *Sir Walter Scott* approached Newfoundland, the sisters may have watched the stately procession of majestic icebergs that visit the waters along the east coast of the island during the spring and early summer. Perhaps they were lucky enough to catch a glimpse of whales in their pursuit of the millions of silver caplin on their annual visit to the beaches of Newfoundland.

Early on the morning of June 3, the wind changed, and a soft westerly breeze turned the restless sea into a blue expanse of water, with waves dancing in the sun.[100] Word went around the ship that land had been sighted some hours before dawn and that the long journey was almost at an end. The sisters went on deck to catch sight of their future home. In the distance they could see the long, rocky face of Newfoundland. Francis Creedon had seen it all before, but for the other three, the sight of the craggy headlands and the seemingly unbroken line of forbidding rock may have filled them with dismay. They were accustomed to the gentle green hills and valleys of Ireland. Now they were faced with what seemed to be a stern, unyielding land. As the ship drew closer, they were aware of small pinnacles of rock thrusting up through the surface of the waves. Ahead of them, the rugged cliffs had been transformed by the sun into a multicoloured wall of blue, gray, silver, and black. Soon they were able to distinguish a narrow opening in the wall of rock that surrounded their new home. One of the sailors may have explained that this opening was called "The Narrows." They must have been disappointed when they were told that, because of the direction of the wind, they could not enter the harbour until the following day. However, the impatient Bishop Fleming was not about to wait a moment longer than necessary to escort his new community to their temporary home. He hired a pilot boat and went out to bring them ashore himself.[101] It is doubtful that his plan

---

99. Carroll, *Leaves*, vol. 3, p. 16.

100. Bishop Fleming's account of the arrival of the Sisters of Mercy states that the wind was offshore, i.e., in a westerly direction. M. Austin Carroll mentions that June 3 was a bright, sunny day. Carroll, *Leaves*, vol 3, p. 16.

101. According to Rosemary Ryan, RSM, the St. John's Harbour pilot who brought the Sisters of Mercy safely to port was her great-great grandfather, Thomas Ryan.

received an enthusiastic response from the sisters. They eyed with consternation the frail rope ladder descending from the deck of the *Sir Walter Scott* to a small boat tossing around on the surface of the restless ocean. While the bishop urged them on with cries of encouragement, one can imagine each sister nervously approaching the rail and cautiously climbing down the ladder into the waiting arms of a brawny sailor. The bishop wrote, "In a short time [we] got all on board the boats, although from the great height of the vessel and the heaving of the sea, it was attained with some difficulty to get the ladies safely and comfortably placed there."[102]

The experience of entering St. John's Harbour is memorable, even today. The towering hills with stunted fir and spruce trees clinging to the rock give no hint of what lies a mile or so ahead. It was not until their boat had entered the Narrows that, suddenly, the sisters could see the whole town of St. John's laid out in the form of an amphitheatre, the streets rising one above the other on the northeast side of the harbour. Bishop Fleming described the town as it was seen by the sisters in 1842:

> The aspect of a fishing hut perched in a nook among hanging and perpendicular rocks which for some time puzzle you to discover a means of approach to the [shore]. The wide spread fish flake, here carried over the rocks and even over the sea, and there with its myriad of props in shores supporting over the dwelling house and extensive stores; again the stages where fish is taken in from the boats running far out upon the sea in sheltered coves.
>
> [The little sheds] with grass on top to keep out the rain and sun—all of these appear in the eyes of the European visitant exquisitely picturesque, and they failed not to excite the greatest interest particularly in the Sisters of Mercy who, not improbably, were filled with the thought that, amid scenes such as these, and amongst the poor who dwelt thus in positions the very approach to which, particularly in winter, was pregnant with danger, their future destinies were cast.[103]

---

102. Letter from Bishop Fleming to an unnamed clergyman, Feast of St. John [June 24], 1842, AASJ, 103/1/ 8.

103. Ibid. Some words and phrases in this letter are illegible. The words in brackets are suggested by the context.

When at last they arrived at the wharf, the sisters were a little over-whelmed, perhaps, at the throngs of people gathered to welcome them. They, and the two young ladies destined for the Presentation Convent, were intro-duced to Mrs. Tobin, who brought them to her home to await the bishop's car-riage. After a brief visit to the Presentation Convent, where they took leave of the Presentation postulants and Maria Supple, the bishop escorted them to the church to offer prayers of thanksgiving for their safe arrival. After that, they were brought to the bishop's own home on Henry Street where they resided until their convent was ready for occupancy. The fact that the Sisters of Mercy were housed in the bishop's own residence is confirmed in a letter from Fleming to Dr. O'Connell in which he stated, ". . . the Sisters of Mercy taking up their abode at my residence which I had given up to them pro temper, until I should have prepared for them a more suitable and comfortable dwelling."[104] In another letter from Fleming to O'Connell, August 1846, the bishop identi-fied his residence as being next to the chapel, "situated a little north of Duckworth Street."[105] On yet another occasion the bishop stated that, for a few months after their arrival, the Sisters of Mercy lived in his own home, which "I gave up altogether to them"[106] until their convent was ready.

That evening as they gathered for the prescribed hour of recreation, the sisters had a special reason to celebrate, for the day that saw the end of one journey and the beginning of a new and exciting future was the Feast of the Sacred Heart.[107] Perhaps in their excitement, they forgot the words of Catherine McAuley to Frances Warde, "If they should have a new foundation—it will not be without the cross."[108]

---

104. Fleming to O'Connell, February 19, 1844, AASJ, 103/2/25.

105. Fleming to O'Connell, August 18, 1846, AASJ, 103/2/27.

106. Fleming, Relatio to Propaganda Fide, November 1846, AASJ, 103/2/27.

107. Catherine McAuley directed the Sisters of Mercy to practice special devotion to the Person of Jesus under the title "Sacred Heart." "Rule and Constitutions of the Religious Sisters of Mercy," part 1, chapter 15, article 3, cited in Sullivan, *Catherine McAuley*, p. 309.

108. M. Catherine McAuley to Sister M. Frances Warde, November 9, 1840. Sullivan, *Correspondence*, p. 316.

CHAPTER THREE

AS IT WAS IN THE BEGINNING

This is your life, joys and sorrows mingled, one succeeding the other.

Catherine McAuley[1]

aturday, June 4, 1842, marked the beginning of the ministry of the Sisters of Mercy in Newfoundland. Already they had lost one member of their group, the prospective postulant, for as noted previously, Maria Supple went to the Presentation Convent. After thirty days at sea they had become so accustomed to the rolling and pitching of the ship that it was difficult for them to adjust to the sensation of being on solid ground. The bishop, a seasoned traveller himself, took this into account when he urged the sisters to take a little time to settle into their temporary home. The fact that their first day in St. John's was a Saturday gave them time to unpack their few belongings and take stock of their new surroundings. The next day, the first Sunday of the month, was by Rule a day of retreat that allowed them time to reflect on the ministry to which they were being called. With the impatience of youth, they were anxious to begin their work without any delay. They were conscious, too, of Catherine McAuley's advice, "Commence the visitation as soon as possible."[2]

---

1. M. Catherine McAuley to M. Frances Warde, May 28, 1841. Sullivan, *Correspondence*, p. 401.

2. M. Catherine McAuley to M. Frances Warde, November 24, 1840. Ibid., p. 323. Catherine's advice was in connection with the foundation at Wexford.

And so, with the bishop's permission and blessing, the sisters began their work on the following day, Monday, June 6.

A few weeks later, Bishop Fleming wrote, "They [the Sisters of Mercy] are now actively engaged in their sacred employ, daily visiting the sick. Indeed, so pressing were they to be permitted to enter upon their labours immediately on their arrival, that I was obliged to consent to it on the subsequent Monday."[3] It was all so new to them. The little streets seemed to meander hither and yon, apparently without rhyme or reason—and always at a perpendicular angle. It was quite different from what they had been used to in Dublin. Until their school was ready, they decided to devote all their time to the visitation. If they could provide some education to the poor in their homes while attending to sick members of a family, then so much the better. The sisters, however, were not the only ones having to contend with a new set of circumstances.

Bishop Fleming, when he arranged with the foundress, Catherine McAuley, to establish a Mercy convent in his diocese, fondly imagined that the superior of the new community, M. Francis Creedon, would be his protege. A passage in a local newspaper stated, "It is expected that the Right Reverend Prelate intends to found a house of that order [i.e. Sisters of Mercy] in St. John's, and that Miss Creeden [sic] . . . is to be the Superioress."[4] It appears that someone at Baggot Street thought the same. The entry in the Register at Baggot Street recorded of M. Francis Creedon, "She left this House on the 2nd of May, 1842, having entered the Order for the purpose of establishing a Convent in that mission."[5] But when preparations for the Newfoundland mission had been completed, it appears that M. de Pazzi Delany ignored any arrangements that may have been made between Catherine McAuley and Bishop Fleming and appointed someone else as the superior of the new foundation.

---

3. Fleming to Rev. and Dear Sir, Feast of St. John [June 24], 1842, AASJ, 103/1/8.
4. *The Patriot and Terra Nova Herald*, July 13, 1842, p. 3.
5. Register, AMIC.

The identity of the first superior of the Newfoundland mission has never been satisfactorily settled. It must be acknowledged that the weight of oral tradition, both in St. John's and in Dublin, identifies M. Ursula Frayne as the first superior of the convent of Our Lady of Mercy in St. John's, Newfoundland. Several historians, quoting the authority of a page from a Register in Baggot Street, support this theory.[6] Conclusive evidence of this is something else.

A careful examination of the few extant documents from that period—and in particular, of the original handwritten Register—casts doubt on the authenticity of the tradition. In the original Register, the entry for Clara (M. Ursula) Frayne gives the names of Ursula's parents; the dates of her entrance, reception, and profession; and her religious name. Then, in what appears to be a subsequent entry, is added, "Having been appointed first Mother Superior of our convent of the Holy Cross, Perth, Western Australia, she left this House September the 8th, 1845."[7] There is no mention of Newfoundland. This original Register, containing information on the women who were professed as Sisters of Mercy in Baggot Street, is kept in the archives of the Congregation of the Sisters of Mercy of Ireland, Herbert Street, Dublin. M. Clare Augustine Moore gathered the information from this Register when she made illuminated copies of the original entries for the Register that is currently held in the archives at Mercy International Centre (MIC).[8] However, the archives at MIC contain a photocopy of this page from the original Register (quoted above). At the end of the photocopied page, in a very different style of handwriting from the rest of the document, some person added, "1842–11th May [sic]–First Superior of St.

6. Killerby, *Frayne*, p. 67; O'Neill, *A Seaport Legacy*, p. 792; and M. Williamina Hogan, *Pathways of Mercy: History of the Foundation of the Sisters of Mercy in Newfoundland, 1842–1984* (St. John's: Harry Cuff Publications, 1986), p. 32.

7. Register of Profession, Archives of the Sisters of Mercy of Ireland. I am indebted to Marianne Cosgrave, archivist for the Irish Sisters of Mercy, for this information and to Patricia March, RSM, for a copy of this document.

8. M. Clare Augustine Moore was born in Dublin, August 1, 1808, and baptized Mary Clare. She entered the convent of the Sisters of Mercy on Baggot Street on August 8, 1837. When she was received into the novitiate in February 1838, she adopted the name, Mary Clare Augustine. M. Clare Augustine Moore was an artist, and among her valuable contributions to Mercy history are the illuminated Registers recording the entrance, reception, and profession dates, the major assignments, and the date of death of members of the community at Baggot Street. Sullivan, *Catherine McAuley*, p. 192.

John's Convent, Newfoundland; 1846–Went to Perth, Western Australia; 1857–7th March–Went to Convent of Mercy, Melbourne, Australia; 1885–Died there."The additions are undated. It is significant that, in the original Register from which this copy was made, there are no additional notes on the page devoted to M. Ursula Frayne. This leads to the conclusion that the additions were made at a much later date, perhaps as late as the twentieth century.

Furthermore, a copy of a beautifully illuminated page, similar to those found in the MIC illuminated Register, was donated to MIC by the Australian Sisters of Mercy. This page provides the same introductory information on M. Ursula contained in the first two Registers but adds, "Was sent in May 1842 to *assist in establishing a Convent of the Order* in St. John's, Newfoundland. Returned to Dublin in November 1844 [*sic*]. Was sent in November 1845 with six Sisters *to establish a Convent of the Order in Perth*, Western Australia."[9] Then, the writer mentions specifically, "Was appointed Superioress of the new community September 14, 1845."[10] It is interesting to note the subtle difference in the words used to describe M. Ursula's position relative to each of these missions. The phrase, "to assist in establishing" suggests that someone other than Ursula was appointed as superior of the Newfoundland foundation.

Some historians, notably Catherine Killerby, noted conflicting statements on the matter, "Sister Ursula was appointed Superioress, a fact confirmed by the Dublin *Register*. The Dublin *Annals* . . . state that not Ursula but rather Sister Rose was the Superioress."[11] Apparently, Killerby was using as her source the photocopied page with annotations kept in the archives at MIC rather than the original document preserved in the archives on Herbert Street that contains no mention of Newfoundland.[12] Unfortunately, the Dublin

---

9. The italics used in the passage quoted are mine. I am indebted to Maureen McGarrigle, RSM, and Patricia March, RSM, for a copy of this document. The original of this copy has been framed and is hanging in the reception parlour of the convent of Mercy in Fitzroy, Melbourne, Australia. This information was supplied by Agnes Gleeson, RSM.

10. Ibid.

11. Killerby, *Frayne*, p. 67.

12. I am indebted to Marianne Cosgrave, archivist for the Sisters of Mercy of Ireland, for a copy of the page from the original Register.

Annals have been lost or mislaid. Consequently, a certain amount of ambiguity surrounds the whole question of M. Ursula's position in the first Newfoundland community of Sisters of Mercy. If indeed she had been named superior, how long did she remain in that office? In May 1843, the accounts book of the convent of Mercy in St. John's was signed, "Sister M. Rose Lynch, Superior."

On the other hand, M. de Pazzi was aware of Catherine McAuley's policy of sending with each new founding group a more experienced sister to guide the new community through the difficult first phase of a mission.[13] Certainly, M. Ursula Frayne had more experience than either M. Rose Lynch or M. Francis Creedon. M. de Pazzi may have continued Catherine's practice by assigning to M. Ursula Frayne the task of assisting the appointed superior for the first few months of the mission. This would explain the confusion surrounding the identity of the first superior of the Newfoundland mission. Also, it would explain why M. Ursula did not scruple to return home to Ireland when she felt that she could no longer be effective in St. John's.

Before leaving the thorny question of the leadership of the community, it should be noted that the original "Rule and Constitutions of the Religious Sisters of Mercy" stated unequivocally that where there were fewer than seven professed sisters in a community, the superior was appointed by the bishop.[14] In the case of the Australian foundation, the Rule was followed when Bishop Brady appointed M. Ursula Frayne to the office of superior of the convent in Perth.[15] As far as we know, the Rule of the Sisters of Mercy was not followed in the appointment of the superior of Mercy Convent in Newfoundland. Did Bishop Fleming have any say in the selection of the person who would govern the little group of Mercy Sisters who came to St. John's? At some time between his arrival in Ireland in December 1841 and his return to St. John's in April

---

13. When Bermondsey was founded in 1839, M. Clare Moore was appointed the temporary superior for a year, and in 1841, M. Cecilia Marmion remained at Birmingham to assist the newly professed superior, M. Juliana Hardmann, for the first few months of the mission.

14. "Rule and Constitutions of the Religious Sisters of Mercy," part 11, chapter 2, article 11. Sullivan, *Catherine McAuley*, p. 321.

15. Killerby, *Frayne*, p. 92.

1842, it is probable that Bishop Fleming visited Baggot Street to finalize plans for the Newfoundland foundation and for the sisters' voyage to St. John's. Was the question of the leadership of the community raised then? Or did the bishop take it for granted that the understanding he had with Catherine McAuley with reference to Francis Creedon's leadership would be honoured? Did M. de Pazzi wait until shortly before the sisters' departure to appoint M. Ursula Frayne as leader of the little group of missionaries? M. Ursula was a dynamic woman who had a mind of her own and the energy, the determination, and the will to take into her own hands the direction of any enterprise involving the Sisters of Mercy. Nevertheless, the tradition at Mercy Convent in St. John's holds that Bishop Fleming bypassed M. Ursula and consulted M. Francis Creedon in all matters relating to the mission.[16] Such a practice might have seemed logical to the busy bishop. After all, M. Francis Creedon had been aware of his plans and was familiar with conditions in St. John's long before M. Ursula knew that such a place existed. Furthermore, it is likely that the bishop was much too preoccupied with the struggle to build his cathedral to worry about the niceties of convent protocol.

While our interest and curiosity may be engaged in trying to solve the question of leadership in the convent in St. John's, our three pioneers, M. Ursula, M. Rose, and M. Francis had other fish to fry. Perhaps their most pressing concern was to become familiar with the geography of the town. St. John's at the time consisted largely of rows of narrow streets and small wooden houses, although a few buildings of stone and brick were beginning to appear. Sir Richard Bonnycastle described St. John's as it appeared in 1842:

> Duckworth Street, the next great parallel to Water Street is also improving . . . by the addition of stone and brick houses; but altogether, St. John's has not yet arrived at much architectural embellishment, and it will be many years before the thickly crowded little wooden tenements will give way to a better and safer class of buildings.[17]

16. The author was told this by senior sisters at Mercy Convent in the 1950s.

17. Sir Richard Henry Bonnycastle, *Newfoundland in 1842*, vol. 2 (London: Henry Colburn, 1842), p. 224.

It was to these little tenements that the Sisters of Mercy went every day to visit the poor and the sick.

The weather in the month of July 1842 turned hot and humid, creating the ideal climate for an outbreak of one of the epidemics that swept through the town at regular intervals. This time it was a particularly virulent form of measles. *The Patriot* reported:

> The Measles still prevails among us and though not so generally as it did some weeks past, as yet retains its force with a tenacity for which this disease is so characteristic. The intense heat of the weather, though it has been oppressive to the hale and healthy, has favoured the patient labouring under this disorder. The brisk showers of rain, which occurred at intervals during the past week, have completely changed the state of the atmosphere, against the *chill* of which the sick cannot be too guarded. The *Sisters of Mercy*—introduced here by that noble Philanthropist, the Right Rev. Dr. Fleming, have ministered with untiring zeal among the poor afflicted, from the very moment of their arrival, and never, we believe, was there greater need for their hallowed services than at this period. But it is when sickness is prevalent—when disease is raging—when death hovers around—that those Sisters—like "Angels of Mercy"—flit from one scene of misery to another, administering to the wants of those who otherwise might suffer without assistance and die for want of it.[18]

During the first months after their arrival, the sisters were kept busy caring for sick children. At the same time, they became involved with liturgical celebrations within the parish. Both M. Ursula Frayne and M. Francis Creedon were skilled musicians, and it is likely that M. Rose Lynch had some musical training since that was one of the accomplishments of well-educated young ladies of the time. With the Feast of the Assumption of Mary drawing near, the local choir was in the throes of preparing appropriate music for the celebration. Early on the morning of August 15, Bishop Fleming celebrated

---

18. *The Patriot and Terra Nova Herald*, August 3, 1842, p. 3.

mass at the Presentation Convent and then proceeded to the old chapel on Henry Street for the parish mass. Once more, *The Patriot* recorded the contribution of the Sisters of Mercy:

> When we witnessed the exertions of the Rt. Rev. Dr. Fleming at the Presentation Convent in the morning and particularly his impressive Sermon on that occasion, we expected to find him, in the Church, exhibiting symptoms of exhaustion, yet at 11 o'clock behold him, once more, at the ALTAR, celebrating High Mass, which he sang with peculiar effect, the Ladies of the Convent of Mercy assisting in the Choir, where they performed in a style of superior elegance Mozart's High Mass, No. 12. The rich and varied harmonies of the exquisite composition expressed by these Ladies with a pathos and tenderness truly impressive, produced upon the dense congregation an effect the most thrilling.[19]

Mozart's Twelfth Mass, even when executed in a simplified version, requires a high degree of skill and plenty of practice. One wonders how they managed it! Perhaps Maria Nugent, sister of John Valentine Nugent, had a hand in the performance. Whether or not she did, the sisters would have welcomed whatever help was available at the time, and Maria was a talented musician.

As summer turned to autumn, the array of colours presented by the changing of the leaves from green to red to gold was a source of delight to these young women from Ireland. Then came winter, with a force and severity they had not experienced before. While they may have been excited over the first fall of soft white snow, they were quickly brought down to earth—in more ways than one—as they attempted to navigate the slippery, snowy streets of the town. Years later, M. Ursula Frayne told of an excursion she made with the diminutive M. Rose Lynch as companion. Catherine Killerby relates the story: "Suddenly the Sister vanished and Mother Ursula saw the top of her bonnet protruding through the snow."[20] There would have been plenty of willing

---

19. Ibid., August 31, 1842, p. 1.

20. Killerby, *Frayne*, p. 64. Killerby cites, X. Bomford, "Recollections of Mother M. Ursula Frayne," MS, Mercy Archives, Melbourne, Australia, typescript in Mercy Archives, Perth.

hands to rescue poor M. Rose from her cold and uncomfortable position in the snowbank for, by this time, the Sisters of Mercy were a welcome sight as they walked to the homes of the poor. Years later, M. Ursula Frayne, on one of the rare occasions when she mentioned Newfoundland, spoke of the kindness and generosity of the people toward the Sisters of Mercy. One occasion when the sisters had no tea, they asked a neighbour if she could spare them a little. "When the Sisters returned from Mass they found the hall lined with chests of tea, bags of sugar, flour and other commodities, enough to last for a long time. The good lady had spread the news that the nuns were in want of provisions and the people responded generously."[21]

Winter had already arrived when the sisters moved into their new convent on Military Road. In a letter to Propaganda Fide, Bishop Fleming wrote:

> I turned my undivided attention to the erection of a comfortable residence for the Sisters of Mercy. In anticipation of their arrival I had purchased the "Fee simple" of a piece of ground immediately adjoining the Cathedral ground. There I proceeded to the erection of a Convent, and before the winter closed I had completed an elegant edifice about 60 feet long and 30 feet wide, terminated Westerly by a tastefully executed Tower upwards of fifty feet high surmounted by a large gilded Cross. This Tower, though not more than fifteen feet square, comprised their respective parlour, their community room, and an Oratory, to each of which apartments one entire floor of it is appropriated, and from that end of the building runs at right angles with it an addition for the accommodation of the School. . . . I may as well mention here that the Building was completed in December following, and on the 12th of which month I had the gratification of inducting the Ladies of that Order into their new and elegant dwelling and in March of 1843 they opened School having devoted every spare moment of their time from the hour of their landing to visiting the Sick, and in a few weeks their school was tolerably fitted. [22]

---

21. Killerby, *Frayne*, p. 67.
22. Fleming to Propaganda Fide, November 26, 1846, AASJ, 103/2/27.

Was it just coincidence that the day they took possession of their new home was December 12, the eleventh anniversary of the foundation of the Congregation of the Sisters of Mercy? Historians who have studied the life and episcopacy of Bishop Fleming claim that it was entirely in keeping with his character and values that he would be sensitive to the significance of such anniversaries in the life of a religious community.[23]

In the letter quoted above, Fleming stated that the Sisters of Mercy opened their school the following March, ". . . and in March of 1843 they opened School having devoted every spare moment of their time from the hour of their landing to the visiting the Sick, and in a few weeks their school was tolerable fitted."[24] However, in another letter, Fleming wrote that the school opened on May 1, 1843,[25] the date confirmed by the local press.[26] Apparently, the bishop was careless about details that he considered insignificant, such as the actual date on which Our Lady of Mercy School opened its doors. He was more concerned to record the fact that it did open.[27] However, it is possible that once the school was ready, perhaps in March 1843, the sisters began to admit some students, even though the formal opening had not been announced.

By this time there were four Sisters of Mercy in St. John's, for during the latter half of 1842, the Sisters of Mercy admitted their first postulant in the person of the erudite and talented Maria Nugent.

Maria Nugent was born in Waterford in 1799. She was highly educated and well versed in the Greek and Latin classics, with a thorough knowledge of French and Italian literature. She spoke and wrote fluently in both languages.

---

23. Brother J. B. Darcy, CFC, has studied the life and times of Bishop Michael A. Fleming. He confirmed that it was entirely in keeping with Fleming's sense of what was proper that the day the sisters occupied the first Mercy Convent in the New World should coincide with the anniversary of the foundation of the Order.

24. Fleming to Propaganda Fide, November 26, 1846, AASJ, 103/2/27.

25. Fleming to O'Connell, February 19, 1844, AASJ, 103/2/25.

26. *The Patriot and Terra Nova Herald*, April 26, 1843, p. 3. *The Newfoundland Indicator*, March 30, 1844, p. 3.

27. I am indebted to Brother J. B. Darcy for this explanation of the conflicting dates given by Bishop Fleming for the opening of Our Lady of Mercy School.

Born into a deeply religious family, it is not surprising Maria felt attracted to religious life. She joined the Ursuline Convent in Waterford, but before making her profession of vows, she was stricken with severe sciatica and was forced to return home. It was shortly after this that her brother, John Valentine Nugent, was encouraged to emigrate to Newfoundland, taking with him not only his wife and children, but also his mother, Mary Nugent; his sister, Maria; and his sister-in-law, Marianne Creedon. Two weeks after their arrival in St. John's, Mrs. Mary Nugent, mother of John and Maria, died.[28] Maria, who by this time was perfectly restored to health, decided to try religious life again. On February 2, 1834, she entered the Presentation Convent in St. John's, receiving the habit of a Presentation Sister on August 5, 1834.[29] The Patriot gave a detailed account of the ceremony of reception at which Bishop Fleming presided.[30] This was the first ceremony of its kind to be held in Newfoundland, and it aroused widespread interest. Because of the large numbers expected to attend, the largest classroom in the school was fitted out as a temporary chapel so that as many as possible could be accommodated. The account of the ceremony mentions that three very young children, nieces to Maria, took part in the procession. One child carried the crucifix, and two others bore lighted wax candles in one hand, while in the other they carried between them a silver basket containing the habit, cloak, and veil, with which their aunt was to be clothed. What happened to Maria's career as a Presentation Sister is related in the Annals of the Presentation Convent:

> At the end of two years being on acct. of continual delicacy, timid about profession, the superiors at the desire and consent of the community allowed her in consideration of her many estimable qualities to try a second noviciate, at the expiration of which for the above mentioned reason they were obliged, tho' reluctantly, to dismiss her.[31]

28. Mrs. Mary Nugent died on June 6, 1833.
29. APSSJ. I am indebted to Sister M. Perpetua Kennedy, PBVM, for this information.
30. *The Patriot and Terra Nova Herald*, August 12, 1834, p. 3.
31. Annals, Presentation Convent, St. John's, APSSJ.

She returned to her brother's house where, we are told, she lived as a recluse, occupying herself with the education of her brother's children.[32]

Maria must have been bitterly disappointed at the failure of her second attempt to follow what she was convinced was a call from God to the religious life. But God was not finished with her yet. The years passed and one fine day in June 1842, the *Sir Walter Scott* arrived outside the Narrows bearing the Sisters of Mercy. The Presentation Sisters of the time conclude their story of Maria Nugent by saying in their Annals that shortly after the arrival of the Sisters of Mercy, Maria Nugent joined them, "feeling that at last she had found her true home."[33] It is unfortunate that no date is mentioned to indicate just when Maria joined the Mercy Sisters. Bishop Howley wrote, "As soon as the Sisters of Mercy came she felt revive in her the strong religious vocation."[34] Although M. Austin Carroll remarked that "Maria Nugent was ready to make her profession the day she entered,"[35] Carroll did not claim that the profession took place on that day. On the contrary, writing from the recollections of the Newfoundland sisters who knew Francis Creedon, she stated that the profession took place *after a few months*. Thus, it seems safe to assume that Maria Nugent spent some time either as a postulant or novice with the Sisters of Mercy. It is probable that she was received as a novice sometime prior to January 1843. The evidence for this is found on the inside cover of a book found in the archives of the Sisters of Mercy of Newfoundland. The book is entitled, *Lettres de S. Francois deSales*. An inscription, which is partly illegible, reads, "Mary Jane Nugent [from her] Aunt, Sr. M. Joseph Nugent, January 13, 1843." It is obvious from this that by January 1843 Maria Nugent had already been given her religious name, a practice that took place at the reception of the candidate as a novice.

Inevitably, the question arose of the need for Maria to spend another two-year period as a novice before her profession as a Sister of Mercy. Catherine McAuley and her companions had passed their novitiate in a

---

32. Carroll, *Leaves*, vol. 3, p. 24.
33. APSSJ.
34. Howley, *Ecclesiastical History* p. 375.
35. Carroll, *Leaves*, vol. 3, p. 24.

Presentation Convent to prepare for their profession of vows as Sisters of Mercy. Taking this as a precedent, Bishop Fleming decided, and the community agreed, that Maria Nugent—having passed one novitiate with the Ursuline nuns and two novitiates with the Presentation Sisters—was more than adequately prepared to pronounce her vows as a Sister of Mercy. Those who have experienced the discipline of even one novitiate would be inclined to agree wholeheartedly with the bishop! M. Austin Carroll summed up the matter as follows:

> The bishop having received from Rome the necessary authority, and the community consenting, Maria, now Sister Mary Joseph, was allowed to make her profession in a few months, the novitiate in the Presentation convent being deemed sufficient. The case of Mother McAuley herself, though so dissimilar, was considered a sort of precedent. [36]

No documents have been found to clarify what is meant by the phrase, "the necessary authority." Neither is there any evidence, other than M. Austin Carroll's statement, to prove that Bishop Fleming asked for and received permission from Rome to dispense Maria from completing the prescribed two years of Mercy novitiate. If such documents existed, they may have been destroyed in the disastrous fire of 1846, when the bishop lost many valuable papers stored in the newly erected Presentation Convent on Long's Hill. In any case, with or without Rome's permission, Maria Nugent, now Sister Mary Joseph, was professed as a Sister of Mercy at the Presentation Convent on March 25, 1843, thus becoming the first Sister of Mercy to be professed outside the British Isles.[37]

Unfortunately, the addition of another professed member, an event that should have been a source of joy and happiness, was a matter of concern to at least one member of the Mercy community. Apparently, M. Ursula Frayne was

---

36. Ibid., p. 25.
37. Paul O'Neill, "Sister Mary Joseph Nugent," *The Monitor*, January 1976, p. 48. It is not clear why the ceremony took place at the Presentation Convent. Possibly the chapel at Mercy Convent was too small or had not been completely furnished at this time.

outraged! She was not convinced that Bishop Fleming had any right to dispense M. Joseph Nugent from making a complete novitiate within the Mercy community. Several years later she was still brooding over the matter. While en route to Australia, she wrote:

> I told him [Bishop John Brady] all about the Newfoundland business. He was perfectly astonished and said 'What would I take and be in Dr. Fleming's shoes?' I said that perhaps he had a dispensation. He said, "No, the Pope himself would not change a Rule once confirmed. *That* Sister is *not* professed—she might return to the world tomorrow without any sin except the scandal of it."[38]

At the time she wrote this, M. Ursula was delighted with Bishop Brady for, on the same voyage to Australia, she wrote to the superior of Baggot Street, "What a contrast there is between Dr. Brady and Dr. Fleming, if any of the Foundations are blessed in a Bishop, we certainly are; he is kind, affectionate and fatherly."[39] Bishop Brady's kindness, however, did not extend to providing accommodations for the sisters on their arrival in Perth. Unlike Bishop Fleming who gave up his own house "altogether" to the sisters, Brady left them to fend for themselves.[40] Nevertheless, within a relatively short time, M. Ursula found herself at serious odds with Bishop Brady. Possibly his lack of administrative ability was a source of annoyance and anxiety to the capable M. Ursula Frayne.

It is not known how soon after their arrival in St. John's that sparks began to fly between M. Ursula Frayne and Bishop Fleming. In a letter to

---

38. M. Ursula Frayne to M. Vincent Whitty, November 25, 1845, cited in Killerby, *Frayne*, p. 39. In light of what is known of Bishop Brady's career, it is highly unlikely that he was competent to pronounce on the validity of another bishop's decision or actions. Undoubtedly, he was a very zealous, holy man, but his appointment as bishop was greeted with serious reservations by his colleagues in Australia. Killerby, *Frayne*, p. 109, in describing Brady's lack of ability, cited V. Tiggerman, "On the Administration of Church Property in Western Australia, 1845–1867," (Ph.D. diss., Pontifical Urban University, 1955).

39. M. Ursula Frayne to M. Cecilia Marmion, November 5, 1845, cited in Killerby, *Frayne*, p. 108.

40. See Killerby, *Frayne*, pp. 138–139.

Archbishop Murray on February 7, 1843, Fleming mentioned that the new Mercy Convent had been completed, and he remarked, "my little community have removed there some two or three months since, and are feeling apparently quite happy. They are doing wonders among the better class of people in the way of Instruction and visiting the sick of all classes."[41] If there were any problems at that time, the bishop either was not aware of them or preferred not to mention them.

In spite of this statement, M. Ursula, at least, was not happy with events as they unfolded in St. John's, and without consulting anybody, she communicated her misgivings to M. de Pazzi Delany in Baggot Street. Somehow or other, Bishop Fleming found out about this and wrote to Archbishop Murray to complain. The first hint that all was not well is found in a letter from M. de Pazzi to Bishop Fleming, dated January 29, 1843:

> I take the liberty of writing to express my great surprise at the charge brought against me in your letter to our Archbishop and am directed to inquire upon what grounds you accuse me to him "of causing breach of discipline in the convent of which you have charge by encouraging clandestine correspondence with some of the Sisters."[42]

Clearly, Archbishop Murray acted on Fleming's complaint and questioned M. de Pazzi on the content of the bishop's letter sometime prior to January 29, 1843.

If M. de Pazzi was expecting the matter to be resolved quickly, she was doomed to disappointment, for her letter did not arrive in St. John's until April when Bishop Fleming was away. On his return, M. Rose Lynch presented him with M. de Pazzi's letter, whereupon the bishop saw red! He deferred action on the matter while he attended to more pressing business and then sat down and penned a hotheaded reply that did nothing to soothe the ruffled

---

41. Fleming to Archbishop Murray, February 7, 1843, cited in FitzGerald, "Conflict and Culture," p. 376.
42. M. de Pazzi Delany to Fleming, January 29, 1843. DDA, Murray Papers, AB 3/32/1, (1843–44) Addenda.

feathers of the mother superior of Baggot Street. In his response to M. de Pazzi, Fleming identified M. Ursula Frayne as the author of the "clandestine" letters. He wrote, "I am not aware that I used the expression 'clandestine correspondence' with reference to Sister Ursula's letters and your reply shortly after they landed here."[43] Furthermore, the bishop made it clear that he viewed content of M. de Pazzi's letters to the sisters as interference in the Newfoundland mission:

> It appears to me that somehow or other you would seem to regard the Convent of St. John's as merely forming a branch of the Baggot Street Institution and as I deem it incumbent on me to disabuse you of that error I beg leave to intimate that the Convent of Mercy of Newfoundland is utterly and entirely independent of every institution of the kind in any country whatever and owing obedience alone to the Vicar-Apostolic of Newfoundland.[44]

Bishop Fleming was, of course, quite correct in claiming that Baggot Street had no jurisdiction over the convent in St. John's, other than the respect in which Baggot Street was held by every Mercy community. In Catherine McAuley's plan, every convent was autonomous. Furthermore, her Rule stated clearly, "This religious Congregation of the Sisters of Mercy shall be always subject to the authority and jurisdiction of the Diocesan Bishop, and the Sisters shall respect and obey him as their first Superior after the Holy See."[45] Apart from the question of his jurisdiction, the good bishop was obviously annoyed that things were not going as smoothly as he had anticipated. He had invested a great deal in the success of this enterprise, even apart from the financial outlay involved. The education of the daughters of the middle and upper classes

---

43. Fleming to M. de Pazzi Delany, June 14, 1843, DDA, Murray Papers, AB 3/32/1, (1843–44) Addenda, letter 208. These documents were unknown to researchers of Mercy history until John E. FitzGerald first discovered them in 1995 in the Dublin Diocesan Archives and presented copies to the Archives of the Mercy International Centre in Dublin.

44. Ibid.

45. "Rule and Constitutions of the Religious Sisters of Mercy," part 2, chapter 1, article 1, cited by Sullivan, *Catherine McAuley*, p. 317.

was crucial to his plan to improve the social and political standing of the Catholic population of the colony. The last thing he wanted was someone writing home to Dublin "groundless and frivolous complaints and accusations"[46] about what was going on in St. John's. The bishop does not identify the nature of the complaints, but in another section of the same letter he wrote:

> I confess to you that sometimes it appears to me impossible that you could have known that Sister Ursula's communication to you had left this [place] without having been subjected to the inspection of her Superior even though I had seen your reply to her and that it contained *not one word of advice upon that subject*, not one word of reproof for the fault she found so unjustly with her Superior but this letter now before me of last January brings me the distressing conviction that in this I was mistaken.[47]

This gives rise once more to the question of the identity of the superior with whom M. Ursula Frayne was finding fault. Was it M. Rose Lynch? There is incontrovertible evidence that by May 1843, M. Rose was the superior of St. John's.[48] The theory that M. Rose was the superior prior to May 1843, is strengthened by the words of Bishop Fleming when he wrote to M. de Pazzi, "your letter was handed to me by Sister M. Rose."[49] This suggests that M. Rose was the person who received all communications that arrived at the convent, i.e. the local superior.

On the other hand, both John FitzGerald and Catherine Killerby assert that Fleming himself claimed to be superior with the right to inspect all incoming and outgoing mail.[50] The statement that Fleming claimed to be the "superior" is well-documented. Equally well-documented is the fact that, according to the original Mercy Rule, he had every right to such a claim: "This religious

46. Fleming to M. de Pazzi Delany, June 14, 1843, DDA, Murray Papers, AB 3/32/1, (1843–44) Addenda, letter 208.
47. Ibid.
48. Accounts Book, Convent of Our Lady of Mercy, St. John's, 1843, ASMSJ.
49. Fleming to M. de Pazzi Delany, June 14, 1843, DDA, Murray Papers, AB 3/32/1, (1843–44) Addenda, letter 208.
50. FitzGerald, "Conflict and Culture," p. 379. See also Killerby, *Frayne*, p. 71.

Congregation of the Sisters of Mercy shall be always subject to the authority and jurisdiction of the Diocesan Bishop, and the Sisters shall respect and obey him as their first Superior after the Holy See."[51] But the distinction between the office of *ecclesiastical* superior and that of local superior of a convent is significant and must be taken into account. The position of this writer is that Fleming assumed jurisdiction over the lives and internal government of the Sisters of Mercy in much the same fashion as did his successors up to the middle of the twentieth century. In this context it is interesting to cite a passage from the letter of the Newfoundland bishops when, in 1915, they forwarded a petition to the Sacred Congregation for Religious requesting permission to amalgamate the independent convents of the Sisters of Mercy (and those of the Presentation Sisters) in Newfoundland:

> Their Lordships are of the opinion that the Institute can be more effectually and more appropriately governed by a Mother-General and her council than under the present system by which each House is independent and the Sisters subject to the Ordinary as their first superior. [52]

In his address to the Presentation and Mercy Sisters, Archbishop Roche explained:

> Hitherto the government and the administration of our two religious communities were almost entirely in the hands of the Bishops. The general effect of the new system of government will be the transfer of very much of the authority hitherto vested in and exercised by the Bishops to a Mother-General and her assistants.[53]

---

51. "Rule and Constitutions of the Religious Sisters of Mercy," part 2, chapter 1, article 1, cited in Sullivan, *Catherine McAuley*, p. 317.

52. Newfoundland bishops to Archbishop Stagni, AASJ, 107/1/1.

53. Archbishop E. P. Roche, quoting from Petition to the Sacred Congregation of Religious cited in "Address to Presentation and Mercy Sisters on Amalgamation of Independent Convents of each Congregation," August 4, 1916, ASASJ, 107/1/1.

Whether the bishops, and in particular Bishop Fleming, regarded censorship of the sisters' mail as one of the rights of governance and administration is debatable. According to M. Xaverius Lynch, Fleming did not presume to open letters addressed to the Presentation Sisters. Writing to Ireland, M. Xaverius mentioned an occasion on which the bishop delivered a letter to her. "He brought me a letter from sweet Ireland . . . I took it out of his hand with the greatest joy and kept looking at it and fiddling with the seal not knowing well what I was doing I was in such joy. He immediately turned round and asked me if I was going to open it though Rev. Mother was present."[54] This states clearly that M. Xaverius received the letter with the seal unbroken. Ordinarily, it would have been given to the local superior who had the right to open all letters. Writing to Ireland in September 1833, M. Magdalen O'Shaugnessey said, "The Bishop by chance opened a box in which there was a parcel directed for us."[55] The use of the words "by chance" indicates that this was not the bishop's normal practice.

The section of Fleming's letter to M. de Pazzi that is open to interpretation is: "Sister Ursula's communication to you had left this [place] without having been subject to the inspection of her Superior, even though I had seen your reply to her and that it contained . . . not one word of reproof for the fault she found so unjustly with her Superior."[56] Both FitzGerald and Killerby use this sentence to support their contention that Fleming censored the convent mail. If Fleming were identifying himself with the "Superior" mentioned in this passage, it would seem logical that he would write, "without being subject to *my* inspection." Presumably, M. Ursula shared with the bishop the content of M. de Pazzi's reply, hoping that the words of the superior of Baggot Street would legitimize her position on whatever dispute had arisen. Unfortunately, it had the opposite effect.

---

54. M. Xaverius Lynch to Ann, January 26, 1834, APCG. To expedite the exchange of mail between Ireland and St. John's, Bishop Fleming had arranged that letters and parcels be sent to "Dr. Fleming, to the care of Messrs Graham & Taylor, Merchants, Liverpool." This information is found in a letter from M. X. Lynch to Galway, September 22, 1833.

55. M. Magdalen O'Shaugnessy to Revd. Mother, September 22, 1833, "Sesquicentenary Souvenir," p. 15, APSG.

56. Fleming to M. de Pazzi Delany, June 14, 1843, DDA, Murrary Papers, AB 3/32/1, (1831–44) Addenda, letter 208.

At any rate, from that point on, matters deteriorated until the decision was made that M. Ursula Frayne should return to Ireland. Because she could not travel alone across the Atlantic, the obvious person to accompany her was M. Rose Lynch. Rose's feelings in the matter are not recorded, and she may not have been consulted! While the bishop might have been disappointed at the loss of two Sisters of Mercy to the mission, he felt he could afford to do without the strong willed and obviously discontented M. Ursula Frayne. Accordingly, he concluded his fiery letter of June 14, with the following words, "Should you in the meantime feel . . . a regret that . . . you permitted subjects of your House to assist in forming this foundation, I shall be most happy at a moment's notice to resign them once more to your care."[57] For her part, M. Ursula, probably feeling that enough was enough, was glad to return to a place where her gifts and talents would be graciously acknowledged and properly utilized. Arrangements were made, and on November 20, 1843, *The Newfoundlander* carried the following news item, "The Rt. Rev. Dr. Fleming accompanied by two Ladies from the Convent of Mercy embarked on board the *Ratchford* for Waterford on Monday last."[58] It was a sad conclusion to a venture that had begun with such noble intentions, buoyed up by the enthusiastic, wholehearted dedication of three young women who had given up everything to follow what they perceived as God's will for them.

After their return to Ireland, the two sisters, M. Ursula and M. Rose, remained at St. Catherine's Convent in Baggot Street until each was assigned to a new mission. In August 1845, Bishop John Brady arrived at the convent begging for sisters to establish a foundation in Perth, Western Australia. M. Ursula Frayne, who was never afraid of trying something new, was among the six who volunteered for this distant land. After two weeks of hurried preparation, the little group journeyed to St. Edward's Convent, London, where, on September 14, 1845, Bishop Brady appointed M. Ursula superior of the new foundation. Two days later they arrived at the pier where the ship was ready to leave for Perth. To their dismay, they discovered that the only

---

57. Ibid.
58. *The Newfoundlander*, November 20, 1843, p. 2.

way they could board the boat was to be lowered to the deck in a herring basket!

During the long voyage from England, Ursula wrote frequently to M. Cecilia Marmion, the superior at Baggot Street. Her letters are full of amusing details of the journey. M. Ursula had a gift for writing with such a delightful sense of humour that characters and events came to life on each page of her prose. After a voyage of just over sixteen weeks, they arrived in Australia to a lukewarm reception.[59] This was in stark contrast to the enthusiastic welcome Ursula had experienced when she landed in Newfoundland!

The first task facing the superior was to find appropriate accommodation for her community, one of whom, M. Catherine Gogarty, was seriously ill. However, M. Ursula was not one to sit down and wring her hands in helpless frustration. Within short order, the resourceful M. Ursula had found a suitable dwelling and fitted it up as well as circumstances and limited resources would permit. M. Catherine's death a few months later was a blow to the new mission and a source of deep personal grief to M. Ursula. As well, there were tensions within the community. The oldest member of the group, M. Ignatia de la Hoyde, was professed just two weeks after the sisters arrived in Perth. M. Ursula's correspondence concerning M. Ignatia is revealing. She writes, "I would not think it right to yield to her on every occasion, and as she is miserable when found fault with, I now leave her entirely to herself."[60] This was indeed a very unhappy state of affairs. It is easy to understand why the constant whining of M. Ignatia about her doubts and fears would exasperate the forthright and assertive M. Ursula Frayne. The gentleness that characterized her later years seems to have been noticeably absent in her youth! The problem within the community was resolved when Ursula opened a branch convent in Fremantle, and M. Ignatia de la Hoyde was transferred to that community.

From the beginning of the Mercy ministry in Australia, M. Ursula and her sisters established a pattern of actively seeking out women in need of help and especially Aboriginal women. It was in the field of education, however,

---

59. Killerby, *Frayne*, p. 113.
60. M. Ursula Frayne to M. Cecilia Marmion, March 1847, MS, AMIC.

that they made the greatest impact on Australian society.[61] There was no doubt in the minds of the authorities in Ireland that, given a free hand, there was little that M. Ursula Frayne could not achieve when she set her mind to it.

Although the Sisters of Mercy in Perth had established a thriving mission, there was trouble brewing between Bishop Brady and M. Ursula Frayne. It is possible that Brady's worsening financial woes contributed to his testiness with M. Ursula. Her outstanding administrative abilities were a reproach to his less than capable management of financial affairs. Things went from bad to worse and Brady's behaviour became more and more erratic. He placed unwarranted restraints on the sisters, and when M. Ursula, without seeking prior approval from Brady, requested a physician to visit one of the sisters, the bishop was so incensed that he placed the sisters under a formal interdict. Although the interdict was removed, the incident was but one of a series of confrontations between M. Ursula and Bishop Brady. Brady's financial troubles continued to accelerate until finally, in 1851, Rome suspended him from exercising his office as bishop of Perth and appointed Bishop Serra as apostolic administrator.

The appointment of a new administrator did nothing to solve M. Ursula's problems, which only increased under Bishop Serra's administration. Eventually, she found a way out of her difficulties by responding to the invitation of Bishop Goold of Melbourne to establish a foundation in his diocese. M. Ursula and two companions left for Melbourne in November 1856, thirteen years after she had sailed from St. John's.

M. Ursula was now beginning the fourth and most successful phase of her life. In contrast to her experiences with Bishops Fleming, Brady, and Serra, M. Ursula got on well with Bishop Goold. During the twenty-eight years that remained to her, she established two branch houses, pension schools, poor schools, a House of Mercy, and a Catholic orphanage. No one could accuse her of idleness, and she seemed to rise above every difficulty. One final trial awaited this intrepid woman—a lengthy and debilitating illness. From 1879 onward her health deteriorated until on June 9, 1885, M. Ursula Frayne's long and

61. Killerby, *Frayne*, p. 125.

tempestuous career came to an end. She died at the convent she had founded on Nicholson Street, Fitzroy, Melbourne.

The story of M. Ursula's companion in Newfoundland, M. Rose Lynch, is not nearly as well-documented. Having spent four years at Baggot Street after her return from St. John's, M. Rose went on the Dundalk foundation with M. deSales Vigne in October 1847. While there are few facts recorded about her life at Dundalk, there is enough written to indicate a certain restlessness in her behaviour. It was still too early for her companions to recognize the symptoms of the serious mental illness that caused so much future pain and distress. In May 1859, the annalist wrote, "Mother M. Rose . . . visited Baggot Street for three weeks . . . It was then Mother M. Rose got her 'foreign notions.'"[62] At the time of this visit, M. Xavier Maguire was planning a foundation in Geelong, Australia. The project was attractive to M. Rose's adventuresome spirit, and she returned to Dundalk full of the idea of volunteering for the new foundation. She was accepted and the community of Mercy Sisters, under the leadership of M. Xavier Maguire, arrived in Australia in December 1859. Five months after their arrival, M. Rose seemed to be quite happy, perhaps too happy. She writes, ". . . as for me, I never felt in the least low-spirited or gloomy no matter what happened, so I say unless I am paid well for it, I'll never fret or be anxious for or about anything in this beautiful old world."[63]

At first M. Xavier was delighted with M. Rose, appointed her bursar of the community and left her to herself to fulfill her duties. A short time later, when M. Xavier examined the books, she discovered to her horror that the sisters were in debt to the tune of £150.[64] Killerby reports that further investigation showed that the actual amount of the debt incurred by M. Rose was closer to £3000.[65] By this time, it was clear to every member of the community that something was seriously wrong. On January 8, 1861, M. Xavier wrote a letter to the superior of Baggot Street:

62. Annals, St. Malachy's Convent, Dundalk, 1859.
63. M. Rose Lynch to M. Aloysius, n.d., AMIC, RG 500–2.3: 210 Aus.
64. M. Xavier Maguire to Rev. Mother, n.d., AMIC, RG 500–2.3: 210 Aus.
65. Killerby, *Frayne*, p. 240.

... Sister M. Rose is very imprudent, nothing can keep her tongue quiet, and when she is in a temper I am always expecting some bitter declaration from her before no matter who. To my surprise I discovered she knows absolutely nothing about arithmetic. I saw by the way she kept the house books she did not know much but still, I thought she could teach the children. She told me they could do any sums in *compound* proportion. Well, I said nothing at the time, but I suspected it might be something like the repeated assurance that we were going on so well—not going into debt—for I was hearing complaints about the sums from the parents. We had examinations last week and I gave the children two sums in simple proportion to do for me ... but such productions you never saw. I had to put every child in the school back. . . . They are hard at work now for a grand premiere, but sums are the things of all others the parents care for. And indeed the only thing they are capable of forming any judgments about except needlework ... and only fancy, a child brought a frock to be made—and without saying anything to me, she told the child to take it out of the school, we were not dressmakers!!! Now, dear Revd. Mother, if I am obliged to depend much on her, the mission in all its parts will be ruined; first, she threw me headlong into debt—she taught Arithmetic by handing the book around to other children to copy their sums with the *Answers as well*, and now she turns a frock out of the school although I am so anxious to have children taught such work.[66]

Finally, the Register of the Sisters of Mercy, Geelong, contains the following entry:

July 1861, The Chapter assembled to decide on sending Sister M. Rose Lynch back to Ireland in consequence of her insubordination and spirit of discontent. She was removed from the office of Bursar which she had held for about two months and left the community with the approbation of the Bishop and full consent of the Sisters on the 28th of August.[67]

66. M. Xavier Maguire to M. of Mercy Norris, January 8, 1861, AMIC, RG 500–2.3: 210 Aus.
67. Extract from Register of the Sisters of Mercy, Geelong, July 1861. I am indebted to M. Ursula Gilbert, RSM, of Tasmania for a copy of this page of the Register.

A month later, Bishop Goold of Melbourne wrote a personal letter to the Baggot Street superior expressing his own feelings on the matter:

> My Dear Rev. Mother,
> Mother Mary Rose will return this month to Ireland. This change in her vocation is the subject of much talk here & to me it has been an unpleasant lesson. I had nothing to say to the selection of the Sisters who came out with Mrs. McGuire & so I am relieved as to personal responsibility but I cannot, I regret to say, view the matter in the same light with reference to my Episcopal responsibility. I have, therefore, informed the superiors of our two religious communities [in Melbourne and Geelong] that in future that no one from Home should join them without my written invitation.
>   Pray for me & believe me, dear Rev. Mother . . .[68]

Apparently, the sisters in Dundalk were aware of trouble in Geelong. The entry in the Annals for May 22, 1861, reads, "Heard a rumour that Mother M. Rose is coming home . . ." and a month later, "It was piously believed that Mother M. Rose was already sailing home. Father Pat Kieran wanted to know if she would be allowed back here if he sent money to her. He was answered in the negative."[69] At that time, when a sister requested a transfer to another convent, she relinquished any claims on her former community. This was necessary, for each convent had very modest financial and household resources, and could support only a limited number of sisters. On October 17, 1861, the Dundalk annalist wrote, "Mother M. Rose actually on the sea."

The next mention of M. Rose is found in the Annals of St. Edward's Convent, Blandford Square, London, dated November 25, 1861, "Sr. M. Rose Lynch arrived from Australia."[70] The entry for January 1, 1862, is significant:

---

68. Bishop J. A. Goold to Rev. Mother, Baggot Street, August 1861, AMIC.
69. Annals, St. Malachy's Convent, Dundalk, 1861.
70. Annals, St. Edward's Convent, London. I thank M. Barbara Jeffrey, RSM, for researching these Annals and providing me with copies of all the references to M. Rose Lynch.

"The Professed Sisters of this community and Sister M. Rose Lynch renewed their Vows . . ."[71] This statement is repeated for the years 1863–1871. Every year M. Rose Lynch is named separately, an indication that she was not considered a member of St. Edward's community.

M. Rose remained at St. Edward's for the next ten years. Apparently, there was no place else for her to go. Dundalk had refused to readmit her, and neither was Baggot Street prepared to accept her. The next appearance of M. Rose's name is in the Annals of the convent in Bermondsey. A member of that community, M. Catherine, had been discontented for several years. In 1870, she left the convent to return to her family, who would not receive her. Reluctant to return to Bermondsey, the unfortunate sister asked to be admitted to St. Edward's community. The kindly superior offered to receive her on condition that Bermondsey accept M. Rose Lynch. A letter written by the assistant of St. Edward's Convent to M. Clare Moore, the superior of the Bermondsey convent, revealed that St. Edward's could not afford to support both M. Catherine and M. Rose. With regard to M. Rose, the assistant wrote, ". . . she cannot regain admittance in Baggot St. or Dundalk and so she has stayed on here year after year."[72] The Bermondsey community rejected the proposal. This decision was recorded by the annalist with the terse phrase, "[it] was not considered advisable."[73]

By November 1871, M. Rose was so ill that she was sent to the convent infirmary. The superior, realizing the gravity of her condition, was unwilling to take responsibility for a sister who had been professed as a member of another community. In consultation with the archbishop of Westminster, she decided that M. Rose would have to return to Ireland. The archbishop confirmed the decision in writing:

> The course to take is to find out Sr. M. Rose's family. Then to write them saying on such a day she will leave London for Ireland. You must give her travelling expenses and about £3 more. Write also to Monsignor Ford, the Cardinal's Vicar General, saying what you

---

71. Ibid.

72. M. de Pazzi, assistant, to Rev. Mother, November 28, 1870. The letter was discovered by the author in the Bermondsey Annals for the year 1870.

73. Annals, Convent of Mercy, Bermondsey, November 19, 1870.

have done and that it has my sanction. When you have written, tell
Sister M. Rose and say that resistance is useless.
I hope she will act rightly—I am very glad about the Inspection.
Yours affectionately in J.C.
+H.E.M. [Henry Edward Manning, Archbishop of Westminster][74]

The final entry concerning M. Rose Lynch in the Annals of St. Edward's
Convent reads, "Rev. Mother and Sister M. Regis accompanied her to the
train."

A glance through the brief notes made in the Dundalk, Geelong, and St.
Edward's Annals suggests that M. Rose Lynch may have been suffering for
years from a progressive form of mental illness. It is clear that her companions
in community did not realize the cause of her erratic behaviour. We can only
imagine the suffering poor M. Rose endured through all these years and especially after her return from Australia. There was no community willing to
accept her; she was isolated and alone. Her presence seems to have been merely tolerated at St. Edward's Convent, but the sisters must be credited with providing for her needs until they could no longer care for her.

The last written account of M. Rose Lynch is a brief reference made by
M. Clare Moore in a letter of September 24, 1874, in which she wrote, "Sister
M. Rose Lynch is now in Toulouse."[75] M. Rose remained in a hospital for the
mentally ill in Toulouse until her death on August 6, 1890. Her burial place is
unknown.

In retrospect, it is logical to question just when the symptoms of M.
Rose's illness began to appear. Although M. Ursula Frayne's written comments
on Bishop Fleming are adequate proof that she and the bishop were—to say the
least—not on good terms, there may have been another reason for her aban-
donment of the Newfoundland mission. If M. Ursula had noticed any erratic

---

74. Ibid.

75. Archives, Convent of Mercy, Bermondsey. It is an oral tradition among Sisters of Mercy
in Ireland and England that religious who suffered from severe mental illnesses were sent
to hospitals in France where religious orders, such as the Franciscans, operated hospitals
specifically for religious. Apparently, there were no hospitals of this kind in Ireland or
England in the nineteenth century. This information was provided by Marion McCarthy,
RSM, archivist for the Institute of the Sisters of Mercy in England.

behaviour on the part of M. Rose after their arrival in St. John's, she would have communicated her concern to M. de Pazzi in Dublin before making her fears known to Bishop Fleming. Naturally, she could not have submitted this communication to the superior, M. Rose. Could this explain the references in the bishop's letter, "Sister Ursula's communication to you had left this [place] without having been subjected to the inspection of her Superior."[76] Is this the reason M. Ursula felt it necessary to return to Ireland with M. Rose?

There may have been several reasons for M. Ursula's decision to return to Ireland. Most of the facts dealing with the foundation have been lost. The little we know has been the source of lively speculation. Historians seem to react to the same events in widely divergent ways—all of which point out the danger of insisting on too personal a version of the past. When all is said and done, we are left with probability, possibility, and conjecture, but no sure answers to the questions that have haunted the Sisters of Mercy in Newfoundland since the beginning.

---

76. Fleming to M. de Pazzi Delany, June 14, 1843, DDA, Murray Papers, AB 3/32/1, (1843–44) Addenda, letter 208.

CHAPTER FOUR

AND THEN THERE WERE TWO

We do pray for mercy, and that same prayer
Doth teach us all to render
Deeds of mercy.

Shakespeare, *The Merchant of Venice*, 4.1.204–06

he departure of Sisters M. Ursula Frayne and M. Rose Lynch in November 1843 must have caused some diminishment in the level of service carried on by the Sisters of Mercy. By way of encouragement, the remaining sisters, M. Francis Creedon and M. Joseph Nugent, may have pondered the words of their foundress, "It commenced with 2, Sister Doyle and I."[1] According to the Mercy Convent accounts book, the school enrolment continued to increase.[2] When school was officially opened on May 1, 1843, forty-two pupils were enrolled. The following year, 1844, fifty-five students attended regular classes at Our Lady of Mercy School. In addition, M. Francis and M. Joseph gave private instruction in music to a number of students and continued the visitation of the sick on weekends and, in cases of emergency, after school hours during the week. In fact, from the early days, the Sisters of Mercy devoted their weekends to visitation. Starting out at ten

---

1. M. Catherine McAuley to M. Elizabeth Moore, January 13, 1839. Sullivan, *Correspondence*, p. 178.
2. Accounts Book, Convent of Our Lady of Mercy, St. John's, 1843–44, ASMSJ.

82

on Saturday mornings, they used to visit the slum areas of old St. John's, bringing food, procuring coal for the poor unheated homes, attending to the sick, and many times cleaning wretched, uncared-for hovels. This poses the question, "How could two sisters accomplish all this and, as well, spend a couple of hours a day in prayer?" There is no doubt about the courses offered at the school in the 1840s. The local newspapers carried advertisements listing the subjects taught, the fees charged, and the "extras" that might interest some of the students: "Reading, Writing, Arithmetic, English Grammar, Geography, Use of the Globes, History, etc., Needlework (Plain and Ornamental) etc., Terms, £5 per annum. Extra Charges: French or Italian £2. Music £8."[3] The advertisement does not specify what was included in the "etceteras"!

Apparently, school activities in the 1840s were carried on at a much more leisurely pace than is the case today. Classes began in the morning at ten o'clock, and the children returned home at noon for dinner. Classes resumed at half past one and concluded at three o'clock.[4] The only surviving sketch of the original Mercy Convent, taken in conjunction with Bishop Fleming's description of the building, suggests that the school may have consisted of two classrooms. In the absence of written records describing the layout of the school, there is no certainty that this was the case. One can only speculate on the division of work. Possibly, the children were separated into levels according to age and competence and worked individually at assigned tasks while the sisters instructed one group or another. This system of teaching in one- or two-room schools was quite common in outports of Newfoundland right up to the middle of the twentieth century.

With the opening of the school, the sisters were no longer financially dependent on the bishop, a circumstance that must have evoked a sigh of relief from the beleaguered bishop, as well as from the sisters themselves. From the modest fees paid by the students, M. Francis and M. Joseph supported themselves and provided for the needs of the poor.

---

3. *The Newfoundlander*, April 16, 1843, p. 1.

4. M. Bernard Dooley, one of the senior sisters at Mercy Convent in the 1940s, was the source of this information. The extended noon break was customary in many Newfoundland schools until the 1930s and '40s.

The Mercy Convent accounts book dates from the formal opening of Our Lady of Mercy School, May 1, 1843, and includes the names of the students and the fees paid by each. There is no record of fees paid during the summer months, suggesting that school was closed in July and August.

The "Expenditures" side of the accounts book provides a glimpse of the lives of the sisters in those far-off days. The simplicity of their style of living is portrayed on every page. The first financial statement, listing receipts and expenditures from May of that year, was signed in October 1843, "Sister Mary Rose Lynch, Superior," and "Michael Anthony Fleming, Bishop of St. John's." Judging by the entries, the sisters had little variety in their diet. The regular food items purchased were milk, potatoes, butter, flour, molasses, and, on rare occasions, pork or meat (beef). During the year 1843, there is only one entry for the purchase of fish. Perhaps some kind fisherman brought them a sample of his catch from time to time so that they did not need to buy it. In the summer months they purchased vegetables that may have been too expensive or not available during the colder seasons of the year. In the absence of electricity, they bought candles and oil for the lamp, and they treated themselves to new boots. The regular schedule of teaching and visitation left no time for them to ensure the almost oppressive cleanliness frequently associated with convents, but periodic entries for "Servants Wages" show that occasionally they hired help to take care of this problem. The accounts book reveals, too, that even though they had moved into the convent six months earlier, the interior was not completely finished. Entries for June 1843 noted payments to a carpenter, expenses for papering, and the purchase of window blinds. The fact that they bought altar linens and altar wine for the chapel suggests that mass was celebrated in the convent, at least occasionally. Entries of varying amounts appear under the heading, "For the sick poor."

After November 1843, the accounts book was signed, "Sister Mary Francis Creedon, Superior." Her first entry, dated November 12, listed: "Expenses for Sisters' departure, £4/18/9."[5] For the next few years, M.

---

5. This amount may seem to be quite a bargain for the passage of two people across the Atlantic. To put it in perspective, £4 was the yearly wage for a labourer in 1843. I am indebted to John FitzGerald for this information. FitzGerald cited John Mannion as his source.

Francis made gradual improvements to the convent as their income allowed. She purchased more chairs, had an altar made and carpeted the floor of the chapel. The literary bent of the two sisters is indicated by regular entries for the purchase of books. Among the items requiring frequent repair were the sisters' boots and the clock, and during the winter months, an occasional entry under "Medicine" suggests that perhaps the stalwart missionaries were not immune to catching colds.

Both M. Francis and M. Joseph had spent enough time in St. John's to know what to expect from Newfoundland weather. Thus, the months between November and April brought no surprises. Today we might be amazed at situations that our hardier ancestors took for granted. One of the Presentation Sisters, M. Xaverius Lynch, left a description of the daily trials of winter in those days:

> You may imagine what the cold is when in our bedrooms we cannot leave a drop of water in the basins or jugs. We must wait ever so long before we can get it to melt. As for our towels you might as well have a sheet of paste board, for after using them and putting them to dry they are frozen quite hard and stiff. I washed my stockings and put them to dry. What was my amazement when going to mend them to see them stiff as a board and icicles hanging from them. . . . As for the milk for breakfast it is like lump sugar and we are obliged to cut it with a knife . . . and the meat is obliged to be sawn.[6]

The severity of the Newfoundland winter created special hardships for the Mercy Sisters, who had to brave the cold and the snow to bring relief to the sick and the poor. An article in *The Newfoundlander* described their activities:

> Ever and anon might these two pious Sisters have been seen, before or after the toils of the day at school, treading through our snows, and pelted by our sleet, to smooth the pillow of the deathbed of the afflicted, and pouring into the ear of the infected the

---

6. M. Xaverius Lynch to "Dearest Ann," January 6, 1834, "Sesquicentenary Souvenir," p. 18, APSG.

words of promise and of hope, either in the wretched hovel of the poor, or in the Hospital.[7]

Nevertheless, the visitation was—and is—a ministry dear to the hearts of Sisters of Mercy everywhere, and the two were young enough to enjoy a brisk walk in the fresh, crisp air of Newfoundland. Despite the comments of the editor of *The Newfoundlander*, the weather was not always miserable! We are indebted once more to M. Xaverius Lynch for providing information on the delights and hazards of going outdoors in winter:

> The sky is beautiful and clear and while the frost is most intense and ready to freeze your limbs off you are cheered by the most beautiful atmosphere and the brilliancy of the sun and it would appear that the frost and sun were contending together. . . . The people here make use of the most curious things for walking according to the weather. In snow they wear a kind of thing called Moggissons [sic]. They are made either like shoes or boots made of wood. They are worn over their shoes. In frosty weather they wear a kind of thing called creapers [sic], something like patens with large iron spikes out of them to stick in the ice and keep them from falling. The gentlemen use long poles higher than themselves to keep them from falling, with spikes in the bottom of them. Bone-setters are in great demand in this country as it is very hard to escape without getting broken limbs and what renders it so very dangerous to walk is the great hills for the whole country is a complete hill and in frosty weather we might as well be walking on glass.[8]

It is curious that neither M. Francis nor M. Joseph left any account of the events of these years, for both women were well-educated, and several of M. Joseph's translations of works by French and Italian writers have been published.[9]

---

7. *The Newfoundlander*, June 24, 1847, p. 3.

8. M. Xaverius Lynch to "Dearest Ann," January 6, 1834, "Sesquicentenary Souvenir," p. 18, APSG.

9. M. Joseph Nugent translated from the original French a book entitled *Eucologue*, or *The Virtuous Scholar*, that was used widely in the Catholic schools in Ireland. As well, she translated from the original Italian several books of devotion. Some of these books are preserved in the Archives of the Sisters of Mercy, St. John's, Newfoundland.

Perhaps the sisters had neither time nor energy after the strenuous work of the day to think of writing their experiences. They realized that, until others joined them, the success of the mission depended on their maintaining their own health and strength. It is clear that Baggot Street had no intention of sending sisters to replace M. Rose Lynch and M. Ursula Frayne. Commenting on the situation, Mercy historian M. Austin Carroll mused:

> It seems strange that those who felt so keenly their lonely, over-worked situation should have sent them no help, and that Bishop Fleming's eloquent appeals to his countrywomen should have evoked no response. True, extremes of climate and difficulties of another nature—which, however, are not of public interest—were great, and rumor more than trebled them.[10]

M. Austin may not have realized how mistaken she was in her assertion that the difficulties experienced "are not of public interest," for the Mercy congregation has not ceased to question the comment since it first appeared in print.

Nothing of great moment occurred until June 9, 1846. On that day one of the most destructive fires in the history of Newfoundland raged through St. John's, destroying approximately two thousand houses and property worth several millions of dollars.[11] One casualty of the fire was the new Presentation Convent on Long's Hill. By rights, because of its distance from the source of the fire, it should have escaped, but people whose homes were being destroyed flocked to the convent for refuge. Embers brought into the building in a bundle of clothing caused the interior to ignite. Once started, the fire burned so rapidly that the sisters had no time to save anything.[12]

As soon as the two Mercy Sisters saw the Presentation Convent in flames they hurried over to Long's Hill to offer assistance. The Presentation annalist described what happened:

---

10. Carroll, *Leaves*, vol. 3, p. 23.
11. Greene, *Between Damnation and Starvation,* p. 198.
12. O'Neill, *A Seaport Legacy,* p. 629.

> The Sisters of Mercy, seeing the Convent on fire, hastened to the place and brought the Religious to their Convent, where they most kindly invited them to remain until a house could be provided. But they, unwilling to give trouble, only rested a few hours, and then proceeded to a little Cottage of the Bishop who was then in Ireland.[13]

The term "cottage" was a euphemism, for the building was, in reality, a barn. Historian Paul O'Neill described the situation in which the sisters found themselves: "For the next five months the Presentation Sisters slept on the floor of the barn at Carpasia and taught in the nearby fields on fine days."[14] Another author claimed that the sisters slept in the hayloft of the barn, and held classes on the ground level when the weather was too bad to go outside.[15] With the advent of cold weather, such an arrangement could not be tolerated. As a temporary solution, Bishop Fleming arranged for Mercy Convent to be partitioned to receive the Presentation Sisters. They moved into Mercy Convent early in November 1846, where "they were received with the greatest affection, accommodated with the greater part of the House, and where a temporary School was built for them adjoining the convent."[16]

The Presentation Sisters remained at Mercy Convent for the next five years until October 21, 1851.[17] On that date they took up residence in an unfinished section of their new school at Cathedral Square until the Presentation Convent was ready for occupancy. Nothing is recorded of their experiences while they lived with the Mercy Sisters. The tradition passed on at Mercy Convent was that each community lived a separate existence under the one roof, each according to its own Rule and *Horarium*. Because space was limited, it is likely the chapel, refectory, and kitchen were shared. Bishop Fleming referred to the crowded conditions in a letter to the Newfoundland House of Assembly:

---

13. Annals, Presentation Convent, St. John's, 1846–53, APSSJ.
14. O'Neill, *A Seaport Legacy*, p. 791.
15. Rev. P. W. Browne, "Nano Nagle's Daughters," Ave *Maria*, (Notre Dame, Ind.) 38, no. 15 (October 7, 1933): pp. 453–54.
16. Annals, Presentation Convent, St. John's, 1846–53, APSSJ.
17. Ibid.

With reference to the former school . . . as well as the dwelling house of the Community destroyed by the Fire of the 9th of June, 1846 . . . since that period the Ladies of the Institution are compelled to be indebted to the Convent of Mercy for an Asylum, where the scanty accommodation, originally intended for four Nuns, is now obliged to serve no fewer than fifteen, an arrangement greatly calculated to militate against the health of the entire community . . . yet my means, crippled by the vast losses of that Fire, render me unable to provide a remedy. [18]

Meanwhile, M. Francis and M. Joseph continued the ceaseless demands of teaching and caring for the sick poor in their homes and at St. John's Hospital, which was located in what is now Victoria Park, about an hour's walk from Mercy Convent. In June 1847, as a consequence of an epidemic of typhus that broke out in St. John's, the Sisters of Mercy were in constant attendance on the sick at the hospital. The accounts book for this period indicates that the school was closed during the month of June, allowing the sisters to devote all their time to the sick. By June 3, thirty-six patients were crowded into the small ward at the hospital, each one requiring all the attention and skill the sisters could bring. Making her rounds, M. Joseph's attention was caught by a critically ill eighteen-year-old boy. Filled with anger and rage at the captain whose ship had brought the disease to the city, the boy spent his day heaping curses on the head of that unfortunate official—hardly an appropriate state of mind for one so near death. M. Joseph stayed with him, trying to ease his fever while all the time begging him to forgive the man whom he called his murderer. Paul O'Neill described what happened: "In the face of such determination he finally turned to the pleading nun and said, 'Well, Madame, for your sake I'll forgive him.' The priest whom the boy had earlier rejected returned to his bedside and the lad died at peace."[19] When she returned to the convent that evening, June 3, 1847, M. Joseph collapsed, another victim of the typhus epidemic.[20] For two weeks she

---

18. Fleming to the Honourable James Crowdy, *JHA*, 1848, p. 368.
19. O'Neill, *A Seaport Legacy*, p. 794.
20. *The Newfoundlander*, June 24, 1847, p. 3.

suffered the torments of that vicious fever while M. Francis remained by her side
providing whatever comfort was available. From the accounts book, we learn
that she obtained the services of two physicians, Drs. Rochford and Walsh, and
hired a nurse so that the patient could have constant attention. The accounts
book lists the cost of "Hops for a pillow," medicine, and washing, but no amount
of medical skill or loving care was effective in halting the progress of the infection. M. Joseph died at five minutes before two o'clock on the afternoon of June
17, leaving M. Francis Creedon to carry on the Mercy ministry alone.[21]

M. Joseph Nugent was one of the outstanding Newfoundland women of
the nineteenth century, a devoted humanitarian who gave her life in the service of others. "Besides being known as Newfoundland's first nurse, M. Joseph
was also the first woman we know of in Newfoundland's history to give her life
while caring for the sick."[22] *The Newfoundlander* published a lengthy editorial
that reflected the grief and shock of the citizens on hearing of the death of this
woman who had done so much good in the short time since her profession as
a Sister of Mercy:

> It has seldom occurred to us, in our capacity of Journalist, to
> have to record a death in the circle of our own community,
> which is at the same time so painfully bitter to her nearest and
> dearest connexions, so sincerely regretted, and fraught with
> such interest to the Catholic inhabitants of St. John's, and its
> more immediate vicinity; for the whole range of the Colony it
> would be difficult to point at a life of more importance to the
> spiritual and temporal interest of the juvenile female portion of
> our Catholic population, while to the more matured, as well as
> to the sick and the infirm of both sexes, her devotedness in
> instructing and administering to the comforts of the diseased,
> whether of body or mind, could only be surpassed by her untir-
> ing assiduity and zeal in the great cause in which her heart and
> soul were engaged.[23]

21. *The Patriot and Terra Nova Herald*, June 21, 1847, p. 4.
22. Hogan, *Pathways*, p. 36.
23. *The Newfoundlander*, June 24, 1847, p. 4.

M. Joseph Nugent was laid to rest in the old Catholic cemetery on land now occupied by the Kirk and extending to Queen's Road and west to Long's Hill.[24]

Although the days and weeks following the death of her friend and companion were particularly difficult for M. Francis Creedon, she did not allow herself to succumb to self-pity or a sense of defeat; rather, she continued her work of teaching and visitation of the sick. Obviously, enrolment had to be limited, but she did not close the school. The accounts book notes that twenty-seven students were registered at Our Lady of Mercy School for the year 1847–48 and M. Francis struggled on alone. M. Austin Carroll, commenting on the situation wrote:

> The vexations which beset the Newfoundland house in its early days would have broken the heart and spirit of an ordinary woman, but Mother Creedon had the indomitable courage of her mother in Christ [i.e. Catherine McAuley]. . . . Again and again did her dear Sisters of the parent house invite her to return and wait till the fog-draped isle was ripe for the experiment.[25]

Hearing of her lonely and difficult plight, several of her novitiate companions, now superiors of flourishing convents, begged M. Francis to give up the mission.[26] M. Agnes O'Connor was particularly insistent, arguing that M. Francis could do more for God in New York.[27] Even the usually optimistic Bishop Fleming doubted that the Mercy foundation in St. John's could survive, and he considered the possibility of M. Francis joining the Presentation Sisters. For advice on the matter he wrote to Cardinal Mai in Rome and received this reply, "Sisters from other Orders may be allowed to join the Presentation with the permission of the Vicar General of the diocese and of the Superior of their previous Order."[28] Whether the bishop bothered to consult M. Francis on the

---

24. O'Neill, *A Seaport Legacy*, p. 691.

25. Carroll, *Leaves*, vol. 3, p. 22.

26. Ibid. Carroll identifies these women as M. Liguori Gibson of Liverpool, M. deSales Vigne of Dundalk, and M. Agnes O'Connor of New York.

27. Ibid.

28. Cardinal Mai to Fleming, n.d., AASJ, 103/7/1.

matter is debatable. In any case, Francis felt that she had been selected and commissioned by Catherine McAuley herself for this work, and she was not about to give up. The enduring presence of the Sisters of Mercy in Newfoundland is due to the perseverance and magnificent courage of this woman who "stayed the course" and kept the fledgling institute alive. Ever since those early days, M. Francis Creedon is revered as the true foundress of the Newfoundland Mercy congregation.

For ten long months, M. Francis struggled on alone until in April 1848, she accepted Agnes Nugent as a postulant. Agnes was the daughter of M. Francis's sister, Ellen, and John Valentine Nugent and so was niece to both M. Francis and M. Joseph. She was born in Waterford on January 17, 1830, and, at the age of three years, came to Newfoundland with her family. Her parents saw to it that she received a good classical education and was fluent in several languages.[29] Inspired by the example of her aunts, from her early teens she was determined to become a Sister of Mercy. Finally, when she was twenty, her parents agreed to her repeated requests, and Agnes entered as a postulant at Mercy Convent on the feast of St. Mark, April 25, 1848. Almost eight months later, on December 8, she received the habit of a Sister of Mercy, with the name, Mary Vincent de Paul. The ceremony took place in the "Old Chapel" on Henry Street. Two of the St. John's newspapers published an account of the event:

> One of the most touching ceremonies that has ever been con-
> ducted before the public in this country, was witnessed at the
> Catholic Chapel in this Town on last Friday morning, when the
> congregation were particularly edified by the performance of
> the first public reception of a Nun that has taken place in our
> community . . .
>   Although the reception of this young lady was public, yet
> owing to there having been no public notification of the intend-
> ed ceremony, and to its occurring at the early hour of seven
> o'clock, it was expected to have passed off in comparative priva-
> cy. Yet we observed a large congregation present, every one of

---

29. Carroll, *Leaves*, vol. 3, p. 26.

whom appeared deeply impressed with the solemnity of the
scene.

Shortly after 7 o'clock, the Rt. Rev. Dr. Fleming . . . ascend-
ed the high altar, and immediately afterwards 25 of the children of
the school, in white dresses, walked from the sacristy through the
sanctuary, two and two, with a single one preceding . . . the Rev.
Superior and the postulant following and kneeling within the choir
and the door of the sanctuary.[30]

This account is important for, despite statements to the contrary,[31] it confirms
entries in the accounts book indicating that the school remained open
throughout the period when M. Francis was alone.

The reception of Agnes Nugent as a Sister of Mercy was one of the last
public functions at which Bishop Fleming presided.[32] After the disastrous fire
of 1846 that destroyed not only the new Presentation Convent but also most
of his important papers and many valuable artifacts, the bishop's health
declined rapidly. Less than two years after receiving Agnes Nugent as a Sister
of Mercy, Bishop Fleming died on July 14, 1850, and was succeeded by his
friend and coadjutor bishop, John Mullock.

Agnes Nugent, now called Mary Vincent, spent the prescribed two years
novitiate under the direction of her aunt, M. Francis Creedon. Toward the end
of the first year of M. Vincent's novitiate, on November 1, 1849, M. Francis
Creedon accepted a young lady from Charlottetown, Prince Edward Island, as
a postulant. Her name was Catherine, daughter of Cornelius Little and Bridget
Costin Little. She was a sister of Philip Little who became Newfoundland's
first prime minister in 1850. It soon became obvious that Miss Little was not
destined to become a Sister of Mercy, for she left the community after three
weeks. Almost a year later, a young lady from Limerick, Mary Catherine
Elizabeth Teresa Bernard, presented herself at Mercy Convent and was accepted as a postulant on September 18, 1850. This young lady was a friend of

---

30. *The Newfoundlander,* December 14, 1848, p. 2.

31. O'Neill, *A Seaport Legacy,* p. 795.

32. The last public function at which Bishop Fleming presided was the celebration of the
first mass in the new Cathedral of St. John the Baptist on January 6, 1850.

Bishop Mullock, and it was at his invitation she came to St. John's to become a Sister of Mercy.[33] Another postulant joined them three weeks later, October 8, when M. Francis Creedon welcomed a young widow by the name of Mary (O'Regan) Redmond. Now there were four.

Catherine Teresa Bernard was born in Limerick in 1827 or 1828, daughter of Christopher Bernard and Lucinda (French) Bernard.[34] According to the County Records at Limerick, there was only one child born to these parents, a girl whose name is given as Matilda. Apparently, the Bernard parents gave their baby the additional names of Mary Catherine Elizabeth Teresa, for in later years she used the name Catherine and dropped the name Matilda. There is no clear picture of her childhood. M. Austin Carroll wrote that Catherine's parents died before she reached the age of ten years, and she was placed in the care of a religious order, the Faithful Companions of Jesus, at Laurel Hill Convent in Limerick.[35] In this, however, M. Austin was mistaken, for the members of that order did not arrive in Limerick until September 1844 and did not purchase the Laurel Hill property until June 1845, when Catherine Bernard was seventeen years of age.[36] If, in fact, the child was only ten when her parents died, there is no information available on where she spent the intervening years before she went to the sisters at Laurel Hill School, possibly in 1845. It is likely that she remained at Laurel Hill and completed her education there before coming to Newfoundland in 1850. This premise is supported by evidence obtained from sisters who lived with M. Xavier (Catherine) Bernard and were acquainted with the circumstances of her life.[37]

33. ASMSJ, MG 2/1/296. Notes taken by M. Basil McCormack in the early 1950s at an interview with some of the senior sisters at Mercy Convent, ASMSJ.

34. M. Xavier Bernard died in February 1882 at the age of 54. This indicates that she was born in 1827 or 1828.

35. Carroll, *Leaves*, vol. 3, p. 30. M. Austin Carroll was given this information by M. Bernard Clune, a close friend of M. Xavier Bernard and who succeeded M. Xavier as superior of Mercy Convent. I am indebted to M. Hermenia Muldrey, the biographer of M. Austin Carroll, for this information.

36. Margaret Lyddy, "History of St. Joseph's Parish, Limerick," p. 7, Limerick County Archives, Limerick.

37. Carroll, *Leaves*, vol. 3, p. 30.

The other postulant who entered in 1850, Mary O'Regan Redmond, was born in Youghal, County Cork, in 1824. She came to Newfoundland sometime prior to 1843, for there is a record of her marriage to Peter Redmond of Wexford on November 20, 1843, in the Old Chapel on Henry Street.[38] A few years later, Peter died and the young widow was left wondering what do to with the rest of her life. She knew about the Sisters of Mercy, for they were a familiar sight as they passed through the streets to visit the homes of the poor. Something about their way of life appealed strongly to Mary, and she decided to join them. She was welcomed on October 8, 1850, by a community of three, M. Francis Creedon; the postulant, Catherine Bernard; and the novice, M. Vincent Nugent.

On December 8, 1850, Bishop Mullock presided at the ceremonies of reception and profession that took place at Mercy Convent when M. Vincent Nugent pronounced her vows, taking for her title "of the Sacred Heart."[39] At the same time, Catherine Bernard was accepted as a novice and given the religious name, Mary Francis Xavier. A little more than two years later, on April 30, 1853, M. Xavier Bernard made her vows as a Sister of Mercy. With the profession of M. Vincent Nugent and M. Xavier Bernard, the future of the Mercy congregation in Newfoundland began to take shape. Both young women were talented, well-educated, and full of enthusiasm. However, the contribution of the third recruit, Mary Redmond, should not be overlooked. After a four-year novitiate, she was professed as a lay sister on September 24, 1855, taking the name Elizabeth.[40] From that time on, like many of those who came after her, Sr. Elizabeth spent her life in hidden service to her sisters in community and to

38. Marriage Register, Cathedral Parish of St. John the Baptist, St. John's, November 20, 1843, AASJ.

39. It was the custom that at the time of profession each Sister of Mercy adopted a title to indicate her commitment to some special devotion.

40. The designation, "lay sister," referred to a sister who was not required to perform the professional duties of teaching or nursing. For the most part, lay sisters devoted their lives to housekeeping duties around the convent, assisting the poor, and visiting the sick. For some strange reason young women who were received as lay sisters were given the name of some saint without the addition of the name "Mary." During her tenure as superior general in the 1950s, M. Imelda Smith eliminated this form of discrimination for the Newfoundland Congregation of the Sisters of Mercy.

the hundreds of children committed to the sisters' care. Her fidelity to the daily chores around the convent provided the support and the freedom for the other sisters to pursue their works of education and charity.

The departure of the Presentation Sisters in July 1851 to take up residence in the new school created more space at Mercy Convent. A few postulants were accepted, but they stayed only a short time, possibly discouraged by the sheer magnitude of the tasks that faced them. As if the sisters had not already enough work to occupy every waking moment, there was still another urgent matter that the bishop wanted them to address, namely, the plight of orphan girls whose parents had succumbed to one or other of the frequent epidemics that afflicted the residents of this seaport town. He proposed that from funds left by Bishop Fleming for this purpose, an orphanage would be built adjoining Mercy Convent to care for girls who had been left destitute. Lack of numbers did not discourage the compassionate M. Francis Creedon when the bishop presented his request. In 1852, the construction of an orphanage was begun at the rear of the convent, facing Cathedral Square. Subsequently, in 1855, an infirmary was erected from the funds of the Orphanage of the Immaculate Conception. This building was attached to the convent and was intended for the use of orphans who were sick.[41]

At the same time, keenly aware that the sisters desperately needed help, Bishop Mullock wrote to Archbishop Paul Cullen of Dublin, asking him to intercede with the sisters at Baggot Street to send help. Early in 1854, Bishop Mullock received a reply:

> . . . I beg to acquaint you that I will do everything in my power to assist in advancing the interests of the Sisters of Mercy in St. John's. I regret that Mrs. Whitty [the superior of the Baggot Street Convent] is at present in Belfast where she is establishing a new convent and that on account of her absence I cannot give you any certain information for the present. She will return in a few days when I will be able to learn from her what she can do. I think it

---

41. ASMSJ, RG 10/1/1i.

will not be difficult to get a few well-educated nuns to join your community and in this way your school will be provided for. [42]

In spite of the intervention of the archbishop of Dublin, Baggot Street remained unwilling to send help to the overworked little community in St. John's. Bishop Mullock, however, did not give up. He enlisted the aid of a Franciscan friend, Brother Bonaventure MacLaughlin. On June 13, 1854, Brother Bonaventure wrote back to Bishop Mullock, in essence suggesting that he forget about seeking help from Baggot Street and try Limerick:

> When I first spoke to Dr. Cullen about the Nuns, he said that he had mentioned the matter at Baggot St., but they had not any to send who would be capable of discharging the duties for which you wanted them. His Grace, however, promised me that he would try elsewhere. In order to give him as much time as possible I did not call on him until this morning. He told me that he had made other applications but without effect. I asked whether he had tried Limerick and he said not. Now I think that Mr. Moore would be the very best person to whom to apply. I would not, however, like to do so without your consent, but if you wish it, I can do so, as I expect (D.V.) to be in Limerick shortly after the receipt of your next. [43]

Notwithstanding the best efforts of Archbishop Cullen and Brother Bonaventure, the sisters in Ireland seemed willing to offer assistance to the beleaguered missionaries in St. John's.[44]

An outbreak of cholera in North America and the West Indies during the spring of 1854 caused the Newfoundland government to impose quarantine on all ships arriving from these countries. But in spite of this precaution, several deaths from the infection were reported in the city during August of that year, and by October the full fury of the epidemic broke. Fortunately, the

---

42. Archbishop Paul Cullen to Bishop Mullock, January 21, 1854, AASJ, 104/1/8.
43. Brother Bonaventure MacLaughlin to Bishop Mullock, June 13, 1854, AASJ, 104/1/17.
44. The influx of a number of young women from Limerick seeking admission to the Mercy congregation may—or may not—have been due to the efforts of Brother Bonaventure.

contagion did not spread to areas outside the city but during the last three months of 1854 a total of more than five hundred deaths were reported in St. John's.[45] Aware of how many were dying in the hospital, people who became ill insisted on remaining at home, thus unwittingly contributing to the spread of the disease.[46]

In light of the seriousness of the epidemic, the sisters closed the school from the end of July until January of 1855.[47] As the disease spread throughout the centre of the city, the four Sisters of Mercy found themselves in constant attendance on the sick and dying. Bishop Mullock and the priests were kept busy administering the sacrament of extreme unction. Some idea of situations encountered by the priests and sisters is revealed in an article written for *The Newfoundlander* by a member of the clergy:

> When the cholera broke out in the city in 1854 he [i.e. Bishop Mullock] was always one of the first ... to administer to the sick and the dying. He always maintained a pocket knife that was most useful to him in administering the Last Rites. The poorer classes in Newfoundland have an unalterable habit of wearing their stockings in bed. Nothing used to try our patience more when we had a long list of calls than to be brought up short in the act of administering Extreme Unction by finding the feet encased in long woolen stockings. The Bishop used to rip the soles of the stockings with his pocket knife and so complete the Anointing.[48]

No doubt the poor, unfortunate people wore the stockings as a protection against the cold and damp that resulted from the deplorable housing conditions that existed at the time. The sisters provided food, medicine, and comfort. Their presence was a sign of hope when even close relatives and friends, ter-

45. According to the Newfoundland Census for 1857, St. John's had a population of 24,851. The 1847 Census lists the population of St. John's at 20,941. Thus, in 1854 the population of St. John's numbered between twenty and twenty-four thousand persons.

46. *ENL*, s.v. "Health."

47. There are no entries in the accounts book of the Convent of Our Lady of Mercy recording the payment of school fees from July 30–December 10, 1854, when an entry "due February 23, 1854," was recorded. School fees were received again in January 1855.

48. *The Newfoundlander*, June 21, 1864, p. 3.

rified of contagion, left the stricken family members to cope as best they could.[49] A local historian wrote of the work of the Sisters of Mercy during this epidemic as follows:

> It was during this terrible epidemic that the few Mercy nuns then in St. John's distinguished themselves by going into cholera-ridden homes to tend the helplessly sick and haul out corpses that nobody else would touch so that they could be placed in coffins that were dumped on the streets.[50]

By the end of the year, "the few Mercy nuns" were making preparations to initiate a new ministry. On December 8, 1854, the Immaculate Conception Orphanage was opened at Mercy Convent.[51] A nine-year-old child was admitted, and by the end of the year, twelve more had joined her. Two months later, the bishop mentioned the orphanage in his annual pastoral letter:

> Since last Lent heavy afflictions have fallen on us. God, for our sins, sent the Angel of Pestilence among us, and many children have been left fatherless, and many homesteads desolate.... An Orphan Asylum containing already twenty female orphans has been opened. The funds for the building and for the support of several orphans have been left by your late pastor, Dr. Fleming. Under the care of the Sisters of Mercy, these children will be brought up in virtuous and industrious habits, educated and qualified for any situations in which they may be hereafter placed.[52]

---

49. Carroll, *Leaves*, vol. 3, p. 27.

50. O'Neill, *The Oldest City*, p. 294.

51. In the Constitution *Ineffabilis Deus* of December 8, 1854, Pius IX declared that the Blessed Virgin Mary "in the first instance of her conception, by a singular privilege and grace granted by God, in view of the merits of Jesus Christ, was preserved exempt from all stain of original sin." The Orphanage of the Immaculate Conception at Mercy Convent may have been one of the first to be thus named after the promulgation of the dogma. The orphanage was built immediately behind the Mercy Convent, facing west toward Cathedral Square.

52. Bishop J. T. Mullock, "Lenten Pastoral Letter, February 22, 1855," *The Patriot and Terra Nova Herald,* February 26, 1855, p. 3.

There was a triple celebration at Mercy Convent on December 8, 1854. With the universal Church, the sisters celebrated this new feast, the Feast of the Immaculate Conception, in honour of the Mother of God. But there was still more cause for rejoicing. Not only did the orphanage open on that day, but also the first Newfoundland-born postulant entered in the person of Anastasia Catherine Mary Tarahan. This young lady had been denied admission by Bishop Fleming because of being "native born."[53] Obviously Bishop Mullock did not agree with the policy of his predecessor with respect to local vocations, and certainly in her situation, M. Francis Creedon would have been glad to accept postulants from just about anywhere! After seven months, Anastasia was received as a novice on July 2, 1855, and given the name, Mary John Baptist, but the kindly superior who received her would not live to see her profession two years later. The hard work in caring for the sick during the cholera epidemic as well as the hardships of the early years combined to shatter the health of this valiant woman.

By July 1, it was obvious that M. Francis was seriously ill, but she was determined to be present for the ceremony of reception on the following day. Not only did she participate in the ceremony, but also at its conclusion, she went with Sr. Elizabeth Redmond to visit the sick, leaving the other sisters to celebrate at home. The next day she was confined to bed. The frightened and sorrowing young sisters tried everything in their power to prolong the life of one who was so dear, but the doctors could do nothing. M. Francis Creedon died at five o'clock on the morning of July 15, 1855, at the age of forty-three years.[54] Recording the event in his *Ordo*, Bishop Mullock wrote, "Mrs. Creedon, Superioress of the Convent of Mercy, died this morning a victim of overwork for the poor and sick."[55] She was the first to be buried in the sisters' plot in Belvedere Cemetery.

53. O'Neill, *A Seaport Legacy*, p. 795. Bishop Fleming refused to accept Newfoundland-born as candidates for the priesthood and religious life. For a discussion of this policy, see FitzGerald, "Conflict and Culture," pp. 100–101.

54. Although M. Francis's headstone in Belvedere Cemetery states that she was forty-four years of age at the time of her death, she was born on December 5, 1811. Therefore, at the time of her death, she was in her forty-fourth year.

55. Bishop Mullock, *Ordo*, 1855, AASJ, 104/2/14. At that time religious sisters were often addressed by the title "Mrs.," an abbreviation for "Mistress," a term which signified any adult woman.

The story of M. Francis Creedon is the story of the foundation of the Newfoundland Sisters of Mercy. Alone, in a land that was not her own, this quiet, unassuming woman struggled against almost insuperable odds to fulfil the task that had been given her. Her commitment to her mission may have been seen as stubborn and foolhardy, especially during the time when the usually decisive Bishop Fleming dithered about whether the convent should be suppressed.[56] She would have rejoiced if she could have had a glimpse of the future and seen her sisters working in St. Michael's Orphanage, St. Clare's Mercy Hospital, Littledale, St. Patrick's Mercy Home, in all corners of Newfoundland and Labrador, and in Peru. But no such vision was hers. Perhaps her own assessment of her life could be summed up in the words of an unknown author:

> We need to keep our eyes fixed on the Lord our God
>   until God lets us rest.
> And then we will know,
>   as we have always known
> That the effort was worth
>   The gift of our lives,
>   The best of our years,
>   The length of our days.[57]

---

56. See chapter four, n. 29. In context, Bishop Fleming's query is an indication that he considered transferring M. Francis Creedon to the Presentation community, thus suppressing the Mercy congregation in Newfoundland.

57. Author unknown.

CHAPTER FIVE

THE SECOND GENERATION

Do not let loyalty and faithfulness forsake you. Tie them
tightly around your neck. . . . Write them on your heart.

Proverbs 3:2

espite their grief over the death of their dearly loved superior, M.
Francis Creedon, the sisters at Mercy Convent could not take time
off to indulge their sorrow. There was work to be done—the duties
of the visitation and, above all, the orphans who needed their care and attention. There was, also, a decision to be made about the governance of the little
community. And so, the first entry in the "Acts of Chapter of the Convent of
Our Blessed Lady of Mercy" was made on July 20, 1855: "There not being a
sufficient number of professed Religious in the community to elect by vote of
Chapter, the Right Reverend Doctor Mullock nominated to the office of
Superioress Sister Mary Francis Xavier Bernard."[1]

Immediately after her appointment, M. Xavier and her little community reflected on their situation. Although she was the oldest of the group, at the
age of twenty-seven, M. Xavier felt ill-prepared to assume the leadership of
the community and the responsibility of the school and the orphanage. The sisters decided to turn to Baggot Street for help. A few days after the funeral of

---

1. "Acts of Chapter, Convent of Our Lady of Mercy, St. John's," 1855–1915, ASMSJ.

M. Francis Creedon, M. Vincent Nugent wrote to the superior of the Baggot Street Convent, M. Xavier Maguire, informing her of the death of M. Francis and pleading with M. Xavier to send help. The grief of the sisters, as well as their anxiety for the future of their convent, is evident in every word of the letter:

> My very dear Rev. Mother,
>
> It is with the greatest feelings of regret that I now for the first time address you to acquaint you of the terrible loss that this Convent has sustained in the death of our dear and venerated superioress which occurred on the 15th inst. after an illness of 15 days, but which confined her to bed but for ten days.
>
> From the commencement the Doctor said she had symptoms of bilious fever and that on account of her very great weakness for the last few years that he feared she had but few resources, however, notwithstanding, all human means were employed to try and prolong even for a short time a life upon which so much depended. But the Lord saw the soul ripe for the harvest and after spending the time of her sickness in the most edifying manner possible, He called her at five in the morning, to reap the fruit of her long labours.
>
> Dear Rev. Mother you can scarcely picture to yourself the desolation of the Convent, since in a large Community such a loss would be felt most severely but can you imagine what it is in one comprised all together of four, two professed, one novice who received the habit on the second of July which we date the second day of her sickness for tho' she was up yet I feel assured it was but the excitement which kept her up and even after the Ceremony she went a short distance on the visitation of the sick with a lay sister.
>
> The oldest Professed is 27 years of age and I am 25. Ought it not now dear Rev. Mother be needless for me to appeal to your charity and to the charity of the whole Order to prevent a Convent which promises to give so much glory to God from falling for want of a few nuns capable of governing it. The convent is you know since its establishment only in its infancy, yet when there were only two in Community the rule was enforced together with the regulations with as much exactness as if the house was full. It was founded on the cross therefore I feel convinced it cannot but flourish. There are the means of carrying on the estab-

lishment, all now that is needed is some competent persons. Since the opening of the Orphanage everything began to assume a more favourable aspect than before; till now again the Lord has been pleased to send the severest of all trials upon us. Let me pray of you now my dear Rev. Mother not to be deaf to my entreaties but to execute them as soon as possible as you see there can be no time lost and if you fail yourself in being able to relieve us you per-haps may make known my application to some other Convent equally charitable as your own. I cannot close this long letter which I fear must have wearied you without recommending to your prayers and to those of your Community the soul of one who loved you all so much and who I feel almost sure is praying for us all in heaven.

Believe me very dear Rev. Mother
Your fond sister
In Jesus and Mary
(Mary) Vincent Nugent. [2]

As far as we know, the letter was never acknowledged. The only thing certain is that Baggot Street again refused to send help, and the four sisters were left to their own resources. Young and inexperienced, they forged ahead, and under their guidance and direction, the Mercy congregation in Newfoundland began to grow and branch out to other communities to a degree that perhaps M. Francis Creedon had not foreseen. In God's Providence, it was a good thing they were left to themselves for, relying only on God, they validated Catherine McAuley's confidence in the enthusiasm, common sense, and dedication of youth.

Exactly one month after M. Francis' death, on August 15, 1855, Ellen Mary Joseph Tarahan entered as a postulant at Mercy Convent. She was the sister of M. Baptist Tarahan and the second of three Tarahan sisters to enter religious life. Seven months later, on a stormy March 25, 1856, she received the habit and the name, Mary Clare Frances.[3]

---

2. M. Vincent Nugent to Rev. Mother (M. Xavier Maguire), Feast of St. Mary Magdalen [July 22], 1855, AMIC.

3. Bishop Mullock noted the event in his *Ordo*, remarking that after a storm of two days the snow had reached the height of twelve feet. AASJ, 104/2/14.

During all these years, in spite of the constant demands of the visitation and the care of the orphans, M. Xavier Bernard and her companions laboured to establish Our Lady of Mercy School as a centre of excellence, but they were hampered in their efforts because of the physical conditions in which they lived and worked. Not only was the 1842 wooden convent run down and dilapidated, it had serious structural problems as well. More important from the sisters' point of view was the fact that it was not capable of housing the number of young women who wished to become Sisters of Mercy. Moreover, the school was far too small to accommodate the increasing number of students. Nevertheless, the sisters worked tirelessly to ensure that their efforts on behalf of their students were successful. At the end of the academic year, 1855–56, the following item appeared in a local newspaper:

> CONVENT OF MERCY: An examination of the Pupils of the Seminary connected with this Institution took place yesterday in presence of a large number of Ladies and Gentlemen. The young Ladies acquitted themselves with great *eclat* in the various departments of Education, and prizes were awarded them at the hands of the Right Rev. Dr. Mullock, according to the merits of their different accomplishments. The school is presided over by Ladies of brilliant acquirements in the varied branches of literature and ornamental needlework, and the Superioress is a Lady of the most benignant and amiable character. The Seminary is one which deserves general and efficient patronage. [4]

It may have been during the prize-giving ceremony described above that M. Xavier made known to the parents of the children the state of the convent and school. Two weeks later both *The Newfoundlander* and *The Reporter* published long articles informing the public that the Sisters of Mercy were to build a new convent and describing in detail the ceremony of the laying of the cornerstone.[5] On July 28, the editor of *The Reporter* wrote:

---

4. *The Patriot and Terra Nova Herald*, July 7, 1856, p. 2.
5. *The Newfoundlander*, July 24, 1856, p. 2.

> The Rev. Superioress having . . . intimated to some of the parents of the children who are receiving their education under those most accomplished and excellent Ladies, her anxiety as to the condition of the building, and its unsuitableness for the purposes to which it was devoted, and her desire that a more substantial and convenient one might be erected, a meeting of some of our most respectable Catholic fellow-citizens . . . was forthwith convened, and a plan of action adopted for the furtherance of the object stated.[6]

On Tuesday morning, July 22, 1856, crowds gathered in the cathedral grounds to witness the ceremony of the laying of the cornerstone. The newspapers reported:

> . . . the sky was beautifully clear, and the sun agreeably bright and warm. At eleven o'clock a long procession consisting of students and Sisters of the school and a number of clergy, with the orphans bearing the crucifix and appropriate banners, wended its way from the Cathedral towards Mercy Convent. The site chosen was immediately east of the original Convent, and embraced part of the ground on which that structure stood.[7]

That evening the cathedral bells were rung in celebration of the event, and a brilliant display of fireworks took place in front of the cathedral. Several discharges of cannon added to the excitement of the occasion.[8] After the last gun was fired and the fireworks had been exhausted, the Catholic citizens went home congratulating themselves on the success of their efforts. They were satisfied that the sisters who had toiled so selflessly on their behalf would finally have a secure and comfortable residence and a school that would be the equal of any other of its kind in the colony. Within a few days, the removal of the old convent made way for construction of the new stone building to begin. The sisters moved into the orphanage infirmary where, once again, they were forced

---

6. *The Reporter,* July 28, 1856, p. 2.
7. *The Newfoundlander,* July 24, 1856, p. 2. The present Mercy Convent chapel and parking lot is on the site of the 1842 convent.
8. Ibid.

to live in very cramped quarters for fifteen months until the new convent was ready for occupancy.

Just as everything seemed to be settling down in a comfortable routine, St. John's was hit once more by a severe outbreak of cholera. The sisters at Mercy Convent hastened to the aid of families stricken by disease and death. They were well trained to respond to this disaster, for they had the experience of working side by side with M. Francis Creedon during a similar outbreak two years earlier. In his book, *The Ecclesiastical History of Newfoundland*, Archbishop M. F. Howley paid tribute to the work of the Sisters of Mercy during this time of crisis:

> In the year 1856 the cholera broke out in St. John's and raged with great violence. Then were seen the Sisters of Mercy in their true element. From daylight till dark, and often through the night, they worked indefatigably. No part of the city slums was too dark or too filthy for them. They entered the houses of the plague-stricken when all others had abandoned them lighting the fires and preparing some humble food; scrubbing and cleaning up the little tenements dressing and washing the sick; and, finally, carrying the dead bodies to the coffins, which were placed at the doors on the streets by fearful officials.[9]

There were five sisters at Mercy Convent at the time,[10] one of whom had to remain at home to care for the twenty or more orphans. The epidemic was brought under control, and the sisters could breathe a sigh of relief that the orphans under their care had been kept safe from the contagion.

Naturally enough, the energetic M. Xavier Bernard was anxious to add new members to her community. Already in 1855 and 1856, two young ladies had been accepted as postulants, one from Quebec and another from Harbour Grace. One stayed for ten months, the other for ten weeks. In each case the reason for their departure was given as ill health.[11] M. Xavier was not dis-

---

9. Howley, *Ecclesiastical History*, p. 376.

10. M. Xavier Bernard, M. Vincent Nugent, M. Elizabeth Redmond, M. Baptist Tarahan, and M. Clare Tarahan.

11. Annals, Convent of Our Lady of Mercy, St. John's, ASMAJ.

couraged. On March 25, 1857, another Newfoundlander, the nineteen-year-old Susanna Mary Joseph Cole from Colliers, Conception Bay, entered, and within a month (April 17, 1857), two young ladies from Limerick appeared on the convent doorstep seeking admission as postulants. Mary Theresa Carmody was twenty-eight years of age and Bridget Mary Guinane, ten years younger. Less than six months later, on the Feast of Our Lady of Mercy, September 24, 1857, all three postulants were received into the novitiate and given the names M. Camillus Joseph Cole, M. Liguori Michael Carmody, and M. Joseph Stanislaus Guinane. Because M. Clare Tarahan had just begun her second year of novitiate training, Mercy Convent was now bulging at the seams with the unprecedented number of four novices and four professed sisters.

Meanwhile, the new convent was nearing completion. On August 1, 1857, a public examination took place in the large classroom on the first floor of the building. *The Courier* reported, ". . . the result certainly was a display of proficiency on the part of the young ladies in their various branches of study, in the highest degree creditable to their instructresses and themselves."[12] But although the classroom sections of the new building had been completed by the summer of 1857, the convent itself was not ready for occupancy until October 15, 1857.[13] The sisters moved in on that day, and ever since, the building has had a special place in the hearts of successive generations of sisters and students of the school. Of all the convents of Mercy in Newfoundland, there is only one "Mercy." Mercy Convent holds within its walls the memories of women whose vision and courage built this congregation, women who risked everything to proclaim the Good News of God's love and mercy. It has witnessed success and failure, laughter and tears; housed women of great holiness and others whose human weaknesses were all too obvious. Mercy Convent stands as a symbol of who we are and what we have tried to accomplish for God and for God's people through all the years since June 3, 1842.

---

12. *The Courier*, August 6, 1857, p. 3.

13. Annals of the Convent of Our Lady of Mercy state that the first mass was celebrated in the choir by the Rev. Dr. Mullock on the Feast of St. Michael, September 29, 1857, and on the same day mass was celebrated in the Chapel of the Blessed Virgin Mary by Rev. Charles Piel, ASMSJ.

None of this was in the minds of M. Xavier Bernard and her companions as they busied themselves with the problems of a rapidly expanding congregation. In the next few years a succession of young women arrived from Ireland to enter at Mercy Convent. It is noteworthy, however, that with one exception, not a single professed Sister of Mercy came from Ireland to join the mission established here.

The year 1858 brought joy to the heart of the zealous superior of Mercy Convent as, one after another, eight young women sought admission as postulants, six of them arrived in May, one in August, and another in November.[14] It is likely that M. Xavier Bernard had corresponded with the young ladies from Ireland before their arrival and arrangements had been made to assist them with their travel expenses. An entry in the accounts book for January 1858 notes, "Travelling and other expenses for Postulants from Ireland, £114.2.11." It is clear from this that M. Xavier was an able financial administrator, for in addition to supplying for the needs of her rapidly expanding community, she made regular payments toward the debt on the new convent.[15] By mid-1859, there were eighteen sisters living at Mercy Convent. Of these, there were seven professed sisters, nine novices, and two postulants. The time was ripe for expansion, and M. Xavier was ready to meet the challenge.

When Bishop Fleming died in 1850, he left the property known as Belvedere to the Sisters of Mercy to support an orphanage for girls. However, when Fleming's successor, Bishop John Thomas Mullock, discussed with M. Francis Creedon the establishment of the orphanage, there were only four sisters in the Mercy community. It was decided that the wisest course was to build the orphanage as an annex to Mercy Convent rather than have it located some distance away on the Belvedere property. Mullock decided to use his predecessor's Belvedere home as a residence for ecclesiastical students. Later it became a boarding hostel for students attending the Catholic Academy.[16] When, in

---

14. Arriving in May were: Ann Cussen, Ellen Banks, Ann O'Reardon, all from Limerick; Ann O'Riordan, and Honora O'Donovan from Cork; Mary Ann Merchant from Waterford; in August, Esther Coady of St. John's entered; and in November, Ann Clune from Limerick.

15. Accounts Book, Convent of Our Lady of Mercy, St. John's, ASMSJ.

16. O'Neill, *A Seaport Legacy*, p. 783.

October 1859, these students moved from Belvedere to the newly completed residence at St. Bonaventure's College, the Belvedere house was left vacant once more. But not for long!

By the beginning of 1859, it was clear to M. Xavier Bernard that the Immaculate Conception Orphanage at Mercy Convent was too small to accommodate the increasing number of children needing admission. With eighteen sisters at Mercy Convent, she could afford to establish a second convent in St. John's, one that would be dedicated entirely to the care and education of orphans. As soon as the Belvedere residence was vacated by the academy students, M. Xavier was ready to take possession of the property bequeathed to the sisters by Bishop Fleming.

The house itself is of considerable historical interest. Its construction dates from 1826 when a lawyer, by the name of Hugh Alexander Emerson, engaged Alexander Norris, a Scots builder and carpenter, to build a mansion on the land Emerson had purchased in 1821. When completed, the house contained two drawing rooms, a dining room, study, breakfast room, and two kitchens with two large pantries on the first floor, and ten bedrooms on the second. In addition, there was a large frost-proof cellar and "a never-failing Well of Excellent Water."[17] On August 15, 1827, Emerson celebrated the completion of his house by holding a private garden party to which all the "elite" of the city were invited. It must have been quite a party, lasting from eleven o'clock in the morning, through the afternoon and concluding with a ball that was held in the spacious rooms of the mansion. After the death of his wife in 1844, Emerson had no further interest in living in his mansion.[18] He put it on the market, where Bishop Fleming purchased it in 1847 with the intention of having it function as a monastery for himself and the four Franciscan Brothers whom he had brought from Ireland to teach in the Orphan Asylum School. Unfortunately, the brothers found the distance from the monastery to their school too much of an inconvenience. Consequently, they moved into an apartment above the school. Bishop Fleming, who was in very poor health by that

17. *The Patriot and Terra Nova Herald*, August 23, 1845, p. 3.
18. Hogan, *Pathways*, p. 85.

time, retired to Belvedere where he died in 1850, having left his property to the Sisters of Mercy. It was to be nine years before the sisters claimed their inheritance.

On November 16, 1859, thirty orphan girls and four sisters left Mercy Convent to take up residence in Bishop Fleming's old home in Belvedere. The newly professed M. Liguori Carmody was appointed superior.[19] She was the second young woman from Limerick to enter the Mercy community in St. John's, the first being, of course, M. Xavier Bernard herself. Accompanying M. Liguori on the new foundation were M. Elizabeth Redmond, M. Clare Tarahan, and M. Bonaventure Cussen (a novice). The sisters named the new convent and orphanage "St. Michael's" in memory of their benefactor, Bishop Michael Anthony Fleming.

At first, M. Xavier Bernard maintained St. Michael's Convent as a branch house under her authority as superior of Mercy Convent. Although M. Liguori Carmody was in charge of the day-to-day events of the convent and orphanage, all major decisions were referred to the mother house, Mercy Convent. However, within a very short time, it was clear that the four sisters at St. Michael's, Belvedere, were more than capable of handling their own affairs, and the new convent became independent.[20]

In September 1860, M. Philomena O'Donovan, a novice, was sent from Mercy Convent to join St. Michael's community. With this addition to the staff of St. Michael's, the sisters decided to initiate another ministry, one that was dear to the heart of Catherine McAuley, the establishment of a House of Mercy where unemployed young women would be given shelter, education, and training. Encouraged by one of the local priests, Rev. Richard O'Donnell, who saw a need for such a ministry, they built a House of Mercy on the Belvedere property in 1864. On December 12 of that year, the following announcement appeared in *The Newfoundlander*:

---

19. Mary Theresa Carmody entered as a postulant at Mercy Convent on April 17, 1857. She was received on September 24 of that same year and given the name, Mary Liguori Michael. Two years later, on April 25, 1859, she made her profession of vows as a Sister of Mercy.

20. ASMSJ, MG 2/1/165.

On the 8th of this month a House of Refuge for females of good character, out of employment, was opened at Belvidere, under the guardianship of the Sisters of Mercy who superintend the Female Orphanage. This valuable institution was much needed in a town like St. John's, where there are many dangers to persons so circumstanced as those for whom it provides. Many girls after returning from the fishery or leaving the places they have served in, cannot easily or in a short time find other situations. Their small earnings are then spent, and they are left totally destitute. This Institution opens to such a home and a refuge where, under the care of the Nuns, they can remain until they are able to obtain a suitable occupation. The time they spend there will be most advantageous to themselves, as they will be engaged in industrial employment, under constant instruction, and will learn many things most useful to them in any position they may obtain.[21]

This, however, was one ministry the sisters had to abandon because there were too few applicants to justify the expense of the upkeep. The actual length of time it was in operation is unknown, but it was still in existence in 1865, for it is mentioned in one of the newspapers: "The Sisters of Mercy of St. Michael's Convent, Belvidere, gratefully acknowledge the receipt of £10 from the Chief Justice, Sir Francis Brady, for the Orphanage and the House of Mercy."[22] Eventually, the House of Mercy became part of the orphanage, and about the same time, a two-storey building was added that supplied more classroom space. Up to this time, the children at the orphanage had been taught in two or three small rooms. The change from the overcrowded, ill-lighted rooms into bright and airy surroundings was a welcome change for sisters and students.[23]

---

21. *The Newfoundlander,* December 12, 1864, p. 3.

22. *The Newfoundlander,* January 16, 1865, p. 3. On August 23, 1845, when Hugh Emerson advertised the sale of his property, he used the spelling, "Belvidere." This spelling was retained through most of the nineteenth century, but in more recent years the accepted spelling is "Belvedere."

23. *Inter Nos,* June 1924, p. 27. Although the author does not mention the source of her material, in 1924 there were a number of sisters at Mercy Convent and at Belvedere who would have learned the facts surrounding the early history of Belvedere from those who were alive in the 1860s. *Inter Nos* was an annual publication produced by the students of Our Lady of Mercy School and printed in St. John's.

With the number of orphans increasing steadily, the care of over forty children was proving too much of a strain for the timid M. Liguori Carmody: ". . . she had not been three years in Religion and she felt the responsibility beyond her power and begged to be freed from it. Her petition was granted and in January 1861, Mother Vincent [Nugent] was appointed Reverend Mother. Sister M. Liguori returned to the Convent of Mercy."[24]

At the time of her appointment as superior of St. Michael's, the thirty-one-year-old M. Vincent was the senior sister by profession in the congregation. She had pronounced her vows on December 8, 1850, the day M. Xavier Bernard was received as a novice. Moreover, she had previous experience in caring for orphans for, according to M. Williamina Hogan, when the Immaculate Conception Orphanage was opened at Mercy Convent in 1854, it was placed under M. Vincent's direction.[25] During the epidemics of 1854 and 1856, M. Vincent was "one of the band of four Sisters who from early morning until 10 or 11 o'clock at night tended the sick and ministered to the dying."[26] After her transfer to St. Michael's Convent, M. Vincent was to live at Belvedere for the rest of her life. A highly educated woman, M. Vincent recognized that education was the greatest need of the time, and she was determined that the girls entrusted to her care should be provided with the same advantages as children attending any of the other schools in the city.

M. Vincent retained the position of superior until 1865, when she resigned and was replaced by M. Bonaventure Cussen. Relieved of the duty of governing the community and of the daily financial struggle to provide for the needs of the sisters and the children under their care, M. Vincent was free to devote her time to teaching and the visitation of the sick. It was written of her: "Many a time she brought comfort to the homes of the poor (and she knew them all) as well as consolation to the sick and dying."[27]

---

24. Ibid.

25. Hogan, *Pathways*, p. 50. I have not been able to find any confirmation of this statement. M. Williamina may have been given this information by one of the senior sisters at Mercy Convent.

26. *The Newfoundlander*, March 7, 1884, p. 2.

27. Ibid.

M. Vincent's reluctance to fill the office of superior was matched by the community's determination to ensure that her considerable learning and experience would be used to benefit the younger sisters. Thus, when she resigned as superior, M. Vincent was by no means off the hook! She was immediately appointed to the position of mistress of novices.[28] The sisters at Belvedere could have chosen no more suitable person to fill this post than M. Vincent, who spent her own novitiate under the direction of M. Francis Creedon.

M. Vincent had inherited the assertiveness of her famous father, John Valentine Nugent.[29] An educator, writer, newspaper editor and proprietor, politician, and finally High Sheriff of Newfoundland, Nugent was prominent in the religious and political squabbles of the mid-nineteenth century in Newfoundland. On the other hand, when adopting the guiding principles of her life, M. Vincent was influenced by her mother's example. Ellen Creedon Nugent, like her younger sister M. Francis Creedon, was noted for her kindness to the poor and the afflicted. On the occasion of her death, October 22, 1862, *The Newfoundlander* published an obituary that mentioned some of the qualities of this gentle lady: ". . . It was impossible to have known her without being impressed by the rare sweetness and benignity of her disposition. The poor and the afflicted will henceforth miss one of their tenderest friends."[30] For her part, Ellen's daughter M. Vincent was tireless in her efforts to improve the lot of the poor and disadvantaged. Apparently, her reputation for showing kindness and compassion to all classes of people was widely known, for when she died at the age of fifty-six, the following tribute appeared in the public press:

> When her death was announced [M. Vincent Nugent], a chord of sympathy was struck that vibrated in the hearts of a wide circle of people not only in the city of St. John's, but throughout the

28. Young women who wish to become Sisters of Mercy are required to spend two years of study and training under the direction of a professed sister.
29. *The Evening Telegram*, March 4, 1884, p. 4. The writer of M. Vincent's obituary mentions some of her traits of character, among them assertiveness.
30. *The Newfoundlander*, October 27, 1862, p. 2.

Island; for it may be well said that there is not a cove or harbour
on our vast coast in which her name was unknown as a synonym
for kindness and charity. . . . To her came all classes for consolation, advice and assistance: The stalwart fisherman, with his
bruised and festered wounds, to have them dressed . . . the young
man, repenting at last of his waywardness, and coming in simplicity to receive correction, advice and encouragement . . . To this ever
active and zealous charity was added an intellect of wide mental
calibre, cultivated by an education of a much higher order than
generally falls to the lot of young ladies. [31]

Meantime, back at Mercy Convent, M. Xavier Bernard, recently reappointed as superior of Mercy Convent,[32] had a new project in view. The
transfer of the orphans to Belvedere in 1859 left the orphanage building
attached to Mercy Convent free for other uses. The zealous M. Xavier saw a
way of reaching out to girls in the Newfoundland outports to provide them
with a more thorough education than would be available at home. With the
approval and support of Bishop Mullock, she decided to convert the orphanage building to a boarding school. Renovations to the building proceeded at a
slow pace, but finally, on June 3, 1861, the local papers announced the opening of St. Clair's Boarding School.[33] The syllabus included, in addition to the
three R's, Christian doctrine, English, French, history, natural philosophy,
botany, astronomy, geography, and, inevitably, "use of the Globes." Apparently,
the sisters of those days considered the acquisition of this skill an essential
component in the education of young ladies, for the subject is listed among
the required elements in most of the courses of study offered in Mercy
schools. "Use of the Globes" included a study of the terrestrial and celestial
globes and was part of the study of geography and navigation, subjects that
were an essential part of the education of a seafaring country such as

---

31. *The Evening Telegram,* Tuesday, March 4, 1884, p. 4.

32. "Acts of Chapter, Convent of Our Lady of Mercy, St. John's," January 27, 1860, ASMSJ.

33. *The Patriot and Terra Nova Herald,* June 3, 1861, p. 2. The spelling, "St. Clair's" was
used to identify the boarding school. In the twentieth century, the more familiar spelling,
"St. Clare's," was used to identify the home for working girls on LeMarchant Road that later
became St. Clare's Mercy Hospital.

Newfoundland.[34] Similarly, astronomy and natural philosophy were related to navigation, botany, and agriculture. In addition to the subjects listed above, classes in dancing and vocal and instrumental music were offered, together with plain and fancy needlework. The public was assured that the utmost attention would be given to the formation of the children's character and that their health, diet, relaxation, and general comfort would be most carefully nurtured.[35]

The first pupil of St. Clair's Boarding School was Selina Browne of Paradise, Placentia Bay. Many years later Selina (Mrs. Patrick Sullivan) wrote an account of her experiences at St. Clair's. The article, entitled "Back in 1861," was included in the 1923 edition of the school magazine, *Inter Nos*. It is worth quoting, for it gives a vivid picture of life in the first boarding school operated by the Sisters of Mercy in Newfoundland.

> On May 19th, the day after the Riot,[36] I came to St. John's and a few days later had the honour of being the first pupil to whom the doors of St. Clair's Boarding School were opened. . . . For three weeks I was the only pupil. During that time I wept much, being very sorry for myself, and gazed for hours at a time from the Novitiate window at passersby on the street below.
>
> Military Road was . . . a residential street. I enjoyed watching the ladies with their crinolines and tiny parasols, and counting the number of hats that passed to compare them with the number of poke bonnets that passed in the same time, for bonnets were just giving way to hats.
>
> . . . As I recall the old days I realize that we were a very merry group of girls, notwithstanding a few material discom-

34. I am indebted to M. Teresina Bruce, RSM, and to John E. FitzGerald for this information.

35. *The Patriot and Terra Nova Herald*, June 3, 1861, p. 2.

36. Selina Sullivan made an error in the date. The 1861 riot occurred on May 13. Paul O'Neill describes the event in *A Seaport Legacy*, p. 462. The riot resulted when the government rejected the claims of two individuals to take their seat in the Assembly as members for Harbour Main. The uprising caused a great deal of damage; several persons were killed and others suffered serious injury. Finally, in the evening the bells of the Roman Catholic cathedral rang out to summon the people to the church. Bishop Mullock mounted the pulpit and, in an eloquent display of episcopal wrath, denounced the riot and sent the rioters home in a chastened mood to nurse their wounds and bury their dead.

forts which I feel sure would have made my own daughters and their generation miserable and unhappy. In the first place, the building was wooden and had no central heating. There was in our recreation room a small grate which was always the centre of interest. As not more than eight at a time could get within a reasonable distance of the coveted fire, those who got there first only yielded their places to others on compulsion or payment . . .

Our daily routine was that of almost any nineteenth century boarding school. Every day at seven a.m. saw us making our way to the Presentation Convent for the daily Mass. In winter an impassive figure awaited us at the door to brush out the snow that came off our overshoes. In spring and fall the same emotionless form met us to remind us to wipe the mud off our boots before proceeding further.

Our recreation consisted usually of a walk in the Bishop's field near St. Bonaventure's College. Some years ago it was sold in building lots and now contains several fine houses. Paddy Brothers, his Lordship's gardener, always greeted us with a broad smile as we walked sedately past him wearing dark cloak and bonnets, brown veils hiding our smiles and brown gloves covering our fingers. One would never suspect that one of the brown gloved hands along the line would slip sixpence into Paddy's grimy fist to be invested in currant cakes, which he straightway hastened to get to us. On occasion, Liza, the Bishop's housekeeper, a good-hearted soul, would give us the leg of a chicken or a wedge-shaped cutting from a pie that had done duty at his Lordship's table. . . . The Bishop did not know that hungry schoolgirls were taking turns to share his meals, but even if he had found out about it I think he would have kept his discovery a secret.

. . . The discipline at St. Clair's was strict. Though the school was on the outskirts of the city, the pupils kept all their interest within its four walls. The course of studies pursued at St. Clair's would compare very strangely with a present day syllabus. Arithmetic and Grammar, supplemented by long hours of readings from the classical authors, a smattering of geography, and a thorough training in religious knowledge composed the sum total of the heavier part of our education. For the rest, we were taught, as were all nineteenth century girls, how to make the daintiest

embroidery and lace work. Dancing and music and singing were
an important part of the school curriculum . . .[37]

The botany and astronomy also mentioned in the course of study do not
seem to have weighed heavily on Mrs. Sullivan's mind! Her comment about
the discipline maintained at St. Clair's is supported by the following excerpt
from an unsigned letter tucked inside one of the old school registers at Our
Lady of Mercy Academy. It appears that the letter was intended for an
erring parent:

> You will kindly forgive me if I complain of Polly's remaining out
> on Sundays beyond Church hours; it was 4:20 last evening when
> she returned, and I must candidly own I was much displeased at
> so gross a violation of school discipline. . . . There is no use in
> making rules if they are to be violated in this manner. I wish, my
> dear Mrs. T. that you would ask Polly not to repeat this manner
> of acting.[38]

Just prior to the opening of St. Clair's Boarding School, the Sisters of
Mercy were saddened by the death of one of the newly professed sisters, M.
Camillus Joseph Cole, who died on April 13, 1860, at the age of twenty-one
years. This young woman was the first from a Newfoundland outport to enter
the Congregation of the Sisters of Mercy. Her parents must have been fairly
well off, for at the time of her profession, on March 25, 1857, the Mercy
Convent accounts book reports that Bishop Mullock deposited in the bank

---

37. Selina Sullivan, *Inter Nos,* June 1923. Mrs. Sullivan's reference to attending mass at the Presentation Convent is important insofar as it highlights the difference in lifestyle between the Presentation and Mercy Sisters of those days. A priest celebrated daily mass in the Presentation Convent chapel rather than in Mercy Convent because of the rule of enclosure observed by the Presentation Sisters at that time. The Mercy Sisters had no such restrictions. They chose to go to the Presentation Convent rather than at the cathedral, probably because mass was celebrated at an hour that would permit them to open school on time. In later years, when the number of priests increased, mass was celebrated daily at both convents adjacent to the cathedral.

38. Sister M. Basil McCormack, "The Educational Work of The Sisters of Mercy in Newfoundland, 1842–1955" (master's thesis, Catholic University of America, 1955), p. 28.

the sum of £150, Miss Cole's dowry,[39] to be held in trust for the community. M. Camillus Cole fell ill and died less than twelve months after her profession. The accounts book listed expenses for Drs. Rochfort and Bunting and the cost of two marble slabs for the sisters' plot in Belvedere cemetery.[40] These were, of course, headstones for the graves of M. Camillus and for M. Francis Creedon. It seems strange that the sisters waited almost six years before erecting a headstone at the grave of M. Francis. This seeming neglect was due, no doubt, to the simple fact that they could not afford it.

Apparently, obstacles such as illness, death, and lack of resources—both human and financial—discouraged neither M. Xavier Bernard nor Bishop Mullock. Already in February 1860, just three months after the opening of St. Michael's Convent and Orphanage, a new Mercy foundation was being planned, this time in one of the outports. On Sunday, January 29, 1860, Bishop Mullock was in Brigus to celebrate the sacrament of confirmation.[41] After mass the bishop addressed the congregation on the subject of establishing a convent and school in the town, and a subscription was opened for the purpose. According to reports, within a week the enthusiastic people of Brigus had committed more than £1,000 toward the construction of a convent and school.[42]

In the 1860s, Brigus was a bustling, prosperous little town. Its sheltered harbour was the home of many ships that made the yearly trip north to engage in the fishery. As a result, Brigus boasted a lucrative trade in cod, seal skins, and seal oil. The first Catholic school in Brigus was opened by Robin Power in 1805.[43] The fact that the school consisted of one room in Mr. Power's home

---

39. When a sister entered the congregation, it was customary for her family to present her with a dowry, a sum of money that would help support the community of which she was a member. This custom applied only in cases where the family could afford it. After the amalgamation in 1916, this requirement was dropped.

40. Accounts Book, Convent of Our Lady of Mercy, St. John's, ASMSJ.

41. Brigus is a small town in Conception Bay, about forty miles from St. John's. It is the birthplace of one of Newfoundland's great explorers, Captain Bob Bartlett, who accompanied Admiral Peary on his historic trip to the North Pole.

42. *The Harbour Grace Standard,* February 1, 1860, p. 2.

43. McCormack, "Educational Work," p. 52.

suggests that the number of scholars was relatively small.[44] Later on, in 1826, the students were transferred to the sacristy of the newly erected church, where classes were held for five years until a school was built on Power Hill. This building was used until the arrival of the sisters in 1861.

Once the bishop had put his seal of approval on the plan to bring the Sisters of Mercy to Brigus, the parish priest, Rev. Edward O'Keefe, applied himself to the task of building a convent. By the summer of 1861, everything was in place, and it remained only for M. Xavier to choose from among the seventeen sisters living at Mercy Convent those who would form the new community at Brigus. She decided to appoint another young lady from Limerick, the twenty-four-year-old M. of the Angels Banks, as superior of the new foundation. It appears that M. Xavier had a special fondness for sisters who came from her own home city! Accompanying M. of the Angels were M. de Chantal O'Keefe, originally from Cork, and M. Gonzaga Coady, a native Newfoundlander. The fourth member of the group was the eighteen-year-old Mary Barron, who had been accepted as a postulant at Mercy Convent on September 10, the day before the sisters left for Brigus. Mary Barron was born in Wexford, Ireland, in 1842. She came to St. John's as a small child to live with her brother and may have witnessed the opening of the new Mercy Convent on Military Road in 1857. No doubt, she would have seen the "walking nuns" going through the narrow, dusty, muddy, or slippery streets on their errands of mercy to the poor and the sick. Beginning in 1851, the Mercy Convent accounts book listed fees paid for regular tuition and an extra fee for French for a Miss Barron. Whether this person was the future sister, M. Joseph Barron, we have no way of knowing. But, in any case, Mary Barron became acquainted with the Sisters of Mercy and decided to become one of them. The fact that Mary was chosen to be a member of the first foundation outside St. John's suggests that she was quite well-known to the sisters, for the astute M. Xavier would be unlikely to send someone on such an important mission unless she had prior knowledge of her character and her poten-

---

44. John Leamon, *Brigus: Past Glory, Present Splendour* (St. John's: Harry Cuff Publications, 1998), p. 67.

tial. By having a postulant accompany the new community, M. Xavier was following a practice established by Catherine McAuley. The idea was that a public ceremony of reception into religious life would take place within a few months after the community had been established. In this way the aims and purposes of the sisters could be presented to young women who might be inspired to join them.

Finally all was ready, and on September 11, 1861, the four members of the new community, all under twenty-six years of age, accompanied by M. Xavier and her assistant, M. Baptist Tarahan, set off on their way to Brigus. They left St. John's with the bishop's blessing and little else—except an unlimited trust in God. A journey that takes about forty-five minutes by car today lasted for several hours. In all probability they took the regular stage coach from St. John's to Portugal Cove, a little fishing village about twelve miles from St. John's, where they boarded the *Ellen Gisborne* for the trip across Conception Bay. On a fine day, the voyage would have been very picturesque and enjoyable, and the account of the celebrations that took place in Brigus suggests that this may have been the case. The newspapers recorded the arrival of the Sisters of Mercy but made no mention of the journey itself:

> As soon as the *Ellen Gisborne* steamer was seen to approach the harbour, up went the green flag on the well-known staff on Tara Hill, and on the Convent itself. All the Catholics and very many Protestant houses showed flags and colours of various devices, giving the whole town a most festive appearance. The Convent bell sounded its voice and the population moved en masse to the wharf to demonstrate their reverence, as well as their glad feelings for the blessing conferred upon them in the landing of the clergy and nuns. A large cannon with a great number of sealing pieces, shot forth volley after volley from the old Battery head, and the shouts and cheers of the whole people spoke their delight and enthusiasm on the occasion.
>
> They then formed a procession and accompanied the Bishop, priest and nuns to the convent, the demonstrations just mentioned continuing the while. From the convent steps, his Lordship addressed the people, thanking them for their reception

> of him and the nuns and then imparting the Episcopal Benediction. On the morning following the Bishop exhorted from the altar on the subject of education, more especially on the necessity of a religious education, the best means for which the people now possessing the Conventual Institution just established there. The flags were kept flying from the houses until Saturday, when the Reverend Mother returned to St. John's amid a renewal of the demonstrations of Wednesday. [45]

Once the visitors had left, and without further delay, the sisters began the visitation of the sick and the poor. Within a few days, the school was opened, and they took up their duties with great energy and a determination to provide the best education possible to the children of Brigus and the surrounding area. For the first few years after the sisters' arrival, they taught both boys and girls until, in 1870, a male teacher took over the boys' schooling. Up to the time of the sisters' arrival in Brigus, they had operated single-sex schools for girls. However, conditions in the outports were quite different from those obtained in the city. First in Brigus, then in Burin, Conception, and St. Lawrence, the sisters were required from time to time to teach the boys as well as the girls.

The sisters of the Brigus community were all well-educated women and there is a tradition that at least three of them spoke French fluently. The fact that well-thumbed French classics were part of the convent library confirms this story.[46] However, life in Brigus was not one that allowed much time for reading and relaxation. We can only imagine the hardships of those early days "around the bay." The sisters kept a cow and hens and drew water from the well—the same well that in later years inevitably went dry in the summer. The cow had to be milked and the eggs collected. It is not hard to imagine the young postulant, Mary Barron, skirts tucked up in her belt, chasing the cow around the convent garden and into the barn for milking. Transportation was no problem, the sisters walked wherever they went. This walking was quite pleasant in summer, but when winter brought sleet and snow, they had to

45. *The Newfoundlander*, September 23, 1861, p. 2.
46. Annals, St. Joseph's Convent, Brigus, ASMSJ.

struggle through the drifts to visit the sick. Evidently, the heat of summer and the hazards of winter meant little to these women, for the older people of Brigus relate stories handed down to them by their parents, stories that tell of the sisters' daily visits to the elderly and the sick.[47] Early in the spring of 1862, the people of Brigus witnessed for the first time the ceremony of the reception of a novice when Mary Barron received the white veil and the name, Mary Joseph Teresa. This was the first of a number of reception and profession ceremonies that took place in Brigus in the years before a central novitiate was established in St. John's.

With the new convent in Brigus off to a good start, M. Xavier turned her attention to the plight of the poor children in the east end of the city of St. John's. The idea of a school in the area predated the plan for a foundation in Brigus. The first mention of this school appeared in the minutes for the Roman Catholic Board of Education, dated October 30, 1858: "His Lordship [Bishop Mullock] informed the Board that he had purchased a piece of Ground in Maggoty Cove and requested their Concurrance in Erecting a School for Females to be attended by the Sisters of Mercy from the Convent."[48] The bishop may have encountered some difficulty in obtaining money to build the school because nothing more is heard of it for four years. Then, on October 30, 1862, Bishop Mullock again brought before the education board the matter of a school for Maggoty Cove. "His Lordship laid before the Board his wishes for establishing a School for Females in Maggoty Cove to be attended by the Sisters of Mercy."[49] The money needed for the construction of the school came from the education grant allotted by the government to the Roman Catholic board for St. John's:

> Erecting School House in Maggoty Cove attended by the Sisters of Mercy, £343.17.4. The expenses incurred by the building of Maggoty Cove School have augmented the outlay. The School is

47. Mrs. Angela Burke, conversation with author, May 10, 2001.
48. "Proceedings of the Roman Catholic Board of Education," October 7, 1858, p. 58, AASJ, 600/1/3.
49. *Ibid.*, October 30, 1862, p. 64, AASJ, 600/1/3.

now in operation and contains daily about 100–120 Children. The
Salary only £50 per Annum and three nuns of the Mercy Convent
teach there.[50]

According to the Mercy Convent Annals for the year 1863, the sisters
were not too happy with the title "Maggoty Cove School." They immediately
supplied the new educational establishment with what they considered to be a
more refined name, "St. Bridget's." The entry in the Annals reads, "Under the
patronage of the Blessed Virgin Mary and St. Bridget, a school was opened for
the education of poor female children in the East End of St. John's."[51] But in
spite of the attempts of the sisters to supply the school with a more polished
title, the school inspector persisted in referring to the establishment as
Maggoty Cove School. This continued until in 1877, when, writing of the
establishment, he used the name, "St. Brides"—not quite correct but nevertheless an improvement! By the year 1881, it had finally dawned on the inspector that the correct name was St. Bridget's and by that time it had been decided to close the school!

St. Bridget's School was built on Hunt's Lane just west of Temperance
Street. The property belonged to the Church and was about thirty minutes
walk from Mercy Convent. It may have been a coincidence that the school register begins with the date of May 1, 1863, exactly twenty years after the first
entry in the register of Mercy Convent School. On that first day, six students
were enrolled at St. Bridget's, but by May 30, there were 105 names on the
register. At the end of the year, 200 students were enrolled with an average
daily attendance of 130. They were all girls ranging from four to sixteen years
of age. The school records give the age; date of entrance; the father's name;
residence, and occupation; and—when a child left school—her reason for
leaving. These entries are of interest because they mention street names and
locations that are no longer in use, such as "Nunnery Hill," "Marsh," "Limekiln

50. Account of monies received by the Roman Catholic Board of Education for the District
of St. John's for the year ending November 22, 1863, "Minutes of the Roman Catholic
Board of Education for St. John's," p. 68, AASJ, 600/1/3.
51. Annals, Convent of Our Lady of Mercy, St. John's, 1863, ASMSJ.

Hill," and "Maggoty Cove," a section of the city that in later years was given the name of "Hoylestown."[52]

In the school register, each child's name was accompanied by a comment. The range of remarks provides an insight into how the sisters of those days rated their students. Entries such as, "an amiable girl," "a good child," "a talented child" are interspersed with less favourable comments, "an indolent child" or "indifferent—left school." All too often a child's name is followed by the sad notation, "needed at home" or "gone into service." Some of the children who were "needed at home" or "gone into service," had reached the venerable age of nine or ten years![53]

Conditions in the school were far from ideal. There were no separate classrooms in the building—just one large room in which all the activities took place. The task of instructing almost two hundred children under such circumstances would strike consternation into the heart of the most stalwart teacher of today. In those days, however, the situation was not unusual, for many schools in Newfoundland were constructed on lines similar to those of St. Bridget's.[54] Furthermore, the overcrowding suggested by such a large enrolment was partially one of perception, for the actual daily attendance was often less than half the total enrolment of the school. In fact, the inspector for Roman Catholic schools in St. John's was more than pleased with the facilities provided for the children of St. John's East:

> I also visited the School lately established at Maggoty Cove, St. John's, and conducted by Ladies from the Convent of Mercy. The Schoolhouse is a very superior one, and the School-room, which is large and lofty, and capable of accommodating a very large number of children, is provided with the necessary amount of School furniture. [55]

52. The area known as Maggoty Cove was in the east end of St. John's, between Temperance Street and Chain Rock. In the nineteenth century, the area was renamed Hoylestown after Newman Hoyles who owned property in the area. See O'Neill, *A Seaport Legacy*, p. 906.

53. Register, St. Bridget's School, ASMSJ.

54. Until quite recently it was not unusual to find schools in the rural areas of Newfoundland in which several grades were accommodated in a single classroom.

55. Michael John Kelly, "Report of Catholic Schools Year Ended 1863," *JHA*, 1863, p. 631 app.

In those days, from 1861 to 1876, the basic curriculum for schools was under the jurisdiction of the school boards, and guides for determining levels of achievement were established rather arbitrarily by the local board. In his study of education in the nineteenth century, *Schooling in a Fishing Society*, Philip McCann described the level of pupil achievement required by the boards from 1861 to 1871:

> The highest standards in the examinations given at the end of every school year were in this, the first decade of such tests, informal and various . . . the rubric for the highest standard in Protestant schools was for reading, ability to read the "Holy Scriptures"; for writing, "from dictation"; and for arithmetic, "compound rules" and the "rules of three and beyond." For Catholics the highest standards are taken respectively as "reading with ease" and "reading with fluency and expression"; writing from "dictation," and "compound rules and rule of three, etc."[56]

This was the basic level of education offered to Newfoundland children prior to the latter quarter of the nineteenth century, although, as McCann pointed out, the convent schools "gave an education superior to that found in the Board schools."[57]

Unlike the Mercy Convent School, which was a private school, St. Bridget's came under the jurisdiction of the Roman Catholic School Board for St. John's, and as such, it followed the curriculum prescribed for the Board schools. But in addition, subjects such as geography and needlework were taught. Furthermore, children as young as three and four years of age came to St. Bridget's, presumably to attend "Infant School."[58] Entries in the school

56. Philip McCann, *Schooling in a Fishing Society: Education and Economic Conditions in Newfoundland and Labrador, 1836–1986* (St. John's, ISER Publications, Memorial University of Newfoundland, 1994), p. 117. McCann explained: ". . . the 'rule of three' is a method of finding the fourth term of a proposition when three are given. By multiplying the second and third terms together and dividing the result by the first, the fourth term is arrived at."

57. Ibid., p. 120.

58. Register, St. Bridget's School, ASMSJ.

register indicate that some girls remained in school until they were fifteen and sixteen years of age before they were "required at home." Regrettably, however, there are relatively few entries that joyfully announce "finished education," in comparison with the sad notations, "withdrawn," "kept at home," or "died."

A new Education Act of 1876[59] instituted formal and uniform grading throughout Newfoundland schools and mandated a list of subjects in addition to reading, writing, and arithmetic:

> The list of subjects—regarded as "essentials"—was, in addition to Reading, Writing and Arithmetic, Grammar, Geography, History and Navigation. These subjects were graded in "standards" from I–V in order of difficulty. The standards were based upon the six standards introduced into English elementary schools under the Revised Code of 1862. . . . In Newfoundland Standard V . . . would appear to be pitched somewhere between the English Standards V and VI . . . It is assumed that pupils who passed in Grades IV and V in the 3Rs would be functionally literate and numerate on leaving school . . . [60]

By the year 1878 there were 370 children in attendance at St. Bridget's, and in addition to the subjects mentioned above, the curriculum included alphabet and easy lessons, reading, ciphering, and history.[61] Apparently, an addition had been built on to the school in 1865 to accommodate the increased enrolment. In that year, the Roman Catholic Board of Education for St. John's reported an expenditure of £502.13.4 for erecting and furnishing St. Bridget's. The same report lists the cost of purchasing a stove (£5.15.14) and painting the school (£33.8.0).[62] By that time the school curriculum had been organized according to "Standards," beginning with

59. JHA, 1876, p. 60.
60. McCann, Schooling, p. 264.
61. McCormack, "Educational Work," p. 50.
62. Account of monies expended by the Roman Catholic Board of Education for the District of St. John's for the year ending November 22, 1865, "Minutes of the Roman Catholic Board of Education for St. John's," p. 76, AASJ, 600/3/4.

standard I for beginners and culminating in standard VI, when it was presumed the scholar was thoroughly prepared to face whatever challenges life should offer.[63]

Unfortunately, the names of the sisters who were assigned to teach in St. Bridget's School are not listed in the Annals of Mercy Convent. Nevertheless, an oral tradition links the name of M. Columba Glynn with the school. According to this tradition, M. Columba, who came from Ireland in 1876, taught at St. Bridget's for several years until it finally closed in 1881. Another Irish sister who taught at St. Bridget's School was M. Patrick O'Farrell who spent most of her religious life teaching the poor of St. John's in St. Bridget's School, Hoylestown (1863–1881) and the boys' classes at St. Peter's School, Queen Street (1881–1903). M. Patrick's obituary notice in *The Evening Telegram* spoke thus of her teaching ministry at these schools: ". . . In the winter's snow and the summer's sun she went alike with loving obedience and without a murmur and labored hard from ten until three each day."[64]

The decision to close St. Bridget's could not have been unexpected, for the plan to build a railway terminal in the east end of the city was well publicized. In her book, *Pathways of Mercy*, M. Williamina Hogan stated that the reason for closing the school was its adjacency to the railway line that was being constructed from Fort William to the Battery waterfront.[65] This statement is verified by the following entry in the minutes of the RC School Board for St. John's: "His Lordship [Bishop Power] acquainted the Board that as the School House in Hoyles Town was required for the Railroad, he had been awarded £500 in compensation for the Building and £250 for the land. Moreover he had paid £240 out of this award to A. McKay Esq., the Railway developer, for a site for another School House."[66]

---

63. Standard VI was introduced by the Education Act of 1887. In addition to the inclusion of the extra level, the standards were raised at every level and in all required subjects. McCann, *Schooling*, p. 128.

64. *The Evening Telegram*, May 18, 1885.

65. Hogan, *Pathways*, p.188.

66. "Proceedings of the Roman Catholic School Board for St. John's," March 21, 1882, AASJ, 600/1/3.

Very little is known about this new school that was to replace St. Bridget's in the East End, and the Mercy Convent records are silent on the matter. However, an insurance map dating from the 1880s shows a schoolhouse on the west side of Hunt's Lane, not far from where the original St. Bridget's School was located.[67] Then, in 1884, the local newspapers carried an advertisement announcing the opening of a sisters' school in the East End, but with a new name: "St. Joseph's School under the charge of the Sisters of Mercy, Military Road, will open on Wednesday, January 23 at ten o'clock."[68]

The two sisters assigned to teach in the new school may have expected to work under better conditions than those they had experienced at St. Bridget's. If so, they were doomed to disappointment. In his report for the year 1887, J. Wickham, superintendent for RC schools, observed that St. Joseph's was a one-room school, in which two teachers attempted to instruct fifty-five boys and sixty-five girls—a total of one hundred and twenty students, a little less than half the number registered. "The confusion arising from the arrangement must be, at times, sufficient to paralyze the efforts of the teachers."[69] In spite of the superintendent's recommendation that the classroom be divided, the RC board did nothing to rectify the situation. At the end of the next year, 1888, Mr. Wickham remarked in his report, "Notwithstanding the patient and persevering zeal of the Sisters in charge, the results . . . showed little improvement over the preceding year—it could hardly be expected to be otherwise."[70] The report concluded, "The children attending are poor, scantily provided with school requisites, often insufficiently clad, idle in their habits, and exceedingly irregular in attendance."[71] For their efforts the sisters received the princely salary of £50 each *per annum*! They continued to teach in this school until it was

---

67. Insurance Plan, City of St. John's, n.d. but sometime in the 1880s, p. 12, Archives of the City of St. John's (henceforth ACSJ).

68. *The Newfoundlander*, January 22, 1884, p. 1.

69. "Report of the Superintendent of Roman Catholic Board Schools," 1887, AASJ, 600/1/5.

70. Ibid., 1888.

71. Ibid.

destroyed in the 1892 fire, and it was not until 1897 that the sisters resumed their teaching ministry in the east end of St. John's. From that time onward, through all the years that followed, the sisters continued to teach in Hoylestown until, in 1988, shortage of personnel forced the Congregation of the Sisters of Mercy to withdraw from the school.

CHAPTER SIX

A TIME OF GROWTH

I remember the devotion of your youth,
How you followed me in the wilderness,
In a land not sown.

Jeremiah 2:2

After all all work involved in preparing the new convent and orphanage at St. Michael's, Belvedere; establishing the boarding school of St. Clair's; negotiating for the foundation in Brigus; and agreeing to send the sisters to teach in the East End; M. Xavier Bernard may have realized that the sisters had enough to keep them occupied. Altogether, there were now twenty-five Sisters of Mercy in Newfoundland: four at Brigus, six at St. Michael's Orphanage, and fifteen at Mercy Convent. Moreover, the demands of the mission put a constant strain on the Mercy Convent community. Three of the sisters were assigned to St. Bridget's, and after school hours, sisters were needed for supervisory duties at St. Clair's Boarding School. At that time, too, there was a sufficient number of novices to require one sister to be released from other duties—at least part-time—so that the young sisters would receive their proper education and training.

Then, shortly before St. Bridget's School opened in May of 1863, M. Xavier Bernard was presented with a request to send a group of sisters to Burin. Mindful of her already depleted staff at Mercy Convent, M. Xavier put her trust in God and agreed to the proposal.

The town of Burin is situated near the foot of a seventy-five-mile penin-sula on the south coast of Newfoundland. The Burin Peninsula thrusts out into the Atlantic in the shape of a boot. In former times, Burin's secluded and land-locked harbour offered a haven for fishing fleets that frequented the area from the sixteenth century onward, and this feature was an important factor in the early settlement of the town. When John V. Nugent visited Burin in 1845 in his capacity as inspector of schools,[1] he reported that fifty-six children were enrolled in the Catholic school. By the year 1857, Burin was a prosperous, bustling town of over two thousand people, and the education of the children was a matter of prime importance to the zealous pastor, Father Michael Berney, who is thought to have played an important part in obtaining the sis-ters for Burin.[2] Shortly before the arrival of the sisters, Father Berney became ill, and the task of introducing the Sisters of Mercy to the parish fell to his assistant and successor, Father John Cullen.

Having made the decision to send the sisters to Burin, M. Xavier Bernard set about selecting the sisters who would go on the mission. In appointing the superior, she turned once more to her friend, M. Liguori Carmody. It will be remembered that when she had been appointed first supe-rior of St. Michael's, Belvedere, M. Liguori felt unequal to the task and resigned after little more than a year. Now, with four years' experience of working closely with M. Xavier at Mercy Convent, she was persuaded to accept the appointment. The newly professed M. Charles McKenna; the

---

1. In 1844 John V. Nugent was appointed by the House of Assembly as Newfoundland's first inspector of schools. He was advised to confine himself to "inspection of Roman Catholic Schools except that where Protestant Boards may desire you should visit schools in their dis-trict." Fred W. Rowe, *The Development of Education in Newfoundland* (Toronto: Ryerson Press, 1952), p. 108.

2. Frances Marshall, *The South Coast Pioneers: 150 Years in the Growth of St. Patrick's Parish, Burin, Newfoundland, 1833–1983* (St. John's, NL: Creative Printers and Publishers, 1984), p. 35.

novice, M. Xavier Tarahan; and a postulant, Mary McAuliffe, were to be her companions.[3]

On the afternoon of July 11, 1863, the four missionaries, with M. Xavier Bernard and M. Gertrude Moore, boarded the steamer *Ariel* that would take them to Burin.[4] It was a journey of at least twenty-four hours in the days before there were any roads connecting St. John's to the more distant parts of the diocese. They sailed south along the coast of the Avalon Peninsula around Cape Race and westward past Cape St. Mary's where they would have seen hundreds of thousands of seabirds of all varieties nesting in the rocky headland, a pattern of behaviour that is repeated every year to the present time. Having rounded the Cape, the *Ariel* would have sailed northwest across Placentia Bay and into Burin. As they drew near to their destination, they might have been dismayed at the sight of the stark, formidable cliffs that surround the entrance to Burin Harbour and the barren, rocky land that was to be their home. After they entered the harbour, a few trees could be seen pushing up through crevices in the rocks along the shore, and they may have distinguished patches of green here and there, witness to the optimistic attempts of the people to grow flowers and vegetables where God and nature had provided only rocks and stones. The arrival of the Sisters of Mercy in Burin was described in a letter written to *The Newfoundlander* on July 13, 1863:

> On yesterday (Sunday) the 12th instant his Lordship the Bishop of St. John's, [i.e. Bishop Mullock] accompanied by the Rev. Mother of the Order of Mercy and four Sisters of the same order, arrived here to establish a Convent and school in this remote portion of his Lordship's Diocese.

---

3. Mary Agnes McKenna of Limerick entered Mercy Convent in her fifteenth year in July 1860. She received the habit and the name, Mary Charles on January 23, 1861, and was admitted to profession on October 18, 1862. Mary Ann Tarahan of St. John's received the habit and the name, M. Xavier, in January 1863. She was professed in Burin in 1867. She was the third of the Tarahan sisters to become a Sister of Mercy. Mary McAuliffe entered at Mercy Convent in 1863 and was received in Burin and given the name, Catherine. She was accepted for profession as a lay sister at Mercy Convent on January 5, 1872, having spent over seven years in Burin. Annals, Convent of Our Lady of Mercy, St. John's, ASMSJ.

4. *The Newfoundlander*, July 13, 1863, p. 2. The identity of M. Xavier Bernard's companion is found in Notes 1854–1863, ASMSJ, MG 2/1/165. M. Gertrude Moore (baptismal name, Margaret Mary Moore) was born in Kilkenny in 1841, entered at Mercy Convent in 1859 and was professed in 1861.

> About six o'clock p.m. our population were warned by the
> announcement that the steamer *Ariel* had appeared in the offing, and
> within a quarter of an hour the government wharf, on which had
> been erected a tasteful Triumphal Arch, and Mount Saint Patrick
> where cannon had been planted in anticipation of the long-desired
> occasion, were thronged with a rejoicing people, each one eager to
> express his heartfelt gratification at this auspicious event.
>
>   On the debarcation [*sic*] of his Lordship and the nuns,
> salvos of artillery rent the air, accompanied by loud shouts of joy-
> ful welcome from the assembled multitude, and bonfires illumi-
> nated the surrounding hills. [5]

Once safely on land, the first act of the new community was to go in procession to the church to receive the bishop's blessing on the new venture. Bishop Mullock did not miss the chance to impress on the people the importance of education and their duty to co-operate with the sisters in ensuring that the children took advantage of the opportunities offered them. After leaving the church, the sisters were escorted to the priest's house for "a collation" and then to the convent. As they walked along, much to their amusement, little girls in white dresses went ahead of them strewing the path with flowers!

The first convent in Burin, named St. Anne's, was a two-storey house with a gable roof, formerly owned by a businessman by the name of Burfitt. The one-room convent school, attended by both girls and boys,[6] was below Shandy Hill, near the convent. Unfortunately, the convent and school were situated some distance from the church and this created considerable hardship for the sisters, especially during the winter when ice and snow made it difficult for them to get to the church. The older people in Burin remember stories of fathers and grandfathers rescuing the sisters from the middle of a snowdrift, or pulling them across the ice on a makeshift toboggan constructed from a few barrel staves![7] The sisters were young enough to enjoy this form of transportation and may have been disappointed when the old house was dismantled in 1879 and a new convent and

---

5. *The Newfoundlander*, July 20, 1863, p. 2.
6. Although the sisters regarded the teaching of girls as their primary educational focus, the Rule placed no restrictions on the teaching of boys if no other teacher was available.
7. Mrs. Marion Manning, conversation with author, April 4, 2000.

school built in the centre of Burin.[8] After this, the sisters proceeded to the church by a more sedate, though less exhilarating form of locomotion—they walked.

The sisters arrived in Burin at a convenient time of year, for children were not expected to be in school during mid-July and early August.[9] This gave M. Liguori Carmody and her sisters an opportunity to take stock of their surroundings, to visit the sick, and to meet the people. When the new school year began, probably in late August, pupils came from all sections of the district as well as from St. Pierre.[10] No doubt the curriculum was identical to that of the sisters' schools in St. John's and Brigus. The fact that students came from so far away to receive instruction indicates that the convent school quickly established a reputation for excellence. In fact, well into the twentieth century, year after year, the reports of the superintendent of education for Roman Catholic school boards gave the Burin Convent School a very high rating.

At the end of June 1864, there was great excitement in Burin in anticipation of the bishop's arrival. This was not just the ordinary visit when the sacrament of confirmation was celebrated. This year, for the first time, the ceremony of reception of the religious habit was to take place. The postulant, Mary McAuliffe, was to be received into the novitiate. The event is noted briefly in the newspaper:

> On the 30th alt. he [Bishop Mullock] received Miss McAuliffe, in religion Sister Mary Catherine, into the Convent of Mercy which he has lately established at Burin, and which, owing to the provident care and zealous Christian labours of the Sisters, is already exercising its holy influence in the instruction of the young, and is carrying consolation and relief to the sick and poor.[11]

In those far-off days, the sisters seemed to have paid little attention to rules or regulations regarding the length of the novitiate. The unfortunate M. Catherine

---

8. Hogan, *Pathways*, p. 145.
9. There was a Catholic school in Burin at the time of John V. Nugent's visit in 1845. The sisters went to Burin specifically to teach the girls and visit the sick, although, as noted, the convent school in Burin was co-educational.
10. Marshall, *South Coast*, p. 37.
11. *The Newfoundlander*, July 21, 1864, p. 3.

McAuliffe waited eight years before being considered for profession. An entry in the Annals of Mercy Convent reads as follows:

> January 5, 1872: Sister Catherine McAuliffe solicited to be admitted to Holy Profession in the quality of Lay Sister with a promise to go to any "out harbour" mission the Superior might require. Votes were in her favour. She spent over seven years at Burin and was received at Our Lady of Mercy [Convent] with the others who came from that mission.[12]

Whether all the sisters in Burin were content with their lot is debatable. Cut off, as they were, from the companionship of other sisters, the members of the Burin community must have suffered from loneliness and isolation. They were a long distance from any other convent, and there is only one mention of any sister travelling to Burin from St. John's during the first eight years of the mission. This occurred in June 1866, when the accounts book at Mercy Convent noted an expenditure of £1.7, "travelling expenses to Burin." There is nothing to show if this was an appointment to the community or if someone from the mother house had been sent up to see how the sisters were faring in this remote mission. True, the sisters had one another, but they had no say in selecting the persons with whom they were to live. It is doubtful that the bishop—who clearly had the final word in the assignment of sisters—considered compatibility of temperament when selecting sisters to form a community. The needs of the mission were paramount, and the main factors considered in making an assignment were a sister's experience and her ability to do what needed to be done—whether that was to teach music, mathematics, or French or to cook nourishing meals. Most sisters accepted the situation and cheerfully overlooked the idiosyncrasies of their companions; others stoically accepted the status quo and obediently "offered up" annoyances and differences of opinion, remembering that the other sister "has a right to her opinion as, obedience apart, I have to mine."[13] And so, year after year, day in and day out, the sisters

---

12. Annals, Convent of Our Lady of Mercy, St. John's, January 5, 1872, ASMSJ.

13. *A Guide for the Sisters of Mercy*, (n.p.: n.d.). Sections of this guide were assigned reading for all Mercy novices. As a result, certain phrases were indelibly printed in our memory.

of St. Anne's community in Burin performed their religious and professional duties faithfully and well. The first major change in the community occurred on August 11, 1871, when Bishop Power, who succeeded Bishop Mullock in 1870, appointed M. de Chantal O'Keefe to the convent in Burin.[14] A few months later, in November 1871, she was joined by M. Vincent O'Donoghue from the Belvedere community.[15]

M. de Chantal was one of the five young girls from Limerick who came to Newfoundland in 1858 to enter the Congregation of the Sisters of Mercy. Although she had been assigned to Brigus in 1861 as a member of the founding community, she stayed there only three years. As noted, in the days before the amalgamation, when a sister was appointed to a community, she remained there for life. This practice seems to have been ignored more than it was observed, for sisters moved from place to place as circumstances required. In M. de Chantal's case, it appears that her help was needed at the orphanage, for in 1864 she was transferred to St. Michael's Convent, Belvedere. Two years later, in 1866, she was appointed superior of Mercy Convent, and she remained in that position until her term of office was completed in February 1871. Although it is not specified in the Annals that she was appointed superior of the Burin community, there is no doubt that the motive for sending her to Burin was to relieve M. Liguori Carmody of the office that she had held for eight years. Apparently, from the beginning, M. Liguori had been a reluctant superior. Of a gentle, retiring nature, she had no confidence in her ability to lead others. On the other hand, M. de Chantal was a natural leader and ideally suited to assume direction of the mission in Burin.[16]

---

14. "Acts of Chapter, Convent of Our Lady of Mercy, St. John's," August 11, 1871, ASMSJ. The entry reads, "A letter was read at a Chapter meeting from Bishop Power appointing Mother M. de Chantal O'Keefe to Burin."

15. M. Vincent O'Donoghue was born at Clogheen, Tipperary, on July 19, 1844. At the age of twenty years she came to St. John's and entered at Belvedere on November 28, 1864, where she was professed in 1867. Four years after her profession, she went to Burin and stayed for nine years before returning to Belvedere in 1880. In 1888, she was sent to St. Lawrence. Some time later she came back to Belvedere and spent the rest of her life there caring for the orphans. She died on January 27, 1920.

16. M. de Chantal O'Keefe was superior of the Burin Convent from 1871 to 1875, ASMSJ.

The appointment of M. de Chantal to Burin was accompanied by an almost complete change in the personnel of the community. As noted above, the novice, M. Catherine McAuliffe, went to the mother house in 1871 to prepare for her profession. There is no extant correspondence, but the Annals noted that at least two others of the Burin community wanted to return to Mercy Convent. The entry for August 28, 1871, reads as follows:

> Bishop Power proposed to the Community to admit as "Temporary Visitors" Mother M. Liguori Carmody and Sister M. Charles McKenna. Such proposals would not be favoured in the future, but Mother M. Liguori and Sister M. Charles would be received as "Temporary Visitors."[17]

It is clear from this that M. Xavier and her assistants understood the difficulties encountered in distant, isolated communities and were prepared to abandon the principle of stability when the "peace and happiness" of the sisters was at stake. The decision to accept sisters as "temporary visitors" obviously carried little weight, for M. Liguori remained at Mercy Convent for the rest of her life. In 1883, she was appointed mistress of novices. She died at Mercy Convent in 1915. Nothing further is recorded of M. Charles, but it is likely that she remained at Mercy, where she died in 1901. In the case of the long-term novice M. Catherine McAuliffe, although she had been accepted for profession, nowhere is it recorded that she pronounced her vows, and she is not listed among the deceased Sisters of Mercy. In the absence of evidence to the contrary, it may be assumed that she left the community before profession.

The community in Burin had lost three sisters, but in addition to M. de Chantal O'Keefe, three others had been appointed. The same entry in the Annals that recorded the arrival of M. Liguori Carmody and M. Charles McKenna at Mercy Convent concluded with a list of appointments to Burin:

> ... Also it was proposed to give the right of returning to the Parent House Sister Mary of the Cross Reardon, Sister M. Stanislaus Taylor and Sister M. Rose Murphy about to leave for

17. Annals, Convent of Our Lady of Mercy, St. John's, August 28, 1871, ASMSJ.

Burin, should their stay there be an obstacle to their peace and happiness.[18]

From this point on the story becomes complicated and unclear. Of the founding group that went to Burin in 1863, only M. Xavier Tarahan was left. All the rest were newcomers unless another sister had been sent there in the meantime. But the changes in the Burin community were not complete. To follow the story with some coherence it is necessary to bypass, for the moment, the chronological sequence of foundations[19] and move to the establishment of the convent at St. Lawrence.

There are no documents or letters remaining that trace the sequence of events leading up to the decision to open a convent and school in St. Lawrence. The Annals simply mention that the sisters arrived in St. Lawrence on September 21, 1871. The sisters appointed to the new foundation at St. Lawrence were: M. Rose Murphy, who was to be the superior; M. Stanislaus Taylor; M. Xavier Tarahan; and a postulant, Mary Burfitt. The strange thing about all of this is that two of the group, M. Rose and M. Stanislaus, had been assigned to the Burin convent less than one month previously. The addition of M. Xavier Tarahan to the St. Lawrence community left Burin with only M. de Chantal O'Keefe, M. of the Cross Reardon, and possibly one more—the unknown traveller of 1866.[20]

This state of affairs must have been less than satisfactory to the new superior, M. de Chantal. The career of M. de Chantal indicates clearly that she was not prepared to put up with an inadequate staff or lack of the facilities necessary to the efficient discharge of her responsibilities. Accordingly, when the bishop, with M. Xavier Bernard and her assistant, M. Francis Doutney, stopped off at Burin on their way to St. Lawrence to pick up the three sisters destined for the new foundation, it is clear that M. de Chantal expressed her dissatisfac-

---

18. Ibid.

19. The Sisters of Mercy went to Petty Harbour in 1866, to Conception Harbour in 1869, and to St. Lawrence in 1871.

20. The accounts book at Mercy Convent for the year 1866 lists the expenses of a trip to Burin.

tion in no uncertain terms. The result was the immediate appointment of M. Joseph Rawlins of Mercy Convent to St. Anne's Convent, Burin:

> On the 22nd of September [1871] his Lordship, the Most Revd. Dr. Power, appointed Sister M. Joseph Rawlins to leave for the Burin mission; and as the Mother Superior and Mother Assistant were then on the Foundation of the St. Lawrence mission, the Chapter as prescribed by the Constitutions was not held for this Sister, who left the parent house on the 27th of September for the above mentioned place.[21]

As far as can be determined, with this appointment the Burin community now consisted of at least three, and probably four sisters. In the absence of accurate records, we can only piece together the few scraps of information available and try to present as accurate a picture as possible of these long-ago events. One member of the group, Sr. Mary of the Cross Reardon, had managed to land herself in hot water at Mercy Convent some years before her transfer to Bruin. A note in the Annals declared that she had been removed from the positions of vicaress and mistress of novices and was to be banned from holding any further positions of authority within that community.[22] Obviously, the Burin sisters did not hold this mysterious misdemeanour against her, for Mary of the Cross Reardon had a distinguished career in that community, and her influence was such that a Burin historian mistakenly lists her as one of the superiors of the convent there.[23] She died in 1885 and is buried in the sisters' plot in the Burin cemetery.

However, long before a second foundation on the Burin Peninsula was considered, and before anybody in St. John's had heard of Bishop Power, M. Xavier and Bishop Mullock had another missionary project in view—this time on behalf of the people of Petty Harbour. Having secured M. Xavier's approval, Bishop Mullock approached the RC Board of Education. The board's enthusiastic endorsement of his plan was recorded in the proceedings of October 24, 1865:

21. Annals, Convent of Our Lady of Mercy, St. John's, ASMSJ.
22. Ibid.
23. Marshall, *South Coast*, p. 37.

His Lordship informed the meeting that having established a
Presentation Convent in Torbay . . . he was anxious to extend to
Petty Harbour the same advantages as far as lay in his power . . .
[and] . . . by a small addition to the salary paid the present Female
Teacher he could provide for two Sisters of Mercy as he should
only have to procure a suitable residence, as the present school
was amply sufficient to accommodate all the scholars the settlement at this time contained, and more if required. His Lordship
further stated that an addition of £15 to the present salary of £25,
making an Amount of £40 would content the Sisters and hoped
the Arrangement would satisfy the Board. The Board expressed
their great gratification at the proposal and hoped His Lordship
would be able in a short time to have so desirable an
Arrangement speedily accomplished.[24]

Petty Harbour is a small, very picturesque fishing village nestled deep in
the head of Motion Bay about ten miles south of St. John's. The steep, bare hills
that surround the harbour provide a shelter from the storms that frequently
batter the east coast of Newfoundland. In former days, the harbour afforded
an excellent base for pirates lying in wait for vessels approaching St. John's.
Back as far as 1675, there were a few permanent settlers in Petty Harbour and
by the end of the eighteenth century, the population had reached 255. The
same census revealed that there were two carpenters, two coopers, two laun-
dresses, and a surgeon. But the centre of activity for Petty Harbour always was,
and is today, the fishery. By 1857, the population of the village had increased
to more than seven hundred, with nearly twice as many Catholics as
Protestants. There were two churches—one Church of England and one
Roman Catholic—over a hundred dwelling houses, and two schools operated
by the Newfoundland School Society,[25] with over one hundred pupils each.
The town was prosperous, for in addition to the activities of the fishermen,
there were three cod oil factories and premises for salting fish.[26] It is easy to

---

24. "Proceedings of the Roman Catholic Board of Education," St. John's, October 24, 1865, p.
77, AASJ, 600/1/3.
25. See chapter two.
26. *ENL*, s.v. "Petty Harbour."

understand, therefore, Bishop Mullock's concern to provide adequate educational opportunities for the children of this thriving centre.

But before the new convent was established, there was a change of superiors at the mother house. M. Xavier Bernard's term of office having expired on January 30, 1866, Bishop Mullock appointed M. de Chantal O'Keefe to the office of superior. It was now her task to select and prepare the sisters for the new mission. Obviously, it did not enter the head of M. de Chantal, or of anyone else, that future generations would be interested in details of their daily lives and activities such as who went where, when, and why. Any available information comes from outside sources, newspapers, and educational reports. Some individual in Petty Harbour, however, using the initials P. H., was excited enough about the sisters' arrival to write to *The Daily Courier*:

> Sir: As an ardent friend of Education I am most grateful for the establishment of a Convent and School of the Sisters of Mercy in our thriving settlement of Petty Harbour. The blessings conferred on the country by these Institutions are invaluable and are justly estimated by the people, who manifested their delight by the cordial reception given to the 4 ladies who undertook the foundation. Whit-Sunday will long be remembered by this good people, who now cherish among them an Institution, destined, I hope, for ages, to disseminate the blessings of a religious education, and afford a living example of the corporeal and spiritual works of Mercy. As no note has been taken of an event of such importance to us, and of which we would like to inform our distant friends, you would oblige the people of Petty Harbour by inserting this notice.
>
> P. H., Petty Harbour, May 28, 1866.[27]

Very little is known of the Petty Harbour foundation—not even the names of the sisters who established the convent! Unlike the foundations in Brigus and Burin, the convent in Petty Harbour remained a branch house, under the direction of M. de Chantal O'Keefe, the superior of Mercy

---

27. *The Daily Courier*, May 30, 1866, p. 3.

Convent. Was it because the sisters assigned to Petty Harbour were too young and inexperienced to be left on their own, or was it that M. de Chantal wanted to keep control firmly in her own hands? The Annals are silent on the matter.

From the beginning there were at least one hundred girls enrolled in the sisters' school in Petty Harbour, and the usual subjects taught in convent schools formed the basis of the curriculum: reading, easy lessons, writing on slates and paper, arithmetic, geography, grammar, sacred history, and needlework.[28] The establishment of the convent school was a source of great satisfaction to the people of Petty Harbour, and they expressed their delight in an address presented to Bishop Mullock on the occasion of his visit in December 1866:

> My Lord, the Catholic people of Petty Harbour . . . are not unmindful of the great and manifold blessing which you have conferred upon us in the establishment of schools, and more particularly do we allude to the establishment of a branch of the Order of Mercy Convent in our midst, whereby we are enabled to obtain for our female children the blessings of a sound religious education.[29]

The Sisters of Mercy remained in Petty Harbour from 1866 to 1870, teaching in the school and visiting the sick. From the accounts book at Mercy Convent, we learn that in May 1866 the sisters paid £1.7.6 to purchase coal for Petty Harbour, and there is a note to the effect that "Petit Hr. School payment of £11.5.0—due April 1, 1867."[30] However, the Mercy mission in that settlement was of short duration. The final entry from Petty Harbour, noting the receipt of fees, appeared in the Accounts Book on November 30, 1870.

According to M. Austin Carroll, the reason for the withdrawal of the Sisters of Mercy from Petty Harbour in 1870 was the fact that there was no resident priest in the settlement.[31] Not only were the sisters deprived of daily

---

28. ASMSJ, MG1/1/28.
29. *The Newfoundlander*, December 20, 1866, p. 3.
30. Accounts Book, Convent of Our Lady of Mercy, St. John's, p. 283, ASMSJ.
31. Carroll, *Leaves*, vol. 3, p. 29.

mass, but during the winter months, it was on rare occasions that Sunday mass was available. The authorities at Mercy Convent perceived this as being detrimental to the spiritual welfare of the sisters, and so, on March 6, 1870, the Petty Harbour Convent was closed.[32]

No doubt M. Xavier Bernard was disappointed at the withdrawal of the sisters from Petty Harbour. At the time the foundation was made she knew that there was no resident priest, and she would have discussed this problem with her good friend and advisor, Bishop Mullock, who had invited the sisters to go to Petty Harbour. But Bishop Mullock died suddenly on March 29, 1869,[33] and his successor, Bishop Thomas J. Power, did not arrive in St. John's until September 9, 1870.[34] The non-involvement of the two persons who made the initial decision in favour of the foundation and the absence of the new bishop sealed the fate of the Petty Harbour Convent. The last mention of the sisters' connection with Petty Harbour was made in 1870 on the occasion of Bishop Power's first episcopal visit to the town. During this visit, the people extracted a promise that he would send the sisters back to them—a promise that was destined to remain unfulfilled.[35]

However, the work of expansion was by no means complete. Just one year prior to the sisters leaving Petty Harbour, M. de Chantal O'Keefe, the superior of Mercy Convent at the time, was asked to establish a convent in Conception Harbour, a small outport in the southwestern part of Conception Bay. Like her predecessor (and successor) in office, M. Xavier Bernard, M. de Chantal had no hesitation in accepting the invitation. On May 24, 1869, the members of the founding community, with M. de Chantal and her companion, sailed from Portugal Cove to one of the most picturesque little harbours in all of Conception Bay.

32. Hogan, *Pathways*, p. 177.

33. Bishop Mullock had just returned from a visit to the Mercy Convent to discuss plans for reception and profession ceremonies that were due to take place when he suffered a stroke and died almost immediately.

34. At the time of his appointment as bishop of St. John's, Thomas Joseph Power was president of Clonliffe College in Ireland. He was consecrated bishop by Cardinal Cullen in Rome on June 12, 1870.

35. *The Newfoundlander*, October 11, 1870, p. 3.

The history of Conception Harbour is not nearly as well-documented as that of some of the nearby settlements. Until around 1870, the village was known as Cat's Cove. Although tradition holds that it was settled in the 1700s, it did not enjoy the prosperity of Brigus, its neighbour to the north. By 1836, the population was around 250 persons, who depended for their livelihood mainly on the herring fishery.[36] By the mid-1800s, the seal hunt became important, and in 1857, no fewer than twelve vessels from Conception Harbour were engaged in the hunt. The economic health of the town, however, depended on the Labrador cod fishery. During the summer months, the men went north while the women cared for the cattle and tended the gardens that provided vegetables for the winter. The children, too, did their part by taking to the hills in summer to gather the wild berries that grow in profusion in the woods and marshes of Newfoundland. The berries harvested by the children were made into jellies and jams to provide treats for the long, cold winter evenings.

It was to this industrious little outport that M. de Chantal brought three young sisters to establish the next Mercy foundation in Newfoundland. The original convent in Conception Harbour was built in 1869—an exact replica of the convent in Brigus.[37] The leader of the little group—the first community to occupy this beautiful building—was a young woman from Kilkenny, M. Gertrude Michael Moore. At the time of her appointment to Conception Harbour, she was twenty-six years of age and had been professed almost eight years. Her two companions, M. Teresa Slattery and M. deSales Meehan, were both from Limerick and were a couple of years junior to her in age and profession. Two of the three, M. Gertrude and M. deSales, remained in Conception Harbour for the rest of their lives and are buried in the sisters' plot in the convent garden. M. Teresa had come from Limerick in 1860 at the age of fifteen and was accepted as a postulant at Mercy Convent. Her younger sister, Catherine, joined her four years later. The two sisters did not have much time together for it was only two years after Catherine (now Mary Francis) was professed that M. Teresa went to Conception Harbour. She remained there

---

36. *ENL*, s.v. "Conception Harbour."
37. ASMSJ, MG 2/1/217.

for the next forty-two years until 1911, when she became superior of St. Joseph's Convent, Brigus. However, at the time of the amalgamation, in 1916, she was asked to return to Conception Harbour as superior. When her term of office was completed in 1919, M. Teresa was assigned to St. Michael's Convent, Belvedere, where she died in 1931 at the age of eighty-six.[38]

There is no description of the arrival of the sisters in Conception Harbour, except that they were "enthusiastically received by the people."[39] It seems inexplicable to us today that those women who established convents in different parts of Newfoundland left no written account of their experiences. The Annals record only the date of the foundation and the names of the sisters who formed the first community. As for the three "founding" sisters of the Conception Harbour Convent, one thing is certain—they planted a love of the Mercy congregation very firmly in the hearts of the people of Conception Harbour, for over the years, more than a dozen young women from that small outport became Sisters of Mercy.

At the time the convent was established, Conception Harbour was a mission of the parish of Harbour Main where Rev. Jeremiah O'Donnell was pastor. His nephew and curate, Father Patrick O'Donnell,[40] made weekly visits to Conception Harbour to celebrate mass and attend to the spiritual needs of the people, almost all of whom were Catholic. It was not until fifteen years after the sisters' arrival that Conception Harbour was made a parish and Father Patrick O'Donnell became the resident pastor. Possibly, the absence of a priest in the settlement was one of the reasons why the Sisters of Mercy played such an important role in the life of the community. The people called on them for just about any and every emergency.[41] Like Sisters of Mercy everywhere, they taught in the school, visited the poor and the sick, assisted the dying, prepared children and adults for the sacraments, and together with

---

38. M. Francis Slattery spent all her religious life at Mercy Convent where she died in 1905.

39. ASMSJ, MG 2/1/217.

40. Three of Rev. Jeremiah O'Donnell's nephews served as priests in Newfoundland, Patrick, David, and Richard.

41. I was told this by Sister M. Barbara Wade who heard her grandparents' stories of the sisters' role in the life of the community.

the women of the town, they prepared the church for the various religious celebrations that took place. One of these celebrations was described in *The Patriot* of April 18, 1874, and signed by a person who called himself "Traveller":

> Sir: Some short time since we happened to be in Conception Harbour. As we were starting for Brigus . . . we found a number of the inhabitants making their way to their "House of Prayer." We enquired the reason of their gathering on this day of work. We were told there was to be a "Reception" in the Mercy Convent. We then learned for the first time that Conception Harbour possessed a Convent of Mercy Nuns. They devote themselves to the instruction of young girls, visiting the sick, helping the needy. They will shortly open a boarding school for young ladies . . .
>
> Hearing of a "Reception" we wished to see what it was like. We went with the crowd; we saw, we felt surprised. There was a young lady, fair and beautiful . . . the young lady is Miss Leamy; we were told she is niece of the Very Rev. Vicar General O'Donnell, P.P., St. Mary's. She was received under the guardianship of the amiable and worthy Rev. Mother Gertrude Taylor. Furthermore, we were told that "since the hills were formed and the land; ever since the tide began to rise and fall in this remarkable harbour; ever since the green trees on the surrounding hills added to the romance of this picturesque place," this was the first "Reception" in Conception Harbour. It was an event![42]

The young lady who was received as a Sister of Mercy in 1874 was M. Philomena Leamy. At the time she was eighteen years of age. Incidentally, nobody else seems to have heard of the planned boarding school noted by Traveller. In addition, the mention of "the amiable and worthy Rev. Mother Gertrude Taylor" is a mistake on the part of Traveller, a mistake that was copied into the Conception Convent Annals.[43] The only Sister of Mercy with the surname "Taylor" at that time was M. Stanislaus Michael Taylor, who was

---

42. *The Patriot and Catholic Herald*, April 18, 1874, p. 3.

43. Annals, Immaculate Conception Convent, Conception Harbour, ASMSJ. In 1874, M. Gertrude Taylor succeeded M. Gertrude Moore as superior of the convent. In fact, the second superior of Immaculate Conception Convent was M. Stanislaus Michael Taylor.

the superior of the Immaculate Conception Convent in 1874.[44] M. Stanislaus Taylor must have moved to different places more frequently than was usual for sisters in those days, for her name appears in the Annals of several convents. She went on to the foundation in St. Lawrence in 1871. Then, in 1874, she was appointed as the superior of the Immaculate Conception Convent, Conception Harbour. The ceremony of reception described above must have taken place shortly after M. Stanislaus arrived to take up her new post. After her term of office had expired she must have returned to St. Lawrence for there is an entry in the Annals of Mercy Convent for May 16, 1885, "Bishop Power requested that Sr. M. Stanislaus Taylor be received back from the St. Lawrence mission. She arrived June 15, 1885."[45] In 1890 she was appointed mistress of novices at Mercy Convent and remained there until her death on May 27, 1895.

The convent school in Conception Harbour followed the curriculum offered in other schools operated by the sisters. School attendance in Conception Harbour was relatively high. For instance, in 1878, the school inspector reported that 136 pupils were present on the day of his visit and were rated excellent in writing, ciphering, geography, grammar, history, and needlework.[46] Although these subjects are listed in the examiner's report, drawing and vocal music were also taught. There seems to have been a very close bond between the sisters and their pupils at Conception Harbour. Older residents tell stories of how they vied with one another to bring messages from the school to the convent. The small messenger was sure of receiving a reward in the form of a cookie or a slice of freshly baked bread with molasses.[47]

Another story handed down through the years concerns a native of Conception Harbour, M. Gertrude Kennedy. Born in 1876, Agatha Kennedy

44. Ann Mary Catherine Taylor of Limerick, age nineteen years, was accepted as a postulant at Mercy Convent on June 7, 1859. She was received three months later and professed on September 8, 1861. Her name in religion was Sister Mary Stanislaus Michael of the Mother of God.
45. Annals, Convent of Our Lady of Mercy, St. John's, ASMSJ.
46. "Report on the Inspection of Roman Catholic Schools for the Year 1878," AASJ, 600/2/1.
47. Catherine Kenny, RSM, a native of Conception Harbour, is the source of this story.

received her early schooling in the local convent school. When she was about fourteen years of age her parents sent her to school in Ireland where she became a close friend of one of the students, Mary Hoey. Born in 1874 in Carrock McCross, County Monaghan, Mary was the eldest of twelve children born to Owen Hoey and Margaret Philips-Hoey. She was a student at St. Louis Convent school in Carrock McCross when Agatha Kennedy arrived from Newfoundland.

Agatha, like many displaced Newfoundlanders, never stopped extolling the beauties of her homeland. She described to her friend, Mary Hoey, the dear old convent in Conception Harbour and confided to Mary her intention of becoming a Sister of Mercy as soon as she returned to Newfoundland. Agatha Kennedy was as good as her word. A few months after she arrived home, she entered the Immaculate Conception Convent in Conception Harbour on September 8, 1892 at the age of sixteen years, but not without a struggle! When Agatha approached the sisters in Conception Harbour requesting to be admitted as a postulant, the sisters suggested that she was too young to make such a decision and told her to wait another year. Agatha went home, packed her suitcase and sat on the convent steps until the sisters reversed their decision and admitted her.[48] On her entrance into the novitiate, she received the name, Mary Gertrude.

There is no doubt that Mary Hoey was influenced by her friend's descriptions of life in Conception Harbour, as well as by Agatha's admiration of the Sisters of Mercy who ministered to the people of the area. In June 1894, Mary Hoey came to Conception Harbour and was accepted by the sisters into the community.

At the time Mary Hoey made her decision to come to Newfoundland, the village of Conception Harbour was going through a difficult economic downturn. M. Gertrude Kennedy wrote to her friend and attempted to dissuade her from coming because of the great hardships and poverty the sisters were experiencing. Mary Hoey was not discouraged. Rather, the challenges

---

48. M. Gertrude Kennedy told this story to Sr. Catherine Kenny, a native of Conception Harbour. Many years later, Sr. Catherine told the story to the author.

inherent in overcoming such difficulties served to strengthen her resolution. She arrived at Conception Harbour, received the religious name, Mary Brigid, was professed and remained at Conception Harbour for the next twenty-two years where she was a great asset to the teaching staff of the convent school. She was a teacher who brooked no nonsense. Gentle and sympathetic with those who found learning difficult, she accepted no excuse for careless, slip-shod work, and woe betide the child who dared to come to school without the assigned homework completed to her satisfaction.[49] Like most of the sisters, she insisted that students who attended school learn more than the three R's, and throughout her life, she had a reputation for instilling in her pupils a strong desire to excel in the various subjects offered in the school curriculum. This ambition was cultivated assiduously by the bestowing of rewards in the form of apples and cookies salvaged from the convent table. It did not occur to M. Brigid that her constant bestowal of these goodies might have been a source of annoyance to the members of her religious community in days when apples and cookies were considered a treat by young and old alike. All that mattered to her was that the smallest step along the path of learning was duly acknowledged and promptly rewarded.

Shortly after M. Brigid Hoey's profession, her friend M. Gertrude Kennedy became very ill. Apparently, she suffered from a type of paralysis caused by injury to her spine. In spite of the best medical attention available, she remained severely disabled. Eventually, her father, William Kennedy, brought her to St. Anne's Shrine in Quebec, praying for a miracle. A plaque in a little grotto on the grounds of the parish church in Conception Harbour records what happened:

> In 1898, Sister M. Gertrude Kennedy was miraculously cured during a pilgrimage to St. Anne's Shrine, Quebec, during Mass. She was cured of a spinal condition which obliged her to wear an iron collar on her neck to support her head. This condition was pronounced beyond medical aid. This cure was recorded in St. Anne's

---

49. Bernard McDonald, a former student of St. Joseph's School, St. John's, conversation with author, August 19, 1998.

Annals, 1899. Sister M. Gertrude Kennedy was the first
Newfoundland Postulant to enter at Conception in 1892.[50]

In the early days Conception Convent School was noted for the exquisite point lace, silk work, embroidery, and other types of needlework the pupils produced.[51] In that period such skills were considered an essential element in the education of young ladies. In addition, as in all schools operated by Presentation and Mercy Sisters, music was an important part of the curriculum. The frequent concerts put on for the public provided an opportunity to teach children to behave in public with poise and self-confidence, as well as to show off their accomplishments before admiring parents, friends, and relatives. While the audiences were generally well-behaved during the performances of their children, this was not always the case if the program included adults. Should members of the audience find the quality of the entertainment less than satisfactory, they were quite capable of providing their own by striking up a rousing chorus among themselves that left the unfortunate cast on stage competing to be heard against the uproar.[52] The sisters, taking all this in their stride, continued to promote public performances by the students—and not only for the personal development of the children, but also to obtain funds to purchase much needed equipment for the school. As a result, Conception Harbour has a long tradition of music making that continues to the present time.

As the decade of the 1860s drew to a close, the sisters at Mercy Convent in St. John's could look back with a sense of accomplishment. In the ten years since 1859, the new orphanage and five new convents had been opened, St. Clair's Boarding School was filled to capacity, and Our Lady of Mercy School had earned a reputation for excellence. Furthermore, the sisters at St.

---

50. Inscription found in St. Anne's grotto located on the parish grounds in Conception Harbour. Mr. William Kennedy erected the grotto in thanksgiving for the cure of his daughter, Sister Mary Gertrude Kennedy.

51. Thomas Hanrahan, "Report of the Roman Catholic Superintendent for Education for the Year Ended December 31, 1901," p. 36, ASMSJ.

52. An account of such an incident in Conception Harbour is found in *The Evening Telegram,* December 11, 1891, p. 4.

Bridget's School were accomplishing wonders for poor children in the east end of St. John's. But there was one more foundation to establish before the first phase of growth was complete.

Reference has been made already to the convent in St. Lawrence. However, before leaving the chapter on the original foundations it is important to present in more detail the story of the early days in what was, at the time, the most remote mission of the Newfoundland Mercy congregation.

There is nothing written in the Annals of Mercy Convent to indicate just when the possibility of a foundation in St. Lawrence was first discussed. Was there a connection between the withdrawal of the sisters from Petty Harbour in 1870 and the decision to send a group of sisters to St. Lawrence in 1871? If it was perceived that St. Lawrence was in urgent need of qualified teachers, the authorities at the mother house may have re-evaluated the foundation at Petty Harbour, especially in light of the fact that the sisters there were deprived of mass and the sacraments. This would provide the number of teachers required for a new foundation without depleting the teaching staff at Mercy Convent. It is true that the congregation was attracting new members every year, but it was crucial to maintain a sufficient number at the mother house to carry out the commitments already made to Our Lady of Mercy School and St. Bridget's. M. de Chantal O'Keefe would have sympathized with M. de Pazzi Delany's complaints made fifty years earlier at Baggot Street that the poor mother house was being depleted constantly in favour of the missions![53] Whatever the circumstances that determined the closing of one mission, Petty Harbour, and the opening of a new mission on the Burin Peninsula, there must have been some lengthy deliberations between the diocesan authorities and the superior at Mercy Convent.

But before the decision on St. Lawrence was finalized, M. de Chantal's term as superior of Mercy Convent expired, and on February 2, 1871, Bishop

---

53. M. de Chantal O'Keefe was superior of Mercy Convent from 1866–1871. Her term of office expired on February 2 of that year. It is not known if she made the decision to send the sisters to St. Lawrence, or if it was made by M. Xavier Bernard who succeeded her.

Power presided over a chapter to select a new superior and an assistant. By this time there was a sufficient number of professed sisters to justify an election, but the "Acts of Chapter" contained the terse statement, "No majority in any scrutiny. Bishop Power appointed Mother M. Francis Xavier Bernard."[54] It is clear from this statement that M. Xavier was not the choice of the majority of the sisters, for the Rule prescribed that if no sister received a majority after the first votes were counted, a second and, if necessary, a third voting would take place. If there was still no majority, the bishop had the right to appoint the superior. Looking back, it seems strange that M. Xavier Bernard was not elected unanimously, for there is no doubt that she was a woman of vision and courage. Possibly, in light of the fact that she had been superior for eleven years already (1855–1866), some of the sisters might have wanted a fresh face at the helm. Even today there is a healthy reluctance in convent circles to having authority in the hands of one person for too long a period. Thus, the votes were divided, M. Xavier was appointed by the bishop, and now it was up to her to finalize plans for the St. Lawrence foundation.

St. Lawrence is a town near the "toe" of the Burin Peninsula. At the time of the sisters' arrival, its economic health depended on the viability of the fishery. One of its main attractions was—and is—its ice-free harbour. The original settlers built their homes along the shore of a harbour surrounded by four hills that they named Cape Chapeau Rouge, Mount Margaret, Mount Anne, and Mount Lucy Anne.[55] The initial isolation of communities such as St. Lawrence that were accessible only by sea forged strong bonds of loyalty and friendship among the original settlers. Life was often difficult, especially when the fishery did not come up to expectations. But these were strong and brave people—men and women who were quick to come to the aid of neighbours in trouble or in need. These qualities have endured through the years and are typical of outport people all over Newfoundland and Labrador, even in this period of instant communication and ease of travel.

54. "Acts of Chapter, Convent of Our Lady of Mercy, St. John's," February 2, 1871, ASMSJ.
55. Ena Farrell Edwards with R. E. Buehler, *Notes Toward a History of St. Lawrence* (St. John's, NL: Breakwater Books, 1983) p. 16.

However in 1871, when the sisters assigned to the new foundation prepared to leave for their mission, they had no idea of what life was like in that
far-away place or the character of the people among whom they were to live
and work. The Annals simply mention that they arrived in St. Lawrence on
September 21, 1871. As mentioned previously, the three sisters sent to establish the mission were M. Rose Murphy, who was the superior; M. Stanislaus
Taylor; M. Xavier Tarahan; and a postulant; Mary Burfitt.[56] As was customary,
the bishop of the diocese, Bishop Power; the superior of Mercy Convent, M.
Xavier Bernard; and her assistant, M. Francis Doutney, accompanied the
founding trio. The journey provided an opportunity for M. Francis to visit her
brother Reverend William Doutney, a curate of the parish of Burin. Father
Doutney lived in St. Lawrence at the time and cared for the spiritual needs of
the people.

The sisters' arrival late in September meant that the school year had
begun, and there was no time to lose in finding suitable classroom space.
Suitable or not, the only place available was a fish shed, and in short order,
the sisters began classes for ninety-five students. Girls and boys attended
together until a regular teacher was secured for the boys, but periodically
down through the years, the education board had trouble finding a competent teacher for the boys, and more often than not, the sisters taught boys as
well as girls.

---

56. M. Rose Murphy, baptized Agnes Mary, came to Newfoundland from Youghal, County
Cork. She was accepted as a postulant at Mercy Convent on August 29, 1862, and professed on March 25, 1865. It is not known how long she remained in St. Lawrence, but
eventually she returned to Burin where she died on October 5, 1904. She is buried in the
sisters' plot in Burin. For M. Stanislaus Taylor, see chapter six, n. 114. Mary Ann Joseph
Tarahan was the third of the Tarahan sisters to become a Sister of Mercy. On March 19,
1863, she was accepted at Mercy Convent as a postulant for the Burin mission; she was
received at Mercy Convent on June 6, 1863, and given the religious name, M. Francis
Xavier. She was professed at Burin on August 22, 1867 and remained there until she was
transferred to St. Lawrence in 1871, where she remained for the rest of her life. She died
on March 2, 1902, and is buried in the sisters' plot in St. Lawrence. Mary Burfitt was accepted as a postulant and member of the founding community at St. Lawrence where she made
her novitiate, having received the religious name, M. Joseph. She made her profession of
vows on August 13, 1876 during the first ceremony of profession held in St. Lawrence. Sr.
Joseph spent her whole religious life at Sacred Heart Convent in St. Lawrence where she
died on December 22, 1937. She is buried in the sisters' plot in St. Lawrence.

For the first five years of the St. Lawrence foundation, the sisters lived in the presbytery while the convent was under construction. Father Doutney, the curate from Burin, resided at the home of one of the parishioners. Finally, on November 13, 1876, the convent was blessed and formally opened by Bishop T. J. Power, although much of the interior of the building was still under construction:

> Owing to the prevailing lean times, the building, though possessing the appearance of a handsome, well-built convent, was far from being a finished product. Its comforts were meagre, and its conveniences few. The furnishings consisted mostly of substitutes of a most primitive nature.[57]

During the first years after the convent was built, the sisters endured real hardship. The refectory consisted of a small room with a board laid across two empty barrels to serve as a table.[58] Should a guest drop in for dinner, an extra "chair" was created by placing a board over a box or a small barrel in the style of a seasaw. This arrangement was only slightly less comfortable than the regular seating accommodation "enjoyed" by the sisters. On one notable occasion, however, the curate, Father Doutney, dropped in for dinner and insisted on sharing the sea-saw with M. Xavier Tarahan. This ever-vigilant sister, noticing that the priest had no milk for his tea, jumped up to repair the deficiency, thereby causing the unfortunate curate to fall sprawling on the floor. His plate soared to the rafters while the remains of his dinner landed on his beautifully pressed black trousers.[59] This anecdote is hardly worth the telling except that it illustrates the sisters' attitude toward what some might consider a spartan lifestyle. Far from considering themselves in the role of martyrs, these women accepted it all with grace and humour, knowing that in their poverty they were

57. M. Francis Hickey, *Mercy Communico* 1, no. 8 (July 1968): p. 2, ASMSJ. *Mercy Communico* was a quarterly journal printed and distributed to Mercy convents throughout Newfoundland by the Congregation of the Sisters of Mercy.

58. Edwards, *Notes*, p. 72.

59. This story was told and retold with embellishments by M. Borgia Kenny who spent many years at St. Lawrence and heard the story from one of the sisters who had witnessed the event.

one with the people they came to serve. Thus, strong bonds of loyalty were forged—ties that have endured throughout all the years, in good times and in bad.

With the founding of the convent in St. Lawrence, the first phase in the expansion of the Mercy congregation in Newfoundland was complete. In spite of the great need that existed in many places, M. Xavier Bernard realized that it was time to call a halt to new foundations. The schools operated from Mercy Convent—Our Lady of Mercy School with St. Clair's Boarding School attached and St. Bridget's in the East End—and the never-ending demands of the visitation of the sick and the poor provided more work than could be handled by the number of sisters available. It was time, now, to consolidate, to renew, and to reinvigorate the foundations already established.

CHAPTER SEVEN

A TIME FOR PUTTING DOWN ROOTS

Consider the generations of old and see;
has anyone trusted in the Lord and been disappointed?

Sirach 2:10

I n the midst of all the flurry of new foundations, M. Xavier Bernard never forgot for one moment the importance of Our Lady of Mercy School in the education of the Catholic girls of St. John's. In 1861, the enrolment had grown to more than one hundred students.[1] The school was gaining an enviable reputation for the excellence of the programs offered and the quality of the teaching. In December 1865, a review of a concert presented by students of Our Lady of Mercy School appeared in the local paper:

> On Thursday and Fridays evenings of last week some of the young ladies attending the Convent of Mercy School gave very agreeable entertainments, at which the bishop and priests and as large a number of ladies and gentlemen of St. John's as the convent schoolroom would hold, attended. . . . The first piece performed was a French play entitled *Le pieur Mensonge*. . . . I am sure that all who had the pleasure of attending these entertainments feel gratitude to the Rev. Superioress and community for providing such an interesting instructive treat, and to all the young ladies who took part in

---

1. *The Patriot and Terra Nova Herald*, January 23, 1861, p. 2. More than a hundred students of Our Lady of Mercy School were present at the ceremonies of reception and profession.

them. The . . . modest demeanor, and clear, distinct elocution of these young ladies testified to the religious and intellectual edification imparted by the Sisters of Mercy—an additional proof, if such were necessary, that the members of that community are as successful in the training of youth as they are unswerving in their efforts to relieve and console the destitute and afflicted.

Spectator.[2]

When M. Xavier Bernard's term as superior had been completed on January 30, 1866, Bishop Mullock appointed M. de Chantal O'Keefe to that office. Apparently, M. de Chantal was a stickler for order and discipline and, according to the oral tradition at Mercy Convent, not too progressive in her thinking. She liked "the old ways"![3] No sooner had she assumed the role of superior than she instructed the bursar, M. Bernard Clune to write to the Mercy Convent in Cork for a copy of the *Guide to the Customs Observed by Sisters of Mercy*.[4] The *Guide* was issued as a result of a general chapter that was held in Limerick in 1864. This was the first general chapter in which the superiors of many Mercy convents in Ireland gathered to discuss the customs and regulations observed in the different communities of the Sisters of Mercy.[5] There was concern that, as time passed, the original spirit and way of life sanctioned by Catherine McAuley might be modified or changed according to the whim of a local superior or, what was more likely in those days, a bishop. Hence, many felt that the publication of a "Book of Customs" would ensure fidelity to Catherine's vision for the Sisters of Mercy, no matter in what part of the world

2. *The Newfoundlander*, December 21, 1865, p. 2.

3. Notes taken by M. Basil McCormack in conversation with senior sisters at Mercy Convent in the early 1950s, ASMSJ.

4. M. Bernard Clune to M. Josephine Warde, July 9, 1866, ASMSJ, RG 10/1/308. M. de Chantal was a native of Cork. Thus it would be expected that she would have more contact with the Mercy convent in that city than with Baggot Street in Dublin. Furthermore, it will be remembered that the Sisters of Mercy in St. John's had not had much luck in seeking assistance of any kind from Baggot Street.

5. It is interesting to note that the Baggot Street convent did not participate in this chapter. Several communities who supported the concept of a general chapter, were unable to obtain permission to attend from their bishops. The bishop of Athlone went so far as to say that he was going to compile his own "Book of Customs" to be observed by the sisters in his diocese—when he had time!

they ministered. The decisions of the chapter were published in 1866 in *A Guide for the Religious Called Sisters of Mercy*. As a companion to this guide, an abbreviated version was issued, entitled *Abridged Edition of the Guide for the Sisters of Mercy*.[6]

Apparently, M. de Chantal was determined that the Newfoundland sisters would follow the same customs as those observed in Ireland, right down to such details as the length of the annual retreat and the reading materials prescribed for this exercise. In her letter to the superior of the Mercy Convent in Cork, M. Bernard Clune wrote:

> Would you have the kindness to mention if our Sisters at home keep eight or ten days retreat in August. Our Sisters here keep ten days, but we do not wish to be different from the other Houses of our Holy Order. And . . . if you would be kind enough to send us the Chapters of the Imitation and New Testament for the August Retreat.[7]

Unfortunately, M. Josephine Ward of Cork had such a hazy idea of the geography of eastern North America that her response was considerably delayed in reaching its destination. In October 1866, M. Bernard wrote back to Cork to inform M. Josephine that the materials she had requested had not arrived. She noted that a letter had been received from M. Josephine addressed to St. John's, Halifax, Newfoundland. Evidently, M. Bernard's repeated requests were beginning to get on M. Josephine's nerves for she complained in a letter that she was "weary and disappointed" that copies of the required materials had not reached St. John's.[8] The problem was settled when Bishop

---

6. The Dublin sisters issued a guide of their own, in 1869. Sisters of Mercy in many parts of the world used this guide, as well as the 1866 *Guide*. Apparently, the Newfoundland Sisters of Mercy followed the 1866 version.

7. M. Bernard Clune to M. Josephine Warde, July 9, 1866, ASMSJ, RG 10/1/310. The *Imitation of Christ* was a devotional work by Thomas à Kempis. It was required reading in all Mercy convents, especially during the novitiate and prior to making profession of vows.

8. M. Bernard Clune to M. Josephine Warde, September 30, 1867, ASMSJ, RG 10/1/312.

Mullock, who had been in Ireland on business, arrived back in St. John's bringing with him the coveted volumes.[9]

Because the approved English translation of the Rule was not published until 1844,[10] two years after the sisters arrived in Newfoundland, they relied on the handwritten copy of Catherine McAuley's original Rule that they brought with them from Baggot Street.[11] This differed in some respects from versions that were published after the Rule was approved by Rome. In addition to changes in wording that occurred during its translation to Italian and then back into English, other alterations were made by an Italian Consultor. Mary Sullivan, RSM, in her book *Catherine McAuley and the Tradition of Mercy* explained:

> ...Paul Gavino Secchi-Murro ...a Consultor to the Congregation for the Propagation of the Faith, had been asked to review the text of the Rule and Constitutions prior to the July 1840 meeting of the Congregation. Secchi-Murro issued his report to the Congregation on March 3, 1840. In it he recommended a number of ways in which the specificity of the document should be increased. He noted in particular, that greater detail should be provided to the members of the Institute about their "conduct" and "the means of perfecting themselves in the service of God."[12]

Some of Secchi-Murro's modifications were incorporated into the "Rule and Constitutions" before the final text was published in Italian in 1841. Catherine McAuley noticed these, in addition to other alterations that occur in the Italian text, when she received a copy in 1841. In a letter to M. Frances Warde, she commented, "The Very Rev. Dr. Kirby . . . called here the day before he sailed. I mentioned to him some evident mistakes in the copy of our Rule."[13] M.

9. M. Bernard Clune to M. Josephine Warde, November 27, 1866, ASMSJ, RG 10/1/309.
10. Sullivan, *Catherine McAuley*, p. 283.
11. This handwritten copy of the "Rule and Constitutions of the Sisters of Mercy" is preserved in the Archives of the Sisters of Mercy, St. John's.
12. Sullivan, *Catherine McAuley*, p. 274.
13. Catherine McAuley to M. Frances Warde, October 12, 1841, Neumann, *Letters*, p. 381.

Elizabeth Moore also noted mistakes in and alterations to Catherine's original Rule. She wrote to Mary Ann Doyle shortly after Catherine's death, "Get no translations of our Holy Rule till I have time to explain further. Our dear Revd. Mother did not sanction the alterations with the exception of one or two. Not certain how they crept in, but I have my suspicions." Unfortunately, M. Elizabeth did not identify her "suspicions."[14] What is clear is that the foundress did not approve of some of the alterations. The whole matter has been researched thoroughly by Mary Sullivan, and in *Catherine McAuley and the Tradition of Mercy*, Sullivan presented a comprehensive history of the evolution of the Rule and its modifications.[15]

The archives of the Sisters of Mercy of Newfoundland contain a copy of "Regulations and Customs of the Sisters of Mercy" in the handwriting of M. Francis Xavier Bernard.[16] The volume consists of two sections, the first of which is a series of meditations for retreat, possibly copied from some book of devotion. The section entitled "Regulations and Customs" is signed by M. Francis Xavier Bernard, 1859, and concludes, "All for Jesus through Mary. Praise to God for ever and ever. Pray for the soul of Sr. M. F. Xavier Bernard." The sequence of chapters is the same as that found in the handwritten copy of the "Rule and Constitutions" that the founding sisters brought from Dublin in 1842. The *Guide* that was compiled in 1864 was based on the approved English translation of the Rule, published in 1844. Thus, when M. de Chantal and the sisters at Mercy Convent received the *Guide*, they would have noted changes from the original Rule, and as well, they saw that customs and regulations contained in this *Guide* differed somewhat from those copied by M. Xavier Bernard in 1859. They realized that if they were to follow the customs observed in the convents in Ireland, they would have to adapt some of their

14. M. Elizabeth Moore to Mary Ann Doyle, November 21, 1841, cited in Sullivan, *Catherine McAuley*, p. 272.

15. Sullivan, *Catherine McAuley*, pp. 258–291.

16. ASMSJ. The customs and regulations identified in this volume are not nearly as detailed as those contained in the *Guide* of 1866. One example is in M. Xavier's section on "Visitors." Although visitors for a member of the community are announced to the mother superior before informing the sister, no length of time or frequency of visits is mentioned except to note that sisters did not receive visitors during Lent or Advent.

practices. In a letter to M. Josephine Warde, M. Bernard Clune wrote: "Dearest Mother, when next you have the kindness to favour us with a line, would you mention particularly if the *Customs and Regulations* heretofore observed are to be laid aside, and the Guide only observed."[17] The anxiety of the Newfoundland sisters to ensure that they followed in every detail the customs observed in Ireland seems to have been shared by Sisters of Mercy everywhere. Up to the time of Vatican II, there was an astonishing similarity of observances in Mercy convents throughout the world.

In the absence of any documentation, there is no evidence that M. de Chantal required the sisters to observe the regulations set down in this new *Guide* while she was superior of Mercy Convent or that she introduced them when she went to Burin in 1871. However, it may be presumed that she did so, because after her appointment as superior of St. Michael's, Belvedere, she lost no time in seeking the bishop's approval to make "great changes." A Christian Brother, Brother Richard Fleming, in a letter to Ireland dated June 3, 1884, noted one of these changes:

> Mother de Chantal, or rather—his Lordship—has made great changes. Visitors remain a quarter of an hour now, at least, some. I met Mary Joseph's sister a few days since just at the gate. She complained of not being allowed to see her, M. J., more than once a month.[18]

The original Rule is silent on the matter of visitors, and even a quick reading of any biography of Catherine McAuley will demonstrate that she welcomed relatives to the convent, even making a home for her nieces at Baggot Street. The *Guide* of 1866, however, spoke sternly of the practice of receiving visitors and laid down strict rules for the length and frequency of visits:

---

17. M. Bernard Clune to M. Josephine Warde, November 27, 1866, ASMSJ, RG 10/1/309.

18. Brother Fleming to Brother Holland, June 3, 1884. Fleming is referring to M. Joseph Kelly who entered at Belvedere on March 31, 1871. It is probable that M. de Chantal effected the "changes" with the bishop's approval, in compliance with the 1866 *Guide*.

Superiors are under a strict obligation to limit secular inter-
course, visits, etc. within the bounds that duty and charity pre-
scribe. . . . The usual time permitted to visitors is a quarter of an
hour; to parents half an hour. The Sisters take a quarter-glass or
watch to measure the time. The Sisters are permitted to see parents about once a month; mere acquaintances very rarely.[19]

In August 1871, M. de Chantal left St. John's to take up the position as
superior of the Burin community, where she remained until 1875 when she
returned to Mercy Convent and was elected bursar. Evidently, she was someone who was in a position of authority for just about all her religious life.[20]
She remained at Mercy Convent as either bursar or assistant until the bishop
appointed her superior of St. Michael's Convent, Belvedere, on July 6, 1883,
where she spent the rest of her life until her death in 1927 at the age of
eighty-nine.

In the meantime, the sudden death of Bishop Mullock on March 29, 1869
was a loss, not only to the Catholic community, but also to the entire population. He was one of the most outstanding churchmen of his time, and his
contributions to the intellectual, political, and scientific progress of the
country are widely acknowledged by students of Newfoundland history. But
one person in particular mourned his passing, perhaps more than all others.
To M. Xavier Bernard, Bishop Mullock had been friend and advisor since her
decision to offer herself to the Newfoundland mission. Given the degree of
control bishops exercised over their lives, both Presentation and Mercy
Sisters must have awaited the announcement of a new bishop with no small
degree of trepidation.

---

19. *Guide for the Religious Called Sisters of Mercy* (London: St. Anne's Press, 1888), pp.
109–110. If the Newfoundland Sisters of Mercy brought a quarter-glass with them to the
parlour to measure the time, the practice died out very quickly for even the oldest members of the Newfoundland congregation (going back to 1918) do not remember having
seen it used. By the mid-twentieth century, visitors usually stayed about an hour, but it is
doubtful that anyone timed the visit.

20. After her return to Belvedere in 1883, M. de Chantal O'Keefe filled the office of superior several times, from 1883–93, 1899–1903, 1907–10, 1912–19, and when she was not
superior, she was assistant.

Whatever fears M. Xavier may have experienced at the loss of her good friend, Bishop Mullock, the new bishop, Thomas Joseph Power, like his predecessors, proved to be a strong supporter of the sisters. Born in Newross, County Wexford, Thomas Power attended university in England and then went to the Irish College in Rome to complete his studies in theology. In Rome, he became a master of church ceremonials. After ordination to the priesthood, Thomas Power returned to Ireland and ministered in the diocese of Dublin. A few years later he was made president of Clonliff College where he remained until he was appointed to succeed Bishop Mullock in the Diocese of St. John's, Newfoundland. He was ordained bishop in Rome on June 12, 1870, and arrived in St. John's three months later on September 9.

Bishop Power was an educator, a scholar, and a liturgist. Archbishop Howley wrote that "he raised to a height of particular grandeur the music and ritual of the Cathedral."[21] In this achievement he had the help of the talented M. Xaverius Dowsley of Mercy Convent, who in 1868 became organist and choir director at the cathedral, succeeding Thomas Mullock, Bishop Mullock's brother, who was the first organist of the cathedral from 1855 to 1868.[22]

Elizabeth Dowsley was born in St. John's in 1841, the only child of Ellen and George Dowsley. She received her early education at Our Lady of Mercy Academy, and later she continued her education in England, specializing in instrumental and vocal music. After completing her studies, Elizabeth returned to St. John's, where as the daughter of a well-known and prosperous family, she was caught up in a whirl of activity, even dancing with the Prince of Wales (later Edward VII) during a party at Government House.[23] Given the prince's reputation, one would suspect that Elizabeth was taking more than her life in her hands! In any case, she soon became tired of the ceaseless round of social engagements, for on September 8, 1864, she was admitted as a postu-

21. J. G. Higgins, "Right Reverend T. J. Power, E.D., Bishop of St. John's, 1870–1893," *The Centenary of the Basilica-Cathedral of St. John the Baptist*, ed. P. J. Kennedy (St. John's, NL: Archdiocese of St. John's), 1955, p. 247.
22. I am indebted to Larry Dohey, archivist for the Archdiocese of St. John's, for this information.
23. McCormack, "Educational Work," p. 54.

lant at Mercy Convent, Military Road. Four months later, on January 11, 1865, the "Acts of Chapter" of Mercy Convent record that "Elizabeth Ann Mary Dowsley (Sister Mary Xaverius Bernard) was admitted to receive the Holy Habit."[24] M. Xaverius spent the first twenty-two years of her religious life teaching at Mercy Convent. She was organist and choir director at the cathedral for more than twelve years, a position that she filled with a great deal of success. In his diary, Bishop Power referred often to the music performed under her direction at different liturgical celebrations: "The music of Mass was particularly beautiful, the singing brilliant."[25] At this time there was no rule against solo singing during mass or other liturgical functions.

The brilliant singing that so delighted Bishop Power was the contribution of M. Bernard Clune, the woman whose foresight and determination brought Littledale into being and so offered the opportunity for education and a better life to thousands of Newfoundland children throughout the length and breadth of the island.[26] M. Bernard Clune was the sixth young lady from Limerick to cross the Atlantic to become a Sister of Mercy in Newfoundland and, like her compatriot, M. Xavier Bernard, was one of the outstanding figures in the history of the Mercy congregation. Those who knew her described her as a strong personality, fifty years ahead of her time. She introduced new vigour into the schools and used her influence to persuade more girls to come from Ireland to Newfoundland, among them, M. Bridget O'Connor and M. Mercedes Lyons. In the opinion of one of her contemporaries, "she was a brilliant woman but unwilling to listen to advice."[27]

M. Bernard Clune was professed on January 23, 1861. Five years later, on January 30, 1866, she was appointed bursar, with the responsibility to manage the financial affairs of the convent, school, and St. Clair's Boarding

---

24. "Acts of Chapter, Convent of Our Lady of Mercy, St. John's," ASMSJ. The ceremony of reception of the habit took place on March 25, 1865.

25. Bishop Power's Diary, August 1877, AASJ.

26. St. Bride's, Littledale, was a boarding school and teacher training institution, founded by M. Bernard Clune in 1883. The beginnings of Littledale are dealt with in the next chapter of this book.

27. Notes taken by M. Basil McCormack in conversation with M. Philomena Walker, *circa* 1950, ASMSJ.

School—quite a challenge for a young woman not yet thirty years of age. She held this position until 1875, when she was appointed mistress of novices. A few years later she was named superior of Mercy Convent. But before she assumed this office, a most unpleasant and awkward series of events occurred.

It all began in October 1878, when the sisters at Mercy Convent agreed to accept a professed sister from Mount St. Vincent Orphanage, Convent of Mercy, Limerick, named M. Ita McSweeney, who wished to transfer from the Limerick community to the Mercy Convent in St. John's.[28] Incidentally, she is the only professed sister from Ireland to volunteer for the Newfoundland mission since the three founding sisters arrived in 1842. During M. Ita's first two years at Mercy Convent, M. Xavier Bernard was the superior. On February 20, 1880, M. Xavier's term of office was completed, and a chapter was convoked for the purpose of electing a sister to replace her. In this case the election process was a disaster. The results of the chapter are summed up in the following terse statement, "Bishop Power presided over a Chapter, assisted by Rev. M. A. Fitzgerald. There was no majority and the bishop appointed Sister M. Ita McSweeney as Superior."[29] The fact that the bishop made the appointment indicates that the sisters were so strongly divided in their choice that they were unwilling to change their votes even when it became clear that a majority was impossible, a decision that they were to regret before many weeks had passed. Unfortunately, the names of those who received the highest number of votes were not recorded in the "Acts of Chapter." And so the stranger, M. Ita McSweeney, assumed the role of superior of Mercy Convent. On the same day, M. Xavier Bernard was elected assistant, and M. Bernard Clune was elected bursar and novice mistress.

Apparently, M. Ita McSweeney was not blessed with the gift of leadership. Furthermore, she had been in Newfoundland less than two years and may not have understood either the sisters or the people to whom they ministered. Even with the advice and help of the wise and experienced M. Xavier Bernard and the

---

28. "Acts of Chapter, Convent of Our Lady of Mercy, St. John's," October 1, 1878, ASMSJ.
29. Ibid., February 20, 1880.

capable M. Bernard Clune, the situation went from bad to worse. Finally, six months later, things came to a head. The "Acts of Chapter" for August 20, 1880, contain the following entry, "A special Chapter was called by the Bishop. The vocals expressed disapproval of the governance of Sister M. Ita McSweeney. The next day the Bishop received her resignation and named M. Bernard Clune as 'Acting Superior for the time being.'"[30] After that, M. Ita McSweeney dropped completely out of sight. As a matter of fact, the entry in the Mercy Convent chapter book is the only evidence that she ever existed. Her name is not found in the Register at Mercy International Centre in Dublin. Nor is it found in the Register of Professed Sisters of Limerick. After her forced resignation, she may have sought admission to one of the Mercy convents in the United States, or she may have returned to Ireland. She is another mystery waiting to be solved.

On December 3, 1880, Bishop Power presided at a chapter of elections and this time, putting aside differences of opinion and taking no chances, the sisters elected M. Bernard Clune as superior. Evidently, they had learned the hard way the wisdom of exercising their right to choose the leader of their community. On the same day, M. de Chantal O'Keefe replaced M. Xavier Bernard as assistant.[31]

For some months M. Xavier's health had been failing. No doubt the troubles associated with the short tenure of M. Ita McSweeney had taken their toll, and in September 1880, "she was stricken with paralysis."[32] For eighteen months she was a helpless invalid until on February 25, 1882, she died. At the time of her death she was fifty-four years of age and had lived in Newfoundland for thirty-two years. M. Xavier Bernard was known throughout the island. Church leaders recognized her as a woman of vision and courage. The poor, the sick, and the little children of all denominations loved her for her tender charity. Lengthy obituaries appeared in both *The Evening Telegram* and *The Newfoundlander*, the latter giving an account of her funeral:

---

30. Ibid., August 20, 1880.
31. M. de Chantal O'Keefe was superior in Burin from 1871–75. She returned to Mercy Convent early in 1875 where, on May 14 of that year, she was elected bursar.
32. *The Evening Telegram,* February 28, 1882, p. 4.

At an early hour the coffin . . . was borne to the Cathedral and
placed on the catafalque, and from then till the commencement of
the Sacred functions was tenderly watched, not only by the
bereaved Sisters . . . but also by an ever increasing throng of faithful souls, many of whom recalled the days of hardship and bitter
cold when she had "taken the hunger off them," or shielded them
from the winter's blast by giving them (unknown to all but God
and themselves) the garments from her own person . . . As the
time approached for the moving of the cortege the congregation
had increased to a dense throng composed of all classes and
denominations of our citizens. . . . It was feared that the great
snow banks blocking the road to the Cemetery since the late falls
would have interfered with the procession; but not so. The good
people had turned out en masse with their shovels and made a
level pathway through the spotless mountains. As the coffin was
lowered to its last resting place a few quivering snow flakes fell
upon it as gently as the tears of angels "weaving a silvery pall."
    While offering this feeble tribute to a memory that will live
in Benediction, we bid her loving friends in her own Green Isle
across the ocean to weep not, for though we have laid her deep
beneath the white snow mantle, yet shall the sunshine of spring
burst forth and the green shamrock and crimson tinted daisy
bloom joyously upon her grave; she shall sleep as sweetly and be
guarded by hearts as warm and prayerful as though she were laid
to rest in the sunny valley of her own native clime on "The Banks
of Shannon's Lordly Stream." May she rest in peace. [33]

M. Xavier Bernard may be regarded as a second foundress. When M.
Francis Creedon died in 1855, there were four sisters at Mercy Convent—two
professed sisters, one lay sister, and a novice. Under the leadership of M.
Xavier Bernard, the congregation grew rapidly until, at the time of her death
in 1882, there were more than forty sisters in six convents in various parts of
Newfoundland.

Back at Belvedere, the struggle to provide for the children in the orphanage
was ongoing. The parishioners responded with characteristic generosity to the

33. *The Newfoundlander*, March 3, 1882, p. 3.

yearly collection taken up in the cathedral. From time to time, concerned individuals made private donations that were acknowledged in the local newspapers; for example, "The Sisters of Mercy of St. Michael's Convent, Belvedere, gratefully acknowledge the receipt of £10 from the Chief Justice, Sir Francis Brady, for the Orphanage and the House of Mercy."[34]

There were close ties between the orphanage and the members of the cathedral parish, and accounts of various religious celebrations mention the participation of the Belvedere children. For example, on January 31, 1871, the citizens of St. John's opened their newspaper to find an account of the celebrations that had taken place on the previous weekend. "The devotion of the *Quarante Ore*, or Forty Hours Adoration of the Most Blessed Sacrament commenced at the Cathedral on Sunday morning. . . . After Mass a Procession was formed at the Altar. It was composed of the Orphan children in the charge of the Sisters of Mercy."[35] Furthermore, the children took part in social activities sponsored by the parish, such as parades and picnics. Participation in events such as these demonstrated to the children of the orphanage that they were members of a wider community. At the same time, their presence at public events served as a reminder that the care and support of these children was a responsibility to be shared by the whole Catholic community—a fact that the bishops were not shy in bringing to the attention of the people. Bishop Mullock, unwilling to depend solely on collections taken up during the Sunday masses, scheduled special church-related events during which a collection was taken up in support of his many educational and social projects. An account of one such collection that took place on September 15, 1865, was published in *The Newfoundlander*:

> A congregation numbering about four thousand assembled at Belvidere cemetery at 11 o'clock yesterday for the purpose of contributing toward the support of the Orphanage in connection with the Convent of Belvidere. After the collection, Mass was offered in the Mortuary Chapel by the Rev. J. O'Donnell—the

---

34. Ibid., January 16, 1865, p. 2.
35. Ibid., January 31, 1871, p. 2.

> nuns singing the usual parts in truly exquisite style, with the
> Harmonium accompaniment. His Lordship, Dr. Mullock, then
> addressed the large assemblage . . . on the eternal recompense
> promised to all who are compassionate and succour those pecu-
> liar objects of her care the orphan children . . .[36]

On January 21, 1871, M. Clare Francis Tarahan was appointed superior
of St. Michael's Convent, Belvedere, succeeding M. Bonaventure Cussen. Ellen
Tarahan (M. Clare) was the second of the three Tarahan sisters who became
Sisters of Mercy. A Newfoundlander by birth, she was accepted as a postulant
at Mercy Convent on August 15, 1855, just one month after the death of M.
Francis Creedon. On March 25, 1856, she was received into the novitiate and
given the name, Mary Clare Francis. Seven months after her profession on
April 25, 1859, she went to Belvedere as a member of the first community of
St. Michael's Convent.

Apparently, for the first year or so after M. Clare's appointment as
superior, things moved along very smoothly. Two new novices were
received, M. Angela Kitchin and M. Joseph Kelly. But the serene, happy days
that marked the first year of her term of office were not to last. In August
1872, there was a severe outbreak of typhoid fever at the orphanage. At that
time eighty-four people lived at Belvedere, ten sisters and seventy-four
children from the ages of three to fourteen years. In spite of the best efforts
of the sisters, forty-one of the children became ill. The fact that four of the
sisters also caught the infection put an additional load on those who were
looking after the sick and attending to the regular duties associated with the
orphanage. The more seriously ill children were sent to the Fever Hospital
in the city. At the orphanage, M. Clare Tarahan worked tirelessly, cleaning,
scrubbing, and nursing the sick until, much to the grief and consternation
of the sisters, she became ill with the fever and died on November 11,
1872. The Belvedere Annals state that she caught the infection washing the
clothes of the children who were sick. Of the forty-one children who contracted the disease, two died. Of the four sisters who became ill, all recov-

---

36. Ibid., September 17, 1865, p. 3.

ered except M. Clare. With the death of M. Clare, the epidemic had run its course.[37]

Within a very short time after the outbreak of the fever the appropriate department within the government made a complete inspection of the convent and orphanage to ascertain the source of the infection. The following letter from the colonial secretary of the day outlines the suggestions made to correct any future contagion. It is worth quoting in its entirety, for it gives an idea of the hardships endured by children and sisters in the days before modern plumbing and at a time when no government support was available to these women who devoted their lives to caring for orphaned children.

RE: INSPECTION OF BELVEDERE, MARCH 19, 1873

We beg leave to report that we have, in accordance with the desire of the Government, visited and examined St. Michael's Convent at Belvedere, used for the reception of orphan children.

The buildings which compose the institution consist of two houses, united by a centre building containing the schoolroom and work room, and are situated on a gentle slope facing to the North about half a mile from the town, the site being in itself all that could be desired. The buildings are commodious and well adapted for the purpose to which they are devoted and afford ample room for the inmates who consisted at the time of the outbreak of fever of ten adults and 74 children of ages ranging from 3 to 14.

At the time of our visit the children were reduced to 49, there being then 17 in the Fever Hospital at River Head. Two having died, and six having been recently discharged.

The appearance of the children proves that they are well fed and cared for, they have, by testimony of both the Sisters of Mercy in charge of them, and of the medical men who have from time to time attended them, been remarkably free from serious disease from the period of the removal of the institution to its present locality in 1858 [sic] up to the month of August last, when the first case of the present epidemic occurred, from which time to the present date 41 children have been attacked of whom two

---

37. Ibid., November 19, 1872, p. 2.

have died, and three of the Sisters, of whom one (the Revd. Mother of the Convent) died, and one is at present ill.

The disease is fever of a gastric or typhoid character such as is specially liable to be produced by imperfect drainage or other sanitary defects.

On examination of the internal arrangements, its condition ...was found satisfactory till we came to the basement where is situated the closet that had served for the use of all the inmates. This closet, adjoining the house and connected with it by a covered passage, is placed over a small cesspool without any attempt at drainage, and with a window in it, which though intended for ventilation, serves, when open, simply to propel the foul air through the connecting passage into the house, where it gradually diffuses itself, poisoning the whole atmosphere, and ready at any time to generate disease. In this arrangement no doubt must be sought the cause of the persistence of the present epidemic.

A commencement has been made towards remedying these defects by building a cesspool at some distance from the house to connect with the closet by pipes, a cistern capable of containing a certain quantity of water being intended to be built at the top of the house for the purpose of flushing the pipes.

These works, we understand, have been stopped for want of means, and we would strongly recommend that the plans for their completion should be submitted to some competent authority.

There is an excellent well of water at a short distance from the house and so situated as to be out of reach of pollution. . . . The water supply of so large an institution ought, however, on the score of both of convenience and health, not to depend merely on what can be conveyed by hand from day to day. [38]

Three years later, the problem of an adequate supply of clean, fresh water was still not solved. Sometime around 1874, M. Ignatius Guinane,[39] the newly elected superior at Belvedere, wrote to the governor of Newfoundland:

---

38. Letter from the colonial secretary, James Noonan, March 19, 1873, ASMSJ, RG 10/2/45.

39. Honora Mary Teresa Guinane of Limerick entered at Mercy Convent on July 31, 1860 in her sixteenth year. She was received on December 23, 1869, taking the religious name of Mary Ignatius.

TO THE HONOURABLE, HIS EXCELLENCY GOVERNOR
JOHN HAWLEY GLOVER AND COUNCIL.

The Reverend Mother Superior and Community of St. Michael's Convent of Mercy and by the inmates, numbering over 80:
The respectful petitioners of the Roman Catholic Orphanage of St. John's would humbly herewith:
That the said Roman Catholic Orphanage has long suffered much inconvenience from the want of a supply of water for the establishment having only a well within the grounds from which the house can be supplied and which occasionally during the summer months becomes dry. At such times the inconvenience suffered cannot be described, besides this, danger to be apprehended from fire breaking out in the establishment. The petitioners humbly pray that his Excellency will in the commencement of his Government display his benevolence by removing this grievance.
Your petitioners in duty bound will ever pray,
Sister Mary Ignatius Guinane and Community. [40]

Whether M. Ignatius ever received a response from the governor is debatable, but the concerns of the sisters for the plight of the orphans did not go unnoticed by Bishop Power. In 1883, he appointed the strong-willed M. de Chantal O'Keefe to succeed M. Ignatius Guinane as superior of St. Michael's Convent. M. de Chantal had no hesitation in pointing out to the bishop that a new and modern building was needed to house the orphans in safety and comfort and to provide better and more modern facilities for their education and training. Bishop Power agreed and decided to entrust the entire work of planning the construction and financing of a new orphanage to his curate at the cathedral, the talented and energetic young priest, Michael Francis Howley. In a letter to *The Evening Telegram*, Dr. Howley explained how the money was raised to begin this important project:

---

40. M. Ignatius Guinane to Governor John Hawley Glover and council. Noted on the copy of the letter, "Sir John Hawley Glover—this was at the commencement of his Government, 1873," [signed] Sister M. Chrysostom, ASMSJ, RG 10/2/48.

> For many years the nuns have cherished the hope of commencing
> a new building on an improved scale, but the many other works
> in progress in the diocese forbade them to take the initial step.
> Having, however, received a certain amount of compensation
> money for land taken by the Railway Company, which was aug-
> mented by the judicious letting out of other land, and by kind
> donations from musical and dramatic performances, and from pri-
> vate friends, amounting altogether to about £1,200 they deemed
> it safe to inaugurate the work. [41]

The amount realized was enough to pay for the initial cost of stone and brick
used in the construction of the building,[42] but it fell far short of what was
needed. With this totally inadequate amount and complete trust in Divine
Providence, construction began in May 1884. The work proceeded rapidly, and
in September, Dr. Howley reported:

> The walls are now completed, consisting of three stories of solid
> stone and brick work, 100 feet long by 44 wide. The roof is now
> being placed in situ and will be completely covered in by the end
> of October. . . . The heating apparatus will cost about between
> £300 and £400, and it is hoped that the entire cost of the build-
> ing, when completed and furnished with all appliances, beds, hot
> and cold water baths, lavatories, laundries, oven, bakery, school
> appurtenances, sewing, ironing, washing machines, fire escapes, etc.
> will amount of about £4,000 all told. [43]

The Irish Christian Brother, Richard Fleming, watched the progress of
the new building with great interest. In his letters to his friend and predecessor, Brother Francis Holland, Fleming gave a blow-by-blow account of events
at Belvedere. Fleming's observations provide an insight into the strengths and
foibles of persons whose achievements we applaud but of whom, in reality,
we know so little. His letters are especially interesting because of the human,
everyday touches he includes. For instance, when reporting the death of M.

41. *The Evening Telegram*, September 26, 1884, p. 4.
42. *Inter Nos*, June 1924, p. 27.
43. *The Evening Telegram*, September 26, 1884, p. 4.

Vincent Nugent, he mentioned M. Bonaventure Cussen's illness and its rather improbable cure: "Mother Bonaventure is getting better. Strange case. Dr. Sims prescribed the drinking of buttermilk. Since then she is getting strong."[44] On June 3, 1884, Fleming reported, "They are working away at the Belvidere Orphanage. Walls about 3 or 4 feet high now. Dr. Howley is man and master."[45]

From the beginning, the struggle to meet the financial demands of such a project placed a heavy burden on the sisters. In September 1884, a collection in support of the new orphanage was taken up in the cathedral, but the failure of that year's fishery made it impossible for the people to respond in their normally generous fashion. Nevertheless, the construction continued, and on September 29, 1885, one hundred and twenty little girls moved into the new orphanage, which was dedicated to St. Michael the Archangel. At the time, eleven sisters made up the community of St. Michael's Convent.[46] Two weeks later, Brother Fleming wrote, "The fires, fire rather, were lit in the new Orphanage today. The heating was a great success. You could not lay your hand on the pipes and yet they do not scorch the woodwork though quite close to it. It seems to be a great invention."[47]

A few months after the new orphanage was opened, the driving force behind the project, Dr. Howley, was appointed prefect apostolic of St. George's on the west coast of Newfoundland. Brother Fleming commented:

> Bishop Power is not sorry to lose the Dr. you may be sure. He thought him a little tart and busy. The Rev. Mother at Belvidere [M. de Chantal O'Keefe] is also rubbing her hands with joy. She too found him a little inconvenient in the planning and regulating of her new orphanage. So you see with all his goodness and activity he did not please everyone.[48]

---

44. Brother Fleming to Brother Holland, March 15, 1884. "The Slattery Papers," Library of Mount St. Francis Monastery, St. John's, NL (henceforth LMSF).

45. Ibid., June 3, 1884.

46. Brother Fleming to Brother Holland, October 12, 1885. "The Slattery Papers," LMSF.

47. Ibid.

48. Ibid., January 20, 1886.

M. de Chantal may have felt some frustration and annoyance when her ideas clashed with those of Dr. Howley, as apparently they did. Nevertheless, at his departure the orphanage was deprived of a most capable and ardent supporter. Over the next few years, the difficulty of raising money to cover the huge debt on the building was a constant source of worry. Finally, the sisters came up with the idea of placing little tin boxes in the banks and other places of business in an attempt to encourage patrons to donate a few cents to help them liquidate the debt.

> The good ladies of St. Michael's Orphanage in their exertions to relieve their building from debt have placed collection-boxes in the banks and principal business establishments where donations may be deposited. It is to be hoped that the boxes will be liberally patronised, especially by the fortunate ones who draw goodly balances and whose remembrances will merit lasting reward. . . . The cost of erecting the brick orphanage which could not, in the interest of the health and safety of the inmates, be any longer delayed, entails a heavy annual interest charge, to meet which taxes the resources of the community to the utmost. They, therefore, ask help through the medium of these little contribution boxes . . .[49]

It is natural to feel a good deal of sympathy for these highly educated and cultured women who were obliged to go from place to place with their little tin cans to beg for a few cents to help pay a debt that, in fact, belonged to society as a whole. Their efforts met with moderate success. On July 8, 1892, *The Evening Telegram* published a note of thanks from the sisters:

> The Sisters of St. Michael's Orphanage gratefully acknowledge the receipt of $67.16 from the patrons of their collection boxes, being the sum deposited in the boxes at the various banks and mercantile offices. It will help materially to pay the annual interest of the debt on the Orphanage, which interest amounts to $300 a year. The ladies of St. Michael's will avail of the courtesy of our Bank managers and merchants to replace the little tin receptacles in

---

49. *The Evening Telegram*, April 21, 1892, p. 4.

their offices; and entertain the hope that the contributions of the
public will again manifest the generous interest they take in performing this, one of the corporal works of mercy—the support of
the orphans of the community.[50]

The sisters did not realize when they wrote this acknowledgement
that the days of the little tin boxes were gone forever. The very day it
appeared in the newspaper, July 8, 1892, St. John's was subjected to one of
the most devastating fires in its history. Almost the entire city was reduced
to ashes. Banks and businesses, shops, stores, warehouses, and wharves were
levelled to the ground. Hundreds of people lost their homes with everything
they possessed, and the need for food and shelter was almost impossible to
meet. At least twelve thousand people had been burned out.[51] Hundreds of
well-to-do families were reduced to poverty and had to begin to build their
homes and businesses all over again. Furthermore, the destruction of St.
John's affected the industry and trade of the whole country.[52] Belvedere's
need was only one among many, and it would be a long time before the citizens of St. John's were in a position to provide assistance to the cash-strick-
en orphanage.

However, right from the beginning, the sisters had relied on Divine
Providence to provide for the orphans under their care. They were not disappointed. To help liquidate the debt on the orphanage, Judge Joseph Little[53]
donated to Belvedere the insurance money on his house and property that had
been destroyed in the fire. This generous act was recorded in the Annals of St.
Michael's Convent, and Judge Little's name was remembered prayerfully and

---

50. Ibid., July 8, 1892, p. 4.

51. O'Neill, *A Seaport Legacy*, p. 642.

52. Ibid.

53. Joseph Little, brother of Philip Little, was born in P.E.I. At age sixteen, he followed his
brothers Philip and John to Newfoundland where he was called to the Bar in 1859. He
spent more than thirty years in public life, as a lawyer, politician, and judge. At the time
when Canada became a federation in 1867, Joseph Little was elected to Newfoundland's
House of Assembly as an Anti-Confederate, and he continued as an elected member of
the House until his resignation in 1883. Newfoundland did not enter Confederation with
Canada until 1949.

with deep gratitude by generations of sisters and children for whom Belvedere was home.

Although Joseph Little's generous bequest went a long way in solving the financial problems of the new orphanage, M. de Chantal could not rest until the entire debt was settled. She realized that she could expect little help from the citizens of St. John's, many of whom had lost everything in the recent fire, and so she decided to turn to friends in the United States. In the autumn of 1892, with M. Ignatius Guinane as her companion, she sailed for New York to seek financial aid.[54] On their arrival in the big city, they discovered that their task had been made much easier through the interest and co-operation of the rector of St. Peter's Church in Brooklyn, Rev. M. A. Fitzgerald. Fr. Fitzgerald, originally from Waterford, Ireland, came to Newfoundland while still a deacon and was ordained to the priesthood by Bishop Power in 1877. He was named president of St. Bonaventure's College in 1881 and served in that capacity until 1888, when he transferred to the Diocese of Brooklyn.[55] While he was in St. John's, he became friendly with the Sisters of Mercy, so much so that they did not hesitate to seek his assistance in promoting their fundraising project. After a successful visit to New York, they travelled to Philadelphia, where Archbishop Ryan, a classmate of Bishop Power of St. John's, made them welcome and gave them permission to solicit help from parishes and religious communities in his diocese.[56] Before returning home, M. de Chantal and her companion visited Boston, where expatriate Newfoundlanders responded generously to their appeal. Although she was successful in raising funds to pay for the orphanage itself, one of M. de Chantal's dreams, the construction of a chapel, was still in the planning stages. Ultimately, the considerable expense involved in such an undertaking, coupled with the economic havoc created by the 1892 fire and the disastrous bank crash of 1894 forced her to abandon this project.[57] One of

---

54. Hogan, *Pathways*, p. 91.

55. I am indebted to Brother J. B. Darcy for information on the career of Rev. M. Fitzgerald.

56. *Inter Nos*, June 1924.

57. On December 10, 1894, the two banks carrying on business in St. John's, the Union and Commercial banks, were forced to close. The result meant ruin to thousands of depositors whose savings had suddenly become worthless.

the large rooms in the orphanage was set aside and served as an oratory. In this Oratory of the Sacred Heart, as it was called, the children celebrated First Eucharist and were received into various sodalities, postulants were accepted into the novitiate, and novices pronounced their religious vows.[58]

In spite of all the planning and activity associated with the construction of and payment for the 1885 orphanage, the sisters at Belvedere never forgot that their first interest and responsibility was the education and upbringing of the children in their care. Until the year 1895, the school at Belvedere received no monetary assistance from the board of education. However, in February of that year, Rev. Michael Francis Howley was consecrated bishop of St. John's, succeeding Bishop Power who had died unexpectedly on December 4, 1893. In spite of ten years' absence from the diocese, Bishop Howley had lost none of his interest in Belvedere. At a meeting of the Roman Catholic School Board for St. John's, April 28, 1895, the new bishop turned his attention to obtaining adequate funding for the school at Belvedere. Up to this time, the sisters had three main sources of income: regular collections taken up in the churches, the proceeds from bazaars, and donations. Bishop Howley proposed to place the school under the jurisdiction of the board, thereby ensuring that it would be entitled to a share of government funding:

> The question of making Belvedere Orphanage a Board School was discussed. The nuns of this Institution have under their charge some eighty orphan children whose training and education they look after, and as teachers they receive no assistance or payment from the Board. It was proposed that the school be made a Board School subject to the supervision of the Government Superintendent, Mr. Wickham, and that the nuns receive the sum of $200 from the grant as the teachers of such a school.[59]

---

58. The first novices to pronounce their vows in the Oratory of the Sacred Heart on December 18, 1887, were M. Philippa Hanley and M. Patrick Flynn, both of Roscommon, Ireland. ASMSJ.

59. "Minutes of Meeting of the Roman Catholic School Board for St. John's District, April 28, 1895," pp. 1–6, AASJ, 600/1/4.

As a board school, Belvedere followed the curriculum approved by the Roman Catholic board for the schools under its jurisdiction and received periodic visits from the superintendent of education. According to reports that were published yearly, the Belvedere School compared very favourably with others in the system. For instance, the report for the year 1899 describes the work carried on in the classrooms at Belvedere:

> There were 94 registered, 93 of whom were present; 59 of these were in the Junior Room, classified in Standards I–III, and 34 in the Senior Room, classified in Standards IV and V. In the former department the pupils read, spelled and wrote remarkably well for children so young; and in the Advanced Department the pupils also passed a creditable examination.
>
> The total number of children in the Orphanage is 105; eleven of these are engaged solely in domestic work. One of the first things which strike a visitor is the order, neatness and cleanliness about the whole institution and the ease and straightforwardness which characterize the answering of the children. Certain hours of the day are set apart for classes in Sewing, Knitting, etc., a room being used exclusively for these purposes. Here they make their own dresses and knit their warm winter clothing, under the guidance and tuition of the Sisters in charge.[60]

Besides following the curriculum prescribed by the board of education, the children at Belvedere enjoyed the same cultural programs as those offered at the prestigious Mercy Convent School, namely, music and drama, drawing and painting, and plain and fancy needlework. Because most of the girls at Belvedere would be obliged to earn their living after leaving school, they were taught to knit and how to make clothing for themselves and others. Other skills, such as cooking, housekeeping, and budgeting formed part of the training so that by the time a girl was ready to leave the orphanage she was equipped with the tools necessary to make her way in the world. In this way, the sisters at Belvedere followed the instructions of the foundress, Catherine

---

60. Vincent P. Burke, "Report of the Superintendent for Roman Catholic Schools for Year Ended December 31, 1899," p. 18, ASMSJ.

McAuley: "The Sisters shall feel convinced that no work of charity can be more productive of good to society, . . . than the careful instruction of women, since whatever be the station they are destined to fulfill, their example and their advice will always possess influence."[61]

Fortunately for the sisters' education ministry, a steady stream of young women continued to come from Ireland to join the Sisters of Mercy as missionaries in Newfoundland.[62] The increasing numbers of young professed sisters in the 1860s and '70s made it possible for the superior at Mercy Convent to co-operate with the bishop in his efforts to look after the educational needs of the people. As the population of St. John's steadily increased, it became obvious that another church and school would be needed to serve the people in the west end of the city. And so, Bishop Power looked around for a suitable building that could serve these purposes until a church could be built in the area. In 1873, he purchased the Fishermen's Hall, located on the corner of Queen Street and George Street in downtown St. John's. This building, erected in 1861, served as the venue for all sorts of entertainments ranging from exhibitions of tightrope walking and flower shows to concerts and plays—complete with costumes and scenery—and performed by professional dramatic troupes.[63] The building itself, constructed of square-cut whinstone, with a slate-covered gable roof,[64] is one of the oldest structures still in use in that part of St. John's. At the present time, it functions as a bar.

Having purchased the Fishermen's Hall, Bishop Power had the interior redesigned to create two storeys. The upstairs was consecrated for use as a chapel dedicated to St. Peter, and the ground floor was fitted out as a school.[65]

---

61. "Rule and Constitutions of the Sisters of Mercy," chapter 2, article 5, cited in Sullivan, *Catherine McAuley*, p. 297.

62. M. Dolorosa Kinney, the last of the Irish-born Sisters of Mercy in Newfoundland, claimed that the Irish women who entered the congregation here came because they wanted to be "missionaries."

63. O'Neill, *The Oldest City*, p. 250.

64. Ibid.

65. Ibid.

In the meantime, the bishop had arranged with M. Xavier Bernard at Mercy Convent for four sisters to staff the new St. Peter's School.[66]

The first mention of St. Peter's School in the education reports for the RC School Board was in 1882:

> St. Peter's: The school for boys is held in the basement storey of St. Peter's Church and for girls in the room overhead. In the Boys' school there were present 39 the day I visited. . . . The principal object of this school is to provide instruction for the younger children in the vicinity. The majority of those present were, consequently, young and in elementary lessons.
>
> The room was well kept and has been made as convenient for the purpose as its location and condition will admit. The ceiling being low, the movements of those attending the school overhead cause much distraction to the children and worry to the Teacher. To teach, therefore, so large a number in a school thus situated is a very laborious and trying task . . .
>
> In the Girls' School, 134 were present, 60 of whom were in the First Book. The most advanced class read in Third Reading Book, and in Reading, Spelling, Dictation, and English Grammar did well. . . . This is a populous and central part of the city, and these schools are always sure to be largely attended.[67]

In the same report, the superintendent noted that there were four teachers at St. Peter's and the school had a registration of 360 students. Obviously, absenteeism was a big problem at St. Peter's.

The opening of St. Patrick's Church in 1883 relieved some of the overcrowding but did little else to improve conditions at St. Peter's School. The classrooms were moved to the upper storey while the lower level was used as a recreation hall for the students. The separation of boys and girls into separate units continued, with two teachers for each unit. In the 1887 education report, the superintendent noted the difficult conditions that continued to plague sisters and students at St. Peter's:

---

66. ASMSJ, RG 10/1/24.
67. Michael J. Kelly, "Report of the Superintendent of Education for Roman Catholic Schools for the Year Ended December 31, 1882," p. 54, AASJ.

> The school is taught by four Sisters of Mercy from the Convent
> on Military Road. . . . School operations . . . are attended with dif-
> ficulties which are not experienced to so great an extent in any
> other school in the City with the exception of St. Joseph's in the
> East End. The pupils are, for the most part, children of the poorer
> classes, are scantily provided with books, often insufficiently clad,
> and attend very irregularly. [68]

During the following years, the complaints about absenteeism at St.
Peter's were repeated by the superintendents. In 1888, the new superintendent, James Wickham wrote:

> . . . so long as poverty exists, accompanied as it usually is with indif-
> ference in matters educational, so long will difficulties of this kind
> have to be met and combated. But taking everything into account,
> I am in a position to state that results were quite up to my expec-
> tations. In the Girls' school particularly the pupils appeared to be
> doing quite well. [69]

The fact that the superintendent's report ended on a positive note was due to
the patience of the sisters and the persistence of the children who attended
school on a regular basis. One of these teachers was M. Mercedes Lyons, who
spent nineteen years at St. Peter's and when it closed in 1903, followed her
students to their new classrooms at St. Vincent's.

M. Mercedes Lyons was born in Kerry on June 24, 1864, and baptized
Catherine Mary. In 1883, with another young girl named Mary O'Connor (M.
Bridget), she crossed the Atlantic and entered as a postulant at Mercy
Convent. During all her religious life, M. Mercedes seems to have lived—

---

68. J. Fenelon, "Report of Superintendent of Roman Catholic Schools for the District of St.
John's for Year 1887," AASJ, 600/1/4. It should be noted that St. Joseph's in the East End
replaced St. Bridget's School and that sisters from Mercy Convent taught at both St.
Peter's and St. Joseph's.

69. James J. Wickham, "Report of Roman Catholic Schools for the District of St. John's for
the Year 1888," AASJ, 106/17/3.

quite happily—in the shadow of her companion and close friend, M. Bridget O'Connor. They were professed together at Mercy Convent on December 8, 1885. M. Bridget went to Littledale and then to Burin before returning to Mercy Convent to become the first superior general (or mother general) at the time of the amalgamation of the convents. M. Mercedes, with the exception of a brief period at Littledale, lived at Mercy Convent and spent much of her teaching career instructing the poor at St. Peter's.

The sisters assigned to St. Peter's had no easy task. On warm, sunny days it would have been quite pleasant to leave Mercy Convent in the morning and walk down to Queen Street. It was not quite so pleasant, even on fine days, to walk back up the steep hills to Mercy Convent after a long, long day spent in the crowded classrooms of St. Peter's. It was still more unpleasant when the wind was blowing in off the ocean, sleet beating on their faces, and snow up to their knees. M. Mercedes never spoke of difficulties in connection with her beloved St. Peter's except the poverty and hardship endured by the children under her care. It was at St. Peter's that she acquired her lifelong concern and compassion for the poor.

Teaching duties at St. Peter's did not absolve M. Mercedes from taking part in activities at Our Lady of Mercy School. In 1892, she was given charge of the after-school lending library, and when the Sodality of the Children of Mary was established at Mercy Convent on June 1, 1900, the bishop appointed M. Mercedes to be director. At the time of the amalgamation in 1916, when her friend M. Bridget O'Connor was elected superior general, M. Mercedes Lyons was elected councillor, a position she held for fifteen years.

December 28, 1935, marked the golden jubilee of the profession of M. Mercedes and M. Bridget. *Inter Nos* published a full account of the celebrations—M. Bridget received eight pages, M. Mercedes two paragraphs! Archbishop Roche, however, in his homily at the mass, was careful to point out M. Mercedes's years of quiet, dedicated service to the poor and the sick, and the hardships of those years when she struggled to provide an education to the poor children of the city.

In her later years, M. Mercedes was confined to bed, but she was rarely alone, for her room was a haven of comfort for young and old—for the dis-

consolate young sister who had just broken the "priest's milk jug," and for others who had weightier problems to solve or sorrows to share. Her wide reading, her knowledge of current events, her wonderful store of memories, and
her Irish wit made her a pleasant and brilliant conversationalist. M. Mercedes
loved to pray the Office of the Blessed Virgin Mary in Latin, and because her
sight was bad, she had memorized it from cover to cover. This is why, after her
memory began to fail and she could no longer remember a sister's name, the
familiar phrases of the Office came more readily to her lips. She would say,
"*Benedicamus Domino* brought me my dinner," and everyone knew the identity
of *Benedicamus Domino*! Sister M. Mercedes Lyons died on December 9, 1951,
at the age of eighty-seven, sixty-seven years after she left Kerry to come to
Newfoundland.

Other Irish sisters who taught at St. Peter's were M. Berchmanns O'Quinn,
who spent ten years at St. Peter's, and M. Columba Glynn, who has been mentioned in connection with St. Bridget's. Apparently, M. Columba had a special
gift for teaching small children, for she was given charge of the younger boys
and girls at St. Peter's and, later on, at St. Vincent's. The Newfoundland-born
M. Pius Mulcahy was another sister who taught for a while at St. Peter's and
St. Vincent's.[70] Her name, however, is more closely associated with Burin and
Littledale. In addition, there were sisters who gave valuable service to the children at St. Peter's whose names are not recorded. The sisters mentioned above
are known only because, in 1950, M. Basil McCormack went looking for information from the senior members of the Congregation of the Sisters of Mercy
whose memories went back to the beginning of the century.
    By 1900, the Roman Catholic board had hired Miss Maher and Miss
Nugent to assist the sisters at St. Peter's. The accounts book for the RC board
of St. John's reveals that Mercy Convent received $400 in the year 1900–01
for the services of four sisters, Miss Maher received a salary of $125 and Miss
Nugent, $90.[71] By December 1902, the bishop and the Roman Catholic

70. Hogan, *Pathways*, p. 57.
71. Accounts Book, Roman Catholic School Board for St. John's, AASJ, 600/2/4.

School Board had been persuaded that the St. Peter's building was unfit for use as a school and too expensive to maintain. The bishop proposed to sell the building and procure another site in the same locality.[72] By July of the following year, 1903, Bishop Howley had changed his mind about the location of a building to replace St. Peter's. According to the minutes of the school board meeting, the bishop reported, "St. Peter's was still in the same position as he [the bishop] had stated at the last meeting [December 1902]. He hoped to sell the place and open a school in a more convenient location."[73] Finally, in July 1904, Archbishop Howley[74] informed the board that St. Peter's had been closed and the pupils and teachers moved to St. Vincent de Paul Hall on the Parade grounds.[75] As a result the name of the school was changed to St. Vincent's.

     The decision to move the school to St. Vincent's must have elicited an initial sigh of relief from the sisters who had been teaching at St. Peter's. They were under the impression that the move was a temporary measure until a new school could be built. In the meantime, the school board decided to make some improvements and alterations to the St. Vincent de Paul building to make it suitable for use as a school. The sum of $472.66 was expended in making sewage connections and "other improvements." Among "other improvements"[76] was the erection of a wooden partition across the centre of one of the larger rooms, dividing it into two rooms. The superintendent of schools was not impressed. In 1909, he wrote his report:

> After my last inspection I reported to His Grace the Archbishop on the unsuitability of the rooms in use. His Grace readily realized the necessity of immediate action being taken, made a formal visit to the school, and ordered the necessary improvements to be commenced at once. There was no money to the credit of the St. John's Board of Education to enable the Board to do anything in

---

72. "Minutes of the Roman Catholic School Board for St. John's, December 9, 1902," p. 28, AASJ, 600/1/ 4.

73. Ibid., July 6, 1904, p. 31, AASJ, 600/1/ 4.

74. In 1904, St. John's was raised to the status of an archdiocese.

75. "Minutes of the Roman Catholic School Board, July 6, 1904," AASJ, 600/2/32.

76. Ibid., July 5, 1905.

the matter, so His Grace very kindly gave instructions to get on with the work on his own responsibility. Enrolment, 278: 208 girls, 70 boys. Standards I–V.[77]

In 1914, the superintendent reported that two sisters and two lay teachers were employed. The enrolment had dropped from 318 in 1910 to 173. He concluded the report with what had become his annual refrain, "The building is unsuitable."[78] But still the sisters and their assistants continued the struggle to educate children who made infrequent appearances in the classroom. Finally, in 1918, the superintendent appears to have given up in disgust. He concluded his report with the curt comment, "The school building is the worst of its kind in the country."[79]

In spite of the deplorable conditions that prevailed at St. Peter's and St. Vincent's, children benefited by the perseverance of the sisters and their assistants. One student at St. Peter's, Matthew Hawco, an exceptionally bright and intelligent boy, went on to more advanced studies and achieved considerable success in life.[80] Matthew was one of a number of ex-pupils of St. Peter's and St. Vincent's who realized the hopes and dreams of those sisters who worked so hard to provide them with the tools for success in this life and the next.

77. Vincent P. Burke, "Report of the Superintendent for Roman Catholic Schools for the Year Ended December 31, 1909," p. 45, ASMSJ.

78. Ibid., 1914, p. xxii, ASMSJ.

79. Ibid., 1918, p. 49, ASMSJ.

80. After leaving St. Peter's, Matthew Hawco went to Wisconsin, USA, and attended Wisconsin State High School in Superior where he studied engineering. Later he became chief of harbour construction on the Great Lakes waterways. On his return to Newfoundland, he was elected to the House of Assembly, and later served for many years as district magistrate for Holyrood. Matthew Hawco was the father of M. Annette Hawco, of McAuley Convent, St. John's.

CHAPTER EIGHT

DARING TO DREAM

Lord, give us the courage to begin tasks
That are longer than our lives.[1]

Unknown

The 1880 chapter at Mercy Convent confirmed the disastrous appointment of Sr. M. Ita McSweeney as superior of the community. But, as we have seen, M. Ita did not last long in that office, and by the end of the year, M. Bernard Clune had been elected to the position. History has shown that it was a wise choice, and today the Sisters of Mercy of Newfoundland revere M. Bernard Clune as a woman of unusual vision and daring.

Ann Mary Bridget Clune (M. Bernard Xavier) arrived in St. John's in November 1858, at the age of twenty-one years, to seek admission as a postulant at Mercy Convent. She was received into the novitiate by M. Xavier Bernard in April 1859 and professed two years later in January 1861. Both M. Xavier Bernard and Ann Clune came from Limerick, and apparently, in spite of a ten-year age difference, they were devoted friends.[2] The fact that M. Xavier Bernard gave an inversion of her own name to Ann Clune by bestowing on her the religious name of M. Bernard Xavier adds credence to this story.

---

1. Author of this passage is unknown.
2. *The Evening Telegram*, February 28, 1882, p. 3.

Early in 1866, just five years after her profession, M. Bernard Clune was appointed bursar of Mercy Convent. This was an important position for a young sister; she became responsible not only for the financial affairs and maintenance of the convent but also of St. Clair's Boarding School and Our Lady of Mercy School, and her responsibilities did not end there. Entries in the accounts book at Mercy Convent show that the bursar managed the expenditures of St. Bridget's School and, after 1866, of the convent and school at Petty Harbour as well. In addition to her duties as bursar, M. Bernard was a full-time teacher at OLM.[3] In this capacity, she was an outstanding success. Not only did she have a natural gift for imparting knowledge, but also, she had a superb education and was fluent in several languages.[4] Her teaching schedule, combined with her office as bursar, kept her busy, but on the plus side, these duties provided her with valuable experience for what was to be the most important work of her life, the foundation of a boarding school at Littledale.

In 1875, M. de Chantal O'Keefe, having completed her term as superior of Burin, returned to Mercy Convent and was elected bursar. M. Bernard Clune was appointed mistress of novices. This illustrates the tendency to re-elect (or reappoint) the same persons to positions of responsibility. It is a matter of debate whether this was because of a desire to stay with the "tried and true" or if it was because certain people were extraordinarily gifted. It was probably a little of each! Then too, the bishop seemed to have had the final say in selecting persons for leadership and, more than likely, the only sisters he knew well enough to trust with responsibility were those already in authority. From the aspect of community life, the practice was unhealthy, to say the least. In days when obedience was sometimes confused with subservience and when permission had to be obtained for the simplest transactions, persons who were too long in charge of the community tended to forget how difficult such an interpretation of religious obedience could be. Fortunately, most of the appointees were blessed with common sense and mercifully free from delu-

---

3. OLM is used as an abbreviation of Our Lady of Mercy School.

4. *Inter Nos*, June 1932, pp. 9–10. M. Mercedes Lyons often spoke to the author of M. Bernard Clune and mentioned her fluency in languages.

sions of grandeur. Nevertheless, there were the few who gloried in the exercise of authority, causing varying degrees of tension and dissatisfaction among the sisters. From the recollections of those who knew her, M. Bernard Clune, on the contrary, was blessed with an appreciation of and the willingness to use the talents and gifts of others, and she was universally loved and respected by sisters and students.[5]

Shortly after M. Bernard's election as superior, her friend and mentor, M. Xavier Bernard, suffered a paralytic stroke and spent the next two years in a sort of "twilight zone," not recognizing anybody and confined completely to bed. Her illness and death occurred at the very time when M. Bernard was planning the most ambitious project undertaken thus far by the Mercy Sisters in Newfoundland.

The sisters in the convent schools outside the city were accomplishing good work in the field of education, and as well, St. Clair's Boarding School offered to outport girls an opportunity to avail of the educational and cultural advantages offered in the city. But M. Bernard had a dream that could not be realized by the limited accommodations offered at St. Clair's. Some Catholic girls were sent to boarding schools in other countries to be educated, and M. Bernard felt that there was a need for a local institution with the space and the facilities to provide young women with the opportunities currently being sought elsewhere. Aware of the improved social and economic conditions of the country, she observed with great interest the various attempts to establish a railway that would connect various important sections of the island.[6] Inevitably, the railway would bring increased travel from the outports to St. John's. M. Bernard envisioned an academic centre for young women who would come from all corners of Newfoundland and bring back to their own regions the advantages of education and culture. At the same time, she hoped that the close association with the sisters provided by a boarding school would encourage some young women to dedicate their lives to God as Sisters of

5. John J. FitzHenry to the editor of *Inter Nos*, May 1943.
6. For an account of attempts to establish the railway see O'Neill, *A Seaport Legacy*, pp. 509–10, pp. 515ff.

Mercy. She had discovered the ideal site for her new school—the estate of Philip Little, the former prime minister of Newfoundland.

Philip Little, a lawyer from Prince Edward Island, came to Newfoundland in 1844 and settled in St. John's. From the beginning, he was active on the political scene and, in 1855, became the country's first prime minister at the age of thirty-one. He served in that capacity until 1858 when he was appointed judge.[7] Sometime after his arrival, he purchased a parcel of land in the Waterford Valley about three miles from the city and proceeded to clear the land and build his house. He called his estate, Littledale. Many years later, in 1938, Philip Little's niece, Mère Louise de la Croix (Eileen Little), recorded her recollections of Littledale for Edward J. Little, Philip's son. Mère Louise wrote:

> Three miles outside of the city, in the Valley of Waterford Bridge, your Father purchased a large piece of land, surrounded with woods, fields, the river running quite near. It was a most beautiful scenic, solitary place. He had great taste for farming and building, got a fine house erected on the spot, the cottage it was called, though much larger and nicer than the house in town. Littledale has eight immense bedrooms, a bathroom, clothes room, wide halls; and downstairs: drawing, dining, and breakfast rooms, kitchen & storeroom. The stairs wide. Lots of air and light came in by the high French windows . . .
>
> Littledale, when he bought it, was but a wilderness. He gave work to all the people about, by having it fenced, trees felled, ornamental plants and even tropical trees planted in artistic forms. . . . The garden had all sorts of vegetables and fruit, even apples which would ripen in September and October.[8]

Philip Little left Newfoundland in 1866 to take up residence in Ireland, but the property remained in the hands of the Little family until it was sold to the Sisters of Mercy by Judge Joseph Little, brother of the original owner. M. Bernard Clune, with the approval of Bishop Power, organized a plan to raise the necessary funds to buy the Littledale property. The purchase price of

---

7. Ibid., p. 439. See also Daniel Woodley Prowse, *A History of Newfoundland From the English Colonial and Foreign Records* (Portugal Cove-St. Philip's, NL: Boulder Publications, 2002), pp. 506 ff.

8. Mère Louise de la Croix to Edward J. Little, 1938, ASMSJ, RG 10/7/95.

£1,300 was financed by loans amounting to £600. The remaining £700 was to be paid in annual installments.[9] And so, on November 13, 1883, the Sisters of Mercy purchased the country estate of Philip Little.[10]

As soon as the sisters took possession of the property they began the work of adapting it to its new purpose. Two additions were made to the original building—a wooden classroom was erected on the eastern side and a small dormitory at the rear. But M. Bernard was concerned for more than the physical plant. Taking M. Teresa O'Halleran with her, she went to Halifax to observe how boarding schools were operated in that city.[11] After about seven months of frantic preparation, everything was in place to receive the first boarders. M. Bernard Clune decided to name the new foundation in honour of the great Irish saint, St. Brigid, since, as she said, it was situated between St. Patrick's Church on one side and Kilbride Church on the other.[12]

On August 20, 1884, St. Bride's Convent, Littledale, was formally established "Under the Patronage of the B.V.M. Mother of God and of St. Brigid, 'The Mary of Erin.'"[13] Because, at the beginning, it was dependent financially on Mercy Convent, it remained a branch house under the authority and direction of the superior of the mother house. Before selecting the founding members of St. Bride's, M. Bernard had to determine which sisters could be spared from the staff of Our Lady of Mercy School.[14] At the same time, she had to

---

9. Accounts Book, Convent of Our Lady of Mercy, St. John's, ASMSJ.

10. M. Philomena Walker claimed that the sum of £1300 was paid from the dowry of M. Xaverius Dowsley and added that the purchase of this property was not favoured by some members of the community at Mercy Convent. M. Philomena Walker, interview by M. Basil McCormack, "Notes," *circa* 1952, ASMSJ.

11. Hogan, *Pathways*, p. 217.

12. Ibid., p. 218.

13. ASMSJ.

14. It should be remembered that every year, up until the beginning of the twentieth century, several young women came to St. John's from Ireland to join the Sisters of Mercy here. This steady increase in numbers allowed the superior at Mercy Convent to supply sisters for new foundations and send extra help to outport convents. The last Irish-born young woman to come to Newfoundland to enter the Congregation of the Sisters of Mercy was M. Dolorosa Kinney. She was born on March 22, 1886, at Newry, County Down, Ireland, and came to Newfoundland to enter the Mercy Order. She was admitted as a postulant at Littledale on September 24, 1907. She spent most of her religious life at the Convent of Our Lady of Mercy on Military Road. She died on February 16, 1979.

take care that those chosen had the requisite educational qualifications. Then, to ensure the academic excellence that would be a hallmark of the new boarding school, M. Bernard hired the best lay teachers available. The sisters selected for the new foundation were the mature and prudent M. Ita Glynn; the practical and astute M. Teresa O'Halleran; a novice, M. Mercedes Lyons; and a postulant, Mary Farrell, who although still a teenager, had been well-educated in Ireland.

Mary Farrell was born in Knocklofty, County Tipperary, in 1867. Sometime before her seventeenth birthday, she joined the Sisters of Mercy in Newfoundland and was accepted as a postulant at Littledale just in time for the formal blessing and opening of the new St. Bride's Academy, Littledale.[15] One reason for Mary's appointment to Littledale may have been that M. Bernard wished to use a part of Mary Farrell's dowry to help meet the payments due. This is confirmed in a letter from Joseph Little to M. Bernard, in which he informed her that Mr. Kent had been instructed to forward the correct amount owing from Miss Farrell's "dower."[16] After serving a five-month's postulancy, Mary Farrell was received into the community of the Sisters of Mercy at Mercy Convent on January 6, 1885, and given the name Mary Genevieve. When she went to Littledale as a postulant, Mary Farrell was not much older than the students whom the sisters hoped to attract to the new boarding school. Although she had duties in the school, M. Bernard Clune realized that the young novice herself needed further education and training, payment for which was included in the terms of her dowry. In a letter to the lawyer, John Kent, who was, presumably, in charge of dispensing interest on the Farrell dowry, M. Bernard reminded him of the fees owing for Mary Farrell's music lessons.[17]

---

15. Although the correct name of the institution was St. Bride's Academy and later, St. Bride's College, it was, and is, known throughout Newfoundland simply as Littledale.

16. Judge Joseph Little to M. Bernard Clune, July 21, no year given, but likely 1888, since the letter is in reply to a request from M. Bernard dated January 28, 1888, ASMSJ, 106/17/10. In the past, the family of a young woman who joined a religious congregation was expected to provide her with a dowry. If the family was not in a position to provide a dowry, the requirement was waived.

17. M. Bernard Clune to John Kent, October 13, 1885, ASMSJ.

The other three sisters who went on to the foundation were also quite young. The senior by age and profession, M. Ita Glynn, was named "senior sister." Originally from Limerick, in 1873 Ellen Glynn (M. Ita) joined the Sisters of Mercy at Mercy Convent in St. John's at the age of nineteen years. She was about thirty when she was appointed to this new and important foundation. Even though the overall direction of the school remained in the hands of M. Bernard Clune, the position of senior sister placed a heavy responsibility on M. Ita's shoulders. She remained in the position for just a year. In December 1885, she returned to Mercy Convent where she was appointed to the position of novice mistress.[18] In 1891, M. Ita asked to go on the mission to Burin.[19] Her younger sister, M. Columba, had been appointed to that community in 1885 or '86, and it is possible that her sister's experience on the mission was a factor in M. Ita's decision to request a change to Burin. Whether this was so or not, her request came at a good time, for in August 1891, M. Angela Kitchin, who had been sent to Burin as superior in 1888, having completed a three-year term, resigned, and the community was looking for someone to fill the position. The bishop, no doubt feeling that if M. Ita Glynn wanted to go to Burin she might as well make herself useful, promptly appointed her to the office of superior of the Burin Convent. After a three-year term in Burin, she moved to St. Lawrence where she remained until 1896, when Archbishop Howley recalled her to Mercy Convent and appointed her superior of the mother house,[20] a position she held for sixteen years with one intermission. After a four-year term back at Littledale (1915–19), M. Ita went to the newly opened St. Clare's Home as superior, serving there until 1922. At that time she became ill and returned to Mercy Convent, where she remained until her death in 1936. During the last years of their lives, the two sisters, M. Ita and M. Columba Glynn, were together at Mercy Convent. Stories abound of their frequent little spats, after each of which M. Columba made her

---

18. M. Teresina Bruce, "Notes for a History of St. Bride's College," ASMSJ.

19. ASMSJ.

20. Although many of the bishops interfered in the appointment of sisters, none more so than Archbishop Howley, who seemed to take a personal interest in the makeup of each community, a practice that was continued by his successor, Archbishop E. P. Roche.

way to the chapel to pray aloud, "Lord, Ita is an impossible woman. Since you made her that way, you had better give me patience to put up with her!"

The other professed member of the first Littledale community, M. Teresa O'Halleran, was assigned to the new foundation just three months after her profession. Margaret O'Halleran (M. Teresa) came from Ballyheige, County Kerry, in 1881 to enter the Mercy Convent in St. John's. Letters she wrote in later years reveal that she never stopped missing Ireland and her family, but this did not diminish her love for and dedication to her adopted land and its people. A year after Margaret received the religious habit and her new name, Mary Teresa Xavier, M. Liguori Carmody was appointed mistress of novices. M. Liguori, although an unassuming, saintly woman, was nevertheless "a stickler for order and discipline."[21] The influence of this woman left a lasting impression on M. Teresa O'Halleran, for her spirit of self-discipline and prayer, and her unbounded trust in God are revealed in letters she wrote her niece and namesake, Margaret "Peggy" Halleran.[22] During the second year of M. Teresa's novitiate, two more young ladies arrived from Ireland and were received into the novitiate on December 8, 1883, M. Mercedes Lyons and M. Bridget O'Connor. Today we talk about prophetic witness and vision. We cannot even imagine what it must have been like to be so closely associated with women who were living examples of these qualities—M. Bernard Clune, the superior of Mercy Convent and the new novice, M. Bridget O'Connor, both of them towering figures in Mercy history.

A couple of months after her profession of vows on May 15, 1884, M. Teresa O'Halleran was sent on her new mission as one of the founding members of St. Bride's Convent, Littledale. It is not hard to understand why she was chosen for this important new foundation. From the beginning, she showed a keen interest in the schools. But it was in the realm of business that M. Teresa evinced a remarkable aptitude. Within a very short time she became the faithful co-worker of M. Bernard Clune, who relied on her advice during the try-

---

21. John FitzHenry, *Inter Nos*, June 24, 1942.
22. After emigrating to the United States, the O'Halleran family dropped the "O" in the surname.

ing days when the Sisters of Mercy were labouring under the heavy debt incurred by the purchase of the Littledale property. M. Teresa was involved, too, in the planning and construction of the Golden Jubilee Oratory of the Sacred Heart at Mercy Convent.[23] She studied its plans, watched its erection, witnessed the pleasure of the senior sisters on its completion and saw in it a monument to the glory of God.

M. Teresa O'Halleran remained at St. Bride's, Littledale, for twelve years until she was appointed superior of Burin in 1896, replacing M. Philomena O'Donovan. The fourth member of the founding community at St. Bride's was the novice, M. Mercedes Lyons, who stayed at Littledale for a few months and then returned to Mercy Convent to complete her novitiate. Another postulant, Bedelia O'Connor (later M. Xavier), who had recently arrived from Roscommon, Ireland, replaced M. Mercedes.

By August 1884, M. Bernard Clune was ready to advertise the opening of the new boarding school:

> St. Bride's Boarding School for Young Ladies will be opened on Thursday, 21st August. . . . The Sisters of Mercy will spare no expense, and leave nothing undone on their part, to make St. Bride's a first-class educational institution. The efficiency of their schools at the Convent, Military Road, where the pupils . . . have displayed a high proficiency in every department of school work, and the distinctions invariably won . . . by their pupils abroad, are a sufficient guarantee to the most critical parents of the success that will be sure to attend their children at Littledale.
>
> Besides the training of Sisters who have obtained the highest certificates of grade from the National Board, the young ladies will be favoured with the immediate superintendence of the energetic and gifted Superioress; and will moreover receive instructions from Professors Ryan, Hancock, and Nichols.[24]

On the first page of the same paper the following advertisement appeared:

---

23. *The Monitor*, February 1937, p. 10.
24. *The Evening Telegram*, August 14, 1884, pp. 1, 4.

St. Bride's Young Ladies Boarding School, Littledale, conducted by the Sisters of Mercy, (under the patronage of the Most Rev. Dr. Power, Bishop of St. John's.)

This Establishment is situated on Waterford Bridge Road, and within two miles of St. John's. It is beautifully sheltered by groves, and at the same time commands a charming view of the picturesque scenery around. The grounds are quite extensive, affording ample room for recreation of every kind.

The course of instruction will embrace all branches comprised in a first-class English education—French, Music, Drawing and Painting, Domestic Economy, Plain and Ornamental Needlework. Masters are engaged to teach advanced and special subjects.

TERMS

Pension for Board and Tuition	£36
Entrance Fee	1
Laundry	1

EXTRAS

Piano Lessons from Master	8
Piano Lessons from Mistress	4
Organette	3
Vocal Music by Master	4
Vocal Music in Class	2
Drawing in Pencil and Crayon	2
Painting in Oils, on Glass, Satin, Velvet & Gelatine	4
Dancing	3[25]

A glance at the fee structure shows that the theory of masculine superiority was alive and well in 1884—and accepted even by the far-sighted M. Bernard Clune! Miss Knowling was engaged to teach dancing and calisthenics; Mr. Ryan taught arithmetic; and Mr. Hancock taught French and provided

---

25. Ibid., p. 1.

instruction in the various branches of music offered in the curriculum.[26] The sisters conducted the regular program of academic courses, as well as drawing and painting classes until the arrival of Bedelia O'Connor (M. Xavier), a talented artist who was given the task of providing instruction in the visual arts.

The beginnings of St. Bride's Boarding School were small, indeed. On the day it opened, a grand total of four young ladies were enrolled as boarders, but by the end of the year, enrolment had risen to thirteen students. To mark the opening of the new convent and school, Monsignor John Scott celebrated mass in the little convent chapel. Incidentally, Monsignor Scott proved to be a staunch supporter of the fledgling institution, and M. Bernard Clune depended on his wise advice and financial expertise in her ongoing struggle to pay the installments due on the purchase of the Littledale property. Evidently, Monsignor Scott was an exception among the priests of the diocese in his support of M. Bernard's plan for a boarding school at Littledale. In a letter to Ireland, Brother Fleming wrote, "Rev. Mother Bernard opened the boarding school at Littledale on St. Bernard's Day. She got five [sic] boarders to commence with. The native priests are against her and make no secret of it. So I fear she will have a hard tug."[27] As well as facing the opposition of the clergy, M. Bernard was aware that she did not have the full support of the community at Mercy Convent.[28] It did, indeed, place a heavy burden of debt on the sisters, not all of whom shared their superior's vision and sublime trust in God's Providence.

By a remarkable coincidence, the first student to register at St. Bride's Boarding School was Mary Sullivan, daughter of Selina Sullivan, who, as Selina Brown, was the first student enrolled at St. Clair's Boarding School in 1861.[29] The other three students were Susan Cole, Caroline Mitchell, and Minnie Fitzgibbon. The latter, having completed her studies at St. Bride's, entered religious life at Mercy Convent and became known throughout St. John's as Mother

---

26. Bruce, "St. Bride's," ASMSJ.

27. Fleming to Holland, August 25, 1884, "The Slattery Papers," LMSF.

28. M. Philomena Walker, interview by M. Basil McCormack, "Notes," *circa* 1959, ASMSJ.

29. McCormack, "Educational Work," p. 72.

Mary Benedicta Fitzgibbon but irreverently referred to by the junior sisters as "Little Benny." Although she was a tiny little woman, her zeal and determination were in inverse proportion to her size. During her years at St. Bride's, Littledale, she studied music with M. Xaverius Dowsley and became an accomplished musician. Many years later, she wrote the music for one of Archbishop Howley's poems, "Dear Old Southside Hills." As a pianist, she was fond of embellishing her accompaniments with all sorts of arpeggiated passages, so much so this habit became known as "Little Benny's musical doodles." She filled many influential positions in the congregation throughout her long life, acting as novice mistress for many years—for so many years, in fact, that she was inclined to treat everyone she met as a novice. For instance, on one occasion, the convent chimney caught fire at two o'clock in the morning. As the firemen, armed with hatchets and hoses, entered the convent, M. Benedicta cautioned them, "Now Sirs, please observe the Great Silence and avoid all unnecessary conversation."[30] Another idiosyncrasy was her habit of ferreting out from obscure sections of the local press various tragedies that had occurred throughout the world. An example of this, handed down through the generations, was the sad tale of the thirty turkeys that blew away in a hurricane in Tibet. Such a catastrophe caused the tender-hearted M. Benedicta much pain, not only because of the misfortune that befell the turkeys, but because some poor farmer had suffered such a loss to his livelihood. As she became older, M. Benedicta became somewhat fixed in her ideas, but in her youth, when she was a student at Littledale, her name was prominent in the list of those who won prizes for academic excellence.

Once the formalities of the opening of the institution were concluded, the sisters and students of Littledale lost no time in getting down to work. Music was given a high profile in the curriculum offered in all convent schools, and Littledale was no exception. It seems that the four sisters on the staff were quite musical and entertained themselves with music at the evening's recreation. M. Joseph Walsh, a Sister of Charity of Halifax, one of the first students of

---

30. The "Great Silence," prescribed by the Rule of many religious communities of women, extended from night prayers to after breakfast. During this time nobody spoke unless on a matter of great urgency. The whole period was one of prayer and rest.

Littledale, remembered studying outdoors under the trees in the evening at twilight and hearing the sound of singing coming from the sisters' community room. They were singing Irish songs.[31]

At the beginning of the second term, in January 1885, *The Evening Telegram* published an account of a concert held at St. Bride's, Littledale. According to the paper's correspondent, "The entertainment provided consisted of pianoforte selections from the ever new and pleasing Irish melodies; songs by some of the young ladies, and a short but delightful operetta, representing some of the most interesting incidents of Gypsy life."[32] The sisters believed that a young lady should be able to present herself in public with dignity, poise, and clarity of speech. Through annual concerts featuring drama, choral recitation, and choral and instrumental music, Littledale students were given the opportunity to acquire these skills.

During the first ten years, the average enrolment at Littledale was about twenty students.[33] Although it was a secondary school, for special reasons, pupils of elementary standard were admitted. In January 1886, the newly professed M. Bridget O'Connor was transferred from the mother house to the staff of St. Bride's and named headmistress of the school. From that time onward, Littledale began to assume more and more significance in the history of education in Newfoundland, and this was due mainly to the genius of the new headmistress. The name of M. Bridget O'Connor holds a special place of honour in our story. Everywhere she went she left a legacy of learning, art, and culture. She was truly one of the most outstanding women of Mercy history.

Mary O'Connor (later, M. Bridget) left her native Kilmainhamn, County Kerry, in the spring of 1883.[34] She was fresh from the classroom and vibrant with the energy of her desire to devote her life as a Sister of Mercy in

31. M. Joseph Walsh to M. Patricia Hogan, July 23, 1972, ASMSJ. At the time M. Joseph was almost 100 years of age.

32. *The Evening Telegram*, January 12, 1885, p. 1.

33. "Chronicle of St. Bride's, Littledale," ASMSJ.

34. M. Bridget O'Connor was the great-aunt of Carroll O'Connor, well-known for his portrayal of the prejudiced Archie Bunker, one of the main characters in the television series *All in the Family*.

Newfoundland. The following tribute appeared in the press after her death in 1945. It is worth quoting in its entirety, for in it the writer captured the essence of this remarkable woman:

> Nature had marked her out as a woman of exceptional genius for she possessed a mind crystal clear and profound, great breadth of vision united to an indomitable will and magnificent courage. To this forceful personality were added in abundant measure the softer traits of womanhood, and that simplicity and directness that are always associated with great purity of heart.... Mother M. Bridget ... identified herself, heart and soul with the people of Newfoundland and no patriot ever sought to raise the standards of achievement in this country more than she sought, within the limits of her sphere, to spread learning and culture in this island of the western seas.
>
> As a young Sister at Littledale she moulded and formed the characters of her youthful charges. With zest she prepared her pupils for the newly established C.H.E. examinations, where they shone pre-eminently.... So widely diversified were her talents that she was equally at home in all departments of learning and her practice was as thorough as her theory was sound.
>
> From Littledale she was sent to Burin, where she is remembered with affection by those whose privilege it was to have been her pupils. Here, with limited facilities, her versatility showed itself not only in providing the best in school equipment but in improvising and painting stage scenery, in exquisitely embroidering linens for the altar and altogether in raising the standard of the schools to unprecedented levels.
>
> Recalled to St. John's as Mother Superior of the Convent at Military Road in 1914, [sic] she was chosen by Archbishop Roche and Their Excellencies of Harbour Grace and St. George's in August 1916, as Mother General of the newly amalgamated Convents of the Mercy Order. In this wider field her dynamic energy found ample scope and she unified and co-ordinated the different Convents of the Order into a Harmonious whole. The young Sisters were her special care, and when they had been solidly grounded in the religious life, she saw to it that they pursued their studies, many of them being sent abroad to receive special training in particular branches of study.

An educationalist of the first rank, she strove to inculcate in her Sisters the principles and techniques she herself employed so successfully in the classroom, insisting always on the paramount importance of character formation and on the necessity of recognizing in each child an individual with a distinctive personality. No teacher ever found her too engrossed in business to attend to her plans and her problems, for the improvement of pupils was a theme dear to her heart. In the schools it was refreshing to see her with the little ones who thronged around her, never annoying or worrying her with their chatter. Older pupils loved her too. She was so broad, so sympathetic, so modern and up-to-date that they never regarded her as being too old to understand their views.

Realizing that teacher and pupils do their best work when housing and equipment are adequate she did not hesitate to embark on a building programme which was climaxed by the addition of the gymnasium-auditorium to the College of Our Lady of Mercy in 1939. The men who worked under her supervision were unanimous in their admiration of her soundness of judgement no less than of her kindness and consideration.

With all her zeal for the development of the child in body, mind, and soul, Mother M. Bridget did not neglect the other works for which the Order of Mercy has been established. She laboured indefatigably for the establishment of St. Clare's Mercy Hospital in 1922, and her enthusiasm was responsible in no small degree for the growth of the hospital to its present proportions. The Sisters of St. Clare's, too, she sent to be trained at the best hospitals and schools of nursing in the USA and Canada.

But it was as a Religious that Mother M. Bridget was pre-eminent. Herein lay her greatest force for good. Her life was beautifully ordered and no matter how great the pressure of work she never allowed it to absorb the time for prayer.... One who knew her intimately said: "She had many of the most enriching traits of St. Teresa of Avila as shown in her capacity for business and administration as well as those—rarest of all—in her spiritual guidance and motherly affection for the associates and subjects. I always thought of her as a silent source of strength, wise and good and holy with the mighty strength of the humble and the selfless." Her visible monuments are all around us and the greatest, perhaps, are those based on the reverence and affection of all the Mercy Sisters.[35]

This was the woman who was sent to St. Bride's as headmistress in 1886. She remained there until 1903. During these seventeen years, Littledale saw many changes.

At the beginning of her tenure as headmistress at Littledale, M. Bridget O'Connor was guided by the experienced and wise M. Bernard Clune, who was in almost daily contact with the boarding school. However, in 1887 M. Bernard became seriously ill and was forced to go to Halifax for treatment.[36] Because of this, she was absent when the students presented a highly successful concert on July 16, 1887. A large number of dignitaries attended, including Bishop Power and one of the leading Catholic politicians of Newfoundland, Sir Ambrose Shea, with his wife, Lady Shea, who distributed awards to the delighted students.

Prior to 1894, the students at St. Bride's, Littledale, sat for private examinations conducted by the professors of St. Bonaventure's College.[37] In 1889, the principal of St. Bonaventure's College, Brother J.L. Slattery, devised a plan to achieve a degree of standardization within the denominational educational system. This plan was implemented in 1893 with the formation of the Council for Higher Education (CHE), which established a common syllabus and uniform examinations for grade VI and the higher grades. Initially, these examinations were set in England and sent there to be marked.[38] M. Bridget O'Connor thoroughly approved of this initiative, and at the first CHE examinations in 1894, she entered eleven students, all of whom were successful. First prizes for all the English subjects, geography, history, domestic economy, and arithmetic were won by Littledale students. The following year, in 1895, a student of Littledale won a scholarship for

---

35. *The Daily News*, January 22, 1945, p. 5. M. Bridget O'Connor was appointed superior of Our Lady of Mercy Convent, Military Road, in 1915, not 1914 as stated in this article.
36. *The Daily Colonist*, July 16, 1887, p. 4.
37. Ibid., August 23, 1887, p. 4.
38. *ENL*, s.v. "Schools."

first place in the country.[39] These successes established a standard that Littledale students worked hard to maintain through the generations that followed.

The year 1895 was significant in the history of Littledale, for in that year St. Bride's Convent became independent of the mother house. After more than ten years of operating as a branch house, the sisters at Littledale, and in particular, M. Bridget O'Connor and M. Pius Mulcahy,[40] were convinced that the institution would operate more efficiently if authority was centred in the local community rather than at Mercy Convent.[41] Two other factors may have added weight to the decision. First, M. Bernard Clune died in October 1894. She had been the inspiration and driving force behind the establishment of the boarding school. M. Liguori Carmody, who, as mentioned in previous chapters, was a rather reluctant superior, replaced her as superior of Mercy Convent. M. Liguori would not have welcomed the responsibility of governing two communities. Second, in February 1895, St. John's had a new bishop, the first native Newfoundlander to hold the office, Dr. Michael Francis Howley. Bishop Howley fully supported independent status for Littledale, especially in light of his plans for the training of teachers. M. Xaverius Dowsley, a Newfoundlander by birth, was transferred from Mercy Convent and named superior of St. Bride's Convent. M. Bridget O'Connor was her assistant and M. Angela Kitchin, another Newfoundlander, was sent from Belvedere to take the position of bursar. In spite of the fact that the majority of Mercy Sisters in Newfoundland were Irish by birth, it appears that Bishop Howley was determined that native Newfoundlanders would fill the positions of authority in the several convents in his diocese.

---

39. James J. Wickham, "Report of Superintendent of Education for Roman Catholic Schools for the Year 1895," AASJ, 106/17/3.

40. M. Pius Mulcahy (Minnie Mulcahy) was born in St. John's, was a student at Littledale in 1885–86, entered in 1886, was received into the novitiate at Littledale in 1887 and professed at Mercy Convent in 1889. She became a member of St. Bride's community shortly after her profession.

41. M. Philomena Walker identified M. Bridget and M. Pius as the most vocal proponents of independence for Littledale. She told this to M. Basil McCormack when the latter was collecting information in preparation for her master's thesis.

The second significant event that occurred in 1895 was the elevation of St. Bride's Academy to the status of a teacher-training institution.[42] Prior to this, many Catholic teachers were graduates of the Presentation and Mercy schools that were scattered throughout the island. It is unlikely that there was much formal training in the outports for the profession of teaching. For the most part, those planning to enter the profession observed their own teachers and brought to their teaching duties the skills assimilated during their school years. In fact, this practice continued for several years after formal teacher-training schools were established. The superintendent of education for the diocese of Harbour Grace reported in 1902, "The convent supplies nearly all the teachers employed by the Brigus Board and the excellent training these have received is very evident in the way they conduct their schools."[43]

The Newfoundland government, however, recognized that teachers needed a more structured course of training than that provided in the regular school system. And so, the Education Act of 1892 designated the Presentation Convent School at Cathedral Square in St. John's as a pupil teachers school (normal school) for female Catholic teachers.[44] The only drawback was the lack of living accommodations for out-of-town students. The Presentation Sisters were planning to address this need as soon as it was possible to do so. But when Bishop Howley was appointed to the diocese, he saw the advantages of establishing a teacher-training centre at Littledale. It was obvious that Littledale had the space to provide living accommodations for the teachers-in-training. The natural beauty of the site and its distance from the distractions of the city were factors he considered to be conducive to study, and the spacious grounds afforded ample opportunities for expansion. Accordingly, within a month of his induction as bishop of the diocese, Bishop Howley sent J. J. Wickham, the superintendent of the RC School Board, to the Presentation

42. "Statement of the Financial Affairs of Littledale Academy," June 5, 1897, AASJ, 106/17/3.
43. Thomas Hanrahan, "Report of the Superintendent for Roman Catholic Schools for the Year Ended December 31, 1902," p. 41, ASMSJ.
44. Education Act, *JHA*, 1892, p. 63.

Convent to present his plans to the superior. On March 23, 1895, Wickham reported to the bishop:

> I have had an interview with the Rev. Mother of Cathedral Square Convent and ascertained that she has no objection to the proposed transfer of the Pupil Teachers to Littledale. This being the case, I see no difficulty in the way of carrying out your Lordship's idea in connection with this business, as soon as the House of Assembly re-opens.[45]

One wonders how the Presentation Sisters really felt about the bishop's interference. With the graciousness that has always characterized this group of women, they accepted his decision and relinquished their ministry of educating the pupil teachers in favour of Littledale. The Government of Newfoundland approved the bishop's proposal, and in 1895, by an amendment to the Education Act of 1892, St. Bride's, Littledale, was recognized as the training school for Catholic female teachers.[46] For almost eighty years, until 1974, Littledale was the designated site for Catholic female teachers to pursue their studies.

By 1897, Bishop Howley had completed his plans for a new wing at Littledale to accommodate the influx of students:

> By an amendment to the Education Act of 1892, the Pupil Teachers or Normal School was transferred ... to Littledale.
>
> In order to meet the requirements of this change a considerable expenditure of money was necessary both to provide accommodation for the pupil-teachers, and for the erection of a New Wing for the Young Lady Boarders, as well as for the introduction of a more perfect sanitary system, with baths, closets, and thorough draining, etc. Several improvements were also made in the Lawn and playgrounds.
>
> ... During the past year I have built and furnished on the Grounds a Board-School to supply the place of the Boggy Hall School, which was taken down some time since. It is capable of accommodating from 50 to 60 children, and is furnished and

---

45. James J. Wickham to Bishop Howley, March 23, 1895, AASJ, 106/17/3.

46. July 1895, Amendment to Education Act of 1892, recognizing Littledale as Training College for Teachers, AASJ, 106/17/3. See also, ASMSJ, RG 10/7/197.

equipped in the best style, with desks, maps, etc. It is in charge of one of the Sisters who is assisted by the Normal teachers as Monitress. Thus it serves the double purpose of giving an excellent school to the large population of Topsail and Old Bay Bulls Roads, and also of giving an opportunity of exercising the pupil-teachers in the work of practical teaching and school management.[47]

The board school to which the bishop referred was built in 1896 on the western side of Littledale grounds. Initially, it was known as the Waterford Bridge School,[48] but later it was dedicated in honour of St. Joseph. Still later, the school was taken down, and a new St. Joseph's School was built by the side of the Waterford River, just across the road from St. Bride's, Littledale.[49] As the bishop suggested, not only did Waterford Bridge (and later, St. Joseph's) School serve as a day school for children in the surrounding area, but also it allowed student teachers to gain practical experience in teaching and classroom management under the supervision of a senior teacher. The superintendent's report for 1899 described the staff and enrolment of the school. At the time, M. Aloysius Lyons was the teacher in charge. With an enrolment of fifty-six pupils, forty-two girls and fourteen boys, Waterford Bridge School was well equipped with sixteen feet of blackboard space. The superintendent remarked that this compared very favourably with other board schools that provided only three, five, seven, and nine feet of blackboard. Furthermore, thirty-two students at Waterford Bridge School were registered for vocal music.[50]

Construction of the new two-storey wing for St. Bride's began in 1899 and was completed in 1902. It was built of brick and stone, measuring sixty by

---

47. M. F. Howley, "Statement of the Financial Affairs of Littledale Academy, Pupil-Teachers Home, Board-School, etc.," June 5, 1897, AASJ, 106/17/3.

48. Vincent P. Burke, "Report of the Superintendent for Roman Catholic Schools for the Year Ended 1899," p. 18, ASMSJ.

49. The new St. Joseph's School was opened in 1923, ASMSJ.

50. Vincent P. Burke, "Report of the Superintendent for Roman Catholic Schools for the Year Ended 1899," pp. 41–42, table C. M. Aloysius Lyons, younger sister of M. Mercedes Lyons, entered in 1885. Professed on January 4, 1887, in the old chapel at Littledale, she taught at St. Bride's Academy before being assigned to Waterford Bridge (St. Joseph's) School. She became ill while accompanying her sister, M. Mercedes, to New York for treatment on her eyes. M. Aloysius died in 1901. ASMSJ.

forty feet, at a cost of $20,000. Half of this amount came from the estate of Thomas Talbot, in whose memory the new building was named "The Talbot Memorial Wing."[51] In consequence of this generous bequest, M. Xaverius Dowsley, on behalf of the sisters, consented to the establishment of the "Talbot Bourses." In a formal document, the sisters agreed to provide a full year's board and education at Littledale to two young women who would be selected annually by the bishop of the diocese.[52]

The Talbot Wing is situated on the east of the Little cottage on the same site as the old wooden building that was erected in 1884 to provide additional classroom space. The second floor of the new wing contains the chapel, which is still in use, four music rooms, and two rooms that serve as the sacristy. An unusual feature of the sacristy is the ornamental winding staircase made of iron that connects the first and second storeys of the building. The chapel is one of the most beautiful of its kind in Newfoundland. It is built in Gothic style, with stained glass windows and an ornate open-work ceiling constructed of pitch pine. The original altar was hand-carved by Dan Carroll at Callahan Glass & Company's furniture factory in St. John's.[53] The panelled walls and the beautifully carved choir stalls are of polished oak. The Littledale chapel holds a special place in the hearts of the Sisters of Mercy, for after 1916, it was in this chapel that most of the sisters received the religious habit and made their profession of vows.[54] The first floor of the Talbot Memorial Wing was used for classrooms, but after the construction of the west wing in 1912, it doubled as a recreation hall and a concert hall. The stage was more than adequate to accommodate moderately large groups of performers, and it was designed especially for the production of plays and operettas. The performers used the

---

51. *ENL*, s.v. "Talbot, Thomas." Thomas Talbot came to Newfoundland from Kilkenny in 1837. He was prominent in the literary, educational, and political life of the country. He died in 1901 at the age of ninety.

52. This agreement was honoured from 1902 until St. Bride's College closed in 1974.

53. Dan Carroll was a local artist and poet.

54. The first ceremony of reception to take place in the new chapel occurred on March 19, 1902, when a former Littledale student, Nellie Gladney, received the habit of a Sister of Mercy and the name, Mary Bernard. M. Josephine Cullen received the habit on the same day. ASMSJ.

"winding stairs" to gain access to the sacristy that was used as a dressing room at concert time. The screen was made of heavy canvas material hand-painted by Dan Carroll. It depicted the entrance to the Narrows and sailboats in St. John's harbour. The screen was raised and lowered by means of ropes handled by two students, one on each side. The success of this operation depended on each student's ability to gauge the speed at which her partner was handling the rope. Otherwise, one side of the screen was apt to land on the stage with a thud, while the other side was suspended somewhere between ceiling and floor. On these occasions the audience was treated to the spectacle of an agitated sister frantically attempting to wrest the rope from the hands of a student who refused to let go! Sometime in the 1950s, the beautiful screen disappeared and was replaced by a red velvet curtain. At that time the stage itself was renovated and proper lighting installed. But somehow the new, modern version lacked the charm of the old stage, and audiences were deprived of the challenge of guessing which side of the screen would hit the floor first.

In 1901, the balance of the Littledale mortgage had been paid and the property was secured. Also in 1901, M. Xaverius Dowsley had completed her term of office as superior of Littledale. In her place, Bishop Howley appointed another Newfoundlander, M. Joseph Kelly from Belvedere. The bishop knew of M. Joseph's literary ability and, no doubt, felt that she had a lot to offer the student teachers at Littledale. M. Joseph was a prolific writer of verse, and several of her poems can be found in Bishop Howley's files in the archdiocesan archives. Some of her poems were published in the local press, identified only by her initials, S.M.J. After her appointment as superior of St. Bride's, Littledale, M. Joseph lost no time in establishing a literary club that flourished for many years. She was responsible, also, for establishing the school journal, *Littledale Leaves*,[55] which provided an opportunity for the students to demonstrate their literary skills to the public. By this time, there were more than fifty boarding students at Littledale and, in addition, ten teachers-in-training. Most of the young women who completed their teacher training at Littledale were destined to fill teaching positions in the outports. And so,

---

55. The first issue of *Littledale Leaves* was published in 1907.

through these young women, the influence of the Sisters of Mercy reached hundreds of little outports that dot the coast of Newfoundland.

The year 1903 saw a significant change in personnel at Littledale. Bishop Howley sent the talented and capable headmistress of St. Bride's Academy, M. Bridget O'Connor, to Burin. M. Bridget, in addition to her other duties, had held the position of novice mistress, thus her departure left two important positions to be filled. It seems strange that, within a short period of time, two of the leading lights of Littledale were appointed to Burin, M. Pius Mulcahy and M. Bridget O'Connor. According to the convent grapevine, they were a little too outspoken for the bishop's liking and thus were "banished to Burin."[56] The bishop filled the position of novice mistress by replacing M. Bridget with M. Philippa Hanley from the Belvedere community. M. Philippa was a gentle, cultured lady, but her heart was in Belvedere. Dutifully, she stayed at Littledale for four years and then was reassigned to her beloved orphanage. For her part, M. Bridget remained in Burin until 1914, the year of Archbishop Howley's death, when she was appointed superior of the mother house on Military Road.

The increasing importance of Littledale in the educational life of the country and the need for highly qualified teachers to staff the institution was a matter of concern to Bishop Howley. It must have seemed like an answer to a prayer when he received a letter from Liverpool, England. The letter, dated February 9, 1903, was from a young man named Daniel O'Callaghan, who wrote to the bishop telling of his desire to enter the priesthood and serve in the diocese of St. John's. In the course of the letter, O'Callaghan mentioned that his sister, too, wished to come to St. John's to enter the Presentation Convent. O'Callaghan explained that his sister was a highly qualified teacher, having obtained diplomas and certificates from reputable centres of learning:

> Probably you will wonder at my wishing to settle this matter at such an early stage in my college career, but I have a serious reason for doing so. . . . I have a sister to whom I am very much attached, and who is my junior by some eighteen months. She is desirous of entering a convent, and having also read, with

56. M. Basil McCormack, conversation with author, September 26, 1999.

great interest, your book on Newfoundland . . . she has become
desirous of entering the Presentation Convent (that attached
to the Cathedral) of St. John's, Newfoundland. My sister is an
accomplished scholar, having gained a very high place in the
"First Class" Government examination for teachers after two
years training with the Sisters of Notre-Dame, Mount Pleasant,
Liverpool. Since leaving college she has also studied for an
examination in connection with St. Andrew's University, and has
succeeded in obtaining the title and Diploma of L.L.A.[57]

Bishop Howley was delighted at the prospect of obtaining such a well-
educated young lady for his diocese. Completely ignoring her request to enter
the Presentation Convent, he saw that she was just what he needed to augment
the teaching staff at Littledale, especially in light of his plan to send M. Bridget
O'Connor to Burin. He was not quite so enthusiastic, however, about her
brother. He wrote back to Daniel O'Callaghan, explaining that he could not
accept him for the diocese, but that his sister would be welcome! On May 20,
1903, Sarah O'Callaghan wrote back to Bishop Howley:

> We were both extremely disappointed that you could not accept
> him [Daniel] for your diocese, and as we are very much attached,
> I had almost resolved to defer making any final arrangements until
> his future abode was also definitely settled. However after much
> prayer and consideration, I have concluded to settle at once, and
> leave Dan's future and all else to the Holy Will of God.
>   My brother also informed you that I had no dowry other
> than my certificates, but from your letter I infer that this would
> not be a great obstacle, and so, My Lord, if you and the Revd.
> Mother would be pleased to accept me for the Convent attached
> to the Cathedral, I should be very grateful.[58]

Bishop Howley, however, had changed his mind about Daniel
O'Callaghan. A few weeks later Daniel received a cablegram with the news

---

57. Daniel O'Callaghan to Bishop Michael J. Howley, February 9, 1903, AASJ, 106/10/24.
58. Sarah O'Callaghan to Bishop Michael J. Howley, May 20, 1903, AASJ, 106/10/24. "The convent attached to the Cathedral" was the Presentation Convent.

that, after all, he was accepted for the Diocese of St. John's. The bishop had no reason to regret this action. After ordination, Daniel O'Callaghan came to St. John's,[59] and for the rest of his life, he ministered in the diocese, serving the people in the various parishes to which he was assigned with energy and devotion.[60] For her part, Sarah O'Callaghan was prompt in thanking Bishop Howley for accepting her brother. At the same time she did not let the bishop's arbitrary decision with regard to her own future pass without comment:

> I was a little surprised to learn that you had accepted me, not for the Presentation Convent, but for the Convent of the Sisters of Mercy. But having placed my future, with perfect confidence and trust, under the guidance of the Sacred Heart and Our Lady, I take your acceptance of me for the Mercy Convent to be God's Holy Will; and so I am only too happy to acquiesce with your wishes and transfer my allegiance to the convent mentioned. I have always admired and liked the Sisters of Mercy, particularly for their kindness to the poor. . . . I shall be grateful if Revd. Mother can let me know all particulars as soon as possible, as I shall have a very short time in which to prepare. We expect to get our vacation about July 10th, and Dan and I are going for a quiet holiday to the north of Ireland where we spent our childhood days with our grandparents. . . . I shall then devote all my time to preparation of necessaries, and hope to be leaving here about the end of August.[61]

Sarah O'Callaghan arrived in St. John's on September 22, 1903, and was accepted as a postulant at St. Bride's Convent, Littledale. At the time she was twenty-six years of age. She was born in Southdown, Ireland, in a family of nine boys and two girls. After completing her education in the local schools,

---

59. Daniel O'Callaghan to Bishop Michael J. Howley, June 15, 1903, AASJ, 106/10/24.

60. After serving in several parishes of the diocese, in 1917, Father Daniel O'Callaghan was appointed first parish priest of St. Francis of Assisi Parish, Outer Cove. He remained there until his death in 1948. While he was pastor at Outer Cove, he built a church, schools, and a presbytery. Those who knew him describe him as a determined shepherd who saw his word and rule as law. Through his leadership and support, he involved Outer Cove and neighbouring communities in the St. John's Regatta, where the success of the rowers is known today both in story and song. I am indebted to Larry Dohey, archivist for the Archdiocese of St. John's, for this information.

61. Sarah O'Callaghan to Bishop Michael J. Howley, June 19, 1903, AASJ, 106/10/24.

she went to Liverpool where her brothers operated a chain of grocery stores.[62] While in Liverpool, Sarah continued her studies and eventually accepted a teaching position with the Sisters of Notre-Dame in Liverpool. Upon her arrival in Newfoundland, she was admitted as a postulant at St. Bride's Convent, Littledale, where after five months, she was received into the novitiate of the Sisters of Mercy at Littledale on February 28, 1904, and given the religious name, Mary Perpetua. Novitiate regulations notwithstanding, almost immediately, she was appointed headmistress of St. Bride's Academy, a position she held for seventeen years. Under her guidance, Littledale not only continued to maintain its high academic record but each year saw an increase of both student achievements and enrolment. This continued until July 1921, when M. Perpetua went to Fordham University, New York, where in 1924, she received the degree of doctor of philosophy. On her return to St. John's, she was appointed to the staff of Mercy Convent, Military Road, for a few years until 1929, when she returned to Littledale as novice mistress. In addition to her duties with the novices, she taught classes in high-school religion and directed the studies of the younger sisters. She died at Littledale in 1933 at the age of fifty-six.

By the year 1910, the increased enrolment at Littledale necessitated another addition to the complex. On November 8, 1911, the sod was turned for a new five-storey building on the west side of the former Little cottage that currently served as the convent. This new structure was made of concrete with granite quoins. It was intended mainly for the use of the students, and contained sleeping quarters, washrooms, a study hall, and classrooms. A bright, well-equipped kitchen, laundries, and storage rooms were located also in the basement of what was called the "West Wing." It was at this time that Brother Boniface Brennan of Mount Cashel Orphanage conceived the idea of obtaining a water supply for the Littledale complex from one of the springs in the Southside Hills. The pure spring water was delivered to Littledale by means of pipes that were laid under the railway track and the Waterford River.[63] By

---

62. Biographical Data, Rev. Daniel P. O'Callaghan, AASJ.
63. "Outline Notes on St. Bride's Convent/Academy/College," ASMSJ.

1912, the new wing was fully completed at a cost of approximately $60,000. The headmistress, M. Perpetua O'Callaghan, faced with a debt of such magnitude, enlisted the help of her brother, Father Dan O'Callaghan, in promoting the garden party that took place annually on Littledale grounds. The popularity of Father O'Callaghan's garden parties at Littledale is a matter of record, for even the Reid Railway Company put on a couple of extra trains to accommodate those who wished to attend:

> In connection with the Littledale Garden Party, on Wednesday next, . . . in addition to the excursion train, which is run at 2:30 p.m. and the ordinary at 6:00 p.m. there will be a special train despatched to Waterford Bridge at 4:00 p.m. The fare is very reasonable—15 cents return, so that all travelling by train as far as Waterford Bridge Station may return by the ordinary train at 9:15 p.m. or by the special, if necessary at 8.00 p.m. for the small sum of 15 cents for the double journey. [64]

Through these garden parties, concerts, and other events, Father O'Callaghan raised more than $12,000 to defray the cost of the new wing. The community itself had $11,000 on hand, and Archbishop Howley[65] arranged for payment of $20,000. Thus, the greater part of the cost of the building was paid off by the time it was ready for occupancy.[66]

The archbishop's plans for Littledale, however, were not yet complete. He noted with concern the increasing deterioration of the old Little cottage that still served as the convent and the connecting link between the east and west wings of the complex. He decided to replace the old wooden cottage and connect the two wings by building a six-storey centre building.[67] However, the outbreak of war in 1914 caused the implementation of the plans to be delayed. And then, on October 15, 1914, after an illness of only ten days, Archbishop Michael J. Howley died.

---

64. *The Evening Telegram*, August 9, 1909, p. 8.
65. When, in 1904, Newfoundland was made an ecclesiastical province, the Diocese of St. John's became an archdiocese, and its bishop an archbishop.
66. "Chronicle of St. Bride's College, Littledale," ASMSJ.
67. Hogan, *Pathways*, p. 228.

The death of Archbishop Howley was a blow to the archdiocese as a whole, and particularly to the sisters and students of Belvedere and Littledale. He had a deep love for the orphans at Belvedere and visited them frequently. It is said that he knew every child by name, and they looked on him as a benevolent "Grandpa."[68] In spite of the archbishop's high-handed treatment of everything to do with the sisters and their ministry, there is no doubt that he was tireless in his efforts to further their work and to improve the conditions under which they operated. He took a keen, personal interest in Littledale and spared no effort to provide the sisters with the support and advice that helped them pay off the heavy debt on the property. And, to be fair, Archbishop Howley was no different in his dealings with the religious under his jurisdiction than were bishops in other parts of the world. A short biography of Archbishop Howley, written on the occasion of the centenary of the consecration of the Cathedral of St. John the Baptist, describes the archbishop as follows:

> Our first Archbishop was a man of broad vision and high intellectual attainments. His fondness for study and research, his gift of easily learning a foreign language and his urge to set down his thoughts and ideas in writing mark him as a scholar. He could write as fluently in Latin or Italian as in English. Fishermen from Spain used to go to him for confession when they were in port. ... he was a good theologian and a member of the Royal Society of Canada and contributed to the meetings of this learned body many articles displaying profound historical knowledge and research.
>
> To state that Archbishop Howley was a poet is not enough: he had the soul of a poet. He was sensitive to beauty and the changing moods of nature. He had a sense of fitness of words, or orderly thought and clear expression. He was devoted to Newfoundland. He loved it and especially the people. ... Always a man of the people, the Archbishop wished to be buried in Belvedere rather than in the Cathedral that he had restored and embellished. The last sermon he preached was to the Catholic members of the Royal Newfoundland Regiment just before they sailed for overseas. ... And so he died in harness,

68. M. Basil McCormack, conversation with author, September 26, 1999.

> leaving to posterity his writings, his songs, the memory of his zeal and devotion . . . [69]

With the appointment of Archbishop Howley's successor, Rev. Edward Patrick Roche, as archbishop of St. John's, a new era dawned, not only for St. Bride's Academy, Littledale, but for both congregations of women religious and, in fact, for the Roman Catholic Church in Newfoundland.

One of the first challenges to face the new archbishop of St. John's was the implementation of his predecessor's plan for a new building at Littledale to replace the old residence of Philip Little. By the time it was completed in 1919, wartime difficulties and increased costs caused Archbishop Howley's original design for a five-storey building to be modified to one of three storeys.[70] There was a tradition at Littledale that Archbishop Roche intended someday to complete the structure according to the original design, but the plan was never realized.

The first two levels of this new centre block contained new and improved facilities for the boarders. A large student dining room, a well-equipped domestic science room, and furnace rooms were located on the ground floor. A bright, spacious study hall was found on the first floor, as well as a music room, library, parlour, and a small room known as "the priest's breakfast room." For many years, a priest from St. Patrick's Parish came to Littledale every morning to celebrate mass. A novice was appointed to serve the reverend gentleman his breakfast, which he consumed in solitary splendour in "the priest's breakfast room." The infirmaries were located on the second floor, as well as several other rooms that served various functions over the years, ranging from sleeping quarters to music rooms. At the front

69. W. J. Browne, "Most Rev. Michael Francis Howley, Bishop of St. John's, 1895–1904, Archbishop of St. John's, 1904–1914," in *The Centenary of the Basilica-Cathedral of St. John the Baptist*, ed. P. J. Kennedy (St. John's, NL: Archdiocese of St. John's, 1955), pp. 270, 271. The mention of Belvedere refers to Belvedere Cemetery, one of the four Catholic cemeteries in St. John's. Archbishop Howley's predecessors, beginning with Bishop Scallan, are all buried under the high altar of the cathedral.

70. Hogan, *Pathways*, p. 216, stated that the plan was for a five-storey building. *ENL*, s.v. "St. Bride's College," stated that a six-storey building was planned.

of the building was a suite of rooms for the use of Archbishop Roche, who lived at Littledale for some time after the episcopal residence was destroyed by fire in 1921. Also, at the front of the building was a beautiful staircase made of polished oak, known as the "Archbishop's Stairs" and therefore not to be used by ordinary mortals, such as novices, students, or in fact, by any-body not entitled to be called "Mother," "Father," or "Your Grace."

With the completion of the centre block, the residents of Littledale enjoyed a rest from the sounds of hammers, saws, thumps, and bumps that had accompanied the construction of the building. At the same time, the new section provided extra space needed to house eighty boarders and twenty sisters.[71] Perhaps nobody was happier to see the finished product than M. Teresa O'Halleran, who was responsible for overseeing the work. As bursar, she had charge of the entire property. In those days, Littledale had a large farm with cows and horses and three men to work the farm. M. Teresa went around every day to see the crops being put in and the men at their work. All of this brought back memories of home and Ireland but also its share of worries. For instance, during the summer of 1923, she was concerned that the many icebergs along the coast were keeping the temperatures so cold that the crops would be affected, for the sisters depended on the crops for food for the winter.[72] A letter to Peggy, her niece, solves another Littledale mystery—the source of "Everlasting Jam." For many years this mysterious concoction was served as a dessert to the boarders at Littledale on Tuesdays, Thursdays, and Sundays. No other jam was known to grace the tables in either the sisters' or the boarders' dining rooms. Hence the sobriquet "Everlasting Jam." Many years later, when M. Teresa's letters came to light, the secret was revealed: "During the summer I made over two thousand pounds of preserves for the sisters and boarders—

---

71. M. Teresa O'Halleran to Peggy Halleran, November 16, 1920, ASMSJ. M. Teresa O'Halleran began writing to her niece Peggy Halleran when the latter was nine years of age in 1914. The letters continued until M. Teresa's death in 1937. Peggy kept all M. Teresa's letters, and many years later, Peggy's nephews, Reverend John and his brother, Mr. Edward Halleran, discovered these letters and made copies for the Mercy Archives. The Sisters of Mercy of Newfoundland are deeply grateful to Father Halleran and Mr. Halleran for this precious gift.

72. Ibid., August 15, 1923.

that kept me busy. Of course I had the novices to help."[73] Another letter reveals the nature of the ingredients used in making these preserves:

> We have lost our gooseberry crop. Something happened them during the retreat. I imagine the man in spraying them gave them an over dose of some stuff to be put on to kill grubs and deprived me of 40 gallons of gooseberries too bad. I put up a lot of rhubarb, strawberries, raspberries etc. etc., in all about 3,000 pounds—that is a great help for both Boarders and Sisters. This work is my own choice and I have done this work for the past 14 years.[74]

The letters of M. Teresa O'Halleran provide a glimpse into what life was like at Littledale during the early part of the twentieth century. They also reveal the heartbreaking sacrifice made by these young Irish women who came to Newfoundland. On one occasion, M. Teresa's niece wrote her, suggesting that her newly ordained nephew would like to visit her in St. John's. She replied:

> Now, child, never think of letting Fred come this way. I want to see you all in heaven and not before—that pleasure would be only temporary, and leave a big want in the heart. Better far to wait for the Eternal. I will go on praying and loving you all the same and then when I depart Fred will be there to remember my poor soul. Is this not the right thing? I am happy and never regretted coming to Newfoundland and I felt it was the place God destined for me. I love the work He has given me to do. I love the school, then keeping accounts, but I do not like debts, and in a big establishment like Littledale, debts will have to come, but I trust to God, and He helps me.[75]

In her letters, M. Teresa wrote of small, everyday events as well as major calamities, such as the tsunami on the Burin Peninsula and its effect on people

---

73. Ibid., September 25, 1925.
74. Ibid., August 1927.
75. Ibid., Dec. 15, 1930.

she had come to know and love during the years she spent in Burin. As well, her letters reveal a woman of strength, faith, and courage. She showed a deep and tender affection for her homeland and family, but she was willing to endure lifelong separation from those she loved because she believed that God had called her to this ministry. M. Teresa O'Halleran was representative of all those young women from Ireland who came to spread the message of God's love and mercy in this land and to whom the Sisters of Mercy, and many other Newfoundlanders, owe so much.

M. Teresa O'Halleran witnessed many changes in her long life, not the least of which was the major structural change that occurred within the Congregation of the Sisters of Mercy in Newfoundland in 1916—the union of all the separate convents under the jurisdiction of a central administration, a development that will be described later. Meanwhile, the sisters in the out-ports also had their share of triumphs and difficulties, and the contribution of these valiant women to the educational and social development of Newfoundland should never be forgotten.

CHAPTER NINE

THE QUIET GROWTH

The very commonness of everyday things
harbours the eternal marvel and silent mystery of God
and of God's grace.[1]

Unknown

In the absence of contemporary documents, it is difficult to piece together in a coherent fashion the story of the foundations outside St. John's. The scanty information available comes mainly from yearly reports of the superintendent of Roman Catholic schools. All the convent schools, with the exception of Our Lady of Mercy School in St. John's,[2] were public denominational schools, termed "board schools," and shared in the district grants for education.[3] Nevertheless, the curriculum in these schools, although including all subjects required by the board, was patterned along the lines established at Our Lady of Mercy School. A fee was charged for extras such as French, drawing, painting, and music. In order to ensure that a sister was available to teach the more specialized subjects, such as music, a degree of co-operation existed between neighbouring convents. In spite of the fact that

---

1. The author of this passage is unknown.
2. Our Lady of Mercy in St. John's received no government or Church assistance but depended entirely on fees paid by the pupils.
3. Hogan, *Pathways*, p. 110.

each convent was autonomous, there is no doubt that sisters were transferred from one to another. For instance, in 1874, Bishop Power wanted to transfer one of the music teachers from Mercy Convent to the convent in St. Lawrence, for as has been shown in the previous chapter, the bishop moved sisters hither and yon as he pleased. In this case, the bishop's request was denied, and unlike some of his successors, he did not insist.[4]

Teaching in the outports brought its share of headaches. A report of the Roman Catholic School Board in 1869 identifies a major problem faced by all teachers:

> The early age at which children in this country can by their labour contribute to the support of the family, tends to the too early withdrawal of the children from school ... but the too early withdrawal of the children is not so injurious as their irregular attendance during the years they are presumed to be pupils of the school.[5]

When the Sisters of Mercy opened their first convents outside St. John's, their primary objectives were the education of girls and visitation of the sick and the poor. However, circumstances of time and place frequently required them to teach boys as well. For instance, in St. Lawrence when the sisters' first school was opened in 1871, boys and girls attended together until a regular teacher was secured for the boys. Even after a teacher had been engaged to teach the boys, it sometimes happened that the teacher became ill or proved incompetent, and the sisters were once again placed in charge of the boys. The inspector of Roman Catholic schools made the following observations in 1874:

> The Boys' School at St. Lawrence was still in charge of the Ladies of the Convent at the time I visited the settlement, owing to the Board failing to secure the services of a male teacher. The atten-

4. His request was denied because no one could be spared. "Acts of Chapter, Convent of Our Lady of Mercy, St. John's," September 5, 1874, ASMSJ.
5. Michael John Kelly, "Report upon the Inspection of Roman Catholic Schools," 1869, AASJ, 600/1/3.

> dance is large—daily average being 64, and the progress made by
> the pupils in their studies under the present teachers is satisfacto-
> ry evidence that the temporary absence of a male teacher is much
> to their advantage. . . . There are 96 returned as daily attending
> the Girls' School so that 160 children are daily attending school in
> this settlement.[6]

The report makes it clear that, by this time, boys and girls were taught separately. This put an additional strain on the small teaching staff of the convent
school, a situation to which the superintendent refers in 1887 and, again, more
than twenty years later in 1899:

> The teacher of the Boys' School at St. Lawrence had resigned a
> few months before my visit, and the nuns, while the Board were
> [sic] waiting for a teacher, took charge temporarily to keep the
> children in attendance. A teacher is wanted for this school imme-
> diately as it is in a decidedly backward condition; in fact, about the
> worst I met with, and it is too great a strain on the good Sisters
> to keep it open, as it weakens the teaching staff at the Convent
> School.
>   A marked contrast to the Boys' School was the Convent
> School. The good nuns have erected a new building, connected
> with the convent, entirely at their own expense. It is 45x25 feet
> and contains two schoolrooms separated by folding doors, having
> ceilings eighteen feet high. It is well ventilated and very nicely fin-
> ished. There were 71 registered. . . . Pupils were classified in
> Standards I to V and with few exceptions, passed a creditable
> examination.[7]

This new building came about because of a legacy from Charles Laughlan (or
McLaughlan) to his sister Catherine (M. Borgia Laughlan), who was a member
of the St. Lawrence community.

Catherine Laughlan was born in St. John's, the only daughter of
Catherine and Charles Laughlan of County Tipperary. Nothing is known about

---

6. Ibid., 1874. See also *JHA*, 1875, p. 644.

7. Vincent P. Burke, "Report of the Superintendent for Roman Catholic Schools for the
Year Ended December 31, 1899," p. 31, ASMSJ.

her early years, except on September 5, 1868, she married John Walsh who had moved to St. John's from his home in County Kilkenny.[8] Two years later, on August 17, 1870, John Walsh died at the age of thirty years.[9] Less than a year after John's death, in 1871, Katie Laughlan-Walsh applied and was accepted as a postulant at Mercy Convent. In October of that same year, she was received as a novice and given the name Mary Borgia. However, the sisters at the mother house felt that her health was not strong enough "to permit her to discharge efficiently the arduous duties of the Parent house."[10] They admitted her to the novitiate on condition that she would agree to go to the Sacred Heart Convent in St. Lawrence as a member of that community. And so, a few days after her reception, she joined the community at St. Lawrence, where she spent her novitiate years. Sometime in 1874, she returned to Mercy Convent to prepare for her profession of vows. Once again, the sisters at the mother house were uncertain about admitting her to profession. The "Acts of Chapter" of August 28, 1874, contain the following entry: "No conclusion about the Profession of Sister M. Borgia Laughlan of the St. Lawrence Convent. Chapter was held at the direction of Bishop Power. No satisfactory account from the Community where she spent her novitiate."[11] A week later, the following entry was made: "Sister M. Borgia should return to her own community and let them decide about her profession."[12] Perhaps the sisters were doubtful that M. Borgia's health was strong enough to withstand the hardships of life in the missions, or maybe they had doubts about her stability in her vocation. M. Borgia, however, defied all negative predictions. She went back to Sacred Heart Convent, St. Lawrence, made her profession of vows and remained in the community for the rest of her life. When she died in 1901, she was sincerely mourned not only by the sisters but also by the whole town of St. Lawrence.[13]

---

8. Register of Marriages, Roman Catholic Cathedral of St. John the Baptist, St. John's, September 5, 1868, AASJ.
9. *The Newfoundlander*, August 21, 1870, p. 2.
10. "Acts of Chapter, Convent of Our Lady of Mercy, St. John's," October 10, 1871, ASMSJ.
11. Ibid., August 28, 1874, ASMSJ.
12. Ibid., September 4, 1874.
13. *The Evening Telegram*, May 7, 1901, p. 3.

When M. Borgia went to St. Lawrence in 1871, she was not going into
any bed of roses. The Annals record that the early years of the Sisters of Mercy
in St. Lawrence were lean ones. The sisters had barely enough to live on and
their material comforts were practically non-existent. In time, the extreme
poverty that the sisters were experiencing became known to Charles
Laughlan, M. Borgia's brother, who was a wealthy merchant living in St.
John's. His response was to send donations of food to the sisters twice each
year when the schooner brought supplies from St. John's. This enabled the sisters to provide for themselves and offer assistance to families who were in
need. At his death in 1896, Charles Laughlan's only living relative, M. Borgia,
inherited his large fortune. With the permission of her superiors and, no
doubt, the encouragement of the bishop, she donated her entire inheritance to
the local community. Her first project was the building of a new parish school,
called St. Anne's, adjoining the convent. The convent itself was remodelled and
renovated. Finally, in 1898, with funds from the Laughlan estate, the construction of a parish church was begun. However, Sr. M. Borgia died in 1901
before the church was completed. She is buried in the sisters' plot in St.
Lawrence.

In contrast to the early days of the convent in St. Lawrence, the sisters at St.
Anne's Convent in Burin appear to have had a rather easy life. That is not to say
that they did not have their share of heartaches, problems, and difficulties, but
certainly, there is nothing to indicate that they suffered the chilling poverty of
their sisters in St. Lawrence. In 1879, when M. Joseph Rawlins was superior,[14]
a new convent was built in a central location, and as well, a new three-room
school was constructed next to the convent. Up to this time, the sisters taught
the boys as well as the girls, but in 1879, the boys were placed in the charge of
a master. The Burin children were bright and enthusiastic, and the reports of
the school inspector reflected the interest of the children as well as the excellence of the instruction they received. In his report for the year ending 1882,

14. M. Joseph Rawlins went to Burin in 1871 and remained there for the rest of her life.
She died in 1918.

the superintendent of the time, James Fenelon, made the following observation after visiting the convent school in Burin:

> Along with the usual plain and fancy needlework, the more grown girls are taught knitting and spinning. This practical instruction given girls in Convent Schools leads to provide to some extent, employment for the female members of families. . . . When girls are taught how to prepare woolen articles of clothing for domestic use, it will naturally follow that the father and sons become more desirous of providing the necessary material. In this way some encouragement, however, small, would be given to the extension of agriculture, especially as regards the rearing of sheep. [15]

Mr. Fenelon made no mention of the academic subjects taught except to say that the pupils are "well-trained and intelligent."[16] He seems to have been more interested in the socio-economic future of the region.

The 1880s were a difficult period for the sisters in Burin. M. Francis Born, a Newfoundlander who had entered and been professed in Burin, died on March 1, 1884, at the age of forty-two years. M. Francis's death was followed a year later, March 2, 1885, by that of the Irish-born Mary of the Cross Reardon. The little community had hardly recovered from these two losses when M. Madeline Stephenson became ill and died in November 1886. She had been professed just ten years. The loss of three sisters in such a short time placed a heavy burden on the few sisters remaining in the community. There are no convent records naming the sisters who were in Burin at the time, but according to the reports of the school inspector, there were three sisters teaching in the school.[17] Two additional sisters, M. Columba Glynn and M. Emeria Cormack, were sent from the mother house to Burin in 1885 or 1886.

The name of M. Columba Glynn is associated usually with St. Bridget's, St. Peter's, and Our Lady of Mercy schools in St. John's. However, she was remem-

---

15. "Report upon the Inspection of Roman Catholic Schools for the Year 1882," AASJ, 600/2/4.

16. Ibid.

17. "Report of the Superintendent of Education for Roman Catholic Schools for the Year 1885," AASJ, 600/2/4.

bered with affection and gratitude by the people of Burin for her efforts on behalf of the sick during a particularly severe diphtheria epidemic that occurred in the late 1880s or possibly in 1890. During the epidemic, a priest from St. Lawrence, Father John Walsh, came to Burin to minister to the people. Unfortunately, he became a victim of the contagion that, at the time, was often fatal. M. Columba cared for him during his illness, but in spite of her efforts, he died. She and other sisters of the community contracted the disease but recovered.[18]

In 1885, M. Emeria Cormack was appointed superior of the Burin community, replacing M. Gertrude Keough who had served in that office since 1880.[19] Although M. Emeria had been professed for only five years, M. Bernard Clune had no hesitation in sending her to Burin as superior. It must have been a difficult task for a young, inexperienced sister and perhaps a little too much to expect of her, for after two years, her health broke down. When the superintendent of schools wrote his 1887 report of the convent school in Burin, he said:

> The Convent was undergoing repairs at the time of my visit, and the Rev. Superioress had been obliged to visit the Capital in the interest of her health, which at the time was rather delicate. These circumstances, as might be expected, tended to disorganize school matters somewhat. The pupils, notwithstanding, passed a very creditable examination.[20]

M. Emeria remained another year as superior and then resigned in 1888. In the following eight years, Burin had no less than three superiors: M. Angela Kitchin, M. Ita Glynn, and M. Philomena O'Donovan. Finally, in 1896, M.

---

18. Marshall, *South Coast*, p. 38.

19. Frances Keough (M. Gertrude of the Sacred Heart) entered at Mercy Convent in 1873. At the completion of her novitiate, her superiors decided that she should return home. Bishop Power interceded and requested that she be allowed a longer period of probation. M. Xavier Bernard agreed, but decided that the young novice was more suited for life in a smaller community. M. Gertrude was professed for the Burin community in September 1876. Four years later, she was named superior of St. Anne's Convent, Burin. She served in Burin for nine years, after which she was transferred to St. Michael's Convent, Belvedere, where she remained for the rest of her life.

20. "Report of the Superintendent of Education for Roman Catholic Schools for the Year 1887," AASJ, 600/2/30.

Teresa O'Halleran was appointed to the position, and by completing two full terms as superior, she returned stability to the mission.

In Burin, M. Teresa found scope for her ability in the enlargement of the convent and the building of a beautiful little oratory. The school, however, was the chief focus of her attention during the six years she spent on the South Coast. As a result, the annual reports of the superintendent of education refer in glowing terms to the convent school in Burin. He noted that there were three teachers in the school, which in 1899 had an enrolment of fifty-five students:

> The pupils of this institution made a splendid showing. In my note-book I find almost every subject marked very good or excellent. The Senior Classes seemed quite at home in Arithmetic. . . . and the Juniors also did remarkably well, according to their standards. The answering in Grammar showed the pupils to have been carefully taught in that subject, as they answered with attention and forethought, and not at random, as is done in many schools. There was an atmosphere of order and neatness about the whole school, and an alertness about the movements of the children, which was refreshing to witness.[21]

In his report for the year 1900, the superintendent claims that the Burin Convent School is ". . . one of our best out-port schools. Every subject is taught with thoroughness as shown by the intelligent and correct answering in subjects of Standards I–VI."[22] Every year the superintendent made reference to the beautiful needlework produced by the pupils. As well, he remarked the clarity of diction and "the atmosphere of . . . refinement and culture" that he found in the school.[23]

When M. Teresa O'Halleran's term of office as superior in Burin expired in 1902, she was appointed bursar at Mercy Convent, Military Road.[24] The

---

21. Vincent P. Burke, "Report of the Superintendent of Roman Catholic Schools for the Year Ended 1899," p. 30, ASMSJ.

22. Ibid., for Year Ended December 31, 1900, p. 61, ASMSJ.

23. Ibid., for Year Ended December 31, 1901, p. 65, ASMSJ.

24. "Acts of Chapter, Convent of Our Lady of Mercy, St. John's," November 1, 1902, ASMSJ, RG 1/3.

name of M. Teresa O'Halleran is not as well-known to the public—or even to
the Sisters of Mercy who came after her—as is that of her novitiate companion, M. Bridget O'Connor. However, because of her administrative and teaching abilities, M. Teresa laid the groundwork in Burin for the splendid achievements of her successors, M. Bridget O'Connor and M. Pius Mulcahy.

M. Pius (Minnie Mulcahy) was born in St. John's in 1868 and went to Littledale
as a student shortly after St. Bride's Boarding School was opened. Together with
another Littledale student, Mary Dooley (Mary Bernard), she was received into
the novitiate at Mercy Convent in 1886 and professed in 1889. During these
three years she spent some time teaching at St. Peter's School. Shortly after her
profession, she was appointed to the staff at Littledale, where she worked closely with M. Bridget O'Connor. In 1902, Archbishop Howley appointed her to
succeed M. Teresa O'Halleran as superior of the community in Burin. A local
author sums up the contribution of M. Pius as follows:

> Mother Pius, a Sister with exceptional ability, business and admin-
> istrative, as well as educational, made extensive improvements in
> educational facilities during her tenure in Burin. She had a modern
> three room school with dressing rooms built and furnished with
> the latest equipment including adjustable desks and seats from
> Boston. The convent property was greatly enhanced by the con-
> struction of a cement wall which prevented collapse of surround-
> ing garden grounds.[25]

In 1903, a year after M. Pius had been appointed to Burin, she was
joined by her good friend, M. Bridget O'Connor from Littledale. Even today,
a hundred years later, the people of Burin recall the name of M. Bridget
O'Connor and the achievements of the children who were fortunate enough
to have come under her influence. Although remembered principally as an
educator and administrator, M. Bridget was also a talented artist. Some of her
paintings have been preserved and may still be found in the older homes of
Burin. There seems to have been no limit to her energy, for she found time to

---

25. Marshall, *South Coast*, p. 39.

paint antependiums to decorate the altar of the church and pictures to adorn the church walls.[26]

After the arrival of M. Pius and M. Bridget, the superintendent's reports on the convent school in Burin became even more positive than in the previous years: "There is no better school outside of the Colleges within my superintendence."[27] The year 1907 saw the students of the Burin Convent School carry off a number of prizes, including the Outport Scholarship, first place in art, and first place in English overall.[28] At the end of 1908, the superintendent reported, ". . . the work done in it [the convent school] is much above the average. I have no better school within my superintendence."[29]

After taking up her position in Burin, M. Bridget O'Connor lost no time in introducing her pupils to the curriculum set by the Council of Higher Education (the CHE). In the year-end report for 1902, the superintendent remarked, "Pupils were examined in subjects varying from the Intermediate Grade Syllabus C.H.E. down, with excellent results."[30] By 1908, M. Bridget felt they were ready for the examinations. In the year-end report, the superintendent remarked on the success of these students: "Four Intermediate candidates (all receiving honours in English, arithmetic, French, book-keeping and shorthand), five Preliminaries, and three Primaries were successful."[31] In 1912, a pupil of the school was one of only four girls outside St. John's who passed junior matriculation examinations.[32]

In 1908, M. Bridget succeeded M. Pius as the superior of the convent. Nevertheless, she did not allow the responsibilities associated with this new

26. Ibid., p. 38. An antependium is often used to decorate the altar during church services. It is a drape that hangs from the altar table to the floor, covering the entire front of the altar. It is usually made of costly material and often decorated by paintings or embroidery.

27. Vincent P. Burke, "Report of the Superintendent of Roman Catholic Schools for the Year Ended December 31, 1907," p. 77, ASMSJ. The reference to "the Colleges" embraces St. Bonaventure's, St. Bride's (Littledale), the Methodist College—all in St. John's.

28. Ibid.

29. Ibid., 1908, p. 58, ASMSJ.

30. Ibid., 1902, p. 63, ASMSJ.

31. Ibid.

32. McCormack, "Educational Work," p. 58, ASMSJ.

position to detract from her work in the schools. A letter from one of her former students gives some idea of the scope of her efforts on behalf of the children of Burin:

> She taught, after school hours, French, painting, drawing, needlework, typewriting and shorthand to both Catholic and non-Catholic girls who had left school. She had wonderful concerts, but two that stand out in my memory were *Mary Queen of Scots* and *Marie Antoinette*. They were heavy plays, and she painted the scenery for them. The Protestant children attended our school and many went teaching from the school. About fifty girls became teachers. There were approximately one hundred children on the roll. The boys came to the convent after school hours for instruction for Confession, Holy Communion and Confirmation.
>
> When I took exams, we had to do four pieces of fancy needlework each. The work had to be sent to England to be examined. When it came back we gave it to the Bazaar. Several of the girls received prizes. It was beautiful work—point lace, Limerick Lace, drawn thread, applique work, silk work, tatting, crochet and embroidery.
>
> The nuns were the first to teach music. Mother Mary Joseph [Rawlins] taught music all day long for years. The non-Catholics love the nuns just as much as the Catholics, and they have asked the pastor several times if he could have the Sisters back. Burin lost so much when it lost the nuns.[33]

Mrs. Rose's statement that the sisters were the first to teach music in Burin is questionable. Perhaps the sisters were the first to offer formal instruction in music, but long before their arrival, the people of Burin were capable of presenting a musical performance that surprised and delighted the bishop of the diocese.[34] Also, every Newfoundland outport has a strong musical tradition that finds expression in the hundreds of songs and dances that enrich the folk

---

33. Mrs. M. Rose, quoted in McCormack, "Educational Work," p. 59. As a result of a downturn in the economy and resulting out-migration, St. Anne's Convent in Burin closed in 1939.

34. When Bishop Fleming visited the area in 1834 (or 1836) he remarked the "excellent choir" that had provided music for mass. See Marshall, *South Coast*, p. 18.

repertoire of our island. Nevertheless, the sisters were happy to build on the skills and culture already established. There is no doubt that M. Bridget O'Connor encouraged the children to develop their natural ability by ensuring that music, dancing, and drama were an important part of the curriculum, and in this she found an enthusiastic collaborator in M. Joseph Rawlins.

When the youthful M. Joseph Rawlins set sail for Burin in 1871, it is not recorded that she had a sister companion for her long sea voyage to her new home. If no sister could be spared to accompany her, the Rule prescribed that she would travel with "a prudent companion," no doubt some lady from "the Coast" who was returning home from the city. As a music teacher with little experience, M. Joseph may have felt some trepidation in facing the challenges of sharing her skills and knowledge with those who had already a strong musical tradition of their own. Whatever her feelings on the long, possibly stormy voyage, it is clear that she very quickly fell in love with the rocky bump on the leg of Newfoundland called Burin. For forty-seven years, she taught music to the children and adults from Burin and the surrounding area. However, the parish choir was her biggest challenge and her greatest joy. She devoted much of her energy to teaching and preparing the choir for the various liturgical feasts of the Church year. She was so successful in this that the Burin choir was known far and wide as one of outstanding excellence.[35]

By the year 1917, M. Joseph was beginning to feel the weight of her years. Born in St. John's in 1846, she had attended Our Lady of Mercy School and, for a short time, had been a boarder at St. Clair's Boarding School. She studied music with Professor Mullock, the first organist at the Cathedral of St. John the Baptist. At age seventeen, she was accepted as a postulant at Mercy Convent and remained there until her assignment to Burin. But the hard years of the early foundation and the unceasing work had caught up with her. Her good friend and co-worker, M. Bridget O'Connor, now the superior general, invited her to return to Mercy Convent, where she would have the best medical attention available at the time. But Burin was home now, and she wanted to spend whatever time was left in the company of her sisters and the friends

35. Marshall, *South Coast*, p. 45.

she had made over the years. Forced to give up teaching, she devoted her time to prayer. In August 1918, the Burin sisters went to St. John's for the annual retreat. One of them, Margaret Mary St. John, remained behind to look after M. Joseph. The following day, August 19, M. Joseph collapsed during evening prayer in the little chapel. During the next few hours, her condition became critical, and at midnight, the convent bell rang out to summon help.[36] We can imagine the alarm and consternation of the people as the pealing of the bell resounded through the dark, sleeping town, shattering the silence of the night. The ladies of Burin responded immediately, but M. Joseph died a few hours later, leaving Margaret Mary St. John with the task of arranging for the wake and the funeral. M. Joseph was the last sister to be buried in the sisters' plot in Burin.

Out in the Conception Bay area, the St. Joseph's Convent School in Brigus had gained a reputation for excellence in music and drama.[37] Although the convent school was intended for the education of girls, when it opened in 1861, both boys and girls attended.[38] In an account of early Catholic education in Brigus, the writer notes, "Patrick Power was educated by the nuns and in 1870 he taught the boys, and the girls were still under the care of the sisters."[39] After Patrick Power's death in 1900, Stephen James took over the school for boys. He taught there until he was pensioned in 1916, when sisters again took over the care of St. Patrick's School for boys, as well as St. Joseph's girls' school.

St. Joseph's School had a relatively small enrolment. In 1887, there were sixty girls registered, and in the following years, the number did not vary to any marked degree.[40] As was the case wherever the Presentation and Mercy

36. Ibid.
37. Records of Sacred Heart Parish, Brigus. See also the yearly reports of the superintendent of education, ASMSJ.
38. "Brigus Notes," unsigned document, ASMSJ, RG 3/10/14.
39. Unsigned, undated account of the history of Catholic education in Brigus. The account was written sometime in the 1940s or '50s for it refers to the parish priest of the time, Dr. Jones, who served in Brigus from 1944–1954. ASMSJ, RG 10/3/27.
40. "Reports of the Superintendent of Education for Roman Catholic Schools, Diocese of Harbour Grace," 1887–1908, ASMSJ.

sisters established convents, there was no shortage of entertainment offered by the school to the residents of the town. In short order, the children were introduced to singing, dancing, and drama. These entertainments were good for the children, but in addition, they brought in much needed revenue for the school. Some of the performances were ambitious, to say the least. In 1898, the young people of Brigus united to produce the operetta *HMS Pinafore*. One of the senior students of St. Joseph's Convent School, Ellen Walker, coached the troupe in the solos and choruses of the operetta.[41] This was no mean accomplishment for a small place like Brigus. After all, only twenty years had elapsed since the first performance of the operetta, on May 28, 1878, at the Opera Comique in Paris.

The school itself had a good academic record, and so it is not surprising to learn that the pupils participated successfully in the first CHE examinations in 1894.[42] Judging by the reports of the superintendent of education, St. Joseph's School maintained its excellent reputation. The 1899 year-end report noted that fifty students were registered, "the majority of whom were classified in the higher Standards. Reading, Recitation and English Composition were fully up to the best in the Diocese. Arithmetic, to discount, was accurate and quick. . . . Vocal and instrumental music were, as on my previous visit, prominent and pleasing features of the school work."[43] At the time, there were four sisters teaching in the school. In 1901, the school superintendent noted an addition to the teaching staff at the convent in the person of a postulant, Ellen Walker.[44] At the time he made his report, this young lady, later known as Mary Philomena, was teaching classes in practical and theoretical music. M. Philomena continued the custom of preparing the students for a public concert at least twice a year—at Christmas and in the spring. These concerts usually consisted of an operetta or a program of vocal

41. "Brigus–Education," unsigned manuscript, ASMSJ, RG 10/3/15.

42. McCormack, "Educational Work," p. 54. McCormack cited the Report of the Council of Higher Education, 1894.

43. Thomas Hanrahan, "Report of the Roman Catholic Schools of the Diocese of Harbour Grace, Year Ended June 30, 1899," p. 83, ASMSJ.

44. Thomas Hanrahan, "Report of Superintendent of Roman Catholic Schools for the Diocese of Harbour Grace for Year Ended, June 30, 1901," p. 37, ASMSJ.

and instrumental solos and choruses. They were so popular that the performances were repeated on several successive evenings in order to accommodate
the people from the neighbouring towns.[45] M. Philomena Walker remained in
Brigus until 1923, when she was appointed to the staff at Littledale, where,
except for short periods at St. George's and Mercy Convent, she spent most
of her remaining years. She had the reputation of being an excellent teacher
and a woman of great wisdom and culture. She was eccentric, forgetful, gentle, and kind—and she was known to the Littledale students as "the nun with
the twinkling eyes."

Evidently, a program for training prospective teachers was offered by
the sisters in Brigus. In 1902, Thomas Hanrahan, the superintendent of education for the Harbour Grace diocese, remarked, "The convent supplies nearly
all the teachers employed by the Brigus Board and the excellent training these
have received is very evident in the way they conduct their schools."[46] In order
to qualify for a teaching position, students were required to obtain a teaching
certificate from a board of examiners. In reference to St. Joseph's School in
Brigus, the 1902 education report notes, "The year's work of the convent
includes six passes in Preliminary of CHE, two in First Division, four in
Second, and four Teachers' Grades certificates secured in July examinations
held by the Board of Examiners."[47]

It is almost impossible to discover the names of more than a few of the
sisters who worked in Brigus during the latter years of the nineteenth century. Of the four women who formed the first community, the superior, M. of
the Angels Banks, remained in Brigus until her death in 1884. She is one of six
sisters buried in Brigus. A second member of the founding community, M. de
Chantal O'Keefe, lived in Brigus for three years and then was sent to
Belvedere. M. Agnes Banks replaced her. Annie Banks (M. Agnes) arrived from

45. This information was provided by Mrs. Angela Burke in conversation with the author.
46. Thomas Hanrahan, "Report of the Roman Catholic Schools of the Diocese of Harbour Grace, Year Ended June 30, 1903," p. 40, ASMSJ. The report for the year 1901 provides the information that, in addition to the convent school, there were seven schools under the jurisdiction of the Brigus Roman Catholic Board. Graduates of the convent school in Brigus staffed six of these schools.
47. Ibid., 1902, p. 40, ASMSJ.

Ireland in 1864 and entered the Sisters of Mercy at St. Michael's Convent, Belvedere. She was sent to Brigus while she was still a novice, where she completed her novitiate and was professed in 1867. Four years later, in 1871, she succeeded M. of the Angels Banks as superior.[48] Ten years later, M. Agnes Banks was transferred to the Immaculate Conception Convent, Conception Harbour, and remained there until her death in 1893. Another member of the founding band, M. Gonzaga Coady, a native Newfoundlander, spent her entire religious life in Brigus. The postulant, Mary Barron (M. Joseph Teresa), was received and professed in Brigus, where she remained for more than forty years. Early in the 1900s, possibly 1909, she was transferred to the Immaculate Conception Convent, Conception Harbour, until around 1919. Some elderly people living in Conception Harbour remember M. Joseph Barron with affection and gratitude. Mrs. Mary Dalton recalled that M. Joseph, who was her teacher in the primary grades, was very concerned for little children who arrived in school with cold, wet feet during the winter. M. Joseph asked some of the men to make small, low stools. The men, who would do anything for "Mother Joseph," promptly set to work. Within a week, they supplied M. Joseph with enough little stools for every child in her class. When the children came to school the next morning, they found a row of little stools arranged around the pot-bellied stove in the classroom. M. Joseph had the children sit around the stove with their feet on the little stools until their shoes and stockings were thoroughly warm and dry.[49] Small acts of thoughtfulness like this endeared M. Joseph Barron to generations of children who carried the memory of her gentle kindness with them through life. She spent the last eight years of her life at Mercy Convent, presumably because of failing health. *Inter Nos* reports that for two and a half years before her death, she was confined to bed. In a few words, the writer sums up the person of Sister M. Joseph Teresa Barron: "gentle, unobtrusive and humble; she spent her life in assiduous work for God's poor."[50] She died on March 3, 1927.

---

48. It is not known if these two sisters were related, although it is likely they were either sisters or cousins, since both came from Limerick.

49. Mrs. Mary Dalton, age ninety-six, conversation with author, May 5, 2004.

50. *Inter Nos,* 1927.

Over the years, a few young women entered at St. Joseph's Convent in Brigus, and some were transferred to Brigus from other convents. There was M. Berchmans Meehan from Limerick, who entered the convent in Conception Harbour in 1874 and transferred to Brigus in 1891. M. Berchmans was an artist who had studied at the Kensington School of Art.[51] It was inevitable, therefore, that she would be given the responsibility of teaching art in the school and to young adults who came to the convent after hours for private instruction. One of M. Berchmans' pupils, Mrs. Mary Hawco, remembers that she was very popular with the students because of her delightful sense of humour.[52] Mrs. Hawco recalled that M. Berchmans produced a number of beautiful paintings and hundreds of pieces of exquisite embroidery, and other types of needlework. Two sisters whose names are remembered by some of the older citizens of Brigus are M. Veronica Crawley and M. Ultan Mullowney. Clare Mullowney (M. Ultan) was a student of Our Lady of Mercy Academy while living at St. Clair's Boarding School in St. John's. When she was seventeen she was accepted as a postulant at Mercy Convent, and after her profession, she was sent to Brigus in 1910, where she became involved in the parish liturgies as organist in the church. She is remembered by some of the older residents of Brigus as a competent and patient music teacher.[53] The fact that two of the sisters were music teachers, M. Ultan and M. Philomena Walker, suggests that the people of Brigus were eager to see that their children received instruction in music. Furthermore, children and young adults came by train from the surrounding towns of Cupids, Clarke's Beach, Bay Roberts, and as far away as Spaniard's Bay to be taught music by the sisters. In fact, in 1904, Brigus was the first town outside St. John's to have its own examination centre for the Trinity College of Music, London.[54] In 1919, Laura Cantwell, a student of the

---

51. Examples of the artistic works of M. Berchmans are preserved in the Heritage Room of the Sisters of Mercy at McAuley Convent in St. John's.

52. Mrs. Mary (Burke) Hawco, conversation with author, May 9, 2001.

53. Ibid.

54. A professor on the staff of Trinity College of Music in London made yearly visits to various centres in Newfoundland to adjudicate the performances of students who had registered for various grade levels in applied music, usually piano. This practice began in 1909 and continued until the latter part of the twentieth century.

sisters in Brigus, won in competition with all of Canada the first Exhibition Award of Trinity College to be gained in the New World. Two years later, the same student, Laura Cantwell, was awarded the Senior Pianoforte Exhibition.[55]

During the years 1910–1920, students from nearby settlements, who could not attend on weekdays, came by train on Saturdays to the convent in Brigus to take business courses. The topics covered were typing, shorthand, English, and bookkeeping.[56] In this way the influence of the Sisters of Mercy was not confined to Brigus but spread through the entire region of Conception Bay North. It may be partly due to the influence of the sisters that Brigus became the cradle of a number of vocations to the priesthood and religious life. Graduates of the Brigus Convent schools include eleven priests, three of whom went to the foreign missions; eleven professed as Sisters of Mercy,[57] three Presentation Sisters; one Franciscan priest; and two Christian Brothers. But the sisters' teaching and influence may have been felt more in the hundreds of Christian homes and families where parents remembered and passed on to their children the faith, hope, and love that formed the heart of what they learned from the Sisters of Mercy during their school days.

Although Brigus is only about fifteen miles north of Conception Harbour, in the days preceding the advent of the automobile, there were few opportunities for the sisters to exchange visits. Such a journey would take several hours by horse and carriage, and the sisters' busy schedule left little time for making visits. After the establishment of a railway from St. John's to Harbour Grace in 1884, sisters from Conception Harbour could take the train from Avondale if they wished to visit the convent in Brigus. Visits between members of the two convents, although rare, provided a means of communication that was benefi-

---

55. Laura Cantwell was M. Philomena Walker's niece.

56. M. Angela Fowler, conversation with author.

57. The eleven young women from Brigus who were professed as Sisters of Mercy were M. Philomena Walker, M. Jerome Walker, M. Lucina Cowley, M. Angela Fowler, M. Raymond Burke, M. Helen Shea, M. Geraldine Morrissey, M. Damien (Rita) Morrissey, M. Pius Shea, Veronica Lidster, and Anne Marie Barry. Several others were received into the novitiate but left the congregation before profession of vows.

cial to both communities. Sisters of both convents welcomed the interchange of ideas, the sharing of teaching and reading materials, as well as interaction with a wider circle of people.[58]

The annual report of the superintendent of Roman Catholic schools presents a very favourable picture of the progress of the students who attended the convent school in Conception Harbour. The report is useful, too, in that it mentions the number of sisters teaching in the school. Conception Harbour School had a full complement of teachers, judged by the standards of those days. In 1883, ninety-two students were registered at the school with six sisters on the teaching staff. Two years later, in 1885, a severe epidemic of diphtheria raged through the settlement and a number of deaths were recorded. At the time of the superintendent's visit, only sixteen children were in school. One of the sisters, M. deSales Meehan, died that year at the age of forty-three years, but it is not known if she, too, was a victim of the diphtheria epidemic.

In 1891, a new parish priest was assigned to Conception Harbour, Father William Veitch. Father Veitch was young, energetic, enthusiastic, and not one to let any grass grow under his feet. Within five years of his arrival, a new church was under construction, and as soon as that was completed, he began work on a new girls' school that was ready for occupancy in 1899. The school superintendent, Thomas Hanrahan, was delighted. He wrote in his report:

> Present 75. A class of 16 grown girls in Sixth Standard, with algebra to simultaneous equations, geometry (Book I), Book-keeping, English Literature, vocal and instrumental music, English and Scripture History, made an intelligent examination in all subjects except Geography. English Literature was particularly strong, the class showing an intimate knowledge of the names of leading authors and their works. The lower classes did equally well according to grade. The nuns are now teaching in their new school. The classrooms are large and well-ventilated, cheerful, and exquisitely clean, affording increased facilities to

---

58. M. Philomena Walker gave this information to M. Basil McCormack when M. Basil was gathering information in preparation for writing her master's thesis in the 1950s.

the teachers and the utmost comfort and convenience to the pupils.[59]

It appears that absenteeism was somewhat of a problem in Conception Harbour, for although the superintendent reported seventy-five students present on the day of his visit, one hundred students were registered.[60]

While the sisters were busy teaching subjects in the regular curriculum, Father Veitch decided to start a program of industrial arts as a means of increasing employment opportunities for the people of Conception Harbour. He arranged for one of the graduates of the convent school, Rachael Gushue, to go to Misgauche, New Brunswick, to learn weaving so that on her return she could teach it to other young women.[61] In 1901, he purchased three hand looms and rented a building where Miss Gushue instructed thirty young women in the art of weaving. At the end of the year, the students had produced materials for carpets, blankets, sheets, towels, and homespun dress material to a total value of $130. By 1903, Father Veitch had transferred instruction in weaving to the convent school and included it as part of the curriculum. The superintendent of education approved: "This arrangement, which places an attendance of about eighty girls in touch with a valuable feature of manual training, is bound to have the effect of interesting the whole settlement in the art of weaving."[62]

Always ready to expand and improve the curriculum, the sisters purchased a typewriter. They had heard of the success of M. Joseph Fox in teaching typing at Our Lady of Mercy School and decided to introduce a similar program of instruction in Conception Harbour. It is possible that one of the sisters went to St. John's and took lessons from M. Joseph Fox at Mercy Convent to prepare herself to teach others. Six young girls expressed interest,

---

59. Thomas Hanrahan, "Report of the Superintendent of Roman Catholic Schools for the Diocese of Harbour Grace for the Year Ended June 30, 1899," p. 82, ASMSJ.

60. Ibid., p. 82.

61. McCormack, "Educational Work," p. 62. M. Basil noted that Miss Gushue later went north to teach at the Grenfell Mission at St. Anthony. One of her pupils took her place at Conception Harbour.

62. Thomas Hanrahan, "Report of the Superintendent of Roman Catholic Schools for the Diocese of Harbour Grace for the Year Ended June 30, 1902," pp. 39-40, ASMSJ.

and classes in typing began at the convent school in Conception Harbour. By the time the superintendent made his visit to the school in 1902, he was able to report that the six budding typists were making progress.[63] By 1902, the students in Conception Harbour Convent School were following the CHE curriculum, but it is not clear from the report of the superintendent if any of them registered for the examinations:

> Classified in all the Standards with the additional programme of Preliminary and Intermediate of the CHE. My examination resulted in the usual high markings. The strongest subject of the most advanced class (12 grown girls) was English history (95%). In the other subjects, including geometry (Euclid I & II) the lowest average was 72%.[64]

Like St. Joseph's Convent School in Brigus, the convent school in Conception Harbour offered a training program for girls who were interested in teaching. The school report of 1913 notes that a great number of teachers employed by the Conception Harbour School Board received their training at the convent school—this in spite of the fact that St. Bride's was recognized as the official training school for Catholic female teachers.

By this time, none of the founding sisters remained in Conception Harbour. As mentioned above, M. deSales Meehan died in 1885, and the first superior, M. Gertrude Moore, passed away in 1891. M. Teresa Slattery was transferred to Brigus at some point prior to 1902, but she returned to Conception Harbour and was appointed superior in 1916. Having completed a three-year term of office, she was transferred to St. Michael's Convent, Belvedere, where she spent the rest of her life. She died in 1931.

After the Immaculate Conception Convent was established in Conception Harbour, the community accepted several postulants, among them M. Berchmans Meehan, the younger sister of M. deSales Meehan; M. Gertrude Kennedy; M. Brigid Hoey; M. Cecilia Joy; M. deSales Galvin; and M. deSales Ahearn. These young women spent their novitiate in Conception Harbour and

63. Ibid.
64. Ibid., p. 39.

made their profession of vows in the parish church. The little cemetery in the convent garden contains five headstones with the names of sisters who died before the amalgamation of the convents in 1916. The headstones bear the names of M. deSales Meehan (1885), M. Gertrude Moore (1891), M. Agnes Banks (1893), M. Philomena Leamy (1893), and M. Cecilia Joy (1910).

By the year 1900, the railway was making regularly scheduled trips from St. John's to the towns around Conception Bay. This provided an opportunity for the sisters in Brigus and Conception Harbour to communicate more regularly with the sisters in other parts of Newfoundland. To a certain degree, this prepared the way for the amalgamation of all the Mercy convents since it allowed more sharing of ideas and resources. With the amalgamation in 1916, of course, came the sharing of personnel, as well. From that time on, the personnel of the convents changed from year to year, as dictated by the needs of each place where the sisters ministered.

In the year 1881, the new superior of Mercy Convent, M. Bernard Clune, turned her attention to the educational needs of the younger children of the city. The stages covered in her plan conformed to what today would be called preschool, kindergarten, and primary grades. On September 13 of that year, an announcement appeared in the local papers that was reprinted a month later in *The Newfoundlander*. It is worth noting that the spelling of the boarding school had been changed from St. Clair's to St. Clare's:

> The Ladies of the Convent of Mercy, Military Road, are preparing to open an Infant School for boys and girls from three to eight years old. The large room of St. Clare's is being suitably fitted up for the purpose, and henceforth will be placed very appropriately under the protection of the Angels Guardian. A great want is thus supplied. The best means will be used to make the lessons pleasing, interesting and instructive. Knowledge will be imparted chiefly by object lesson, and after a little time, the Kindergarten system so popular and successful in America will be introduced. School will be open on the 19th inst. Terms paid in advance, 10s per quarter. (September 13, 1881).[65]

---

65. *The Newfoundlander*, October 14, 1881.

The Angels Guardian School opened on September 18, 1881, and accepted both boys and girls, beginning with what would be today known as preschool, through kindergarten and up to grade IV or V. When the boys had completed grade V, they were transferred to the Christian Brothers schools; the girls moved to Our Lady of Mercy School, to the "lower school" that was located on the first floor of Mercy Convent.[66] When it opened in 1881, Angels Guardian School had an enrolment of thirty-four children. However, by September 1882, this number had doubled to sixty-eight. Sixty years later, in 1942, on the occasion of the centenary of the arrival of the Sisters of Mercy in St. John's, some of the "graduates" of Angels Guardian School sent letters of congratulation. Former student John FitzHenry mentions in his letter the names of sisters who taught him at Angels Guardian School:

> Sister Mary Francis [Slattery], vivacious and competent; Sister Mary Joseph [Fox], thoughtful and considerate; Sister Mary Madeline [Stephenson] a girlhood friend of my mother; Mother M. Liguori [Carmody] who was a stickler for discipline, and the gracious, kindly Reverend Mother Bernard [Clune] who always carried herself with a regal air which inspired respect and esteem.[67]

At the time John FitzHenry attended Angels Guardian School, M. Joseph Fox must have been a novice or a very young professed sister, for she was received into the novitiate in 1882. M. Madeline Stephenson was professed at Mercy Convent in 1876. Evidently, M. Madeline did not remain at Angels Guardian for any length of time, for she died in 1886 in Burin.

The Angels Guardian School remained in existence until October 1896. Two years later, in 1898, M. Joseph Fox opened Newfoundland's first business education school for women at Our Lady of Mercy Academy.[68] M. Joseph had

66. Hogan, *Pathways*, p. 53.
67. John J. FitzHenry to Reverend Mother General, July 29, 1942, ASMSJ, RG 1/16/4.
68. M. Joseph Fox was born in Sligo, Ireland. Her baptismal name was Mary Jane. She was accepted as a postulant at Mercy Convent in the autumn of 1881 and was received into the novitiate with M. Teresa O'Halleran in March 1882. Both novices were professed in 1884. M. Joseph Fox spent most of her religious life at Mercy Convent.

never heard of "women's lib," but she was a firm believer in the ability of women to compete on an equal footing with men as employees in the world of business. Her ambition was to introduce women stenographers and secretaries to the working world. M. Williamina Hogan, describing M. Joseph's contribution to women's struggle for equality, wrote, ". . . more than any other woman in Newfoundland [she] was responsible for thrusting women into the business world of the 20th century."[69]

M. Joseph Fox began her venture into the field of business education with five students and one typewriter. Gradually her equipment and the number of students increased. But the businessmen of St. John's were reluctant to accept the novelty of a female stenographer, still less a female secretary. A number of M. Joseph's pupils were hired as typists, a few found employment as stenographers, but it was almost ten years before any of the young women trained by M. Joseph found employment as secretaries. In April 1909, the Bank of Montreal advertised for a new stenographer/secretary, never dreaming that the all-male preserve of the banks was about to come to an end. M. Joseph persuaded the manager, Mr. Paddon, to interview one of her students, Isabelle (Belle) Kelly.[70] Mr. Paddon was so impressed that he hired her on the spot, and so Belle Kelly had the distinction of being the first woman employed by a bank in Newfoundland.[71] Not to be outdone, the Bank of Nova Scotia promptly hired not one, but two of the graduates of M. Joseph's business school. When the businessmen of St. John's saw that neither of the banks had collapsed after the unheard-of step of employing female secretaries, they were anxious to follow suit. Soon M. Joseph had all she could do to keep up with the demand for graduates from her school. Within a very short time, the business education department at Our Lady of Mercy School became known throughout Newfoundland for its excellent courses, and students came from many parts of the island to prepare for a job as stenographer or secretary. M. Joseph continued her work, taking advantage of every new technique and

---

69. Hogan, *Pathways*, p. 76.

70. Belle Kelly married Joseph Darcy in 1917. They are the parents of Brother J. B. Darcy, CFC, a well-known historian in St. John's.

71. *The Daily News*, August 7, 1917, p. 4.

method of instruction available. Soon her students were taking part in international competitions. In 1907, in competition with the British Isles and fourteen other countries, Belle Kelly, a student of M. Joseph, won the gold medal awarded by the Sloan-Duployan Society of Ramsgate, England.[72] In 1909, again in international competition, students of Mercy School won two of the five medals that were granted by the same society.[73]

The gifted director of the commercial department of Our Lady of Mercy School, M. Joseph Fox, made many friends in every walk of life, and through her connections with the business world, she was able to direct her students to jobs that they found challenging and fulfilling. Some of M. Joseph's former students are still alive, and they remember her with gratitude and affection. Inevitably, there are stories that have been handed down about her—that she ruled her adult students with "an iron hand in a velvet glove." One such story concerns her love for flowers. The commercial room at Our Lady of Mercy School was one of the brightest, most attractive rooms in the building, for M. Joseph had the hands and the soul of an artist. She knew how and where to place her flowers to the best advantage of the plants themselves and, as well, to add beauty and colour to the appearance of the room. Apparently, M. Joseph was convinced that the best medicine for an ailing plant was a hefty dose of tobacco juice. Every Friday afternoon, she dispatched two of her students to the tobacco factory, located a short distance from Mercy Convent, to procure a quantity of this "sure cure." The fact that twenty-year-old young ladies might be embarrassed to be seen toting a bucket of this evil-smelling brew through the streets of the city did not enter M. Joseph's head.[74]

When she died unexpectedly on September 1, 1930, expressions of sympathy poured in to Mercy Convent from all over Newfoundland, Canada, the United States, and England. Several lengthy tributes were published in the

---

72. Hogan, *Pathways*, p. 78.
73. *The Daily News*, July 27, 1909, p. 5.
74. This story was told to the author by her sister-in-law, Mabel Bellamy, a graduate of M. Joseph's business school.

local press, all of them acknowledging her contribution to education and to society in general:

> The passing of Sister M. Joseph Fox removes an educationist of more than usual note from our midst, one to whom the commercial life of the city owes a great deal, for three generations of stenographers and secretaries and female accountants have passed through her capable hands. She may be said to have initiated modern stenography in the city and was the first to adopt the typewriter here and train pupils in its use. Her list of successful pupils who have graduated into prominent places in the business life, not only of Newfoundland but abroad as well, must be very large and her influence has been very great.[75]

However, there was another aspect of M. Joseph's career that was remembered with appreciation and gratitude—her artistic ability in producing drawings, paintings, and illuminated addresses:

> Of Sister Joseph's work the Press has highly spoken, and all classes and creeds have approved of their eulogies. . . . But there was one particular feature of Sister Joseph's life's work that seemed to be overlooked—a feature by which she became known to the business and commercial community. It was her rare artistic skill in the etching, engrossing, and illuminating of public addresses presented to eminent people on special occasions. . . . Such documents called for delicacy of touch, and for chaste execution in their design. . . . Only people of soul can accomplish such tasks. . . . Hence it was the parchments which came from Sister Joseph's gentle touch that revealed her real self—revealed her soul.[76]

In June 1892, the Sisters of Mercy celebrated the golden jubilee of the establishment of the congregation in Newfoundland. The event seems to have had the wholehearted support of the Catholic population and particularly of the artistic community. Two weeks before the event, a lengthy write-up

---

75. *The Evening Telegram*, September 4, 1930, p. 3.
76. I. C. Morris, Ibid., September 6, 1930, p. 5.

appeared in the local press, notifying the public of the celebrations planned to mark the occasion. The writer included the information that sisters from Brigus and Conception convents would be coming to St. John's for the celebrations and staying at Mercy Convent and St. Michael's, Belvedere. Notice was given of two concerts to be presented in honour of the occasion, the proceedings of which would be donated to the building fund for a new chapel or oratory at Mercy Convent.[77]

Several years prior to the anniversary, it was decided to mark this milestone in the history of the congregation by building an oratory attached to the convent.[78] The new oratory was dedicated to Our Lady of Good Counsel; it is one of the most beautiful little chapels to be found in Newfoundland. In early July, *The Evening Telegram* carried a description of its design and architecture. In spite of the extravagance of the language, typical of the time, the writer conveyed the pride of the citizens of St. John's in the new chapel and their appreciation of the skill and artistry of those who built it:

> The beautiful oratory of the Mercy Convent was . . . built under the personal supervision of the Rev. John Scott . . . The architect of the Sisters of Mercy's oratory was Mr. John Coleman, and in it he has combined the strength and gracefulness of two chaste orders of architecture, the Byzantine interiorly, the Corinthian exteriorly. . . . The stonecutter was Mr. William Hay, whose chiseled work in stone is beautifully executed. Mr. William Ellis was the mason, and the solidity of the massive walls are a testimony to the excellence of his workmanship. Mr. Michael Stapleton did the stuccoing in a style so beautiful in its snowy sheen as to be faultless. The painting was executed by Mr. George Gamberg, his artistry appearing to conspicuous advantage, and the excellent heating apparatus (of hot water) was finished by Messrs. Gear & Co. The roofing of galvanized plates was placed on by Messers R. Callahan & Co. and most creditably finished. The various workmen have contributed their craftsmanship to a gem of

---

77. *The Evening Telegram*, June 8, 1892, p. 4.

78. Up to this time, one of the rooms on the second floor of the convent was used as a chapel. It was called the Chapel of the Blessed Virgin Mary. Since 1892, this room serves as the convent community room.

architecture which will long attest their taste, skill and good work.[79]

The ceremony of dedication of the new oratory took place on June 23, 1892, with Bishop Power officiating. Later on the same morning, solemn High Mass was celebrated by Father John Scott in the Cathedral of St. John the Baptist. Present in the sanctuary were the archbishop of Halifax, and the bishops of St. John's; Charlottetown; P.E.I.; and Harbour Grace. According to the newspapers, a considerable number of priests attended as well as the Sisters of Mercy and a large congregation of Catholics from St. John's and nearby places. The cathedral choir, under the direction of Charles Hutton, a former music student of the sisters, provided the music for the mass and for the ceremony of benediction that followed.[80]

As they looked back over the fifty years between 1842 and 1892, the sisters who gathered at Mercy Convent had reason to be thankful. From such small beginnings, the congregation now had over sixty sisters in seven convents—Our Lady of Mercy, St. Michael's, and St. Bride's in St. John's; St. Joseph's (Brigus) and the Immaculate Conception (Conception Harbour) in Conception Bay; and St. Anne's (Burin) and Sacred Heart Convent (St. Lawrence) on the Burin Peninsula. A lengthy passage in *The Evening Telegram* reviewed the history and the ministry of the Sisters of Mercy as follows:

> During the first year of its existence, from June, '42, to the 1st of May, '43, the three ladies of the Order devoted their attention to this work of mercy—visiting and consoling the sick and dying, and on the latter date their first school was opened. From this nucleus have spread branches of fifteen scholastic institutions, in full life and vigour at the present time, being an establishment of one new school in almost every three years since their foundation a half century ago. . . . The work of visiting the sick and suffering being the primal rule of their life, ladies of the various convents in the city accordingly minister in this respect to the necessities of the Inmates of the Hospitals, the Poor Asylum, the Asylum for the

79. *The Evening Telegram*, July 1, 1892, p. 4.
80. Ibid., June 23, 1892, p. 4.

Insane and the Jail; and in each they find a field of good to be done. ...As far as the limited means of their funds will allow, and often aided by the thoughtful care of charitable friends, the Sisters are enabled to give relief to the sick poor in their homes. One of the noblest labours of the Order is that of their care of female orphans. Where their faculties of benevolence are so many and unselfish, it is, indeed, difficult to pronounce which is the grandest; yet, this distinctive achievement is one of so inestimably precious a type, that it shines with lustrous brilliancy from the galaxy of good deeds which beam in the diadem of the Order of Mercy.[81]

After all the celebrations of the jubilee were over, the sisters returned to the regular routine with renewed energy and enthusiasm for the ministry entrusted to them. This was true especially for the sisters from Brigus and Conception Harbour who had so few opportunities to meet with sisters from the other communities. As they exchanged stories of their experiences and speculated about what the next fifty years might bring, they may not have been aware that very soon four Sisters of Mercy from Providence, Rhode Island, would establish a community on the west coast of Newfoundland.

---

81. Ibid., June 15, 1892, p. 4.

CHAPTER TEN

BEGINNINGS IN THE WEST

The human mind plans the way,
But the Lord directs the steps.
Proverbs 16:9

The impetus for the establishment of the Sisters of Mercy on the west coast of Newfoundland came not from the mother house of the Sisters of Mercy in Newfoundland but from a group of sisters of Providence, Rhode Island, in the United States. As far as the sisters in St. John's were concerned, the west coast of the island was a vast, little-known territory.

Many of the people who settled in western Newfoundland were French-speaking Acadians from Cape Breton, and Irish and Highland Scots from the same area.[1] The latter settled in Codroy, attracted by stories of the fertility of the soil in that region. Other settlers on the West Coast were descendents of French fishermen who came during the summer months to fish the waters of Newfoundland. Eventually some of these fishermen settled

---

1. Reverend Thomas Sears, "Report of the Missions, Prefecture Apostolic, Western Newfoundland, 1877," p. 1.

permanently, although illegally, many of them in the region of Bay St. George and the Port au Port Peninsula.[2]

While numerous permanent settlements were established all along the coast in the eighteenth and nineteenth centuries, there were no roads connecting these communities and, until the latter half of the nineteenth century, no government services. The reason for this apparent neglect by the Government of Newfoundland can be traced to centuries-old disputes between Britain and France. In 1713, the Treaty of Utrecht gave the French unlimited rights to fish off a large part Newfoundland's coast.[3] Later, the rights of the French were modified to embrace the entire eastern shore of the Great Northern Peninsula and the west coast of the island.[4]

The privileges accorded to the French by these treaties were an obstacle to Newfoundlanders who wanted control over the island's fishery and, as well, prevented the orderly growth of settlements and the development of industry. The Newfoundland government had, on many occasions, attempted to obtain greater control over the western part of the island but to no avail. After almost a century of struggling to settle what was called the "French Shore Problem," an Entente Cordiale was signed between Britain and France in 1904. According to this agreement, Newfoundland acquired complete jurisdiction over and rights to the land and territorial waters that had comprised the "French Shore," thus eliminating obstacles to the development of the region.[5]

When permanent European settlement began in western Newfoundland and for many years thereafter, no provision was made to care

---

2. Very Reverend Michael Brosnan, *Pioneer History of St. George's Diocese, Newfoundland*, ed. The Catholic Teachers Guild of St. George's Diocese (Toronto: Mission Press, 1948), p. 4. Article XIII of the Treaty of Utrecht made it illegal for the French to stay in Newfoundland "beyond the time necessary for fishing and drying of fish," quoted in Prowse, *History*, p. 258. As a result, many French-Canadians settled there. and French became the predominant language. Today some families on the Port au Port Peninsula speak only French when at home. Some of the older people have never learned to speak more than a few words of English.

3. Ibid., p. 258. According to Article XIII of the Treaty, the French were given the right to catch fish and to dry them in the area that stretches from Cape Bonavista in the east to Point Riche on the west. Commenting on this Treaty, Prowse wrote, "No condition was more disgraceful than the surrender of the Newfoundland fishery to the French." Prowse, *History*, p. 256.

4. Treaty of Versailles, 1783, see Prowse, *History*, p. 353.

5. *ENL*, s.v. "Entente Cordiale."

for the spiritual needs of the Catholic people.[6] Nevertheless, these Catholics clung to their faith with admirable tenacity and depended on the occasional visits of French and Canadian chaplains to celebrate the sacraments.[7]

Not until 1850 did Catholics on the West Coast have their first resident priest when the French-speaking Father Alexis Belanger from the Magdalen Islands arrived at Bay St. George and took up residence in Sandy Point. A small peninsula in St. George's Bay, Sandy Point, until 1951, was connected to the mainland of Newfoundland by a strip of land except at high tide when the sea covered this isthmus.[8] At the time of Father Belanger's arrival, Sandy Point was the largest year-round community on the West Coast and the principal English settlement in the area with a population of about seven hundred. Because of its central position in a bay that boasted a thriving herring fishery, it was the major port and supply centre for much of the coast.[9]

As the only resident priest in all of the West Coast, Father Belanger visited outlying places, as well as the Bay of Islands and Codroy.[10] In describing the last of these visits, Belanger's successor, Reverend Thomas Sears, noted:

---

6. The first known inhabitants of St. George's Bay were Mi'kmaq, and by the mid-1700s, the area was a major centre of Mi'kmaq activity. By 1783, there were a few settlers of Jersey extraction, and by 1800, there were about one hundred settlers in the Bay St. George area. In 1820, W. E. Cormack reported twenty families and one hundred people at Sandy Point itself. See *ENL*, s.v. "Sandy Point."

7. Brosnan, *Pioneer History*, p. 6. Father Brosnan mentions that the Canadian government occasionally sent boats to check on the lighthouses on the coast (p. 5). These boats usually carried a Catholic chaplain who ministered to the needs of the people in the area visited.

8. Eventually, the erosion caused by the sea widened the gap, making the isthmus no longer passable even at low tide, so that Sandy Point is now an island about three miles long and a half a mile wide. It is partly wooded but mostly grass meadow.

9. *ENL*, s.v. "Sandy Point." In 1872, a severe storm resulted in much destruction of homes and property on Sandy Point, so much so that, rather than rebuild their former homes, people moved across the bay, and the population of Sandy Point dropped to around four hundred people. The demise of Sandy Point was determined in the 1890s when the railway passed through the town of St. George's on the south side of the bay directly opposite Sandy Point. Within a few years, the churches, clergy residence, and schools had been moved "across the bay," and with them many of the inhabitants of Sandy Point.

10. Brosnan, *Pioneer History*, p. 10.

This poor missionary had to take up his abode in a small fishing hut on the shore. In this he spent several days, the poor people coming from different places to see him. So exhausted was he from labor that he was often known to be obliged to give up several times before he could get through the ceremonies of baptizing a few children. This was the condition in which he was when he had to undertake the voyage homewards, some one hundred miles, pent up in the uncomfortable cabin of an old schooner used in the fish trade.[11]

A few days after his return from this voyage, on September 7, 1868, Father Belanger died alone in his little log cabin at Sandy Point, thus leaving the West Coast once more without a resident priest. Bishop Mullock, aware of the critical need of the Catholics in this remote section of his diocese, immediately visited Canada to try to obtain priests to serve the region only to find that no bishop would take the responsibility of sending a priest to such an isolated area.[12] However, the parish priest of Port Mulgrave, Nova Scotia, Father Thomas Sears, offered himself for the mission and almost immediately set sail for Newfoundland, arriving in Sandy Point on December 14, 1868.[13]

Father Sears was quick to see the potential for development on the West Coast, in the fertile soil, the magnificent forests, and the rich fishing grounds just a few miles offshore. However, he deplored the lack of even the most basic government services. Shortly after taking up his duties in Newfoundland, Father Sears sent Bishop Mullock a report of his first impressions. He wrote:

It would be most desirable that the Government of St. John's do something towards establishing some sort of civil authority and something for the cause of Education on this Coast. Another great want is felt here—they have no roads, not even pathways. I

11. Ibid., pp. 10–11.

12. Ibid., p. 18.

13. Reverend Thomas Sears, "Report of the Missions, Prefecture Apostolic, Western Newfoundland, 1877," p. 15.

> hope the day is not far distant when some Government will take
> charge of the place . . . and look after the interests of the poor
> people who are now at the mercy of cupidity or caprice of heart-
> less traders or merciless petty merchants.[14]

Until 1870, western Newfoundland was attached to the St. John's diocese, but in 1870, it was constituted a prefecture apostolic, and Father Sears
named prefect apostolic with the title of monsignor.[15] Within a short time of
his arrival, he had won the trust and affection of the people. However, the
obstacles he faced would have daunted a less stalwart soul. In a report to
Rome, Monsignor Sears wrote:

> Without the aid of teachers, religious orders, or any other means
> of educating the young except through the sole efforts of the
> poor missioner, how can it be expected that his single efforts can
> do much when he has to travel several hundreds of miles to visit
> the whole of his flock, and then no means of travelling except in
> an open boat or when he chances to meet a small craft or vessel
> trading from one harbour or Bay to another. [16]

This total absence of roads and the lack of any formal civic organization
shocked the missionary from Nova Scotia. He was convinced of the necessity
of "road building as a civilizing and reassuring influence on the lives of the
people,"[17] and he was tireless in petitioning the Newfoundland legislature to
assume its responsibilities to the people on the western shore of the island. In
1881, the government realized, finally, that the residents of the West Coast
were entitled to send two representatives to the House of Assembly. After the

14. Rev. Thomas Sears to Bishop Mullock, November 29, 1868, cited in Brosnan, *Pioneer History*, pp. 29–30.

15. "The last official act performed by Bishop Mullock was to advocate with Rome the appointment of Father Sears as Prefect-Apostolic of the West." Brosnan, *Pioneer History*, p. 51. The new prefecture consisted of the whole of the western seaboard, and it extended as far as Cape La Hune on the South Coast, covering approximately five hundred miles.

16. Sears to the Society for the Propagation of the Faith, cited in Brosnan, *Pioneer History*, p. 34.

17. Ibid.

railway was completed in 1897, development of the West Coast began in earnest.[18]

From the moment of his arrival in Newfoundland, Monsignor Sears set about trying to recruit priests. To enable young men to study for the priesthood, he procured bursaries in All Hallows Seminary, Dublin; Propaganda, Rome; and several others. He received donations from the Society for the Propagation of the Faith and from friends in other parts of Newfoundland,[19] but he did not meet with much success in persuading priests to help him in his lonely mission. Some came and gave temporary assistance, ranging from a few months to a few years. Another problem was securing funds to support any priests who might come to the West Coast. However, Monsignor Sears quickly discovered that the people were prepared to make sacrifices to secure the presence of a priest. In addition to providing free labour in the construction of churches and chapels, one funding initiative of the people that became a tradition was "the day for the Church."[20] On a certain specified day, every fisherman sold his fish to the local merchant and the sale was credited to the priest. Similarly in winter, one day was set aside when all the men of the town went to the woods to cut trees to provide fuel for the presbytery and the school.[21]

The state of education was another major concern for the zealous missionary. The amount provided by the government for education in his mission was about $1,000.[22] With this paltry amount at his disposal, he was expected to build schools and pay teachers. Although schools were built, thanks to voluntary labour and the generosity of the people, the scarcity of trained teachers was a serious problem. But this was a man who was not afraid to dream. In a report to Rome, Monsignor Sears expressed his desire to attract to the prefecture a group of nuns so that he could open a school for girls: "Could we

18. Brother J. B. Darcy, "Msgr. Thomas Sears (1824–1885)," 2000, AASJ. The first passenger train made the trans-Island run in 1898. Leaving St. John's on the evening of June 29, it arrived at Port aux Basques 28 hours later. See also *ENL*, s.v. "Railway."

19. Darcy, "Sears," AASJ.

20. Ibid., p. 96.

21. Later on, the convents shared in the benefits provided by "the day for the Church."

22. Brosnan, *Pioneer History*, p. 107.

afford to establish a good seminary of instruction for females as the first beginning we would soon gain much. A convent of five or six well-educated nuns would be of the greatest importance."[23] He explained to the Society for the Propagation of the Faith that, from money left by the late Bishop Mullock, he had renovated a "fine house" for this purpose.[24] The dream was not realized in his lifetime. It was the work of his friend and successor, Reverend Michael Francis Howley, to bring a community of Sisters of Mercy to the west coast of Newfoundland.

Michael Francis Howley had been ordained to the priesthood at the Cathedral of St. John Lateran in Rome on June 6, 1868. A few months after his return to St. John's, Dr. Howley was appointed assistant to Monsignor Sears, whom he accompanied on a visitation of the prefecture of the west coast of the island. During this period, the two men formed a lasting friendship and Michael Howley began to take a keen interest in the development of the west. In 1879, he was recalled to St. John's and assigned to the cathedral parish. However, by the year 1885, the tasks involved in caring for the vast prefecture of St. George's were proving to be beyond the strength of Monsignor Sears. He asked for an assistant and recommended Dr. Michael Howley for the position, but before Dr. Howley took up his new duties, Monsignor Sears died on November 7, 1885.[25]

Dr. Michael Howley arrived on the West Coast on January 5, 1886, and in July of that year he was confirmed as prefect apostolic. Six years later, the Prefecture of St. George's was declared a vicariate. Howley was named vicar apostolic and consecrated titular bishop of Amastris on June 24, 1892, the first Newfoundlander to attain episcopal rank in the Roman Catholic Church.[26]

The new bishop was a man of brilliant intellect and with the vision and courage to initiate great and worthwhile projects. It helped, too, that his fam-

---

23. Ibid., p. 39.

24. Ibid. The house was in Sandy Point, Bay St. George.

25. Brosnan, *Pioneer History*, p. 136.

26. *ENL*, s.v. "Howley, Most Rev. Michael Francis." Titular bishops are those who have been appointed by the Holy See to a diocese which, in former times, had been canonically established but which is no longer in existence.

ily had connections with influential political and financial interests in St. John's, and Howley did not hesitate to call on these friends for assistance in furthering his efforts for the people in western Newfoundland. His priority, however, was to promote religion and education throughout the scattered population of his vicariate.[27] Shortly after his arrival, with the help of the people, he erected a pro-cathedral, and a presbytery at Sandy Point,[28] but he was acutely aware of the unrealized dream of his predecessor, to establish "a convent of five or six well-educated nuns." Help came from an unexpected source through a series of coincidences that some recognize as a direct intervention of Divine Providence.

A wealthy American lady, Mrs. Henrietta Brownell,[29] while travelling on a riverboat in Massachusetts during the mid-1880s, entered into conversation with some Sisters of Mercy, one of whom was M. Juliana Purcell of St. Xavier's Convent, Providence, Rhode Island.[30] Shortly after this, Mrs. Brownell picked up a medal of the Virgin Mary. As a Protestant, she had no use for such an object, but realizing that it might be of value to someone else, she decided to give the medal to the Sisters of Mercy who had made such an impression on her during her previous trip. Her association with the sisters, and especially with M. Juliana, soon developed into deep and lasting friendship. Henrietta Brownell was an accomplished musician and violinist. In return for the sisters' kindness to her, she offered to teach violin to any of them who were interested. The superior of the time, M. Germaine Thomey, was delighted to accept her offer. It was a decision M. Germaine was to regret, for it led

---

27. In a letter to the Society for the Propagation of the Faith, August 3, 1894, Bishop Howley reported that there were no native Newfoundlanders serving as priests in the vicariate, but the area had the assistance of six visiting missionary priests. AASJ, 106/10/2.

28. At that time Sandy Point was the centre of the Prefecture of St. George's. With the coming of the railway, Howley's successor, Bishop Neil McNeil, moved his residence and the church buildings to the south side of the bay, which became the town of St. George's, the centre of the Prefecture (later, Diocese) of St. George's.

29. According to Records of Births and Deaths for the State of Rhode Island, 1850-1860, Henrietta Brownell was born in Bristol, Rhode Island, to Stephen and Henrietta Hunt on July 2, 1855. Henrietta Hunt married a man named Pearce, by whom she had a daughter and a son. After the death of Mr. Pearce, Henrietta married Charles de Wolf Brownell.

30. Carroll, *Leaves*, vol. 3, p. 439.

to frequent contact between Henrietta Brownell and the sisters and particularly with M. Antonio Egan. In a document dated November 19, 1892, M.
Germaine wrote:

> Mrs. Brownell offered to give the Sisters violin lessons. I regret
> deeply having given her permission to teach five or six Sisters, as
> it gave Sister Antonio an opportunity of meeting her more fre-
> quently and brought Mrs. Brownell more in contact with the
> members of the Community. Sister Antonio often went to the
> parlor and remained with Mrs. Brownell without permission when
> she came to see about her pupils. Several Sisters expressed very
> strong disapproval of the familiarity that existed between them,
> but Mrs. Brownell insinuated herself into their good graces by giv-
> ing presents etc. so that these very Sisters became admirers of
> herself and Sister Antonio.[31]

Sometime during the 1880s, Henrietta Brownell was received into the
Roman Catholic Church, and in thanksgiving for the gift of faith, she resolved
to devote some of her wealth to establishing a convent in a missionary country. Mrs. Brownell discussed her plans with M. Juliana and also with M.
Antonio Egan, to whom she had taken a liking because "she fancied the Sister
resembled a daughter who had left her."[32] After M. Juliana's death in February
1888, it was M. Antonio to whom Mrs. Brownell turned for friendship and
advice:

> She confided to Sister Antonio her desire to provide the financial
> backing for a foundation of Sisters to go to a missionary land.
> Through M. Corsini Dempsey, . . . she learned of the desperate
> plight of Catholics on the West Coast of Newfoundland . . .
>   When the decision was made to establish a Convent of
> Mercy on the West, Sister M. Antonio Egan was chosen as the
> Superior of the band of four Sisters from St. Xavier's.[33]

---

31. Sister M. Germaine Thomey, statement signed before Thomas Doran, Notary Public,
November 19, 1892, Archives of the Sisters of Mercy, Providence (henceforth ASMP).
32. Notes of Bishop Harkins regarding election of 1892, Archives of the Diocese of
Providence, R.I. (henceforth ADP).
33. ASMP.

This account is an abbreviated and heavily censored version of the confusing
and turbulent period that preceded the establishment of the first Mercy
Convent in western Newfoundland. Although there are many gaps, it is possible to trace the sequence of events preceding the foundation in Sandy Point.
The story begins with M. Antonio Egan.[34]

Elizabeth Egan was born in England on December 5, 1852. At the age of seven
or eight she came to the USA with her father, brothers, and a sister and lived
there with an aunt who raised the children. On May 20, 1868, at the age of fifteen years, Elizabeth Egan entered the convent of the Sisters of Mercy at St.
Xavier's, was professed on January 1, 1871, and given the name Mary Antonio.
At the chapter of elections of 1886, the sisters elected her as superior by a
majority of votes, but she was unwilling to accept the office and M. Thomasine
O'Keefe was appointed.[35]

In 1888, another election was held at St. Xavier's, and once more M.
Antonio Egan was elected mother superior.[36] This time she accepted the decision of the community and was prepared to assume the responsibility, but the
bishop of the diocese, Bishop Harkins, intervened. He refused to confirm the
election and ordered the sisters to hold a second and then a third vote, but in

34. Most of the information on events concerning M. Antonio Egan and M. Corsini Dempsey
was found in the Archives of the Diocese of Providence, R.I., and in letters and depositions
preserved in the Archives of the Sisters of Mercy of Providence. I am indebted to Rose Marie
Rocha, RSM, archivist for the Sisters of Mercy of Providence, R.I.; to Veronica Lima,
archivist for the Diocese of Providence; and to Edward Halleran of Providence for much of
this information.

35. Ibid., The entry for August 1886, contains the following statement, "M. M. Thomasine
O'Keefe appointed. Sr. M. Antonio Egan having the plurality of votes was first appointed but
refused to take the responsibility. The above mentioned had the next numbers." ASMP.

36. Sister M. Matthew, provincial of the Sisters of Mercy of Rhode Island, to the mother general of the Union of the Sisters of Mercy, Bethesda, Maryland, June 15, 1933. In 1888, the
Sisters of Mercy in Providence were a diocesan congregation. The major superior, or reverend mother, was elected at a chapter over which Bishop Harkins presided. Other convents
in the diocese each had a local superior who supervised the ordinary transactions of the
community, but who was ultimately responsible to the reverend mother in St. Xavier's. It
appears that M. Antonio's election was for the position of reverend mother. I am indebted to
Rose Marie Rocha of the Sisters of Mercy of Providence for this information.

spite of the bishop's opposition, M. Antonio Egan continued to receive a plurality of votes. The bishop, however, was adamant in his refusal to confirm M.
Antonio's election and appointed another member of the community, M.
Mechtilde Brennan, to the office of superior. Bishop Harkins made notes outlining the sequence of events, giving his reason for refusing to confirm the
election: "She (M. Antonio Egan) was certainly unqualified for the office of
Superior."[37] Some of the sisters in the community felt that the bishop had overstepped his authority and wrote to Rome complaining of his actions.
Apparently, no reply was sent to the sisters, but sometime later, in a letter to
the current superior, M. Mechtilde Brennan, Bishop Harkins stated that he had
received a communication from Rome supporting his right to refuse confirmation of the election.[38] One of the sisters of the community described the
unhappy affair as follows: "Some years later, she (M. Antonio) was again elected Superior of St. Xavier's; but the bishop, who was an Irishman, would not
accept her. It is said that after this she was sent to another house with all the
cranks."[39] A document found in the Mercy archives at Providence suggests that
the house "with all the cranks" was St. Mary's Seminary, Bayview.[40] A less
biased reading of contemporary accounts suggests that M. Antonio's friendship
with Henrietta Brownell was the bone of contention between M. Antonio and
the superior, M. Germaine Thomey, and was the main reason for the bishop's
refusal to confirm her election as superior.[41]

These were the days when any kind of real friendship with another community member or a professional colleague was prohibited. There was a puzzling inconsistency in the religious formation of individuals that, on the one

---

37. Notes from Bishop Harkins regarding elections, ADP.

38. Bishop Harkins to Mother M. Mechtilde, March 7, 1893, ADP.

39. ASMP. The writer of this comment assumes, unfairly, that Bishop Harkins' refusal to
accept the results of the election came from the Irishman's dislike of the English-born M.
Antonio Egan.

40. "In September 1888 Sr. M. Antonio Egan was changed from the Convent at Fall River
where she had been local Superior, and sent to the Seminary." Deposition of Sister M.
Thomasine O'Keefe regarding Sister M. Antonio Egan, ASMP.

41. Matthew Harkins, "Report of the 1888 Election of the Superior." Although it is not dated,
it must have been written late in 1888 or 1889, for in it, the bishop refers to the election of
"last July," ADP.

hand, spared no expense or effort in fostering the spiritual and intellectual development of the individual but, on the other hand, totally ignored the whole area of human relationships and the need for emotional and psychological maturity. The young religious was taught that, although charity was the greatest of virtues and was to be cultivated beyond all others, this kind of charity meant "a nonemotional, general acceptance of and benign affection for all other members among whom, ideally, no distinctions were to be made."[42] Unlike Catherine McAuley, who certainly had close friends both within and outside the circle of her religious community,[43] the superiors who succeeded her either forgot or were unaware that friendship is not only natural but also important to the psychological health of individuals. The fact that one has a few close friends does not detract from the love and loyalty that a religious owes to every member of the community—and to associates and colleagues as well. Fortunately, most sisters realized this very early on in their religious life and, ignoring the taboos and restrictions, quietly formed wonderful friendships both within and outside religious life, friendships that were essential to their maturity as social and professional persons. Today the harsh rules and regulations of the past that governed the relationships of religious with other persons have been discarded in favour of a more realistic, healthy attitude.

However, for poor M. Antonio Egan, this more enlightened stance had yet to be developed. Her friendship with Henrietta Brownell was regarded by her superiors with frowning suspicion:

> On July 23rd, 1889, I took charge of the Community and the following August brought Sister Antonio from St. Mary's Seminary, Bayview, to the Mother House for the purpose of checking as much as possible the great intimacy that existed between herself and Mrs. Brownell by restricting the visits of the latter. [44]

---

42. Sandra M. Schneiders, *Selling All, Commitment, Consecrated Celibacy, and Community in Catholic Religious Life* (New York: Paulist Press, 2001), p. 245.

43. For example, Catherine McAuley's friendship with M. Frances Warde and her reliance on the support and advice of her friends, Fathers Armstrong and Blake, are endearing features of her character.

44. Statement of Sister M. Germaine Thomey, November 19, 1892, ASMP.

Documents obtained from the archives of the Sisters of Mercy of Providence and of the Diocese of Providence show that although M. Antonio had friends and supporters among the sisters, these did not include the bishop's hand-picked superior and other senior members of the community. Apparently, M. Antonio's every action was scrutinized and notarized reports sent to Bishop Harkins.[45] However, to be fair to Bishop Harkins and the superiors of the Mercy community, it appears that they were quite sincere in their opinion that M. Antonio's friendship with Henrietta Brownell had overstepped the limits set by convent rules and regulations of the time. It was alleged, also, that the time the two friends spent together was to the detriment of M. Antonio's religious and professional duties.[46] In retrospect it seems that, on the one hand, the bishop and the superiors overreacted to the situation and, at the same time, the experience of being mistrusted—and probably misjudged—served to increase M. Antonio's reliance on the support and encouragement of her friend. Eventually she became so distraught that she considered leaving religious life altogether, and it appears that Henrietta Brownell encouraged her to do this by offering her a home with the Brownell family.[47] But God had other plans for M. Antonio Egan. Perhaps through these long years of doubt and suspicion, God was fine-tuning the character of this gifted woman to prepare her for the greatest challenge of her life—the founding of a convent of the Sisters of Mercy on the west coast of Newfoundland.

Through all these troublesome times, there was in the Mercy community of Providence a sister who, although Irish by birth, had lived in St. John's, Newfoundland, for some years before her family moved to the United States. This young lady, whose baptismal name was Kate Dempsey, entered the Sisters of Mercy in Providence on August 18, 1865. At her reception into the

---

45. Bishop Harkins' file in the Archives of the Diocese of Providence, R.I. contains four statements witnessed by Thomas F. Doran, Notary Public, that were made by members of the Providence Sisters of Mercy relating to the relationship of M. Antonio Egan and Mrs. Brownell.

46. Ibid.

47. Deposition of M. Thomasine O'Keefe regarding Sister M. Antonio Egan, ADP.

novitiate she was given the name Mary Corsini. After her departure from St. John's, M. Corsini kept in touch with her Newfoundland friends and, through their letters, she learned of the needs of the people of western Newfoundland where Bishop Howley was vicar apostolic. When M. Corsini Dempsey approached Henrietta Brownell with the idea of establishing a convent of the Sisters of Mercy in the missionary territory of western Newfoundland, Mrs. Brownell was delighted.[48] On November 17, 1892, M. Corsini wrote to Bishop Howley and outlined a proposal for the establishment of a convent in his vicariate.[49] Unlike other foundations made by the Sisters of Mercy, it appears that the impetus for the foundation in western Newfoundland came solely through the initiative of a few individual sisters rather than by a decision of the community. There is no doubt, however, that the foundation in Sandy Point was made with the permission, if not the encouragement, of the religious superiors of the sisters who volunteered for the mission.

For Bishop Howley, M. Corsini's letter of November 17, 1892, was indeed, an answer to prayer. As soon as the Advent and Christmas celebrations were over, he travelled to the United States. In his diary, the bishop noted that he visited Mrs. Brownell on January 31, 1893, and discussed arrangements for the new convent.[50] He met the sisters who had volunteered for the mission and called on Bishop Harkins of Providence to discuss the process of transferring the sisters from one jurisdiction to the other.[51] A few days later, Bishop Howley, Mrs. Brownell, M. Antonio, and M. Corsini signed an agreement about the new convent and the bishop noted, "Mrs. Brownell made over to me Bonds and Bank deposits amounting to $11,858.44."[52]

Having concluded all the business connected with the new foundation, Bishop Howley hurried back to Newfoundland, leaving M. Antonio Egan to deal with the legalities of removing herself and the other three volunteers from

48. See n. 34 of this chapter.
49. M. F. Howley, "Notes of Correspondence," November 21, 1892, AASJ, 106/12/3.
50. M. F. Howley's Diary, January 31, 1893, AASJ, 106/12/3.
51. Ibid., February 1, 1893. See also Bishop Harkins' Diary, February 1, 1893, ADP.
52. Ibid., February 4, 1893.

the Diocese of Providence to the Vicariate of St. George's. Apparently, Bishop Harkins complained that M. Antonio had not given him a formal statement of her intention to leave his diocese, for on February 14, 1893, she wrote to him as follows, "You will kindly pardon my delay in notifying you of my intention of going on the Foundation, preparing to leave your Diocese. I supposed at first that my informing the Reverend Mother was sufficient. . . . Your unlimited consent about the Sisters leaving, of course included me."[53] A month later, M. Antonio sent Bishop Harkins the names of those sisters who were accompanying her on the mission. She wrote:

> Rev. Mother has notified you of the Sisters who wish to go to Bishop Howley. I should have written before this but was obliged to delay as there was one Sister from whom I expected an answer to a letter I had written to her on the subject. Now I consider the matter closed with her and can only add my name to those you have already received, Sr. M. Corsini, Sr. M. Veronica, Sr. M. Sylvester, Sr. M. Antonio.
> Bishop Howley told me you have given your consent that four or five might go to him as they so wished. I feel sure, my Lord, that you will believe me when I say that I have not influenced the Sisters in this matter. On the contrary, I have put before those who did not know the place the hardships and privations they might expect. I trust time will prove that our motives and intentions are for the greater glory of God. Should you kindly feel an interest in our welfare and be pleased to hear of us, may you hear with truth that we are striving to become perfect religious. [54]

But there was no satisfying this bishop. In spite of the conciliatory tone of the letter quoted above, Bishop Harkins complained that M. Antonio was proceeding without the necessary authority. M. Antonio quickly set matters straight:

---

53. M. Antonio Egan to Bishop Harkins, February 14, 1893, ADP.

54. M. Antonio Egan to Bishop Harkins, March 12, 1893, ADP. The sister from whom M. Antonio expected an answer was probably M. Vincent Sullivan, whose name appears in error on a list of sisters who came to Newfoundland in 1893. This document is kept in the Archives of the Sisters of Mercy of Providence.

It was not the case that you stated all the conditions referred to at Visitation. I applied in the name of several Sisters for permission to leave the Community: 1st through the Vicar General, 2nd personally, and 3rd through Bishop Howley, receiving permission in all instances, the first being conditional that another Bishop should receive us, etc. Bishop Howley certainly understood that he had your full consent and that the matter was quite settled. [55]

Apparently, M. Antonio Egan was beginning to lose patience with the petulant prelate.

For his part, Bishop Howley was fully aware of the difficulties being put in the way of his little band of missionaries. On May 9, a week before the above letter was written, Howley wrote to Bishop Harkins as follows:

In my interview with your Lordship last winter concerning the transfer of the Nuns who had consented to come to my Mission, your Lordship stated that you would procure all the necessary papers drawn up in due canonical form to be signed by all parties concerned. As the Sisters informed me that they would not be able to leave the Diocese till the end of the Educational Year in June, I promised to go to fetch them at that time, and I thought it would be time enough then to sign the documents and that by that time your Lordship would have them all prepared.

Some time ago I received a letter from Sr. Antonio enclosing a copy of a paper sent to her by the Rev. Mother to be signed. She thought it better to submit it to me before signing. I have just written her saying I did not think there was any hurry about her signing and anyway, the document did not quite come up to my idea of what is required. It is rather harsh and unsisterly in tone and besides, does not express the true status of the Sisters in the business ...

Lest your Lordship may not have received the papers or forms of which you spoke to me, I am enclosing a form for your Lordship's consideration. It is partly adapted from the approval given some sixty years ago by the Bishop of Galway on the occasion of the foundation of the Presentation Nuns in Newfoundland.[56]

55. M. Antonio Egan to Bishop Harkins, May 16, 1893, ADP.
56. Bishop Howley to Bishop Harkins, May 9, 1893, ADP.

On the same day, May 9, Bishop Howley wrote to Reverend Mother Mechtilde Brennan:

> I hereby promise and declare that I shall make ample provision financially and in every other respect for the Sisters, so that they shall be able to carry out their good work, and shall not be a source of any anxiety to you.
>
> I also promise and agree that the Sisters, after having been transferred to my jurisdiction, shall not have any further claim of any sort whatsoever upon your Community or any other Community in the diocese of Providence.[57]

This statement was confirmed by each one of the sisters in a signed document in which they renounced all claims upon the Diocese of Providence or the Providence community of the Sisters of Mercy, as well as all rights to re-admission to the Sisters of Mercy of Providence. Because two of the four sisters who volunteered for the Newfoundland mission wanted to return to the Sisters of Mercy of Providence, the content of the documents is significant:

> I, the undersigned professed Religious of the Order of Mercy of the diocese of Providence, R.I., having been at my request released in canonical form, Chapter having been held, from the obedience which I have hitherto used to the Ordinary of the Diocese and to the Mother Superior of said Community, in order to proceed to the Community established by Rt. Rev. M. F. Howley, Vicar Apostolic of St. George's in Western Newfoundland—do hereby renounce all claims upon the said Diocese or any Religious Community therein, and all right of re-admission thereto.[58]

Meanwhile, Bishop Howley and the people of Sandy Point were working frantically to have everything in readiness for the arrival of the sisters. On June 20, construction of a new residence for the bishop began, while at the

---

57. Bishop Howley to Reverend M. Mechtilde, May 9, 1893, ADP.
58. These documents of release are preserved in the Archives of the Sisters of Mercy in Providence.

same time, his own residence was being adapted to the needs of the sisters.[59] Ten days later the bishop took possession of fifteen acres of land on the south side of the bay to which he gave name "Mount Amastris" and declared that it was to be the future site of convent, schools, church, and episcopal residence. On July 3, he left Sandy Point for Providence to accompany the sisters to Newfoundland. Immediately on his arrival, he went to visit Bishop Harkins only to discover that the latter was not at home! On July 18, Bishop Howley, accompanied by M. Antonio Egan, M. Corsini Dempsey, M. Veronica Payne, M. Sylvester Carver, and Mrs. Brownell sailed from Boston on the *Olivette*, and after a six-day stopover in Halifax, they boarded the SS *Harlow*, arriving in Sandy Point on Friday, July 28.

The four missionaries must have been delighted with their first sight of this new land. *The Evening Telegram* of August 12 provided a glowing description of their arrival:

> The beautiful and picturesque settlement of Sandy Point was all en fete on Friday, July 28th in preparation for the reception of the Right Rev. Bishop Howley with the first installment of the Sisters of Mercy.... The noble outline of the lofty mountains, rising in rich purple on either side, seemed to vie with the far-famed scenery of the Bay of Naples ...
>
> As the steamer neared the wharf a great crowd gathered, and salvoes of guns were heard on every side. The line of procession from the wharf to the Bishop's residence (where the nuns are to be temporarily located) was spanned by several arches of evergreens ... and decorated with wreaths, mottoes and flags, among which the tri-colour of France was particularly conspicuous ...
>
> The nuns will take charge of the public school immediately after vacation, and will very soon open a branch for higher education. The site for the new Convent, to be named Mount Amastris, is on the south side of the harbour, and preparations for the building will be commenced during the coming winter, so that

---

59. In an entry in his diary, June 20, 1893, Bishop Howley wrote: "Started to build a new house on Sandy Point—preparing my own for reception of Nuns." AASJ, 106/10/2.

by the time the railway shall have been finished, it is hoped the new building will be fully completed.[60]

During the few weeks after their arrival, the sisters had an opportunity to meet the people, visit the sick and elderly, and prepare to open their school. Many years later, one of the sisters who was living with both M. Antonio and M. Corsini recorded their memories of these early days:

> On arrival at Sandy Point the Sisters received a whole-hearted welcome, but the festivities were soon over and the Sisters found themselves face to face with the stern difficulties of mission life in a new and poor country. The out-look was far from bright. The tyrannies of the "Treaty Days" had killed all initiative in the people and the children were imbued with a spirit of apathy inherited from parents who had known only the harder side of life. The contrast between the school environment of Sandy Point and that of Providence, R. I. can be better imagined than described. The inadequacy of the school building which was but a small rude structure serving also as a Church, and the lack of modern equipment were by no means the only obstacles in the way of progress.
>
> Whilst among the settlers there were several families of educated people whose industry and enterprise had placed them in comfortable circumstances, yet the majority were poor and many were destitute; consequently the greater number of the children who filled the schools were ill clad and underfed. Many were without even the most rudimentary knowledge of their Faith. There were difficulties connected with language, too; the children of French extraction spoke a dialect which was neither French nor English but a sort of "patois" very difficult to understand, and this did not facilitate the work of instruction. But the Sisters were undismayed. Under their skillful management things began to improve.[61]

---

60. *The Evening Telegram*, August 12, 1893, p. 4. In light of the references to the Bay of Naples and the style of writing, it is interesting to speculate whether Bishop Howley himself wrote this description of the arrival of the sisters.

61. M. Fintan Downey, "Jottings from the Annals of St. Michael's Convent, St. George's," ASMSJ. M. Fintan suggested that either M. Agnes Doyle or Margaret Mary Collins was the author of this account.

When school opened in September, about fifty children presented themselves to be taught. All instruction was in English, and that posed a difficulty for most of the young scholars. However, the sisters managed to devise ways of communicating with their students, and slowly, month by month, the academic level of the children improved. Besides the usual academic subjects of the day, great attention was paid to music, painting, and needlework—plain and fancy. The latter courses, painting and needlework, were the domain of M. Corsini Dempsey. Many years later, M. Corsini taught art at St. Michael's College, St. George's, and the design and colour of her exquisite embroidery were unequalled anywhere in the country.[62]

For the first few years after the sisters' arrival in Sandy Point, it was Mrs. Brownell's custom to come to Newfoundland for the winter months while her husband, Charles, was in Florida. Apparently, she lived in the convent with the sisters—an arrangement that may have been necessary in the circumstances, but one that was most unusual, to say the least! Mrs. Brownell shared in the work of the mission by teaching violin, piano, and painting. In addition, she taught singing to groups of schoolchildren and trained and directed a choir for the church.[63] Within the first year of their arrival, Mrs. Brownell and the sisters had prepared the children to present a concert:

> On Wednesday . . . we were treated to a very successful musical and dramatic entertainment by the children of the nuns' school, the programme being filled out by some assistance from some of the young men and ladies of the place.
> The performance of the children was altogether of a superior quality. Indeed, the universal verdict was, that considering the short time the school has been under the charge of the Sisters, and the very juvenile ages of the youngsters, it was simply won-

---

62. Hogan, *Pathways*, p. 254.

63. Monsignor Roderick White told the author that his father sang in Mrs. Brownell's choir. For the celebration of midnight mass of Christmas 1893, the convent piano was carried to the church. Mr. White recalled that it was returned to the convent immediately after mass at two o'clock on a snowy winter's morning!

derful. . . . The musical portion of the performance was under the
management of Mrs. Brownell.[64]

The program consisted of a number of choruses, skits, and recitations performed by the schoolchildren. Violin duets and compositions for piano and
violin were presented by Mrs. Brownell and a Mrs. Bishop. The men of Sandy
Point, not to be outdone by either the children or the ladies, sang, danced, and
presented satirical debates on the "American Constitution" and "The French
Shore Question Settled," much to Bishop Howley's delight.

Henrietta Brownell used not only her musical talents but also her wealth
to assist the people of the area. Every year before leaving the United States, she
filled several trunks with clothing for the poor and Christmas gifts for the children. On Christmas Eve, a large tree was erected in the school, and every child
on Sandy Point received a bright, shining new toy as well as warm winter
clothing: "No child or poor person went away empty-handed."[65]

The early days were difficult for these women accustomed to the higher
living standards of the United States. The bishop's house, where they lived until
the convent was built in 1899, lacked many of the conveniences that were taken
for granted in more prosperous and developed areas of North America.
However, even in later years, M. Antonio did not allude to the loneliness or the
privations they experienced. She remembered her excitement at the coming of
the mail by dog team that was their only means of communication, for during
the winter months the ports were closed to shipping. She recalled, also, that
during the long winter evenings when there was little else to do, she passed the
hours working difficult problems in mathematics to "redeem the time."[66]

The severity of the winter and the isolation were not the only problems
faced by the new mission. By the end of their first year in Sandy Point, M.
Corsini Dempsey had convinced herself that she had made a mistake in leaving

---

64. *The Evening Telegram*, April 21, 1894, p. 4.

65. Hogan, *Pathways*, p. 252. After Mrs. Brownell's death in 1897, the sisters continued
this Christmas tradition until after the amalgamation in 1916.

66. Notes made by M. Basil McCormack in preparation for a master's thesis, *circa* 1950s,
ASMSJ, MG 2/1/331.

the community at Providence to come to Newfoundland. In spite of her signed declaration renouncing any right to rejoin the Sisters of Mercy of Providence, on July 2, 1894, she wrote to M. Mechtilde Brennan, the superior at St. Xavier's Convent, asking to be received back into the community:

> Things here have not turned out as we had hoped. There is not work for two in the school, nor is there occupation of any kind for a Sister of Mercy, visitation of the sick, etc. and it may be years ere an increase can be hoped for. . . . Now if this can be, forget, please, my willfulness and reply in charity at your earliest convenience.
>
> . . . The Sisters ere we left told us that should we desire to return we could do so. However, I know His Lordship, Bishop Harkins, would have something to say about that. I am not writing him until I hear from you.[67]

M. Corsini's statement about lack of work for the sisters is open to question. The poverty that prevailed among some sectors of the population of Sandy Point as well as the lack of knowledge of the essentials of the Catholic religion would have provided more than sufficient work for the four Sisters of Mercy in the area. However, in light of her future career, it appears that M. Corsini was gifted in the area of fine arts. Therefore, it is easy to understand why she felt there was nothing for her to do in a school where children came to learn the basic skills of reading and writing. But, whatever the reasons given for her request to leave Sandy Point after less than a year, the evidence suggests that M. Corsini had a habit of changing her mind! A report written by the superior of the convent in Valley Falls, R.I., states, "Sister M. Corsini Dempsey has a very unsettled disposition and while a member of our Community applied on different occasions for admittance to other communities."[68]

M. Mechtilde lost no time in answering M. Corsini's letter of July 2. It is clear from M. Corsini's second letter (August 21, 1894) that M. Mechtilde had refused her request to re-enter the Providence community and advised her

---

67. M. Corsini Dempsey to M. Mechtilde Brennan, July 2, 1894, ASMP.
68. Account of the problems with Sister M. Corsini, written by the superior of Valley Falls, R.I., n.d., ASMP.

to try and settle into her new surroundings. M. Corsini, however, was not prepared to take this advice. She informed M. Mechtilde of her decision to return to the United States to visit her family and asked if she might visit the convent at that time.[69]

Her first attempt to return to the Providence community having failed, M. Corsini persuaded M. Antonio Egan to write Bishop Harkins. In this letter M. Antonio explained that M. Corsini was "most unhappy" and begged the bishop to allow her to re-enter the Sisters of Mercy of Providence. The tone of this letter suggests that M. Antonio had a good deal of sympathy for M. Corsini in her distress.[70] Bishop Harkins, however, refused. He wrote, "It was good of you to write in Sister M. Corsini's behalf. But considering everything connected with the matter, I do not think it advisable that she should return to the Community of Providence."[71]

After this letter was received in Sandy Point, M. Corsini, with Bishop Howley's permission, decided to apply to the Sisters of Mercy in Missouri. Her presence in Boston in early January 1895 suggests that she left Sandy Point in late November or early December 1894, but before leaving Newfoundland she expressed her intention to visit the Sisters of Mercy in Providence.[72] This prompted Bishop Howley to write to Bishop Harkins of Providence:

> I know your Lordship is aware that Sister Corsini has not been happy here, and I am also aware that Mother Antonio has asked for her re-admission at Providence. I have not done so because I gave you my word of honour I would never ask your Lordship to take any of them back. I did, however, on her behalf, seeing her so unhappy and out of harmony with the rest, ask Bishop Tierney to take her, but he could not. Seeing, then that it was utterly impossible for her to get on here, she has decided of her own free will, and of course with my consent, to go to Missouri. On her way she will pass through Providence and there may be

69. M. Corsini Dempsey to M. Mechtilde Brennan, August 21, 1894, ASMP.

70. M. Antonio Egan to Bishop Harkins, September 17, 1894, ADP.

71. A note in Bishop Harkins' handwriting at the end of M. Antonio's letter of September 17, 1894, ADP.

72. M. Corsini Dempsey to M. Mechtilde Brennan, August 21, 1894, ASMP.

in her mind a faint hope that her former Superior or Your
Lordship may relax when she is on the spot and receive her
again. I only wish to assure your Lordship in all sincerity and
honour that I am not sending her counting on this hope. That
she must go somewhere is both her and my mature conclusion,
and as no other place nearer offers, I suppose the poor thing
will have to go out west. She is truly to be pitied. I have no fault
whatever to find in her, only firstly, I have no work for her;
2ndly, there is an insuperable incompatibility between her and
her present surroundings. I may add all the others, and affairs
generally, are going well.[73]

In January of 1895, M. Corsini, who was now in Boston, wrote to
Bishop Harkins, begging him to reconsider his refusal. When her appeal was
denied she wrote to the apostolic delegate to the United States, Archbishop
Datulla, who, in turn, interceded with Bishop Harkins on her behalf:

I have received several letters from Sister M. Corsini exposing to
me the unfortunate state she is in, having no house of her order
which she can call home. She is now in the Convent of Mercy,
Providence. Prescinding altogether from the merits of the case, I
beg Your Excellency to give the matter your kind and charitable
attention and to take such measures as may best serve to place
the poor woman in a bearable position.[74]

But even the plea of the apostolic delegate could not move Bishop Harkins.

Meanwhile, M. Corsini had been in touch with the Sisters of Mercy in
Leopolis, Missouri, to request affiliation with that community.[75] In January
1895, she was received as a visitor by the Sisters of Mercy at St. Patrick's
Convent in Fall River, where she remained for a little over two months while
awaiting a reply from the convent in Leopolis. When the letter of acceptance
arrived, M. Corsini was asked to leave St. Patrick's Convent and given money

73. Bishop Howley to Bishop Harkins, November 12, 1894, ADP.

74. Archbishop Datulla, apostolic delegate to the United States, to Bishop Harkins, May 22,
1895, ADP.

75. In her letter of August 21, 1893, to M. Mechtilde Brennan, M. Corsini mentioned that
she was going to Missouri.

to help defray the expense of travelling to Missouri.[76] Nothing is known about her attempt to join the Sisters of Mercy in Missouri except that, once more, she changed her mind, or someone else changed it for her! After three weeks, she was on her way back to St. Patrick's Convent.[77] Certainly her peregrinations during this period of her life lend credence to the superior's comment on her lack of stability.

Very little else is known about M. Corsini's troubles in the United States or, in fact, the precise cause of her leaving Sandy Point. Bishop Howley's letter of November 12, 1894, mentions that she was "out of harmony with the rest" and that "there is an insuperable incompatibility between herself and her present surroundings." M. Corsini herself wrote to Bishop Howley on June 4, 1895, and in the course of the letter she made this curious statement, "Come to Providence and learn the result to Mrs. Brownell's family of the life she has been leading."[78] This suggests that Mrs. Brownell's presence in the convent in Sandy Point did not meet with M. Corsini's approval and may have been the cause of some of her dissatisfaction.[79] In this same letter M. Corsini asked Bishop Howley, who was by this time bishop of the Diocese of St. John's, to transfer her to some convent in that diocese.[80] This letter was written when she was staying with a friend, Dr. Smith of Valley Falls, and still trying to be readmitted as a member of the Mercy community of Providence. It was another two years before M. Corsini's future was settled.[81] The exact date of her

---

76. An account of the problems with M. Corsini Dempsey, written by the superior of St. Patrick's Convent, Valley Falls, R.I., August 1895, ASMP.

77. The Mercy Convent in Leopolis, Missouri, is something of a mystery. The Sisters of Mercy in Missouri have no records of there having been a convent established there during the 1890s, although the Archives of the State of Missouri mention that there was a convent of the Sisters of Mercy in the Roman Catholic parish of St. Patrick's in Leopolis.

78. M. Corsini Dempsey to Bishop Howley, June 4, 1895, AASJ, 106/12/3.

79. Henrietta Brownell died on October 15, 1897. It may be a coincidence that M. Corsini Dempsey returned to Newfoundland in late 1897 or early 1898. Whether there was a connection between Mrs. Brownell's death and M. Corsini's return is a matter of speculation.

80. M. Corsini to Bishop Howley, June 4, 1895, AASJ, 106/12/3.

81. M. Corsini was still in Providence in August 1897, according to a letter, August 1, 1897, from M. Germaine, superior of St. Patrick's Convent, Providence, to Bishop Harkins. In this letter M. Germaine begs the bishop not to allow M. Corsini to reenter the community of Sisters of Mercy of Providence.

return to Newfoundland is not known. All that is certain is that M. Corsini came back to St. Michael's Convent at Sandy Point, settled down there—apparently quite happily—and led a long and very useful life as a member of that community. She died on December 12, 1919.[82] A week later a tribute appeared in *The Western Star*:

> Death came on Friday evening and left the Diocese of St. George's poorer for its loss of a great teacher, who for over thirty years without band or blow quietly did the Master's work among the children of the people. She had at the time of her demise reached the ripe old age of eighty-two years—years which were full of good works and Benediction. The funeral service was largely attended, some of her old pupils coming a long distance to be present.[83]

What was it that caused such unhappiness to M. Corsini Dempsey? In none of her letters does she identify any specific reason for her dissatisfaction. After the passage of so many years, perhaps it does not matter. In the end, M. Corsini put all her troubles and difficulties behind her and gave the rest of her life in dedicated service to the people of the area and to her religious community. The fact that she did this shows the power of the human spirit to overcome spiritual and psychological difficulties at a time when there was little understanding of the root causes of such conditions and, certainly, no professional help available to address the problems.

M. Corsini Dempsey was not the only member of the band of four who had trouble adjusting to missionary life in Newfoundland. The youngest of the group, M. Sylvester Carver (Alice Carver), had entered the Sisters of Mercy in Providence in 1880 and was professed as a lay sister in 1882.[84] M. Sylvester Carver was born in Halifax, Nova Scotia. At the time of the foundation in

---

82. M. Corsini was described by one of the senior sisters as "a real darling," and by one of the students, as being "a wonderful teacher but a bit on the strict side." Notes taken by M. Basil McCormack in conversation with M. Philomena Walker.

83. *The Western Star*, December 17, 1919.

84. I am indebted to Rose Maria Rocha, RSM, archivist for the Sisters of Mercy of Providence, for this information.

Sandy Point, she was about thirty-two years of age.[85] In her book, *Pathways of Mercy*, M. Williamina Hogan wrote that the severity of the Newfoundland winter was too much for M. Sylvester's frail constitution, and she returned to the United States in the late 1890s.[86] While she may have been correct in giving the reason, M. Williamina was mistaken in the approximate year of M. Sylvester's departure. As a matter of fact, M. Sylvester may have gone into a state of shock after experiencing the first Newfoundland snowstorm! An entry in the accounts book fixes the time of her departure, not in the late 1890s but barely five months after her arrival, in December 1893, for in that month the sisters spent $12 for "passage for Lay Sister."[87]

After her return to the United States, M. Sylvester made repeated but unsuccessful attempts to rejoin the Mercy community in Providence. Even when she was about seventy-eight years of age, she was still trying to be readmitted. Early in 1933, she applied to the mother general of the Union of the Sisters of Mercy in the United States who, in turn, wrote to Providence for information. A copy of M. Mechtilde Brennan's reply to the mother general has been preserved in the archives of the Sisters of Mercy of Providence:

> The foundation was made in Newfoundland in 1893 and some years later Sister M. Sylvester abandoned the Community returning to the world. After an elapse of some time she tried to return to the Providence Community, but Bishop Harkins refused to allow her to remain. After a space of several more years she again tried to return to Providence but Bishop Hickey, having consulted the records of the case kept in the Episcopal Archives, also refused.[88]

---

85. A note in the *Halifax Chronicle,* July 21, 1893, reads as follows: "Four Sisters of Mercy arrived by steamer *Olivette* . . . accompanied by Bishop Howley of Newfoundland, where they are to establish their order. Among them is a Haligonian . . . Miss Alice Carver, daughter of the late Thos. Carver, of this city."

86. Hogan, *Pathways*, p. 253. According to the accounts book of the Sandy Point Convent, M. Williamina was mistaken when she dated the time of M. Sylvester's departure.

87. Accounts Book, Sandy Point Convent, 1893, ASMSJ.

88. M. Mechtilde Brennan to the mother general, Sisters of Mercy Generalate, Bethesda, Md., June 15, 1933, ASMP. There is a discrepancy in M. Mechtilde's statement that "Some years later" M. Sylvester left the community, and the time noted in the accounts book of the Convent in Sandy Point. This can be explained by the forty-year period that had elapsed between the events of 1893 and the date of M. Mechtilde's letter to the mother general.

The phrase quoted above, "Bishop Harkins refused to allow her to remain," suggests that the Sisters of Mercy of Providence had received M. Sylvester back into the community, but Bishop Harkins intervened and dismissed her. Obviously, the bishop in those days ruled the roost! No other information on the unfortunate Alice Carver is available.

The fourth founding member of the Sandy Point community was M. Veronica Payne, who was born in Kilkenny, Ireland, and baptized Margaret.[89] She entered the Sisters of Mercy at St. Xavier's Convent in Providence on August 3, 1868, and was professed on August 15, 1871. When the opportunity arose to work in a missionary country, M. Veronica had no hesitation in volunteering to be a member of the founding group. Her life was singularly free of the turmoil that marked the early careers of her companions. A woman of deep faith and boundless charity, she was a rock of stability for the little community at Sandy Point. Her advice was sought, not only by M. Antonio Egan, but also by the children she taught, the people she visited, and even by the bishop himself.[90]

In 1895, word was received that Bishop Howley, the vicar apostolic of St. George's had been appointed bishop of the Diocese of St. John's. At this time there were only two of the original four sisters left in Sandy Point, M. Antonio Egan and M. Veronica Payne. M. Corsini Dempsey was trying to sort herself out in the United States, and M. Sylvester Carver had left permanently. Mrs. Brownell was, of course, still spending six months of the year with them. Thus, when they learned that Bishop Howley was leaving, they felt cut adrift at the thought of losing their friend and patron at a time when the future looked so uncertain. Furthermore, with the departure of Bishop Howley, the sisters in Sandy Point lost an important link with the Sisters of Mercy in eastern Newfoundland and their history. Michael Howley was closely associated with the Sisters of Mercy in St. John's not only during his tenure as curate at the cathedral but also as a boy growing

89. *The Western Star*, April 14, 1909, p. 3.
90. This information was provided by Monsignor Roderick White, whose father was about twenty years of age at the time of the foundation in Sandy Point. Mr. White knew the Sisters of Mercy well, but M. Veronica Payne held a special place in his love and esteem.

up in the city. Born in 1843, just a year after the arrival of the Sisters of Mercy in St. John's, the young Michael Howley was sent to the catholic academy that was under the direction of John V. Nugent, a close friend of the Howley family.[91] Michael Howley, therefore, would have known John Nugent's wife, Ellen Nugent, M. Francis Creedon's sister, and possibly M. Francis herself. It was in 1888, during his tenure as vicar apostolic of St. George's, while he was living in Sandy Point, that Howley's *Ecclesiastical History of the Church in Newfoundland* was published. This being so, it may be assumed that he would have discussed the history of the St. John's Mercy foundation with the members of his Sandy Point community. There are no documents in existence to show if M. Antonio or anyone in the new foundation at Sandy Point picked up on this and communicated with the mother house in St. John's. As far as we know, Bishop Howley was the thread that connected the two convents. With his departure, even this tenuous link was severed. They need not have worried. With the arrival of Bishop Howley's successor, Bishop Neil McNeil from Antigonish, Nova Scotia, a new and exciting chapter in the history of the Church on the west coast of Newfoundland was about to begin.

The new vicar apostolic of St. George's, Bishop Neil McNeil, was born in Hillsborough, Nova Scotia, in 1851. He had learned as a boy how to use his hands, for his father was a blacksmith, a farmer, and a merchant. Ordained a priest in 1879, McNeil was vicar apostolic of St. George's Diocese in Antigonish, Nova Scotia, when he was unexpectedly named vicar apostolic of St. George's, Newfoundland, in 1895.[92] One of his first decisions after arriving in Newfoundland was to move the seat of the vicariate from Sandy Point to the south side of the bay, which was soon afterwards officially renamed, St. George's. Like his predecessor, McNeil recognized that St. George's had the advantage of being directly on the railway line. He could see that when the railway was completed, St. George's would become an

91. Browne, "Michael Francis Howley," p. 260.
92. *ENL*, s.v. "McNeil, Neil."

important centre of communication for the whole area of Bay St. George. Consequently, a relatively rapid and sizeable increase in the population of the settlement could be expected, and in the bishop's mind, the church should move with the people.

Bishop McNeil lost no time putting his ideas into action. The first task was to prepare the physical foundation for the church buildings that were to be erected in St. George's. It was a huge project for the time and the place. When completed, the complex would include a church, presbytery, convent, and schools. The bishop worked alongside the men of the settlement in clearing and draining the land and set up a workshop, sawmill, and stone quarry with skills he learned as a boy in his father's forge.[93] During the initial building stages, the bishop crossed over from Sandy Point every day to join the men in their work. Eventually, he decided to move to St. George's so that he could be on hand for every stage of the construction. While waiting for his own house to be built, he lived in an apartment in a hotel owned by Captain LeRoux.[94]

In the meantime, the sisters continued teaching in the school at Sandy Point. In 1896 they were joined by Brigid Sears, their first postulant. Brigid Sears had been educated in Paris, and among her other accomplishments, she was a fine pianist and an artist.[95] Brigid had come from Ireland to visit her brother, Father Andrew Sears of the Bay of Islands, an area of the West Coast just north of Bay St. George. She knew of the Sisters of Mercy and asked to be admitted as a postulant at Mercy Convent in St. John's, but Bishop Howley, recently appointed bishop of that diocese, would not accept her.[96] Subsequently, she applied to the Sisters of Mercy in Sandy Point, where she was received with open arms. Perhaps Bishop Howley's refusal to accept her in St. John's was prompted by his interest in securing postulants for the Sandy

93. Ibid.
94. M. Xavier Wadden, "Reminiscences," circa 1956, ASMSJ, MG 2/1/328a. This "hotel" was a house large enough to accommodate businessmen who were in St. George's in connection with the building of the railway. Another source said he built a small log cabin in St. George's and he lived in this until his own house was ready. ENL, s.v. "McNeil, Neil."
95. Hogan, Pathways, p. 253.
96. ASMSJ, MG 2/1/329.

Point community. In any case, Brigid Sears completed her novitiate and was professed in St. George's on May 9, 1899. Her religious name was Mary Cecilia.[97] Sadly, her life as a Sister of Mercy was very short. She contracted tuberculosis and died on May 9, 1904, at the age of thirty-two years.[98] It was the fifth anniversary of her profession.

However, M. Cecilia Sears was not the only young lady who entered the community at Sandy Point. Jane de Bourke was admitted as a postulant on September 8, 1898. Jane came to Newfoundland from D'Escousse, Nova Scotia, to work as a housekeeper for Bishop McNeil. In Sandy Point, she met the Sisters of Mercy and promptly decided to join them. Jane was received as a novice on March 25, 1899, and given the name Teresa Joseph. Unlike her novitiate companion, M. Cecilia Sears, M. Teresa Joseph enjoyed good health and spent forty years as a Sister of Mercy. She was one of the pioneer sisters who helped weave strong and vibrant threads in the tapestry of Mercy in western Newfoundland. She died on March 26, 1942.

In the meantime, construction of the new school in St. George's was nearing completion, but the convent was still only half finished. This problem was no match for the ingenuity of Bishop McNeil. He decided to have his own house at Sandy Point towed across the ice to St. George's to provide a temporary residence for the sisters. With the aid of horse and sled and some good, strong rope, the men were successful in moving the house from its original site and onto the thick ice that covered the bay. By all accounts, it was strenuous going. When they were about halfway across, the sled became stuck on a patch of rough ice, and in spite of the herculean efforts of the men and the horses, it would not budge an inch. House and sled remained firmly impaled in the middle of the bay for two days. This posed quite a dilemma, for if the wind shifted in an easterly direction, the ice would move out the bay into the Gulf of St. Lawrence, house and sled along with it. The bishop considered his options and then turned for advice to Captain LeRoux. LeRoux sized up the situation and advised the bishop to call on every man in the community for assistance. The

---

97. Ibid.
98. Wadden, "Reminiscences," ASMSJ.

response was immediate and universal. It is said that every male within a radius of twenty miles, ranging in age from eight years to eighty, turned up to lend a hand. They pushed and shoved and finally the house began to slide slowly to its destination. Once it was established firmly on dry ground, the sisters moved in and lived there until the new convent was completed.[99]

Nothing else is recorded of the sisters' departure from Sandy Point, but the report of the school superintendent for the year 1899 confirms the fact that they moved to St. George's in the spring of that year:

> The nuns, who from the time of the establishment of the convent at Sandy Point . . . in 1893, until the spring of the present year had been teaching there, have now removed their convent and school to the south side of the harbour (St. George's). A new school, separated from the convent building, has been erected here by His Lordship, Bishop McNeil. It is 44x24 feet, with high ceilings, and has two rooms, a junior and senior department, provided with ample blackboard surface.
>
> There was a total enrolment in this school, during the year, of 75, of whom 32 were boys and 43 girls. I was pleased with the proficiency shown by the pupils, according to their different standards. Under the management of the zealous and energetic ladies in charge, this school will, no doubt, produce very gratifying results in the near future. The Mother Superioress informed me that it is her intention to have resident students a little later on. Good and ample accommodation will be provided in the new and beautiful convent now nearing completion.[100]

Once installed in their new home, the five sisters lost no time in preparing a section of the spacious building to receive the first boarding students in the persons of Sarah Blanchard of Searston and Sarah Doyle of the Codroy Valley who arrived in 1900. Incidentally, St. Michael's Boarding School was the only one of

---

99. ASMSJ, RG 10/8/13a.

100. Vincent P. Burke, "Report of the Superintendent of Roman Catholic Schools for the Year Ended December 31, 1899," p. 33, AASJ. The sisters who moved from Sandy Point into the new St. Michael's Convent and School were M. Antonio Egan, M. Corsini Dempsey, M. Veronica Payne, M. Cecilia Sears, and M. Teresa Joseph de Bourke.

its kind in Newfoundland outside St. John's. One suspects that most of the work of caring for the physical comfort and material needs of the boarders was assigned to M. Teresa Joseph de Bourke, who had been professed as a lay sister.

Over the years the boarding school recorded a small but steady growth in the number of girls requesting admission. The numbers varied from year to year, ranging from about an average of fifteen in the early 1900s to a maximum of forty-nine in later years.[101] Initially, the boarders attended school with the boys and girls from St. George's and the surrounding area, but in later years they attended classes in the convent while the day students attended the nearby St. Joseph's School, also under the direction of the sisters.[102] The schools were the recipients of glowing reports by the superintendent of Roman Catholic schools after his yearly inspection. For instance, in 1900 the following report was published:

> Convent St. George's. Taught by an efficient and zealous staff of teachers who are doing excellent work. This school continues to advance rapidly and the progress made during the year is very marked. Reading has improved considerably. The French element being so large, the Sisters have much uphill work, as English is the language taught in the school. Enrolled, 62; present 40 (of whom two are resident students) classified in Standards I–V.[103]

In 1901, M. Antonio Egan was satisfied that the students were ready to enter the CHE examinations. This decision prompted a comment by the superintendent of schools, "The language of the school is English, a tongue foreign to the majority of the pupils. That such an advance could be made in the short space

---

101. Annals, St. Michael's Convent, St. George's, ASMSJ, RG 10/8/ 4.

102. In the absence of any documentation, it is impossible to be precise about when a separation was made between the boarding school and the day school. M. Michael Power said that when she went to St. Michael's as a boarder in 1935 there were three classrooms in the convent in which the boarders attended classes. The school comprised three rooms, a junior room, a senior room, and a commercial room. Commercial students included young women and men from St. George's as well as the boarders. Other students who lived in or near St. George's attended the day school. Still later, in the 1950s and '60s, boarders and day students (boys and girls) attended the senior high school classes in the convent.

103. Vincent P. Burke, "Report of the Superintendent of Roman Catholic Schools for the Year Ended 1900," p. 65, AASJ.

of two years is indeed a matter which may warrant one in predicting brilliant results . . . in the not too far distant future."[104] By the year 1906, St. Michael's Academy, St. George's, was ranked by the superintendent of schools as being among the best in the outports.[105] In the following year, 1907, the enrolment at St. Michael's Academy had reached one hundred. In the CHE examinations the students received honours in arithmetic, algebra, bookkeeping, shorthand, and typewriting, with one student placing first in Newfoundland in typewriting.[106] That same year the superintendent, Vincent P. Burke, advocated the establishment of Teachers' Guilds of Normal School Institutes, citing the successful teachers' convention held at St. Michael's by Bishop McNeil that same year.[107]

In the year 1905, the St. George's community accepted two more postulants. Both young women were from St. John's, Ellen Holden and Stella Wadden. They had heard of the shortage of sisters on the West Coast, and decided to offer themselves to the mission. M. Francis Holden and M. Xavier Wadden were received in 1905 with the distinction of being the first two Newfoundlanders to join the Sisters of Mercy in St. George's.[108] The following year one of the first boarding students of St. Michael's, Sarah Doyle, and another young lady from St. John's, Mary Doyle, came to St. George's asking admission to the community. Sarah Doyle became M. Dominic,[109] and Mary Doyle

---

104. Ibid., 1901, p. 70.

105. Ibid., 1906, p. 17.

106. Ibid., 1907, p. XI.

107. Ibid. This was not the first meeting of Catholic teachers but it was the first Catholic teachers' convention.

108. While collecting material for her master's thesis (1955), M. Basil McCormack noted that, previous to going to St. George's, M. Francis Holden had entered the community of St. Michael's Convent, Belvedere, as a lay sister and stayed for a short time before leaving. I have found no confirmation of this. M. Francis was professed as a choir sister in St. George's and was known as a successful teacher in many places throughout Newfoundland.

109. Sarah Doyle was admitted as a postulant at St. George's in November 1906 and given the religious name, Mary Dominic. She died in 1924. According to her obituary, M. Dominic Doyle spent her life teaching the children of the poor. She was the last sister to teach in St. Vincent's School in St. John's before it closed. Many years later, one of M. Dominic's grandnieces, Sylvia Doyle, became a Sister of Mercy and received the religious name, Mary Dominic, in memory of her great-aunt. Later on, in 1973, Sylvia resumed her baptismal name. After retirement, Sylvia worked in pastoral care at McAuley Convent and at St. Patrick's Mercy Home. At the time of writing, she is preparing for ministry in Stephenville Crossing.

was given the name M. Agnes. In the same year, 1906, M. Antonio Egan having completed almost thirteen years as superior of the community, felt it was time for a change. Accordingly, Bishop McNeil made the wise decision to appoint M. Veronica Payne as superior.[110]

The new superior was a woman of remarkable courage and strength. In the first difficult years of the foundation in Sandy Point, she saw the departure—and return—of M. Corsini Dempsey, the departure of M. Sylvester Carver, and the death of the sisters' friend and supporter, Henrietta Brownell, in October 1897.[111] For M. Antonio Egan, M. Veronica was like a solid rock of perseverance and loyalty when everything else seemed to be falling apart. She endeared herself to bishop, priests, and people, and her kindness to and compassion for the poor was known throughout the entire region. She witnessed the great social changes that had occurred since her arrival in 1893—the coming of the railway and the move from Sandy Point across the bay to the new St. Michael's Convent in St. George's. She was part of the celebrations when, in 1905, the prefecture was elevated to a diocese, the Diocese of St. George's, and she assisted M. Antonio Egan in the opening and subsequent operation of a boarding school for young women of the West Coast in 1899. M. Veronica was not only an extraordinarily kind woman, she was also an astute leader, quick to recognize the special abilities of both students and sisters. Consequently, soon after the musically talented M. Xavier Wadden had been professed in 1908, M. Veronica made arrangements for her to continue her studies in the Conservatory of Music in Montreal so that the students at St. George's would have the advantage of first-class instruction in music.

M. Veronica Payne barely completed her three-year term of office as superior. She became ill and died on Good Friday, April 9, 1909, when the

110. The usual term of office for a superior was three years with the possible re-election for another three. After this, another sister had to be elected to the office. However, in the case of new foundations, this rule was relaxed.

111. *The Providence Visitor*, October 17, 1897, contains a short obituary of Henrietta Brownell. She died suddenly in Providence, R.I., on October 15, 1897, while making preparations to sail for Newfoundland. Some weeks after her death, her trunks, containing gifts for the children of Sandy Point, arrived in the settlement. The sisters distributed these gifts according to Mrs. Brownell's wishes.

priests of the diocese were in St. George's for the Holy Week ceremonies. It is said that during her last hours Bishop McNeil remained by her bedside until she died.[112] She was buried on Easter Sunday in the sisters' cemetery in St. George's. An editorial in *The Western Star* paid tribute to the deceased sister:

> One of the sweetest and most lovable women in Newfoundland passed peacefully away at St. George's after a life of unselfish devotion to the cause of religion and humanity.
>
> Reverend Mother Veronica came to St. George's from the United States where she had been superior of various convents. She was born in Kilkenny, Ireland, her worldly name being Payne, and was a member of an old and highly connected family in the green isle. She brought to the West Coast a zeal for teaching, combined with some of the noblest of feminine traits which has borne fruit in the present splendid condition of Catholic education at St. George's.
>
> Mother Veronica was loved by all classes. All creeds and denominations respected her for a good and true woman whose life had been devoted to the task of making the world a better place to live in and the prospect of eternal happiness more alluring to frail humanity.
>
> There were many sad and sorrowful hearts in St. George's Sunday when all that was mortal of this noble woman was laid to rest to await the final summons into eternal glory. To her associates in religion and to the bereaved community of St. George's the STAR extends its sincere sympathy.[113]

The death of M. Veronica Payne left the community with only two of the original group of four sisters who had arrived in Sandy Point in 1893, M. Antonio Egan and M. Corsini Dempsey. The other four sisters at St. Michael's Convent were M. Teresa de Bourke, M. Agnes Doyle, M. Xavier Wadden, and M. Francis Holden.

In 1911, a new wing was added to St. Michael's Convent to provide more accommodation for boarding students. At the same time, the day school

---

112. Monsignor Roderick White, conversation with author, May 16, 2002. Monsignor White's father recalled that Bishop McNeil admired M. Veronica and was very distressed by her death.

113. *The Western Star,* April 14, 1909, p. 3.

was enlarged. M. Fintan Downey, who was a student-boarder at the time, recalled that prior to these renovations, St. Michael's Convent had no modern facilities such as hot and cold running water. Water had to be carried from the "Bishop's Well" and heated on the huge stove in the kitchen. This was the same stove in which M. Teresa de Bourke baked dozens of loaves of bread—so delicious that students of St. Michael's remembered "Sister Teresa's bread" for the rest of their lives. M. Fintan spoke often of the kindness of M. Agnes Doyle who, on cold nights, used to bring hot gruel to every one of the students after they had retired for the night. Renovations to the convent were completed during the Christmas vacation of 1911, so that in January 1912, the students returned to a warm and comfortable house.[114]

Every year students were given a rigorous preparation for the CHE examinations. M. Corsini Dempsey's students entered the advanced needle-work examinations set by the CHE and won several prizes for their entries in Professor Nicholl's art exhibition in St. John's.[115] Besides providing a good education to the children of the region, St. Michael's trained future teachers for the Catholic schools in western Newfoundland.[116]

Meanwhile, in 1904, the Vicariate of St. George's had undergone a significant change when the Catholic Church in Newfoundland became an independent ecclesiastical province. Coincidental with this change, the vicariate[117] was elevated to the status of a diocese, and Bishop Neil McNeil became bishop of St. George's. For the clergy and people of the new diocese this "promotion" was something like the proverbial "kick upstairs," for it had serious finan-

---

114. M. Fintan Downey, "Recollections," ASMSJ.

115. Professor Nicholls, RDS, FSA, was the official delegate for Newfoundland to the Third International Art Congress and Exhibition held in London in 1915. He organized art exhibitions in St. John's. The superintendent's report of 1921–22 made special mention of the art exhibition held every year at St. Michael's Academy, St. George's. ASMSJ, MG 2/1/318.

116. McCormack, "Educational Work", p. 92. McCormack cites "Annual Report of the Department of Education, 1921–22."

117. Vicariate apostolic was the name given to an ecclesiastical administrative district under the jurisdiction of a bishop. In 1904, when the Ecclesiastical Province of Newfoundland was established, it consisted of the Archdiocese of St. John's, the Diocese of Harbour Grace, and the Diocese of St. George's.

cial implications for this underdeveloped region of the country. Prior to 1904, the Vicariate of St. George's was looked upon as missionary territory and thus entitled to a certain degree of support from the Society for the Propagation of the Faith.[118] As a diocese, however, it was expected to be self-sufficient.[119] By skillful management and sound financial practices, Bishop McNeil was able to continue to provide schools and churches to meet the needs of the growing population of the area, but the problem of adequate financing was an ever-present headache for many years.

Year after year, the bishop continued to endear himself to the people. The people loved and respected him as a simple, humble man who was equally at home in the stone quarry, in the classroom, or in the company of the learned and wealthy. "An amateur mathematician and astronomer, Neil McNeil had a keen interest in technology. He is said to have brought the first flashlight, the first gasoline motor, the first electrical installations, and the first modern plumbing to the West Coast."[120]

In 1910, Bishop McNeil received word that he had been appointed archbishop of Vancouver, British Columbia.[121] McNeil had no idea that he was being considered for this position, and it was with a heavy heart that he accepted Rome's decision.[122] The Sisters of Mercy and the people of the diocese were stunned by the announcement, and it was with a great deal of sadness and disappointment they prepared to say goodbye to their popular and talented leader.

Although the people of St. George's diocese were convinced that there could never be another like Bishop McNeil, they were pleasantly surprised when the news came that the former parish priest of Harbour Breton,

---

118. The Society for the Propagation of the Faith is an international association established in Lyons, France, in 1822. Its objective is to provide financial assistance to priests, brothers, and nuns engaged in preaching the Gospel in missionary countries.

119. I am indebted to Monsignor Roderick White for this information.

120. *ENL*, s.v. "McNeil, Neil."

121. Two years after his appointment to Vancouver, Archbishop McNeil was named archbishop of Toronto, Ontario. He died in Toronto in 1934.

122. I am indebted to Monsignor Roderick White for this information. Monsignor White heard the story from his father.

Father Michael Power, was to be their new bishop. At the time of his episcopal ordination, Bishop Michael Power was only thirty-four years of age.
He realized that he was succeeding men of outstanding ability and dedication. As he took stock of his diocese, the youthful bishop realized that his
most urgent task was to attract priests to the area. He was successful beyond
anything he had anticipated. Within a few years a number of youthful, energetic priests had arrived, among them the Newfoundlanders, Walter
Brennan, a native of Bay Roberts in Conception Bay, and John Kirwan, with
two Irishmen, Michael Brosnan and Michael O'Reilly, who later became
bishop of the diocese.

By this time St. Michael's Boarding School was known up and down the
shores of the West Coast and beyond. Girls came from different sections of
western Newfoundland to stay at St. George's. Codes of conduct were established to which the boarders were expected to adhere. M. Veronica Payne, and
the Newfoundland-born sisters were happy to turn a blind eye to occasional
lapses in deportment, but M. Antonio Egan and M. Corsini Dempsey had the
reputation for being strict.[123] For example, one of the most exhilarating winter sports in Newfoundland was tobogganing, or "sliding" as it was called. One
day after school, a number of the boarders took their slides and headed for a
nearby hill. In a few minutes they were off, lying face down on the slides with
their legs bent upwards at the knees, so as not to impede their speed as they
catapulted down the hill. As it happened, M. Antonio chose this moment to
glance out the window of the convent. Thoroughly shocked at the sight of a
half-dozen pairs of legs waving joyously in the air, she immediately sent for the
offenders and lectured them soundly on what was expected of a student of St.
Michael's Boarding School for Young Ladies. After all, St. Michael's, in addition
to offering a superb education, promised to "provide moral training for young
girls"![124] The girls were astonished to learn that the proper position for a young

123. Helen Southcott, IBVM, to Nellie Pomroy, RSM, 1992. Helen's mother Geraldine (Joy)
Southcott attended St. Michael's Boarding School in the early 1900s. The letter contains
some of Geraldine's reminiscences of her school days, ASMSJ, RG 10/2/68.
124. Prospectus, Michael's Boarding School for Girls, 1900, ASMSJ.

lady while sliding was to sit upright on the slide with her legs tucked modestly beneath her.[125]

Many parents saved for years to allow their children to attend St. Michael's. "The sisters were flexible, though, accepting turnips or a lamb in lieu of cash."[126] Parents felt that the education provided at St. Michael's was well worth the sacrifice. But, on occasion, even more was being asked of them, for some of the students, motivated by the example of the sisters and inspired by the grace of God, left home forever to be professed as Sisters of Mercy.[127] As the years passed, other young ladies, attracted by the prospect of working in what was still considered missionary country, came from St. John's to offer themselves as postulants in St. George's. But the isolation that had surrounded this foundation in western Newfoundland was soon to come to an end. M. Joseph Byrne from St. John's and M. Michael Gillis from the Highlands (west coast) made their first (temporary) profession as members of St. Michael's Convent, St. George's, but a year later they pronounced perpetual vows in the chapel of the general novitiate at Littledale. In fact, they made history, for they symbolized the union of the foundation in the west with Mercy communities in the east. Furthermore, they bridged the transition between the days of autonomous communities and the creation of the Congregation of the Sisters of Mercy of Newfoundland seventy-four years after Francis Creedon, Rose Lynch, and Ursula Frayne established the first Mercy Convent in North America.

---

125. Letter from Helen Southcott, IBVM, ASMSJ, RG 10/2/68.

126. Joan Sullivan, *The Sunday Telegram*, March 12, 1993, sec. B, p. 9.

127. Former students at St. Michael's who became Sisters of Mercy include M. Michael Gillis, M. St. Joan McDonnell, M. Fintan Downey, M. Emeria Gillis, M. Loretta McIsaac, Marie Michael Power, Marie Alma O'Gorman, Margaret O'Gorman, Rona O'Gorman, and Theresa Boland.

CHAPTER ELEVEN

THE SECOND SPRING

There is in them but one heart and one soul in God.

Catherine McAuley

ll through the years, since the opening of Our Lady of Mercy School in 1843, the sisters had been able to support the school and provide for their own needs from tuition paid by the students.[1] As well, extra fees were charged for private instruction in various subjects, principally instrumental music.[2] To provide additional sources of income, the students and teachers at Our Lady of Mercy School organized public performances of concerts, operettas, and plays. According to the local papers, these events were well patronized. The amazing sum of twenty cents was charged for admission "throughout the hall," for the Mercy Sisters did not believe in reserved seats—except, of course, for the clergy! For those patrons who desired it, a program was provided at an extra cost of three cents.[3]

Another fundraising effort was the annual Christmas Tree. This popular attraction during the Christmas season and the activities associated with the two-week event raised much-needed funds to maintain the school and the con-

---

1. Our Lady of Mercy School, because it was a private school, received no support from the government. Convent schools elsewhere in Newfoundland were board schools and each teacher received a stipend from the local board of education.

2. Accounts Book, Convent of Our Lady of Mercy, St. John's, ASMSJ, RG 1/4.

3. *The Evening Telegram*, December 26, 1883, p. 4.

vent. *The Evening Telegram* described what a patron could expect at the Mercy Convent Christmas Tree:

> The Christmas Tree in the class hall of the Mercy Convent was opened to the public this evening. The Tree is very artistically decorated, and a good selection of toys and useful articles are upon it and the tables attached—toys, wool-work, and bric a brac. The refreshment table, presided over by Miss Casey, bids you, "Welcome," and offers tempting delicacies.
>
> Professor Bennet's Band discoursed sweet music; and there is a piano in the room for the use of players.... The ladies in charge have been energetic in their efforts, and they should be encouraged by the patronage of the public, and, at the same time, the good Nuns would be very materially assisted.[4]

In sponsoring these concerts and bazaars, the sisters had more in mind than simply fundraising. They felt that an important aspect of education was to teach a child to assume a degree of civic and social responsibility and how to speak and act in public. There was, too, the added incentive to study and practice that was presented to a student by the prospect of performing in public. The annual spring concert that took place toward the end of the school year provided an opportunity for the students to parade their achievements before admiring parents and friends, and—more than that—before the public, as well. Every year the St. John's newspapers carried accounts of successful performances of the pupils of various city schools. For instance, *The Evening Telegram* of July 23, 1897, published a lengthy account of a "Closing Exhibition" performed in St. Patrick's Hall by the students of Mercy School.[5] The program consisted of four parts: music, reading and recitation, physical exercises, and a finale that included various styles of dancing. While the writer had high praise for the performers in each section, he had this to say of the music, "In this branch of education the nuns of the Mercy Convent may be said to excel."[6] As early as 1855, music formed an important part in the education of the

4. *The Evening Telegram*, December 28, 1891, p. 4.
5. Ibid., July 23, 1897, p. 3.
6. Ibid., July 27, 1897, p. 3.

young sisters at Mercy Convent. An entry in the accounts book, dated November 1855, mentioned that £22.5s.6½ was spent on music lessons for the sisters.[7] This appreciation of the place of music in education was a trademark of Our Lady of Mercy School until its closing on June 19, 1992. Since the 1920s, this was due, in large measure, to the efforts of M. Baptist McDermott.

The name of M. Baptist McDermott holds an honoured place, not only in the history of the Sisters of Mercy but also in the development of music, dancing, and drama in Newfoundland. For M. Baptist is one of the founders of modern music education in our province. Her untiring quest for new and better methods of instruction and performance and her uncompromising demands for accuracy of interpretation and performance influenced her own students and through them successive generations of music teachers in Newfoundland.

M. Baptist was born in St. John's on September 27, 1889, and given the name Margaret Mary. Her father's name was John Prim Davis, and her mother was Anastasia Flannigan. When she was a very young child, her parents died and she was placed in Belvedere orphanage. From there she was adopted by Mr. P. McDermott, St. John's, and McDermott was the surname she used for the rest of her life. Mr. and Mrs. McDermott sent her to Mercy Convent School on Military Road where the example of the sisters made a deep impression on young Margaret Mary McDermott, and on January 6, 1907, she was accepted as a postulant at Mercy Convent. In July of the same year, she was received into the novitiate and given the religious name, Mary Baptist.

Recognizing her exceptional musical ability, the superior of Mercy Convent, M. Ita Glynn, engaged for her the best teachers in the city. M. Baptist was one of the first students in Newfoundland to be awarded an associate diploma in piano and teaching from Trinity College of Music of London. M. Ita's successor as superior was M. Bridget O'Connor.[8] M. Bridget, too, was quick to

---

7. Accounts Book, Convent of Our Lady of Mercy, St. John's, ASMSJ, RG 1/3.
8. M. Bridget O'Connor returned from Burin at the end of the school year, 1914–15, and was appointed superior of Mercy Convent, Annals, Convent of Our Lady of Mercy, St. John's, ASMSJ, RG 1/20/4.

see the potential of this young musician and made arrangements for her to study at the Boston Conservatory of Music. Subsequently, M. Baptist attended the Pius X School of Liturgical Music in Manhattanville, N.Y., where she gained much of her knowledge of Gregorian Chant. This was only the beginning. Throughout the forty-three years of her religious life she was never satisfied with the status quo. Forever, she was searching out new ways, new methods and insights that would benefit her students and provide them with the knowledge and skill to achieve their highest musical potential. In all of this she was supported by her friend and mentor, M. Bridget O'Connor, who encouraged her to make frequent visits to universities in the United States to study the best and most modern methods of imparting her vast store of knowledge.

In 1921, M. Baptist McDermott organized the Mercy Convent String Orchestra—the first of its kind in the city.[9] Some of her students who played in the orchestra, and others who came later, distinguished themselves in the associate and licentiate examinations of Trinity College. M. Celine Veitch, a pupil of M. Baptist, was one of the first musicians in Newfoundland to receive a fellowship in piano from Trinity College. Dr. David Peters, a long-time organist at Cochrane Street United Church, was another of M. Baptist's students. In 1929, from money provided by a legacy from her adoptive parents, M. Baptist was given permission to purchase a harp for the Mercy orchestra. Among the first students to study the harp was Carla Emerson (Mrs. Richard Furlong). Carla had a natural gift for music. Under Sister M. Baptist's careful coaching, she became so proficient that she was accepted as a student at Julliard School of Music and, eventually, became a professional harpist, playing in London, England, with the Royal Philharmonic Orchestra under the direction of both Sir Thomas Beecham and Sir John Barbaroli.[10] The reason for mentioning all of this is to point out how M. Baptist shared all she had with others. She incessantly sought to increase her own skill and knowledge,

---

9. Among the students who played in the first orchestra under M. Baptist's direction were three future Sisters of Mercy, Marie Norris (M. Cecilia Agnes), Alice Slattery (M. Mercedes Agnes), Madeline McGrath (M. Bernardine). M. Bernardine was one of the foremost music teachers in St. John's.

10. Mrs. Carla Furlong, interview by author, March 5, 2002.

not only to satisfy her own thirst for learning, but so that she could be more effective in her teaching and thus make a real contribution to the development of music in her homeland.

M. Baptist's activities, however, were not confined to music, for she shared in every phase of the education offered at Our Lady of Mercy and in particular, the area of drama. It was through the plays she put on for the public, as well as through the orchestra, that her name became known throughout the city and beyond.[11]

In September 1949, M. Baptist went to Boston to consult with a specialist about her eyes. After recovering from successful eye surgery, she was about to return to St. John's in April 1950, when she became ill and died.[12] Her remains were brought to St. Xavier's Convent in Providence to be waked before burial. The quirk of history that saw M. Baptist's body being brought for burial to the very convent that released the four missionary sisters to come to Sandy Point, Newfoundland, was not the only coincidence connected to M. Baptist's death. More than eleven years later, M. Assumpta Veitch[13] received a letter from M. Flavia of the Mercy Generalate, Bethesda, Maryland. On behalf of the Mercy congregation in Newfoundland, M. Assumpta had sent a generous gift for the support of the Mercy mission in Belize. M. Flavia wrote:

> How strange are the ways of God! The night your Sister Baptist was brought to St. Xavier's, M. Bernard and I waited for the undertaker and helped to dress Sister for burial. M. Bernard, the present superior of St. Catherine's in Belize, put her own church cloak on Sister Mary Baptist. How strange it is that Sister's community would come so quickly to Sister M. Bernard's aid at a time when she so truly needs it![14]

---

11. In 1923, with Mrs. John Baxter, M. Baptist McDermott directed the public performance of the drama *Pilate's Daughter*, presented at the Casino Theatre with music provided by the Mercy Convent Orchestra. This was the orchestra's first public performance.

12. M. Baptist McDermott is buried in St. Francis' Cemetery, Pawtucket, Rhode Island.

13. At the time M. Assumpta Veitch was superior general of the Sisters of Mercy of Newfoundland.

14. M. Flavia to M. Assumpta Veitch, December 28, 1961, ASMSJ.

While M. Baptist McDermott was a leader in music education in the early twentieth century, prior to her time other teachers were accomplishing splendid work in the music field.[15] After its formation in 1893, the Council of Higher Education inaugurated examinations in practical and theoretical music, and local professors were appointed as examiners. In 1902, however, a new chapter in music education began when the Trinity College of Music of London, England, held its first examinations in Newfoundland.[16] The examinations were conducted by members of the Faculty of Music of Trinity College, who came from England to Newfoundland every year thereafter and travelled to different parts of the island to conduct the examinations. The sisters' pupils from Mercy Convent, Littledale, and Brigus were among the first students in Newfoundland to enter and successfully complete these examinations.[17]

And so the years continued to unfold. The death of M. Bernard Clune on October 6, 1894, was a severe blow to the sisters at Mercy Convent and at Littledale. M. Bernard's health had been a source of worry for about eight years prior to her death. The debt due on the Littledale property weighed heavily on her mind and possibly contributed to her death at the age of fifty-six. Back as far as 1886, Brother Richard Fleming commented in one of his letters:

> Mother Bernard has been very unwell for the past eight or ten days. Poor Nuns have been very anxious about her. They would be almost as helpless as orphans if anything happened to her. No one among them fit to take her place, so says Father Scott. Poor women have been very much worried for some time past between Littledale and Military Road. And worst of all not being

---

15. Another well-known musician was Sir Charles Hutton, a pupil of M. Xaverius Dowsley, who was an accomplished musician. Sir Charles continued his musical education in England and subsequently returned to St. John's where he became the acknowledged leader in the field of education and musical entertainment in Newfoundland. A contemporary of Hutton was D. A. O'Flynn, organist, composer, and teacher.

16. McCormack, "Educational Work," p. 39. M. Basil's reference was to the records of Trinity College of Music, London, England. Trinity College is a teaching school of the University of London. In 1876, it launched a system of local examinations, practical—i.e. performance—and theoretical, throughout the British Empire.

17. Ibid. The practice of entering students for the Trinity College examinations continued every year until the second half of the twentieth century when, gradually, it was replaced by programs offered by the Royal Conservatory of Music in Toronto.

able to meet her demands. The school at Littledale is going on
pretty well. She has as many boarders as she can accommodate.[18]

In spite of Father Scott's doubts, both Littledale and Mercy Convent flourished under new leadership. The death of M. Bernard Clune cleared the way
for St. Bride's, Littledale, to become autonomous, and under the direction of
M. Xaverius Dowsley, the institution continued to expand. M. Bernard
Clune's successor at Mercy Convent was M. Liguori Carmody, and it was during her term as superior (1894–1899) that the trees were planted in the garden and the iron railing enclosing the garden was erected (1896–97).[19] The
introduction of business education by M. Joseph Fox in 1898 added a new
dimension to the curriculum of Our Lady of Mercy School and also an influx
of adult students.[20]

The sisters, however, were interested in more than academic excellence. They never lost an opportunity to contribute to the spiritual development of their pupils as well. Shortly after membership in the Sodality of the
Children of Mary had been made available to young girls anywhere in the
world, the first Sodality of Children of Mary in Newfoundland was formally
established by Bishop Howley at the Mercy Convent School on June 1,
1900.[21] Father Edward P. Roche, parish priest of Topsail (later archbishop of
St. John's) was appointed spiritual director and M. Mercedes Lyons was the
first directress, a position she held for twenty-five years.

By 1913, it was obvious that more space was needed in both the school
and the convent. There was only one problem—the sisters had no money to
undertake the necessary renovations. Although the debt on the Littledale

18. Fleming to Brother Holland, June 7, 1886, "The Slattery Papers," LMSF.
19. Howley Papers, AASJ, 106/13/1.
20. See chapter nine.
21. A sodality is a pious association formed to advance the spiritual welfare of its members through prayer and charitable activities. The Sodality of the Children of Mary originated in Paris, France, in 1830, and associations were formed made up of young girls
who were students of the Sisters of Charity. In 1876, Pope Pius IX extended membership
to young women everywhere and this permission was given final approval by Pope Leo
XIII in May 1897.

property had, by this time, been paid in full,[22] the cost of the new chapel (1892) demanded careful and competent management of the convent finances. Also, the west wing at Littledale (1912) had just been completed at considerable expense, and the mother house was expected to lend a helping hand where necessary. But in 1913, the need for more classroom space and additional living accommodations at Mercy Convent itself had become critical.

Given the tradition of being completely self-supporting, it was with a good deal of soul-searching and after exploring every other avenue, M. Ita Glynn, the superior of the mother house, and her competent bursar, M. Teresa O'Halleran, reluctantly decided to look for outside help. Early in 1913, a number of former students and friends met with the sisters at Mercy Convent to discuss ways and means of raising the money required for necessary repairs and additions to the existing building. A committee, spearheaded by Lady Isabelle Morris[23] and chaired by Monsignor J. Scott, decided that the easiest and most straightforward means of addressing the problem was to inform ex-pupils of the situation. M. Ita and M. Teresa agreed to put their heads together and compose a letter that would be signed by Monsignor Scott:

> The Sisters of the Convent of Mercy . . . find themselves in a position which obliges them to make an appeal to the public . . . Nothing but sheer inability to effect imperative repairs and improvements to their Schools and Convent . . . forces them to depart from the line of conduct which they have hitherto pursued—of maintaining their community and schools by their own efforts, with no call on an already taxed congregation.[24]

The plan was to build an extension to Mercy Convent that would house a new dining room, a kitchen, and new, improved sanitation for the Angels Guardian

22. Copies of letters from M. Bernard Clune and her assistant to Judge Little give a clear picture of the struggle to meet the debt on the original purchase of the Littledale property. Apparently, M. Bernard had used up all the monetary resources of the community to further this endeavour.

23. Lady Isabelle Morris was the wife of the prime minister of Newfoundland, Sir Edward Morris.

24. Rev. J. Scott to ex-pupils and friends of the Mercy Convent School, ASMSJ, RG 10/1/26.

School. It was pointed out that the sleeping accommodations for the sisters were seriously overcrowded—four sisters occupying a room designed for two. The letter continued:

> To do this, it is the intention to utilize that portion of the house which connects the Military Road Convent with the building in Cathedral Square known as St. Clare's. Through want of funds and reluctance to solicit them, this building has fallen into such a state of dilapidation as to be almost unfit for occupation. It will now be restored and will contain kitchen, refectory, sleeping rooms, baths, etc., but the restoration will entail considerable outlay.
>
> To devise some plan whereby a fund might be raised to cover the cost of these expenses, a meeting of ex-pupils and friends was called. . . . It was suggested . . . to approach the friends and supporters of the Convent, and the Catholic people generally, and ask them to consider the advisability of straight giving.[25]

The letter included an envelope addressed to the reverend mother, Mercy Convent, and each recipient was asked to donate whatever amount she could afford. When the envelopes were collected on May 20, 1913, by one of the forty-two ladies who had volunteered for the task, the response was more generous than anyone had anticipated. With the necessary funding in place, work on the convent began almost immediately. In addition to the renovations, accommodation was provided for eighty additional students.

The year 1915 witnessed another phase in the evolution of Our Lady of Mercy School. Because of a change in government legislation, the school was brought within the jurisdiction of the Roman Catholic Board of Education. This had financial implications, for now the teaching sisters in the school were entitled to a salary from the board. The school had changed in other ways, too, since it first opened its doors in 1843. First of all, it was now called, "The Academy of Our Lady of Mercy," and through the years there had been changes in the curriculum to reflect the new emphases of each succeeding decade. In the nineteenth cen-

---

25. Ibid.

tury, girls were trained along cultural lines. After they had passed through the equivalent of primary and elementary grades, in which they mastered the arts of reading, writing, and basic arithmetic, the emphasis turned to the arts in general and in particular, French and German, drawing, painting, vocal and instrumental music, elocution, and fancy needlework. It is true that, year after year, the course of studies mentioned subjects such as geography, navigation, and astronomy—subjects that reflect the maritime heritage of Newfoundland. But newspaper reports of exhibitions held at the end of the scholastic year continued to emphasize the quality of musical and dramatic performances and also the excellent artwork created by the students.[26] Gradually, the curriculum at Mercy School began to shift in favour of a broader-based syllabus, similar to that used in the Christian Brothers' Schools. In fact, Christian Brothers from St. Bonaventure's College conducted the year-end examinations at Our Lady of Mercy School. For instance, in the year 1891, the results of the school examinations at Mercy School appeared in *The Evening Telegram*. The report, which gave the names of all the students and the percentages obtained, included a list of the subjects covered in the examinations:

Geography	mathematical, physical, and political;
History	English, Roman, Modern, Newfoundland;
Grammar	Analysis, Syntactical, Parsing, and English composition;
Arithmetic	interest, vulgar and decimal fractions and book-keeping;
Christian Doctrine	DeHarbe's Catechism, Ecclesiastical History, Bible History;
Reading	Sixth Royal Reader;
Writing	Ornamental Penmanship.[27]

The advent of the CHE found students in convent schools well-prepared to compete with any other school in the island, for in 1894, the first year the CHE examinations were held, girls from Mercy Convent, Littledale, and Brigus were successful candidates. Within a few years, the other convent schools were following the syllabus prescribed by the CHE.

---

26. See, for example, *The Evening Telegram*, December 23, 1891, p. 4. See also *The Daily News*, January 10, 1902, p. 5.

27. *The Evening Telegram*, December 31, 1891, p. 3.

Students from St. Lawrence were successful in the public examinations as early as 1902. The superintendent of Roman Catholic schools reported in 1903:

> Classes are preparing for the Preliminary and Primary examinations of the Council of Higher Education. A candidate, who entered last year, was successful in obtaining a Preliminary Diploma. The entering for the examinations has already created a certain amount of emulation and interest among the pupils, which gives promise of much good.[28]

In 1907, a student of the convent school in Burin, Gertie Virgus, won the Outport Scholarship, another student of the same school won first place in the art section, and still another, first place overall in English.[29] In the years that followed, the curriculum prescribed by the council was followed throughout the whole educational system, and annual examinations were the yardstick by which the students' progress was measured.

The commercial and music departments of the Academy of Our Lady of Mercy in St. John's were singled out for special mention in successive yearly reports of the superintendent of education:

> The Gold Medal for speed and accuracy in stenography in the world wide competition for 1917 was awarded by the Sloan-Duployan Society to Lillian Sullivan of the Commercial Class. There were 147 students in the Commercial Classes and of these fifty-one obtained employment already.
>
> In the Music Department there were 150 students enrolled in all grades of Trinity College Examinations. In the 1918 international competitions, this department took first place. Three gold medals and three silver medals were awarded, and special mention was given to six pupils whose papers were excellent but could not be awarded medals owing to the limited number offered.[30]

---

28. Vincent P. Burke, "Report of the Superintendent of Education for the Year Ended December 31, 1903," p. 64, ASMSJ.

29. Ibid., 1907, p. 77.

30. Ibid., 1918, p. 44.

However, in the years immediately preceding the First World War, a series of events occurred that had far-reaching implications for the Sisters of Mercy. Strangely enough, the Mercy Sisters played no part in the initial transactions that led eventually to the establishment of one of their principal ministries in Newfoundland.

In the early years of the twentieth century, a large piece of property on LeMarchant Road in St. John's came into the possession of the Presentation Sisters of St. John's through M. Clare Waldron, who had inherited the land on the death of her brother, Father Thomas Waldron. In the early years, the sisters used the property, called "Waldron's Farm" as a grazing ground for cattle.[31] Sometime later, the sisters sold part of the Waldron property to the Honourable E. M. Jackman, minister of finance for the government, better known as "Jackman the Tailor."[32] Jackman built a large, private home on his piece of land and called it, the "White House."

Some years later, another Presentation Sister by the name of M. Clare English entered the picture. M. Clare English was interested in providing a hostel for young girls who came from the outports to work in the city of St. John's.[33] To this end, she had raised funds from the sale of knitted goods, from school concerts, the sale of cancelled stamps, and donations from friends. It was a slow, tedious process, but M. Clare persevered. And then there occurred an event that must have seemed to her like a miracle. She received a visit from a man by the name of John Funchion who had been, at one time, a boarder in her mother's house on Water Street in St. John's. Funchion went to work in the Yukon during the time of the gold rush and, as a result, had become very wealthy. His purpose in returning to St. John's was to marry a childhood friend of M. Clare English, and shortly after the wedding, the bride and groom visited her at the convent. During the visit,

31. M. Fabian Hennebury, "Notes on the History of St. Clare's," ASMSJ.

32. O'Neill, *The Oldest City*, p. 305. See also Hennebury, "Notes," ASMSJ.

33. It will be remembered that the same motive inspired Catherine McAuley to build the House of Mercy on Baggot Street in Dublin.

Funchion presented M. Clare with the gift of a rosary made of forty gold nuggets.[34]

At this point, the Knights of Columbus enter the story. In 1911, the Supreme Master of the Fourth Degree Knights of Columbus John H. Reddin came to St. John's and was introduced to M. Clare English. During their conversation, M. Clare asked Mr. Reddin to find a buyer who would be willing to pay one hundred dollars for the "Golden Rosary." The following year, the Supreme Knight James A. Flaherty visited St. John's and informed her that the Knights of Columbus wished to purchase the Golden Rosary as a gift to James Cardinal Gibbons of Baltimore on the occasion of his golden jubilee.[35] M. Clare accepted his proposal, and to her delight and astonishment, he presented her with a cheque for one thousand dollars, a considerable sum of money in those days. This large sum of money, together with the funds she had collected through her small fundraising efforts, was enough to permit M. Clare English to act on her dream of establishing a hostel for working girls. She purchased a piece of land on LeMarchant Road adjoining the Jackman home and the Waldron Farm, but before she could go any further, Archbishop Howley intervened. What transpired between the archbishop and M. Clare is described by Paul O'Neill in *The Oldest City*:

> She [M. Clare English] was called to a lengthy private meeting in the convent parlour with Archbishop Howley. When she returned to her room it was obvious from the crestfallen look on her face that something unpleasant had transpired. She turned to her secretary and said, "Send it all to the Mercy Order." When the secretary protested ... she was told it was the Archbishop's wish and she must obey. Despite the fact that Sister Clare had drawn from the prelate the promise that her original purpose would not be forgotten, the order seems to have come as a severe shock to her. Already in poor health, she began to fail and died shortly afterwards.[36]

---

34. O'Neill, *The Oldest City*, pp. 304–05.

35. Ibid.

36. Ibid., p. 305.

O'Neill claims that the cordial relations between the Presentation Sisters and the archbishop that had marked their association during his years as a young priest at the cathedral had soured after he became bishop. O'Neill suggests that perhaps the young superior of the Presentation Order "did not make a proper fuss over him on his attainment of churchly rank" adding "Great men have been known to be hurt by insignificant slights."[37] On the other hand, the early records of St. Clare's Mercy Hospital noted that M. Clare English, a former student of Our Lady of Mercy School, requested "that the Home purchased by the archbishop be placed under the direction of the Sisters of Mercy since, at that time, the Presentation Sisters were not involved in Social Work of this type."[38]

In any case, by adding to the amount M. Clare English had received from the sale of the Golden Rosary, Archbishop Howley bought the "White House" from E. M. Jackman for five thousand dollars and renovated it as a hostel for working girls. In the meantime, he had arranged that the hostel should be operated by the Sisters of Mercy. The Mercy Convent Annals pick up the story:

> Saint Clare's Home in the city of St. John's was opened by His Grace, Archbishop Howley on the Feast of Saint Michael, the 29th of September in the year of our Lord, one thousand nine hundred and thirteen under the patronage of Our Blessed Lady of Mercy and the great Saint Clare, as a "Home for Working Girls."
>
> The first Mass was celebrated in the little chapel of the Convent by His Grace, Archbishop Howley on that day.
>
> The Sisters who went to establish this Convent were Mother M. Pius Mulcahy, Mother Superior, Sister M. Berchmans Quinn, Sister M. Bernard Gladney.[39]

The Sisters of Mercy named the home "St. Clare's" in honour of the Presentation Sister M. Clare English, whose sacrifice and generosity had prepared the way for this new ministry.

---

37. Ibid.
38. Hennebury, "Notes," p. 2, ASMSJ.
39. Annals, Convent of Our Lady of Mercy, St. John's, ASMSJ.

St. Clare's Home was meant to be self-supporting, but the salaries of the young women who became residents were so small that only fifty cents a week was charged for room and board. It was clear that St. Clare's Home would have to offer additional programs to provide enough income to keep it in operation. A morning kindergarten class was opened for children in the area, and classes in business education—typing, shorthand, accounting—were offered in the evening by M. Catherine Greene, who was assigned to St. Clare's to teach these courses. In addition, a music teacher, M. Gerard O'Reilly, was transferred from Mercy Convent to provide lessons in piano. In this way, the sisters were able to offer affordable housing to grossly underpaid young women who were working in the various business establishments of St. John's. St. Clare's Home continued to operate in this fashion for nine years when a more urgent need for the services of the sisters became apparent.

In addition to the progress of education in the schools and the establishment of a home for working girls, more radical changes were in store for the Sisters of Mercy in Newfoundland—this time affecting their lifestyle and form of governance. Ever since the first convent had been established outside St. John's, the sisters in the outports had grappled with some very serious problems. One, of course, was the isolation of the smaller communities outside St. John's, some of which were accessible only by sea. Also, because each convent was autonomous, with a few exceptions, the personnel of most of the communities remained unchanged for years. Moreover, it was reported that some sisters were reluctant to leave the convent in which they were professed to go elsewhere, even if some other community was in need of help.[40] Another serious problem faced by the Sisters of Mercy, especially in the outports, was the lack of adequate novitiate facilities and programs, for it was difficult for communities with one or two novices to provide thorough training in religious life. In small convents, there was always the temptation to allow the novices to take over some of the duties of an overworked staff of professed sisters, thus cutting into the time that should have been spent in prayer and study. More than anything else was the fact that each local community was on its own to sink or swim. The unity and strength that come from concentrated effort, from collaboration, from the exchange of ideas, information, and materials—none of this was possible under the existing structure.

The new archbishop of St. John's, Edward Patrick Roche,[41] was well aware of these problems. Almost immediately after his appointment in February 1915, the archbishop turned his attention to what he perceived to be the weaknesses of the religious communities in the country. He had a strong ally in the newly appointed superior of Mercy Convent, the talented and visionary M. Bridget O'Connor who had just returned to St. John's after an eleven-year posting in Burin.[42] If the archbishop's proposal for amalgamation was to be adopted, it would mean an end to the almost total control over the lives of religious hitherto exercised by the bishop of the diocese.[43] Authority within the congregation would, in future, be exercised by a General Administration made up of sisters elected from among the professed members of the congregation. Each convent would have a local superior appointed by the General Administration, and individual sisters no longer would belong to just one local community but could be moved according to the needs of the different ministries of the congregation.

Most of the sisters realized that the current policy of autonomous communities had outlived its usefulness. Thus, when it was suggested that all the local convents should amalgamate under one general administration, the idea gained almost unanimous approval with, apparently, only two communities

41. Edward Patrick Roche was born in Placentia, Newfoundland, on February 19, 1874, and ordained to the priesthood at All Hallows in Dublin. Ordained archbishop in St. John's on June 29, 1915, he won the respect and admiration of all Newfoundlanders for his efforts on behalf of education and health care. However, he is remembered today especially because of his strong opposition to Confederation with Canada. He died in September 1950.

42. M. Bridget O'Connor was appointed to Burin in 1903 by Archbishop Howley. It may be a coincidence that she returned to St. John's after Howley's death. Does this lend substance to the rumour that he "banished her to Burin"?

43. Ironically, Archbishop Roche continued to exercise an unwarranted degree of control, even after amalgamation.

expressing doubt as to the wisdom of such a plan.[44] No doubt it was the topic
of conversation in every community room, and the pros and cons were thoroughly discussed. For instance, the story is told that one objection to amalgamation was voiced by M. Xavier Wadden of St. George's, a native of St. John's
who, rather than enter the convent at home, had entered at St. George's to
escape the attentions of an overzealous admirer. With the prospect of amalgamation, she feared she might be sent back to St. John's and be subjected once
more to the pleadings of the disappointed but persistent suitor.[45]

However, before a decision on amalgamation could be made, every sister had to be consulted. For this purpose, representatives of the Presentation
and Mercy Convents throughout Newfoundland were called to St. John's by
their respective bishops.[46] On July 3, 1915, these sisters, together with all
the professed sisters residing in St. John's, assembled in the Episcopal
Library and were addressed by the apostolic delegate, Archbishop P. F.
Stagni. The delegate explained fully the implications of amalgamation and the
advantages of such a union.[47] The sisters were given the fullest opportunity
to state any difficulties or objections, but it is doubtful that anyone had the
nerve to do so.

On the day following the delegate's address to the sisters, each one of
them was interviewed individually by her bishop and given an opportunity to
state her views. After this a secret vote was taken, which resulted in forty-two
Sisters of Mercy pronouncing in favour of union of their convents. Two were
against it. Who were the two? Because this was a secret ballot, the names of the
two dissenters will never be known for certain. However, the convent

---

44. M. Basil McCormack, "Notes in Preparation for M.A. Thesis," ASMSJ, MG 2/1/335. In
conversation with M. Agnes Doyle who belonged to St. Michael's Convent, St. George's,
in 1915, M. Basil learned that the two communities who expressed some doubts were St.
Michael's Convent, St. George's, and Sacred Heart Convent, St. Lawrence.

45. This story is told by Sr. Maura Mason who heard it from her mother, Mrs. Alice Mason,
a childhood friend of M. Xavier Wadden.

46. ASMSJ, RG 1/6/38. Since not all the sisters in the outports came to St. John's for the
meeting, it must be presumed that they communicated their ideas to the local superior
or the second community representative.

47. Petition for Amalgamation of the Mercy Convents in Newfoundland, ASMSJ, RG
1/6/38.

grapevine has a way of ferreting out such information. According to rumour, M. Corsini Dempsey from St. George's and M. Brigid Hoey from Conception Harbour were the two who held out for autonomy.[48]

It was the task of the local superiors to formulate a petition to the Holy Father for a radical change in the Rule to allow the proposed amalgamation. Nevertheless, one may suspect that the petition had been prepared in advance by an impatient Archbishop Roche who was not one to leave important matters on the long finger. The decision for amalgamation was heartily endorsed by all three bishops of Newfoundland in a separate petition. The documents were forwarded to Rome where the Sacred Congregation of Religious, for once, was prompt in sanctioning the proposal in a decree dated November 25, 1915.[49]

On July 26, 1916, one hundred and thirty-two sisters (Mercy and Presentation) from all over Newfoundland assembled in St. John's for their annual retreat of ten days.[50] The retreat, directed by a Jesuit priest from New York, was held in the Episcopal Library that had been converted to a temporary chapel.[51] At the conclusion of the retreat on August 4, the decree uniting all the houses of the Congregation of the Sisters of Mercy was promulgated. The first article of the decree read:

> We canonically unite all the Houses of the Sisters of Mercy which up to this time have been independent of each other in the Island of Newfoundland so that they all form one and the same Congregation which We constitute under the supreme rule of one and the same Superior General. The title of the Congregation thus constituted will be "The Congregation of the Sisters of Mercy of St. John's, Newfoundland."[52]

48. M. Basil McCormack heard this story from M. Philomena Walker who was a professed sister at the time of amalgamation. M. Basil related it to the author on September 2, 1999.

49. Fr. Peregrine Francis Stagni, OSM, delegate apostolic to Canada, "To all whom these letters concern," July 14, 1916, ASMSJ, RG 1/6/46.

50. Notes from the diary of Archbishop Roche, August 4, 1916, AASJ, 107/17.

51. ASMSJ, RG 1/6/468.

52. Ibid.

The second and third articles of the decree set out the structure of the administrative body. This consisted of a superior general (or mother general) and four councillors, a general treasurer, and a secretary, all of whom, like the superior general, were to be elected for a term of six years by a general chapter of the congregation.[53]

On August 4, 1916, a solemn Mass of Thanksgiving was celebrated by Bishop John March of Harbour Grace and benediction administered by the Bishop Michael Power of St. George's. Archbishop Roche addressed the members of both congregations, the Sisters of the Presentation and the Sisters of Mercy. He read the decree confirming the amalgamation of the convents after which he spoke at length, explaining the implications of the new union. He explained that this union involved a radical and essential change in the Constitutions of each congregation in order to bring them more in line with the spirit of the Church's legislation for religious orders. He pointed out that under the former system, because of the isolation of some communities, customs had crept in that were contrary to the well-being of the community. The archbishop stressed the advantage to the smaller communities, who would, in future, secure more experienced teachers for their own schools. At the same time, the new union would provide opportunities for postulants entering from isolated places to come to the city for further education and training in a central novitiate especially equipped for study and prayer. Finally, there was the question of authority. The explanation given by Archbishop Roche, quoted below, sheds an entirely new light on what has been interpreted as high-handed actions of Newfoundland bishops respecting the Sisters of Mercy. Bishop Fleming, in particular, has been accused of exceeding his authority.[54] According to this statement, the sisters had been, in fact, subject to the bishop as their "First Superior":

> Their Lordships are of opinion that the Institutes can be more
> effectually and more appropriately governed by a Mother General

---

53. By the same decree and at the same time, all the Presentation Convents in Newfoundland were amalgamated.
54. Killerby, *Ursula Frayne*, p. 69.

and her Council than under the present system by which each
House is independent and the Sisters subject to the Ordinary [i.e.
the Bishop] as their First Superior. . . . The general effect of the
new system of government will be the transfer of very much of
the authority hitherto vested in and exercised by the Bishops to
a Mother General and her assistants. The general effect of the
change will be to give the Sisters throughout the Island at large a
voice in the administration of the Institute.[55]

The archbishop informed the sisters that, until such time as they could
get used to the new organization, the Sacred Congregation, after consultation
with the bishops, had appointed the first superior general and her councillors
for a period of three years. Finally, he announced the names of the sisters of
the General Council of the Congregation of the Sisters of Mercy of
Newfoundland for the period 1916–1919. To no one's surprise, M. Bridget
O'Connor, the superior of Mercy Convent, was named superior general. Her
novitiate companion and close friend, M. Mercedes Lyons, also of Mercy
Convent, was appointed first councillor. The other councillors were M.
Joseph Kelly from St. Bride's Convent, Littledale; M. Philippa Hanley from
St. Michael's Convent, Belvedere; and M. Brigid Hoey, from Immaculate
Conception Convent, Conception Harbour. The new bursar (or treasurer)
general was M. Bernard Dooley of Mercy Convent, and M. Genevieve
Farrell, also of Mercy Convent, was appointed secretary general. Finally, a
general novitiate was erected for the whole congregation in St. Bride's
Convent at Littledale, and M. Benedicta Fitzgibbon was appointed the first
novice mistress.[56]

At one of the first meetings of the General Council, the discussion
revolved around the profession of two novices from St. Michael's Convent, St.
George's. The Constitution that came into effect at the amalgamation mandat-

55. Archbishop E. P. Roche, Address to the assembled Sisters of the Presentation and
Mercy congregations, August 4, 1916, ASMSJ, RG 1/6/470.

56. It is interesting that this group of seven appointees included four Irish and three
Newfoundland-born sisters. M. Joseph Kelly, M. Bernard Dooley, and M. Benedicta
Fitzgibbon were born in St. John's and the latter two were students at Littledale before
being accepted as postulants at Mercy Convent.

ed annual vows for a period of time before a person could be admitted to per-petual profession.[57] This required a change in the Act of Profession, which was approved by the General Council on August 12, 1916.[58] Three days later, on August 15, 1916, at St. Michael's Convent, St. George's, M. Joseph Byrne and M. Michael Gillis became the first Sisters of Mercy in Newfoundland to make annual vows.[59] For the first period after amalgamation until the approval of the new Constitutions, sisters made vows annually for three years. After that, they made a three-year commitment before being admitted to perpetual vows.[60]

Other decisions of the new General Council resulted in the transfer of some sisters from one convent to another. This was the first time in the histo-ry of the Newfoundland Mercy Sisters that there had been such wide-ranging changes of personnel. Hitherto, one or two sisters occasionally transferred from one place to another. Now, seventeen sisters had to pack their bags and join another community in new and strange surroundings. Two sisters who had been born in St. John's but who had elected to join the sisters in St. George's were transferred back to the East Coast—M. Francis Holden went to St. Joseph's Convent, Brigus, and M. Agnes Doyle, to Mercy Convent in St. John's. Happily, M. Xavier Wadden—who feared unwanted attentions from her disappointed suitor should she return to the capital city—was left in peace to continue her work at St. Michael's Convent, St. George's. Perhaps the biggest upset happened in St. George's where M. Aquin Gormley was appoint-ed superior to replace M. Antonio Egan, who had been superior of St. Michael's Convent from its foundation in 1893, with the exception of the three years when M. Veronica Payne replaced her in that position. It must have been

57. Prior to the amalgamation, upon completion of the prescribed novitiate, sisters were admitted to perpetual profession.

58. "Minutes of the First Meeting of the General Council of the Sisters of Mercy, August 12, 1916," ASMSJ.

59. ASMSJ, MG 1/4/365. M. Evangelist Walsh was the last sister to be admitted to per-petual profession according to the old Constitutions.

60. The ninth general chapter decreed that the formation policy of our congregation should be brought in line with the document from Rome, "Instruction on the formation of Modern Religious" (IRF). According to this instruction, the time of temporary profession would be no less than three and no more than nine years, (IRF, Article 37:1).

a difficult situation for both M. Aquin and M. Antonio, but one that lasted a very short time, for within the year, M. Antonio was reassigned to St. John's, July 7, 1917.[61]

One of the newly appointed councillors, M. Joseph Kelly, had been superior of Littledale for a period of fourteen years (1901–1915) before she was replaced by M. Ita Glynn. In spite of the fact that a number of sisters at Littledale were qualified for the office of superior, it appears that Archbishop Howley had little confidence in anyone other than his lifelong friend, M. Joseph.[62] Not long after her appointment to the General Council, she became ill and died on May 14, 1917. M. Joseph is remembered as a woman of culture and sensitivity, qualities that were appreciated by Littledale students as well as by the highly literate archbishop.

In this period of transition, it was important that someone be found to take M. Joseph's place. By and large, the different ministries of the congregation were represented on council. M. Bridget O'Connor had taught both at Littledale and on the Burin Peninsula. M. Philippa Hanley's years at Belvedere provided her with insight into the needs of the orphanage. M. Brigid Hoey had spent most of her religious life in the Conception Bay area. M. Bernard Dooley was aware of the needs of the inner city of St. John's. Only the West Coast lacked representation on the General Council. In their wisdom, the three bishops of Newfoundland appointed M. Antonio Egan as second councillor to take the place of M. Joseph Kelly.[63] M. Antonio returned to St. John's and took up residence at St. Bride's Convent, Littledale.

It is hard to understand why M. Antonio was not appointed to the General Council in the first place, for she was the logical choice to represent an area of Newfoundland that was relatively unknown to the other appointees. After her appointment, however, she brought to the deliberations of Council her unique experience as a member of the Sisters of Mercy of Providence as well as her knowledge of the needs of the west coast of Newfoundland. With

61. "Minutes of the Meeting of the General Council, July 7, 1917," ASMSJ.
62. The writer of M. Joseph Rawlins' obituary referred to the friendship between M. Joseph and Archbishop Howley. See *The Daily News*, May 17, 1917, p. 5.
63. "Minutes of the Meeting of the General Council, June 8, 1917," ASMSJ.

the addition of M. Antonio to the council, every sector of the mission of the Sisters of Mercy was represented. This was the group that was to guide the destinies of the institute through the difficult period of transition from a group of autonomous convents to a congregation, united in the spirit of Mercy. How well they did their work was acknowledged by M. Joseph Kelly when she wrote, "The generalate so long contemplated and, I may say, so dubiously regarded in the beginning, is now an accomplished fact, and . . . we hail this important event as one freighted with blessings for the Order of Mercy in Newfoundland."[64] M. Bridget O'Connor added her testimony to the success of the amalgamation when she wrote:

> Immediately after the amalgamation of the convents, I visited all the houses of the Congregation and found them working in perfect accord with the new state of things and in perfect harmony with the views of the Church in constituting the Generalate.
>
> There were nine houses between three Dioceses, and seventy-nine Sisters, and among them there was not one member dissatisfied either with the Generalate itself or with the wishes of the Bishops regarding the appointment of the officials for the term of three years.[65]

Another important task facing the General Council was the adaptation of the original "Rule and Constitutions" to reflect the changes brought about by amalgamation. During the three-year period, 1916–1919, the Council prepared a document called "Supplement to the Rule and Constitutions for the Government of the Amalgamated Houses."[66] To provide all members of the congregation with plenty of time to review the changes and offer suggestions, the document was sent to all the convents in June 1917.[67] However, M. Bridget O'Connor was nothing, if not thorough. She had little confidence in the readiness of her sisters to give prompt attention to documents that arrived

---

64. M. Joseph Kelly, "Our Generalate, 1917, Amalgamation," Minutes of meetings of the General Council of the Sisters of Mercy, 1916–1952, pp. 39-40, ASMSJ.

65. M. Bridget O'Connor, Ibid., p. 35, ASMSJ.

66. "Minutes of the General Council, April 15, 1917," ASMSJ.

67. Ibid., June 6, 1917.

by mail. Long experience taught her that sisters were (and are) inclined to postpone the examination of such materials until more immediate tasks were accomplished. Aside from the issue of a ready response, it was as democratic as it was diplomatic to consult with each community and its members in order to inform herself of the problems each one faced. Consequently, M. Bridget began a visitation of all the convents and discussed proposed changes in the Constitution with every sister in the congregation. At a subsequent meeting of the General Council, M. Bridget presented the opinions expressed by the sisters and amendments were made to the original document.[68]

The establishment of the central novitiate at St. Bride's, Littledale, was a major innovation that resulted from amalgamation. It would have placed a heavy financial burden on the local community of St. Bride's Convent if the whole congregation had not shared the cost. Financial records of the local convents indicate that each one was required to send a certain percentage of its income to the generalate (or General Administration) for the support of the novices. The triennial report to the Holy See, dated August 15, 1919, records that in the three-year period 1916–1919, as many as nineteen novices had been received. As a matter of interest, at the time the report was compiled there were twelve sisters with temporary vows[69] and sixty with perpetual vows.[70] In some cases, postulants and novices were asked to provide their own clothing, beds, and bedding, but this requirement was waived more often than not, depending on the applicant's financial circumstances. Once a sister was professed, however, she was completely dependent on the community for all her needs.

When a young woman had been accepted as a postulant, she was assigned to some ministry within the congregation and lived in one of the convents as a member of that community for a period of six to nine months. If the

68. "Minutes of the Meeting of the General Council, November 10, 1917," ASMSJ.

69. After amalgamation, the Rule was changed so that, on completion of the novitiate, sisters made temporary vows annually for three years before committing themselves to perpetual vows.

70. Congregation of the Sisters of Mercy, Newfoundland, "Triennial Report to the Holy See, 1916–1919," ASMSJ, RG 1/6/56.

experience was mutually satisfactory, she was admitted to the novitiate for a period of two years, at least one of which, the "canonical year," had to be spent in the novitiate house. The canonical year was a period of study and preparation under the direction of an experienced religious, the novice mistress. During this year, the studies consisted entirely of subjects related to the spiritual development of the novice, such as the theology of the religious vows, scripture, moral theology, and the history of one's own religious congregation.

The selection of St. Bride's Convent, Littledale, as the general novitiate made a lot of sense because of the fact that St. Bride's College was the authorized teacher training institution for Catholic female teachers. The young woman who aspired to be a Sister of Mercy would, in all likelihood, spend the rest of her days as a teacher in one of the convent schools. Thus, it often happened that the novice spent either the first or second year of her novitiate pursuing the course of study required for a teaching certificate. Novices who were already certified as teachers spent time either helping out in one of the schools or pursuing studies leading to a higher degree of education. But it was not just the classroom that provided training for junior members of the community. Novices were taught how to care for the sick, and in the days before St. Clare's Mercy Hospital existed, these nursing skills were in great demand.

The two years spent by each sister in the novitiate provided enough storytelling material to last a lifetime. There was, first of all, the requirement that a person own up to any breach of discipline of which she may have been guilty, and novices were notorious for being guilty of every imaginable infraction of the Rule. One of the most frequent violations of "holy poverty" involved the handling of dishes, for novices seemed to be incapable of picking up a dish without dropping it. This unfortunate tendency created havoc at meal times when, frequently, the sister-servers scrambled to find enough cups, saucers, or plates to go round. M. Benedicta Fitzgibbon, the first general novice mistress, thought she had found a way to impress on her novices the necessity of handling the goods of the community with gentle care. She ordained that, in future, any novice who broke a cup or a dish must collect the pieces and bring them to the chapel where, in the presence of the whole community, she would declare her "breach of poverty." A few days later, when the community had gathered to pray vespers, two of the novices were conspicuously absent. The superior, who happened to be M. Ita Glynn, waited patiently for everyone to assemble. After a few minutes, the chapel door burst open and the two missing novices staggered in carrying a large clothes basket full of pieces of broken crockery. When questioned by the superior, one of the novices acknowledged with some pride, "Yes, Mother Superior, I broke them all myself!" Then there was the novice whose duty it was to serve the priest's breakfast whenever mass was celebrated in the convent. Unlike the sisters, who were served porridge and beans as the first meal of the day, the reverend gentleman breakfasted on steak and bacon. When the novice returned to clear the table, she discovered that Father had left half his breakfast untouched. Reluctant to see all this good food go to waste, the hungry novice devoured the lot and returned the empty plates to the kitchen. Later on, suffering qualms of conscience, she owned up to her offence by admitting that she had "eaten the priest's remains"! Finally, there was the novice whose duty it was to sweep and dust the chapel. Sad to say, she was not always overly conscientious in performing this duty. On one occasion she was prompted to declare her negligence by admitting that she had "failed to remove a dead mouse from under Reverend Mother's *prie-dieu.*" Whereupon, reverend mother, who was terrified of mice—dead or alive— was seen to beat a hasty retreat from the chapel.

Stories like these provide a small glimpse into what life was like for novices in the days before Vatican II. Sisters today tell such stories over and over again in an attempt, perhaps, to recapture some of the joyous simplicity of those earlier years when life was uncomplicated, when there was "a place for everything, and everything in its place." Novitiate discipline was often strict but always kind. Novices learned habits of order and neatness; they learned not to squander either time or material goods; they learned to listen to others with respect and to realize that "every Sister has as much right to her opinion as— obedience apart—I have to mine."[71]

The sisters chosen to direct the novices in those early years had no training in "sister formation." For the most part, they were women of compassion

---

71. A novitiate maxim from the 1940s inculcated in the novices trained by M. Camillus Dunphy.

who understood the impulsiveness of youth and who had that most valuable of all qualifications—common sense. It is significant that most, if not all, sisters remember their novice mistress with respect, love, and gratitude. When they came to Littledale to ask to be accepted as postulants, most of these women were unsophisticated young girls, accustomed to racing freely up and down the hills of Newfoundland, climbing over the rocks of the seashore, and playing on the ice pans in the harbours. The sisters appointed to the office of novice mistress welcomed each young lady with open arms and managed somehow, gently and with great kindness and understanding, to turn these unlikely prospects into Sisters of Mercy.

CHAPTER TWELVE

NEW BEGINNINGS

Without counsel, plans go wrong;

but with many advisers they succeed.

Proverbs 15:22

At the time of the amalgamation in 1916, there were seventy-nine professed sisters in nine convents scattered throughout Newfoundland. Consequently, very early in their term of office, the newly appointed General Council of the Sisters of Mercy came to the conclusion that it was time to branch out. Priests from all over Newfoundland were looking for sisters to staff the schools, and so it was not easy to determine where the need was greatest. Having examined the requests presented by different parishes and the qualifications of the sisters available for new missions, the council decided to establish two new convents, one in the mining town of Bell Island and another one on the West Coast. The council had good reason to consider having another community of sisters on the West Coast. From the beginning, the convents in the east had maintained a degree of communication, one with another, even to the extent of an occasional interchange of personnel. But prior to 1915, there was very little—if any—contact with the lonely convent in the west. After amalgamation, it was important for each sister to understand that this change had implications beyond the mere enactment of a piece of Church legislation. It required that the love and loyalty pledged by each person to the community she had chosen at profession be enlarged and broadened to encompass the persons and the ministry of the whole Congregation of the Sisters of Mercy. It was crucial to the survival of the congregation that the words of the foundress become a reality, "There is in them but one heart and one mind in Christ."[1] Thus, the sisters in the west needed to know that they were not alone nor separate from the rest of the congregation and that the needs and concerns of their area were being given equal consideration with those of the east. And so, in 1917, eight sisters in different parts of Newfoundland were preparing to pull up stakes and leave for parts unknown. Four of them were preparing for their ministry on Bell Island, while another group of four was making similar preparations to establish the second Mercy convent in the parish of the Bay of Islands on the west coast of Newfoundland.

Like other parts of the West Coast, a permanent settlement was slow in coming to the shores of the Bay of Islands, but throughout the nineteenth century, there was a gradual increase in the number of families who came to live in the area. When settlement did occur, it was concentrated largely in the southern arm, although there were smaller settlements dotted around the shores of the entire bay and on the islands that gave the bay its name. Some of the original settlers to the area came from Sandy Point and from other parts of Newfoundland, while some others came from as far away as the West Country of England and Ireland. They were encouraged to move to this area of Newfoundland because of its rich herring fishery and also for the apparently limitless wood supply found in the surrounding countryside.

By the end of the nineteenth century, the settlement of Birchy Cove, a sheltered inlet at the bottom of the bay, had become a thriving, prosperous little town. Local herring factories salted the catch and exported it to Canadian and American markets. Other species of fish, such as cod, salmon, and lobster,

---

1. "Rule and Constitutions of the Sisters of Mercy," cited in Sullivan, *Catherine McAuley*, p. 308.

provided important sources of income. In addition to the riches of the sea, people exploited the resources of the land—agriculture, logging, hunting, and trapping. The coming of the railway in 1899 meant increased business with the rest of Newfoundland, and companies from St. John's, such as Ayre & Sons, established branches in Birchy Cove.[2] The 1911 census returns showed that the settlement was the largest community in the Bay of Islands with 1,047 inhabitants. Prior to this census, in 1904, the name "Birchy Cove" was changed to "Curling" to honour Reverend James Joseph Curling, a well-loved Anglican priest who had served the people of the area from 1873 to 1886.[3]

On the south side of Curling (Birchy Cove), a neighbouring community called Petries had existed since the 1870s when a Nova Scotian by the name of Alexander Petrie settled there.[4] When the railway went through the settlement, two of Petrie's relatives built a hotel near the rail line at what was called Petries Crossing. Along with Curling, the community of Petries continued to grow and prosper, and with the resulting increase in population came the demand for schools and churches.[5]

In 1890, the newly ordained Father Andrew Sears, recently arrived from Ireland, was appointed parish priest of the Bay of Islands. At that time, the parish included the whole of the bay and as far east as Grand Lake. One of Father Sears's first projects was to move the residence of the parish priest to Curling—or Birchy Cove, as it was called at that time. Until his arrival, there had been no Catholic school in the settlement. Catholic children received their education in the school established by the Church of England. Another of the first projects of the new parish priest was to provide a Catholic school for these children. The fact that the only available building was a one-time shed did not discourage this

---

2. *ENL*, s.v. "Corner Brook."

3. According to Bert Riggs, *The Evening Telegram*, November 18, 1997, p. 12, the renaming of Birchy Cove to honour this dedicated priest, J. J. Curling, was at the instigation of Bishop Michael F. Howley.

4. When Curling was incorporated in 1947, Petries was included within its boundaries.

5. Sr. Edward Mary Roche grew up in Curling in the 1920s and '30s, and at that time, Petries was looked upon as a community, distinct from Curling, which began "on the other side of the church." When the parish was established in 1884, it was the Parish of the Bay of Islands, and it included the area known as Petries. Eventually, both Petries and Curling became part of the city of Corner Brook.

vigorous young man. With the help of the women and men of the area, the building was scrubbed, painted, and renovated into some semblance of a classroom. The converted shed was the settlement's first Catholic school.[6] Father Sears, however, was far from satisfied with this makeshift arrangement, and within a short time, he set to work to complete a building, St. Patrick's Hall, the construction of which had been started by one of his predecessors. As soon as the roof was finished, Father Sears moved the classes from the former shed into the new building. Students of those days told of the wind howling through the half-finished walls as they sat shivering in their seats,[7] but through the efforts of the men of the settlement, the new school was finished in short order. By existing standards, St. Patrick's Hall was a very fine school, indeed, and it continued to serve the Catholic children of Petries and Curling until 1925.[8]

In the meantime, the prefect apostolic of St. George's, Dr. Michael Howley, visited Father Sears in Petries, and together they selected a site for a rectory, the foundation stone of which was laid in 1892.[9] Within a year the rectory was completed and ready for occupancy.[10] Father Sears called the site Mount Cecilia in honour of his sister, M. Cecilia Sears, who had entered the community of the Sisters of Mercy in St. George's. Now that he had a place to live, Father Sears turned his attention to the construction of a church. The beautiful new Sacred Heart Church, erected near the rectory on Mount Cecilia, was formally dedicated on September 16, 1900. A month prior to the dedication, on August 19, 1900, Bishop McNeil of St. George's diocese celebrated the first mass in the new church and blessed the church bell, which was christened St. Francis Xavier Bell.

The period from 1900 to 1916 was a time when the west coast of Newfoundland was experiencing unprecedented growth. Much of the pros-

---

6. Hogan, *Pathways*, p. 242.

7. Ibid., p. 264.

8. In letters and documents dating from the 1920s, the names, "Curling" and "Petries" are often used interchangeably, although at that time, Petries had its own identity. However, both Curling and Petries belong to the Roman Catholic Parish of the Sacred Heart, Curling.

9. McCormack, "Notes," ASMSJ, RG 10/11/56.

10. This rectory was destined to become the first convent of Mercy in the Bay of Islands.

perity happened because the railway opened up the country to new business opportunities and also because the problems associated with the French Shore treaties had been finally settled.

It was now twenty-four years since the sisters' arrival in Sandy Point. Their work in education and in their care for the sick and the poor was well-known up and down the coast. Consequently, the priest and the people of Bay of Islands were eager to have the sisters establish a convent in their area. Furthermore, prior to 1915 M. Antonio Egan of St. Michael's Convent, St. George's, planned to establish another convent on the West Coast.[11] The prospect of amalgamation caused her to defer this enterprise until the changes consequent on such a union could be determined. However, Bishop Michael Power, bishop of the Diocese of St. George's, continued to pursue the prospect of having a second Mercy convent in his diocese. Eventually, the dream became a reality. On June 14, 1917, the bishop wrote the following jubilant letter to Dean Matthew O'Rourke who was, at the time, pastor of the Bay of Islands:

> I beg to notify you that I have concluded the deal whereby the Sisters of Mercy will take over the educational work at Petries Crossing. They have agreed to send four Sisters, one of whom is to have a First Grade certificate and another of whom is to have a First Class Musical certificate.
>
> On our part we convenant to pass over the present presbytery and schools to the Order and to prepare the Presbytery for occupancy by September. We further agree to give $400.00 per annum from the Bay of Islands Board of Education.
>
> In view of this arrangement it will be necessary to make arrangements to vacate the present presbytery by the first of August next.[12]

Two months later, on August 17, M. Bridget O'Connor, the superior general of the Sisters of Mercy, arrived by train at Petries Crossing "to exam-

---

11. McCormack, unpublished manuscript, 1955, ASMSJ.

12. Bishop M. F. Power to Dean O'Rourke, June 14, 1917, Archives of the Diocese of St. George's in Corner Brook (henceforth ADSG).

ine the site of the new Convent about to be erected."[13] On her arrival she discovered that there was to be no new convent but rather a hasty patching up of the old rectory. By this time, Father John Kerwan had been sent to Petries as parish priest to replace Dean O'Rourke. Perhaps Dean O'Rourke was less than happy at being ousted from his presbytery for the sake of a group of sisters! When Father Kerwan arrived, he was faced immediately with the problem of having no place to live. Until he could arrange for a suitable house to be built, he lived in a temporary apartment built on a piece of land separating the convent and the church.[14]

Back in St. John's, the sisters selected for the new convent in the west were making preparations for their mission. M. Brigid Hoey, who had been appointed to the first General Council in 1916, was named superior of the foundation in the Bay of Islands. Accompanying her were three young sisters, M. Francis Hickey from St. Michael's Convent, Belvedere; M. Agnes Baker, a graduate of St. Bride's Academy, Littledale, who was to be the music teacher; and M. Agnes Doyle who had been appointed to Mercy Convent in 1916. No doubt M. Agnes Doyle was happy to be returning to the West Coast, having spent the first eleven years of her religious life in St. Michael's Convent, St. George's. According to newspaper accounts, the new community of sisters arrived at Petries on Sunday, September 24, the Feast of Our Lady of Mercy. Gathered at the station to meet them was a very large crowd of people headed by Bishop Power, Father Kerwan, and other priests of the diocese. The superior of St. Michael's Convent, M. Aquin Gormley,[15] and M. Michael Gillis came from St. George's to greet the new arrivals and welcome them to the West Coast and to the new convent of St. Mary's on the

---

13. *The Western Star*, August 22, 1917, p. 2.

14. After their arrival, the sisters used this apartment as a classroom for students in the higher grades.

15. M. Aquin Gormley, succeeded M. Antonio as superior of St. Michael's Convent, St. George's, in 1916. Born in Roscommon, Ireland, in 1873, she came to Newfoundland, arriving on October 24, 1891, and was admitted as a postulant at Mercy Convent. She served as superior of St. Anne's Convent in Burin, Immaculate Conception Convent in Conception, and St. Michael's Convent, St. George's. In 1925, she returned to Mercy Convent where she spent her remaining years. Her special work was teaching in the commercial department.

Humber.[16] Two days later, *The Western Star* published an account of the arrival of the sisters:

> During this week great events have transpired in our midst. By Sunday's Express there arrived from St. George's His Lordship, Bishop Power, Rev. Dr. Greene of the Cathedral in St. John's, and a number of priests of the Diocese of St. George's in order to be present at the Reception of the Sisters on the following day . . .
>
> Under perfect weather conditions with sunshine lighting up the classic hills of the Humber, with the glorious river sleeping at the foot of the sun-kissed hills, without a ripple on the water nor a disturbing breath on the land, the Feast of Our Lady of Mercy was ushered in. It was a historic occasion for the Bay of Islands Parish for it marked the long-promised and much desired day of the good Sisters' coming . . .
>
> The Sisters were met at the Humber by some of the priests who accompanied them to Petries where they were detrained and where a multitude had gathered to bid them welcome.[17]

On the following day, after mass had been celebrated for the children in the parish church, the sisters began their teaching in the thoroughly renovated St. Patrick's Hall.

Once the school schedule and the convent *Horarium* had been established, life for the new missionaries settled down to a regular routine. For the first year, at least, there were no surprises, and the authorities at Mercy Convent in St. John's pronounced themselves pleased with the state of affairs in the west. In a letter to Bishop Power, M. Bridget O'Connor wrote:

> St. Mary's on the Humber is going on all right. . . . They do not seem to be keen on School Fees; their totals were only $18.75 against $206.50 in Bell Island, whilst the Music Fees of the latter are double. Perhaps the circumstances of the people are

---

16. The convent was named in honour of Mary, the Mother of God, and the magnificent Humber River that empties into the Bay of Islands a few miles from where the convent was built. The Humber River has its headwaters in the Long Range Mountains and flows into the Bay of Islands near Corner Brook. It has a total watershed area of 5,033 miles and is the second largest river in insular Newfoundland. It is one of the world's great salmon rivers.

17. *The Western Star*, September 26, 1917, p. 2.

between [sic], or perhaps there is more Mercy in the individual
at the head of affairs in Bay of Islands. Both Superiors are laying
down a precedent for their successors and I would like it to be
correct.[18]

In the same letter, M. Bridget commended M. Aquin Gormley, the superior of
St. Michael's Convent, St. George's, for her management skills in catering to
the boarding school in difficult economic times. She pointed out that the prudent superior had managed to achieve a balance of $471 and that, she wrote,
"proves good housekeeping."[19] Apparently, everything in the west was off to a
good start!

Toward the end of the school year, 1917–1918, M. Bridget O'Connor
and her council planned to send two sisters to Montreal to study French,
particularly conversational French. Always sensitive that sisters on the other
side of the island be included in whatever programs that were available, M.
Bridget wrote to Bishop Power suggesting that one of the sisters at St.
George's, M. Michael Gillis, might benefit by going to Montreal with the sisters from St. John's. In his response to this letter, the bishop also recommended that the talented M. Xavier Wadden should continue her studies at
the Montreal Conservatory of Music during the summer months, and he
suggested that M. Agnes Baker from St. Mary's on the Humber might benefit from programs offered at that institution. M. Bridget, however, felt that
M. Agnes, who was still very young, would profit more by studying with
some of the congregation's experienced teachers in St. John's, before being
sent away to a Canadian conservatory. It may have been this suggestion by
Bishop Power that prompted the General Council to decide to bring all outport music teachers to St. John's during the summer months to avail of fur-

---

18. M. Bridget O'Connor to Bishop Michael F. Power, March 4, 1918, ADSG. The reference to Bell Island is in connection with St. Edward's Convent that was founded on the
same day as St. Mary's on the Humber. The third sentence, ". . . circumstances of the
people are between . . ." suggests that M. Bridget must have written this letter in such
a hurry that her thoughts raced ahead of her writing, and thus some word or words
were omitted.

19. M. Bridget O'Connor to Bishop Michael Power, March 4, 1918, ASMSJ.

ther coaching by more highly qualified sisters in the city.[20] But plans for M. Agnes' further musical education never materialized. Even from her reception into the novitiate, her health had been a cause of concern, and the strenuous routine of teaching, visitation, and community duties proved too much for her frail constitution. At the end of the school year, 1918–19, she was recalled to St. John's and in September 1919, her position as music teacher on the staff of St. Mary's on the Humber was taken by M. Xavier Wadden.[21]

During her years at St. Michael's Convent, St. George's, M. Xavier had been a popular and very successful teacher. In addition to her teaching duties, she was organist and choir director in the cathedral. In 1917–18, she entered a group of students in the Trinity College of Music examinations. All these students were successful, and their results, published in *The Western Star*, May 1, 1918, were a source of satisfaction to children and parents alike.[22] Certainly, the music program at St. Michael's Academy was well established. Now M. Xavier who, since her postulant days in 1905, had been largely responsible for this success, was asked to leave St. Michael's Academy and move to a new community and begin all over again the task of building a music program in the school. With a readiness and good humour that was typical of this gentle, but determined woman, M. Xavier quickly settled into her new home. Little did she realize in September 1919 that, in spite of the goings and comings associated with the demands of amalgamation, she would remain at St. Mary's on the Humber for thirty-seven years.

Sometime prior to this change in the personnel of St. Mary's on the Humber, and quite unknown to the people of Petries, there appears to have been trouble brewing in the convent.[23] Apparently, the younger sisters found

20. "Minutes of the Meeting of the General Council, June 11, 1918," ASMSJ.

21. Not long after being recalled to St. John's, M. Agnes Baker became very ill. Even with the best medical treatment available, her condition continued to deteriorate. At the request of her parents who lived in the United States, she was sent to that country for further treatment but died on February 19, 1924, in the Sisters of Providence Hospital, Seattle, USA.

22. *The Western Star*, May 1, 1918, p. 4. As early as 1914, M. Xavier had begun to register students for the Trinity College of Music examinations. All were successful.

23. In conversation with the author, Sr. Edward Mary Roche noted that her mother, Mrs. Edward Roche of Curling, who worked with the sisters in 1918, had no idea that there was anything but perfect harmony reigning in the convent.

the superior, M. Brigid Hoey, too stern and unbending. They must have communicated their dissatisfaction to Bishop Power, who in turn wrote the superior general, M. Bridget O'Connor. In the context of M. Bridget's reply, it appears that the bishop asked her to make a change in the personnel of the community for she wrote to Bishop Power as follows:

> I was aware that a certain dislike for the Superior [M. Brigid Hoey] had crept in among the Sisters; but on their own word, that I need have no worry, and that there was nothing whatever in community life to disturb charity or interfere with religious discipline, I was reassured that at least until next June, there was no necessity for making any change . . .
>
> If there was [sic] anything serious, my Lord, disturbing the peace and happiness of St. Mary's community, in fact of any community, difficulties would not come in my way of finding a remedy. . . . I shall ask you, my Lord, to think the matter over again. . . . At the general change next summer a more suitable selection can be made for the Bay of Islands . . .[24]

However, within a very short time the sisters of St. Mary's on the Humber had more to occupy their minds than dissatisfaction with their superior. Toward the end of the First World War, Spanish Influenza broke out in Asia and Europe, and its subsequent spread to North America by returning soldiers affected many places in Newfoundland. When the epidemic spread to the Bay of Islands, the sisters at the convent of St. Mary's on the Humber immediately volunteered their services. At their own request, there was no publicity given to it, but their self-sacrifice and courage in the face of this life-threatening epidemic won the gratitude and admiration of the whole settlement.[25] They visited and nursed the sick, irrespective of religious affiliation, brought food and clothing where necessary, and prepared the dead for burial. Unable to provide the necessary care for the sick in their own homes, the sisters con-

---

24. M. Bridget O'Connor to Bishop Michael F. Power, December 3, 1918, ADSG.

25. In spite of the sisters' reluctance to have their efforts acknowledged, a letter appeared in *The Western Star*, April 18, 1919, in which the writer paid tribute to the generosity, self-sacrifice, and courage of the Sisters of Mercy during the epidemic.

verted one of their classrooms into a makeshift hospital. Day and night, assisted by the parishioners, they ministered to the needs of the sufferers.[26]

The Bay of Islands was only one of the many areas of Newfoundland
affected by the Spanish Flu. When the people of St. George's fell ill, the sisters
of St. Michael's Convent were quick to respond to the needs of the sick. The
superior of St. Michael's Convent at the time was M. Aquin Gormley. There
were, by that time, eight sisters in the community.[27] Many years later, M.
Xavier Wadden wrote an account of the tense days when so many people, especially the poor, were suffering and dying:

> The Sisters in St. George's and Curling cared for the sick poor in
> their homes. All denominations were cared for during this epidem-
> ic that the people called, "The Bad 'Flu." I was in St. George's during
> the time (1918–1919) and the Sisters took turns visiting the sick.
>
> Bishop Power got the Court House fitted up as a temporary
> hospital. Long carts, covered by blankets, were fitted up to bring the
> sick to the hospital. Father O'Reilly (later Bishop) used to go to the
> 'hospital' in the early morning, long before Mass, to bring Holy
> Viaticum to the dying in the Court House Hospital.
>
> The Sisters took turns in the hospital during the day and in
> the early morning. We also visited the sick in their homes, bringing
> hot soup, clothing, etc. Every day we washed and dressed the chil-
> dren—these families were very poor. We visited one family, I
> remember, where the seven children were all stricken with the 'Flu.
> They were just lying around—the mother died. While we were
> there, the father [entered], coming from the woods where he was
> looking for rabbits to make soup for the children. No central heat-
> ing in those days![28]

A few months after the events just described, M. Xavier Wadden was
transferred to St. Mary's Convent in Petries. She was not the only new member
to be assigned to the Bay of Islands community. The superior general, M. Bridget

---

26. Hogan, *Pathways*, p. 271.

27. The eight members of St. Michael's Convent in 1918 were: M. Aquin Gormley, M.
Corsini Dempsey, M. Teresa de Bourke, M. Joseph Byrne, M. Xavier Wadden, M. Michael
Gillis, Margaret Mary Collins, and M. Alphonsa Walsh. ASMSJ.

28. M. Xavier Wadden, unpublished manuscript, ASMSJ, MG 2/1/354.

O'Connor, had not forgotten Bishop Power's concern over the tension existing in the convent. She transferred every sister in the community! In August 1919, M. Brigid Hoey was sent as superior of St. Anne's Convent, Burin, and in her place, the recently professed Sr. M. Carmela Fitzgerald (1915) from St. Bride's, Littledale, was appointed superior of St. Mary's on the Humber. M. Xavier Wadden, Margaret Mary Collins, and M. Joseph Byrne—the three of them from St. Michael's Convent, St. George's—are named in the archives of the Sisters of Mercy, along with M. Carmela Fitzgerald, as forming the second community of St. Mary's on the Humber.[29] At the conclusion of her three-year term as superior, M. Carmela was recalled to St. Bride's Convent, Littledale, where she was appointed novice mistress, and M. deSales Ahearn assumed the leadership of the community of St. Mary's on the Humber.

M. deSales had been born in Bay de Verde, a fishing village at the top of the northwestern arm of the Avalon Peninsula. As a young girl, she attended St. Bride's College, Littledale, where she was awarded her teaching certificate. She taught for some years in various parts of the island before being accepted as a postulant at Immaculate Conception Convent, Conception Harbour, in 1909. After her profession in 1911, she remained in Conception Harbour for another ten years. However, the superior general, M. Bridget O'Connor, recognized and appreciated M. deSales' ability as a teacher and administrator. When the office of superior of St. Mary's on the Humber was vacant, with the consent of the General Council, she appointed M. deSales Ahearn to that position in August 1922.

When M. deSales arrived in Petries she found that the sisters' living accommodations were far from ideal. She discovered to her horror that the only room in the house with running water was the kitchen. Furthermore, except for "Old Faithful," the sisters' affectionate title for the ancient King Edward range in the kitchen, there was only one other stove in the house and that was in the parlour. During evening recreation,[30] the sisters huddled around the small grate in

---

29. ASMSJ, MG 2/1/335.

30. Evening recreation in the convent (up until 1967) was from eight o'clock to nine o'clock. At nine o'clock, night prayer was recited in the chapel, and the sisters were expected to be in bed with all lights out by ten o'clock. Since morning prayers began at quarter after six, no sister objected to the relatively early hour of retiring.

the community room in a futile attempt to warm themselves before facing the piercing cold of the second floor where their bedrooms were located. There was no basement, as such, but a short stairway in the kitchen led underneath to a large dugout where coal was stored. Reflecting on the discomfort endured by her uncomplaining companions, M. deSales decided immediately that somehow, somewhere she would find enough money to make their lot a little more comfortable and a great deal healthier. And so, toward the end of her second year as superior, in November 1924, she had a central heating system installed in the convent. Other improvements followed.

Everyday the sisters at St. Mary's walked down a long avenue leading from the convent to St. Patrick's Hall on Mount Cecilia where two sisters taught a total of about ninety students, covering all grades from grade I to grade VII, inclusive. Because the hall was used for all parish activities, the desks were moveable. On frequent occasions, whenever some social event was scheduled—such as a concert, a sale of work, bingo, or a similar function—sisters and students, known as the "Desk Brigade," carried the moveable desks up the long avenue and stacked them on the convent verandah. On the morning after the function, the "Desk Brigade," led by M. Liguori Wade (who bore the nickname "Sergeant Major"), carried the desks back and arranged them row by row in the classrooms.

The higher grades, VIII to XI, inclusive, were taught in a building adjoining the convent that, years ago in the 1890s, had been used by the priest as temporary living quarters until the presbytery was completed. Space in this building was so limited that not more than thirty pupils could be accommodated. The commercial class and the music pupils were taught in the parlour of the convent—the music pupils during the morning session and after school hours, the commercial class in the afternoon session and evenings. Lest M. Xavier Wadden entertain for a moment the notion that her afternoons from one o'clock to half past three were free, the superior, who was also the school principal, arranged that she teach classroom singing during these hours. In the 1920s, M. Catherine Greene taught the commercial classes. Their courses consisted of typing, shorthand, business English, bookkeeping, and accounting. Late afternoon and evening classes were made more available when the

Newfoundland Light and Power Company set up business in Curling in the 1920s. The superior of the convent, M. deSales, was quick to avail of this new service, and within a few months of the arrival of the company, the convent was wired for electricity.

One problem that the capable superior was unable to solve was the over-crowded condition of the schools. At the time of M. deSales' appointment to Petries, the Bay of Islands area was on the threshold of unprecedented pros-perity with the imminent establishment of a paper mill in nearby Corner Brook. In 1923, the paper mills were up and running, and the consequent influx of population led to serious overcrowding in all the schools. This was particularly true for the convent school. It seemed that everyone wanted to send their children to the sisters. Parents, not only from Petries and Curling, but also from outlying places, begged M. deSales to admit their children to the school, and she was tired of having to continually refuse these requests. She decided to write to the new bishop of the Diocese of St. George's, Henry T. Renouf, and explain the situation.[31] The bishop, who was at his wit's end to provide more priests, more churches, and more schools to accommodate the population explosion, uncharacteristically gave M. deSales a favourable reply.[32] The site chosen for the new school turned out to be a marsh, and the problem of draining it required hours and hours of free labour contributed by the men of the place and also by sisters and schoolchildren. Every day after school, the sisters and the children helped drain the land by transferring the topsoil in small wheelbarrows. The soil was deposited in the green field in front of the convent where, eventually, the sisters created an attractive flower garden.[33] Many years later, writing of this garden, M. Liguori Wade recalled, "On one occasion we picked over one hundred roses of different shades from this beau-tiful garden to decorate the altars."[34] Many years later, in 1975, the new con-

31. Bishop Michael Power died on March 6, 1920, at the early age of forty-three years. He was succeeded by the former pastor of St. Patrick's Parish, St. John's, Rev. Henry T. Renouf.
32. As will be seen, Bishop Renouf's dealings with the Mercy Sisters were often less than cordial. However, he seemed to have taken a fancy to M. deSales Ahearn.
33. M. Liguori Wade, "Memories of the 1920s in Curling," ASMSJ.
34. Ibid.

vent of St. Mary's on the Humber was built in the very spot where M. Liguori had her rose garden. Work on the new school proceeded rapidly, and in January 1925, Holy Cross School opened its doors to receive the more or less eager students of Petries and Curling. It was an all-grade school with four large classrooms, an attractive, bright commercial room, and a music room. But even this extra space soon proved insufficient. After a few years, extra classrooms were added to take care of the growing population of the area.

After the completion of Holy Cross School in 1925, M. deSales turned her attention once more to the inadequacies of the convent. Up to this time, one of the rooms on the second floor of the convent had been used as a chapel. It was barely large enough to accommodate the sisters for community prayer, but when a priest came to celebrate mass there was room only for the priest and the server. The sisters knelt in the corridor outside—a situation hardly conducive to devotion! M. deSales, however, looked on this not as a problem to be endured but a challenge to be faced. She felt that they should investigate the cost of adding an extension to the convent. Through the generosity of relatives and friends of the sisters, money was put aside for the "Chapel Fund."[35] By the year 1927, M. deSales was ready to act. She got in touch with a skilled carpenter from Harbour Main, Conception Bay, and engaged him to come to Petries and build a two-storey extension to the convent. When completed, the extension provided not only a more spacious and beautiful chapel, but also a couple of extra sleeping apartments and—much to M. Xavier Wadden's satisfaction—a music room.[36]

The year 1928 brought more changes to the convent of St. Mary's on the Humber. M. deSales' term of office as superior had been completed, and she was replaced by Sr. M. Alphonsus McNamara. However, the General Administration in St. John's, having discovered the unusual administrative ability of the young M. deSales Ahearn, were not about to allow her to slip back

35. The names of donors to this fund can be found in the Annals of the Convent of St. Mary's on the Humber, 1917–1929, ASMSJ.

36. M. Liguori Wade, "Petries, Bay of Islands, 1923–1945," ASMSJ. Sr. M. Liguori was a member of the community of St. Mary's on the Humber during this period. At the request of M. Chrysostom McCarthy, she wrote an account of the early days in Petries.

into the ranks where she would have little scope to exercise her natural talents. They immediately appointed her superior of St. Michael's Convent, St. George's. The departure of M. deSales from Petries marked the conclusion of the first phase of the ministry of the Sisters of Mercy in the region of the Bay of Islands. There had been significant improvements—economically, socially, and culturally—since the arrival of the Sisters of Mercy in 1917, and there was reason to be confident that their ministry and their presence provided a source of comfort and satisfaction to the people they served.

The convent in Petries, however, was only one of the foundations initiated by the new General Council of the Sisters of Mercy in 1917. The idea of establishing a convent on Bell Island originated in 1915 when Archbishop Roche made his first official visit to the island. The archbishop was quick to see the advantages of establishing in this rapidly growing community a convent school with well-trained personnel. Unfortunately, though, during the same period of time, he was busy with plans for the amalgamation of the convents in Newfoundland, and so all other major decisions relating to the religious congregations of Sisters had to be put on hold. Consequently, it was not until 1917 that the new General Council of the Sisters of Mercy was in a position to approve the opening of a convent on Bell Island.

Bell Island is the largest of three islands in the middle of Conception Bay, the other two being Little Bell Island and Kelly's Island.[37] Bell Island itself is about six miles long and a little more than two miles wide. A three-mile stretch of water known as the Tickle separates the island from the eastern side of the Avalon Peninsula; transportation across the Tickle is provided by regularly scheduled ferries to Portugal Cove.[38] Although the distance is short, occasionally the boat trip can be quite rough, depending on the winds and tides. Strong winds and stormy weather occasionally disrupt the operation of the ferry; in

37. Kelly's Island was the source of some of the stone that Bishop Fleming used in the construction of the Cathedral of St. John the Baptist. The bishop himself lived for many weeks in a makeshift camp on Kelly's Island. He worked alongside the labourers to quarry the materials that subsequently were loaded onto small boats to be transported to St. John's.

38. The road from Portugal Cove to St. John's was constructed in 1831 and was one of the first built in Newfoundland.

addition, slob ice coming down from the north in springtime frequently blocks the Tickle and prevents the boats from operating. As a rule, though, commuters can depend on reliable service back and forth to the island.

As early as the sixteenth century, European fishermen and the pirates who sailed the North Atlantic stopped at Bell Island to obtain fresh water.[39] The first recorded permanent settler on the island was a native of Jersey in the Channel Islands named Gregory Normore, who built his home there around the year 1740. Normore was followed by other English and Irish settlers who made their living by farming, fishing, raising cattle, and harvesting the wild berries that grow in profusion on the island. But the settlement had another resource that eventually turned a predominantly farming community into what became known as the "Iron Isle." Throughout Bell Island, and for many miles under the sea, there are deposits of rich iron ore. Since the days of the earliest settlers, people had suspected that there was something unusual about the red earth found on the island. Around 1628, John Guy[40] visited Bell Island and, being curious about the type of rock he saw lying around, sent a sample home to England for analysis.[41] But more than three hundred years passed before the content and value of the rock was identified. In 1893, the Nova Scotia Steel Company bought the lease on the iron-rich land and named the site "Wabana," an Indian word meaning "place where the light first shines."[42]

The beginning of mining operations brought a huge increase in the population of Bell Island. In 1901, the island was home to 1,320 persons. By 1923, it had surpassed Harbour Grace as the largest town outside St. John's, and in 1956, the population had climbed to 11,724.[43] As the population grew, so did the need for services—law enforcement, health services, and above all, education.

---

39. *ENL*, s.v. "Bell Island."

40. John Guy from Bristol, England, established a plantation at Cupids in Conception Bay in 1610. It was the first settlement in Newfoundland to be authorized by the English Parliament.

41. *ENL*, s.v. "Bell Island."

42. Ibid., p. 168.

43. Ibid.

The first mention of a school on Bell Island was a Church of England school in Lance Cove, one of the small communities into which Bell Island is divided.[44] The school was attended not only by Anglican children but also by Roman Catholics. In 1875, the Catholics had their first resident priest in the person of Rev. Richard Dunphy, and three years later, in 1878, a Catholic school was opened.[45] However, in 1875, three years before this school was opened, a lady in the East End taught some Roman Catholic children in her own home.[46] In 1891, a total of 164 children attended the two schools, but with the opening of the iron ore mines in 1895, everything changed. There was an influx of workers and their families from Conception Bay communities, and as well, experienced miners arrived from Nova Scotia to fill positions that required technical training and education. This led to a veritable uproar when people suspected that the mining company would bring in additional workers from Nova Scotia, thus bypassing the local men. The people realized that they needed education and training to avail themselves of new job opportunities offered by the mining company.[47] At the urging of Bishop Michael J. Howley, the first Roman Catholic School Board for Bell Island was appointed by the government on May 31, 1898, and on February 17, 1901, the first Catholic high school, the Superior School, was opened.[48] Incidentally, the newly composed "Ode to Newfoundland" was sung for the first time on Bell Island for the opening of this school.[49] At the time of Howley's death in 1914, there were four Catholic schools on the island. Three years later, the new archbishop, Edward Patrick

---

44. L. C. Reese, "Lance Cove, Bell Island. A Brief History of the Early Inhabitants," p. 18, 1972. Bell Island is divided into several small communities: Lance Cove, the Front, East End, the Green, the Mines, and West Mines.

45. Records of St. Michael's Parish, Bell Island, AASJ.

46. Mary Craig, *Pictorial History, Roman Catholic Schools, Bell Island, 1875–1983*, (St. John's, NL: Memorial University of Newfoundland, 1983), p. 4.

47. Ibid., p. 6.

48. Ibid., p. 7.

49. Ibid. The words of the *Ode to Newfoundland* were composed by Sir Cavendish Boyle, governor of Newfoundland. The music was composed by Sir C. Hubert H. Parry and approved and officially recognized for the *Ode to Newfoundland* by Minute of the Committee of the Honourable the Executive Council of Newfoundland on May 20, 1904.

Roche, succeeded in persuading the Sisters of Mercy to establish a convent school in this prosperous mining town.

By this time, the number of Newfoundland-born sisters was beginning to equal, if not exceed, the number of those born in Ireland. Of the four sisters who were assigned to the new foundation, only the superior, M. Consilio Kenny, was Irish.[50] It was a wise decision to appoint M. Consilio superior of this new foundation on Bell Island, for she was, above all, a woman of great kindness and gentleness. She possessed a genuine Irish wit that gave verve and sparkle to her conversation, but at the same time, she was a woman of sound judgment, and her wide range of knowledge gave worth to her opinion on a variety of subjects. She was a gifted teacher, and one who put up with no nonsense from her students—such as haphazard attendance, neglected homework, or untidy workbooks. She demanded the best they could give, and they usually gave it! At the same time, she was a firm believer in the efficacy of rewards. Her former students recalled with affection how they were lured along the precipitous paths of learning by the prospect of some tempting and immediate prize—usually in the form of rather squashed candy bars produced from the depths of M. Consilio's seemingly bottomless pockets.[51]

The second member of the founding community, M. Cecily O'Reilly, was born in Argentia, a settlement near the old French capital of Newfoundland, Placentia, where she received a first-class education from the Presentation Sisters. A few years after completing her education, Monica O'Reilly joined the Sisters of Mercy as a postulant in St. Lawrence. Although at her reception into the novitiate she was given the name M. Cecilia, she was never known by anything other than Mary Cecily. This corruption of the name

50. M. Consilio Kenny was born in Castlerea, Roscommon, the youngest of eleven children, and at baptism, given the name, Agnes. She came to St. John's early in 1892 to join the Sisters of Mercy at Mercy Convent, Military Road. Before her appointment to Bell Island, she taught the senior grades at the Academy of Our Lady of Mercy. After a six-year term as superior on Bell Island, she returned to Mercy Convent for a short time before being appointed as bursar of St. Michael's Convent and Orphanage at Belvedere. In 1937, she was elected treasurer general of the Mercy congregation, and continued to hold this office until her death on November 2, 1945.

51. This story was told to the author by M. Celine Veitch who was a member of M. Consilio's class at Our Lady of Mercy School in St. John's.

"Cecilia" began possibly with Bishop Howley, for he wrote in his diary, "May 17, 1903 . . . Reception of Sister Cecily (Monica O'Reilly)."[52] M. Cecily remained in St. Lawrence until after the amalgamation, when, in 1917, she became one of the founding members of St. Edward's Convent, Bell Island.[53]

The third member of the founding group, M. Alphonsus McNamara, was from Low Point, Conception Bay. At the age of seventeen years, she became a postulant at Mercy Convent and was professed at Littledale on July 8, 1917. Two months later, she went to Bell Island where she remained for two years. Her next mission was Burin (1919), and from that point on, she served in a number of places. Apparently, M. Alphonsus was a person who could adapt well to changing circumstances. Certainly, any qualities of leadership that she possessed were fully utilized by successive General Councils, for she filled the office of superior in seven different communities between 1928 and 1943 when she became ill. After a very painful illness, she died at Belvedere in 1945.

M. Aloysius Rawlins was a native of St. John's. She attended St. Bride's Boarding School at Littledale and later joined that community as a postulant. She was professed with M. Alphonsus McNamara in 1917 and was assigned to the new foundation on Bell Island. M. Aloysius Rawlins began her ministry as a Sister of Mercy by filling the role of music teacher, parish organist, and choir director on Bell Island, but before many years had passed, she found herself in a new and challenging career as hospital administrator.[54]

The parish priest of Bell Island at the time of the sisters' arrival was Father James McGrath (later Dean). Father McGrath was only too pleased to welcome a community of Sisters of Mercy to his parish and immediately set to work to build a convent near the parish church of St. Michael's. It was a difficult time to start building, for World War I was still raging, and materials were in short supply. Also, there was the problem of obtaining competent carpen-

---

52. Howley Papers, AASJ, 106/8.

53. For the remainder of her active ministry, M. Cecily O'Reilly remained on Bell Island. In 1927, she was transferred to the newly opened Immaculate Conception Convent at the Mines. From that time until her retirement, she alternated between the two Bell Island convents. In 1941, failing health forced her to retire to Belvedere where she died in 1945.

54. The story of M. Aloysius Rawlins can be followed in more detail in the following chapter dealing with St. Clare's Mercy Hospital.

ters. Thousands of young Newfoundlanders were fighting overseas, and most of the able-bodied men remaining on the island worked in the mines. Despite these drawbacks, the optimistic Father McGrath gathered whatever materials were available, hired anyone who could drive a nail and set to work to build his convent. Realizing that it could not be ready in time, he made arrangements for the sisters to live in one section of a double house that was in his possession.

An account of the arrival of the sisters on Bell Island was described by M. Consilio Kenny:

> On Wednesday afternoon, 19th September, 1917, four Sisters, M. Cecily [O'Reilly], M. Alphonsus [McNamara], M. Aloysius [Rawlins] and M. Consilio [Kenny] left the Motherhouse on Military Road in a motor car kindly provided by the Archbishop and drove to Portugal Cove where they met their new pastor, Rev. J. J. McGrath, accompanied by Father T. Gough of the Cove.[55]

After the introductions had been completed, the sisters boarded the boat for the thirty-minute journey across the Tickle to the island. The hospitable Father McGrath invited the four of them to the presbytery where he had arranged for them to have dinner and spend the night before moving into their temporary residence. For the next three days, they worked hard, unpacking furniture, books, pots, pans, and dishes to convert their side of the house into a convent. While these preparations were under way, the sisters and their housekeeper were invited to the presbytery for their meals.[56] Finally, everything was in place, and M. Consilio, who thoroughly enjoyed a good dinner, recorded that they cooked their first meal in their temporary convent on Saturday, September 22. That evening, Archbishop Roche arrived to inaugurate the new

---

55. Annals, St. Edward's Convent, Bell Island, ASMSJ.
56. In those days, young girls who had very little education were often employed as housekeepers. These young ladies were referred to as "maids." In the case of outport convents, if there was no sister in community who was free to fill the role of housekeeper, some young girl from the settlement was hired for this duty. The sisters encouraged these young ladies to complete their education, and if they were interested, one of the sisters provided private tutoring.

mission. On Monday morning, September 24, the Feast of Our Lady of Mercy, St. Michael's Church was packed to the doors as the archbishop celebrated mass and prayed for God's blessing on the people of Bell Island and the sisters who came to serve them. After mass, the congregation, clergy, parents, and schoolchildren accompanied the sisters in procession from the church to the school where the archbishop blessed the former Superior School, renamed St. Edward's Convent School in honour of the archbishop's patron saint.

Before the excitement had time to cool down, Father McGrath presented the sisters with a new piano. Unfortunately, it was to be another two years before the new convent was ready to house either the sisters or the piano. The sisters, however, did not need a convent in order to begin their work of teaching and visitation of the poor and the sick. Because St. Edward's School was so far away from the convent, the pastor, Father McGrath, decided that they should teach in St. Joseph's Hall for the time being. In fact, they continued to teach in St. Joseph's Hall until 1928, when the new six-room St. Edward's School was built opposite St. Michael's Parish Church. For her part, M. Aloysius Rawlins lost no time in introducing the children of Bell Island to music. The accounts book for St. Edward's Convent, September 29, 1917, to March 31, 1918, reported that music lessons provided the sisters with an income of $216.[57] An additional $15 was paid to the sisters for the services of M. Aloysius who, in addition to teaching music in the schools, was organist and choir director in the parish church.

By October 1918, the exterior of the new convent was completed, but the interior of the building was still unfinished. This posed a problem for Archbishop Roche. The archbishop took great pride in the first Mercy foundation of his episcopate and decided to name the new convent in honour of his own patron, St. Edward, whose feast day is celebrated on October 13. His dream of escorting the sisters to their new home—where his patronal day would be recognized with due solemnity and appropriate celebrations—was doomed to disappointment. Nevertheless, he was determined that the convent would be dedicated on "St. Edward's Day," and so he set off for Bell Island on

---

57. Accounts Book, St. Edward's Convent, Bell Island, March 31, 1918, ASMSJ.

October 12, 1918, to open the convent—finished or not. M. Consilio described the event in some detail, concluding her account with more than a hint of Irish patriotism:

> On October 12th, 1918, the Archbishop arrived to open the new convent. Mass was celebrated in the church after which the C.C.C. Band played Mozart's "Gloria" in great style, after which the procession was formed to the Convent. The Archbishop blessed the house and addressed the vast congregation from the steps of the front door, urging them to co-operate with Father McGrath in hastening the completion of the interior.
>
> Three days before these ceremonies the Superior General, Mother Bridget [O'Connor] accompanied by Sister M. Pius [Mulcahy] and Sister M. Xavier O'Connor came to assist in preparations for the concert and the reception of guests. On the feast of St. Edward, October 13, they were joined by Sisters M. Philippa [Hanley] and Patrick Flynn. Other visitors were Father Callan O'Reilly and Monsignor McDermott. Thus the opening ceremonies of St. Edward's were honored by representations from Ulster, Munster, Leinster, and Connaught.[58]

Apparently, M. Consilio was more impressed by the presence of visitors of Irish origin than she was by the episcopal rank of other distinguished guests, for both Bishop John March of Harbour Grace and Bishop Michael Power of St. George's were present, the latter having been homilist at the Pontifical Mass.[59] The presence of such a large number of visitors provided an opportunity for the sisters to show off the talents of their students:

> The largest crowd that ever gathered in any building on the Island, attended the Musicale and entertainment given by the Pupils of St. Edward's Convent on the evening of October 12th ... the children excelled themselves in the Programme. Vocal Selections,

---

58. Annals, St. Edward's Convent, Bell Island, ASMSJ. The initials, CCC Band, referred to the Catholic Cadet Corps Band. The representatives of the counties of Ireland: Father Callan (Ulster), Father O'Reilly (Leinster), M. Bridget O'Connor, (Munster), and Monsignor McDermott (Connaught). M. Consilio was from Roscommon. The CCC Band had travelled from St. John's for the occasion.

59. *The Evening Telegram*, October 16, 1918, p. 4.

Recitations, Pianoforte selections, and Drills, all of which showed
the excellent training that is being given . . .[60]

It was an appropriate conclusion to the celebrations, for it demonstrated the
fact that wherever the sisters went, they encouraged the children to grow in
an appreciation of the arts, and Bell Island children took to music like ducks to
water. M. Consilio, a woman who had little tolerance for second-rate performances, pronounced—with a great rolling of *rs*—that it was, indeed, "a
very fine concert."[61]

After the excitement of the opening of the new St. Edward's Convent
and the departure of all the visitors, the regular routine of teaching, visitation,
and community life resumed in earnest. The sisters had to wait another seven
months before they could move into their convent, but in the meantime, they
collected materials to furnish each room. Their friends and relatives helped,
particularly in providing for the chapel. M. Consilio scrupulously recorded the
names of their benefactors. For instance, two weeks before the blessing of the
convent, a new altar for the chapel arrived—the gift of Archbishop Roche. The
general manager of the Nova Scotia Company, Mr. Gillis, ordered a fireproof
brick pumphouse to be erected in the garden for the use of the convent.[62] On
May 24, 1919, the four sisters moved into the new St. Edward's Convent. In
recording this event, M. Consilio added:

> I feel it a duty to record the munificent donations given this
> Convent by the Dominion Company under the management of
> J. J. McDougall. It was he who gave orders to have the Convent
> lighted by electricity and saw that the plant was installed as well
> as the water supply which he superintended personally, and
> under his kind regime we obtained an ample supply of coal—
> *gratis*. We trust that future generations will remember the name
> of J. J. McDougall as our first benefactor.[63]

---

60. *The Daily News*, October 16, 1918, p. 2.
61. Annals, St. Edward's Convent, Bell Island, ASMSJ.
62. Ibid. This work was completed July 2, 1920, ASMSJ.
63. Ibid.

Within a short time after the sisters' arrival, parents from other parts of Bell Island were eager to have their children attend the sisters' school. This meant a long walk to school for many of the children from the section of Bell Island called "the Mines." After a year or two of greeting small children who were tired out after such a long walk, the sisters questioned why they did not go to the students rather than have the students come to them. The pastor, Father McGrath, thought this was a brilliant idea. As a result, beginning in 1919, in addition to teaching at the Front, the sisters took over the direction of the school at the Mines. Every day of the school year, two of the sisters travelled by horse and carriage across the "Track," from the convent to the Mines school. During the winter, when the weather was piercingly cold and the roads blocked by snow, the sisters travelled to and from school by horse and sleigh. Most of the time, they looked forward to these sleigh rides as the horse jogged across the "Track," bells jingling in the crisp winter air. However, it was not always so pleasant, especially when the not-so-skilful driver turned the sleigh on its side, thus depositing the sisters and all their paraphernalia into a cold, wet bank of snow. More often than not, the driver and his horse trotted along happily, completely unaware of the plight of the unfortunate passengers who were struggling to extricate themselves and their belongings from the depths of a snowdrift.[64] As a matter of fact, the hardships and difficulties of commuting from the Front to the Mines in winter prompted the superior general to write to the archbishop.[65] In her letter, she noted that the health of the sisters was being seriously undermined by the repeated colds and chills suffered as a result of their frequent exposure to rain, snow, sleet, and high winds—not to mention the effects of frequent immersion up to the neck in banks of snow. She suggested that during the winter months, the parish might hire lay teachers who lived closer to the school. In response to this request, the archbishop promised to build a small convent near the Mines school. In fact, the Mines school had become too small to accommodate all the Catholic children of that section of Bell Island. The pastor, Father McGrath, having examined the fiscal

---

64. M. Assumpta Veitch to M. Basil McCormack, January 14, 1955, ASMSJ.
65. M. Philippa Hanley, unpublished manuscript, ASMSJ, RG 1/7/15.

health of the parish, decided to build a new school at the Mines, to be financed almost totally by parish funds. On September 24, 1920, Archbishop Roche arrived to open the sisters' new school at Wabana (the Mines). It was called the "Immaculate Conception School."[66] Classes began three weeks later, on October 11. In addition to the two sisters, M. Bernadette O'Rourke and M. Rita Coady, who commuted from St. Edward's Convent, two other teachers, Miss Bessie Craig and Miss Adele Flynn, conducted classes in the new school. Within a short time of its opening, attendance had risen to almost three hundred children. Successive reports of superintendents of education for the RC School Board remarked the high quality of instruction and the conduct of the school. Shortly after it opened, the inspector for the Roman Catholic School Board visited the Immaculate Conception School and reported, "The school has been lately erected and was opened officially on September 24, by His Grace the Archbishop. Under the direction of the Sisters of Mercy, I hope for great results from this centre of learning in this important locality."[67] M. Bridget O'Connor, who took a keen interest in education, made yearly visits to all schools conducted by the sisters. In 1921, she commented on the Mines school as follows:

> It was very gratifying on my first visit to the Convent Schools (The Mines) to find four spacious rooms well filled with bright, intelligent pupils, all clean and well kept. That the Sisters have worked hard during the two terms this school has been in session was evident from the satisfying answering of the Pupils in the school tests which I had the pleasure of giving during these days."[68]

In 1922, the children of the Immaculate Conception School presented an ambitious public performance, which was duly reported by The Daily News.

---

66. The Mines comprised that part of Bell Island surrounding Town Square. St. Edward's Convent and School were located at what was known as the Front—the section facing Portugal Cove.

67. Thomas J. Flynn, assistant superintendent of Catholic schools, Report, 1921, AASJ.

68. M. Basil McCormack, unpublished notes, taken from the records of the Immaculate Conception Academy, Bell Island, ASMSJ. The original records were lost in a fire that destroyed the school and convent on December 13, 1969.

"An operetta in three acts, *Princess Ju Ju* was presented in the Star Hall under the Direction of the Sisters of Mercy, St. Edward's Convent."[69] However, events such as this further emphasized the inconvenience to the sisters of living so far away from their work. Archbishop Roche had not forgotten his promise to provide a convent for the sisters who taught at the Mines, but it was several years before he found a solution. He was aware that the Bell Island Council of the Knights of Columbus enjoyed a very healthy financial situation, and so he decided to approach the Knights and ask for their help. On October 5, 1926, he received a positive response from the recorder of the council meetings, Michael A. Dunne:

> Following the conversation of our Grand Knight with Your Grace re the erection of a Home for the Sisters at the Mines:
> I am instructed to inform Your Grace that same met with unanimous approval of our Council at its regular meeting and that you can therefore take the necessary steps to have work started at as early date as you deem wise.[70]

The new convent was to be dedicated in honour of the Immaculate Conception of the Blessed Virgin Mary in acknowledgement of the assistance provided by the Bell Island Council of the Knights of Columbus. The work of construction began almost immediately. According to the Annals, the Pastor, Rev. J. J. McGrath, assisted by Fathers E. J. Rawlins and G. F. Bartlett, turned the first sod on October 13, 1926. R. Costigan and J. Morley represented the Knights. Five days later, the work of excavation began and, as the annalist remarked gratefully, "All the labour for this part of the work was free."[71] Obviously, winter weather mattered very little to Bell Island workmen, for in spite of frequent storms and the ever-present cold winds that always seem to embrace Bell Island, construction of the Immaculate Conception Convent was completed by the end of January 1927:

---

69. *The Daily News*, October 17, 1922, p. 4.
70. Michael A. Dunne to Archbishop E. P. Roche, October 5, 1926, AASJ, 107/29/4.
71. Annals, Immaculate Conception Convent, Bell Island, ASMSJ.

> On the Eve of the Purification, February I, 1927, the Sisters attending the Schools at the Mines drove from St. Edward's Convent for the last time, and that night slept in the Convent of the Immaculate Conception. Those who remained that first night were Sister M. Rose Power (Superior at St. Edward's), Sr. M. Cecily O'Reilly, Sr. M. Alphonsus McNamara, Sr. M. Gabrielle Carter, Sr. M. Mercedes Slattery (novice). [72]

The first community of the new convent consisted of M. Cecily O'Reilly (superior), M. Alphonsus McNamara, M. Gabrielle Carter, and M. Madeline Sophie Aylward. [73]

The opening of the Immaculate Conception Convent saved a good deal of time for the sisters who were teaching in school, for they were spared the long walk back and forth to St. Edward's Convent. At that time, there were approximately four hundred children registered in Immaculate Conception School, a building that boasted four classrooms. M. Alphonsus McNamara taught in the senior room, M. Gabrielle Carter taught primary, preliminary, and intermediate (corresponding to grades VI, VII-VIII, IX-X) in a second room, and Miss Adele Flynn taught grades IV and V in the third room. M. Madeline Aylward and M. Cecily O'Reilly shared the remaining larger class-room that accommodated one hundred and twenty children in grades I, II, and III. Many years later, M. Madeline described the system she and M. Cecily devised to bring some order of what might otherwise have been a chaotic situation:

> We used to take them [i.e. the children] on the corridor in groups to teach them in order to give the other teacher a chance to

---

72. Ibid.

73. M. Gabrielle Carter was born in Witless Bay, and shortly after her profession in 1924, she was stationed at St. Edward's Convent, Bell Island. A few years after her transfer to the Immaculate Conception Convent, she became ill. Because she was unwilling to leave Bell Island and the children and sisters she had grown to know and love, the sisters of her community cared for her until her death on May 10, 1936. She is buried in the Catholic cemetery on Bell Island. M. Madeline Sophie Aylward was from St. Lawrence. She taught in several convent schools throughout Newfoundland and spent many years at St. Michael's Convent, Belvedere. She died at McAuley Convent in 1993. M. Madeline Sophie is remembered especially for her sense of humour and dry wit.

work with the remaining group. Sr. M. Cecily had monitors and any other helps she could procure. There was no time for extra subjects, but special emphasis was put on reading, writing, spelling, arithmetic and religion.[74]

From the beginning, both St. Edward's and the Immaculate Conception Schools were coeducational. In 1926, the assistant superintendent for Catholic schools, after his visit to the Immaculate Conception School, mentioned the large class of boys in "the Senior Room who were preparing for Primary."[75] In the same report the superintendent remarked the excellence of the classroom singing and the precision of the boys' performances in drill.[76] Furthermore, from the first year the Immaculate Conception School opened, capable students were registered for the CHE examinations. For instance, in June 1921, six students wrote the preliminary examinations and two wrote intermediate. In the following year, however, one young student successfully passed the junior associate examination, the equivalent of grade XI. At the time, the grade XI certificate from the CHE was sufficient for admission to university. In 1927, the Immaculate Conception School presented twenty-two successful candidates for the June CHE examinations.

During all this time, the music program continued in both convent schools on Bell Island. Until the arrival of M. Emeria Gillis in 1930, the sister who taught music at St. Edward's walked to the Mines twice a week to give lessons at the Immaculate Conception School. M. Emeria, a former student of St. Michael's Boarding School, St. George's, was appointed to the staff of the Immaculate Conception School in 1927. M. Emeria was a great advocate of the Trinity College of Music examinations, and immediately on taking up her new

74. M. Madeline Aylward, "Early Years at the Immaculate Conception School, Bell Island," ASMSJ, RG 10/15/12.

75. Thomas J. Flynn, assistant superintendent of Roman Catholic schools, Report for October 12, 1926, AASJ. In those days, primary, the equivalent of grade VI, was looked upon as the first year of high school. From that level through junior and senior associate, students wrote the CHE examinations every June.

76. St. Kevin's Boys' School opened in 1938 for boys from grade IV to grade XI. This school was taught by male teachers. St. Edward's and the Immaculate Conception Schools continued to teach boys up to and including grade III.

duties, she introduced her piano students to the program of studies prescribed by Trinity College. She found that her predecessors had been quite successful in inculcating good practice habits and the correct technique of piano performance. As a result, M. Emeria found that she could register more than enough students for the examinations to allow the Immaculate Conception School to have its own examination centre.[77] M. Emeria Gillis was the first of a series of gifted music specialists who taught in the convent schools on Bell Island. The names of those who succeeded her were well-known in educational and musical circles of Newfoundland as being among the finest teachers of their time.

In 1933, Archbishop Roche appointed a newly ordained, energetic young priest, Rev. George Bartlett, as curate in St. Michael's Parish, Bell Island. At the time, the pastor, Very Rev. Dean McGrath, was nearing retirement and did not realize the deplorable conditions that existed in certain sections of the parish. Not long after his arrival in the parish, Father Bartlett noticed poorly clad, undernourished children playing in the streets when they should have been in school. He decided to take a census of the Catholic families on the island. He found that one hundred and eighty-six children, ranging from ten to fifteen years of age, had never been to school, had received no religious instruction and had never been brought to church. In explaining this situation, M. Madeline mentioned that this was the time of the Great Depression, many men had been laid off, and the mines were working only two days a week. Thus, the reason for the children's absence from school and church was because they had nothing to wear. Under the leadership of M. Alphonsus McNamara, the sisters organized card games and sold needlework in an effort to alleviate the situation. From the proceeds, they purchased material and, with the assistance of a number of ladies of the parish, made enough suits and dresses to clothe every child identified in Fr. Bartlett's survey. But the provision of clothing was only the first step in solving the problem. M.

---

77. According to Trinity College of Music policy, a school was allowed to have its own centre if twelve or more students of the school had registered for the examination. This meant that the examiner visited the designated centre and students did not have to travel elsewhere to be examined.

Madeline wrote that the sisters organized after-school religion classes to prepare these children to receive the sacraments. "Then," she added, "we had to
have more card games to dress them to receive Holy Communion."[78]

By the year 1936, the downturn in Bell Island economy was over. The
mines resumed full production and from that time until the late 1950s, the
island knew prosperity and growth.

But all of this was in the future. Turning back to the first three years of amalgamation of the convents, 1916 to 1919, one cannot help but marvel at the flurry of activity that marked this period of Mercy history. Not only had two new
convents[79] and the general novitiate been established, but also the "Supplement
to the Guide to Customs and Regulations" that reflected the changes brought
about by amalgamation had been prepared for presentation to the 1919 general chapter. In addition, the lengthy triennial report to the Holy See had been
compiled. This was the first time that the Newfoundland Sisters of Mercy had
been required to submit such a document, the preparation of which required
much time and research. More important, perhaps, than all of this was the fact
that sisters from many different convents were able to make the transition from
an autonomous organization to a united congregation that required a great deal
of detachment from persons and places. The three-year experiment had seen an
unprecedented interchange of personnel from one convent to another. For the
most part, the sisters, unused to such changes, took them all in good part and
may have enjoyed the challenge of working with new people and in new surroundings. Thus, as the General Council approached the end of its three-year
mandate, the councillors could feel assured that the first difficult years had been
negotiated successfully. Now it was time that the whole congregation prepared
to elect a new General Council.

---

78. Ibid.
79. St. Mary's on the Humber in Petries and St. Edward's on Bell Island.

CHAPTER THIRTEEN

COMING OF AGE

We can never say, "It is enough."
Catherine McAuley, Familiar Instructions

On June 18, 1919, Archbishop Roche wrote to M. Bridget O'Connor to announce that according to the decree of the Sacred Congregation, August 15, 1919, was the day appointed for the election of a new superior general and council. M. Bridget, of course, was aware of this, and had already convoked a general chapter for August 15 of that year. Superiors of larger communities, such as Mercy Convent, St. Michael's, Belvedere, and Littledale were ex officio delegates to the chapter. In addition, the sisters of these convents elected a delegate from their community. Smaller convents were grouped together, and the sisters elected one superior and one professed sister from the group. It was the duty of these delegates to elect the members of a new General Administration. In addition, they were required to examine and make any necessary modifications to the "Supplement to the Guide to Customs and Regulations of the Sisters of Mercy of Newfoundland." The members of chapter were required, also, to study and approve the triennial report on the affairs of the congregation from 1916–1919 that had to be sent to Rome. The first chapter of elections for the General Council was held on August 15, 1919. The results showed that the sisters of the congregation were satisfied with the performance of the sisters who had been appointed by their bishops in 1916. M. Bridget O'Connor was elected superior general (or mother general) and, with the exception of M. Brigid Hoey, all the former councillors were returned to office. The new member of council, M. Teresa O'Halleran, was elected treasurer general to replace M. Bernard Dooley, who became first councillor. M. Mercedes Lyons, M. Philippa Hanley, and M. Antonio Egan resumed their positions as councillors, and M. Genevieve Farrell was confirmed in her position as secretary general.

The term of office for the General Council was six years. The superior general could be re-elected for a second term of six years, but there was no limit on the number of times that councillors could be re-elected. In fact, M. Teresa O'Halleran and M. Genevieve Farrell remained in their respective positions for the rest of their lives.[1] M. Bridget O'Connor filled the positions of superior general and first councillor alternately until her death. M. Bernard Dooley was re-elected to every council up to the year 1943. However, when the death of M. Bridget O'Connor in January 1945, left a vacancy on council, M. Bernard Dooley was appointed to the position of first assistant. She remained in that position until the general chapter of 1949.

It was a wise decision on the part of the members of the congregation to maintain a stable membership on the first few councils. These were the years of rapid growth, and the challenges of the post-war period required the wisdom of experience. Already there were more requests for the services of the sisters than could be considered in the immediate future. However, one priest, Father Patrick O'Brien from Bay Bulls, was particularly insistent, and in 1921, the Sisters of Mercy agreed to establish a convent in his parish.

Bay Bulls is a small fishing settlement on the east coast of the Avalon Peninsula about nineteen miles south of St. John's. It is one of the earliest settlements on the island, for its name appeared on a manuscript map by Thomas Hood in 1592.[2] The name may derive from a species of bird known as "bull bird" or,

---

1. M. Genevieve Farrell died on May 19, 1935. Since only two years remained in the Council's six-year term, the superior general, M. Philippa Hanley, recorded the minutes of council meetings. M. Teresa O'Halleran died on February 4, 1937. Because there was such a short time before the next chapter the position was left vacant. Six months later, at the 1937 chapter, M. Consilio Kenny was elected as treasurer general. ASMSJ, MG 1/6/72.
2. *ENL*, s.v. "Bay Bulls."

more correctly, the dovekie, which is found along the coast of Newfoundland in winter. Other historians have suggested that the name came from Jersey fishermen who called the place "Baie Boulee" or "Buley Bay."[3] Before the Treaty of Utrecht (1713) decided England's claim to Newfoundland, England and France waged constant battles over possession of the island and its rich fishing grounds, St. John's being the focus of the French attacks on the colony. However, in spite of repeated attempts, St. John's was practically invulnerable to attack from the sea because of the unique contour of the surrounding cliffs. Bay Bulls, with its sheltered, deepwater harbour, provided the French with an ideal anchorage spot for their warships and a direct overland route for an assault on the capital. In the century between 1696 and 1796, the French attacked Bay Bulls five times.[4] In 1796, during their last attack on the colony, Bay Bulls was totally destroyed and some of the inhabitants taken prisoner. Nevertheless, by the beginning of the nineteenth century, the population of Bay Bulls was once more on the increase. Those who had fled the invasion returned and rebuilt their homes, and as well, a number of settlers arrived from Ireland.

In 1831, Bishop Fleming appointed the Irish priest, Father Patrick Cleary, as first pastor of the parish of Bay Bulls, an area that stretched from Bay Bulls Big Pond to La Manche.[5] Father Cleary established his own residence in Witless Bay, a settlement a few miles south of Bay Bulls.[6] He immediately set to work building churches, schools, and finally, in 1860, a convent in Witless Bay for the Presentation Sisters. It was that same year, 1860, that Father (now

---

3. Paul O'Neill, *The Seat Imperial: Bay Bulls, Past and Present* (St. John's, NL: Harry Cuff Publications, 1983), p.10.

4. *ENL*, s.v. "Bay Bulls." In 1696, a British frigate, *Sapphire*, was sunk in action in Bay Bulls harbour. The *Sapphire* is thought to be the oldest of three ships buried in silt in the harbour.

5. O'Neill, *The Seat Imperial*, p. 34.

6. Witless Bay remained the parish centre until 1921 when the newly appointed parish priest, Patrick O'Brien, caused an uproar when he decided to move the centre to Bay Bulls. The people of Witless Bay complained to Archbishop Roche, who settled the controversy by creating two separate parishes of Bay Bulls and of Witless Bay. See Queen Maloney, *Trail Wanderings: A Folk History of Bay Bulls, Newfoundland* (St. John's: Creative Book Publishing, 1994), pp. 40–41.

Dean) Cleary was given an assistant in the person of the newly ordained Nicholas Roche. However, it was not until 1879 that Bay Bulls had its own resident priest when Dean Cleary's assistant, Father Roche, took up residence in the town. By 1890, in order to accommodate his large congregation, Father Roche replaced the church of Sts. Peter and Paul in Bay Bulls with a new and larger building that is still in use. Many years later, several eighteenth-century cannons were discovered in one of the old battle sites in Bay Bulls. The cannons had rested there undisturbed for more than a century until Father Roche's successor and a group of men transferred them to the church grounds to be used as gate posts. They serve as pedestals for statues of Saints Peter and Paul, St. Patrick, and St. Thérèse of Lisieux.

As was the case in other settlements, the education of the children was of prime importance to the parish priest. As early as 1850, there was a Roman Catholic School Board at Bay Bulls, over which Dean Cleary presided with six of his male parishioners as board members. It was the women of Bay Bulls, however, who initiated and carried on the real work of education. Back as far as 1818, a few women had begun teaching a group of children during the summer months.[7] By the year 1870, over forty young girls paid £1.2.6 a year to attend a school taught by Miss Williams. A gentleman named Terrence Morrissey collected the same fee from about sixty boys who attended his "Commercial School." The subjects taught were the same in each school— writing on slates, and "easy lessons" that consisted probably of basic reading, writing, and arithmetic.[8] However, the remuneration provided by the government to the teachers depended on the sex of the individual. For his labours, Mr. Morrissey received an annual salary of £50, while Miss Morrissey had to be content with the munificent sum of £25 per year. Nevertheless, the efforts of these pioneer educators should not be undervalued. Paul O'Neill paid tribute to them and pointed out the hardships that accompanied their work when he wrote:

---

7. O'Neill, *The Seat Imperial*, p. 39. O'Neill cites as his source Margaret Chang's unpublished manuscript held at the Centre for Newfoundland Studies, Memorial University of Newfoundland.

8. Ibid.

While the masters and the mistresses who taught in the one and
two room schoolhouses prior to World War I often did excellent
work, poverty in the purse dampened their spirits. They carried
out their shunned and thankless burden with meagre funds and on
starvation wages. In 1921, however, matters improved considerably
at Bay Bulls when the Parish Priest, Father Patrick O'Brien ... invited the Sisters of Our Lady of Mercy to open a convent and school
there.[9]

Father O'Brien was not alone in his anxiety to have the sisters come to Bay
Bulls to take charge of the school. The people were unanimously behind their
parish priest in his efforts to persuade M. Bridget O'Connor to establish a convent in the town. As early as 1915, in spite of limitations and shortages due to
the war, the people were preparing to receive the sisters. The convent was built
through the free labour of the men of the village. Mrs. Queenie Maloney, who
was a small child at the time, recalled that:

The men hauled the frame from the woods and helped to build it
[the convent]. We had a dance in it just before it was consecrated and all the mothers and fathers and their children were there
and people took turns playing the fiddle, as it was called then, not
violin, also the accordion.[10]

The building of the convent took five years, but by 1921, the people had erected a new school, a hall, and a convent, confident that even the most obdurate
reverend mother would not be able to refuse their repeated requests. Finally,
in September 1921, their hopes were realized.

On the morning of September 24, 1921, the Feast of Our Lady of
Mercy, the superior general of the Sisters of Mercy, M. Bridget O'Connor, and
the four sisters who were to form the first Mercy community in Bay Bulls
arrived by car to an enthusiastic welcome from the people of the town. Father
O'Brien, his curate, Father Michael Kennedy, and every parishioner who was

9. Ibid.
10. Queen Maloney, "Recollections," ASMSJ, RG 10/12/44. A handwritten account of the
arrival of the sisters in Bay Bulls.

the owner of a car escorted the sisters from St. John's. When the motorcade rounded the top of the hill approaching Bay Bulls, it was greeted by a volley of gunfire and the cheers of the people who lined both sides of the road. Two days later, on September 26, school began with a total enrolment of 170 boys and girls.[11]

Father O'Brien had planned well, for when the sisters arrived, the convent was finished and ready for occupancy. It was unusual for Sisters of Mercy going on a foundation to be able to move immediately into a beautiful new convent. St. Patrick's Convent was a spacious building next to the parish church. It had a large chapel on the second floor, the chief adornment of which was a magnificent stained glass window. The pastor, Father O'Brien, designed the window himself and sent the plan to Dublin to a company that specialized in making stained glass windows. The window depicted St. Patrick preaching to the King of Tara, St. Bridget of Ireland, and the patrons of the sisters who formed the first community, St. Winefride, St. Michael, St. Paul, and St. Rita.

The superior of the new community was M. Winefride Greene, a native of St. John's. She was educated at Our Lady of Mercy School, and at the age of nineteen, she made up her mind to become a Sister of Mercy. She completed her novitiate at Mercy Convent under the direction of Margaret Mary Lynch and was professed June 16, 1900. Three years later, she spent a year in St. Anne's Convent, Burin, before being transferred to Sacred Heart Convent, St. Lawrence, where a few years later, she was appointed superior. M. Winefride remained in St. Lawrence until the amalgamation in 1916 when she was recalled to St. John's. Clearly, she had a good deal of experience before being appointed as superior of St. Patrick's Convent, Bay Bulls. From that time on, for almost the rest of her life, M. Winefride filled the office of superior in different convents in Newfoundland. Finally, she was elected to the General Council of the Sisters of Mercy.

M. Winefride was a woman who demanded a good deal of herself and of others. Some sisters who lived with her perceived her as being strict, with little understanding of or patience with the impetuosity and inexperience of

---

11. ASMSJ.

youth. Others spoke of her as a woman who showed kindness and consideration for the sisters in her community. But in spite of differing opinions, all
agree that when trouble came, or if encouragement and advice were needed,
M. Winefride Greene was always available with reassuring words and wise
counsel.

When M. Winefride Greene was appointed to St. Patrick's Convent in
Bay Bulls she faced a workload that, if offered to many of her less stalwart successors, would frighten them out of their wits. In addition to being superior
and principal of the school, she was also the music teacher. Like all outport
music teachers, she was responsible not only for teaching music during the
school day, after hours, and on Saturdays, but also for training and directing the
church choir and playing the organ for church functions. Moreover, she organized and directed several concerts every year. An important and by no means
insignificant reason for these concerts was to raise funds to supplement the
pitifully small government subsidies for school maintenance, for M. Winefride
was determined to provide the best and latest equipment for the young scholars of Bay Bulls. Furthermore, the people looked forward to these events,
especially in the outports, as a welcome form of entertainment. However, M.
Winefride had to overcome a major obstacle before she could continue her
concerts. Father O'Brien did not approve of the sisters spending their evenings
preparing for these entertainments. He decreed that it was not appropriate for
them to be seen traipsing back and forth to the parish hall after dark. No
amount of persuasion could change his mind until M. Bridget O'Connor
stepped in and declared that if the sisters were prepared to undertake the extra
work, the concerts should go ahead as planned. When faced with M. Bridget's
gentle insistence, Father O'Brien's thundering edicts were muted to a subdued
pianissimo.[12] During her three years in Bay Bulls, M. Winefride directed several operettas and laid a solid foundation for what became a successful music
program in the school.

A glance at the lives of these pre-Vatican II women suggests that they
gave no thought to seeking a ministry or a community that would satisfy their

12. M. Teresa Williams to M. Basil McCormack, March 3, 1955, ASMSJ.

own needs, or be "life-giving" to themselves. Rather, they appear to have been completely self-forgetful, trusting God—to whom they had given their lives—to be with them wherever they went, and they asked for nothing more. Looking on their assigned tasks as God's will for them, they gave themselves unstintingly to the ministry assigned them. In their unshakeable belief in God's loving Providence they found spirit and life in abundance and, incidentally, brought these gifts to others.

The second member of the community of St. Patrick's Convent, Bay Bulls, M. Michael Gillis, had spent most of her life on the West Coast before being transferred to Bay Bulls. The severity of the storms and the piercing cold of the easterly gales blowing in directly off the Atlantic Ocean were new and difficult experiences for M. Michael. Nevertheless, the rugged beauty of the East Coast, so different from the mountains and lush, quiet valleys of the west, was a source of wonder and inspiration to this imaginative young woman.

M. Paul Ryall, the third member of the community, was born in St. John's on December 29, 1894, the daughter of Samuel Ryall and Louise Kennedy. She received her education at Mercy Convent and was accepted as a postulant at Littledale on September 24, 1915. In 1921, three years after her first profession (July 16, 1918), she was sent to Bay Bulls as a member of the founding community. Many years later, sisters who lived with M. Paul remember her as one who was never heard to utter an unkind word about anyone. During the twenty-seven years she spent at St. Michael's Convent, Belvedere, the orphans referred to her as "the smiling nun."[13] When she went to Bay Bulls, in addition to teaching regular classes during the day, M. Paul taught commercial classes several evenings a week and on Saturdays. These sessions were held for the benefit of young men and women who were unable to attend during regular school hours. The students were charged a fee of twenty-five cents a quarter,[14] an amount that did not swell the convent coffers to any notable degree. In any case, M. Paul was not overly conscientious about collecting the twenty-five cents from the commercial students, and the superior, M.

---

13. Annals, St. Michael's Convent, Belvedere, ASMSJ.
14. Annals, St. Patrick's Convent, Bay Bulls, ASMSJ.

Winefride, in spite of her somewhat austere bearing, was prepared to overlook M. Paul's lack of diligence in this regard. On Saturday afternoons, as a change from her regular duties during the week, M. Paul occupied herself by teaching art to some interested and talented young people of Bay Bulls.

The junior member of the community, M. Rita Coady, was born in Burin where she received her early education from the Sisters of Mercy. Later on, as a teenager, she became a boarding student at Littledale where, in 1918, at the age of eighteen, she asked to be admitted as a postulant. Less than two months after her profession on July 16, 1921, she became one of the foundresses of St. Patrick's Convent, Bay Bulls. It was the beginning of a long life of service to the young people of Newfoundland.

However, it was not "all work and no play" for the sisters in Bay Bulls. Mrs. Queen Maloney remembered that in August, after they returned from summer school in St. John's, the sisters often brought the children on picnics. Parents provided transportation, and Father Michael Kennedy, the curate, went along to supervise the boys. They spent part of the day picking berries and playing games, such as "Farmer in the Dell." But the most important event of the outing was the "boil-up," when the priest made a fire, and the sisters boiled the kettle and treated the children to a lavish lunch consisting of beans, bread, and cookies.[15]

Prior to the arrival of the sisters, grade XI was not taught in Bay Bulls. In fact, it was not until 1926 that a pupil was ready for this level of the CHE examinations when a student named Mary Mulcahy was a successful candidate.[16] Beginning in 1930, and every year thereafter, Bay Bulls students registered for the CHE examinations up to and including grade XI matriculation. As a rule, the results were a source of pride and satisfaction to the whole community. The sisters taught these high-school students in a room that connected the convent to the parish church. Primary and elementary classes were taught in a three-room school at the rear of the convent. There was no running

---

15. Maloney, "Recollections," ASMSJ.

16. M. Teresa Williams to M. Basil McCormack, January 28, 1955. ASMSJ. The Mary Mulcahy to whom the letter referred was not the future M. Nolasco Mulcahy who would have been only nine years old at the time.

water in this school and no central heating. Each child, in turn, brought a bundle of wood to school and, under the eagle eye of the sister in charge, lit the fire in the big pot-bellied stove in the middle of the room. The parish hall, where the concerts were held, also lacked any modern conveniences. On one occasion the sisters held the concert in the large music room of the convent. In this case the financial returns amounted to $90. Obviously, members of the audience were extraordinarily generous, since the admission fee was twenty cents for adults and five cents for children.[17]

In spite of the fact that, for years, the ladies of the parish had provided voluntary and expert service in caring for the church, the sacristy, and the altar linens, when the convent opened the sisters were expected to take over these duties. This was true, not only in Bay Bulls, but also everywhere else in Newfoundland. Invariably, the sisters enlisted the help of the senior girls. In Bay Bulls, along with the students, the ladies continued to lend a hand, especially in preparing for big celebrations. By working together on a weekly basis, sisters and parishioners formed a close, friendly, and co-operative relationship that continues to the present day.

Another chore that the pastor required of the sisters in Bay Bulls was the direction of the Sodality of the Children of Mary. Apparently, the sodality did not contribute much to the parish or the community, at least in the early days, for M. Teresa Williams wrote, with brutal honesty, "The only activity of the Children of Mary I remember was the tatting of a surplice for Father O'Brien."[18] Apparently, the sisters had plenty of time to carry on all these extra assignments for, according to M. Rita Coady, Father O'Brien was a most unusual man. An early riser, his first obligation of the day was to celebrate mass for the sisters—at five o'clock in the morning.[19] Thus, an extra hour was added to the *Horarium* of St. Patrick's Convent, for the working day began at six o'clock in every other convent.

---

17. Annals, St. Patrick's Convent, Bay Bulls, ASMSJ.
18. Ibid.
19. Hogan, *Pathways*, p. 180.

During the summer months, most of the sisters in outport convents were required to go to St. John's to attend summer school. One or two remained behind to provide sisters from St. John's, who were not attending school, with a few weeks rest and relaxation away from the city. In any case, someone had to stay home to look after the church, play the organ for liturgical celebrations, help "make the hay," and look after the convent cow.[20]

A Delco engine supplied electricity to both church and convent in Bay Bulls, and although more than a little temperamental at times, the Delco was a great help to the sisters during the long, dark evenings of autumn and winter. By the 1920s, the convents in St. John's were connected by phone. In Bay Bulls, however, if the sisters needed to use the phone, they walked to the public pay station that, according to M. Scholastica Flynn, was "up the road a piece."[21] As a matter of fact, the sisters had to go "up the road a piece" for reasons other than to use the telephone. For example, according to canon law at that time, all religious were required to present themselves to the regular confessor once a week to receive the sacrament of penance. Because the regular confessor in Bay Bulls was also the parish priest, it was often embarrassing, to say the least, for a sister to have to tell the holy man that she had sinned by entertaining uncharitable thoughts about the pastor![22] As a result, it was more convenient for the erring one to go to Witless Bay, a community about five miles south of Bay Bulls, to receive the sacrament of penance from the pastor there—who also may have entertained uncharitable thoughts about his reportedly autocratic colleague in Bay Bulls and therefore could be expected to be somewhat lenient in the penance he imposed.

Nevertheless, Father Patrick O'Brien appreciated the ministry of the sisters and spared no effort or expense to provide them with whatever they needed to further their work for the parish. He was particularly supportive of their efforts to enhance the liturgy. In 1930, he purchased a Casavant pipe organ for

---

20. M. Scholastica Flynn, "Memories of St. Patrick's Convent, Bay Bulls," November 1982, ASMSJ.

21. Ibid.

22. Ibid. Evidently, uncharitable thoughts about the pastor were thought to be more sinful than uncharitable thoughts about anybody else.

the church, and at the same time, he had an eight-bell chime installed in the church tower. This chime was operated from a keyboard near the organ. It was an investment greatly appreciated by the people of Bay Bulls, especially during the Christmas season when, every evening, the music of the carols rang out through the quiet little village.

Even with all the inconveniences associated with lack of facilities, inadequate heating, and multi-grade classrooms, the convent school at Bay Bulls produced a number of very successful graduates, such as Dorothy (Fanning) Wyatt. After leaving school, Dorothy became a registered nurse and later received a university degree in social work. For two successive terms she was mayor of the City of St. John's, and in later years, she was voted in as a member of city council in successive elections up to the day she died.[23] Another former student, Kevin Melvin, is a leading heart surgeon in St. John's, and many graduates of the sisters' school in Bay Bulls hold influential positions at the university, in various government departments, in the arts community, and in the business world. Another brilliant student who graduated from the convent school in Bay Bulls was Mary Mulcahy. Mary entered the novitiate of the Sisters of Mercy at Littledale at the age of sixteen years. Known throughout Newfoundland as Sr. M. Nolasco, she became a towering figure in educational circles in the province and, in fact, throughout Canada. Two students of the convent school in Bay Bulls, Francis Mullowney and Albert O'Driscoll, were ordained to the priesthood, and eight young women from the town entered the Congregation of the Sisters of Mercy.[24] The fact that eight students in such a small school chose to enter religious life is a tribute to the sisters who lived and worked in Bay Bulls.

The sisters had a good deal of sympathy for young men and teenage boys who, because of family circumstances, did not complete high school. Most of these young lads went fishing at the age of fourteen or fifteen to help augment

23. Dorothy Wyatt was critically ill in hospital at the time of the election for St. John's City Council in 2001. Elections were held September 4, and when the results were announced, Dorothy had been reelected to her seat on council. Sadly, she had died early that morning.

24. Srs. M. Teresa Williams, M. Borgia Kenny, M. Nolasco Mulcahy, M. Patrick O'Driscoll, M. Theophane O'Driscoll, M. Uriel O'Driscoll, Margaret Williams, and Margaret Mulcahy were all professed as Sisters of Mercy in Newfoundland.

the family income. The convent Annals of 1925–1930 show that "Evening Classes for Boys" were well attended and met with considerable success. Because of the interest and dedication of the sisters, these young men graduated from high school, and most of them went on to enjoy considerable success in their chosen careers.

After the death of Father P. J. O'Brien in 1940, the front section of the spacious convent was partitioned and made into a residence for the parish priest. Although this required the sisters to make some rather radical readjustments in their part of the house, the arrangement worked quite well. As well, some additions were made to the school.

A few years later, in 1949, the sisters' school received a sudden increase in enrolment when the children from the Anglican schools in Gunridge and Bread and Cheese were sent to St. Patrick's School.[25] In 1958, a school opened at Bread and Cheese for children from grade I to VI, but students from grades VII to XI continued to attend the Catholic school. However, the school at Bread and Cheese closed in 1965, and all the students returned to St. Patrick's. Two years later, the parish priest of Tors Cove, Father William Lawton, succeeded in persuading the General Council of the Sisters of Mercy to send a couple of sisters to take charge of the Catholic school in his parish. Tors Cove is a small fishing village about fifteen miles south of Bay Bulls on the Southern Shore. The two sisters assigned to the new mission belonged to the community of St. Patrick's Convent and commuted from Bay Bulls. The first two sisters to teach in Tors Cove were M. Francis Xavier Turpin (principal) and M. Rona O'Gorman. They were welcomed officially to the parish after mass on Sunday and presented with a Volkswagon. Evidently, the people of Tors Cove wanted to make sure that the sisters would not have to depend on others for transportation. The sisters served in Tors Cove for eleven years until, in 1978, the General Council of the Sisters of Mercy found it necessary to withdraw them from the school. The people of the parish were very disappointed when the announcement was made, but they showed their appreciation by inviting all the

---

25. Gunridge and Bread and Cheese were tiny communities on the north shore of Bay Bulls Harbour. Most of the people belonged to the Anglican faith and, up until 1949, had their own little school.

sisters who had taught in the school to a special Mass of Thanksgiving in the parish church, followed by a reception in the parish hall. The decision to withdraw the sisters was a source of sorrow to all concerned. In order not to sever all ties with people who had shown them so much affection and co-operation, two sisters gave voluntary service in the school and visited the sick and elderly of the parish until June 1980, when circumstances compelled them to retire permanently from ministry in Tors Cove.

In 1968, the trend toward consolidating high-school education reached the Southern Shore. The Roman Catholic School Board for the district opened a central high school in Mobile, a town about ten miles from Bay Bulls. Students of high-school age from Bay Bulls and other villages in the area were transported by bus to the new school. St. Patrick's School in Bay Bulls was now a primary/elementary school.

Back in Bay Bulls, the sisters continued to teach in the old St. Patrick's School that, over the years, was beginning to show its age. Eventually, a new elementary school was built, and the students began classes in the new school on January 3, 1978. By a strange coincidence, the new school, located some distance from the convent, was built on the site of the school that was in use before the sisters went to Bay Bulls in 1921. During the decade of the 1980s, there were five sisters in the community of St. Patrick's Convent. Three sisters taught in the school, and the other two spent their days visiting the sick and shut-ins and assisting in all kinds of activities that took place in the parish. By the end of the 1990s, there were only two sisters left in the school. It was no longer feasible to maintain a large convent for two people, and the Leadership Team of the Sisters of Mercy[26] suggested that Srs. Ann Normore and Patricia Gallant investigate the possibility of leasing a smaller house. This posed no problem, for new houses were appearing almost overnight in Bay Bulls. Within a short time, the sisters were warm and snug in a new, modern bungalow, conveniently located about five minutes' drive from the school. In addition to

---

26. At the general chapter of 1997, the name of the administrative body of the congregation was changed from "General Council" to "Leadership Team." In future, the superior general would be called "congregational leader," except in special circumstances when it might be advisable to retain the title "superior general."

their school duties, they continued to be involved in parish activities, particularly in the liturgy, and, of course, visiting the sick and the bereaved.

With only one sister left in the school at the time of writing, it seems that the happy story of the Bay Bulls foundation will shortly come to an end. But sisters who have served in Bay Bulls over the past eighty years will remember always with gratitude and affection the kindly people among whom they lived and worked.

Meanwhile, just before the first sisters left for Bay Bulls in 1921, important changes were taking place in other convents. In spite of the extension built in 1913, Archbishop Roche was concerned about the lack of space at Our Lady of Mercy School. Now he saw a way to remedy the situation. The Knights of Columbus were anxious to build a school as a memorial to those killed in the war. When informed of their intention, Archbishop Roche made the following suggestion to the Knights:

> There is another educational work of very great importance to which I have been giving consideration for a long time past, and that is the building of new schools in connection with the Academy of Our Lady of Mercy, Military Road. This School—one of the leading centres of training for our Catholic girls—has been lamentably deficient in accommodation for years past . . . the schools are overcrowded, the classrooms congested, and the Sisters who do such excellent work for our girls are handicapped by these unfavourable conditions . . .
>
> It is proposed to erect in the Convent grounds a three-storey building containing twelve classrooms, music rooms, cloak rooms, aula maxima, etc., all planned and laid out on the most approved modern educational principles. This building when finished will be . . . a Memorial with which the Knights of Columbus will be proud to be associated.[27]

---

27. Archbishop E. P. Roche to C. J. Cahill, Grand Knight, Knights of Columbus, November 12, 1919, AASJ, 107/29/6.

The archbishop reminded the Knights that they could expect the support of their wives in this undertaking. This may have been a veiled threat that if they should refuse his request, they would bring down on their heads the wrath of their spouses—all loyal alumnae of Our Lady of Mercy Academy! As further encouragement, the archbishop reminded the Knights of the well-known fundraising abilities of Mercy graduates. The Knights agreed to the archbishop's proposal, and construction of the new wing began immediately.

The new Knights of Columbus Memorial School opened on September 14, 1921. It contained fourteen new classrooms, seven music rooms, six dressing rooms, and a modern commercial department where more than eighty-five young men and women were enrolled in the business education courses. Unfortunately, however, after a few years the Knights of Columbus found themselves in financial straits, and the sisters were forced to assume responsibility for the debt on the school. In a letter to the Knights, Archbishop Roche made the following remarks:

> As you know, an unexpected obligation of $22,000.00 had to be assumed by the Sisters of Mercy, and this, with the $4,000.00 outstanding which the Council has been unable to pay to the [Episcopal] Corporation, makes a total indebtedness on the K. of C. School approximately $26,000.00. It seems clear that this obligation will now have to be assumed, directly by the Sisters of Mercy . . .[28]

To assume responsibility for a debt of this magnitude was serious commitment for the Sisters of Mercy, especially in view of the requirements of other institutions owned by the congregation. Undoubtedly, M. Bridget O'Connor had inherited the unlimited confidence and trust in Divine Providence that was one of the legacies of Catherine McAuley to her sisters. However, through wise administration and the conscientious sacrifices of all the sisters, eventually the debt was paid in full. In 1942, Archbishop Roche outlined the sequence of events for the information of the new Grand Knight:

28. Archbishop Roche to James Gibbs, Terra Nova Council of the Knights of Columbus, October 10, 1936, AASJ, 107/29/5.

Unfortunately ... owing to general worldwide conditions, here and elsewhere, the Council found it impossible to meet the annual obligations ...

An account has been opened in the West End Branch of the Royal Bank of Canada ... in which deposits will be made from time to time by the College of Our Lady of Mercy to meet the Interest and liquidate the Principal. I would also say on behalf of the College of Our Lady of Mercy that they have been glad to assume this comparatively small outstanding obligation in view of the great work which was done by the Council in erecting this Memorial School.[29]

Pupils of the Academy of Our Lady of Mercy continued to reap the benefits of the improved facilities provided in the new K of C Memorial wing. They consistently achieved very satisfactory results in the CHE examinations, but M. Bridget O'Connor knew that there was no standing still in the field of education. Therefore, she was determined to provide opportunities for the sisters to continue their studies and obtain even higher academic qualifications. Under the wise administration of M. Teresa O'Halleran, the financial health of the congregation was looking brighter. With this in mind, the General Council decided to send a sister away for postgraduate study. M. Perpetua O'Callaghan, the brilliant headmistress of St. Bride's College, Littledale, was the obvious choice.[30] In fact, M. Perpetua had been suffering for some time from fatigue and overwork. This influenced the decision to release her from her duties as headmistress. However, M. Perpetua could not see herself doing absolutely nothing. Characteristically, she persuaded the council that further studies at a recognized university would be a welcome change from her former occupation. M. Perpetua was accepted at Fordham University in New York where she completed the requirements for both the bachelor and master of arts degrees. In 1923, she was awarded the degree of doctor of philosophy, the first—but by no means the last—Newfoundland Sister of Mercy to achieve such a distinction.

---

29. Archbishop E. P. Roche to J. Duffy, Grand Knight, Knights of Columbus January 28, 1942, AASJ, 107/29/7.

30. In 1917, an amendment was made to the Education Act whereby St. Bride's Academy was permitted to share in the grant for colleges; and so, Littledale became recognized as the Roman Catholic college for women, "Report of the Department of Education," 1918, p. 49.

Other sisters in their turn were sent to American and Canadian universities to pursue graduate degrees in different academic disciplines.

Neither did M. Bridget O'Connor neglect the arts. An artist herself, she encouraged sisters to develop their gifts and provided opportunities for them to do so. Furthermore, she was determined to maintain the excellent reputation of the Sisters of Mercy in the field of music. Sisters in St. John's and in the outports were brought to Mercy Convent where, through the genius of M. Baptist McDermott, they were taught the knowledge and skills needed to continue to develop the gift of music with which a loving Creator has so generously endowed the children of Newfoundland. Then, when sisters were thoroughly grounded in knowledge and technique, M. Bridget sent them off to universities in the United States and Canada to earn a degree.

Another problem brought before members of the General Council shortly after their appointment in 1916 was the fact that St. Michael's Orphanage at Belvedere was in urgent need of repair, renovation, and new equipment for the classrooms. The superior of St. Michael's Convent, M. de Chantal O'Keefe, was not hesitant in reminding the council that educational standards throughout Newfoundland had improved considerably since the beginning of the century. She insisted that the students at Belvedere have the same educational advantages as children in other schools operated by the sisters. In 1917, more than 130 girls were being cared for at the orphanage. Without hesitation, the council gave approval for the necessary work to be done and new equipment purchased. Before the end of the following year, the renovations had been completed. The report of the superintendent of education for that year contained a description of the improvements effected:

> The Orphanage has been thoroughly renovated; hard-wood floors laid, and many improvements effected. The spacious school-room ... is now divided into separate class-rooms, well-lighted and ventilated ...In addition to the usual school subjects taught, 8 pupils are receiving lessons in shorthand, typewriting, and book-keeping ...
>
> The room devoted to the infants is ideally situated—facing south, it has the benefit of sunlight for many of the school hours. This department is also supplied with handsome dual-desks, wall black-boards, ball frames, reading charts, attractive pictures—

everything calculated to make school-life interesting and happy for the "babies." The tiny tots of three and four are learning to read from the Beacon Chart, and their proficiency in a short period is amazing. The play-hall is in close proximity to the infant room, and at intervals the little ones are granted a five minutes recess to run and romp around. . . . Action songs and musical drill are important features in the Infant-room work, and are much enjoyed.[31]

The superintendent mentioned also that the school library was well-stocked with books of interest to children of all ages. Furthermore, although it did not come within his mandate, he remarked that along with their academic duties, the sisters supervised meals, recreation, study, and household chores in the orphanage. His report concluded with the statement, "In addition . . . the Sisters attend to the making and mending of the vast amount of clothing required for such a number of children."[32]

The ceaseless round of duties took its toll on the health of many of the young sisters in Belvedere. M. Angela Christopher, who had been professed in 1915, died nine years later at the age of twenty-nine. Others became seriously ill and were incapacitated for long periods of time. Over and above the physical demands, sisters who were assigned to the orphanage had little time for themselves. At Belvedere, the needs of the children took precedence over everything else, even community prayer and recreation. As a result, it often happened that sisters went for days without any opportunity to relax from the unceasing demands of loving and caring for over a hundred children. As every parent knows, a child needs much much more than food and lodging. There were hurt and lonely children to be comforted; excited and happy children to be encouraged; puzzled teenagers to be counselled; scraped knees to be bandaged; cut fingers to be inspected, kissed, and cured; night prayers to be heard; stories told and children tucked into bed for the night.

Nevertheless, those in charge did their best. While the focus seems to have been on the comfort and security of the children, the sisters, too, benefit-

---

31. "Report of the Superintendent of Education for Roman Catholic Schools for the Year Ended December 31, 1918," p. 49, ASMSJ, MG 34/1/122.

32. Ibid.

ed from the improvements made to the building itself, to the sleeping accommodations, and to the classrooms. In 1922, at a cost of $10,000, a recreation
hall was erected to provide facilities for dramatic and musical performances, for
physical training, and—most important—for the enjoyment of the children. In
that year there were 180 children registered at Belvedere. Three years later, in
1925, the General Council authorized the construction of a new wing to provide additional classrooms, dormitories, dining rooms, workrooms, and a
chapel. It was in 1925, as well, that the popular superior of St. Michael's
Convent, Belvedere, M. Philippa Hanley, was elected to succeed M. Bridget
O'Connor as superior general of the Sisters of Mercy in Newfoundland.

M. Philippa Hanley was born in Roscommon, Ireland, on January 12,
1866. She and her friend, Catherine Frances Flynn (later M. Patrick), came to
St. John's on August 15, 1885, and, having spent seven months as postulants at
St. Michael's Convent, Belvedere, they were received into the novitiate on
March 8, 1886. By this time the new orphanage, completed in 1885, was
almost filled to capacity, so that the advent of these two young ladies from
Ireland was a godsend to the overworked staff of St. Michael's Convent. The
two new novices were professed together on December 28, 1887, and as far
as they were concerned, they would spend the rest of their lives caring for the
orphans. But God had other plans for M. Philippa Hanley. In 1904, Archbishop
Howley decided she was needed at St. Bride's Convent, Littledale. With a
heavy heart, she packed her few belongings and left her beloved Belvedere for
Littledale where, in addition to serving as novice mistress, she taught the senior students and the teachers-in-training. Four years later, the impulsive archbishop decided that M. Philippa's talents could be put to better use elsewhere.
Accordingly, in January 1908, she found herself on the high seas en route to
the Sacred Heart Convent in St. Lawrence.[33] During her three years in St.
Lawrence, M. Philippa gave herself unstintingly and generously to her work in

---

33. It is possible that M. Philippa was sent to St. Lawrence to succeed M. Antonio Kelly as
superior of the Sacred Heart Convent. M. Antonio was appointed superior in 1904, but
there is nothing to indicate when her term of office expired. In light of M. Philippa's appointment, it is possible that M. Antonio Kelly resigned in January 1908, was succeeded by M.
Philippa who, in turn, was succeeded by M. Winefride Greene in December 1910.

the schools and in the settlement. In the Annals of the Sacred Heart Convent, it is written, "Her three years of missionary work in the pioneer centre won the love and gratitude of the beneficiaries of her kindness and charity."[34] In December 1910, M. Philippa's years of exile came to an end, and she was transferred back to Belvedere, to her dearly loved orphans and her close friend, M. Patrick Flynn. During the next fifteen years, she filled the offices of novice mistress and superior of St. Michael's Convent and Orphanage.

These years passed quickly, and at the beginning of 1925, a letter was sent out from the superior general, M. Bridget O'Connor, convoking the second general chapter of the Sisters of Mercy. M. Bridget reminded the sisters that as she had served two successive terms as superior general, she was ineligible for re-election. When the elected delegates gathered at Mercy Convent in August 1925, it is probable that M. Philippa Hanley had no idea of what was in store for her. She was a gentle, quiet lady who asked for nothing but to be left in peace at Belvedere. But once more, she was asked to put aside her own desires and embrace a new ministry—one that would demand all that she had to give in the form of wisdom, understanding, patience, and fortitude. On the first ballot she was elected to the office of superior general.

It was during M. Philippa's tenure as superior general that the Congregation of the Sisters of Mercy petitioned Rome for approval of the new "Rule and Constitutions." Although Archbishop Roche was the lead figure in negotiations with Rome, the preliminary study and the collating of pertinent documents were the tasks of M. Philippa and her first assistant, M. Bridget O'Connor.

When M. Philippa's first term of office of six years had expired, the sisters re-elected her for a further six years.[35] These were the years of the Great Depression, but notwithstanding the strain of financial uncertainty, under M. Philippa's administration, the congregation continued to grow both numerically and intellectually. Summer schools to provide advanced studies for the

---

34. Annals, Sacred Heart Convent, St. Lawrence, ASMSJ.

35. M. Philippa Hanley was elected to the office of superior general on August 15, 1925. At the general chapter of August 15, 1931, she was re-elected for another six years, concluding this ministry on August 15, 1937. Minutes of general chapters 1925 and 1931, ASMSJ.

sisters were inaugurated with the assistance of the Sisters of Charity of Mount St. Vincent College, Halifax, and the practice of sending sisters to pursue graduate studies at mainland universities was continued. M. Philippa was scrupulous in carrying out regular visitation of the convents so that every sister in the congregation would have an opportunity to speak to her privately. Never very robust, M. Philippa would not permit ill health or severe weather conditions to prevent her from carrying out her duty. On one occasion, when she was crossing Placentia Bay by boat to visit the convents on the Burin Peninsula, a sudden violent storm erupted. For several hours, the sailors struggled to keep the boat afloat, and it was only through superb seamanship that the passengers landed safely in Burin.

In 1937, M. Philippa completed her second term as superior general, and at the general chapter in August, M. Bridget O'Connor was chosen once more to lead the congregation. M. Philippa Hanley was elected first assistant. At this time in her life, M. Philippa had a little more leisure. She began a project that she had thought about for many years—to write the history of the Sisters of Mercy in Newfoundland. Regrettably, she did not live to complete the work. She died at Belvedere on November 4, 1941.

St. Bride's Convent, Littledale, was another large complex that required constant attention not only to the physical structure but more especially to the educational advancement of the sisters assigned to the staff of the school. In the early days, gifted teachers like M. Bridget O'Connor and M. Pius Mulcahy had established St. Bride's Academy at Littledale as one of the leading educational centres on the island of Newfoundland. The addition of the scholarly M. Perpetua O'Callaghan to the staff of St. Bride's further enhanced the reputation of the institution. In addition to M. Perpetua, there was the talented young student of Littledale, Bride (M. Augustine) O'Connor, whose outstanding ability and specialized training, together with unlimited dedication, kept the name of St. Bride's high on the academic honours list of that time. Throughout the years that followed, Littledale was blessed with many highly qualified, capable, and dedicated teachers. But it should be recorded that these two sisters, M. Perpetua O'Callaghan and M. Augustine O'Connor, guided the destinies of the school in the days when funds were pitiably low, equipment necessarily meagre, and the problem of maintaining high standards an ever-present and urgent need.

In 1917, St. Bride's Academy, Littledale, was raised to the status of a college with an expanded curriculum and facilities, new departments, and more specialty teachers. St. Bride's College was not only recognized as the teacher-training college for Catholic female teachers, it offered, as well, the regular academic program for primary grades through high-school matriculation. In 1918, the first two students to take senior matriculation examinations passed with honours. Furthermore, in that same year, a Littledale student, Mary Bruce, won the Junior Associate Scholarship, having obtained first place in the country in the CHE examinations, and another Littledale student was awarded a scholarship in the intermediate examinations. Mary Bruce, who came to Littledale from the Codroy Valley, subsequently became a Sister of Mercy and was given the religious name, Mary Teresina. Through her dedicated work as a teacher, and especially through her contribution to teacher education and formation, M. Teresina Bruce made an invaluable contribution to education in Newfoundland. This contribution was recognized many years later when she received the degree of doctor of laws, *honoris causa*, from Memorial University of Newfoundland.[36]

Although shorthand and typing had been offered from the early days, in 1918, a department of business education was opened at Littledale. The new department offered the complete program of studies required to prepare a student for a career in the business world. Initially, this department was placed in the care of M. Gerard O'Reilly. Four years later, in 1922, M. Agatha Bonia succeeded her. M. Agatha had been a student of M. Joseph Fox in the business education department at Mercy Convent, and before her entrance into religious life, she had been secretary to the minister of finance in the Newfoundland government. M. Agatha reigned over the business education department—and all its students—from 1922 until 1958, when she was transferred to Holy Heart of Mary Regional High School in St. John's.

---

36. M. Teresina Bruce received the degree of doctor of laws, *honoris causa*, on May 29, 1982.

In June 1940, "St. Bride's College Annual" published a summary of the academic work for the years 1933–1940:

> During the past seven years, an average of twenty-five pupils have annually taken the Junior Matriculation examinations. Of this number eighty-one percent passed, forty percent obtaining distinction in all subjects. Twice during these years the Junior Jubilee Scholarship was won by this class, Miss Mary Mullowney being winner in 1933 and Miss Rita Mullowney [her sister] scoring in 1936 the largest number of marks yet obtained in Grade XI. The King George V Jubilee Scholarship of five hundred dollars, founded in 1935, was awarded to Miss Helen Kehoe in 1936, and was again won by Miss Mollie McCarthy in 1937. The Memorial University Scholarship of six hundred dollars was carried off by Miss Mary Mullowney in 1935, and the Senior Jubilee of one thousand dollars was won by Miss Rita Mullowney in 1938. In the same year Miss Helen Kehoe merited the Mount St. Vincent Scholarship.[37]

Following her graduation from St. Bride's College, Mary Mullowney studied at Memorial University of Newfoundland and at the University of Toronto where she received a B.A. degree. After her return to Newfoundland, she entered the Congregation of the Sisters of Mercy and was given the religious name, M. Thaddeus. Because of the awards M. Thaddeus Mullowney had earned during her high school years and at university, her superiors saw to it that she was given the opportunity for further study. Throughout her career, she earned several master's degrees, beginning with M.A. in philosophy from the University of Ottawa.

By 1940, the demands for more space at Littledale became so imperative that, in spite of the difficulties of procuring materials in wartime, Archbishop Roche decided to construct a new building on the campus. This involved the sacrifice of the gooseberry patch—the main source of ingredients for the "everlasting jam" that had nourished the boarding students and the sisters at St. Bride's since the days of M. Teresa O'Halleran. Construction

---

37. "St. Bride's College Annual," June 1940, p.109.

was completed in 1943, and the building formally opened in February 1944. It was named St. Augustine's Hall in memory of M. Augustine O'Connor, a woman who spent her life in service to the students of Littledale.[38] The new school provided classrooms for 450 students from kindergarten to grade XII, under the administration of M. Teresina Bruce, the first principal. In addition, St. Augustine's Hall included a commercial department, general science laboratory, and domestic science room. A large music room doubled as a lounge for student-teachers in the evenings. Furthermore, there were classrooms and dormitories for student-teachers and sleeping apartments for supervising sisters.[39]

In the years between 1944 and 1958, all grades between kindergarten and grade XII were accommodated at St. Augustine's. Then, with the opening of regional high schools, it became an elementary school. Through funds provided by the federal Department of Regional Economic Expansion (DREE) a new high school was built in 1973 by the Roman Catholic School Board on land adjoining Littledale. High-school students from St. Augustine's were transferred to this new Beaconsfield High School and several Sisters of Mercy taught in the school from 1973 to 1979.[40] Subsequently, during the 1980s and '90s, new and larger schools were built to accommodate the growing population of the Kilbride area of St. John's. In 1986, St. Augustine's Elementary Girls' School became co-educational, accommodating children from kindergarten to grade V. The neighbouring Beaconsfield Elementary Boys' School became Beaconsfield Junior High School for students from grades VI–IX. At the time, Sr. Loretta Chafe was the only sister assigned to the staff of Beaconsfield Junior High. She remained there until 1991, when she was assigned to Holy Heart of Mary High School. However, Sisters of Mercy continued to teach and administer St. Augustine's School until 1988, when Sr. Maura Mason was assigned to

---

38. M. Augustine O'Connor died in July 1942, after a relatively brief illness. She was forty-four years of age at the time of her death.

39. *The Monitor*, March 1944, p. 3.

40. Sisters who taught at Beaconsfield High School were: M. Michelle Gibbons, M. Williamina Hogan, Charlotte Fitzpatrick, M. Jerome Walker, and M. Evangelista Bolger. M. Evangelista was the last sister to teach in this school.

St. Lawrence. Sr. Madeline Kehoe was the last sister to teach in St. Augustine's School, and after her retirement from a salaried position in 1996, she continued to give voluntary service until the school closed.

By the year 2000, rather than invest in the extensive repairs required for St. Augustine's, the St. John's RC School Board decided to close the school. In May of that year, students, former pupils and teachers of St. Augustine's gathered to celebrate the fifty-six years during which the school had served the children of the area. The speaker for the occasion was a former student, Janet Henley-Andrews. She recalled that, in 1961, her kindergarten class numbered fifty children, boys and girls. However, as children moved into grade II, the boys moved to other schools. In recalling the contribution of the sisters, Mrs. Henley-Andrews said:

> The Sisters of Mercy shaped the culture of St. Augustine's and every other school in which they taught. The education of the whole child, spiritual, intellectual and artistic was the objective. Every child, rich or poor, had equal opportunity. There were no breakfast programs and no school lunch programs but no child knowingly went hungry. The Sisters fed them and clothed them if necessary. Universality ruled. Every child had a music education second to none, and gifted children had private piano and voice instruction whether or not they could afford it. If the school needed resources, the Sisters provided them. No child missed a field trip because she couldn't pay. Every child, even in very large classes was valued as a person, an individual with individual gifts, needs and abilities.
>
> As the number of Sisters at St. Augustine's declined over the years, other dedicated teachers filled the hole left by the women whose entire lives were dedicated to God and to our needs. Ultimately the caring culture created by the Sisters of Mercy at St. Augustine's and other schools did live on and is reflected in ... our own individual values.[41]

The closing of St. Augustine's School marked the end of a ministry in education that had been carried on at Littledale since 1884. The old wooden build-

---

41. Janet Henley-Andrews, Address given at the celebration of the closing of St. Augustine's School, May 28, 2000, ASMSJ.

ing that bore the name, "St. Augustine's Hall," was demolished in 2002, and in its place there is a surprisingly small area of green grass. One wonders will the gooseberry patch, which had supplied "everlasting jam" to so many generations of Littledale students, take root once more?

While generations of students entered and left educational facilities on the Littledale campus, the sisters on the West Coast were labouring diligently to promote the cause of education in that region of the country. From the beginning of the amalgamation of the convents in 1916, the superior general, M. Bridget O'Connor, had been sensitive to the feelings of sisters on the West Coast. She was particularly concerned for the members of St. Michael's Convent, St. George's, a community that had survived on its own for thirty-three years before amalgamation took place. To strengthen the unity of the congregation and to eliminate any feeling of isolation that might have been experienced by the sisters in the west, M. Bridget initiated an exchange of personnel. Sisters from the east were transferred to convents of St. Michael's and St. Mary's on the Humber on the West Coast, while members of these communities found themselves on the train heading east to fill positions that had been vacated because of the transfers.

    However, all was not smooth sailing in M. Bridget O'Connor's dealings with the west coast hierarchy. When Bishop Michael Power of St. George's died suddenly in 1920, the Sisters of Mercy lost more than a staunch friend and supporter. The cordial relations that had existed between the mother house in St. John's and the episcopal palace in St. George's took a turn for the worse with the advent of Michael Power's successor, Bishop Henry T. Renouf.

    Henry Renouf was born in St. John's and educated at St. Bonaventure's College before attending Propaganda College in Rome. After his ordination in 1895, he served in parishes belonging to all three Newfoundland dioceses before being appointed bishop of St. George's in 1920.[42] Within a short time of his arrival in St. George's, he found himself at odds with the Sisters of

---

42. Rev. Henry Renouf served in Sandy Point and Harbour Breton (St. George's diocese), in Harbour Grace (Harbour Grace diocese), and at the time of his appointment as bishop, he was pastor of St. Patrick's Parish, St. John's.

Mercy. The first indication that the bishop intended to keep a tight rein on the sisters and their pupils occurred about a year and a half after his arrival in St. George's, when he objected to the boarders at St. Michael's Academy, St. George's, staging an operetta in Grand Falls during the summer holidays. The operetta had been presented as part of the annual spring concert in St. George's, but a railway strike had prevented the parents of the students from attending. Bishop Renouf's main objection to the performance was that Grand Falls was not in his diocese but part of the Diocese of Harbour Grace.[43] Responding to this objection, the superior of St. Michael's Convent, M. Aquin Gormley, who was not in the habit of mincing her words, pointed out that when the Grand Falls girls returned home for their holidays they were no longer the responsibility of the sisters. Unfortunately, she did not stop there. She pointed out that neither were they under the jurisdiction of the bishop of St. George's.[44] One may only guess the bishop's reaction to this statement!

In a letter of July 28, 1922, the bishop informed the superior general, M. Bridget O'Connor, that he had decided to close the boys' school in St. George's and return these children to the care of the sisters in St. Joseph's School. In her reply to this letter, M. Bridget assured him that the newly appointed superior of St. Michael's Convent, M. Agnes Doyle, would support him in any initiative to improve conditions in the schools in St. George's. In conclusion, she mentioned that M. Antonio Egan, who had been living in St. John's since 1917, would be returning to St. Michael's. Her next piece of information, however, did not please the bishop. She informed him that Miss Clara Downey (later, M. Fintan) had been accepted as a postulant for St. Michael's Convent. M. Bridget felt that because of her experience as a teacher in Stephenville Crossing, the new postulant would be competent

---

43. Bishop H. T. Renouf to M. Aquin Gormley, June 14, 1922.

44. M. Aquin Gormley was born in Roscommon, Ireland, as were her schoolmates and life-long friends, M. Philippa Hanley and M. Patrick Flynn. She came to Newfoundland in October 1891 and was accepted as a postulant at Mercy Convent. She was an efficient administrator and a kind, understanding, and generous superior and teacher. She was direct and forthright in dealing with others, and she would have been incapable of playing petty politics in order to curry favour with either superiors or bishops.

to take charge of the boys' department.[45] Bishop Renouf replied by return mail:

> The new Superior is as big a stranger to me as was Mother Aquin, but I am hoping she has good common sense. The return of Mother Antonio is a bit of a surprise, and I trust that there won't be two Superiors instead of one. . . . I am looking for co-operation. . . . I am afraid that Miss Downey hardly suits my idea, and the people will look on her as the teacher from Stephenville. . . . I don't think I am hard to please but I shall not bear with the attitude shown me in the past two years.[46]

Apparently, Bishop Renouf and M. Aquin had been at loggerheads from the time of the bishop's arrival in St. George's.

For her part, M. Bridget was at her wit's end trying to satisfy bishops and priests who demanded only the best, the most experienced, and the most highly qualified teachers for their schools. As usual, M. Bridget tried to do her best to supply sisters with training and qualifications to meet the needs of the schools in St. George's. In her next letter to Bishop Renouf, she included the names of the sisters assigned to St. Michael's Convent for the following year. Of one of them she wrote, "Sr. M. Edward [Murray] is no doubt an excellent little Sister; she has brains and determination, but she is young, [and] inexperienced."[47] Then, possibly in an attempt to lighten the tone of their communication, the usually circumspect M. Bridget was imprudent enough to add that M. Edward Murray had a "prettier face" than the sister whom she was to replace. Unfortunately, this comment served only to add fuel to the bishop's dissatisfaction with the Sisters of Mercy. Immediately he fired back a curt reply:

> Acknowledging your letter of 17th I can only state plainly, that any member of the late regime could not be acceptable to me. I also feel that your first appointment would not have been decided

45. M. Bridget O'Connor to Bishop H. T. Renouf, August 7, 1922, ADSG.
46. Bishop H. T. Renouf to M. Bridget O'Connor, August 10, 1922, ADSG.
47. M. Bridget O'Connor to Bishop H. T. Renouf, September 17, 1923, ADSG.

> upon if S.M.P. [M. Patricia Hogan] had been a success at
> Hoylestown. As to Sr. M. Edward, she is a stranger to me as are
> most of your Sisters. . . . As far as I am concerned the ugliest Sister
> of the Order can be sent as long as she is capable and able to
> impart what she knows.[48]

But even the most long-suffering mother general can reach breaking-point. Upon reception of this missive, M. Bridget wrote back a spirited defence of M. Patricia, declaring in no uncertain terms that this young sister was one of the bright lights of the teaching profession—intelligent, dynamic, talented, and in great demand on the East Coast. She concluded the letter by insisting that the members of the General Council were just as interested in the schools and convents in the Diocese of St. George's as in any part of the island.[49]

Unfortunately, relations between the mother house in St. John's and the bishop of St. George's did not undergo any noticeable improvement over the years of Bishop Renouf's episcopate. Letters preserved in the archives of the Diocese of St. George's[50] and in the archives of the Sisters of Mercy indicate that the superior general and council in St. John's and the sisters in St. George's and in Petries tried their best to accommodate the bishop's arbitrary demands. Apparently, he was unwilling to admit that anyone could misunderstand his often contradictory directions. For instance, on May 20, 1924, he wrote to M. Bridget as follows:

> I fail to understand your line of action after my settling with you
> as to when you could see me on business and your own request,
> and hope it is not meant to be grossly insulting, for there has not
> been conveyed to me the slightest excuse for not keeping the
> appointment. . . . My experience so far of the Mercy Order in the
> diocese is not such as one might be glad of.[51]

---

48. Bishop H. T. Renouf to M. Bridget O'Connor, September 21, 1923, ADSG.
49. M. Bridget O'Connor to Bishop H. T. Renouf, September 24, 1923, ADSG.
50. As new population centres emerged, the seat of the Diocese of St. George's was transferred to Corner Brook although the name of the diocese remained unchanged.
51. Bishop H. T. Renouf to M. Bridget O'Connor May 30, 1924, ADSG.

M. Bridget O'Connor replied to this letter, explaining that she was under the impression that her interview with his Lordship was to take place in the convent, and she apologized to him for the misunderstanding. Bishop Renouf refused to accept this apology and added further words of reproof.

Throughout all this correspondence, in addition to the specific complaints of the bishop, there was the constant threat of his objection to the presence of M. Antonio Egan. He claimed that she interfered with the smooth running of the convent; that she tried to overrule the wishes of the superior, who was, at the time, M. Agnes Doyle, and also, that as one of the general councillors, M. Antonio should be in St. John's where she could be consulted. M. Bridget explained to him that there was nothing to prevent councillors living at a distance from the mother house since business requiring their presence was transacted only at times when it was convenient for them to attend. And she added, "With regard to Mother Antonio, my Lord, I cannot well deny her the right to St. George's."[52] Nevertheless, there may have been some justification for the bishop's complaint that M. Antonio's presence in St. Michael's detracted from the authority and position of the appointed superior, M. Agnes Doyle. After all, M. Antonio Egan was the foundress of the Sisters of Mercy in the west, she had received M. Agnes into religious life and had been M. Agnes' superior until 1916. M. Agnes might have felt somewhat inhibited by M. Antonio's presence, especially when, in order to meet the needs of students and sisters of the 1920s, she felt it necessary to change policies and procedures initiated by M. Antonio during her time as superior. In any case, M. Bridget's explanation of M. Antonio's presence did not satisfy the disgruntled bishop of St. George's. He continued to fire off blistering letters to the mother house, informing M. Bridget that he wanted "simple straight honest dealing without insincerity and insulting remarks."[53] Once again, M. Bridget tried to placate the angry prelate, "I am most unfortunate in my correspondence with your Lordship. I feel that I am not insincere but not explicit enough."[54]

---

52. M. Bridget O'Connor to Bishop H. T. Renouf, July 20, 1924, ADSG.
53. Bishop H. T. Renouf to M. Bridget O'Connor, August 1, 1924, ADSG.
54. M. Bridget O'Connor to Bishop H. T. Renouf, August 23, 1924, ADSG.

The dissatisfaction of the bishop of St. George's with the Sisters of Mercy reached new heights in 1926. During the previous year, Archbishop Roche met officials of the Sacred Congregation of Religious in Rome to secure approval for changes in the "Rule and Constitutions" of the Presentation Sisters and the Sisters of Mercy of Newfoundland that were necessary because of the amalgamation of the convents. In a letter to the apostolic delegate to Canada, Roche informed him that the Sisters of Mercy of San Francisco had set a precedent by amalgamating several years previously, and the consequent changes in the Rule of the Sisters of Mercy for that province had been confirmed absolutely by Rome. Roche explained further, "By following as closely as possible the Rules approved for this amalgamation I was informed that the Constitutions of our Sisters of Mercy would be approved as a matter of course."[55] Included in the documents required by the Sacred Congregation before granting approval of the new Rule was a testimonial concerning the sisters' conduct and work from each bishop in whose diocese they were working. Archbishop Roche continued:

> With regard to the third requirement, I wrote to their Lordships, the Bishops of Harbour Grace and St. George's . . . requesting from their Lordships the necessary testimonial letters. I received a reply from the Bishop of Harbour Grace warmly commending the work of the Sisters of both Institutions in his Diocese and authorizing me to transmit his recommendation to the Sacred Congregation. The Bishop of St. George's replied, making no reference whatever to the Sisters of the Presentation, but stating definitely that he could not at present recommend the works of the Mercy Order in his Diocese. In view of this attitude of His Lordship of St. George's, and in view of the requirement of the Sacred Congregation, I do not see that I can proceed any further. . . . I am placing these facts before Your Excellency, and would be glad to have your advice on the matter. [56]

---

55. Archbishop E. P. Roche to His Excellency, Most Reverend P. DeMara, April 11, 1926. Changes to the Presentation Rule presented more difficulty since there was no precedent for this amalgamation.

56. Ibid.

The refusal of Bishop Renouf to provide the necessary testimonial letter came as a nasty shock to the General Council of the Sisters of Mercy. In spite of the stormy relationship that had existed between this bishop and the congregation, the disputes were of a personal nature, usually over inadvertent or imagined slights rather than over matters of policy or discipline, for the bishop's wishes were carried out to the letter. The superior general, M. Philippa Hanley, who succeeded M. Bridget O'Connor in 1925, wrote Bishop Renouf, asking him if he would state the reasons for his refusal to supply the required testimonial letter.[57] Bishop Renouf refused to do this, stating that since Archbishop Roche had placed the matter before the apostolic delegate, he (Renouf) would deal only with the delegation. What transpired subsequently between the delegate and the bishop of St. George's was a well-kept secret. However, three weeks after Bishop Renouf's letter to M. Philippa, he wrote Archbishop Roche as follows:

> I am in receipt of your communication of April 11th with a copy of enclosure sent to the Delegation at Ottawa.
>
> I shall shortly send to the S.C. Congregation my approval and recommendation for both Mercy and Presentation Orders....
> I shall also suggest to the Sacred Congregation that in the event of these Constitutions being approved by Rome and ecclesiastical Superiors have to be appointed for each Order, that they be selected outside the Archdiocese in which both Mother Houses are located.[58]

This final comment was a direct insult to Archbishop Roche who was, after all, the archbishop of St. John's where both mother houses were located and, as well, the metropolitan of the ecclesiastical province of Newfoundland. Perhaps Bishop Renouf resented the close and friendly relations that existed between Archbishop Roche and the Sisters of Mercy. In his correspondence with the sisters, Bishop Renouf frequently jotted notes on the back of a letter as a

---

57. M. Philippa Hanley to Bishop H. T. Renouf, May 2, 1926, ADSG.

58. Bishop H. T. Renouf to Archbishop E. P. Roche, June 5, 1926, ADSG. There was no greeting or salutation included at the beginning of this letter.

reminder, presumably, of any detail that needed his attention. On the back of one of these letters he wrote in pencil, "Sept. 3/24. At night recreation Sr. X. [Xavier Wadden] openly stated that E. P. R. [Edward Patrick Roche] ran the Mercy Order—before Sisters. HTR." The letter itself was from M. Bridget O'Connor in response to the bishop's request for a book: "I should be most happy to give you the book you need, but I do not know what it is you want."[59]

For a couple of years after the required testimonial letters were sent to Rome and the new "Rule and Constitutions" approved, there seems to have been a truce of sorts between St. John's and St. George's. At any rate, no letters from that period have been preserved. However, in 1928, the correspondence began again with this letter from Bishop Renouf:

> I unreservedly condemn and object to any Sisters in my diocese going motor driving—leaving their convents at 8:00 p.m. and returning 9:45 advanced time. You will be good enough to issue instructions <u>at once</u> in accordance with my desires. [60]

By the end of that same month, July 1928, Bishop Renouf finally had something positive to say of the Sisters of Mercy when he wrote of the superior of the convent of St. Mary's on the Humber, "Mother deSales deserves great credit for what she has done."[61] It was just about this time that M. deSales Ahearn had completed her second three-year term as superior of the convent of St. Mary's on the Humber in Petries. According to the Constitutions, she could not be reappointed superior of the same convent. But there was nothing to prevent her being named superior of another convent. No doubt, the members of the General Council in St. John's appreciated her ability as an administrator, but also they saw their way clear to doing something at last that might please the bishop of St. George's. They promptly appointed M. deSales Ahearn superior of St. Michael's Convent, St. George's.

---

59. M. Bridget O'Connor to Bishop H. T. Renouf, n.d., but probably during the late summer of 1924, ADSG.
60. Bishop H. T. Renouf to M. Philippa Hanley, July 4, 1928, ADSG.
61. Bishop H. T. Renouf to M. Philippa Hanley, July 29, 1928, ADSG.

Unfortunately, it was not long before the usually diplomatic M. deSales ran afoul of the hot-tempered bishop. As was his custom, Bishop Renouf wrote himself a note on the back of a letter he had received from M. deSales in January 1929: "This is an apology for entering my dining room whilst I was at my dinner—without permission. HTR." In the letter, M. deSales had written, "I must ask you to kindly pardon my intrusion today and you taking your dinner. . . . Honestly, My Lord, I was in the Dining Room before I realized it. So many things are going wrong in this old patched up house that really I do not know what to do. Please pardon my going to your dining room today."[62] Apparently, after this breach of protocol, relations between M. deSales and Bishop Renouf continued on a more even keel. At the conclusion of her second three-year term of office as superior, the bishop wrote to M. Philippa Hanley demanding that a dispensation from Rome be requested to permit M. deSales to serve a third term as superior of St. Michael's Convent, St. George's. He explained the reasons for this request: "Peace and harmony reign in the Community. She has the confidence of all her subjects and it would be very difficult to replace her. Moreover, she met with wonderful success in financing the Convent here. And in the present time this is a consideration of great importance."[63] The General Council agreed to petition the Holy See to permit M. deSales to serve an additional three-year term as superior of St. Michael's Convent. They made it clear, however, that the petition was being forwarded at the request of Bishop Renouf, and not on the initiative of the Congregation of the Sisters of Mercy.

Eventually, in 1938, M. deSales was replaced as superior of St. Michael's by M. Alphonsus McNamara, and it was not long before the sisters were once more in trouble with Bishop Renouf. In February 1939, the bishop had occasion to remind the new superior of what he regarded as his rights in respect of the convent:

---

62. M. deSales Ahearn to Bishop H. T. Renouf, January 14, 1929, ADSG. The reference to "this patched up old house" suggests that the bishop was having his dinner in a room in the convent set aside as "the bishop's dining room". M. deSales may have rushed in after the morning school session, not realizing that the bishop had already begun his noon meal—the hour at which dinner was served in Newfoundland in those days.

63. Bishop H. T. Renouf to M. Philippa Hanley, July 14, 1933, ADSG.

> The Bishop has the full use of the Recreation room for Mass, for anything he wishes for any time. He hasn't to ask anyone for it, he has full authority to use any part of any convent in his diocese for any purpose he wishes. You are to make no conditions whatever and if you made any, cancel them immediately.... Were the floor of the Recreation room done over with gold, much less hard wood, it is to be placed most willingly at the disposal of the Bishop.[64]

Unfortunately, the tension between the bishop of St. George's and the Sisters of Mercy continued right up until the time of his death in 1941.

Although it is easy to write off Bishop Renouf as irritable, testy, and unreasonable in his dealings with the Sisters of Mercy, it should be remembered that he became bishop at a challenging time in the history of the West Coast. He succeeded the youthful and charismatic Bishop Michael Power, who as priest and bishop was revered throughout the diocese. It was inevitable that the reserved, aristocratic Henry Renouf would be compared to his popular and dearly loved predecessor. Furthermore, Bishop Renouf had been given the responsibility of the diocese at the very time the paper mill in Corner Brook was beginning operations, bringing rapid social change to the whole area. The demand for churches and schools, with priests, teachers, and support workers to staff these institutions, was a constant challenge to the bishop. The amalgamation of the convents and the status of the Sisters of Mercy as a pontifical rather than a diocesan institute was new in Bishop Renouf's experience.[65] Obviously, he did not understand the implications of the changes whereby authority in the congregation was vested in the superior general and her council rather than in the bishop of the diocese. Thus, when the superiors exercised their right to decide on issues affecting the life of the congregation, he perceived it as an act of defiance against his authority. Nevertheless, M. Angela

---

64. Bishop H. T. Renouf letter written on the bishop's official note paper and signed in ink by Bishop Renouf, ADSG.

65. Pontifical institutes were directly under the jurisdiction of the Holy See. They were subject to the local bishop in the exercise of their ministry within his diocese. The bishop had no jurisdiction over the internal affairs of the Institute. In a diocesan institute, the life and ministry of the institute was under the jurisdiction of the local bishop.

Fowler, who spent many years in St. George's, remembered that Bishop Renouf was kind and understanding in dealing with individual sisters and that he showed a tender concern for the poor and for persons in trouble. Overall, Bishop Renouf effected many changes for good in his diocese, particularly by establishing the Presentation Sisters in Corner Brook and the Redemptorist Fathers in St. George's.

Bishop Michael O'Reilly, who succeeded Bishop Renouf, had served in the Diocese of St. George's for many years before his ordination as bishop. He knew the sisters and had worked closely with them. Consequently, there was a noticeable change of tone in the correspondence between the mother house of the Sisters of Mercy and the episcopal palace in St. George's that boded well for the future.

Important developments had taken place during the tenure of the sisters' first elected General Council (1919–1925). In that period, forty-three young women had been received as novices, and when the second triennial report was sent to Rome in 1925, there were thirty-two sisters with temporary vows and seventy with perpetual vows.[66] Furthermore, during the six-year term period, two more convents were founded, and with the guidance and encouragement of Archbishop Roche, the Sisters of Mercy had undertaken the momentous task of establishing Newfoundland's first Catholic hospital.

---

66. Triennial Report, 1935, ASMSJ.

CHAPTER FOURTEEN

ST. CLARE'S MERCY HOSPITAL

Misericordia Super Omnia (Mercy Above All)
Motto of St. Clare's Mercy Hospital

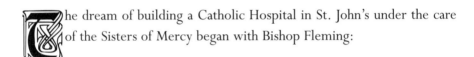he dream of building a Catholic Hospital in St. John's under the care of the Sisters of Mercy began with Bishop Fleming:

> Until the pious Sisterhood of Mercy, judiciously and usefully augmented, shall become capable of attending, not only to ... the duty of continuing to soothe the pallet of the wretched and diseased in the abodes of the poor, as well as in the hospital, which it will be my care to add ... to that happy institution, I shall not consider my mission accomplished.[1]

Unfortunately, the death of M. Joseph Nugent and the refusal of the superiors at Baggot Street to commit any more sisters to St. John's put an end to any hope the bishop may have entertained for the fulfillment of his plans.

Nevertheless, Bishop Fleming's dream was not forgotten. Many years later, one of his successors, Archbishop Michael F. Howley, took the first step in bringing it to fruition. With characteristic foresight, Howley recognized that St. Clare's

---

1. Bishop Fleming, Fifth Letter to Dr. O'Connell, 1844, AASJ, 103/2/27.

Home for Working Girls, although it provided a valuable service to young women, was at too great a distance from the business district of the city to have long-term viability. Furthermore, the archbishop saw the building as ideal for use as a small Catholic hospital—something he felt was urgently needed.

It is true that hospitals for military and naval personnel had been in existence in Newfoundland since the seventeenth century, but it was not until 1814 that the first civilian hospital for the "indigent poor" was built at Riverhead in St. John's.[2] Known as St. John's Hospital, it depended for its support on grants from the governor and on public donations. By all accounts, conditions in the hospital were chaotic. Not only was the building overcrowded, but in addition to those who were acutely ill, it also served patients who suffered from chronic and severe mental illness. Of the nurses who staffed the hospital: "Most of them were illiterate women of humble origin, whose names were included among the 'domestic employees' on the payroll of the hospital."[3] Consequently, when the typhus epidemic broke out in 1847, the two sisters at Mercy Convent were quick to offer their help in the current emergency, for both had experience in caring for the sick.[4] It was while attending the patients at St. John's Hospital that M. Joseph Nugent contracted the infection that cost her life.

Yet, in spite of the distress caused by the epidemic of 1847, conditions at the hospital continued to deteriorate. Because the government seemed unwilling or unable to take steps to rectify the situation, the Roman Catholic bishop of St. John's decided to take a stand. Grieved by the death of two of his priests and concerned for the safety of the sisters and priests who visited the hospital, Bishop Mullock forwarded a petition to the Newfoundland government. The bishop did not mince his words when he described the deplorable conditions that existed in the institution:

2. Joyce Nevitt, *White Caps and Black Bands: Nursing in Newfoundland to 1934* (St. John's, NL: Jesperson Press, 1978), p. xxxi.

3. Ibid., p. 1.

4. M. Francis Creedon had experience in caring for the sick in their homes and in the hospitals during her novitiate in Dublin. M. Joseph Nugent had cared for her sick mother for some time.

That the horrible state of St. John's Hospital is a disgrace to the community and a source of pestilence to the entire people. That typhus fever is so fixed in it that no one can approach it without danger of death. That most of those whom accidents or other diseases oblige to have recourse to the Hospital get typhus fever while there . . . That already three Catholic Clergymen have got typhus by attending the patients in said Hospital, two of whom died; several Sisters of Mercy and two Protestant Clergymen also got the same sickness while on duty.[5]

The bishop begged the government to provide a separate building to care for people with contagious diseases so that other patients and those who attended the sick would be protected. His plea fell on deaf ears.

Eventually, in 1871, the government took over the abandoned military hospital on Forest Road, and the staff and male patients from the St. John's Hospital at Riverhead were transferred to that building—the female patients were sent to the wards of the Poor Asylum![6] Three years later, in 1874, large-scale renovations and improvements to the Forest Road hospital were begun, and a new wing for female patients was constructed. The hospital was renamed, and henceforth it was known as the General Hospital. In the years that followed, further extensions were added to the original building and consistent efforts were made to improve equipment and facilities.

Early in the twentieth century, a training school for nurses was established at the General Hospital. This provided a small but steady supply of nurses to the hospital itself as well as to other smaller hospitals that sprang up in St. John's and in other parts of Newfoundland.[7] In 1913 or 1914, just prior to

---

5. Bishop John T. Mullock, Petition to House of Assembly, *JHA*, 1868, p. 18.

6. Nevitt, *White Caps*, p. 11. Nevitt pointed out that the hospital at Riverhead continued to be used for more than a decade after this, in spite of the dilapidated condition of the building.

7. Among the civilian hospitals in St. John's that predated St. Clare's Mercy Hospital were the Waterford Hospital for Nervous and Mental Diseases (1854), the Salvation Army Rescue Home for Girls (1894), the Cowan Mission Convalescent Home (1902), the Fever Hospital (1906), Jensen's Camp for Tuberculosis (1916), the Southcott Hospital (1916), and the Tuberculosis Sanatorium (1917). There were other smaller buildings used for the care of the sick, but these lasted for only short periods of time as other, more appropriate facilities became available.

the outbreak of the First World War, a young doctor from St. John's, William Roberts, returned from Scotland to set up medical practice in his hometown. Roberts had specialized in the treatment of medical problems experienced by women, and in order to practice his specialty, he adapted the top floor of his residence as a small hospital for women.[8]

Dr. Roberts' initiative prompted Archbishop Howley to act on his plan to establish a Catholic hospital in St. John's. But before he could do this, he needed nurses. In July 1914, on his way home from Rome, Howley visited the Mercy Hospital in Cork, Ireland, where he arranged for a Sister of Mercy from St. John's to begin nursing studies at that institution. On his return to St. John's, he visited M. Pius Mulcahy, the superior of St. Clare's Home, and informed her of the arrangement he had made with Mercy Hospital in Cork. According to St. Clare's records, M. Pius told two of the sisters in St. Clare's community, M. Berchmans Quinn and M. Bernard Gladney, of the archbishop's plans to send a sister to Ireland to train as a nurse. M. Berchmans was a teacher by inclination and training and saw no reason to embrace a new career. On the other hand, M. Bernard was so enthusiastic about the archbishop's proposal that she volunteered immediately to go to Ireland to study nursing. She saw in it the realization of her dream of being of service to sick and suffering humanity. It was fortunate, indeed, that M. Bernard felt this way, for she discovered later that Howley had already selected her as the sister to be sent away for nursing studies![9]

Having notified the St. Clare's community of his plans to close the home for working girls and adapt the building for use as a hospital, Archbishop Howley finalized arrangements for M. Bernard to sail for Ireland to begin her studies in Cork. Unfortunately, before she was ready to leave, war broke out in Europe. The activity of submarines around the coast of Newfoundland and in the Atlantic Ocean made travel extremely dangerous, and so, rather than put M. Bernard at risk, it was decided to defer her training until a later date. She continued her work at St. Clare's Home.

---

8. Nevitt, *White Caps*, p. 146.
9. M. Francis Hickey, *Mercy Communico*, January 1969, p. 2, ASMSJ, RG 37/2/226.

The home continued to attract young working girls to the extent that, within a couple of years, the building could not accommodate all the applicants and many were refused admission. By this time, Archbishop Howley had died[10] and his successor, Archbishop Edward Patrick Roche, was not at all happy that people were being turned away from the home because of lack of space. M. Francis Hickey commented, "The archbishop could not brook this state of affairs. He formulated plans for an addition, which gave a dormitory and twelve more beds, an adequate dining room, and other facilities."[11]

The war dragged on for four years, and it was not until 1918 that M. Bernard Gladney was released from duties at St. Clare's Home to begin her studies, not in Ireland as originally planned, but at Mercy Hospital in Pittsburgh, USA. In June 1920, M. Bernard returned to St. John's for a short vacation. When she sailed for Pittsburgh a few weeks later, she was accompanied by M. Aloysius Rawlins who had expressed an interest in studying dietetics and office management. By this time, amalgamation of the convents had taken place and authority was now in the hands of the superior general and her council. M. Bridget O'Connor was aware of M. Aloysius' ability as a musician. She suggested that, in addition to courses already selected, she pursue studies in vocal and instrumental music at Mount Mercy, which was also in Pittsburgh—presumably, in case the archbishop's plans for St. Clare's Mercy Hospital did not materialize![12]

On October 21, 1921, M. Bernard Gladney returned to St. John's as a registered nurse. In addition to the regular program of studies, she had completed special courses in radiography, anesthesia, and a medical students laboratory course. Immediately on her return, she was appointed superior of St. Clare's Home that continued to operate without interruption for the next six months.[13] Nevertheless, by this time, the date for converting the home into a hospital had been finalized.

---

10. Archbishop Howley died on October 15, 1914. He had been ill only a few days before his death.
11. M. Francis Hickey, *Mercy Communico*, p. 3, ASMSJ, RG 10/9/31.
12. Ibid., p. 4.
13. During the nine years the home was in operation, in addition to M. Pius Mulcahy and M. Bernard Gladney, M. Antonio Egan, M. Ita Glynn, and Margaret Mary St. John held in turn the office of superior.

Early in May 1922, the St. Clare's Home closed its doors. As soon as the last resident moved out, an army of carpenters, painters, plumbers, and electricians moved in. The men worked all day and through the night in their efforts to adapt St. Clare's Home to a twenty-bed hospital. It was a tribute to their skill and perseverance that in three weeks, the hospital was ready to receive the first patient. On May 21, 1922, mass was celebrated by Archbishop Roche in the temporary chapel, and St. Clare's Mercy Hospital was declared officially open. In his address, the archbishop noted that care of the sick is one of the most important ministries of the Sisters of Mercy and voiced his hopes for the future growth of the institution:

> We feel that this work, so eminently in harmony with the spirit of their Order will grow and prosper. They are beginning in a very humble way, a philanthropic work which has vast possibilities for good; they are planting a tiny grain of mustard seed, which we hope will grow into an immense tree, throwing its healing branches over different sections of the country.[14]

He could not have foreseen that before fifty years had passed, the little hospital in the "White House" would grow into a huge, 375-bed institution with a staff of health-care professionals numbering in the hundreds and operating on a budget totalling millions of dollars.

As M. Bernard Gladney surveyed her little staff, she must have experienced a certain degree of trepidation. She had assumed a heavy responsibility, but, on the other hand, she was a woman of great inner strength and courage. Furthermore, she had the assistance of another registered nurse, Alice Casey.[15]

---

14. Archbishop E. P. Roche, Address given at the opening of St. Clare's Mercy Hospital, May 21, 1922, cited in M. Fabian Hennebury, "St. Clare's Mercy Hospital," p. 5, ASMSJ.

15. Alice Casey was born in Harbour Grace, Newfoundland. She was a graduate of the School of Nursing at the General Hospital in St. John's. She married John Higgins, a noted St. John's lawyer. Her younger sister, Carmel Casey, followed her example in choosing nursing as a career. Carmel, too, was associated with St. Clare's Mercy Hospital for a number of years.

Two sisters, M. Catherine Greene and M. Gabriel Fleming, assisted the two nurses. Even though the nursing staff was small, the fledgling hospital was fortunate in having the services of twelve of the most competent physicians in the city.

In light of the origins of St. Clare's, it was appropriate that the first patient to be admitted to St. Clare's Mercy Hospital was a Presentation Sister, M. Benedict MacKenzie. M. Benedict was greeted with open arms and treated with tender care until she was well enough to return home fully cured. The first surgery to take place in the new hospital was a thyroidectomy performed by Dr. N. S. Fraser.[16] The first baby to be born in St. Clare's was Arthur Morris who, more than twenty years later, graduated from medical school and practiced in St. John's for many years as a successful physician. The first baby girl to be born at St. Clare's was Margaret Armstrong Kearney.

The little hospital soon gained a superb reputation for its care of the sick, and within a short time it was functioning at full capacity. Then, just over a year later, disaster struck when the director, M. Bernard Gladney, contracted tuberculosis. Immediately, the superior general, M. Bridget O'Connor, made arrangements for M. Bernard to go to Saranac Sanatorium in New York for rest and treatment. None of the sisters who had been helping the two registered nurses had formal training and the youthful Alice Casey could not be expected to take the responsibility alone. Reluctantly, the archbishop agreed to close the hospital while M. Bridget O'Connor and her council looked to the Sisters of Mercy in the United States for help.

As a first step in her campaign to secure a nursing staff for the hospital, M. Bridget sent M. Consilio Kenny[17] to visit the Sisters of Mercy of Philadelphia to inquire if that community would be willing to release a nurse until two Newfoundland sisters could be trained as nurses. The Philadelphia sisters, however, had no sister-nurse to spare, and so M. Consilio decided to try the Mercy Hospital in Baltimore. It should be noted here that M. Consilio was a very wise woman. This time, instead of going directly to the sisters, she

---

16. Hennebury, "St. Clare's," p. 6, ASMSJ.
17. M. Consilio had just completed her term as superior of St. Edward's Convent, Bell Island.

arranged an appointment with the archbishop of Baltimore and explained to him the plight of St. Clare's and the purpose of her visit to the United States. Archbishop Curley was sympathetic to her request, and armed with his approval and support, she set out for Baltimore Mercy Hospital. The sisters there received her with great kindness and, acting on Archbishop Curley's suggestion, it was agreed that M. Carmelita Hartman, the superior of the Mount Washington community of the Sisters of Mercy in Maryland,[18] and one of the sister-nurses from Mercy Hospital in Baltimore would travel to St. John's to assess the situation. A few weeks later, on October 24, 1923, M. Carmelita and a registered nurse, M. Teresita McNamee, arrived in St. John's to reopen St. Clare's Mercy Hospital.[19]

As soon as they heard of the impending arrival of the sisters from Baltimore, the staff at St. Clare's went into action. The hospital was scrubbed, cleaned, and polished from top to bottom, the beds made, and the equipment inspected and prepared for use. Upon their arrival, the two sisters from the United States participated enthusiastically in these activities. M. Teresita McNamee supervised all aspects of the preparations for reopening the medical and surgical wards, while M. Carmelita Hartman assumed the duty of "chief cook and bottle washer" as she prepared meals, answered the phone and door bell, and bought the supplies for various hospital departments. Within a matter of days after the arrival of the Americans, the hospital was ready for the reception of patients.

At the reopening of St. Clare's Mercy Hospital, M. Aloysius Rawlins was appointed superior and administrator and M. Teresita McNamee, director of

---

18. M. Carmelita Hartman was a significant figure in the history of the Sisters of Mercy of Baltimore, Maryland. She was superior, administrator, and treasurer of Mercy Hospital, Baltimore, from 1904–1917. Subsequently, she filled the offices of bursar and superior of the Mount Washington community in Maryland. She was instrumental in effecting the amalgamation of the Mercy convents in the United States to form the Sisters of Mercy Union, and she was elected first superior general of the Union. She served two terms (twelve years) as superior general and then as vicar general of the Union until her death in 1952. This information was provided by Paula Diann Marlin, RSM, Archivist for the Sisters of Mercy Regional Community of Baltimore, December 4, 2002.

19. *Inter Nos*, February 1924, ASMSJ, RG 10/9/84. M. Carmelita remained in St. John's for almost three weeks, returning to Baltimore on October 20, taking with her M. Stanislaus Parsons and M. Joseph Byrne who were to begin nursing studies at Baltimore Mercy Hospital.

nursing service. To complete the professional staff, the hospital hired several young graduates from General Hospital Training School. Many years later, the sisters who lived at St. Clare's in those early days told stories of the joys and difficulties encountered in nursing the sick in a hospital that was still in its infancy. Much depended on the natural ability and inherited knowledge of the sisters who worked beside the few trained nurses on staff. Nevertheless, these sisters were by no means unskilled novices in looking after the sick. Aside from on-the-job training they had received from M. Bernard Gladney, most of them had grown up in outport Newfoundland where there was no doctor available and people depended on the women of the settlement to care for their sick. A great deal of medical folklore had been passed down from generation to generation, and in addition, many young girls were accustomed to helping their mothers look after sick and elderly relatives. Writing of this period in the history of St. Clare's, M. Fabian Hennebury noted:

> If the methods used for sterilizing in the Operating Room and for conveying patients back to bed following Surgery are difficult for us to envisage, the Sisters had an efficiency born of knowledge, skill, and necessity. They knew what improvising meant.[20]

Some of the improvisations would cause raised eyebrows in these days of modern technology and sophisticated, computerized equipment. For instance, methods of sterilization might fall far short of what might be considered essential today. The sisters and nurses in St. Clare's in the early 1920s depended on the efficacy of boiling water and vigorous scrubbing to ensure that no trace of contagion remained on instruments or other materials used in treating patients. So well did they boil and scrub that nobody picked up an infection as a result of being in St. Clare's. The wheeled, cushioned, and many-gadgeted stretchers of today's hospitals were unheard of in those days. Patients at St. Clare's who could not walk were transported in one of two ways, in a blanket, or—when necessary—on a board well padded with folded blankets. On the maternity floor, when infants arrived in greater numbers than had been antic-

---

20. Hennebury, "St. Clare's," p. 7, ASMSJ.

ipated, makeshift bassinets were constructed of Carnation Milk cartons, well lined with the softest of warm woolly blankets.[21] Undoubtedly, these hastily improvised cots, crafted by loving hands, provided their tiny occupants with just as much warmth and comfort as the professional bassinets supplied by some impersonal manufacturing company in Montreal. In any case, judging by repeated visits to the maternity wing, parents seemed to be quite content with the sleeping accommodations provided to their offspring. Sometimes, however, an impatient baby would decide to arrive ahead of time. If this happened when all the maternity beds were occupied, a sister would give up her own bed to the new mother.[22] The sister, thus deprived, would most likely spend the night in a comfortable chair in the parlour—for in those days, chairs in sisters' community rooms were not designed for comfort.

While M. Teresita McNamee and her staff were attending to the needs of the sick, the General Council of the Sisters of Mercy was making plans to ensure that there would be a sufficient number of sisters trained as nurses to carry on the work of the hospital. Already, in 1923, M. Joseph Byrne and M. Stanislaus Parsons had left for Baltimore Mercy Hospital to begin a program of nursing studies that would be completed in September 1926. However, by that time, M. Teresita McNamee, having given two years of service to St. Clare's Mercy Hospital, had returned to Baltimore. Archbishop Roche and the Mercy Sisters in Newfoundland were well aware of the generosity of the Mercy Sisters in Baltimore in allowing one of their most capable nurses to remain for such a long period. And so, when M. Teresita returned to Baltimore early in 1925, she took with her the undying gratitude of the Congregation of the Sisters of Mercy of Newfoundland.

The departure of M. Teresita McNamee might have left St. Clare's once more without a competent director of nursing services except that a young Newfoundlander, Marcella O'Connor, had recently graduated from St. Vincent's Hospital in New York. When she returned to St. John's early in 1925,

---

21. I am indebted to M. Fabian Hennebury for this information.

22. M. Loretta McIsaac quoted by M. Fabian Hennebury in an address given at the annual meeting of St. Clare's alumnae, 1992. ASMSJ, MG 31/2/27. The sisters' sleeping quarters were on the third floor, actually in the attic of the hospital.

she was offered the position of director of nursing services at St. Clare's Mercy Hospital just in time to take over that position from M. Teresita McNamee. Miss O'Connor held this position until September of 1926, when M. Joseph Byrne and M. Stanislaus Parsons returned home as registered nurses. According to the plan of the General Council of the Sisters of Mercy, the return of the two Sisters of Mercy from Baltimore signalled the departure of another two to begin training at Baltimore Mercy Hospital, M. Magdalene Baker and M. Loretta McIsaac. Both sisters had worked at St. Clare's for a couple of years after their profession, and for each, the experience had confirmed her desire to pursue a career in nursing.

When Janie (M. Loretta) McIsaac travelled from her home in Grand River on the west coast of Newfoundland to seek admission to the novitiate of the Sisters of Mercy at Littledale in 1917, she was prepared to spend her professional life as a teacher. Although the plan for a hospital was on the agendas of both the archbishop and the superior general, such talk had not filtered down to the level of a lowly novice. If the announcement in 1918 that M. Bernard Gladney was going to Baltimore to train as a nurse triggered a response in the mind of the young novice, M. Loretta McIsaac, she made no mention of it in later years. In 1919, she was assigned to Belvedere, and after her profession in 1920, she continued teaching in the orphanage until 1923, when she was transferred to St. Clare's.[23] After observing M. Loretta's interest in the work in the hospital, the astonishingly perceptive M. Bridget O'Connor invited her to consider a career in nursing. In accepting this invitation, M. Loretta made a wise decision that more than justified M. Bridget's confidence in her ability.

In September 1926, M. Loretta McIsaac and her companion, M. Magdalene Baker, sailed for Baltimore. Both sisters were young, intelligent, and eager to make the most of the opportunities offered them. They worked long hours in the hospital, and in their free time, they pored over books, wanting to extract every ounce of information that would help them in their profession. Before returning to Newfoundland in 1929, they had completed post-

---

23. Annals of St. Michael's Convent, Belvedere, ASMSJ, RG 10/2/1f.

graduate training at Mary Immaculate Hospital in New York—M. Magdalene in radiology and M. Loretta in anaesthesia.[24]

On her return to St. Clare's Mercy Hospital in 1929, M. Loretta was appointed supervisor of the operating room and anaesthetist. She was also part-time supervisor of surgical patients, a small department at that time, consisting of only twenty-five or twenty-six patients. After the new St. Clare's Mercy Hospital was opened in 1939, she continued her duties in the operating rooms and, as well, took on the duties of supervisor of an eighteen-bed surgical unit. She continued in these positions until 1949, when Newfoundland joined Canada. However, because Canada did not recognize nurse anaesthetists, M. Loretta's long association with this branch of medicine came to an end—one of the casualties of Confederation with Canada! It must be recorded, however, that in all her years as anaesthetist, not one of M. Loretta's patients died as a result of an anaesthetic. Prevented by law from using her considerable training and experience in this field of medicine, M. Loretta continued as supervisor of the operating rooms and of an eighteen-bed surgical floor for another ten years. Then, after twenty years of such heavy responsibilities she was ready for a change. M. Loretta, however, was not willing to give up her work in the hospital. She was appointed supervisor of central supply where her knowledge of the requirements of surgical and laboratory procedures was an invaluable asset. Then, in her retirement, she continued her service to St. Clare's by volunteering at the information desk.

M. Loretta was a woman who inspired a good deal of awe in those who saw her only in her role as a professional nurse. Because so many years of her life were spent in the operating room, the typical patient remembered only the few moments when M. Loretta urged, "Take a deep breath"—and then, oblivion. She was a brisk, no nonsense woman whose approach to life was intelligent, direct, and totally compassionate.[25]

---

24. Hennebury, "St. Clare's," p. 8, ASMSJ.

25. On June 17, 1976, M. Loretto McIsaac completed her volunteer service in the hospital as usual. Shortly after returning to the convent, she became ill and died within a few minutes.

When M. Magdalene Baker returned to St. Clare's, she worked as a supervisor of the patient units. Then, when the radiology department opened in 1939, M. Magdalene Baker was appointed supervisor of the department.[26] She was, in fact, the first registered X-ray technologist in Newfoundland and a founding member of Radiological Technologists. She reigned supreme over the X-ray department at St. Clare's for more than forty years, and she shared the experience she had gained over these years with many young X-ray technicians, who owe much of their skill and knowledge to her instruction and guidance.[27]

The return of M. Loretta McIsaac and M. Magdalene Baker to St. Clare's in 1929 signalled the departure of the next pair of sisters to travel to Baltimore Mercy Hospital, M. St. Joan McDonnell[28] and M. Aloysius Rawlins. Their graduation in 1934 made a total of seven sisters who had completed the required studies and qualified as registered nurses in the United States. But there was still one more.

When M. Aloysius Rawlins and M. St. Joan McDonnell went to the Mercy Hospital School of Nursing they discovered there another young Newfoundlander by the name of Catherine Kenny. The two Sisters of Mercy were delighted to meet someone from home, a bright, vivacious young woman who regaled them with stories of her escapades during the few holidays permitted to student nurses of those days. Catherine's joyous approach to life and her delight in parties and entertainments would have deceived someone less observant than M. Aloysius Rawlins. M. Aloysius saw in this apparently scatterbrained youngster a woman of steely determination and one who would not be easily discouraged from pursuing any objective she had set for herself. Also, to her surprise, M. Aloysius noticed that Catherine was present at daily mass, even on mornings after she had worked a twelve-hour shift on night duty. M.

26. In addition to supervising the radiology department, M. Magdalen Baker was supervisor of pediatrics for a few years.

27. After her retirement in 1972, M. Magdalen remained at St. Clare's Convent until ill health required that she move to the nursing unit at St. Catherine's Convent where she died in 1985.

28. M. St. Joan McDonnell was born in Salmonier, St. Mary's Bay. She was a graduate of St. Bride's College, Littledale, where she was accepted as a postulant in 1919. After her profession in 1922, she taught in the convent schools in St. George's, Burin, Bell Island, and Our Lady of Mercy in St. John's before she began her studies for nursing.

Aloysius wondered if perhaps this young woman was searching for something deeper than her experiences of the social life of Baltimore. Eventually, Catherine Kenny approached M. Aloysius to ask for advice on how to become a member of the Congregation of Sisters of Mercy of Newfoundland. Not surprised by this announcement, M. Aloysius went into action. She wrote to M. Philippa Hanley, the superior general in St. John's, and in short order, arrangements were made for Catherine Kenny to be admitted as a postulant. Shortly after her return to Newfoundland, Catherine entered the Mercy congregation at Littledale where she was given the religious name, Mary Xaverius. She worked as staff nurse at St. Bride's College, Littledale, for a few years before being appointed to the nursing staff at St. Clare's. Her first appointment at St. Clare's was as scrub nurse in the operating room. After "scrubbing" for a period of time, M. Xaverius Kenny assumed the position of supervisor in the nursing units of the hospital.

Some of the first sister-nurses of St. Clare's Mercy Hospital remained there all their lives; others moved to different convents in the congregation. M. Joseph Byrne served as staff nurse at St. Bride's College, Littledale, and at St. Michael's Orphanage, Belvedere, but for the greater part of her life she was a supervisor at St. Clare's Mercy Hospital. M. Aloysius Rawlins' ability was recognized by her appointment, in 1937, as administrator of the hospital, a position she held until her death in 1951. M. St. Joan McDonnell held several positions in the hospital, director of nursing services, director of the School of Nursing, and day supervisor. Later, she was appointed administrator of St. Patrick's Mercy Home, a position she filled for six years. M. Stanislaus Parsons was the first director of the School of Nursing at St. Clare's. Later she was elected superior general of the Sisters of Mercy and served a term as superior of St. Michael's Convent, Belvedere.[29] These women were the pioneers of St. Clare's Mercy Hospital. Few in number and working in less than ideal conditions, they laid the foundation that saw St. Clare's become one of the principal health care facilities in Newfoundland. More than that, they established a philosophy of care whereby the Sisters of Mercy and their co-workers at St.

---

29. Hennebury, "St. Clare's," pp. 8–10, ASMSJ.

Clare's "endeavoured to transform medical science in its complex organization into love and healing, generously and freely given."[30]

Within a few years, other young sisters chose nursing as a career and began their training at St. Clare's where, under the guidance of these first sister-nurses, they discovered much more than the science contained in medical texts. They were taught that the powerful concern of Jesus for the whole person was to be their guide. As nurses and as Sisters of Mercy, they learned that their vocation was "to bring physical, spiritual, and social health to God's creation and to enrich life wherever their ministry called them."[31]

As a private hospital, St. Clare's Mercy Hospital had no government funding. It was intended to care for patients who were in a position to pay for hospital treatment. When a small extension was planned in 1929, *The Daily News* commented:

> St. Clare's, though small, is thoroughly and modernly equipped, and having regard to its size, has all the appointments that make for efficiency in hospital treatment, and that can conduce to the comfort of the patients. It is competently staffed, with two trained Nursing Sisters, Registered Nurses under the Maryland State Board; a Sister Dietitian, trained at Mercy Hospital, Pittsburgh, two lay graduate nurses, and probationers. Two other Sisters have just graduated at the Mercy Hospital, Baltimore, and will be attached to the staff of St. Clare's in September. The hospital . . . is intended to provide accommodation for patients in a position to pay for hospital treatment, but from the beginning it has been an absolutely open hospital—open to all denominations and all members of the medical profession. The hospital is not privately endowed, nor does it receive a government grant, but is altogether financed by the fees from its patients.[32]

The sister-dietitian, to whom this article referred, was the multi-talented M. Aloysius Rawlins who was, at the same time, superior of the convent and business administrator of the hospital.

---

30. Ibid., Introduction.
31. Ibid.
32. *The Daily News*, May 25, 1929, p. 3.

In spite of the fact that St. Clare's received no help from government grants, it sometimes happened that the hospital was asked to admit urgent cases when there was no space available at the General Hospital. *The Daily News* pointed out that St. Clare's accepted government-subsidized patients at the rate of $3 per day, with an extra operating room fee for surgical cases. These rates covered all expenses—board, medicine, drugs, and surgical and medical attendance. Needless to say, the fee charged these patients was sufficient only to cover the actual cost of treatment. *The Daily News* continued:

> It would be impossible . . . to accept patients at these low rates but for the fact that the Sisters, whose life work it is, receive no remuneration for their services, and also for the further fact that the members of the medical profession generously give their medical and surgical services at reduced rates to patients paid for by the Department of Public Charities.[33]

It should be noted that the sisters at St. Clare's continued to work without remuneration until national health insurance was introduced in 1958. M. Fabian Hennebury, long-time administrator of St. Clare's, explained, "The Sisters' cost of living was included in the operating costs of the Hospital; this was mainly for room and board."[34] For all other expenses, the sisters at St. Clare's depended on the Congregation of the Sisters of Mercy for their support. With the introduction of the National Health Insurance Program, sisters were paid as other staff according to their qualifications and position; but the Congregation of the Sisters of Mercy used the sisters' salaries to pay off the hospital debts.[35]

As the years passed, demands for admission to St. Clare's increased until by 1937, the lack of space could no longer be ignored. On October 31, 1937, a letter from Archbishop Roche was read in all the parishes of the archdiocese announcing his decision to build a new hospital. The Catholic people greeted

---

33. Ibid.

34. M. Fabian Hennebury, "Historical Summary of Financial Operation, St. Clare's Mercy Hospital (1922–1982)," p. 1, ASMSJ.

35. Hennebury, "St. Clare's," p. 26, ASMSJ.

the announcement with enthusiasm, so much so that approximately seventy-two thousand dollars was realized through parish collections and donations from individuals and businesses.[36] The Congregation of the Sisters of Mercy mortgaged the Littledale property and arranged a loan from the Eastern Trust Company.[37] In order to avoid further borrowing, Archbishop Roche requested that funds saved by the sisters over the years for emergencies be used for the construction of the hospital, "which is to all intents and purposes the property of the Mercy Order in Newfoundland."[38] The total cost of this building was approximately $300,000, a very large amount in those days. Construction began in May 1938, and sixteen months later, on October 29, 1939, the hospital was blessed and formally opened. It was with a great deal of pride that Archbishop Roche, recalling the small beginnings of 1922, declared:

> Today, after seventeen years, we are assembled in this splendid new Hospital to see the completion of the work which was then begun. We are opening a large modern Hospital, with accommodation for one hundred patients, built on the most approved scientific lines, equipped with everything that modern hospitalization requires, under the management of a staff that comprises eight trained Nursing Sisters, competent and experienced lay graduates, and a training school of some thirty nurses. Verily, my dear Sisters, the acorn has developed into a mighty oak; the tiny grain of mustard seed has grown, as we hoped it would, into a mighty tree.[39]

There was general rejoicing over the opening of the modern, new hospital and widespread appreciation of the contribution of the Sisters of

36. For several years prior to the construction of the 1939 hospital, an annual collection was taken up on Easter Sunday in all churches of the archdiocese. After this practice ceased, some people continued to contribute anonymously to the support of the hospital. I am indebted to M. Fabian Hennebury for this information.

37. Hennebury, "Historical Summary," p. 1, ASMSJ. In addition, the Congregation of the Sisters of Mercy provided a loan of $56,000 at 2½ % interest.

38. Archbishop Roche to the Superior General of the Sisters of Mercy, August 12, 1938, ASMSJ.

39. Archbishop E. P. Roche, Address at the Opening of St. Clare's Mercy Hospital, October 29, 1939, ASMSJ, RG 10/9/62.

Mercy to the institution. Shortly after the hospital opened, the following article appeared in *The Monitor* under the caption, "Soul of the New St. Clare's":

> Completed, equipped, and running at practically full capacity, St. Clare's Mercy Hospital is designed to play an important part in the life of the community, not only because it represents the best that modern architecture and hospital science can provide, but as well because it is staffed by the Sisters of Mercy, an Order whose work in this field is famed all over the American continent. The building is only the body, they are the soul. Indeed, in this city, they have established themselves as something more than merely capable, scientifically trained competent nurses, they bring to hospital administration more than efficiency. They bring an atmosphere created by their own consecrated lives of devotion to the sick and the suffering. It is this that makes the difference between a hospital and a Catholic hospital, and their presence is the surest guarantee of the fine services St. Clare's will render to Newfoundland.[40]

In November 1939, Sir Humphrey Walwyn, the governor of Newfoundland, and Lady Walwyn paid an official visit to the hospital. Lady Walwyn presented St. Clare's with a picture of the Virgin Mary in a frame of hard wrought brass of ancient design. This picture had been in Lady Walwyn's family for over seventy years and was purchased in Italy in 1872 by her great-aunt, who was wife of the governor of Malta at the time.[41]

The year 1939 was a landmark for St. Clare's. Not only was the new hospital opened, but also St. Clare's School of Nursing accepted its first class for a three-year diploma program. Nineteen nursing students, with their director, M. Stanislaus Parsons, moved into the new School of Nursing at St. Clare Avenue. Five of these students had already completed a year's training at the original hospital. Thus, in 1941, after two additional years of study, they became the first graduates of St. Clare's Mercy Hospital School of

---

40. *The Monitor,* November 1940, p. 3.
41. This picture hung in the board room of St. Clare's Mercy Hospital for many years. It is now preserved in the Archives of St. Clare's Mercy Hospital.

Nursing.[42] The first two Sisters of Mercy to graduate from St. Clare's School of Nursing and qualify as registered nurses were M. Fabian Hennebury and M. St. John Norris.

M. Calasanctius Power, who wrote the history of St. Clare's School of Nursing, describes the program of studies as follows:

> The Nursing Program in the first ten years consisted of three full years of study, including a probationary period of five months, at the end of which the students received their Cap and Bib. . . . [This] marked their admission in the School of Nursing as junior students.
>
> The probationary period completed, the most important part of instruction was now at the bedside. . . . The Sister Supervisor or Head Nurse was responsible for teaching and supervising the student. This was not always the best method, but it was the only one possible at the time.[43]

In spite of the drawbacks of such a program of instruction, M. Calasanctius mentioned that students benefited greatly from the individual attention and guidance provided by the supervisors of the different departments. For instance, in the operating room they learned skills that can be mastered only by practice, which was carried out under the vigilant eye of M. Loretta McIsaac. In the pediatric department, the student nurse came under the discerning supervision of M. Fabian Hennebury and, later, M. St. Clare Maddigan.

In those days, there were no full-time instructors at the School of Nursing. Student nurses attended lectures presented by members of the medical staff. The required subjects included anatomy, physiology, surgical and medical nursing, nursing arts, psychiatry, infectious diseases, pediatrics, obstetrics, and tuberculosis.[44]

---

42. M. Calasanctius Power, *The St. Clare's Mercy Hospital School of Nursing, 1939–1979*, n. p., 1982), p. 1. The names of these graduates were Ethel Goff, Anne Hogan, Lillian Coleman, Eileen O'Brien, and May O'Reilly.

43. Power, *School of Nursing*, p. 2.

44. Hennebury, "St. Clare's," p. 25, ASMSJ.

In 1943, M. Xaverius (Catherine) Kenny was appointed director of the School of Nursing. Relying largely on experience and natural ability, for the next seventeen years she administered the School of Nursing in a manner that earned her the respect of visiting lecturers, colleagues, and, most of all, the students themselves. During these years, the majority of the sister-nurses were released, in turn, to study at different universities to earn degrees in the various disciplines required for the efficient operation of the hospital. It was not until 1960 that M. Xaverius Kenny was given leave of absence to return to the United States for further study. During her absence, M. Calasanctius Power acted as director of the school, a position for which she was well qualified, having previously earned the degree of bachelor of science in nursing. However, M. Calasanctius was already director of nursing education at St. Clare's, having been appointed to the position in 1956; her consent to assume the added task of director of the School of Nursing was an indication of great generosity of spirit and her dedication to the hospital. For two years, M. Calasanctius filled the dual role until M. Xaverius, having successfully completed the requirements for the degree of bachelor of nursing education, returned to St. Clare's. Later, M. Calasanctius was appointed director of personnel at the hospital. At the same time, she continued to fill the post of director of nursing education for a number of years.

It must have been with a huge sigh of relief that M. Calasanctius surrendered the position of director of the School of Nursing into the hands of M. Xaverius, who held the position for another fourteen years until her retirement in 1974. Despite her diminutive size, for she was a little wisp of a woman, M. Xaverius had no problems with discipline in the School of Nursing, not because she was a stern authority figure, but because she was a warm, approachable human being. Her practice of signing all memos to the students with her initials, SMX, earned her the nickname, "Smix," the name still used by St. Clare's graduates in referring to their former director, in spite of the fact that she reverted to her baptismal name, Catherine, in 1973.

Following the opening of the new hospital in 1939, the sisters and staff continued to work hard to provide a high standard of care. M. Fabian Hennebury remembered that they worked twelve hours a day—and sometimes more—

seven days a week. In addition to the sisters, there were only five graduate nurses on staff, with a sister supervisor on each floor. The duties of the supervisor included not only nursing care but also serving meals. While members of the lay staff were given a free afternoon once a week, the sisters continued to work as usual.[45]

During the period from 1922 through the 1940s, the sisters, for the most part, were the only supervisors. Graduate nurses assisted them in the operating room, delivery room, pediatrics, and nursery. M. Joseph Byrne and M. Xaverius (Catherine) Kenny rotated on night duty for periods which lasted initially from several months to a couple of years. However, as other sisters graduated, they were included in the rotation. This meant that the night supervisor worked three- to six-month periods at a time.

It is doubtful that sisters who lived in other convents realized or appreciated the almost ceaseless labour of the nursing sisters at St. Clare's. While there was a certain amount of visiting back and forth by sisters to neighbouring convents in the city, these visits rarely included St. Clare's Convent, not because sisters were not welcome at St. Clare's, but because work and recreation schedules of hospital and schools did not coincide. Thus, for some years, the overworked sisters at St. Clare's had only occasional social contacts with other members of their congregation. Furthermore, teaching sisters were frequently changed from one convent to another according to their qualifications and the needs of the schools in different parts of Newfoundland. Most sisters lived with dozens of different people in the span of ten or fifteen years. St. Clare's, however, was a more static community. The only changes occurred when sisters destined for the School of Nursing came to live at St. Clare's Convent. This might have led to a feeling of isolation on the part of the sister-nurses except that, having the good sense to realize that this is the way things were at the time, they accepted their lot with good-humoured grace. Opportunities for the St. Clare's sisters to forge closer bonds with other members of the congregation occurred when a sister from another community required hospitalization. The joy with which the sister-nurses greeted the sis-

---

45. Later this free time for the lay staff was increased to a full day off once a week.

ter-patient often caused the poor sufferer to wonder at the peculiar attitude of St. Clare's sisters who, apparently, regarded the illness of another sister as an occasion for celebration! Nonetheless, there was no place in the rigid schedule of a nurse to permit her to spend much time at the bedside of another member of her congregation. M. Stanislaus Parsons, in particular, was adamant in insisting that the time of the nurse not be wasted in paying visits to her friends.

Because St. Clare's Mercy Hospital was completely self-supporting, there was a tight control on all spending and strict supervision of the supplies that were available. In her "History of St. Clare's Mercy Hospital," M. Fabian Hennebury wrote:

> It was not unknown . . . for the Student Nurses and others to bring in a supply of dresses and diapers from home for the Nursery and Pediatric Departments. Preparation of formulas was also a part of the nurses' daily routine. . . . Bottles and nipples were boiled after each feeding. It was not uncommon to get the aroma of burnt up nipples, or to see a student or orderly running to the nearby drugstore to purchase a replacement.[46]

Shortly after the new St. Clare's opened in 1939, Archbishop Roche made one stipulation to the sisters—no mother who wanted to be admitted to St. Clare's to deliver her baby would be refused because of inability to pay. This was a laudable sentiment, and one with which the Sisters of Mercy heartily agreed. The only hitch was that the sisters depended on the income from fees paid by the patients to support the hospital; provide equipment, supplies, food, heat, etc.; and to pay the staff. As it was, they just managed to pay the bills and keep solvent. The archbishop understood this and decided to approach the government, knowing that other hospitals were reimbursed for the expenses involved in caring for those who could not afford to pay for themselves.

---

46. Hennebury, "St. Clare's," p. 26, ASMSJ.

In 1944 a request was made to the Department of Health by Archbishop E. P. Roche, that a portion of the grant then paid to the Grace General Hospital for the care of obstetrical patients be given to St. Clare's for poor mothers who preferred to come to St. Clare's.[47]

Apparently, Archbishop Roche had requested help at a time when money was more than usually scarce, and his request was denied. The sisters at St. Clare's put their heads together to try to solve the problem of how to cover the costs involved in caring for these young mothers and their babies. In short order they came up with a brilliant idea—the creation of a "Burse." The superior of St. Clare's Convent, M. Benedicta Fitzgibbon, wrote a letter to friends of St. Clare's to explain the sisters' plan and to elicit support:

His Grace, the Archbishop . . . gave to the Sisters one special injunction that no maternity case was to be refused admission because of inability to pay. This desire of His Grace has been faithfully carried out even in the case of mothers presenting, from the Department of Health, admission slips to other institutions. Acceptance of such cases has never been refused even though the Hospital must care for them without government remuneration. It will be seen, however, that such demands weigh heavily upon an institution dependent entirely on its income from private sources. . . . These reasons impel us to begin in a small way the creation of a fund for this purpose. . . . We are placing this project under the patronage of the powerful protector of the Holy Family, St. Joseph, naming the fund, "St. Joseph's Burse."[48]

The creation of St. Joseph's Burse met with an immediate response, and through the generosity of the benefactors of St. Clare's, hundreds of young mothers had the satisfaction of delivering their babies in the hospital of their

47. Hennebury, "Historical Summary," p. 3, ASMSJ.
48. Hennebury, "St. Clare's," pp. 32–33, ASMSJ. From St. Joseph's Burse, the attending physician was given a fee of $25 for delivery and care, and the hospital was paid the munificent sum of $2.50 a day.

WEAVERS OF THE TAPESTRY

choice. Many of these young women required more than ordinary care because they had not visited a doctor at any time during their pregnancy.

At that time, too, all Roman Catholic babies were baptized in the hospital chapel before their mothers were discharged. This was an especially joyous celebration. Proud parents, doting grandparents, and an assortment of fond relatives and friends assembled in St. Clare's Chapel for the event. At the appointed time, the babies were carried in, each one attired in a long white garment adorned with the multiple frills and flounces characteristic of christening robes at that time. No infant was ever deprived of the luxury of a christening robe. If the mother could not afford one, it was provided to her by means of St. Joseph's Burse.[49] Frequently, after the ceremony was over and the wailing stars of the occasion were brought back to the nursery, the families celebrated with wine and a christening cake. St. Joseph's Burse was discontinued in 1958 when the National Health Insurance Program was available to all citizens in Canada. Until that time, St. Clare's Mercy Hospital continued the practice of providing free accommodation and care to pregnant mothers who could not afford to pay a fee.

In addition to providing care for Newfoundlanders, St. Clare's cared also for seamen from many other countries, especially those from the Spanish and Portuguese fishing fleets. This was because two physicians, who worked mainly at St. Clare's, were also the doctors employed by the Port of St. John's. During the Second World War, St. Clare's admitted many sailors from ships that had been torpedoed off the coast of Newfoundland. On one occasion, eleven seamen were admitted with severe frostbite, having been in lifeboats for several days before they were rescued. At the time of this occurrence, the hospital was working at peak capacity. In order to provide the special treatment that was needed, the office and the doctors' lounge were speedily transformed into nursing units to care for the injured sailors.[50]

---

49. St. Joseph's Burse, which allowed St. Clare's to provide free accommodation and care to needy pregnant mothers, began in 1939 and was continued until the advent of National Health Insurance in 1958.

50. Hennebury, "St. Clare's," p. 27, ASMSJ.

In 1947, on the occasion of Archbishop Roche's golden anniversary of ordination as a priest, the people of the archdiocese presented him with $83,000, which he donated for the completion of a new chapel for St. Clare's Mercy Hospital. The extension contained also a new dining room and cafeteria, a twenty-eight bed pediatric unit, and an extension to the obstetrics department. This left more space for male patients on the first floor of the hospital and an enlarged nursery. The total cost of the new wing was $235,000. In addition to the archbishop's donation, money was raised through bonds and bank loans.[51] It speaks well for the fiscal prudence and wise management of those women who directed the affairs of the Congregation of the Sisters of Mercy as well as of the administrators of St. Clare's that these loans were paid in full by 1968 without any outside assistance. The administrator of St. Clare's during the greater part of this period was M. Fabian Hennebury (1955–81).[52]

M. Fabian Hennebury was born in the historic town of Bonavista, the traditional landing place of John Cabot. At her baptism, she was named Mary, which was also her mother's name. When she was just nine years of age, her mother died. As the oldest girl in a family of eight children—the youngest just seven months old—Mary learned how to accept responsibility at an early age. When she was sixteen, she went as a student to St. Bride's College, Littledale, and during her two years at boarding school, Mary began to think about the religious life. She saw that the sisters who taught her were happy, contented women, who had dedicated their lives to helping others through a variety of ministries. Consequently, at the age of nineteen, Mary asked to be accepted as a postulant at Littledale. On July 16, 1936, Mary Hennebury was received into the novitiate

<hr>

51. St. Clare's Convent contributed a further $54,000 from a savings account called the "Chapel Account." The money in this account was accumulated over the years from gifts by relatives and friends to the convent and to individual sisters, as well as from special projects.

52. The administrators of St. Clare's Mercy Hospital who preceded M. Fabian Hennebury were M. Bernard Gladney (1922–23), M. Aloysius Rawlins (1923–31; 1937–51), M. Stanislaus Parsons (1931–37), M. Carmelita Hartigan, (1952–54), and M. Loretta McIsaac (1954–1955).

and from that time on she was known by her religious name, Mary Fabian. After her profession in 1938, M. Fabian spent a year teaching before she entered St. Clare's School of Nursing in 1939. A few years after graduating as a nurse in 1942, she completed postgraduate work at the Toronto Hospital for Sick Children (1945), and on her return to St. Clare's, she was appointed instructor in pediatrics and supervisor of the pediatric department of the hospital.

In 1954, M. Fabian was asked to move to nursing education. Although she loved her work in pediatrics and had no desire to return to teaching, M. Fabian accepted the decision of her superiors and enrolled as a student at the University of Toronto. She completed the prescribed courses, received her certificate in nursing education and was looking forward to another year's study to fulfill the requirements for the degree of bachelor of science in nursing when word came from the General Council of the Sisters of Mercy asking her to return to her former position as supervisor of pediatrics. Several other sisters had a keen interest in nursing education, but it was not so easy to find someone with M. Fabian's qualifications and experience in pediatrics. M. Fabian was by no means disappointed with this decision, in fact, she was elated. She much preferred nursing in the pediatric unit to teaching in the School of Nursing, and so, in 1955, she returned to her first love—caring for sick children.

All during this time, since 1923, with the exception of a six-year period (1931–37), M. Aloysius Rawlins had served as administrator of St. Clare's. But early in the 1950s, her health began to fail. M. Carmelita Hartigan was sent away to Mercy Hospital in Baltimore to study administration, and after M. Aloysius died in 1951, M. Carmelita was appointed administrator (1952–54). Sadly, M. Carmelita was not destined to fill the position for any length of time, for six months after her appointment, it was discovered that she had an aggressive form of cancer. Ten months later, on October 15, 1954, M. Carmelita Hartigan died, leaving the position of administrator vacant. The archbishop and the General Council of the Sisters of Mercy did not hesitate. Early in 1955, M. Fabian Hennebury was appointed administrator of St. Clare's Mercy Hospital. In the interim, between the death of M. Carmelita and until M. Fabian was ready to assume the position, M. Loretta McIsaac agreed to act as interim administrator of the hospital.

Shortly before her appointment as administrator, M. Fabian Hennebury had been asked to enroll in a two-year correspondence course in hospital organization and management given by the Canadian Hospital Association (CHA). At this time, there was no degree program in hospital administration offered in any Canadian university. The only courses available were offered by correspondence. Having received her certificate from the CHA, she enrolled in a similar program with the American Hospital Association (AHA). After completing written and oral examinations in Chicago, she was admitted as a member of the association and later qualified for a fellowship from the same association. M. Fabian continued to be a member of both the Canadian and American Health Associations and was active in the AHA as a regent and examiner for the American College for over sixteen years.

During the years 1922–1955, the administrator and sisters of St. Clare's Convent directed the operation of the hospital. There was no board of directors nor organized medical staff. "The Archbishop appeared to have jurisdiction over much of the financial operation and was a regular visitor to the Hospital."[53] It was not until the 1950s that the need for formal organization of a board and medical staff was obvious. On March 15, 1956, the newly formed Board of Directors of St. Clare's Mercy Hospital held its first formal meeting with Archbishop P. J. Skinner as chairman.[54] Two months later, the board appointed five members of the medical staff to form the first Medical Advisory or Executive of the Medical Staff, with Dr. J. B. Murphy as the first president.

With the appointment of the Executive of the Medical Staff, the importance of medical records was brought to the board's attention. As a result, M. Brenda Lacey, a registered nurse who had been on the staff of St. Clare's for several years, was sent to Halifax Infirmary where she enrolled in a course for medical records librarians. After her graduation in 1957, she was appointed

53. Hennebury, "St. Clare's," p. 34, ASMSJ.

54. Archbishop Patrick James Skinner succeeded Archbishop Roche who died in 1950. Members of this board were M. Imelda Smith, superior general of the Sisters of Mercy; Monsignor Harold Summers, vicar general of the Archdiocese of St. John's; M. Loretta McIsaac; M. Fabian Hennebury; R. S. Furlong; Dr. E. L. Sharpe; and M. Xaverius Kenny (secretary).

director of the Medical Records Department, a post she held until her retirement from St. Clare's in the fall of 1989. It should be noted here that the term
"retirement" is used loosely when applied to a Sister of Mercy.[55] In M. Brenda's
case, she moved from the Medical Records Department at St. Clare's to the
general office of the Sisters of Mercy where she employs her considerable skill
by recording the income and expenditures of the Congregation of the Sisters
of Mercy of Newfoundland.

With the appointment of the new, dynamic administrator, M. Fabian
Hennebury, the establishment of an active board of directors, and the counsel
of the Medical Advisory Committee, the financial administration of St. Clare's
underwent a thorough reorganization. Liability insurance was taken out for the
first time in October 1956. To prepare for the introduction of the National
Health Insurance Program, a new accounting system was put in place in
January 1957.[56] At this time, too, the importance of accreditation was being
discussed. Because of the inadequate system of keeping medical records that
had been in place prior to M. Brenda Lacey's appointment and the lack of formal organization, the board realized that St. Clare's was not ready to meet the
standards required for full accreditation. Nevertheless, it was decided to apply
to the Joint Commission on Hospital Accreditation for a preliminary survey to
identify deficiencies and suggest improvements. This survey was completed in
July 1958, and St. Clare's was given a one-year accreditation with recommendations. So carefully were these recommendations implemented that the following year the hospital was given full accreditation for three years, a status
that has been maintained to the present day.[57]

---

55. Some sisters claim that the term "recycled" more aptly describes a member of the community who no longer occupies a salaried position.

56. The Canadian National Health Insurance Program came into effect on July 1, 1958.

57. Because the author of the only complete history of St. Clare's Mercy Hospital is M.
Fabian Hennebury, the account makes no mention of her role in the reorganization and
almost miraculous expansion of the hospital. However, the rapid improvements and the
new and compassionate outreach programs initiated by St. Clare's for the benefit of the
community at large coincide with the period during which M. Fabian was administrator. It
is safe to conclude that she was the person with the vision and courage behind these initiatives that make St. Clare's one of the leading hospitals in Newfoundland.

Meanwhile, St. Clare's Mercy Hospital School of Nursing was attracting more and more students. When it opened in 1939, students were housed in residences on St. Clare Avenue and LeMarchant Road adjacent to the hospital. As nursing education became more organized there was an urgent need for additional classroom facilities. At this time, 1957, federal-provincial grants were available for such projects, and for the first time in its history, St. Clare's Mercy Hospital applied for a federal grant to help finance a new student residence. Unfortunately, funds were not available at the time, and the hospital was told that the request would be reviewed the following year. Without the grant from the government, it was impossible to proceed with the plan for a student residence. At the same time, the problem of providing accommodations for student nurses needed an immediate solution. Having exhausted all earthly avenues, the sisters sought heavenly assistance! A novena in honour of Our Lady of Lourdes was begun in St. Clare's Convent, and for nine days, the sisters stormed heaven.[58] The novena concluded on February 11, the day on which the Church celebrates the Feast of Our Lady of Lourdes. That morning, M. Fabian, the administrator, received a phone call from Dr. James McGrath, the minister of health, informing her that the government had reconsidered and that the grant was available to St. Clare's after all.[59] The residence, known as Our Lady of Lourdes Hall, was officially blessed and opened in September 1958, and in November of that year, a marble statue of Our Lady of Lourdes was erected in front of the residence.[60]

By 1960, St. Clare's Mercy Hospital was operating at full capacity and the demands for admission were increasing every day, especially now that people had the freedom to choose their own hospital under the National Health

58. A novena consists of a prayer that is offered to God for nine consecutive days. It is usually offered in honour of the Virgin Mary or some saint.

59. The federal-provincial grant amounted to $220,000. An additional $61,256.50 was contributed by the Sisters of Mercy from a savings account, and a loan of $290,000 was arranged through the Bank of Nova Scotia. The final payments on this loan were made in 1972.

60. The statue was purchased in Italy and was the gift of the architect, John Hoskins. In 2002, the statue was relocated and it stands now in front of McAuley Convent on the Littledale campus.

Insurance Plan.[61] Because the loan for the 1939 building on LeMarchant Road had been completely paid, St. Clare's was in a position to consider further expansion. In April 1959, the announcement was made that a new wing would be added to St. Clare's that would provide additional facilities for obstetrics, pediatrics, and emergency services. Financial arrangements were made for a bank loan to cover approximately sixty percent of the cost, the remainder being obtained through federal-provincial grants. The loan was fully repaid by taking five thousand dollars monthly from the sisters' salaries and through income from the private room differential.[62] The new seven-storey extension, made of brick, was opened on January 8, 1962. While it supported Newfoundland Bricklayers Industry, it caused problems for many years because of frequent major leaks. Eventually, the structural problems were corrected, but not without additional expense.

In June 1967, M. Aiden Howell, the laboratory supervisor, spearheaded the formation of the St. Clare's Mercy Hospital Auxiliary. M. Aiden Howell was truly loved and respected by her colleagues in health care and by her sisters in community. Born in Northern Bay, Newfoundland, she received her early education in the Catholic school in her hometown before going on to St. Bride's College, Littledale, where she made her decision to enter the Congregation of the Sisters of Mercy. Shortly after her profession in 1942, she enrolled in the School of Nursing at St. Clare's, graduating as a nurse in 1945. Subsequently, she attended the University of Toronto where she obtained a degree in laboratory technique. Within a few years, she was appointed Supervisor of Laboratory Services where her sense of humour and her optimistic outlook on life made St. Clare's lab the most popular department in the hospital. Timorous individuals, who visited her laboratory to be poked and prodded with needles of all sizes and shapes, emerged from the ordeal with smiling faces! In 1971, while studying for a master's degree in Baltimore, M. Aiden became very ill. Immediate surgery was required, and it was discovered

---

61. Hennebury, "St. Clare's," p. 39, ASMSJ. Before 1958, patients from the outports, who were participating in the Cottage Hospital Plan, could be referred to St. John's for free treatment but only to the government hospital, which was the General Hospital.
62. Ibid., p. 41.

that she was suffering from terminal cancer. The sisters in Newfoundland, and particularly her colleagues at St. Clare's, were shocked at this unexpected news. Immediately on receiving the report, M. St. Clare Maddigan, one of the nurses on the staff at St. Clare's, left for Baltimore to be with M. Aiden at this difficult time. Naturally, M. Aiden was anxious to return to St. John's, but her condition was such that the American commercial airlines could not accommodate her. The administrator of Mercy Hospital in Baltimore had a brother who was a high-ranking officer in the United States Army. He obtained transportation for the sisters on a medically equipped army plane that was en route to Goose Bay, Labrador. It was arranged that the plane would stop at Gander where they could connect with the regular Air Canada flight to St. John's. M. Aiden died a few weeks later on January 12, 1972. The organization that she established, the St. Clare's Mercy Hospital Auxiliary,[63] continued under the leadership of M. Mark Hennebury, and within fourteen years of its establishment, it had donated more than $350,000 to the hospital.

Within the hospital things were changing rapidly. Reluctantly, the administrator, M. Fabian Hennebury, agreed to discontinue the department of pediatrics. She perceived that the new Janeway Child Health Centre was better prepared to care for children, and furthermore, the city's best pediatricians were attached to the staff of the Janeway. New technology required sophisticated, expensive equipment that was out of date almost as soon as it arrived. For practical reasons, dietary and cleaning services were contracted out to businesses in the city, and laundry services were transferred to the Central Laundry. A policy of group purchasing through the Newfoundland Hospital Association was begun. More significantly, a formal affiliation agreement was signed with the Memorial University's Medical School. In-service education was initiated, and conferences on various topics were held on a biweekly basis.

---

63. The St. Clare's Mercy Hospital Auxiliary consisted of volunteers from the community at large. These people worked to support the hospital through fundraising activities such as the operation of a gift shop, located on the main floor of the building, and the annual Sale of Work.

In spite of all the new initiatives and the rapid expansion that had already occurred, M. Fabian was concerned that there was, as yet, no long-term plan for the future of St. Clare's. She brought her concerns to the board of governors, and as a result, a hospital consultant firm from Toronto was engaged to complete a survey of the hospital and the acute health care needs of the city. As a result of this survey, the urgent need for a service wing and acute-care beds was confirmed, and a request was made to the provincial government for assistance. The Department of Health agreed that the request was reasonable, and in April 1968, construction of the new exten-sion to St. Clare's, including the complete renovation of the 1960–62 build-ing, was announced. The project was completed in 1972, just fifty years after the first St. Clare's Mercy Hospital was opened. The new St. Clare's was a "state of the art" modern hospital, the whole complex providing accommo-dation for 375 patients. The most up-to-date equipment was provided in every department of the hospital. When writing an account of this ambitious project, M. Fabian acknowledged the invaluable assistance of Monsignor Harold Summers:

> Over this difficult period, Msgr. Harold A. Summers, as chairman of the Board, gave much of his time and effort to the various proj-ects. As Chairman of the Finance Committee, he took responsi-bility for the financial planning which he outlined in detail for the Hospital. His schedules covered the whole period for repayment of loans and as a result, payments of interest and principal were always on the date noted. Monsignor retired shortly after arrangements were finalized for the Service Wing, but he main-tained an interest in its progress. The Sisters of Mercy will always be grateful for his assistance.[64]

Much of the money for the expansion of the hospital came from the personal sacrifices of all the Sisters of Mercy in Newfoundland who, in order to support St. Clare's and other ministries of the congregation, lived on a very small per-centage of their salaries. In addition, grateful patients, as well as relatives and

---

64. Hennebury, "St. Clare's," p. 46, ASMSJ.

friends of the sisters, made bequests to St. Clare's. The almost continual changes and renovations carried out in the hospital to meet changing needs were funded, for the most part, from St. Clare's funds and from the Congregation of the Sisters of Mercy rather than from government grants. Many items of major equipment were obtained without government funding. Some of this equipment was purchased from funds donated by the Sisters of Mercy and St. Clare's Mercy Hospital Auxiliary.[65]

Throughout her years as a nurse and especially in her role as administrator, M. Fabian Hennebury was aware of the helplessness of many men and women who were trying to fight an addiction to alcohol. She discussed her concerns with St. Clare's Board of Directors who approved her suggestion to initiate plans for a detoxification centre. The provincial government welcomed the idea and agreed to finance the centre, and on May 1, 1978, the facility known as Talbot House was blessed and opened by the chairman of the St. Clare's board, Monsignor David Morrissey.

Talbot House was formerly a school operated by the Presentation Sisters. It was purchased from St. Patrick's Parish by the Congregation of the Sisters of Mercy and given to St. Clare's. Then, with the help of a grant from the federal government, the building was renovated to make it suitable for its new purpose. "Talbot House is a non-medical residential facility that provides a quiet, non-threatening refuge for people needing help when intoxicated."[66] In addition to providing a detoxification centre, St. Clare's offered treatment for the alcoholic both in the psychiatric in-patient unit and in the day care. Other self-help programs were offered at Talbot House and through this centre, St. Clare's Mercy Hospital continued for many years to offer sanctuary to people fighting the disease of alcoholism.[67]

65. Hennebury, "Historical Summary," p. 6, ASMSJ.

66. Ibid., p. 48.

67. Talbot House was replaced in 1999 by a new detoxification centre called "The Recovery Centre" in the area of St. John's known as Pleasantville. This centre, in addition to providing a residential facility for people needing shelter when intoxicated, provides educational and treatment programs.

Another area of health care in which St. Clare's Mercy Hospital led the way was the care of the terminally ill. Through the compassion and vision of M. Fabian Hennebury and with the financial assistance of the Sisters of Mercy,[68] St. Clare's opened a palliative care unit on October 1, 1979—the first facility of this nature to be established in the Atlantic Provinces. Palliative care provides palliative and supportive care for terminally ill patients and their families. M. Fabian explained:

> In order to assist them [the patients and their families] at this time, we believe in total supportive care of the patient, by our reverence for life—not necessarily by prolonging terminal illness, but by assisting the terminally ill patient to live fully, to preserve mental alertness and to experience the support of the family and a caring community.
> There are two main goals for this unit:
> 1) To maintain a family oriented program apart from the acute care hospital setting, and
> 2) To free the patient from pain and its associated mental anguish and anxiety by a program of pain control.[69]

Over the years the palliative care unit has given comfort and hope to hundreds—perhaps thousands—of people during their darkest hours. Not only have the sick been relieved of much suffering, but also the pain of relatives and friends has been alleviated by the loving concern of medical staff and volunteers especially trained for this ministry. It is one of the ironies of life that the first Sister of Mercy to die in the palliative care unit was M. Fabian's younger sister, M. Mark Hennebury, who died of cancer on January 14, 1984. M. Mark was a registered nurse who spent most of her religious life after profession caring for the sick. With the exception of six years when she was administrator of St. Patrick's Mercy Home, she lived and worked at St. Clare's. All those who worked with her, especially members of St. Clare's Auxiliary, remember M. Mark Hennebury with affection and gratitude. The sisters in St.

---

68. The Congregation of the Sisters of Mercy contributed $100,000 to cover the cost of the Palliative Care Unit during its first six months of operation.
69. Hennebury, "Historical Summary," p. 49.

Clare's community recall her matter-of-fact attitude toward an illness that she accepted with uncomplaining patience. She continued her work with the Auxiliary until one day she announced quietly to the sisters that it was time for her to move to the palliative care unit. She died the next day.

More than one hundred Sisters of Mercy have worked at St. Clare's Mercy Hospital in a variety of ministries—nursing, administration, pastoral care, housekeeping, office management, medical records, laboratory, X-ray, dietary, and education. The contribution of each one has been essential to the growth and development of St. Clare's and to the ministry of the Sisters of Mercy. There is no record of the thousands of ways in which the sisters and the nurses brought renewed hope and comfort to suffering people. For instance, few people know the story connected with the picture that hangs in the sixth-floor lounge, a story rooted in the ordinary, everyday small acts of kindness that were part and parcel of the ministry of St. Clare's. The picture was painted by a German immigrant, Volkmar Rosenberg, who came to Newfoundland after the Second World War. He was admitted to St. Clare's on two occasions, once to undergo an operation for cancer and the second time when he was terminally ill. While he was in hospital, Srs. Mary Manning and Carmelita Power befriended him. The two sisters visited him frequently, even after he was discharged from hospital. During these visits, Volkmar spoke of his life in Germany and Russia. One day he arrived at the hospital with a painting as a gift for those who had taken care of him during his illness. His explanation of the painting is as follows:

> The painting has a black background with a bright yellow sunflower in the centre. He said, "I will explain why I painted this picture. The black background represents all the suffering I experienced in my past life through two world wars and afterwards. I saw my own little sister die of hunger. I lost my faith in humanity. The sunflower represents all the loving care I received while I was in hospital. The nurses on the Sixth Floor East restored my faith in humanity."[70]

---

70. Unsigned document, April 1977, ASMSJ, RG 10/9/75.

The period from 1955 to 1982 was a time when St. Clare's knew phenomenal growth, not only in the size of the physical plant, in the services offered, in its outreach programs, but especially because of the qualifications, expertise, and reputation of the people who staffed the hospital. This period coincided with M. Fabian's tenure as administrator of St. Clare's. Her constant aim was to maintain the position of St. Clare's as a general hospital with the highest accreditation. For her progressive stance and her contribution to health care, she received national and international recognition. Included in her many awards is the Order of Canada that was presented to her on December 17, 1984, in recognition of her outstanding achievements in service to humanity.

Of course, M. Fabian Hennebury did not work alone. She had the advice, co-operation, and dedication of the sisters and staff of St. Clare's Mercy Hospital, the support and encouragement of the successive General Councils of the Sisters of Mercy, and the confidence of the archbishop and administrative board of the Archdiocese of St. John's. However, it must be said that throughout her tenure as chief executive officer (CEO), M. Fabian established at St. Clare's a standard of excellence in the delivery of care that was a model for her successors. M. Fabian retired from St. Clare's in 1981.

After M. Fabian's retirement, M. Lucy Power succeeded her as administrator and CEO of St. Clare's Mercy Hospital. M. Lucy continued to implement the far-sighted policies of her predecessor. In 1985, St. Clare's laboratory had the distinction of becoming the first computerized laboratory in Newfoundland and Labrador and one of the first in Canada. The laboratory was fully accredited and participated in the training of laboratory personnel with the Memorial University of Newfoundland Medical School and the Cabot College of Applied Arts, Technology, and Continuing Education.

M. Lucy Power remained as executive director of St. Clare's until 1986. In 1983, three years prior to her resignation from her position at St. Clare's, she requested a dispensation from her religious vows and married a short time later. After leaving St. Clare's, Lucy was appointed chief executive officer of the General Hospital at the Health Sciences Complex in St. John's. All through the years, Lucy Power Dobbin has kept in close touch with the Sisters of Mercy, but especially with her former colleagues at St. Clare's Mercy Hospital.

Meanwhile, in April 1985, St. Clare's assumed responsibility for the administration of the Dr. Walter Templeman Hospital on Bell Island.[71] This was in response to a government policy of placing small hospitals under the administrative structure of larger regional facilities. Lucy Power Dobbin remarked that the changes would involve making available various types of expertise and helping to provide some services that were not readily available on Bell Island. Furthermore, ongoing education and training programs at St. Clare's would be extended to personnel at the Bell Island hospital. After Lucy Power Dobbin's resignation, Sr. Elizabeth Davis was appointed as executive director of St. Clare's.

When Elizabeth Davis decided to join the Sisters of Mercy in 1966, she looked forward to a future in teaching. After graduating from the Memorial University of Newfoundland with bachelor's degrees in arts and education, she decided to study for a master's degree in theology from the University of Notre Dame in Indiana. Meanwhile, she pursued an active career as a teacher in schools administered by the Sisters of Mercy in Newfoundland. Then, in 1982, she was asked to leave teaching, which she thoroughly enjoyed, and study at the Institute of Religious Formation (IRF) in St. Louis, Missouri, to prepare for the position of director of formation. However, before the end of that academic year, in March 1983, the superior general, Sr. Patricia Maher, asked her to consider administration at St. Clare's Mercy Hospital. She completed the IRF program and, in September 1983, went to the University of Toronto to begin a master's program in health science (administration). At the beginning of each of her two years of study in Toronto, she received an Open Master's Fellowship in recognition of previous academic achievement. Then, during the first year of her studies, she was awarded the Foster G. McGaw Medal and Scholarship in recognition of past achievements. As a requirement for the degree, at the conclusion of each academic year, Elizabeth engaged in a practical experience and received the R. Alan Hay Memorial Prize, the first student to receive this award two years in succession. In May 1985, Sr. Elizabeth accepted the Robert Wood Johnson Award that is presented to the

---

71. *The Evening Telegram*, March 31, 1986, p. 3.

graduating student judged by the faculty as the one most likely to contribute valuable service to the health administration discipline. On November 27, 1985, Sr. Elizabeth Davis graduated from the University of Toronto with the degree, master of health science (administration).[72]

On her return to St. John's, Sr. Elizabeth was appointed assistant executive officer of St. Clare's Mercy Hospital, and on June 16, 1986, she became the CEO of St. Clare's Mercy Hospital. A few days later, a reporter for *The Evening Telegram* wrote:

> "Mercy above all" is a long-standing tradition at St. Clare's Mercy Hospital and it will be maintained under the hospital's new executive director, Sister Elizabeth Davis . . .
>
> The new executive director at St. Clare's has the onerous task of running the 323-bed facility that provides direct health care service to 10,000 in-patients per year. Last year 214,000 used the out-patient facilities and another 38,000 were seen in the emergency centre.
>
> St. Clare's boasts the busiest general surgical facility in the province and has the only palliative care unit. In addition to a rheumatic disease unit, it supervises diagnosis and treatment of about 80,000 arthritics and operates a psychiatric program. It is also a major referral for chest surgery and medicine, general orthopedics and reconstructive surgery, obstetrics and gynecology.[73]

Sr. Elizabeth was not long in establishing herself as a capable and compassionate administrator. Less than a year after her appointment, St. Clare's was awarded the highest level of accreditation available for hospitals in Canada. The Canadian Council on Hospital Accreditation rated the health care facilities at St. Clare's "above average." Because this was the ninth time that St. Clare's had received this award, the Newfoundland hospital was regarded as having one of the consistently highest standards of care in all of Canada.[74]

---

72. *The Monitor*, December 1985, p. 3.
73. Emily Dyckson, *The Evening Telegram,* June 19, 1986, p. 9.
74. *The Sunday Express*, January 25, 1987, p. 3.

In August 1990, the St. Clare's School of Nursing moved to the buildings formerly occupied by St. Bride's College on the Littledale campus, thus providing space for the hospital to expand into the areas formerly occupied by the student nurses. For their part, the teachers and nursing students had the advantage of the spacious lecture rooms, audiovisual room, and library that were available at the former college.

Health care in Newfoundland, however, was becoming more and more costly. In 1992, the Newfoundland government announced that hospitals in the province would be restructured and some services centralized in order to keep costs down. As a consequence of this, the obstetrics department at St. Clare's was closed on April 7, 1992, and transferred to the Grace General Hospital. On May 3, 1992, one of the local papers carried a headline, "The Stork Doesn't Call Here Any More." The reporter, Moira Baird, explained:

> The sign on the fourth floor of St. Clare's Mercy Hospital says OBSTETRICS, but newborn babies and bassinets are nowhere to be seen. These days the floor houses an expanded psychiatric unit.
>
> On April 7, just six weeks away from the hospital's 70th anniversary in May, the St. Clare's obstetrical unit moved down the road to the Grace General Hospital. For St. Clare's, that was the end of an era—one that began in 1922 when the first baby was born in what was then called the "White House". . . . Since that day more than 83,000 babies have been delivered at the hospital and St. Clare's has gone from 20 beds to over 300.[75]

When the announcement was made that St. Clare's was to lose its obstetrical department, M. Fabian Hennebury, former executive director of the hospital remarked, "I feel sad about it. There's something about new birth and new life that makes for something positive in an atmosphere of suffering and pain and sadness."[76] In a statement to the press, Sr. Elizabeth Davis, the current executive director, explained, "Our obstetrical unit was occupied maybe 60 percent

75. Moira Baird, *The Evening Telegram*, May 3, 1992, p. 3.
76. Ibid.

of the time, as was the Grace. So, we knew the time had come to create one obstetrical unit."[77] But there were other considerations. The article in *The Evening Telegram* continued:

> According to Sister Fabian Hennebury, these [considerations] included trends in medicine toward sterilization, genetic engineering and an increasing demand for abortions. This was bound to present an ethical dilemma for St. Clare's if it became the only centre for obstetrics in St. John's.[78]

Sr. Elizabeth agreed, stating in a press release:

> St. Clare's had to consider the possibility of the service being fully centralized at this hospital. The Hospital's owners [the Congregation of the Sisters of Mercy] and Board of Governors, in consultation with the Archbishop of St. John's, accepted the fact that, given its ethical tradition, St. Clare's could not provide the full scope of services to which the community was entitled. This meant that if the service had to be centralized, it could not be centralized at St. Clare's.[79]

On the same day that the obstetrical unit at St. Clare's was transferred to the Grace General Hospital, the twenty-six bed psychiatry ward at the Grace was closed, and all the patients transferred to St. Clare's. However, as well as taking over mental health services, the role of St. Clare's was enhanced in other areas such as musculoskeletal diseases, respiratory diseases, gastrointestinal and abdominal disorders, internal medicine, and ambulatory care.

In 1994, St. Clare's continued its tradition of reaching out to suffering people in the community by opening a mental health care centre. This centre, named LeMarchant House, was formally opened by Aiden Maloney, chairman of the board of governors, and by the chief executive officer of St. Clare's, Sr. Elizabeth Davis. LeMarchant House offered individual and group interventions

77. Ibid.
78. Ibid.
79. Sr. Elizabeth Davis, *The Monitor,* March 6, 1991, p. 3.

and a variety of services from stress management to relaxation therapy. It allowed many people to receive help through outpatient services rather than spend time in hospital.

However, the talented executive director of St. Clare's was about to take on heavier responsibilities. In 1994, the Health Care Corporation was established to integrate hospital services in the St. John's region. In July of that year, Sr. Elizabeth Davis was appointed chief executive officer of the Health Care Corporation. "Leading the corporation—with its 7,000 member staff, and $320 million annual budget—is, to say the least, daunting, difficult, and dynamic."[80] During her tenure as CEO of the Health Care Corporation, Sr. Elizabeth was faced with many difficult decisions. One of her hardest tasks was that of restructuring the St. John's health care system, in the course of which management positions were reduced by forty percent. As part of a massive reorganization of the system, Sr. Elizabeth was forced to announce the closure of the Grace General Hospital and the relocation of the Charles A. Janeway Children's Hospital and the Children's Rehabilitation Centre. Nevertheless, in spite of harsh criticism, Sr. Elizabeth was convinced that these decisions were the right ones, and she moved ahead. Toward the end of her mandate as CEO she remarked, "While I never doubted the direction was the right move for us in the future, the price we had to pay to go in that direction was very difficult. . . . You can't have it both ways. You can't be saying you want to make this world better, but then not be ready to work at the hard thing required to make it better."[81]

After six years as CEO of the St. John's Health Care Corporation, Sr. Elizabeth announced her resignation on March 14, 2000. In a letter to the staff members, physicians, and volunteers, Elizabeth wrote:

> Most of you are aware that I had signed a five-year contract with the Board in October, 1994. I have remained an extra year to finish the work the Board asked me to do in 1994—to provide leadership to enable all of us together to achieve three goals: (1) to

80. Steve Bartlett, *The Express*, March 17, 2000, p. 5.
81. Sr. Elizabeth Davis, *The Express*, March 17, 2000, p. 5.

bring our new organization together in administrative and support areas (2) to integrate our direct care clinical services and (3)
to complete our site redevelopment project. With the transfer of
services from the Salvation Army Grace General Hospital and
Janeway Child Health Centre during this summer, I will have fulfilled the mandate the Board gave me. Together we have
redesigned and developed a new administrative, clinical and physical infrastructure.[82]

When announcing her resignation from the Health Care Corporation, Sr.
Elizabeth indicated that she wanted to return to the field of study and teaching the Hebrew and Christian Scriptures, a field that she had left when the
Congregation of the Sisters of Mercy asked her to enter health administration. Subsequently, Sr. Elizabeth began her studies at the University of
Toronto. However, after a short time, her work was interrupted again when
the Government of Newfoundland asked her to act as one of three members
of a Royal Commission to study Newfoundland's place in Confederation.
This was a year-long task and involved a great deal of travel to many communities in Newfoundland and Labrador as well as the work of summarizing
the hundreds of briefs that had been addressed to the Commission and writing the final report. However, when the report had been completed and presented to government, Sr. Elizabeth was free to return to her books and her
study. Nevertheless, because of her wide experience in many areas, she is in
constant demand as a speaker at conventions, not only in Canada but also in
other parts of the world. Sr. Elizabeth's contribution to health care received
national recognition when she received the Order of Canada on May 13,
2004.

Meanwhile, back at St. Clare's, major changes were about to take place. As
part of the restructuring of health care in the province, the Government of
Newfoundland and Labrador decided that the large hospitals in St. John's
would all come under the jurisdiction of the newly established Health Care

---

82. Sr. Elizabeth Davis to staff members, physicians, and volunteers, March 14, 2000,
ASMSJ.

Corporation of St. John's. In order to allow the government to proceed with its restructuring program, the Sisters of Mercy agreed to transfer St. Clare's Mercy Hospital to the government. On December 8, 1994, the Congregation of the Sisters of Mercy signed the agreement to sell the hospital buildings to the government and transfer the operation of the hospital to the Board of Directors of the Health Care Corporation of St. John's. Under the agreement, the mission, values, philosophy, and ethical principles of St. Clare's would be continued and the ministry of the Sisters of Mercy and their presence in the hospital would continue. Furthermore, the agreement gave the Sisters of Mercy the right to nominate two persons to the Board of Directors of the Health Care Corporation.[83] In addition, the Sisters of Mercy retained the right to approve the person who has direct management responsibility for the St. Clare's Mercy Hospital site. As well, the Sisters of Mercy have the right to maintain the names and symbols at the hospital and the right to remain at St. Clare's Convent under the same conditions as obtained at the time the agreement came into effect, April 1, 1995. This coincided with the change of governance from the Board of Governors of St. Clare's to the Board of Directors of the Health Care Corporation of St. John's.[84] Perhaps the most important statement related to the agreement is the following:

> The Sisters recognize that, with the many technical and financial changes in health care, there had to be changes in the organization of tertiary care for the province. However, they also felt that they wished to remain part of the ministry of healing at St. Clare's. Therefore, the Agreement the Sisters signed with the Government of Newfoundland and Labrador allowed the structural changes to happen while at the same time ensuring that the Sisters continued to influence health care delivery not only at St. Clare's but within

---

83. The first two persons appointed under this agreement were Sr. Charlotte Fitzpatrick and Ms. Eleanor Bonnell. Subsequently, Sr. Charlotte was replaced by Sr. Patricia Maher who, at the time of writing, continues as a member of the Board of Directors of the Health Care Corporation of St. John's.

84. Agreement between the Sisters of Mercy and the Government of Newfoundland and Labrador, ASMSJ, RG 10/9/ 221.

the Health Care Corporation of St. John's and within the province.[85]

In May 1995, Sr. Phyllis Corbett succeeded Dr. Sean Conroy as the on-site administrator of St. Clare's, a position she held for a year. Sr. Phyllis was the last Sister of Mercy to hold the post of administrator of St. Clare's Mercy Hospital.

Although St. Clare's is operated under the jurisdiction of the Health Care Corporation of St. John's, the Sisters of Mercy continue to minister to the sick in the hospital. Sr. Diane Smyth is the divisional manager of the Pastoral Care Department and is assisted by Srs. Betty Morrissey, Mary Manning, Madonna O'Neill, and by several other sisters who work part-time as volunteers. The religious/spiritual care of patients, staff, and family is coordinated through this department. Although it was not formally established until 1975, pastoral care was always one of the primary services provided by St. Clare's. From the beginning, the sisters who administered and staffed the hospital were mindful of the mission of Jesus to "heal the sick," and they recognized that spiritual care was a key component of healing. For many years, St. Clare's had a resident chaplain, a Roman Catholic priest, up to the time when Msgr. James Fennessey retired in 1990.

When the hospital was smaller and a large number of Sisters of Mercy ministered to patients, St. Clare's had a distinctive religious ambience. Clergy from many religious denominations were frequent visitors. However, along with all the other changes that have taken place at the hospital, there is no longer a resident chaplain, but chaplains from several religious denominations care for the spiritual needs of the patients at St. Clare's. The four or five Sisters of Mercy who work with the divisional manager of pastoral care, Sr. Diane Smyth, are "on call" seven days a week. The Anglican, United, Salvation Army, and Pentecostal Churches have appointed chaplains to St. Clare's. Contact persons from other religious groups are called as needed. Sr. Diane described the function of the Pastoral Care Department at St. Clare's as follows:

85. Ibid.

> Pastoral Care at St. Clare's is like the soul of St. Clare's, that spiritual dimension that gives it life, the bonding agent that ensures a connectedness in the many complex and technical aspects of a modern hospital. Pastoral Care is the spirit of St. Clare's that is a manifestation of God's Spirit and God's presence.[86]

The story of St. Clare's Mercy Hospital resembles the parable of the mustard seed.[87] From very small, uncertain beginnings, it has grown into a large, modern hospital. Although it is no longer owned and administered by the Sisters of Mercy, it continues to bear the name St. Clare's Mercy Hospital as a perpetual reminder of the sacrifice and dedication of a handful of women who devoted their lives in service to sick and suffering humanity. M. Fabian Hennebury summed up the story of St. Clare's when she wrote:

> Someone has said that the pioneers of any great venture spin the golden threads which weave an undying tradition. The tradition that the . . . Sisters of St. Clare's have left the Hospital is one of dedication, mercy, kindness and hard work. To them and to all who have assisted them may be applied the words of the Lord Himself, "I was poor and hungry, sick and lonely and you cared for Me." And may St. Clare's continue its mission of Mercy to the sick, the poor, the alcoholic, and the aged with care, concern and compassion.[88]

---

86. Diane Smyth, unpublished manuscript, ASMSJ, RG 10/89/168.
87. Matthew 6:15–19.
88. Hennebury, "St. Clare's," p. 56, ASMSJ.

CHAPTER FIFTEEN

NEW BRANCHES ON THE MERCY TREE

There has been a most marked Providential Guidance which the
want of prudence, vigilance, or judgment has not impeded, and
it is here that we can most clearly see the designs of God.

M. Catherine McAuley[1]

The amalgamation of the convents in Newfoundland under one central
administration had far-reaching effects on the life and ministry of the
Sisters of Mercy. The adage "strength in numbers" injected new life
into the local communities, while the foundations established at Bell Island, Bay
of Islands, Bay Bulls, and the institution of St. Clare's Mercy Hospital provided
the whole congregation with a new and broader sense of mission.

Encouraged by the success of the Bell Island foundation, Archbishop
Roche urged the General Council of the Sisters of Mercy to establish a convent
in Hoylestown—the name given to a section of the east end of St. John's.
However, before tracing the sequence of events that led to the establishment of
the convent, it might be helpful to outline the educational difficulties experienced after the 1892 fire that destroyed much of St. John's, as well as to trace
the history of the building that eventually became St. Joseph's Convent.

---

1. M. Catherine McAuley to Sister M. Elizabeth Moore, January 13, 1838, cited in Sullivan,
Correspondence, p. 179.

Originally, the property on which St. Joseph's Convent stands was named Castle Rennie and was the home of a St. John's businessman, John Dunscombe. In 1844, Dunscombe's business was destroyed by fire, and he left Newfoundland permanently.[2] A year later, on September 29, 1845, Castle Rennie was rented for the sum of £100 and opened as the non-denominational academy under the direction of Headmaster C. D. Newman of Wadham College, Oxford, with John Valentine Nugent and Thomas Talbot as assistant masters.[3] The academy was not a success, and in 1850, it closed.[4] Subsequently, Dunscombe's estate changed hands and eventually, on May 11, 1872, came into the possession of a St. John's jeweller, John Lindberg, who renamed the estate, "Castle Lindberg."[5] The deed of sale provides clear evidence that the titles "Castle Rennie" and "Castle Lindberg" refer to the same property.[6] In addition to his other business interests, Lindberg operated the Bavarian Brewery located just below his house on Signal Hill Road.

Lindberg lived in the house until the Great Fire of 1892 that destroyed his entire property in the area. However, the shell of the house remained standing and Lindberg rebuilt the interior.[7] In doing so, he left one of the architectural gems of St. John's, a home with high ceilings, decorative moldings, rooms with long, elegant windows that catch both the morning and evening sunlight, and a relatively narrow staircase with a mahogany railing on either side. A persistent legend makes a connection between the double railing on the staircase in Mr. Lindberg's house and his brewery. According to this story, frequent tasting of the produce of his brewery—undoubtedly in the interests of ensuring its excellent quality—had an unfortunate effect on the ability of the owner to navigate the stairs leading to the second storey of his house. For this reason, so the story goes, the staircase was equipped with a sturdy mahogany railing on each side to provide adequate support to Mr. Lindberg as he headed toward his bed to rest from

2. O'Neill, *A Seaport Legacy*, p. 778.
3. Prowse, *History*, p. 657. See also James Murphy, ed., *From the Colony of Newfoundland, England's Oldest Possession* (St. John's, NL: James Murphy, 1925), p. 10.
4. Ibid. Subsequently, John V. Nugent opened St. John's Academy, a private school on Monkstown Road.
5. Registry of Deeds, 1844–1884, vol. 22, p. 28, Government of Newfoundland and Labrador.
6. Ibid., April 29, 1892.
7. O'Neill, *A Seaport Legacy*, p. 880.

his labours. It should be pointed out, however, that the only evidence to support this story is the construction of the staircase itself.

Evidently, the Lindbergs were part of the social fabric of the little community around the Signal Hill area. Some years ago, one of the senior residents of Hoylestown, Rose Brophy, wrote her memories of the Lindberg family:

> In the early 1900s Mr. & Mrs. John Lindberg and their son John occupied the Lindberg Castle. Mr. & Mrs. Lindberg were middle-aged at the time I remember, and were very quiet and gentle in their dealings with us children, and if we had a party, would help us out by the loan of chairs etc. and take an interest in our work.[8]

In 1907, Lindberg sold his property to the Roman Catholic Archdiocese of St. John's.[9] Subsequently, it was used as a residence for the local parish priest before it passed into the possession of the Sisters of Mercy, who established a convent there in 1922. As a matter of fact, the sisters had been active in that part of the city almost without interruption since the opening of St. Bridget's School in 1863, walking to school every day from Mercy Convent on Military Road. Unfortunately, after the destruction caused by the 1892 fire, the sisters had to discontinue their educational work in the area because of the difficulty of finding a suitable place in which to conduct classes.

Apparently, it was several years before the Roman Catholic board was able to rent a building to use as a school for the Catholic children in Hoylestown. It was not until 1897 that a temporary solution was found: "During the year several earnest applications have been made by the people of Hoylestown to have a school opened there. A room has been rented and Miss Williams is at present teaching some children of the area."[10] At the same meeting, Bishop Howley identified the location of this makeshift school, "In November 1897, I agreed with T. Kent for his room, No. 20 Forest Road for

8. Rose Brophy, handwritten document, ASMSJ, RG 10/13/2.

9. Bills and Receipts, 1907, AASJ, 106/4/11. See also Registry of Deeds, October 16, 1907, p. 153.

10. "Minutes of the Roman Catholic School Board for St. John's," July 12, 1897, pp. 11–13, AASJ, 106/1/4.

$30 per annum. Kent to put the room in proper condition."[11] A few years later the bishop referred to the same property owned by Thomas Kent as, "No. 20, Hoylestown."[12] This arrangement remained in place until 1902, when the bishop informed the school board that a school under the direction of Miss Doyle had been provided for the children of Hoylestown.[13] Under this agreement one room was set aside as a classroom, while a family by the name of Pike occupied the remainder of the building. Receipts dating from the years 1902 to 1907 confirm the existence of this arrangement, although a Mrs. Glascow replaced the Pikes as tenant in December 1905.[14]

It may seem strange that the sisters did not return to Hoylestown in 1897 when the board succeeded in renting a schoolroom. However, the demand for teaching sisters was so great that the superior of Mercy Convent could not afford to allow sisters to twiddle their thumbs during the five years (1892–97) that it took the board to find a classroom in the East End. By that time, the sisters who had been teaching at St. Joseph's School had been assigned to other schools.

The problem of finding a suitable school building in Hoylestown continued to haunt the RC board. The minutes of a meeting held in 1906 reflect the discouragement of the board members:

> The Hoylestown School was still conducted in the rooms lend [sic] from Mr. A. O'Hayward for which $5.00 a month was paid as rent. His Grace hoped to be able to buy Lindberg's place on Signal Hill Road. If he succeeded he would build a chapel there which would be used for school purposes.[15]

---

11. Ibid. The reference to Forest Road is puzzling, for according to the Registry of Deeds, the property owned by Thomas Kent was a parcel of land on Quidi Vidi Road between Signal Hill and Howe Place. Later references confirm that the property to which the bishop referred was, indeed, at the corner of Quidi Vidi Road and Howe Place, a site not far from Forest Road.

12. Ibid., October 31, 1899, AASJ, 106/1/4.

13. Ibid., December 9, 1902.

14. Ibid.

15. Ibid., July 4, 1906.

In 1907, conditions seemed to take a turn for the better when Archbishop Howley informed the board: "On April 21, 1907, opened School at Castle Lindberg, Hoylestown, East End St. John's in future to be termed St. Joseph's (two Sisters of Mercy teaching there)."[16] This statement is amplified in the year-end report of the superintendent of education:

> A change has taken place in the management of this school, the Board having secured the services of the Sisters of Mercy. His Grace, the Archbishop has had the old building which was used as a school-room a few years ago, enlarged and renovated. It is now capable of accommodating over 100 pupils. [17]

A notation made on an unpublished manuscript indicates that M. Mercedes Lyons was one of the two sisters who returned to teach in St. Joseph's School in 1907.[18] The identity of the other is unknown.

In spite of the information supplied above, it has been difficult to determine the precise location of this school. On an insurance map of St. John's, dated 1907, the former Lindberg house, known as Lindberg Castle, is labelled, "Convent and School."[19] However, this is incorrect, for the convent on Signal Hill was not established until 1922. Neither is there any evidence that Lindberg's house matched the description of "an old building that had been used as a schoolroom."[20] This leads to the conclusion that the label, "Convent and School" was added to the 1907 map at a much later date. An interpretation of the archbishop's statement of April 21, 1907, is that the entire estate on Signal Hill was known as Castle Lindberg, not just the house itself.[21] If this

---

16. Ibid.

17. Vincent P. Burke, "Report of the Superintendent for Roman Catholic Schools for the Year Ended December 31, 1907," p. 68, ASMSJ.

18. "St. Joseph's Convent and School Hoylestown," ASMSJ, RG 10/13/9. The notation was made by M. Chrysostom McCarthy, former archivist for the Sisters of Mercy, St. John's. M. Chrysostom was a close friend of M. Mercedes Lyons.

19. Insurance Plan of the City of St. John's, surveyed September 1893, revised to July 1911, p. 12, ACSJ.

20. Vincent P. Burke, "Report of the Superintendent of Education for Roman Catholic Schools for Year Ended December 31, 1907," p. 68, ASMSJ.

21. I am indebted to Shane O'Dea for this suggestion.

explanation is correct, then the school could have been located on any part of the property.

Another map from this period shows a wooden structure labelled "St. Joseph's Old Church, School and Hall" at the corner of Howe Place and Quidi Vidi Road, immediately behind the brewery.[22] A further identification of the location of this school was provided in a newspaper account of the blessing of the new St. Joseph's Church that described the church as "situated on the elevation at the rear of the old schoolhouse."[23] This was the most probable site of the school to which the Sisters of Mercy returned in 1907. Sr. M. Stanislaus Parsons recalled that when she taught there, circa 1915, the building served the triple function of church, school, and hall. M. Stanislaus did not mince her words when she spoke of the building that was used as a school. She described it as "a shack!"[24] M. Francis Hickey, the editor of the "in-house" journal *Mercy Communico*, described the school as "an old building with a basement that served as the nightly residence of Tommy Kent's spare-boned horse."[25] Furthermore, the superintendent of education complained in successive reports that the school building was used as a church as well as for instructional purposes. These same reports presented a most unflattering picture of conditions in the school:

> The Sisters of Mercy are doing all that can reasonably be expected, and more, considering the conditions under which they work. ...While the enlarged school-house gives much greater and better accommodation than that heretofore provided, yet the site is far from ideal. The three teachers employed conduct classes at the same time in the same room ... and this room is also used as the parish chapel, *pro tem.*[26]

---

22. Map H 373 (*circa* 1890s), Insurance Plans of the City of St. John's, ACSJ.

23. *The Evening Telegram*, November 19, 1917, p. 2.

24. ASMSJ, MG 34/1/122.

25. M. Francis Hickey, *Mercy Communico* 2, no. 13 (December 1968), ASMSJ. This story may be considered accurate, as M. Francis, professed in 1915, had first-hand knowledge of the location of St. Joseph's School in the years between 1907 and 1918.

26. Vincent P. Burke, "Report of the Superintendent of Education for Roman Catholic Schools for the Year Ended 1908," p. 45, ASMSJ.

This wooden structure served as a temporary church and school until a permanent parish church could be built on land purchased June 21, 1912, by the archdiocese from John Lindberg.[27] A few months later, at a meeting of the RC School Board, Archbishop Howley informed the board of his intentions to build a school on the property: "He also referred to the land recently acquired by him at Hoylestown. This is Church property now and it is his intention to build a School House as soon as possible on land fronting on Howe place."[28] In spite of the archbishop's good intentions, he did not live to fulfill this promise.

When he purchased this parcel of land on Signal Hill, the erudite Archbishop Howley positioned the church buildings of St. Joseph's Parish in one of the most historic areas of the old city of St. John's. Signal Hill itself, besides being a familiar and prominent landmark of St. John's, is "a site of local, national, and international significance in the fields of communications and military and medical history."[29]

Signal Hill rises precipitously about five hundred feet from the Atlantic Ocean. At its summit is Cabot Tower, built to commemorate the 400th anniversary of the discovery of Newfoundland in 1497, and to serve as a memorial of Queen Victoria's Diamond Jubilee.[30] As early as 1704, the British garrison used the summit of the hill as a lookout site. In the 1790s, they decided to develop Signal Hill as a citadel for the defence of the Narrows, and by the 1830s, the entire British garrison was concentrated there. The garrison used morning and evening guns to regulate its daily activities, and even after the military left in 1870, the firing of the noonday gun continued right up through the middle of the twentieth century.

---

27. "Archbishop Howley purchased the whole plot of land, which was the site of the Brewery owned by the German brewer, John Lindberg, and situated off the old Castle Rennie Property." Cited in "Minutes of the Roman Catholic Board," June 27, 1912, AASJ, 106/4/11.

28. Ibid., November 12, 1912. AASJ, 106/17/4. St. Joseph's Church was opened November 1917 and, according to a note in the Archdiocesan Archives, "at rear of old schoolhouse."

29. ENL, s.v. "Signal Hill." On May 22, 1958, Signal Hill was designated as Newfoundland's first National Historic Park and has the distinction of having a greater number of yearly visitors than any other park of its kind in Canada.

30. The cornerstone of Cabot Tower was laid by Bishop Howley on June 22, 1897.

Although Signal Hill was strictly a military base, the commanding officers permitted St. John's to use George's Pond, located halfway up the hill, to supply water to the city. Permission was also given to the Newfoundland Ice Company to get its ice from the pond.[31] Later on, after the withdrawal of the military in 1870, the Newfoundland government used the vacant buildings on Signal Hill as a quarantine hospital.[32] The two-storey stone barracks near George's Pond became known as St. George's Hospital and proved its worth during the diphtheria epidemic of 1888 and 1890. This hospital was one of the casualties of the Great Fire of 1892, and subsequently, medical activity on the hill shifted to a barracks near the summit that became known as the Diphtheria and Fever Hospital.[33] It was in an unoccupied section of this unpretentious building on Signal Hill that history was made when, on December 12, 1901, Guglielmo Marconi received the first transatlantic wireless signal. Later, in 1920, three engineers made the first wireless transmission of the human voice across the Atlantic Ocean from Cabot Tower on Signal Hill.[34]

The historical significance of Signal Hill was not lost on the people of Hoylestown, who took great pride in their little corner of the city. Furthermore, in the area there was—and continues to be—a strong sense of community that was nurtured and strengthened when, on August 14, 1907, Archbishop Howley established St. Joseph's Parish. Initially, the pastor Father William Kitchin lived in the cathedral residence.[35] Apparently, this was a short-term arrangement, for, as noted earlier, some time prior to 1910 the Lindberg house was taken over for use as a presbytery.[36]

The new pastor recognized immediately the inadequacy of the little wooden chapel to serve the needs of the population of Hoylestown. A St. Joseph's committee was formed under the leadership of Father Kitchin, and a

31. *ENL*, s.v. "Signal Hill."
32. This hospital was in addition to the former military hospital on Forest Road where routine surgical and medical cases were handled. See chapter fourteen.
33. *ENL*, s.v. "Signal Hill."
34. Ibid.
35. St. Joseph's Parish Records, AASJ.
36. In 1910, the archdiocese paid water assessment bills and the cost of light and power for "St. Joseph's Presbytery on Signal Hill." AASJ, 106/17/4.

petition to build a new church was presented to the newly consecrated arch-bishop of St. John's, E. P. Roche.[37] On November 19, 1916, Archbishop Roche laid the foundation stone of the first St. Joseph's Church, and within twelve months, on November 17, 1917, the new stone church was opened for wor-ship and replaced the old school-chapel.

But the completion of the church was only the first step in the arch-bishop's plans for St. Joseph's Parish. Edward Patrick Roche was convinced that education was the key to spiritual growth and material prosperity. In spite of the financial constraints due to the war, he was determined that the children of his archdiocese would have the schools, teachers, and equipment necessary to achieve these ends. Therefore, as soon as St. Joseph's Church was complet-ed, Roche began construction of a new school. In less than a year after the ded-ication of the church, the new St. Joseph's School was opened on Signal Hill on the former site of the Bavarian Brewery. In his address to the people of the parish, Archbishop Roche recalled the many years during which the Sisters of Mercy had been present in the area:

> It is true, indeed, that our Catholic people generally owe a great deal, more than they can ever repay, to all our teaching institutions … but the people of St. Joseph's have obligations of a special nature toward the Sisters of Mercy. For more than half a century, as I have said, they have been, practically without interruption, teaching the children of this end of the town. … The Sisters in the cases of our other schools in the city have had their school-rooms adjoining their convents, but the Sisters of Mercy have had to come here day after day under all weather conditions in order to impart the prin-ciples of education to the children of this end of the city. … I hope that it may not be too much to expect that in the not too distant future the Sisters may have a home in this Parish, so as to be near their work and to be able to do for the children what they cannot possibly do under the present conditions. … I hope the new Parish of St. Joseph's will be completed within the next few years by hav-ing a suitable residence for the Nuns adjoining their School.[38]

37. Bernard McDonald, conversation with author, August 8, 1998. Bernard's father, Peter McDonald, was a member of this committee.
38. *The Daily News*, September 10, 1918, p. 4.

Four years later the archbishop's hopes were realized when, on December 3, 1922, St. Joseph's Convent was formally blessed and opened in the old Castle Lindberg on Signal Hill Road. That afternoon the archbishop, the clergy, and many parishioners attended a "very pleasing programme" that was presented by the pupils of St. Joseph's School in the parish hall.[39] Indeed, St. Joseph's School had come a long way since the days of the despairing complaints of the superintendent of education.

The sisters who formed the first community at St. Joseph's Convent were M. Benedicta Fitzgibbon, M. Michael Gillis, M. Ignatius Molloy, and a postulant, Margaret Kent, who left the congregation on the expiration of her temporary vows in 1925. M. Benedicta, who was named superior of the small community, came to St. Joseph's from Littledale upon the completion of her six-year term as the first novice mistress after the amalgamation. No doubt this quiet woman, who was conservative by nature, looked forward to the change. It provided her with a chance to recuperate from the trauma of trying to tame the high spirits of impetuous young novices, many of whom had curious ideas of what religious life was all about.

Next in seniority to M. Benedicta was M. Michael Gillis who had been transferred from St. Patrick's Convent, Bay Bulls, where she had spent one year as a member of the first community in that convent. Thus, she was no stranger to new foundations. M. Michael, with her experience of life on the West Coast, her sense of humour, and her dry Scottish wit, was a decided contrast to the serious-minded M. Benedicta. This was fortunate because it brought a balance to the community. The third member of the community was M. Ignatius Molloy, a native of St. John's, who had been accepted as a postulant by the Sisters of Mercy in St. George's. With the establishment of the general novitiate, she returned to Littledale to prepare for her profession. In 1917, she began her ministry as a professed sister on the staff of St. Clare's Home. After one year at St. Clare's, she was assigned to St. Joseph's Convent School in Brigus, where she spent four years before returning to St. John's as a member of the new community of St. Joseph's, Hoylestown. M. Ignatius was

---

39. Ibid., December 5, 1922, p. 4.

a woman of many talents. She was a competent and kindly classroom teacher, but also she was qualified to teach music and commercial subjects.[40]

In those days, the needs of the various missions determined the placement of sisters. Consequently, every year there was a more or less drastic turnover in membership of local communities, and St. Joseph's was no exception. Furthermore, St. Joseph's was an ideal location for young sisters to gain experience in the principal ministries of the congregation because both the General Hospital and the penitentiary were within a few minutes' walking distance from the convent. It was true that the sisters at the mother house had the responsibility of visiting these institutions weekly. Still, this did not hinder the sisters who lived at St. Joseph's from visiting the same institutions, especially when someone from the parish was sick—or was enjoying the King's (or Queen's) hospitality in the "Hotel by the Lake," a popular pseudonym for the penitentiary.

As was the case with other foundations, the sisters did not think it worthwhile to keep an account of their activities. The only item of interest noted was that, in 1924, for the first time in the history of St. Joseph's School, the Trinity College examiner visited the school. This indicates that St. Joseph's had twelve or more students registered for music examinations—probably in piano performance. The music teacher was M. Benedicta Fitzgibbon. In addition to her teaching duties in the school and convent, she had responsibilities in the local church, for it was the custom that wherever the sisters were stationed, the music teacher looked after music for parish liturgies.[41]

At the beginning of 1929, St. Joseph's students numbered 273 in classes from kindergarten to grade IX. It was time to build an extension. The construction was completed that same year under the watchful supervision of

---

40. M. Ignatius Molloy taught in several different convent schools throughout Newfoundland before returning in September 1944 as superior of St. Joseph's, Hoylestown. She died four months later, in January 1945, at the age of forty-eight years.

41. There were a few exceptions to this custom. For example, in the larger city churches of the cathedral and St. Patrick's, organists and choir directors were hired from among professional musicians in the city. It should be remembered, however, that M. Xaverius Dowsley was organist at the cathedral for many years; and in the recent past another Sister of Mercy held the position of organist and choir director at the Cathedral of St. John the Baptist for twenty-five years.

Archbishop Roche, who was determined that the children of Hoylestown would never again be exposed to the miserable, overcrowded conditions that had existed in former years. Like the new St. Joseph's School of 1918, the extension contained four large, airy, and well-lighted classrooms that, together with the original four, served the children of the area until 1955.

The increase in the school population made it necessary to add to the number of teaching sisters on staff. In 1928, M. Benedicta Fitzgibbon, having completed a second three-year term as superior, was replaced by M. Winefride Greene. Four other teaching sisters completed the community: M. Brigid Hoey, M. Gonzaga Henley, M. Angela Fowler, and a postulant, Mary Newbury, who subsequently left the congregation. Each of these sisters stayed only a year or two at St. Joseph's, with one exception. M. Brigid Hoey remained at St. Joseph's until her death.

Whatever other talents she possessed—and they were many—it was obvious that M. Brigid had not been a success as superior. After she was removed from office in St. Mary's on the Humber, the General Council decided to try her somewhere else. She was appointed superior of St. Anne's Convent at Burin, but even there, she did not complete the usual three-year term of office. After two years, M. Agnes Doyle replaced her. From Burin, M. Brigid went to Brigus, this time as a member of the community. In 1924, she was assigned to St. Joseph's, Hoylestown, where at last she found her niche. She was given charge of teaching the boys, for at the time, the boys and girls were taught in separate classrooms. Her former students remember her well, and stories abound of her dealings with her beloved boys who admired and respected her because "she was strict but fair." There was no task too burdensome when M. Brigid needed their help: "Mrs. Evans, will you ask Jackie to come over and clean out the furnace," and Jackie, suitably attired, would present himself without complaint for this less-than-attractive chore.[42] The girls, however, remember her as being "terribly religious" and one who put up with no nonsense when homework was neglected or uniforms less than immaculately clean, so much so that she earned the nickname "Mother Clean." She was also a bit of a fresh air fiend, and many a young sister

---

42. Wilhelmina Evans, wife of Jack Evans, told these stories to the author in May 2000.

shivered through morning office as the bitter east wind from the North Atlantic assaulted her unprotected neck via the wide-open chapel windows. Nevertheless, M. Brigid Hoey was known to her students and their parents for her gracious ways and her love for the children under her care. When she could no longer work in the classroom, she continued to visit the sick in their homes and in the hospitals. In the days before spiritual direction was in vogue, M. Brigid spent many hours sharing the word of God with those who sought her help in their personal difficulties. She had a great deal of sympathy for the poor and for those who turned to alcohol to find refuge from their misery. One of the assistant priests in St. Joseph's Parish was aware of M. Brigid's sympathy for poor unfortunates who had imbibed—not wisely, but too well. He decided to play a joke on the sisters. One evening, he showed up at the door wearing false whiskers and pretending to be in the maudlin stages of intoxication. The young sister who answered the door was less than sympathetic and closed the door in his face. Whereupon, M. Brigid exclaimed, "Well, bless us and save us, dear child, let the poor man in and lie [*sic*] him down on the floor to sleep it off."

In December 1956, M. Brigid celebrated the diamond jubilee of her profession. All during the summer and autumn she had been ill, so much so that M. Barbara Wade pronounced that M. Brigid would go to heaven "with the falling of the leaves." But M. Brigid had no intention of going anywhere before she had a chance to celebrate her jubilee. The day of the jubilee was one of great joy for all the sisters, for in spite of her brusque manner, everybody loved, "Mother Brigid." Her Irish-American grandnephew and his fiancée came from the United States to spend the day with her, and messages of congratulation arrived from relatives in Ireland. Dozens of sisters came to pay their respects to this woman who had devoted her life to the people of Newfoundland. M. Brigid lingered on for several months, determined to stay at St. Joseph's until her death. Her wish was not granted, for when the other sisters left for summer school, M. Brigid went to St. Clare's Mercy Hospital where she died on August 23, 1957.

Another sister who spent many years at St. Joseph's and who is remembered with gratitude and affection is M. Kevin Kennedy. In addition to teaching subjects in the regular curriculum, M. Kevin provided lessons in typing and shorthand to the more senior students. She was a jolly little woman who combined a delightful sense of humour with an all-embracing charity. The chapter of the Mercy Rule that mandates the visitation of the poor and the sick was one that M. Kevin took to heart and made her own. Almost every day after school, rain or shine, snow or sleet, M. Kevin would be seen trotting up Signal Hill, out Battery Road, or down to Quidi Vidi Village to visit someone who needed help. She had her own unobtrusive methods of discovering those persons who were experiencing troubles of one kind or another, and nobody was ever neglected. Of course, these were the days when sisters did not leave the convent without the companionship of another sister. It is not known by what means M. Kevin coaxed or bribed the sisters who accompanied her on these occasions. On the other hand, M. Kevin had an unlimited fund of stories with which she entertained her companion during the often strenuous walks to the homes of the poor. In spite of the fact that the *Guide*[43] required that the sisters abstain from conversing with one another when going on visitation, M. Kevin pointed out that nowhere was it written that a sister was forbidden to talk to herself. Clearly, sisters considered a request to accompany M. Kevin to be a treat rather than an imposition.[44]

Within ten years of its opening, St. Joseph's Convent was too small to accommodate the number of sisters required for the school. Consequently, in 1931, the General Council authorized the construction of an addition to the convent. In contrast to the original "Castle Lindberg," which was made of brick, the extension was a wooden building. It provided a full basement, consisting of laundry, furnace room, trunk room, storage rooms, and another room that in later years acquired the title the "Glory Hole."[45] The first floor provided a large kitchen, pantry, dining room, community room, and music room. The top floor of the extension contained a beautiful new chapel and a couple of extra bedrooms.

---

43. The *Guide* was a set of regulations that were intended to pass on customs and patterns of behaviour that—supposedly—interpreted the spirit of the Rule.

44. M. Ambrose Woodrow, conversation with author, November 3, 1998.

45. The Glory Hole is the most fascinating room in the house. Over the years, it provided storage for all sorts of strange and interesting artifacts that nobody knew how to dispose of. These ranged from outmoded pieces of bedroom furniture, curiously shaped pieces of decorative metal, framed pictures of somebody's bewhiskered relations and of saints whose identity remains a mystery to this day, a few dozen pairs of eyeglasses, and even a set of false teeth.

From the early days when St. Joseph's School consisted of one room where two teachers attempted to teach one hundred and twenty boys and girls whose ages ranged from six to sixteen years to the late 1960s, the progress of the school was truly remarkable. This was particularly the case for music education. It is true that, back in 1863, when the sisters came to St. Bridget's School, singing was included in the curriculum. But after the sisters came to live in the area in 1922, the children who attended St. Joseph's School were provided with a comprehensive music program that quickly became an integral part of the daily school activities.

When M. Benedicta Fitzgibbon left St. Joseph's in 1928, she was replaced by M. Winefride Greene who, in addition to her musical ability, had a flair for drama. As a result, the Christmas plays and spring operettas put on by the pupils of St. Joseph's School became annual events in the life of the parish. Naturally, not all the music teachers who succeeded M. Winefride had the same ability to capture the interest of the children, but each one did her best to develop the musical and dramatic talents of the youth of Hoylestown. Every year the music teacher at St. Joseph's prepared her students for the different levels of the Trinity College of Music examinations in piano and theory. These examinations were valuable, for not only did they provide a graded program of studies, but also they introduced students to various styles of music from the different periods of history.

The institution of the Kiwanis Music Festival in 1952 was, perhaps, the most important initiative in the history of music in Newfoundland. Students were invited to participate at different age levels ranging from "seven years and under" to "over-eighteen" years. Schools were encouraged to register instrumental, vocal, and choral groups in competitive performances that were open to the public. Initially, the instrumental classes consisted mainly of piano and string solos with a smattering of performances on wind instruments. The instrumental section also included performances by small ensembles, school bands, and eventually school orchestras. In the choral music category, classroom choirs from grades I to VIII predominated, but there was provision made for special choral groups such as church choirs, sacred music, girls' choirs, and boys' choirs to compete at their own age level. Another important category included in the festival syllabus was choral speech in which school classes from grades I to VIII participated. Over the years, the numbers of participants in the festival grew from about two thousand to over thirty-five thousand partici-pants. And as the numbers grew, so did the different categories of music included in the festival syllabus.

From the first, the children at St. Joseph's School were eager partici-pants in the festival. Not only were they enthusiastic, they were successful as well. In 1955, one of the choirs from St. Joseph's School tied for first place, receiving ninety marks. Another choral group received eighty-five, and seven children who entered the vocal solo category received over eighty marks. The music teacher at this time was M. Gabriel Fleming, who com-bined her duties as superior with those of organist and choir director for the parish church, as well as putting in a full day's work as music teacher in the school.

M. Gabriel Fleming was one of those capable women who, once having been appointed superior, seemed destined to remain in office for the rest of her life. In actual fact, after the amalgamation no sister could be superior of the same convent for more than two successive terms (a total of six years). However, the General Council members managed to skirt the spirit of the leg-islation simply by transferring a sister they favoured to a different communi-ty. Thus, the unfortunate M. Gabriel found herself occupying the office of superior for twenty-four successive years. At the same time, M. Gabriel was one of those rare persons who had the ability to see things from the point of view of those who were not in authority. As a result, the convents over which she presided were real communities in spirit as well as in name. Blessed with practical common sense and a delightful sense of humour, M. Gabriel was popular among the general rank and file of the congregation. Always straight-forward and outspoken, she was fearless in upholding the rights of her sisters, whether she was dealing with the superior general, the parish priest, or the archbishop. She and Archbishop Roche had many spirited arguments, for M. Gabriel was by no means intimidated by the imposing and authoritative pres-ence of the aristocratic prelate. Many years later, when her health was very frail, the sisters used to stimulate her memory by asking questions. One day

M. Gabriel was asked, "Do you remember Archbishop Roche?" She chuckled, "God bless us all! How could I ever forget him? We had many a little 'spat,' but I always had the last word!"

Because all the sisters at St. Joseph's were teaching, there was nobody to prepare the meals. Therefore, M. Josepha Young, who was the superior at the time, hired a cook. The only person available was an elderly lady who was very deaf and who had her own idea of her responsibilities. When the sisters walked in to dinner, the cook walked into the pantry off the kitchen and sat down to her own dinner. The sister-server rang, called, knocked, but no soup appeared, and neither did the cook. Eventually, M. Gabriel Fleming went to the kitchen and served the community and the cook as well. This state of affairs continued for several months, for the sisters were reluctant to hurt the cook's feelings by firing her. But when it became obvious that M. Gabriel had so little time for her own dinner that she often went without it, the community was forced to terminate the cook's employment.

Meanwhile, the whole east end of the city had experienced a population explosion in the years immediately following World War II. Accordingly, the pastor, Monsignor Edward Maher, decided that St. Joseph's Church needed to be replaced by a larger and more modern building. In 1955, the new St. Joseph's Church was opened on Quidi Vidi Road, and the stone building that had served as the parish church since 1917 was renovated and made into a boys' school with accommodation for 220 students. Male teachers were hired for the boys. The only sister on staff of the boys' school at that time was M. Gabriel Fleming.

The success achieved by the students of St. Joseph's School at the 1955 music festival encouraged the General Council of the Sisters of Mercy to take a closer look at the staffing of the school. By this time, M. Gabriel had been transferred to St. Bride's Convent, Littledale, and been replaced as music teacher at St. Joseph's by Sr. Marie Aidan Murphy. Young, talented, and well-prepared for her new assignment, Sr. Marie Aidan had already received an associate diploma in teaching and vocal performance from Trinity College in London. Also, she continued to spend successive summer holidays at different universities in the United States pursuing studies in liturgical music as well as in choral and vocal music.[46]

After her first practice with St. Joseph's Girls' Choir, Sr. Marie Aidan's popularity with the students was secured. She took an interest in each individual child, and through the schoolchildren, she arrived at the stage where she knew just about every man, woman, and child in the parish. The people of St. Joseph's had complete confidence in this friendly young sister, who had time to listen to their worries and who shared their joys and sorrows. For her part, Sr. Marie Aidan appreciated the community spirit that characterized St. Joseph's Parish and, in later years, remarked that the seven years she spent in Hoylestown were the happiest of her life.

In September 1962, there was an unexpected change in personnel at St. Joseph's. Sr. Marie Aidan was transferred to Stephenville Crossing,[47] and M. Edward Hodge, who had been teaching at Holy Heart of Mary High School, was sent to St. Joseph's. The change was difficult for both sisters. As news spread through St. Joseph's Parish that Sr. Marie Aidan was leaving, the convent phone and doorbell rang constantly. Instead of gathering up her few belongings, poor Sr. Marie Aidan spent her time consoling the dejected who came to the convent parlour to say goodbye. This left little time for packing. As the time of her departure approached, Marie Aidan became more and more frantic. Eventually, she snatched everything in sight, threw it in her suitcase and sat on the lid. It proved to be a strong suitcase, for in spite of dire predictions that it would burst open, the hinges and lock held.

It was an even more difficult change for M. Edward Hodge. She had lived in communities of over twenty-five sisters for most of her religious life; now she had to get used to a small community of seven. Furthermore, she was accustomed to dealing with high-school girls. At St. Joseph's, she had to face boys and girls from kindergarten to grade IX. M. Edward greeted the prospect of constant association with the very young with a good deal of trepidation. To

---

46. Subsequently, Marie Aiden Murphy completed the requirements for the degrees of bachelor of music and master of music with a major in voice.

47. The Convent of the Assumption at Stephenville Crossing, a town near St. George's on the West Coast, had been established in 1950.

compensate for this, she had a number of adult students whom she taught on Saturday mornings and, in addition, she was the director of the choir at St. Clare's Mercy Hospital School of Nursing. Every Tuesday evening she went over to the hospital for choir practice.

The big event of each year for St. Clare's Choir was the graduation that took place in May or June. St. Clare's School of Nursing graduation was an important social event of the year in the city of St. John's. Everybody who was anybody attended, including the lieutenant-governor, the premier of the province, assorted cabinet ministers, the archbishop and vicar general, the superiors general of the religious congregations and their councils, the mayor, other dignitaries, and the parents of the graduates. These events provided M. Edward with a familiar challenge and a welcome change after a week of dealing with young children.

When she arrived at St. Joseph's, M. Edward found that M. Aidan Murphy had done a superb job in training the girls' choirs, but the same standard of performance did not apply to the boys' school. M. Aidan, a gentle, soft-spoken lady, found the boys difficult to handle and not very receptive to her methods of dealing with them.[48] Wisely, she decided to do what she could for the boys, but to devote most of her time and energy in the area where she could provide the best service—the girls' school and the church choir.

M. Edward was not long in sizing up the situation. She decided that the boys would learn to sing, whether they wanted to or not. On the first day of the school year, she faced a class of squirming, snickering young lads with the order, "Stop your nonsense, do what I tell you—or else!" There was a moment of shocked silence as the boys realized that they had met their match—and this, in spite of the fact that M. Edward did not specify what "or else" implied. But from that moment there was no more trouble. To their amazement, St. Joseph's boys realized that not only could they sing, they actually enjoyed making music. As a result, St. Joseph's Boys' Choir, under M. Edward's direction, took first place in the music festival for many years and were constantly in demand to perform at functions held in the city.

---

48. M. Aiden Murphy, conversation with author, February 3, 2003.

Of course, M. Edward did not neglect the girls. An indefatigable work-er, she trained the classroom choirs, the girls' choir, and the church choir. She taught piano and violin to individual students after school and on Saturdays. Many of her senior students achieved high honours in Trinity College exami-nations and in the Royal Conservatory of Toronto examinations. Year after year, M. Edward's piano, violin, and vocal students won awards at music festivals. One of the leading music teachers in St. John's, M. Edward Hodge is remem-bered with affection and gratitude by former pupils, some of whom are num-bered among Newfoundland's finest musicians. M. Edward's contribution to music and music education was recognized when she was inducted posthu-mously into the Hall of Honour of the Kiwanis Music Festival Association on May 28, 2003.

The well-publicized successes of the young musicians of St. Joseph's School tended to overshadow some of their academic accomplishments. Because music is a performing art, it often attracts more attention than equal-ly favourable results in mathematics, language, or history. It is true, however, that no school music teacher, however knowledgeable or talented, can accom-plish much without the co-operation, interest, and active involvement of other members of the faculty, and particularly of the school principal. The sisters assigned to direct the music program at St. Joseph's were fortunate in having the support and encouragement of a succession of principals who understood and promoted the place of music and art in education.

Meanwhile, in 1958, St. Joseph's lost all its high-school students to the new single-sex regional high schools. The girls attended Holy Heart of Mary Regional High School that was under the joint administration of the Presentation and Mercy Sisters. The boys in grades X and XI were sent to Brother Rice High School under the direction of the Christian Brothers, while the younger boys, up to grade IX remained at St. Joseph's. However, in 1959, a year after St. Joseph's high-school students had been transferred to the regional high schools in the centre of the city, the school board decided to close Quidi Vidi School and send the students to St. Joseph's.[49]

---

49. ASMSJ, RG 10/13/108.

As time passed, it became obvious that St. Joseph's needed extra space and more up-to-date equipment and facilities. Consequently, in 1968, when a new St. Joseph's Junior High School opened, it was among the most up-to-date schools in the city. At that time it was an all-girls school, accommodating children from grades IV to grade IX. In addition to a well-equipped music department, it had a spacious gymnasium that functioned also as an auditorium. The new and well-stocked library had a catalogue of over two thousand books and the most modern audiovisual equipment. Furthermore, it had the services of a full-time librarian, M. Constance Travers, who was the first certified librarian to work at St. Joseph's School. M. Constance remained at St. Joseph's until failing eyesight brought about her retirement from the work she loved.

In 1967, M. Rosalita Power was named principal of St. Joseph's School. She was the envy of all the sister-principals in St. John's as she moved into the bright and spacious principal's office—equipped with an intercom that actually worked! The new technology saved her the necessity of walking through long, long corridors to communicate with students and teachers. But, even with the modern equipment and new and up-to-date educational resources, M. Rosalita had a very heavy workload. Conscientious to the core, she was constantly on the move as she made herself available to teachers and students in all three buildings that comprised St. Joseph's School. Fortunately, the Roman Catholic School Board realized the enormity of the task faced by the principal of St. Joseph's and decided to make some changes. In 1970, the school was divided into primary, elementary, and junior high. Sr. Teresa Boland was named principal of the primary school, and M. Pius Shea replaced M. Rosalita as principal of the junior high school. However, M. Rosalita must have left her heart at St. Joseph's, for she returned the following year (1971), and remained as principal for the next two years. In the year 1973, St. Joseph's Junior High became a distinct entity with Sr. Helen Harding as principal. The following year, 1974, there were so many students enrolled at St. Joseph's that the school board was forced to add portable classrooms to the primary school building on Signal Hill Road. At the same time, the policy of providing separate buildings for the boys was discontinued; instruction at St. Joseph's School became entirely coeducational. But this was not the end of changes at St. Joseph's.

In 1982, the grades IV and V French immersion classes, with an enrolment of sixty-five students, were transferred from Holy Cross Primary School to St. Joseph's elementary building. Three French immersion teachers joined the staff at St. Joseph's. The practice of transferring the French immersion students continued for the next two years until, in 1984, there were approximately 150 students enrolled in French immersion classes at St. Joseph's. By this time, it was necessary to accommodate the grade VII French immersion students in the junior high building. Six teachers and one assistant joined the staff at St. Joseph's. At the same time, the rest of the students enrolled at St. Joseph's followed the regular curriculum. At that time (1982–84), Sr. Ruth Beresford was the principal of St. Joseph's. When Sr. Ruth was assigned to St. Teresa's School, Mundy Pond, at the end of the school year, 1983–84, the Congregation of the Sisters of Mercy relinquished the administration of St. Joseph's School (June 1984). However, one sister remained on the staff.[50] In 1986, Sr. Gladys Bozec was appointed to St. Joseph's School to teach the grade VIII French immersion classes. Gladys remained in this position for only one year, for in 1987, she was appointed education consultant with the Department of Education for francophone programs. With the departure of Sr. Gladys from St. Joseph's, the long ministry of the Sisters of Mercy to the schoolchildren of the East End came to an end. However, the Congregation of the Sisters of Mercy did not relinquish the option to appoint a sister to the staff of the school until June 1988.[51]

In spite of the fact that the Sisters of Mercy were no longer members of the teaching staff of St. Joseph's School, the association between school and convent continued. Sisters who lived in St. Joseph's Convent were invited to attend concerts and games at the school. What was more important, through contact with the principal and the teachers, the sisters continued to assist the children of parents who suffered from unemployment and poverty.

---

50. ASMSJ, RG 10/13/1f.
51. Ibid.

During the years when the Sisters of Mercy were withdrawing gradually from St. Joseph's School, the convent itself was alive with activity. The seven
or eight sisters who lived in St. Joseph's Convent were involved in a variety of
ministries.[52] For a period, the convent had been designated as the formation
house of the congregation, but when the last novice, Pamela Quirk, had been
professed, St. Joseph's became just, "St. Joseph's Convent," as it had been since
1922.[53]

Meanwhile, the provincial government was planning far-reaching
changes in the educational system of Newfoundland and Labrador.
Newfoundland had enjoyed a publicly funded denominational system since the
mid-1800s. When Newfoundland became a province of Canada in 1949, the
denominational system of education was guaranteed under the Terms of
Union. However, after two provincial referenda on education in 1995 and
1997, the system changed to a public non-denominational system.
Government moved swiftly to establish regional, elected school boards. In the
process of educational reform, a number of existing schools were closed and
students assigned to schools in central locations. When the reorganization of
schools was announced the parents, teachers, and students of St. Joseph's
school held their breath. For some it was unthinkable that the school board
would consider closing the bright, well-equipped, and relatively new St.
Joseph's Junior High. They were shocked and disappointed when it was
announced that St. Joseph's was one of the schools slated for closure. However,
because of overcrowding in some of the schools designated to remain open, St.
Joseph's was given a year's reprieve. When the school year began in September
1998, teachers and students suspected that this would be their last year in a
school that had served the community so well. Finally, on February 3, 1999,

---

52. Sr. Gladys Bozec worked as education consultant; Sr. Celine Veitch taught music at
the convent and provided music therapy at St. Clare's Mercy Hospital and the Miller
Centre; M. Immacula O'Leary was assistant in the Nursing Unit at St. Catherine's Convent;
Sr. Helen Caule was a social worker with the Department of Health; Sr. Diane Smyth was
a social worker and director of Mercy Residence for Girls; St. Phyllis Corbett was director
of nursing at St. Clare's; Sr. Brenda Peddigrew was director of the Faith Development
Commission for the Archdiocese of St. John's.

53. Subsequently, Pamela Quirk left the Congregation of the Sisters of Mercy.

the convent annalist wrote, "This is a sad day for the students and teachers at St. Joseph's school and for the Sisters at St. Joseph's Convent. Today it was announced that the school would not reopen in September, 1999."[54] In June 1999, St. Joseph's students and faculty invited the sisters to the annual closing concert. However, this year there was a special poignancy attached to the event. This time it was, indeed, a "closing concert." When the performance was over, the sisters visited the classrooms of St. Joseph's School for the last time. When the school year began in September 1999, the playground outside the convent was strangely silent. For the first time in eighty-one years, it no longer rang with the voices of children playing.

As the years passed, Hoylestown experienced a shift in population from the old part of the city to new housing developments that were popping up all over the place. Gradually, year by year, the number of parishioners of St. Joseph's Parish declined. Eventually, the Archdiocese of St. John's decided to amalgamate St. Joseph's Parish with the Basilica Parish of St. John the Baptist, although St. Joseph's Church remained open for a weekend mass. But the writing was on the wall. On February 21, 1998, the final parish mass was celebrated in St. Joseph's Church. The beautiful, forty-year-old building was crowded with parishioners and former parishioners who gathered to mourn the loss of parish identity. Although people had been aware of the possibility that the church would close, most people thought that, somehow or other, the building could remain open. However, the number of regular parishioners was not sufficient to maintain the building. This fact, together with the shortage of ordained priests forced the Archdiocese of St. John's to implement this painful decision.

After St. Joseph's School was closed in September 1999, all the buildings on St. Joseph's Parish property near the convent were empty, with the exception of the former primary school. For a few years, this building had been used to house the School Lunch Program. However, on March 14, 2000, *The Evening Telegram* reported that St. Joseph's Church, presbytery, and schools were to be sold and demolished.[55] Subsequently, the property was purchased

---

54. Annals, St. Joseph's Convent, St. John's, 1999, ASMSJ.
55. *The Telegram*, March 14, 2000, p. 3.

and a number of houses built where the primary and elementary schools once stood. The interior of the former junior high school, which is directly behind St. Joseph's Convent, is being redesigned for use as executive suites. St. Joseph's Convent still stands as the last reminder of what was once a vibrant, active parish community.

After the establishment of St. Joseph's Convent, Hoylestown, the next foundation of the Sisters of Mercy took place in Marystown in 1927. The settlement is built around both sides of a wide harbour that is part of the greater area of Mortier Bay, a large inlet about twenty miles north of Burin on the Burin Peninsula. Originally, the settlement was known as Mortier Bay and, until 1909, was part of the parish of Burin. In light of the growing importance of Mortier Bay to the economy of the peninsula, Archbishop Howley agreed to establish a separate parochial district in the Burin area and appointed Father E. J. Wilson pastor of the Sacred Heart Parish of Mortier Bay. Within a short time of his appointment, Father Wilson decided to change the name of the settlement to Marystown. He also set to work to build a large parish church, and, with the co-operation of all the people of the parish, the building was completed in time for him to celebrate midnight mass in the new Sacred Heart Church on Christmas Eve 1910. During the next few years, the energetic young priest succeeded in building a presbytery, a sturdy school, and a parish centre that he named St. Gabriel's Hall.

Father Wilson had spent the first few years after his ordination as a curate in Burin, where he observed the work of the Sisters of Mercy not only in the school but also in the parish where they visited the poor and the sick. He was determined to obtain the same services for his parishioners in Marystown. Therefore, shortly after St. Edward's Convent was opened on Bell Island in 1917, Father Wilson extracted a promise from M. Bridget O'Connor that as soon as she had enough sisters, possibly in 1919, she would establish a convent in his parish. This was enough to spur the enthusiastic pastor to a flurry of activity in preparation for the arrival of the sisters. In 1918, he began construction of the convent that he hoped would be ready for occupancy the following year. Unfortunately for Father's hopes and dreams, the building was destroyed by fire before it was completely finished.[56]

In the meantime, events were happening rapidly in St. John's. Convents established in Bay Bulls (1921) and in Hoylestown (1922) depleted the number of experienced sisters who could be entrusted with the responsibility of a new and distant mission. Moreover, with the opening of St. Clare's Mercy Hospital, several qualified sister-teachers found themselves transplanted to American hospitals to train as nurses. Even though increasing numbers of bright, intelligent, young sisters were being professed, Father Wilson would have to wait until some more experienced sister was free to take the responsibility of establishing a new foundation.

Several years passed, and still there was no sign of a convent in Marystown. Meanwhile, in 1919, Father Wilson was transferred to Trepassey and was succeeded by Rev. Dr. Francis J. McGrath. Apparently Dr. McGrath made no further efforts to encourage the establishment of a Mercy convent in Marystown—possibly because he was faced with a financial problem of major proportions. The first presbytery, built by Father Wilson in 1910, was destroyed by fire in 1921. Dr. McGrath, unwilling to incur the expense of building a new presbytery, decided to buy a house—the former residences of a local doctor.[57] This was the building that would eventually became the Convent of the Holy Name of Mary.

In 1926, Father John W. McGettigan succeeded Dr. McGrath as parish priest of Marystown. By this time, Marystown was a sizeable community with two schools, a telegraph office, and a steamer service to St. John's.[58] Father McGettigan was just as anxious as was Father Wilson to see a Mercy convent established in his parish. Aware that Father Wilson had made futile appeals to successive General Councils of the Sisters of Mercy, he decided to enlist the help of Archbishop Roche. Obviously, this was the right approach, for within a short time, Father McGettigan received a letter from the archbishop. Reading between the lines of this letter, it appears that the archbishop had taken up the cudgels on behalf of Marystown with no holds barred!

---

56. ASMSJ, RG 10/14/1d.
57. M. Gabriel Fleming provided this information to the author many years ago.
58. *ENL*, s.v. "Marystown."

> Referring to our conversation about the establishment of a Convent of the Sisters of Mercy in Marystown, I am now in a position to state that the Sisters will be in a position to open a house in Marystown next September. . . . I represented to the Mother General of the Mercy Order, very strongly, the urgent need for a foundation in Marystown, and the claims which the Parish had on the consideration of the Order, in view of the preparations that were made for the Sisters a few years back. . . . In view of the evident desire of the people and yourself to have the Sisters in the Parish, and in view of my very strong representation, they have decided to undertake the work and to send Sisters to Marystown in September.[59]

Rather than build a new convent, the parish turned over the presbytery to the sisters and built a new and smaller residence for the parish priest.

The Sisters of Mercy greeted the proposed foundation in Marystown with a good deal of interest and enthusiasm. After 1922, the flurry of activity that marked the first six years after the amalgamation seemed to have come to a standstill. The prospect of a new foundation set the convent rumour mill into full production. It was the custom to release the yearly list of changes in personnel on August 15, a date that was awaited with much anxiety. A sister who was quite satisfied with her lot in life dreaded seeing her name on "The Changes," as the list was called. Another sister might have greeted the sight of her name on "The Changes" with a sigh of relief. In the case of a foundation, most sisters welcomed the opportunity to be part of a new venture. Thus, at the end of the school year in June 1927, conversation at recreation in most convents centred around the identity of the lucky ones to be chosen for Marystown. M. Francis Hickey wrote an account of her memories of those days in which she confessed that she had engaged in all sorts of vocal exercises and a multitude of throat medications to improve her singing voice, hoping by these means to be chosen for the new foundation. "The Pastor," she explained, "ranking as a second John McCormack, will be satisfied with nothing less than the best." She was doomed to disappointment.[60]

---

59. Archbishop E. P. Roche to Reverend J. W. McGettigan, March 8, 1927, ASMSJ, RG 10/14/2.
60. M. Francis Hickey, *Mercy Communico* 1, no. 4 (May 1968): p. 2.

Nevertheless, it was true that Father McGettigan, who possessed a fine tenor voice, was looking for an experienced and talented music teacher.

The congregation did not have to wait long. Within a few weeks, the announcement was made that in mid-August, three sisters would be leaving for Marystown: M. Gabriel Fleming, who fulfilled the pastor's dream of obtaining a first-class music teacher; M. Camillus Dunphy; and M. Anthony Wade. A fourth sister, the nineteen-year-old M. Paschal Dwyer, would join the group at a later date.[61] And so, early in the morning of August 17, M. Camillus Dunphy and M. Anthony Wade, boarded the SS *Portia* in St. John's for the voyage "up the coast." The superior general, M. Philippa Hanley, accompanied by M. Genevieve O'Farrell, and the superior of the new mission, M. Gabriel Fleming, drove to Salmonier by car and connected there with the *Portia* for the trip that would bring them across Placentia Bay to Marystown. En route to Salmonier, their car, speeding along at twenty miles an hour, caught up with a line of traffic headed by a horse pulling a cartload of hay. Given the narrow, unpaved roads in Newfoundland at the time, this was not an unusual occurrence during the summer months. As they drove along toward Salmonier, the line of cars, interspersed with a few more horse-drawn loads of hay, grew longer and longer. When the sisters arrived at their destination, they were preceded by a retinue of vehicles that the people of Salmonier interpreted as a motorcade in honour of the departure of the nuns to Marystown.[62]

Meanwhile, Father McGettigan and the people of Marystown, who expected the sisters to arrive in early September, were blissfully unaware that they were already on their way. Through some misunderstanding, the team had set out for their destination two weeks ahead of time. They would have surprised the pastor and the people by arriving on the scene unannounced and unexpected if it had not been for the foresight of M. Pius Mulcahy. A veteran of the Burin mission, M. Pius left nothing to chance but as soon as the sisters left St. John's, wired a message to Father McGettigan, informing him of their imminent arrival. This message caused consternation and a great deal of hustle

---

61. At the time, M. Paschal was in St. Clare's Mercy Hospital recuperating from minor surgery.
62. M. Gabriel Fleming told this story to the author many years ago.

and bustle in order to accomplish in twenty-four hours what would have taken, under normal circumstances, about two weeks. Word spread quickly around the town, and women came with mops, dusters, and buckets to polish every nook and cranny of the convent. The men hurried to put up arches of evergreen boughs all along the route that the sisters would take on their way to their new home. In a few hours, preparations were complete and everything was in readiness for the arrival of "the nuns."[63]

The people in Marystown had waited for years for the day when they could welcome the sisters. Consequently, on Thursday, August 18, practically the entire population of the settlement gathered near the wharf where the SS *Portia* was due to dock. As the boat entered Mortier Bay and approached the Marystown harbour, the surrounding hills echoed with the sounds of musket fire, and hundreds of flags fluttered in the breeze as the boat slowly made its way toward land. As the *Portia* gently nudged the wharf, the sisters, who were standing on deck, were greeted with loud cheers. Recalling the scene many years later, M. Camillus Dunphy remarked, "We were pleased and delighted to be welcomed with such enthusiasm. At the same time, we were a bit anxious—wondering if we would measure up to the people's high expectations."[64]

The sisters were not long in making friends with the people of Marystown. The day after their arrival they were invited to a motorboat tour around Mortier Bay. This provided an opportunity for them to admire and appreciate the spectacular beauty of their surroundings. They had good neighbours, too, for on Saturday morning, they received a visit from a lady of the parish who brought chicken, potatoes, and cabbage for their Sunday dinner. There was a lot of work to be done to prepare for the formal opening of the convent, which was dedicated to the Holy Name of Mary. M. Bridget O'Connor and M. Pius Mulcahy, who had been invited to attend, were due to arrive August 25 on the SS *Glencoe*. But one of the worst storms on record, known locally as "the August Gale," occurred on that day, causing the *Glencoe* to toss about all night in the middle of Placentia Bay. The sisters in Marystown paced the floor,

63. M. Francis Hickey, *Mercy Communico* 2, no. 17, p. 3.
64. M. Camillus Dunphy, conversation with author, November 25, 1999.

praying for the safety of all those at sea. At half past six the following morning, Father McGettigan came over to the convent with the news that the *Glencoe* had entered Mortier Bay and would be at the wharf by seven o'clock.[65]

In those days, there was no running water in the convent, or electricity, or central heating. The annalist recorded, "Youthful neighbours, Joseph and Raymond Baker, Sylvester Baker and Paddy Flannigan [were] very good to bring water and cut wood for the sisters." Then, a few days later, "Cyril and Paddy Brake cut enough wood for three or four days."[66] The visiting sisters made themselves useful by helping to prepare the convent and the parish church for the ceremony of the dedication of the convent. In anticipation of the arrival of Archbishop Roche, the men of the parish decorated the route from the wharf to the convent with arches of evergreen boughs. Eventually, everything was ready for the official opening of the convent on September 4. The sisters from Burin and four priests were present for the solemn High Mass celebrated by Father John McGettigan at ten o'clock in the morning. It was a formal occasion, during which the local justice of the peace, J. Long, read an address to the archbishop. The latter, never at a loss for words, "responded at length."[67]

The coeducational school in Marystown opened on Tuesday, September 6, with an enrolment of 220 children. M. Bridget O'Connor remained to help in the school until September 15, when the fourth member of the Marystown community, M. Paschal Dwyer, arrived to take up her new duties. The following day, M. Bridget returned to St. John's, and the sisters in Marystown settled down to the regular routine of convent life. The superior of the convent, M. Gabriel Fleming, was principal of the school and was responsible, also, for teaching classroom singing. Neither was she exempt from the fate of all outport-convent music teachers, after-school hours and on Saturdays, she gave private lessons to ten students in piano and theory, trained the parish choir, and played the organ for all the church services. The two-room school was located in St. Gabriel's Hall, where M. Paschal Dwyer and M. Anthony Wade taught

---

65. Ibid. See also Annals, Holy Name of Mary Convent, Marystown, ASMSJ, RG 10/11/5.
66. Ibid., August 28, p. 1, ASMSJ, RG 10/11/5.
67. Ibid.

the primary and elementary grades in the larger of the two rooms, while M. Camillus Dunphy was responsible for the high-school students. For the year 1927–28, classes in the convent school included all grades from I to X.

The school was heated by a pot-bellied, wood-burning stove, the wood for which was brought by the children in turn. At that time a series of *Royal Readers* was prescribed for the primary and elementary grades, but beginners used a little book called *The Primer*. From this book, they learned the letters of the alphabet, then picture words, and later whole sentences. After that they graduated to the first *Royal Reader* and continued until the fifth *Royal Reader* was mastered. In the senior grades, M. Camillus followed the curriculum pre-scribed for the CHE examinations. Other text books in use at the time were a table book that contained the multiplication tables and other mysteries of mathematics, a spelling book, an expositor, a geography book, and, of course, *The History of Newfoundland*. The school day began with prayer and then reli-gion, taught from *Butler's Catechism*—the standard text at that time. Every day, the children in the lower grades were assigned a certain number of questions, the answers to which were to be memorized in preparation for the next day's lesson. The children stood in a row as the sister asked the questions. If a child missed the answer, her place was given to the pupil who did know the answer, while the disgraced scholar was relegated to the last place in the line. Losing one's place was a distinct "loss of face," and it was likely that the child studied even harder to regain the lost place. Copybooks were used as a method of teaching good penmanship. For this exercise, the students used a nib pen which was dipped in ink. Children who lived near the school went home for lunch, but those who lived at a distance had to bring their lunch to school. On cold winter days, the sisters brought hot cocoa over to the school for the benefit of those children who could not go home.[68]

A year after the sisters' arrival, a two-room school was constructed and as the enrolment increased, a third classroom was added. From 1928 onward, classes were extended to include grade IX. Because of the layout of the settle-ment, children from the south side of the harbour travelled to school by tak-

---

68. Mrs. Julia Baker, conversation with author, April 20, 2000.

ing the government ferry across to the north side, where the convent, school, and church were located. This continued until the time of the Depression when, for reasons of economy, the ferry was discontinued. Consequently, the school enrolment dropped to about 180 students.

Although not directly affected by the 1929 tidal wave that caused such havoc in many settlements on the southern part of the Burin Peninsula, Marystown was devastated by the subsequent collapse of the fishery.[69] The Depression of the 1930s added to the misery and hardship of a people who traditionally had made their living from the sea. Needless to say, this reacted unfavourably on the schools. There was no money to purchase books and other items needed for the classroom, also, children often came to school suffering from hunger and cold. The sisters welcomed the opportunity to share the little they had with the people who were in desperate need. M. Pauline Foster, a native of Marystown, remembered with gratitude the care and concern shown by the sisters for children who came to school cold and hungry.[70]

In later years, M. Camillus Dunphy, who spent nine years in Marystown (1927–36), spoke to her novices of the Depression.[71] She recalled days—and sometimes nights—when she and M. Anthony Wade ploughed through deep snowdrifts to visit the sick. M. Camillus recalled that they always brought along soup for the patient. Better still, when somebody donated meat to the convent, this would be used to make broth for the sick. At the time, tuberculosis was rampant not only in Marystown but also in many places in Newfoundland. Young people were particularly vulnerable to the disease. Their deaths seemed to have an enduring effect on the tender-hearted M. Camillus. Years later her sense of loss was still evident as she recounted stories of visits to children who were dying of the disease that in those days was called "consumption."[72]

The sisters, too, experienced their share of physical and material hardship. It was not until 1940 that a water system was installed in the convent. Up

---

69. For an account of the tidal wave on the Burin Peninsula, see chapter sixteen.

70. Hogan, *Pathways*, p. 163.

71. M. Camillus was appointed mistress of novices in 1941, a position she held for the next six years.

72. M. Camillus Dunphy in conversation with the novices, of whom the author was one.

to that time, the sisters depended on an outdoor well. A cooking range in the kitchen plus a smaller stove in the community room heated the convent. Wood was used for fuel, but in later years, a small supply of coal was bought for the coldest part of the winter. In order to provide some heat to the bedrooms, a small oil stove was purchased. Because the upstairs hall was too narrow to accommodate the stove, it was placed in one of the bedrooms. Every afternoon, the sister whose bedroom housed the stove lit the fire and left her bedroom door open so that the heat would circulate through the hall and into the other rooms. Then, before the sisters retired for the night, the stove was turned off.[73] This situation continued through the 1950s. There was no electricity. In the evenings, the sisters prepared their lessons for the next day and corrected students' homework by the light of a kerosene oil lamp. It was not until 1954 that a Delco was purchased to produce the first electric light for the convent. The Delco, however, was not very reliable, and, more often than not, the sisters had to fall back on the trusty old kerosene lamps to provide enough light to prepare their schoolwork. Finally, on September 21, 1959, the first pole was erected in the convent garden for hookup with the electric system that was to be installed in the town. For four months, that lonely pole stood dark and empty, a promise of better days to come. Then, on January 23, 1960, the annalist noted, "At 6:35 p.m. lights came on for the first time."[74]

Through all the years of hardship and adversity, the sisters continued to work quietly and effectively to provide an education for the children of Marystown. In 1943, another extension was added to the school. Nobody begrudged the expense of this construction in the difficult war time period, for the pupils continued to maintain an excellent record in the public CHE examinations, winning the Electoral Scholarships in grades IX and X on two different occasions. All the students participated enthusiastically in special programs for Christmas, St. Patrick's Day, and annual Prize Day concerts. In 1952, Trinity College music examinations were held for the first time on the Burin Peninsula. At the time, M. James (Madeline) Reid was the superior of

---

73. I am indebted to M. Michael Power for this story.
74. Annals, Holy Name of Mary Convent, Marystown, ASMSJ, RG 10/11/5.

Holy Name of Mary Convent and the music teacher. M. James, herself a native of Marystown, had looked forward for many years to the time when the young musicians of the town could participate in these examinations that had proved to be such a challenge to students in other parts of Newfoundland. All fifteen of her students were successful in the examinations. It was the beginning of the yearly participation of Marystown in the Trinity College of Music examinations. In 1955, M. James Reid was reassigned, and Sr. Anita Petrie took her place. By this time, the Kiwanis Music Festival in St. John's was providing an opportunity for young musicians to compete at their respective age levels and to learn from the comments and suggestions of experienced and qualified adjudicators. Sr. Anita decided that distance should not be an obstacle to children who wanted to take part in the festival. Accordingly, several young musicians from Marystown travelled to St. John's to participate in the 1955 music festival. All received good marks with an excellent adjudication, and one of them won first place and a prize of fifty dollars.[75] Eventually, the Burin Peninsula held its own competitive music festival in which the students from Marystown played a prominent part.

But Sr. Anita Petrie was interested in more than music festivals. She worked hard to promote Newfoundland folk music and encouraged her students to learn to play instruments used traditionally in the performance of the music of our people. Every summer she attended summer school at an American university. One summer, she decided to purchase an accordion so that she could help her students to become more proficient in playing this instrument that is so popular in Newfoundland. All summer, Sr. Anita applied herself assiduously to perfecting her own technique, and at the end of six weeks, she felt prepared to start teaching her students. There was only one problem—Canada Customs. She dutifully filled out a form declaring that she had purchased the instrument in the United States, but when she presented herself to the official at the border, she discovered, to her dismay, that her beautiful new accordion was being eyed with considerable suspicion by the customs officer. When questioned, she explained the nature of the object and the pur-

75. ASMSJ, RG 10/14/15.

pose for which she was bringing it into Canada. Her travelling companions watched in consternation as Sr. Anita—clad in the traditional habit of the Sisters of Mercy—was escorted from the line by two stony-faced, uniformed officials to explain to higher authority her possession of this dubious object. Eventually, Sr. Anita returned to the line without a stain on her character but minus her accordion. It was being held in captivity for further examination by Canada Customs. Six weeks later, the accordion was delivered, free of charge, to Marystown Convent, with profuse apologies from Canada Customs for the embarrassment caused to an innocent victim of Canadian bureaucracy.

Meantime, in 1959, Canning Bridge, connecting both sides of Marystown harbour, was opened, and buses were provided to transport students from the south side to Marystown North. The Holy Name of Mary High School was moved to the parish hall, grades I, VI, and VIII were moved to the town hall, while the other grades remained in the old school until the new Holy Name of Mary Elementary School for grades I–VIII opened on September 13, 1960.

Because of the increase in the school population, additional sisters were sent to Marystown. The convent that had housed four sisters at the beginning was too small to accommodate the six sisters who were assigned to Holy Name of Mary Convent. Consequently, on May 1, 1962, the cornerstone was laid for a new convent on land directly in front of the old one. On December 4 of the same year, 1962, the six sisters left the old convent and moved into the new.

The growing importance of Marystown as the industrial centre of the Burin Peninsula was linked to the increasing need for bigger and better boats. As far back as the 1800s, there was an interest in boat building, and in the early twentieth century, Hugh Reddy built bankers and schooners. In 1942, the men of Marystown built four warships (magnetic minesweepers), and in 1949, the government established a centre for building longliners.[76] The latter half of the 1960s saw a dramatic increase in employment opportunities for the people of the area with the construction of a shipbuilding and repair facility to service the trawler fleet on the Grand Banks. This facility employed two hundred men.

76. *ENL*, s.v. "Marystown."

Furthermore, in 1967, a large fish plant, employing over 400 people, was built in Mooring Cove. It was during the construction of these two facilities that the boundaries of Marystown were enlarged to include the adjacent settlements of Creston, Mooring Cove, and Little Bay.[77]

The opening of a new shipyard and a large, modern fish plant injected new life into what was once a quiet little settlement. Hundreds of people moved into the area to find employment at one or other of these new facilities. Large shopping malls, hotels, radio stations, and medical clinics sprang up to create a large, modern town. Obviously, the schools had to keep pace with the progress of the town. In 1967, the elementary school, built in 1960, was enlarged, and in September 1972, the new, modern Marystown Central High School was opened. By this time there were nine sisters teaching side by side with a number of lay teachers in the schools in Marystown.

In the years after the sisters' arrival, seven young women from Marystown became Sisters of Mercy. M. James (Madeline) Reid was the first graduate of the sisters' school to enter the Mercy congregation. Then followed M. Pauline Foster, M. Tarcissius (Mary) Power, Margaret Pittman, Margaret Rose, Cecilia Lambe, Lydia Kelly, Mary Kelly, and Mary Baker. They were all present when, in September 1977, Holy Name of Mary Convent celebrated the golden jubilee of the coming of the Sisters of Mercy to Marystown. This anniversary was unique in that the four founding sisters, M. Gabriel Fleming, M. Camillus Dunphy, M. Anthony Wade, and M. Paschal Dwyer, were present for the occasion. Msgr. J. W. McGettigan, the parish priest who welcomed them in 1927, came from St. John's to take part in the celebrations. It was a time for remembering, for rejoicing, and for giving thanks to God for the blessings of fifty years.

---

77. Ibid.

Mother M. Catherine McAuley.
Foundress of the Sisters of Mercy.

Our Lady of Mercy School Orchestra, *circa* 1930.
1st row L–R: Mary Fitzhenry-Drayton, Mary Irwin-Ryan, Ruth Davis, Mercedes
Kennedy, Madeline Veith (Sister M. Celine, RSM); 2nd row L–R: Mary
Keough-Callanan, Margaret Fitzhenry, Mary Cooper-Stack, Joan Kavanagh; 3rd
row L–R: Pauline Martin-Dawson, Mary Martin, ?, ?, Kathleen Kennedy-Frazer-
Hanley; 4th row L–R: Tessa Hutton-Shea. Marjorie Grouchy-Redmond, ?, Mary
Trainor (Sister Teresa-Madeline, SC); 5th row L–R: Stella McDonald, Eleanor
Coady-Warren; Kathleen Robin-Quigley.

Our Lady of Mercy Glee Club in front of the Indian Pavilion at Expo '67 in
Montreal. The choir presented six concerts at the Expo.

Presentation of the Mathieson Trophy to Our Lady of Mercy Glee Club, 1964.
L-R: Sister M. Camillus Dunphy, Sister M. Assumpta Veitch, Mrs. Peggy O'Dea
(wife of Lt. Governor Fabian O'Dea), Sister Kathrine Bellamy (Choir Director),
Sister Imelda Smith.

Our Lady of Mercy School Grade X class (1958) reunion thirty years later (1988).
1st row, 5th from left, their teacher, Sister M. Assumpta Veitch;
2nd row, 3rd from left, Sister Rosemary Ryan, member of the class.

Coolock House, Dublin.
Catherine McAuley lived here with the Callaghans from 1803 to 1828.

House of Mercy, Baggot Street, Dublin.
In 1831, it became St. Mary's Convent. After the death of Catherine McAuley, it
was renamed St. Catherine's Convent.

In 1994, St. Catherine's Convent, Baggot Street, Dublin, became Mercy International Centre. It is a place of pilgrimage where Sisters of Mercy and visitors from all over the world come to reflect on the charism of Mercy as manifested in the life of Catherine McAuley.

Mercy Convent today.

The Kiwanis Club Grand Award for the most outstanding performance of the music festival was won by Our Lady of Mercy Glee Club. Tessa Hutton (left) and Janet Myler (right) accepted the $200 cash award and a mahogany shield on behalf of the choir. (Courtesy of *The Telegram*.)

Sister M. Francis Creedon's headstone, Sisters' Cemetery, Belvedere.

St. John's Hospital (1814-1888).
(Courtesy of Paul O'Neill.)

The old Catholic Cemetery, Long's Hill, St. John's.
(Courtesy of the Archives, City of St. John's.)

Sketch by Willie Brandts showing the Sisters of Mercy caring for the victims of the
cholera epidemic of 1856.
(Courtesy of CBC, St. John's.)

St. Peter's School, Queen Street, St. John's.
(1881–1903.)

The Cathedral of St. John the Baptist (left). Mercy Convent (right). St. Clair's
Boarding School is behind Mercy Convent. The Presentation Sisters' school is on
the right of the cathedral, *circa* 1878.
(Courtesy of the Archives, Archdiocese of St. John's.)

The *Sir Walter Scott*, the ship that brought the first Sisters of Mercy to
Newfoundland.

The Narrows, or Entrance to St. John's Harbour. Drawn by Lt. A. Thompson, 1842.

Drawing of the Old Chapel and Palace. The Sisters of Mercy lived in this residence from June 3–December 12, 1842. The building is dated from *circa* 1753. (Courtesy of the Archives, Archdiocese of St. John's.)

St. John's from Government House. Drawing by W.R. Best. Lithographed by W. Spreat's Litho Establishment, England, 1851. The building with the tower in front of the cathedral is the first Mercy Convent in the New World (1842).

Sketch of the first Mercy Convent (1842). Drawn by Nelson White according to the specifications given by Bishop Fleming.

Bishop Michael Anthony Fleming.

SUPERIOR GENERAL (CONGREGATIONAL LEADERS) SINCE AMALGAMATION (1916)

Sister M. Bridget O'Connor, first superior general of the Sisters of Mercy of Newfoundland (1916–1925; 1937–1943).

Sister M. Philippa Hanley (1925–1937).

Sister M. Stanislaus Parsons (1943-1949).

Sister M. Imelda Smith (1949-1961).

Sister M. Assumpta Veitch (1961–1973).

Sister Marie Michael Power (1973–1981).

Sister Patricia Maher (1981–1989).

Sister Marion Collins (1989–1997).

Sister Charlotte Fitzpatrick (1997–2001).

Sister Helen Harding (2001–present).

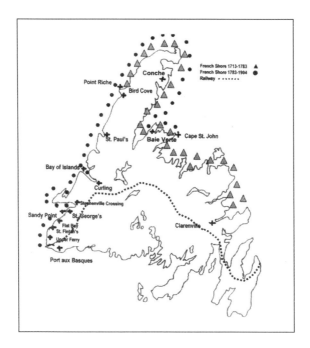

The island of Newfoundland showing the French Shore as designated by the treaties of Utrecht and Versailles. Places where the Sisters of Mercy ministered outside the Avalon and Bonavista peninsulas are indicated by +.

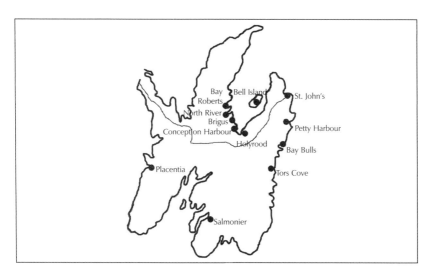

The Avalon Peninsula.

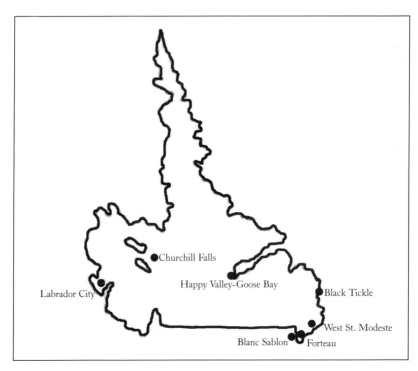

Map of Labrador.

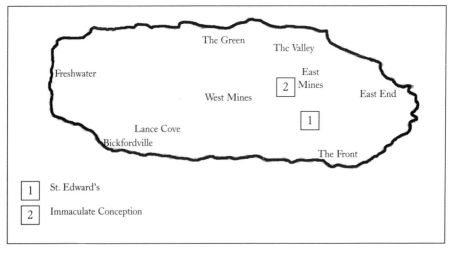

Map of Bell Island.

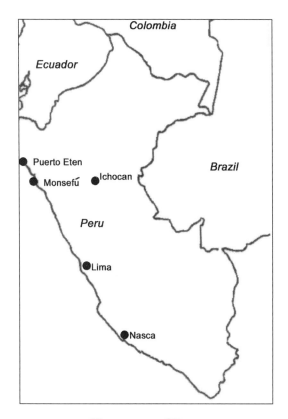

The country of Peru.

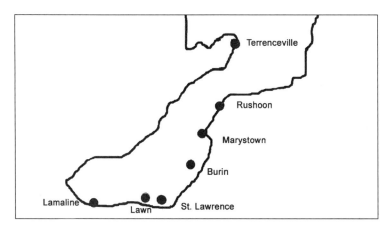

Map of the Burin Peninsula.

SOME "WEAVERS OF THE TAPESTRY"

Sister M. Bernard Clune.
In 1884, she founded St. Bride's Boarding School at Littledale.

Henrietta Brownell and Sister M. Antonio Egan.
With the help of Mrs. Brownell, M. Antonio founded the first convent of Mercy
on the west coast of Newfoundland.

Sister M. Corsini Dempsey.
With Sister M. Antonio Egan, she transferred from the Sisters of Mercy of
Providence, R.I., to establish the congregation on the west coast of Newfoundland.

Sister M. Teresa O'Halleran.
Educator and, for many years, the business manager for the Sisters of Mercy in
Newfoundland.

Sister M. Perpetua O'Callaghan.
Scholar and educator, she was the first Sister of Mercy from Newfoundland to earn
the degree of doctor of philosophy.

Sister M. Baptist McDermott.
M. Baptist holds an honoured place in the development of music, dancing, and
drama in Newfoundland and was one of the founders of modern music education in
Newfoundland. M. Baptist founded Our Lady of Mercy School Orchestra in 1921.

Sister M. Augustine O'Connor.
Principal of St. Bride's College,
Littledale, 1921-1944.

Sister M. Francis Hickey.
Honoured for her ministry to the incar-
cerated. Known as "The Friend of the
Prisoners."

Sister M. Nolasco Mulcahy.
Educator and first principal of the new St. Bride's College, 1967-1970. She exerted significant influence in educational circles, not only in Newfoundland, but also
throughout Canada, particularly in Ontario where she served for a number of years
as head of the Graduate Studies Division at the University of Ottawa.

ST. CLARE'S

Sister M. Bernard Gladney.
First administrator of St. Clare's Mercy Hospital (1922–1923).

Sister M. Fabian Hennebury.
Administrator of St. Clare's Mercy Hospital (1955–1981).

St. Clare's Mercy Hospital, 1922.
From 1913 to 1922, the building was used as St. Clare's Home for Working Girls.

Architect's drawing of St. Clare's Mercy Hospital in 1939.
(Courtesy of the Archives, Archdiocese of St. John's.)

St. Clare's Mercy Hospital and LeMarchant Road buildings:
(left) St. Clare's Nurse's Residence (1958); (centre) St. Clare's Mercy Hospital
Chapel (1947); (right) St. Clare's Mercy Hospital (1938 building). The high building (left rear) is the 1962 extension on St. Clare Avenue.

St. Clare's Mercy Hospital *circa* 1972. The smaller, wooden building (far right) is
the original hospital. It is now St. Clare's Convent.

SISTERS IN THE MINISTRY

Sister Loretta Chafe with altar boys. Bell Island, *circa* 1960s.

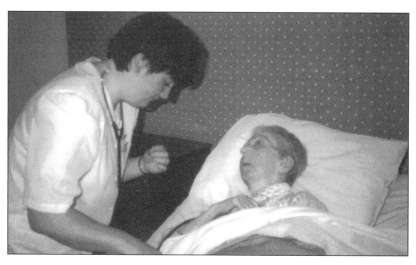

Sister Eileen Penney cares for Sister M. Alacoque McDonald.

Sister M. Annett Hawco caring for Sister M. Benignus Mullowney, St. Catherine's Convent, Nursing Unit.

Sister M. Chrysostom McCarthy, classical scholar, first archivist for the Newfoundland Congregation of the Sisters of Mercy.

Sister Bridget Patterson assisting a hearing-impaired child.

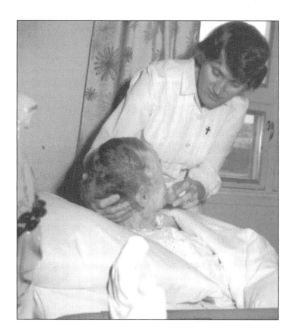

Sister M. Alverna Harnett with patient.

The first community of Holy Name of Mary, Marystown, 1927.
L–R: Sister M. Anthony Wade, Sister M. Gabriel Fleming, Reverend John
McGettigan (pastor), Sister M. Paschal Dwyer, and Sister M. Camillus Dunphy.

First community, Holy Name of Mary Convent, Marystown, taken on the fiftieth
anniversary of the Sisters. Seated L–R: Reverend J. W. McGettigan and Sister M.
Gabriel Fleming. Standing L–R: Sister M. Camillus Dunphy, Sister M. Paschal
Dwyer, and Sister M. Anthony Wade.

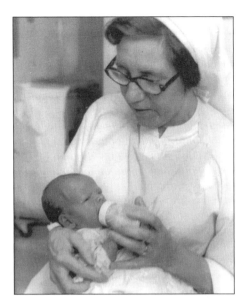

Sister M. Antonia Carroll, St. Clare's Mercy Hospital, caring for a newborn.

Sister Marie Michael Power with high-school class, Marystown, 1957. Brian Peckford, future premier of Newfoundland and Labrador, can be seen in the back row on the far left.

First Communion Class, Fort Pepperrell, St. John's.
(left) Sister M. Colette Ryan. (right) Sister M. Pauline Foster.

Sister M. Edwardine Furlong with cello class, Our Lady of Mercy School, St. John's.

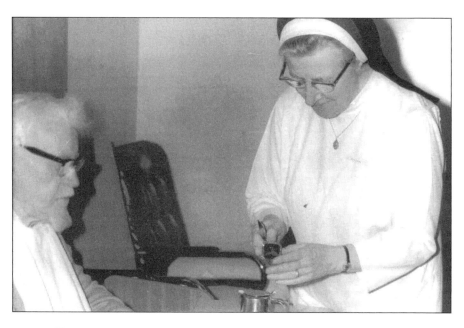

Sister M. Julien Giovanni assists guest at St. Patrick's Mercy Home.

Part for the toddlers at St. Michael's Orphanage, Belvedere.
Standing L-R: Sister M. Noel Croke, Sister M. Alexius St. George, and Sister M. Clare Lawless.

Sister M. Anthony Wade's class, Marystown, *circa* 1927.

Sister Margie Taylor (standing back row) with class in Rushoon.

Sister Kathrine Bellamy, music ministry, Basilica-Cathedral of St. John the Baptist, St. John's.

St. Pius X Girl's School, St. John's, grade VII class, 1967.
Teacher on far right is Sister Rosemary Ryan.

Sister Sheila O'Dea directing a session in Adult Catechesis, Dublin, Ireland.

Sisters and schoolchildren on steps of church, Conception Harbour, *circa* 1904. Standing L–R: Monsignor Wm. Veitch (pastor), Sister M. Gertrude Kennedy, Sister M. Cecilia Joy, Sister M. Joseph Barron, Sister M. Bridget Hoey, and Sister M. Berchmans Meehan.

Sister M. Madeline Aylward and co-workers preparing clothes to distribute to the poor.

Sister Mona Carew (director, back row) with St. Teresa's School Orchestra, Mundy Pond, St. John's.

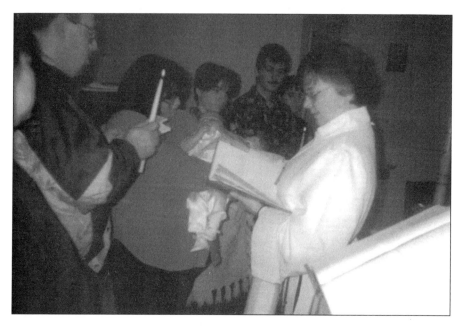

Sister Mona Rumboldt celebrating baptism, Black Tickle, Labrador.

St. Bride's College Orchestra, *circa* 1956.

Transportation in Black Tickle, Labrador.
L-R: Sister Verna Aucoin and Sister Ellen Marie Sullivan.

First Mercy Associates with sponsoring community.
Front L-R: Barbara Bradbury, Kay Daley, Marie Higgins, Flora Fowler, and Sister
M. Celine Veitch. Back L-R: Sister Kathrine Bellamy, Sister Monica Hickey,
Sister Ruth Beresford, Elaine Oostenburg, and Sister Loretta Chafe.

Sister M. Kevina Snook (left) with Sister M. Stanislaus Parsons.

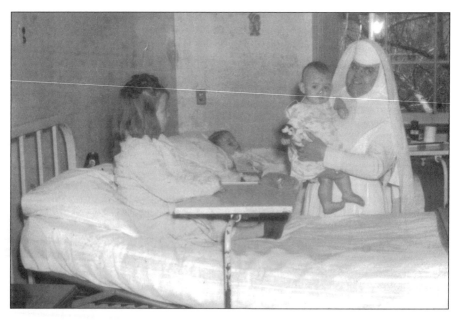

Sister M. Aiden Howell with sick child at St. Clare's Mercy Hospital.

The kitchen, The Gathering Place.
Sister Gertrude Bennett (left) and Sister Maura Mason "cooking up a storm."

Sister Monica Hickey (right), director of Pastoral Care at St. Patrick's Mercy
Home, speaking with one of the guests.

Sister Barbara Kenny and friends, Black Tickle, Labrador.

Sister Rosaline Hynes with self-help book prepared for persons living with HIV
and AIDS.

MEMBERS OF THE SAME FAMILY WHO WERE PROFESSED AS SISTERS OF MERCY

The Carroll sisters.
L–R: Sister M. Dorothy, Sister M. Eugenio, and Sister M. deLourdes.

The Reddy sisters.
L–R: Sister M. Anita, Sister M. Clarissa, and Sister M. Philippa.

The Wade sisters.
L–R: Sister M. Liguori, Sister M. Anthony, and Sister M. Barbara.

The Dunphy sisters.
Sister M. Camillus (left) and Sister M. Hildegarde (right).

The Brennan sisters.
Sister Mildred (left) and Sister Dolorosa (right).

The Beresford sisters.
Sister Ruth (left) and Sister Marie (right).

The Gosse sisters.
Sister Perpetua (left) and Sister Marie (right).

The Hennebury sisters.
Sister M. Fabian (left) and Sister Mark (right).

The Mason sisters.
Sister Geraldine (left) and Sister Maura (right).

The O'Gorman sisters.
Sister M. Alma (left) and Sister Margaret (right).

The Pomroy sisters.
Sister Nellie (left) and Sister Ida (right).

The Power sisters (Bell Island).
Sister M. Rosalita (left) and Sister M. Calasanctius (right).

The Power sisters (Branch).
Sister M. Consilio (left) and Sister Carmelita (right).

The Veitch sisters.
Sister M. Assumpta (left) and Sister M. Celine (right).

CONVENTS

St. Michael's Orphanage, Belvedere, 1884–1969.
St. Michael's Orphanage opened in 1859 in a section of St. Michael's Convent.

St. Michael's Convent/Boarding School, St. George's, 1899–1973.
In 1973, the old convent was demolished. St. Michael's Convent housed student boarders over the years, drawing its pupils from nearby communities. All of the students received a solid education, and many went on to distinguish themselves— such as the renowned Newfoundland writer Cassie Brown, and her siblings Vera and Freda, from Rose Blanche, on the island's southwest coast.

St. Patrick's Convent, Bay Bulls, *circa* 1920s, with the Reverend Patrick O'Brien
standing in front of the famous eighteenth century canons, relics of the battles
between the English and the French during that century. The statues surmounting the
canons are: L-R: Saint Patrick, Saint Peter, Saint Paul, and Saint Thérèse.

St. Michael's Convent, St. George's, 1973-1985.

St. Patrick's Mercy Home, St. John's, built in 1958.

Sacred Heart Convent, Goulds, 1949-2000.
In September 2000, Sacred Heart Convent became Creedon House, Mercy
Spirituality Centre.

The opening of the Convent of St. Mary's on the Humber, 1917-1976. In 1976, the old convent was demolished.

The second Convent of St. Mary's on the Humber, 1976-1994.

"Moving House."
The two houses that were to form Holy Trinity Convent, Upper Ferry, being transported from their original location.

Holy Trinity Convent, Upper Ferry, 1967–1981.

Kilcash, 1965-present.

St. Catherine's Convent / McAuley Hall, St. John's, 1960-1991.

St. Michael's Convent, Belvedere, 1859–1999.

St. Edward's Convent, Bell Island, 1917–1991.

Sisters' Residence, Black Tickle, Labrador, 1984–2002.

McAuley Convent, Littledale, St. John's, 1991–present.

St. Joseph's Convent, Brigus, 1861-1991.

The first St. Anne's Convent, Burin, 1863-1879.

The second St. Anne's Convent, Burin, 1879-1939.

Sacred Heart Convent, St. Lawrence, 1876-1926.
The Sisters of Mercy went to St. Lawrence in 1871. They lived in the presbytery
for five years until the convent was built.

The second Sacred Heart Convent, St. Lawrence, 1927–1969.

Immaculate Conception Convent, Conception Harbour, 1869–1930.

Holy Name of Mercy Convent, Marystown, 1927–1962.
In 1962, the sisters moved into a new convent that stands a few feet from where the original convent was situated.

Immaculate Conception Convent, Conception Harbour, 1931–present.

LITTLEDALE 1884-2005

St. Bride's Boarding School, Littledale, *circa* 1884.

St. Bride's Academy, Littledale, *circa* 1912.
L-R: West Wing, the original house, and Talbot Memorial Wing.

St. Bride's College, Littledale *circa* 1930s. (Left) Corpus Christi Church.

St. Bride's College, Littledale, *circa* 1958.
(Left) St. Augustine Hall, 1943; (2nd left) West Wing, 1912; (3rd left) Centre Block, 1919; (4th left) Talbot Memorial Wing; (right) Our Lady of Mercy Novitiate, 1956 (now St. Bride's Convent). The Littledale farm buildings can be seen on the far left.

St. Bride's College Campus, 1966.

A group of postulates, 1960–61.

A group of novices around the altar, St. Bride's Convent, Littledale, 1958.

St. Bride's Convent, Littledale Chapel, 1902–1958.

Front parlour, St. Bride's Convent, Littledale, *circa* 1930s.

PERU

The first group of Mercy missionaries to Peru with Sister M. Dolorosa Kinney, the last Irish-born member of the Newfoundland Mercy congregation. L–R: Sister Helen Best, Sister Maura Mason, Sister M. Dorothy Carroll, Sister M. Dolorosa, Sister M. Immacula O'Leary, Sister Marion Collins, and Sister Bernetta Walsh.

Sister Patricia Maher and friends, Reque, Peru.

Convento de la Misericordia, Monsefú, Peru.

Sisters Residence, Ichocan, Peru.

Rhythm Band, Our Lady of Mercy School, Monsefú, Peru.

Sister Helen Best's little dancers, Monsefú, Peru.

A lady at the graves of Sister M. Dorothy Carroll and Sister M. Aquin English in the convent garden, Monsefú, Peru.

Early in March 1997, the bodies of Sister M. Dorothy Carroll and Sister M. Aquin English were transferred from the convent garden to the town cemetery in Monsefú, Peru. (8th from left) Sister Mildred Brennan; (11th from left) Sister Carmelita Power.

Transportation, Ichocan, Peru.
L-R: Sister Verna Aucoin, Sister Lily Ferrero, and Sister Rosa Silva Cumpa.

Sister Brenda Phelan (left) and co-workers organize distribution of mattresses to
flood victims, Peru, 1998.
The mattresses were supplied by the Sisters of Mercy of Newfoundland.

Sister Mildred Brennan and assistant pack medical supplies for cholera victims, Peru, 1991.

Sister M. Carmelita Power and assistant packing food for flood victims, Peru, 1998.

Sister Marion Collins being greeted on her return to Peru.

Sister Rosa Mercedes Silva Cumpa pronounced her religious vows in the parish church of Puerto Eten, March 29, 1992. L–R: Sister Marion Collins (superior general), Sister Patricia March (assistant), three priests, and Sister Rosa Silva Cumpa.

CHAPTER SIXTEEN

TIMES AND TIDES

> Say to those who are fearful of heart:
> "Be strong, do not fear!"
>
> Isaiah 35:4

ong before Father Wilson dreamed of bringing the Sisters of Mercy to Marystown, further down the Burin Peninsula, the sisters were hard at work preparing children for life in the twentieth century. When the first CHE public examinations were held in St. Lawrence in 1905–06, six pupils registered and were successful.[1] The high-school teacher of the time was M. Cecily O'Reilly.[2] Another member of the community of the Sacred Heart Convent was M. Cecilia Jordan, a musician who spent most of her time teaching piano and singing. Her duties included preparing the children to participate in operettas and plays to entertain the public during special seasons of the year, especially at Christmas, St. Patrick's Day, or whenever the pastor needed some extra money to purchase new equipment for the school or the church. Apparently, M. Cecilia was a capable and dynamic woman. She filled the office of superior of Sacred Heart Convent, St. Lawrence, for a number of years, and at her death, the correspondent to *The Evening Telegram* wrote of her: "She was an

---

1. Vincent P. Burke, "Report of the Superintendent for Roman Catholic Schools for the Year Ended December 1906," p. 16, ASMSJ.
2. See chapter twelve, p. 334.

accomplished musician and an able administrix. By her death St. Lawrence has lost a benefactor, the poor a friend, and the Convent a wise and good superior."[3]

In 1894, a few years after M. Cecilia had been appointed superior of the Sacred Heart Convent, her niece, Mary Kelly, asked to be admitted as a postulant. Born in St. John's in 1870, Mary Kelly, whose religious name was Mary Antonia, was received and professed in St. Lawrence where, except for a few years spent at St. Anne's Convent in Burin, she passed her entire religious life of almost fifty years. Because of defective eyesight, M. Antonia was forced to retire from teaching but not from active ministry, for she spent many hours in the convent parlour listening to the problems and worries of those who came to her for counsel and advice.[4]

School enrolment at St. Lawrence was small by today's standards. In 1914, the superintendent reported that seventy-four children were present on the day he visited the school, and this seemed to vary only slightly over the years.[5] This number, however, should be viewed in the context of the total population of the area for, according the 1911 census, the population of Greater St. Lawrence was 842.[6] In 1919, the sisters once again took over the boys' school with M. Annunciata Heffernan as teacher. Miss Crescentia Murray, who later became a Sister of Mercy with the religious name of Mary Edward, assisted her. At that time, the boys were taught in the parish hall. After Miss Murray left to join the Congregation of the Sisters of Mercy, M. Francis Holden was sent to replace her.[7]

3. *The Evening Telegram*, March 5, 1904, p. 4.

4. This information was provided by Mrs. Fitzpatrick, mother of Sr. Charlotte Fitzpatrick. Mrs. Fitzpatrick spoke often to her children of M. Antonia Kelly's kindness and gentleness.

5. Vincent P. Burke, "Report of the Superintendent of Education for Roman Catholic Schools, Year Ended 1914", p. xxxviii, ASMSJ.

6. Greater St. Lawrence was made up of St. Lawrence itself and a few small neighbouring settlements.

7. Crescentia Murray was born in St. Lawrence in 1901 and entered the Congregation of the Sisters of Mercy at Littledale on September 24, 1920. At her reception into the novitiate, she received the religious name of Mary Edward. After her profession in 1923, she was assigned to St. Michael's Boarding School, St. George's, where she died in 1924 at the age of twenty-three years. Her sister, Cecilia, also became a Sister of Mercy and was known as Mary Laurentia.

According to Herbert Slaney, M. Francis was an instant "hit" with the boys. Herbert was one of the lads who came under M. Francis' influence, and in his later years, he loved to recall stories of the pranks he and his companions played on the sisters. The boys' school (i.e. the parish hall) was located at the foot of a hill that in winter was covered with snow. Every morning a group of M. Francis's boys waited at the convent door to bring her down to school on a slide, lest she slip on the ice, for M. Francis was a rather large lady. Occasionally, the more mischievous among them might deliberately upset the slide and deposit poor M. Francis in the snow.[8] However, according to Mr. Slaney, she took it all in good part, but at the same time, she was not above "getting it back" on the perpetrators of her misfortune. Mr. Slaney remembered that she could throw a snowball with the best of them, and that her aim was excellent.[9]

M. Francis Holden was assigned to Sacred Heart Convent in St. Lawrence in August 1920. At that time, there were five sisters in the community with the gentle, Irish-born M. Berchmans Quinn as superior. After M. Berchmans' second three-year term of office had expired in 1922, M. Madeline Trahey succeeded her. M. Madeline, born in Conception Harbour, grew up in a prosperous, well-to-do family before she joined the Sisters of Mercy at St. Michael's Convent, Belvedere. Hence, she had little experience of living in an old, draughty building where the roof threatened to sail out over the Atlantic Ocean every time there was a northwest gale. After almost fifty years of weathering the wind and the rain, the old convent in St. Lawrence, which had been opened in 1876, was beginning to show its age. Although it had been renovated and remodelled in 1896, the main structure had deteriorated beyond repair.

In 1926, when the new superior general, M. Philippa Hanley, arrived in St. Lawrence, she was looking forward, no doubt, to spending a couple of relaxing weeks with the sisters and renewing old acquaintances in her former

---

8. These homemade slides were made of a piece of wood, three to four feet in length and a little over two feet wide, supported by a wooden runner on each side, about four inches high. They were usually painted brown and varnished.

9. Herbert Slaney, conversation with author, St. Lawrence, April 17, 2000.

mission. Instead, she received a shock that set her back on her heels—the forthright M. Madeline met her with a request for a new house! A couple of years earlier, there had been extensive renovations to both Mercy Convent and Belvedere and the consequent depletion of the congregation's limited financial resources. And now, M. Madeline was looking for nothing less than a new house! Nevertheless, M. Philippa was a reasonable woman, and she could see that the convent was in deplorable condition. Accordingly, she went back to St. John's and discussed the matter with M. Teresa O'Halleran, the treasurer general, and with other members of the General Council. All agreed that the convent had seen the best of its days and money would have to be found somewhere to replace the dilapidated old building. M. Philippa, a woman who believed in the efficacy of prayer, put aside her doubts and fears, placed her trust in Providence (and in M. Teresa O'Halleran) and informed M. Madeline that she could have her new house. Subsequently, the lovely old convent, with most of its beautiful garden of flowers and trees, gave way to a more modern residence with a two-room school attached, St. Anne's Girls' School. The boys, however, continued to attend classes in the parish hall. And so, things continued without too much change until 1929.

On the afternoon of November 18, 1929, an earthquake that would have measured 7.2 on the Richter scale occurred in the ocean, south of the Burin Peninsula. A couple of hours after the first tremors were felt, a tsunami of between sixteen and fifty feet washed ashore on the Burin Peninsula. The wave reached land at a speed of sixty-five miles per hour and created exceptionally high seas until around ten o'clock that evening. Twenty-seven people lost their lives as a result of the tsunami, and damage in excess of one million dollars was reported from the lower portion of the peninsula. A local historian, Ena Farrell Edwards, described her experience of the event:

> Around 4:30 in the afternoon the ground began to shake, build-
> ings rattled.... The tides were quite high but no particular atten-
> tion was paid to that. Then about 8 o'clock things began to hap-
> pen. The water drained completely out of the harbour and boats
> reeled over on their sides, a strange sight indeed. Then came the
> first wave, a wall of water thirty feet high. Receding, it met an

incoming wave and returned with increased violence to the land, to be followed by a third and final wave. The noise was deafening as fishing stages, flakes and stores left their foundations and were swept out through the harbour ...[10]

The same scene was witnessed in dozens of small settlements on the southern part of the peninsula. In St. Lawrence, the people sought refuge on higher ground so that church, presbytery, and convent were crowded with people, as these buildings were quite a distance from the shoreline. The sisters worked around the clock to provide comfort and shelter for those who had lost their homes. Years later, M. Scholastica Flynn who was in St. Lawrence at the time, recalled her feelings as she watched people struggling up the hill toward the convent, carrying small children or sick and elderly relatives to a place of safety. Children, frightened by the noise and confusion, were crying hysterically, while their parents were trying frantically to discover the whereabouts of missing relatives. Father Augustine Thorne, the parish priest, spent the whole night going from house to house offering encouragement and hope. Even after the waves had settled down, conditions were far from normal. And to add to the confusion, everything was in total darkness. People whose homes were still standing were afraid to return and spent the night in the church, convent, or presbytery, or with neighbours whose homes were still standing.[11]

The aftermath of the tsunami as it affected St. Lawrence was described in the St. John's newspapers:

Next morning sad beyond description was the sight which greeted the wretched people, all their fishing premises, stages, stores, boats, nets, and other gear, as well as the barns of hay, and even their cattle swept away by the pitiless sea, or strewn in fragments upon the shore. Houses, fishing stores, and wreckage of all kinds floated upon the still swollen and raging sea. In a blinding storm of wind, sleet and snow, men and boys were trying at the risk of

---

10. Edwards, *Notes*, p. 38.
11. M. Scholastica Flynn in conversation with the author many years ago. M. Scholastica was a member of Sacred Heart Convent, St. Lawrence, at the time of the tidal wave.

> their lives, to rescue some planks or sticks the only remnants of
> their little property, which represented their all and was the result
> of their lifelong labors and thrift. All the fishing premises . . . with
> the exception of two stores were destroyed, many of them filled
> with fish. All the boats and fishing gear were carried off or thrown
> in a shapeless mass of wreckage upon the shore. Added to this,
> the provisions for the winter, flour, molasses, meat etc., which
> were in their stores were also carried off, several homes were
> destroyed and the people are reduced to a very pitiable condi-
> tion. As the fishery this year was a poor one only the barest nec-
> essaries of life were procurable, and now all is lost.[12]

When morning dawned and the people of St. Lawrence saw the extent of the damage, they were shocked into inaction and despair. They were fortunate, indeed, in having as their parish priest a man who was capable of quick and practical action at times of crisis. The next evening, Father Thorne called the people together and urged them to begin immediately the work of rebuilding. He pointed out that much of the wreckage could be recovered and reused. As a result of the priest's optimism and encouragement, the men of St. Lawrence set to work to salvage what was left of their town.

Unfortunately, the destruction caused by the tsunami was not restricted to the land. It caused widespread damage to the ocean floor, and the fishery around that part of the coast was seriously affected. With the failure of the fishery—the economic basis of the region—interest was revived in deposits of fluorspar that had been discovered in St. Lawrence in the previous century.[13] In 1932, an American named W. E. Seibert visited the settlement and made plans to search for ore in the area. Six men were employed as prospectors and several veins of ore were discovered.[14] Seibert and his associates agreed to hire the local men to explore the ore body. However, there was a condition attached: ". . . provided that

---

12. *The Daily News*, November 22, 1929, p. 3.

13. Fluorspar is a non-metallic ore which, depending on the proportion components, is used in the manufacture of such things as aluminum, glass, and the refrigerant Freon. At the time of its discovery, the St. Lawrence deposit was described as the largest in North America.

14. Edwards, *Notes*, p. 58.

the miners, the people of the area, would agree to mine the ore and handpick the product to bring it up to market specifications; if and when the ore was sold the workers would be recompensed."[15] All through 1933, the men of St. Lawrence dug down deep into the earth to excavate the precious ore. Finally, when the ore was produced and sold, the miners received the wages for which they had worked all year—the paltry sum of fifteen cents an hour![16] Nevertheless, in spite of low wages, the mines provided steady employment. Subsequently, the miners formed a union and made efforts to improve working conditions and wages.

With the opening of the mines came the ever-present fear of accidents. St. Lawrence, like many outports in Newfoundland, did not have the luxury of a resident medical doctor. The nearest doctor lived in Burin, a trip that had to be made by boat since, at that time, there was no road linking the two communities. The people of St. Lawrence petitioned the government for medical assistance, a request that, according to historian Ena Farrell Edwards, was answered in an unusual way.[17]

Shortly after the St. Lawrence people had forwarded their request to government, M. Bernard Gladney was appointed superior of Sacred Heart Convent in August 1934. M. Bernard, the first administrator of St. Clare's Mercy Hospital, had fallen ill with tuberculosis a year after the hospital opened.[18] After a period of treatment in New York, she recovered, and on her return, she was appointed staff nurse, first at St. Michael's Orphanage, Belvedere, and then at St. Bride's College Boarding School at Littledale. The appointment of M. Bernard to St. Lawrence at the very time that the government was looking for a medical resident in the town was coincidental, to say the least. Farrell Edwards wrote, "She was asked to take over the medical needs of the community. She responded to the challenge instantly."[19] It is not clear if the

---

15. Ibid., p. 59. So that families would not starve, merchants of the settlement agreed to stake the men during the period of exploration.

16. Ibid., p. 60.

17. Ena Farrell Edwards, *Billy Spinney, the Umbrella Tree and Other Recollections of St. Lawrence* (St. John's, NL: Breakwater Books, 1990), pp. 48–50.

18. See chapter fourteen.

19. Edwards, *Billy Spinney*, p. 48.

request was made by the government, by the General Council of the Sisters of Mercy, or by the people of St. Lawrence. In any case, given her nursing knowledge and skill, M. Bernard felt it her clear duty to care for the sick in St. Lawrence and the surrounding areas. She had as her assistant a young sister, M. Borgia Kenny.

Shortly after her arrival in the community, M. Bernard converted a small room in the convent for use as a clinic where people with minor ailments came at specified hours for medical advice and attention. Several hours of the day were devoted to home visitation, and as there were few cars available, the sisters walked the length and breadth of St. Lawrence. Several times a week they travelled by small boat or dory to places that were inaccessible by road to care for someone who needed medical attention. Describing M. Bernard's work in St. Lawrence, Farrell Edwards wrote:

> Sister Bernard endeared herself to the people with her kind, loving ways, her closeness with them and the true humanity that flowed from her very being. There were many remarkable recoveries under her care, some of which would rival the advanced medical achievements of today. I've heard one instance many times. A baby girl was severely ill with a hopeless case of mastoids. The mastoid bone pushed its way through her skin and left her with a permanent hole behind her ear. Sister took the child to the Convent, assigned her a room, began intense treatment and kept an almost constant vigil at her bedside. With loving care and attention, little Tessie began to show signs of improvement. . . . After a period going into months ... Tessie was well enough to go home.[20]

Quite frequently, M. Bernard was called upon for help in delivering a baby. Because babies often decide to arrive in the middle of the night, this ministry was having a serious effect on the frail health of the devoted nurse. Accordingly, she decided to train a group of women in the art of midwifery. Many of these ladies had previous experience but no formal training. The training program was quite successful, and so, through M. Bernard's interest and

---

20. Ibid., p. 50.

initiative, the mothers of St. Lawrence were assured of competent care for the months and years ahead. Some maternity cases, however, posed difficulties. Farrell Edwards recalled one situation:

> I can remember when a premature baby was given up for lost by everyone except Sister Bernard. She took that baby to the Convent, set up a sick room and, with the scant means at her disposal, succeeded in saving the child. After an extended period of time he could be taken home to his parents and he grew into a healthy boy and man.[21]

Because there was no doctor, M. Bernard had to set broken bones, stitch open wounds, pull teeth, and treat all sorts of illnesses. She did this with skill and gentleness—and with astonishing success. In later years, M. Bernard's faithful assistant and companion, M. Borgia Kenny, often spoke of those days in St. Lawrence. She recalled instances of clambering down into a tossing dory in the middle of the night, M. Bernard holding the skirts of her white habit, which she always wore, and fighting the rough waves to deliver a baby or to attend someone who was sick.

M. Bernard Gladney remained in St. Lawrence for six years before being recalled to St. John's. According to the convent grapevine, the sisters in the St. Lawrence community worried about M. Bernard's neglect of her own health in her efforts to care for the sick in St. Lawrence and the nearby settlements. Furthermore, a few of the sisters were unwilling to have the convent turned into a quasi-hospital whenever M. Bernard felt that her patient needed care that could not be provided in the invalid's home. In any case, for whatever reason, M. Bernard went back to St. John's where she spent the rest of her days caring for the children at St. Michael's Orphanage, Belvedere. Summing up M. Bernard's contribution to St. Lawrence, Farrell Edwards wrote:

> She faithfully cared for the miners through all their illnesses and was always present when an accident of any kind occurred. Besides her nursing duties, Sister ran the affairs of the Convent

---

21. Ibid.

> community, finding time to participate in the cultural events of the
> community. She staged many concerts and her production of the
> Operetta, "Pearl the Fishermaiden" is still fondly recalled.
>
> Sister Bernard Gladney was indeed a shining light in this
> town during the very unstable thirties. Our present day wonder-
> ful Mother Theresa is often called the living saint of Calcutta. I
> think we can call Sister Bernard Gladney the Mother Theresa of
> St. Lawrence. Sister has gone to her eternal rest now and we think
> of her reverently.[22]

With the mines in full production, almost every man in St. Lawrence was working and people moved from all over the Burin Peninsula to find work in the town. The school population began to grow rapidly. As more classroom space became necessary, additional classrooms were added on the side of the convent. In the early 1940s, St. Augustine's School was constructed to accommodate the boys, and classes in the parish hall were discontinued. These three areas of classroom space were in use from the early 1940s until 1954. The superior of the convent was in charge of all three.

The evolution of the Roman Catholic school buildings in St. Lawrence from that time until the 1970s proceeded almost haphazardly, for in those days the local parish priest did his best with limited funds to provide adequate facilities for the education of the children in the parish. In the case of the burgeoning population of St. Lawrence, almost as soon as a new school was in use, it was found to be too small, and students were hastily assigned to whichever building was large enough to accommodate that particular age group. In September 1954, the new Marian High School was opened with an enrolment of 364 students. By the end of the first year, the number had risen to 418.[23] By that time, there were eleven teachers employed in the school, five of them Sisters of Mercy. For the next few years, the superior of the convent was principal of the Marian High School and also the unofficial supervisor of the whole educational district of St. Lawrence, including schools in Little St. Lawrence, Lawn, and Roundabout.

---

22. Ibid.
23. ASMSJ, RG 10/6/51.

For a while, matters seemed to be under control, but by September 1959, all the classrooms in the Marian High School were filled to capacity. The school board scrambled to find classroom accommodation for the hundreds of children who presented themselves to be educated. St. Augustine's Boys' School, St. Anne's Elementary, and the parish hall were used to accommodate the overflow from Marian High. Every couple of years there was a change in the classification of the school buildings. Eventually, in 1976–77, the Canadian government, through the Department of Regional Economic Expansion, put an end to all the confusion about school accommodation in St. Lawrence by building a large, modern high school called St. Lawrence High School. The new Marian High School (built in 1964) became the Marian Elementary School, and eventually, St. Augustine's was demolished.

Meanwhile, in 1969, the Mercy congregation agreed to send two sisters to Lawn, one as principal of St. Paul's Primary School and the other as a classroom teacher in Holy Name of Mary Elementary School.[24] However, the tenure of the sisters in Lawn was relatively short. In 1976, they withdrew from St. Paul's Primary, and for the next four years, two sisters taught at Holy Name of Mary Elementary until June 1980, when the congregation decided to withdraw altogether from the schools in Lawn.

From the beginning, music went hand in hand with academic subjects in all convent schools, and St. Lawrence was no exception. M. Cecilia Jordan, a gifted musician, was a novice when the sisters moved into the first convent in 1876. Through M. Cecilia's efforts, music became an integral part of the school day so that when M. Winefride Greene arrived in St. Lawrence in 1904, she found a strong musical tradition that had been flourishing there for years.[25] These two sisters, M. Cecilia and M. Winefride, were the first of a succession

24. Lawn is a settlement located on the southern part of the Burin Peninsula, a few miles from St. Lawrence. At the time the Sisters of Mercy taught in the schools, the population of the town was slightly more than one thousand. High-school students from Lawn attended Marian Central High in St. Lawrence.

25. M. Cecilia Jordan died on March 5, 1904. At the time of her death, she was superior of the Sacred Heart Convent in St. Lawrence. A short time later, M. Winefride Greene was transferred from St. Anne's Convent, Burin, and appointed to replace M. Cecilia as superior and music teacher at Sacred Heart Convent in St. Lawrence.

of musicians who worked hard to foster in the children of St. Lawrence the love of music and song that is part of the tradition of outport Newfoundland.[26]

The St. Lawrence school choir was a source of pride to the school and to the town, but never more so than on June 6, 1954. On this date, the United States government presented the communities of St. Lawrence and Lawn with a fully-equipped new Memorial Hospital. The hospital was built as an expression of gratitude to the people of these towns who risked their lives to save the crew of two American ships, the *Pollux* and *Truxton*, that ran aground on desolate cliffs near the southern part of the Burin Peninsula.[27] High-ranking officers of the United States Navy; the Honourable Joseph R. Smallwood, premier of Newfoundland; and other dignitaries were in St. Lawrence for the occasion. The convent school choir provided the music for the celebration of mass for those who had died on the night of the shipwrecks. The choir's performance of the Gregorian Chant caught the interest of the reporters from the Canadian Broadcasting Corporation and they recorded the music for broadcast over the CBC network.

The increase in the numbers of young women who were professed during the 1950s and early '60s proved to be a boon to the overworked staff in schools administered by the sisters. During the 1960s, there were eight sisters teaching in the schools at St. Lawrence, and adequate living space in the convent was only a dim, distant memory. It was clear to M. Assumpta Veitch, the superior general, that something had to be done about the situation as soon as possible. Within a short time, plans were finalized and construction of the new convent began. It took over a year to complete work on the building, but eventually everything was in place, and the sisters moved in on March 15, 1969.

---

26. Among the sisters who taught music in St. Lawrence were M. Olivera Abbott, M. Regina Carbage, Mona Carew, M. Scholastica Flynn, M. Julien Giovannini, M. Ita Hennessey, Maureen Lawlor, Marie Aiden Murphy, Anita Petrie, Madeline Reid, and M. Shawn Hannon.

27. On February 18, 1942, a convoy of two United States destroyers (the *Wilkes* and the *Truxton*) and a supply ship (the *Pollux*) were on their way to Argentia, Newfoundland. Due to extremely rough weather, the radio silence imposed by war regulations, and a miscalculation by the navigator of the *Wilkes*, the three ships were grounded. The men from Lawn and St. Lawrence risked their lives to save the American sailors. For an account, see Cassie Brown, *Standing Into Danger* (St. John's, NL: Flanker Press, 1999).

Meanwhile, the mining operation in St. Lawrence continued to provide full employment for the people of the town and nearby settlements. It was not until the 1950s that the appalling truth about the mines was discovered. In 1948, it was noticed that an unusually large number of miners had to leave work because of a mysterious illness that the people of St. Lawrence called the "Miners' Disease." In 1967, a Royal Commission investigated the fluorspar mines at St. Lawrence. It was revealed that over 150 miners had died and approximately 100 men were permanently disabled with lung cancer and silicosis contracted from conditions in the mines. "These mines, which had been seen as a godsend by the people of St. Lawrence, brought a period of economic prosperity to the town, but at an awful cost; the lives of the young men of the town."[28]

Nevertheless, work went on in the St. Lawrence mines until 1977 when the company, ALCAN, announced that operations would cease. The reasons for ALCAN's withdrawal centred on the high cost of producing ore at St. Lawrence compared with cheap labour costs in Mexico. The Newfoundland government tried unsuccessfully to negotiate agreements with ALCAN and the federal government to keep the mine open. Archbishop P. J. Skinner of St. John's wrote to the president of the company to plead with him to consider the plight of the people of St. Lawrence:

> . . . by the principles of social justice it would be regrettable for a corporation which has derived considerable economic benefit from St. Lawrence to abandon a community and its people, without doing its utmost to aid them to obtain another means of livelihood.[29]

Clearly, neither the board of directors nor the president of ALCAN was about to lose any sleep over questions of social justice. When the mines finally shut down in 1978, three hundred and fifty men were thrown out of work.[30] With the

28. Edwards, *Notes*, p. 65.
29. Archbishop P. J. Skinner to David Calver, President of ALCAN, AASJ.
30. Edwards, *Notes*, p. 68.

closure of the mines, the people returned to their traditional means of livelihood, the fishery. A fish-processing plant established in the town provided a certain amount of work, but the prosperous days of the mining operation were over.

From the time of their arrival in St. Lawrence, the Sisters of Mercy had shared in the joys and sorrows of the community. Because of the economic setback that followed the shutdown of the mining operation, many families moved away from St. Lawrence; those who stayed lived in constant fear of the failure of the fishery. It was at a time like this that the people appreciated the presence of the sisters, who continued to visit them at home and offer what little encouragement they could.

In the early 1960s, the parish priest, Father Gregory Hogan, decided to inaugurate the celebration of the Mardi Gras. It was an attempt to bring some sense of joy and celebration to a people who were living with the devastating effects of the "Miners' Disease" and dismal economic prospects for the town. Concerts, dances, and other forms of entertainment were organized to take place in the three days prior to Ash Wednesday. At first, the sisters were involved in the usual behind-the-scenes activities, such as planning and practicing for the concert, providing needlework for sale at the fair, preparing food for the community supper, and helping in many other ways. However, after 1967, changes in religious discipline as a result of the Second Vatican Council allowed the sisters to take a more prominent role in these activities. It was not long before Mardi Gras concerts included performances by the sisters. Over the years, it became unthinkable that the celebration would take place unless the sisters took a prominent and active part in all the festivities. The event attracted much attention, and people from outlying settlements came to attend the various functions—among them the sisters from Marystown, who had no intention of missing all the fun associated with the Mardi Gras. Every day after school, the Marystown sisters drove to St. Lawrence and made themselves available to help with preparations and to participate in the three-day celebrations.

Sadly, as time passed, the General Council of the Sisters of Mercy found it more and more difficult to fill the vacant places left by sisters who retired or chose to transfer to other forms of ministry. The number of sisters living in St. Lawrence decreased gradually from eight in the early 1960s to six, then to two. In June 1992, Sacred Heart Convent was closed and the two sisters, M. Lucia Walsh and Patricia Gallant, took up residence in a small house.[31] From 1992 until June 2001, there was only one sister teaching in the school at St. Lawrence. The last sister to teach in St. Lawrence was Sr. Sheila Grant, who taught there from 1996 to June 2001. At the time of writing, M. Lucia Walsh lives alone in the sisters' residence. She is pastoral assistant in the parish church of St. Thomas Aquinas, and in addition to her parish duties, she cares for the poor and visits the sick and the elderly of the community.

In nearby Burin, the events of the first half of the twentieth century brought sweeping changes. Up until 1929, Burin had enjoyed a fairly stable economy, but the tsunami that had devastated St. Lawrence and other places on the southern end of the peninsula took nine lives in the Burin area and all but destroyed the town itself and its surrounding settlements. News of the disaster did not reach St. John's for three days. The first official message to the government was sent to the Department of Justice by Magistrate Hollett of Burin:

> Burin, Nov. 21.—Burin experienced very severe earth tremors at 5:05 p.m. Monday, followed by an immense 15 foot tidal wave which swept practically everything along the waterfront from Port au Bras to Great Burin. There is scarcely a waterside premises left standing. Seven dwelling houses in Port au Bras were carried to sea with a loss of seven lives. Four houses at Kelly's Cove and Stepaside disappeared to sea in an instant with loss of two lives. None of the bodies yet recovered, there are many hair-breadth escapes and many people are suffering from shock and privation. . . . The loss of property is terrible and hundreds of people will be destitute. As yet can get no particulars from St. Lawrence to Garnish inclusive. A severe S. E. Gale and rainstorm is raging. Everything possible at present is being done. —M. Hollett.[32]

---

31. On August 28, 1992, Sacred Heart Convent was sold to Mr. Walter Loder of St. Lawrence to be used as a bed and breakfast, ASMSJ, RG 10/6/1b.
32. *The Daily News*, November 23, 1929, p. 3.

When the first large wave swept out of Burin Harbour taking with it houses, sheds, and fishing stages, the people of the town were concerned for the safety of the sisters. At the time, there were three professed sisters in the convent and one novice. Even though the convent was on higher ground than many of the surrounding homes, the men decided to remove the sisters from the convent to be on the safe side. As for the sisters, after the tremors caused by the earthquake had subsided, they resumed their regular routine and at half past seven they were at their desks correcting papers and preparing lessons for school the next day. It was about that time that the first huge wave roared into Burin Harbour. The noise of buildings being torn from their foundations and the crashing of huge rocks and boulders against the side of those buildings still standing was a terrifying experience. There was only one thing the sisters could do. They immediately went to the chapel to pray for the protection of the people of the town. A short time later, several men arrived in small boats to take them to the church, where the people had gone to take refuge from the encroaching waters. When the sisters arrived at the church, they found that their immediate task was to try and restore some calm to the terrified women and children. Fortunately, they knew all the children—and most of the adults—by name. Since there is nothing like a cup of hot tea to soothe the nerves of a Newfoundlander, the sisters set to work immediately to provide this simple remedy. They spent the rest of the night helping with the children and caring for the sick and elderly who had been forced from their homes.[33]

When dawn broke the following day, it was accompanied by a strong southeast gale with rain and sleet, making the task of salvaging what remained of the wharves and fishing stages next to impossible. However, once news of the devastation caused by the tsunami had reached the outside world, help poured in from all over Newfoundland as well as from England and the United States. Individuals and organizations banded together to send help to the stricken communities. But in spite of assistance that poured in from all sides, it took many years before the town of Burin recovered from the havoc caused by the disaster

---

33. M. Anita Reddy in conversation with the author many years ago. In addition to M. Anita, M. Annunciata Heffernan, M. St. Joan McDonnell, and a novice, M. Celine Lannon, were living in Burin at the time.

of 1929. Not only had people lost their homes and businesses, but the tsunami also had devastating ecological impacts on the fishery. For the next few years, during the early '30s, the squid, used as bait for codfish, were scarce. Coupled with this, prices for dried codfish declined during the Depression. Unlike its neighbouring town, Burin had none of the rich veins of ore discovered in St. Lawrence. Many people moved away from the area during the 1930s, seeking employment wherever they could find it. Consequently, there was a significant decrease in school enrolment. Combined with this, the unity that had existed previously between presbytery and convent was noticeably absent.[34]

As the school enrolment dropped, changes took place both in the school and in the sisters' living accommodations. Historian Frances Marshall explained, "They [the sisters] went to live in the priest's house, and school was also taught there. The old convent and our beautiful school were dismantled to build a school in Fox Cove."[35] By 1935, there were only three sisters left in St. Anne's Convent—the superior, M. Bonaventure Reddy, and her two companions, M. Carmela O'Brien and M. Ambrose Woodrow. These three bravely struggled to bring a sense of optimism and hope to the people in the midst of the poverty and hardship of the 1930s. Nor were the sisters shielded from the effects of the Depression. Like the people they served, the sisters suffered from hunger and cold. M. Ambrose Woodrow spoke occasionally of some of the difficulties that they experienced. For example, during the winter months, the convent chapel was so cold that they used to don heavy winter boots before leaving their bedrooms to attend morning prayers. There was a coal stove at the front entrance that was intended to heat the whole house but succeeded in radiating warmth only as far as the foot of the stairs, a distance of about four feet.

Nevertheless, the sisters were happy in Burin. Reciprocal commitment and respect united convent and town. M. Ambrose Woodrow loved to tell amusing anecdotes of her experiences in Burin. One of her favourite stories dealt with her encounter with a horse. One bright, frosty winter's day, the three sisters were out for a walk when they noticed a neighbour's horse, by the name

---

34. Marion Manning, conversation with author, April 18, 2000. According to Mrs. Manning, "Father did not like nuns!"

35. Marshall, *South Coast*, p. 41.

of Duchess, tethered to a fence not too far from the convent. M. Ambrose, who liked horses, went over to have a few words with Duchess but, unfortunately, slipped on an icy patch and fell, slithering right underneath the animal. Her two companions, instead of coming to her assistance, were doubled over with laughter, leaving their fallen associate to fend for herself. Duchess stood perfectly still, wondering, no doubt, what all the fuss was about, while M. Ambrose rolled around the ground trying to find a foothold on the icy slope. Within seconds a group of interested spectators—all male and under the age of ten years—had gathered. Eventually, the owner of Duchess returned and quickly rescued M. Ambrose from her uncomfortable and somewhat dangerous position. It was a fortunate circumstance that the pastor, who is reported to have disapproved of the sisters in any case, was not around to witness this spectacle.

Whatever problems the parish priest had with the convent, the three sisters did their best to support the people during this very difficult period in the history of the town. M. Carmela was determined that the interest in drama and music that had been nurtured by her predecessors would continue. Accordingly, in conjunction with her main task of teaching the high-school students, she organized concerts and plays to raise money for school and parish projects—and she did this without any encouragement from the pastor.[36]

Whether it was the pastor's lack of interest in the sisters' work or the congregation's need for sisters elsewhere, in June 1939, the General Council made the decision to close St. Anne's Convent in Burin. Writing of the Sisters of Mercy who served in Burin, historian Frances Marshall commented:

> There is still deep affection and many a silent prayer of admiration and gratitude for their imprint on Burin's past history....No wonder one of the saddest days in that history was the day the Sisters left Burin in 1939. Changing populations and greater need elsewhere probably made it necessary but that did not console the citizens, even those of other beliefs who had gown up with memories of highly respected, educated ladies.[37]

36. Manning, conversation with author, April 18, 2000.
37. Marshall, *South Coast*, p. 41.

The sisters had left Burin, but the people of the town never forgot them and continued to pray that someday they would return. Subsequently, conditions improved in Burin and other outport towns. With the outbreak of the Second World War, Newfoundland's strategic geographical position was recognized, and the island became the site of several large naval and air force bases. These bases provided work for thousands of Newfoundlanders, and the influx of American and Canadian personnel brought a level of prosperity that the country had not experienced for many years. After the war came Confederation with Canada (1949), and the face of rural Newfoundland began to change. The government's policy of resettlement saw many remote communities disappear, their inhabitants forced to move to the larger centres to avail of basic services such as health and education. During the 1950s and '60s, with the help of the federal government, the first trans-island highway was constructed, and over the next few years, almost all communities in Newfoundland had a road link to the main highway and to nearby communities.

The improved road conditions made travel to Burin from the neighbouring small settlements a matter of minutes. This fact was not lost on the newly appointed parish priest, Rev. William Lawton (1957). He felt that a central school in Burin could employ a sufficiently large teaching staff to offer the children of the area a more comprehensive education than that which was currently available. This central school would replace the numerous one-room, multi-grade schools that served the children of the smaller settlements. Consequently, he began the difficult task of centralizing the schools in the Burin area. When completed, the new school was named St. Patrick's Central School.[38] But Father Lawton had more in mind than a large central school. A graduate of the Immaculate Conception Academy on Bell Island, he appreciated the education he had received at the hands of the Sisters of Mercy, and he wanted no less for his young parishioners. In the early 1960s, he paid a visit to the superior general, M. Assumpta Veitch, and begged her to send a few sisters to staff the school in Burin.

---

38. Hogan, *Pathways*, p. 149.

The request did not come as a surprise to M. Assumpta and the members of the General Council. The fact that the sisters had been withdrawn from this, the first foundation outside the Avalon Peninsula, had left a lingering sense of regret—and even of guilt—that was felt by many in the congregation. The bonds of loyalty and friendship between the people of Burin and the Congregation of the Sisters of Mercy had endured all through the years when the sisters were absent. The link with Burin was strengthened by the fact that six women from Burin had become members of the congregation.[39] With all of this in mind, M. Assumpta assured Father Lawton that his request would be given serious consideration. And with that he had to be satisfied. This vague promise, however, did not suit Father Lawton's successor.

When Father Lawton was assigned to another parish in 1964, Father John Wallis was appointed pastor of Burin and immediately established as his first priority the completion of St. Patrick's School and the return of the sisters. He was told that the Mercy congregation was not in a financial position to build a convent in Burin.[40] Thus, if the parish wanted the sisters, it would have to provide a place for them to live. Unfortunately, the expense involved in the construction of the new St. Patrick's School had exhausted the resources of the parish. With no money available to build a convent, it seemed very unlikely the people of Burin would see the sisters return in the foreseeable future.

However, the new parish priest was not only a zealous pastor, but also he had a very persuasive manner and the ability to couch impractical proposals in such a way that they sounded completely reasonable. Father Wallis assured M. Assumpta that he understood her position perfectly, but he really needed the sisters "NOW." He reminded her that the new Holy Name of Mary Convent in Marystown, opened in 1963, boasted eight bedrooms—more than enough to accommodate the number of sisters in Marystown. He pointed out

39. The six were: M. Stanislaus Parsons, M. Imelda Smith, M. Rita Coady, M. Paula Penney, M. Ricarda Kavanagh, and Marcella Grant.

40. At this time the congregation was struggling to pay the costs associated with the building of Holy Heart of Mary Regional High School, St. Catherine's Convent/McAuley Hall, establishing the mission in Peru, and building a convent in Monsefú.

that under these circumstances there would be no need for the congregation to build a new convent in Burin, because sisters could commute quite easily from Marystown over the new high road—a drive that would take no more than fifteen or twenty minutes. M. Assumpta was won over to his cause and promptly appointed three sisters to Holy Name of Mary Convent, Marystown, with teaching duties at St. Patrick's School in Burin.

Accordingly, in August 1966, Sr. Anita Best was appointed the first sister-principal of the new St. Patrick's Elementary School.[41] On September 17, 1966, the sisters were officially welcomed back to Burin by Archbishop P. J. Skinner in a ceremony held in the parish church in Burin. It was a red-letter day for the people of Burin, who were overjoyed to have the sisters back with them again.[42] The blessing of the new St. Patrick's School that took place two days later on September 19 was a moving experience for the Sisters of Mercy, for it was built on a section of the meadow where the first convent school in Burin was located in 1863.[43]

The arrangement of having sisters commute to Burin from Marystown continued for four years while Father Wallis, who from the beginning had every intention of having the sisters return to live in Burin, bided his time. In 1968, the Roman Catholic School Board decided to build a two-apartment house for teachers. Father Wallis immediately seized the opportunity to rent this house. Two days later, he drove to St. John's and informed M. Assumpta that her objections to having the sisters live in Burin had been eliminated. Consequently, in September 1970, four sisters moved into the house that was now designated, not as a convent, but as a "Sisters' Residence." M. Josephine Ryan was named superior of the group. She was also the first sister to teach in the Father Berney Memorial High School. Father Wallis was delighted with his little community of Mercy Sisters and could not resist bragging about his success in having them return to Burin. On one of these occasions, M. Assumpta was present. Turning to Father Wallis, she reminded him, "Well, you started by

41. The other two sisters on the staff were Rita Fitzgerald and Doris Walsh.
42. Marshall, *South Coast*, p. 54.
43. Hogan, *Pathways*, p. 150.

asking for three; I wanted it reduced to two. You kept at it until you got four, and now I hope you're satisfied!" To this, Father Wallis replied, "Ah, yes! But there are five bedrooms in the house!"[44]

Sadly, the sisters were not destined to remain very long in their new residence in Burin. During the 1970s, many religious congregations experienced a veritable exodus of professed members, and the Sisters of Mercy of Newfoundland were no exception. Because of diminishing personnel during these difficult years, the new superior general, Sr. Marie Michael Power, was obliged to close the residence in Burin. The last three sisters to live in Burin were Srs. Madonna Gatherall, the last sister to teach in Father Berney Memorial High School; M. Uriel O'Driscoll; and Sr. Barbara Kenny. Both Sr. Barbara and M. Uriel taught in St. Patrick's Elementary. But although they no longer lived in the town, two sisters continued to teach in the elementary school, commuting from Holy Name of Mary Convent in Marystown. For another ten years, they taught in St. Patrick's School, but eventually the teaching ministry of the Sisters of Mercy in Burin came to an end. The last sister to teach in the town was Sr. Sylvia Doyle, who taught there from 1983–91.

During the first sixty years after the sisters arrived on the Burin Peninsula, illnesses were treated at home. The sisters were no exception. When a sister became ill, the local community looked after her and nursed her back to health. But in some cases, recovery was not possible. The sisters mourned the death of one of their own and buried her in the local cemetery among the people to whom she had ministered. In the Roman Catholic cemetery in Burin stand six identical headstones engraved with the Mercy cross—silent reminders of more than one hundred years of Mercy ministry to the people of that town.[45]

The convent of the Holy Name of Mary, the third foundation of the Sisters of Mercy on the Burin Peninsula, continues its ministry of Mercy in the

44. Ibid., p. 151.
45. The six Sisters of Mercy buried in Burin are M. Francis Born (1884), Mary of the Cross Reardon (1885), M. Madeline Stephenson (1886), M. Agnes Walsh (1902), M. Rose Murphy (1904), and M. Joseph Rawlins (1918).

Burin/Marystown region. By the 1980s, Marystown had firmly established itself as the business centre of the Burin Peninsula. It had the largest population of any town on the peninsula, and in spite of periodic tribulations and uncertainties experienced by the shipyard, there were other opportunities for employment in the town, particularly in the fish plant. In 1981, the new Sacred Heart Elementary School was opened in the vicinity of the Central High School, but by this time, the number of sisters teaching in the school had been reduced to four. By 1989, only two sisters, Ruth Beresford and Dolorosa Brennan, remained on the teaching staff. Finally, at the end of the school year 1990, the Sisters of Mercy relinquished the administration of Sacred Heart Elementary School. However, two sisters continued to teach in the school until 1999, when the last sister to teach in Marystown, Sr. Rona O'Gorman, retired from teaching.[46]

The winding-down of the sisters' teaching ministry in the schools signalled the beginning of a diversity of Mercy ministries in Marystown. In 1991, Sr. Colette Nagle was appointed coordinator of pastoral care services in the Roman Catholic parishes on the Burin Peninsula, with emphasis on regular hospital visitation at the Burin Peninsula Health Care Centre. Sr. Colette filled this position until 1999, when she was appointed director of pastoral care at St. Patrick's Mercy Home in St. John's. After Sr. Colette's departure, another Sister of Mercy, Sr. Theresa March, was appointed to carry on the visitation of the Burin Health Care Centre. The sisters of Holy Name of Mary Convent provide a variety of services that were not possible when they were responsible for the schools. In 1993, Sr. Mary Manning, who had spent most of her life as a nurse at St. Clare's Mercy Hospital, was assigned to Marystown, where she was responsible for pastoral care in the parish. Sr. Mary spent three years initiating a home visitation program that continued after she was recalled to St. Clare's Mercy Hospital. Adult religious education programs, directed by Sr. Margaret Pittman, are offered at the convent, and Sr. Edward Mary Roche, a religious education specialist, spent a year in Marystown developing sacra-

---

46. By a strange coincidence, Sr. Rona O'Gorman was also the last sister to teach at Sacred Heart School in Curling. In 1993, the Sisters relinquished all positions in that school.

mental preparation programs to be used in the parish. In the midst of all the changes and the letting go of old, familiar ways, the one enduring ministry of the Sisters of Mercy is the visitation of the sick and the care of the poor. This ministry continues in Marystown and, in fact, wherever a Sister of Mercy is to be found.

The sisters' work in educating the young people of Marystown had succeeded beyond their dreams. Many years after the convent had been established, M. Camillus Dunphy, one of the founding sisters, paid a visit to Marystown. She was invited to the school and discovered that almost all the teachers were her former students. In the midst of this joyous reunion, M. Camillus was told, over and over again, that her example was the inspiration that had prompted the decision to choose teaching as a career. Recalling the occasion, she remarked, "Isn't this what it's all about? We teach the few so that they can take up the torch and reach out to the thousands."[47]

---

47. M. Camillus Dunphy, conversation with author, November 27, 1999.

CHAPTER SEVENTEEN

NOT TO FALTER.
NOT TO BE FOUND WANTING.

They turn round and round by God's guidance,
To accomplish all that he commands them.
Job 37:12

fter the establishment of two new convents in 1927, there were no new foundations for almost twenty years.[1] However, in 1931, the congregation agreed to establish a convent and school in Cape Broyle, a settlement about thirty miles south of St. John's on the east coast of the Avalon Peninsula in the region known as the Southern Shore. By August 1931, all the arrangements had been completed, and M. Gabriel Fleming was named superior of the community. M. Jerome Walker was assigned to accompany M. Gabriel, but the names of the other member—or members—of the community are unknown.[2] Until three years ago, not much was known of this proposed foundation, but in March 2000, Edward Halleran provided copies of letters written by his great-aunt, M. Teresa

---

1. The Immaculate Conception Convent on Bell Island and Holy Name of Mary Convent in Marystown were established in 1927.

2. M. Gabriel Fleming supplied this information in conversation with the author many years ago.

O'Halleran, to her niece, Peggy Halleran. One of these letters confirms the fact that such a foundation was in the building stages. In the following letter, M. Teresa mentions a visit to the site of a new convent and school. Her references to Lady Anna Cashin, whose home was in Cape Broyle, identified this town as the site of the new foundation. Furthermore, Cape Broyle is about thirty miles south of St. John's, the distance mentioned in M. Teresa's letter:

> We had another picnic 30 miles in the country—a gentleman's house which our Reverend Mother General purchased this summer for a Convent and School. It is an ideal spot. 16 rooms furnished ready for a Convent, beautiful grounds. 24 Sisters went off in motors. I could not refuse. The day was beautiful—dinner and lunch were all that could be desired. Lady Cashin whose home it was, joined us in the afternoon and is delighted that her grand house is to be converted into a convent.[3]

Further confirmation was found in the minutes of a meeting of the General Council of the Sisters of Mercy: "House (Cashin Residence) purchased. $7,000 at rate of 5% for loan."[4] For some unknown reason, the plan was never implemented. According to the minutes of the council meeting of October, "Some difficulties have arisen. The foundation could not be accepted. (Someone had blundered)."[5] The secretary general at the time was M. Genevieve Farrell, who did not reveal the identity of the person who had blundered! Subsequently, the whole episode was forgotten—except by M. Gabriel who was bitterly disappointed at the abandonment of the project. A further note in the minutes explained that this foundation was to be a rest house and a summer residence for sisters who needed it. The question remains, what happened that the plans did not materialize? Who blundered? It is unlikely that the General Council of the Sisters of Mercy, having pur-

---

3. M. Teresa O'Halleran to Peggy Halleran, September 12, 1931. I am indebted to Rev. John Halleran and his brother, Mr. Edward Halleran, for copies of M. Teresa's letters to her niece, Peggy Halleran. These letters cover the period from 1914–1934.

4. Minutes, General Council of the Sisters of Mercy, August 13, 1931, ASMSJ.

5. Ibid., October 24, 1931, ASMSJ.

chased a house and grounds and assigned sisters to the new convent, had a change of heart. According to M. Gabriel Fleming, Archbishop Roche withdrew his consent for the foundation to proceed, and in such matters, the archbishop's word was law.

After the plans for Cape Broyle were dropped, the superior general, M. Philippa Hanley, and her successors, M. Bridget O'Connor and M. Stanislaus Parsons, and their councillors seem to have developed cold feet when presented with requests for foundations. It was another twelve years before the administration was ready to consider establishing a new convent, this time in the northwest section of St. John's known as Mundy Pond.

Mundy Pond itself is a small pond that lends its name to the surrounding residential area.[6] In the early years of the nineteenth century, many of the wealthier residents of downtown St. John's built summer homes around the shores of Mundy Pond. Also, there were a few permanent residents who owned large tracts of farmland in the vicinity. In 1882, the establishment of the Colonial Cordage Company near Mundy Pond signalled a period of rapid industrial growth. The company, known locally as the "Ropewalk," attracted an influx of workers from various parts of Newfoundland, notably from Placentia Bay.[7] Thus, the character of the district changed to that of a working-class neighbourhood.

By 1923, Mundy Pond had become a mission of St. Patrick's Parish. That same year, 1923, a young man by the name of Harold Summers was ordained to the priesthood and appointed assistant priest at St. Patrick's. The parish priest of the time, Monsignor William Kitchin, made his new curate responsible for the Mundy Pond mission. The mission chapel was located in a small

---

6. In Newfoundland, an inland body of water is often called a pond, even when it is of considerable size. For instance, Twenty-Mile Pond, so called because of approximate length of its circumference, was renamed Windsor Lake in 1812. However, local people still call it by its original name. It is one of the main sources of the St. John's water supply.

7. *Historical Highlights of St. Teresa's Parish (1930–1980)* (St. John's, NL: St. Teresa's Parish, n.d.), p. 10. As a reminder of the days of the Cordage Company, one of the busy streets in the area is known as Ropewalk Lane.

building that served also as a school and hall.[8] In 1928, Father Summers took a census of the Roman Catholic population of Mundy Pond and reported to the archbishop that the mission served approximately 750 persons.[9] In light of this, Archbishop Roche decided to establish St. Teresa's Parish for the convenience of the residents of the three areas that had comprised the mission, and on July 14, 1930, he appointed the popular curate, Father Harold Summers, as its first parish priest.[10]

The new parish grew by leaps and bounds under the wise and capable leadership of the dynamic young pastor. Within a relatively short time, there was a cluster of parish buildings consisting of the church, presbytery, and schools located on a parcel of land near the north shore of the pond. In the pastor's mind there was only one thing missing—a convent. Father Summers was not one to let any grass grow under his feet. A few years after the new parish church was finished (1938) and extensions made to the schools, he approached Archbishop Roche and M. Stanislaus Parsons, the superior general of the Sisters of Mercy, and requested a community of sisters to staff the schools of St. Teresa's Parish. This time nobody blundered! The archbishop approved the request and gave permission for a convent to be established at Mundy Pond. The land on which the convent was to be erected had been donated by Vincent Summers, the pastor's brother.[11] The first sod for the new St. Teresa's Convent was turned on May 9, 1944. Four months later, on September 12, the sisters took over the management of the schools.

When the Sisters of Mercy assumed the administration of St. Teresa's Schools in 1944, they taught in two separate buildings, one near the convent

8. Monsignor Harold A. Summers, "Jottings from a Now Hazy Memory," an account of the early days of St. Teresa's Parish written at the request of Maura Mason, RSM, for the golden jubilee of St. Teresa's Parish, 1980. The multi-purpose building was located at the eastern end of the pond near the junction of Campbell Avenue and Pearce Avenue.

9. Ibid.

10. The three areas that comprised St. Teresa's Parish were Mundy Pond, Freshwater Road, and Thorburn Road.

11. Annals, St. Teresa's Convent, St. John's, 1944–1964, p. 1, ASMSJ. The Summers family was connected by marriage to the Sisters of Mercy, Vincent Summers having married Mary Catherine Veitch who had two sisters in the Congregation of the Sisters of Mercy, M. Assumpta and M. Celine Veitch.

and the other, called "the old school," a short distance away.[12] From the beginning, St. Teresa's schools were coeducational, and at the time of the sisters' arrival, there were 294 children attending classes from grades I to XI. At the end of the school year in June 1945, the number of pupils had increased to 437. In addition to the five sisters, there were four lay teachers, Anna Madden, Regina Reddy, Mary Kelly, and Rose Roche.

The members of the first community of St. Teresa's Convent were M. Benignus Mullowney (superior), Margaret Mary Collins, M. Anthony Wade, M. Constance Travers, and M. Clarissa Reddy. Because construction of the convent at Mundy Pond was still in progress, the sisters stayed at St. Clare's Convent and commuted back and forth to school. For some strange reason, or possibly because M. Benignus placed great value on a substantial repast at noon as a means of sustaining the sisters' health, they did not take a lunch to school but returned to St. Clare's every day for the midday meal. It must have been a hurried luncheon, for the noon break lasted one hour, and the fact that none of the five complained of indigestion ranks as a minor miracle.

By Christmas 1944, the new St. Teresa's Convent was almost ready for occupancy, and elaborate plans were being made to celebrate the formal opening, scheduled to take place on the Feast of Our Lady of Lourdes, February 11, 1945. The sisters moved into the convent on February 7, with just three days to put the finishing touches on an already immaculately clean and furnished residence. As soon as they had settled in and unpacked their few belongings, M. Benignus sent them scurrying around to inspect every inch of the place to make sure that there was not one single grain of sawdust left behind by some careless carpenter. A cook was hired with orders to bake enough cookies to feed all those invited to attend the reception that was to follow the blessing of the convent. A list of the starving masses expected to attend included the superior general, M. Stanislaus Parsons, and her council, a number of sisters from nearby convents, the archbishop, and the priests of the city.

---

12. This building was destroyed by fire in 1967. Sr. Theresa Boland was the last Sister of Mercy to teach in the old school.

When M. Benignus arose from her slumbers at six o'clock in the morning on February 11, the sight that met her eyes must have sent her heart plummeting to her bedroom slippers. As far as she could see, which was not very far, the world was covered with snow. Mighty gusts of wind caused the snow to swirl around, creating huge drifts that blocked the convent lane. Plans for the blessing and formal opening of the convent had to be postponed. Since it was unthinkable that such an event should take place on any other than a very significant anniversary, the affair was rescheduled for Archbishop Roche's birthday, February 19. It was, therefore, a holiday in all the Catholic schools of the archdiocese, which left the sisters free to entertain the guests.[13]

Fortunately, on Monday, February 19, the weather co-operated, and the archbishop and his entourage arrived safely to celebrate the first mass in St. Teresa's Convent Chapel. Many of the visiting sisters remained for the day; in fact, the annalist reported eighteen sisters stayed for dinner and fifty-five for supper.[14] To accommodate parishioners who were anxious to visit and tour the new convent, a general invitation to an "open house" was issued for the afternoon. Consequently, there was a steady parade of visitors, all of whom were delighted with the fine new convent their pastor had prepared for the sisters.[15] Two weeks later, the sisters at St. Teresa's received a visit from Lady Walwyn, wife of the governor of Newfoundland. Other distinguished guests included the superior general and councillors of the Presentation Sisters and the apostolic delegate to Canada. Much to the delight of children and teachers, the delegate declared a school holiday on the day after his visit.

M. Benignus was an excellent principal and administrator. Within a year of her arrival in the parish, some important initiatives had been realized. Although her priority was the spiritual and intellectual development of the children, her interest and concern were not confined to the school, but

---

13. It should be noted that the formal opening of St. Edward's Convent, Bell Island, took place on October 13, the feast of St. Edward who was Archbishop Roche's patron saint. See chapter twelve.

14. This must have required several sittings, for the dining room at St. Teresa's is not very large.

15. The Congregation of the Sisters of Mercy repaid the cost of building and furnishing St. Teresa's Convent. See Summers, "Jottings," p. 5.

embraced the whole parish, and nothing escaped her attention. Convinced that important occasions should be given appropriate recognition, M. Benignus turned her attention to M. Clarissa Reddy's First Communion class. M. Benignus arranged that, for the first time in the history of the parish, a Communion breakfast would be served to the seventy-eight children and their families. In October of the same year, 1945, three hundred and thirty-one young men and women received the sacrament of confirmation.

The ministry of the sisters of St. Teresa's Convent was not confined to the school. The visitation of the poor and the sick occupied much of their free time. As the months passed, the people grew to know the sisters, and many came to the convent for advice and help in times of trouble and distress. On one occasion, the trust and confidence placed in the sisters landed poor M. Clarissa in trouble with her kind but exacting superior. M. Clarissa taught the primary classes in the old school, which was almost ten minutes' walk from the convent. Her classroom was always a joy to behold, for she spared no trouble in decorating it with brightly coloured pictures of animals, flowers, vegetables, and all sorts of objects designed to stimulate the imagination of the children. All of this required a lot of after-school effort, and as a result, M. Clarissa was always the last to leave the building. As a rule, one of the other sisters waited to accompany her back to the convent for, in those days, sisters were not permitted to walk alone on the public street. On one occasion, by some oversight, M. Clarissa discovered that she was left alone in the school. She locked the doors and was walking toward the convent when a gentleman caught up with her. The poor man was in deep distress because of the recent death of his wife. M. Clarissa listened to his story and offered words of consolation and hope as they walked slowly, heads together, side by side along Mundy Pond Road. M. Benignus chose this moment to look out the convent window and was shocked to the depths of her being. Not only was M. Clarissa violating the Rule by walking the street without a sister-companion, but also she was accompanied by a member of the opposite sex with whom she appeared to be having a heart-to-heart conversation. When at last M. Clarissa arrived in the convent—adding to her offences by being late for the four o'clock recreation period—M. Benignus called on her to give an account of her actions. The scandalized superior, in ringing tones, laid the list of M. Clarissa's misdemeanours before her. When, finally, M. Benignus stopped for breath, M. Clarissa made no excuses but told her of the gentleman's loss. M. Benignus, a woman who hid a tender heart behind a brusque, business-like manner, was full of sympathy for the poor husband. She hurried off to the kitchen with instructions for the cook and arranged for M. Clarissa—accompanied this time by another sister—to bring a hot meal to the bereaved household. M. Benignus held the theory that even the most grevious sorrow could be alleviated somewhat by the consumption of a good, hot dinner.

Long before the sisters' arrival, school concerts were held at Mundy Pond, at least occasionally. In the 1920s, a young lady named Nellie Veitch, a teacher in the Mundy Pond School, organized concerts that included dancing, singing, and acting.[16] For her part, M. Benignus was firmly convinced that there was no better way to teach the children how to conduct themselves in public than to have them participate in a concert. Although there was no music teacher assigned to St. Teresa's School during the year 1944–45, M. Benignus had her heart set on having a concert. She reviewed the qualifications of her staff and decided that the most likely candidate to fill the post of director of music was M. Anthony Wade, who had an excellent singing voice. Furthermore, having been educated by the Sisters of Mercy in Conception Harbour, M. Anthony could be presumed to have some knowledge of music. Consequently, M. Benignus called a meeting of the staff and announced her decision. All the children in the school would have a role to play, and the teachers were encouraged to put their heads together to come up with suggestions for the program. As far as the music was concerned, M. Benignus declared that M. Anthony could take care of that by teaching the children a few songs and dances. This announcement was the first that M. Anthony had heard of her new role. But whatever misgivings she may have felt mattered very little. M. Benignus operated on the principle, "It must be done!" Lacking an auditorium and a stage, the sisters improvised by placing the wooden desks in the shape of

---

16. Subsequently, Nellie Veitch became a Sister of Mercy and given the name, Mary Assumpta. In 1961, M. Assumpta was elected superior general of the congregation, a position she held for twelve years.

a platform and then nailed them together to make a stage. After a couple of months' rehearsal, everything was ready. Two sets of folding doors in the largest room were opened to provide space for the audience. On the appointed evening, the parents—or as many as could fit into the limited space—paid the ten-cent admission fee and took their places. The concert was a huge success in spite of the difficulties involved in its preparation and presentation. One item was a rather intricate march that required twenty-four performers, only twelve of whom could fit on the "stage." The problem was solved by closing the curtain in the middle of the march routine. While M. Constance hustled the first group off the platform, M. Clarissa was busy lining up the second. Meanwhile, M. Anthony continued to pound out the music of the march on a "rattle-trap" piano located in the front of the room. The marchers wore black trousers and white shirts, with red capes and red pillbox caps, the latter two items made by the capable hands of Sr. Margaret Mary Collins. When the performance had concluded, the boys marched off the stage and into the dressing room (a neighbouring classroom) where M. Benignus was waiting. Swiftly, caps and capes were collected, and the twenty-four erstwhile soldiers received their final marching orders, "Children, follow me." Keeping strictly to the tempo and rhythm of the music, M. Benignus marched them to the front door of the school, opened the door wide and ushered them out with the caution, "Now dearies, run home as fast as you can, but be on time for school tomorrow." The same fate awaited members of the speech classes and solo performers, for there was no room in the audience for children. Only M. Anthony's choirs were permitted to stay until the end, for one of their duties was to close the concert with the singing of the "Ode to Newfoundland" and "God Save the King."[17] Subsequently, the congratulations heaped on the young performers and their teachers attested to M. Anthony's ability as a teacher of singing and

---

17. M. Clarissa Reddy, "St. Teresa's School, Mundy Pond: Recollections of My Years at the Old School on Mundy Pond Road, September 1944–December 1965," ASMSJ, RG 10/16/13. For the account of M. Anthony Wade's singing class, I am indebted to Srs. Geraldine and Maura Mason, both of whom were members of the class. Subsequently, the two sisters entered the Congregation of the Sisters of Mercy in St. John's.

dancing. However, these activities were in addition to her duties as a classroom teacher.

Why St. Teresa's had not been supplied with a full-time music teacher was a mystery, but an omission that M. Benignus was determined to rectify before the next year's assignments were posted. As she surveyed the list of second year novices who were to be professed in July 1945, she noticed the names of two musicians, M. Ita Hennessey and M. Regina Carbage. After making an appointment to see the superior general on a matter of urgent business, M. Benignus hired a taxi and headed for Mercy Convent. She did not leave until she had extracted a promise from M. Stanislaus Parsons, that in September, one of the two newly professed musicians would be assigned to St. Teresa's. As a result of this visit, M. Regina Carbage had the distinction of being the first music teacher on the staff of St. Teresa's School, where she remained for the next six years. So persuasive was M. Benignus that, in addition to M. Regina, she was successful in securing two experienced classroom teachers, M. Loyola Power and M. Uriel O'Driscoll, from the group of the newly professed. There were now six sisters on the school staff.[18]

In the next few years after the arrival of the sisters, the population of Mundy Pond continued to mushroom. This resulted in some serious overcrowding in the schools. Writing her recollections of this period, M. Clarissa Reddy noted:

> One year I had 100 Grade I's in a small classroom. I had four in each double desk. One day I looked down and one little boy was doing his work with his scribbler leaning on another boy's back. . . . When it was time for copy books, I had to put one group out to recess in the yard while the other group did their copy. When they were finished, the groups changed places. Sometime in the spring . . . Sr. M. Loyola . . . would take out 45 pupils who would stand on the corridor while she taught them.[19]

---

18. M. Loyola Power replaced Margaret Mary Collins. M. Uriel O'Driscoll was sent as an extra teacher to relieve the overcrowding that was beginning to occur.
19. Reddy, "Recollections," p. 2, ASMSJ.

Although the fiscally prudent Father Summers was reluctant to incur the expense of building another school, by the year 1948, it was clear that he could no longer defer the decision. Construction was begun in August 1948, and the new extension was opened in September of the following year. During the same period, extensive renovations were made to the older section of the school. The number of pupils enrolled that year was 618. By this time there were nine professed sisters and three postulants living in St. Teresa's Convent, a state of affairs that required some "doubling-up" on the part of the junior sisters, for the convent had not been built to accommodate twelve.

The year 1950 witnessed the first major change at St. Teresa's. M. Benignus completed her second three-year term of office and was replaced by M. Hildegarde Dunphy. Only M. Clarissa Reddy remained of the original community. The year 1952 was a momentous year for the whole parish of St. Teresa's, for it was in June of that year that their pastor and friend, Father Harold Summers, was appointed administrator of the Cathedral Parish and raised to the rank of monsignor. Recalling this transfer, Monsignor Summers wrote, "I left not too happily for I had spent twenty-two happy years in St. Teresa's amongst a kindly, generous and co-operative people."[20]

The election of the forward-thinking M. Imelda Smith as superior general of the Sisters of Mercy in 1949 signalled the beginning of the end of a "fortress mentality" that characterized most religious congregations of women, including the Sisters of Mercy. Consequently, in 1953, word passed quietly from M. Imelda to the local superiors that teaching sisters should attend meetings of the Newfoundland Teachers' Association (NTA). But although they attended, they were not permitted to speak at the meetings or hold an executive position. Even at the time, sister-teachers objected strongly to these restrictions, which were withdrawn a few years later. However, the annalist at St. Teresa's Convent was perceptive enough to appreciate the significance of this initiative. She was careful to note the date on which the sisters joined their professional colleagues at a public meeting

---

20. Summers, "Jottings," p. 6. Rev. Randall Greene replaced Monsignor Summers as pastor of St. Teresa's Parish.

when she wrote, "On October 12 (1953) the Sisters attended their first NTA meeting."[21]

As St. Teresa's School expanded, so too did the range of extracurricular activities offered to the students. In the area of sports, the boys showed a special aptitude for football and hockey. Every winter since people settled in the area, boys had played hockey on Mundy Pond. In 1954, the first hockey team was formed in St. Teresa's School, and on January 13, 1955, it made its debut by playing Curtis Academy. After the teams battled through three periods, the score remained tied at three goals each. A year later, St. Teresa's team had improved to the degree that the boys held off the mighty St. Pat's team through two overtime periods, the game ending finally in a tie.[22]

Meanwhile in May 1953, work began on an extension to the school that, when completed in 1955, would provide eight new classrooms, an auditorium, and gymnasium. At the same time, three new bedrooms were added to the convent, providing accommodations for twelve sisters. When classes began in September 1955, there were 1,006 pupils enrolled—an increase of over 600 children in the ten years since the arrival of the sisters. St. Teresa's School was now one of the prominent participants, not only in the sports arena, but also in cultural activities of the city. For instance, ten groups of children under the direction of Sr. Anita Petrie participated successfully in the Kiwanis Music Festival of April 1956. Then, two months later in June, more than sixty students from St. Teresa's wrote the high-school public examinations. When the results were released later in the summer, three pupils from St. Teresa's won scholarships, including an Electoral Scholarship. It was during the same year (1956) that the priests of the Redemptorist Order took over the administration of St. Teresa's Parish.

The year 1958 saw another major change in St. Teresa's School. Regional high schools were just coming into vogue in Newfoundland. Educational authorities decided that by bringing all high-school students together on one site, the school boards would be able to provide a better education at less cost.

21. Annals, St. Teresa's Convent, St. John's, p. 27, ASMSJ.
22. Ibid., p.32. ASMSJ.

The Roman Catholic board for St. John's proposed to build at least two regional high schools in the city, one for girls and the other for boys. However, the
cost of building schools large enough to accommodate all the Roman Catholic
high-school students of the city was a major hurdle. The problem was solved
when the Presentation and Mercy congregations agreed to pool their financial
resources and build a regional high school for girls. In due course, when Holy
Heart of Mary Regional High School for Girls opened on November 20, 1958,
girls who were enrolled in various Roman Catholic high schools in St. John's
moved to Holy Heart. Forty-four of them were from St. Teresa's.[23]

For the next few years, the boys of the area continued to attend St.
Teresa's up to and including grade XI, but the loss of the high-school girls was
a traumatic experience for the teachers and pupils who were left behind.
Previously, the girls in grade VIII had been treated with condescending tolerance by their elders in grades IX and X and totally ignored by the elite in grade
XI. Now, suddenly, they were the senior girls in the school hierarchy and
enjoyed the same lofty status as the former occupants of the grade XI classroom. Teachers, too, found it strange to be surrounded by girls all under the
age of fourteen years. When special school celebrations were planned, teachers missed the participation and help of the more mature students. This was
true in all the schools affected by the opening of Holy Heart.

Nevertheless, a concerted effort was made to maintain and strengthen
school spirit. The annual Kiwanis Music Festival was an opportunity to measure talent and skill against students from other schools. The pupils of St.
Teresa's and the new music teacher, M. Genevieve Drake, were determined
that the absence of the senior classes would not lower the standard of their
school's record of achievement. Much to the delight of the entire student
body and staff, the grade VI choral group was awarded first place in the classroom choir competition, and several other groups from St. Teresa's placed

---

23. In 1960, the boys from grades X and XI left St. Teresa's and went to St. Patrick's Hall
School operated by the Christian Brothers. In 1962, Brother Rice High School and
Gonzaga High School were opened to accommodate high-school boys of the city. Brother
Rice was under the direction of the Christian Brothers, and Gonzaga was administered by
the Jesuits.

second and third in their respective classes. By the time school closed in June, the former high-school graduation celebrations were all but forgotten in the excitement of farewell celebrations for members of the grade VIII class who would be attending Holy Heart in September. The twelve sisters were busy at home, too, for the convent had to be cleaned from attic to basement before they departed for the summer—some to attend the annual retreat at Littledale and the majority to study at a university, either in St. John's or on the mainland.

The practice of sending about ninety percent of the Mercy congregation to summer school began in the 1950s. Prior to this (1916–1952), summer began with a ten-day retreat, offered at Littledale, which all the sisters were expected to attend. This retreat was held during the time immediately preceding the ceremonies of reception and profession, celebrated annually on July 16. During the six weeks following July 16, each sister was sent on a two-week vacation to another convent in Newfoundland. Although no sister had a choice as to where and with whom she spent her vacation, it was taken for granted that she would be assigned to a convent located near her family home so that her parents and relatives could visit her.[24] For the rest of the summer there were no scheduled activities—except for the musicians of the congregation, who were expected to spend several hours a day teaching other sisters or perfecting their own technique on various musical instruments.

With the election of M. Imelda Smith as superior general in 1949, all this changed. M. Imelda was a far-sighted, intuitive woman who, in the words of Pope John XXIII, read the "signs of the times." It is true that, before being assigned to a school, every teaching sister had obtained a teaching certificate at St. Bride's College or Memorial University. When the financial resources of the congregation permitted, sisters who evidenced exceptional ability were given the opportunity for further education at colleges and universities

---

24. Regulations governing visitors were relaxed during this two-week vacation to allow a sister more frequent contact with her parents and family members. During the year, social visits were permitted once a month. In the case of illness, a sister was encouraged to visit a family member as often as necessary.

in other countries.[25] On their return home, these sisters were expected to share their knowledge and expertise with others in the congregation. Moreover, for a few years the Sisters of Charity from Mount St. Vincent College, Halifax, conducted summer schools for the sisters in Newfoundland, but the serious pursuit of a graduate university degree was the exception rather than the rule.

M. Imelda, however, saw that it was not enough that her sisters should be certified as teachers and continue informal studies under the guidance of other sisters who had earned degrees. She understood that they needed the challenge of meeting university standards and the experience of exchanging ideas with other young women and men who held widely varying and divergent points of view. Another, and by no means insignificant, consideration was that sisters should earn the academic credits that M. Imelda foresaw would be required by the Department of Education in the very near future.

Early in her first term of office, M. Imelda determined that the long, easy days of summer were a thing of the past for the teaching sisters. In future, every sister who could be spared would be required to attend summer school. Therefore, in 1952 most of the younger members of the congregation flocked to St. John's to register at the Memorial University College to begin studies for a bachelor's degree in arts, education, or science. Sisters who had completed a bachelor's degree were sent to graduate school at universities in the United States or Canada. Those who worked in specialized areas such as nursing, music, or French went to universities that offered degrees in these disciplines. However, during the first few years of M. Imelda's plan, about ninety percent of the sister-students registered for summer school at Memorial University. For the convenience of these sisters, a ten-day retreat was held during August, which left barely enough time in the summer for the two-week annual vacation to which all sisters were entitled.[26]

---

25. For example, M. Perpetua O'Callaghan obtained a Ph.D. from Fordham University, N.Y., and M. Baptist McDermott travelled extensively in the United States and studied various branches of music with renowned teachers in that country.

26. After McAuley Hall residence was opened in 1960, the retreat for sisters attending summer school was held during the Easter vacation.

Many sisters remember those days of the early 1950s and '60s when all the beds were filled in every convent in St. John's. The junior sisters were accommodated on mattresses spread on the floors of the classrooms attached to Mercy Convent. Although this might seem to be an example of undue hardship, most of the young sisters took it in their stride and rather enjoyed the experience of "roughing it" for six weeks. It must be admitted that sleeping in the classrooms was not without its perks, for in such close quarters it was impossible to observe the rule of the Great Silence. Frequently, while the rest of the convent was wrapped in silence, sounds of hilarity were heard wafting from the open windows of the Grade V classroom just outside the third floor of the convent. Nightly visits from Poppy, the Mercy Convent cat, provided an additional source of mirth. Poppy took his duties seriously, and every night he patrolled the classrooms to make sure that they were free of unwanted, four-legged intruders. Unfortunately, Poppy had his own sense of direction, and if his appointed path happened to be occupied by a slumbering student, he simply walked over her face.

In the days before the new Memorial University was established on Prince Philip Drive, the old campus was a short walk from Mercy Convent. This was convenient, for it allowed the sisters to return to Mercy Convent for their meals and also to study in the well-stocked school and convent libraries. After the new Memorial University was opened in 1961, sisters availed of the opportunity to earn credits toward a degree during the school year by attending afternoon and evening classes. At the same time, M. Imelda, and her successor, M. Assumpta Veitch, recognized the advantage of having sisters attend universities in other parts of the world. Thus, for the next thirty years, sisters spent at least six weeks of summer in classrooms and lecture halls all over North America, England, and France in an endless quest for knowledge. As well, the yearly list of assignments contained the names of sisters who had been given a leave of absence from teaching to pursue studies at some university. All of this effort was so that sisters would be better equipped to instruct the children and youth who attended the schools administered by the congregation.

In September 1962, the senior boys from St. Teresa's were moved to grade XI in the newly erected Brother Rice High School under the direction of the Christian Brothers.[27] Boys in grades IX and X were accommodated at Gonzaga High School, administered by the Jesuits. St. Teresa's reverted to the status of a primary/elementary school. But in spite of the departure of all the high-school students, in September 1963, enrolment at St. Teresa's exceeded 1,000 children, with thirty teachers, twelve of whom were sisters.

The 1970s saw the start of the decline in the number of sisters available for teaching. Fewer young women were choosing to enter religious life, others were leaving the congregation to pursue a different path, and a number had reached the age of sixty and were forced to retire. Nevertheless, many sisters chose to provide voluntary service in the schools by organizing the library; coaching students who were having problems with certain subjects, especially mathematics and reading; working in the school office; or wherever extra help was needed. St. Teresa's School was fortunate in having a number of sisters willing to provide these volunteer services.

In 1996, the Sisters of Mercy relinquished the administration of St. Teresa's School when Sr. Helen Harding resigned as principal to take up duties in the offices of the General Administration of the Sisters of Mercy. Helen had been elected to the General Council by the general chapter of 1993, but had continued to serve as principal of St. Teresa's School until June 1996. In 1998, Helen became treasurer general of the congregation and held this position until she was elected as congregational leader in 2001. The departure of Sr. Helen Harding as principal, however, did not mean the departure of the sisters from St. Teresa's School. Srs. Joan Gosse and Mary Kelly continued to provide remedial teaching on a volunteer basis for several years.

Nevertheless, the relinquishment of salaried positions in the school signalled the beginning of new ministries through which the sisters served both the parish and the wider community. To accommodate these new ministries, St. Teresa's Convent underwent a significant facelift in the spring of 1990. The basement was completely renovated for use as a spirituality centre. Programs on prayer, spiritual direction, women's spirituality, and personal growth are

27. Subsequently, boys graduating from grade VIII at St. Teresa's were accommodated at Gonzaga High School.

offered. The centre is under the direction of two Sisters of Mercy, Loretta Dower and Irene Neville, both highly qualified in the fields of theology, scripture, and spiritual direction. Programs of spiritual growth, such as Myers-Briggs and the Enneagram are offered on a regular basis. Furthermore, the sisters at St. Teresa's Convent continue to be deeply involved in parish activities, and the unity and co-operation between parish and convent that existed from the beginning have deepened and solidified through the years.

In 1949, five years after the foundation at Mundy Pond, the Sisters of Mercy agreed to take over the administration of the schools in Goulds, a residential and farming community close to the city of St. John's.[28] Because the chapter of elections was scheduled for August 15, appointments for the school year 1949–50 had to wait for the approval of a new General Council before being released. Therefore, although the rumour mill was in full production, nobody knew the names of those chosen for the new foundation—except the person appointed to be the superior, M. deSales Ahearn. As a member of the outgoing General Council (1943–49), M. deSales had been party to the decision to establish a foundation in Goulds. In accepting the appointment as superior, M. deSales played a major role in selecting the sisters to accompany her on the foundation. Her choices were M. Madeline Trahey, M. Liguori Wade, M. Rita Coady, M. Dolores Garland, M. Monica Matthews, and M. Thaddeus Mullowney. Because of a delay in announcing the names, these sisters had only a short time to pack. However, these were the days when each sister's wardrobe consisted of two habits, two veils, two pairs of shoes, two outdoor shawls (there were no coats), and three of every other item of clothing. Thus, packing did not pose the problems that it does for their post-Vatican II successors.

In some ways, the establishment of the convent in Goulds was like many of the foundations that preceded it. The sisters moved into the former presbytery, which had been purchased by the Congregation of the Sisters of Mercy from the parish.[29] However, the actual foundation differed from others in that

28. In the 1980s, Goulds ceased to be an independent municipality and was incorporated into the city of St. John's.
29. Annals, Sacred Heart Convent, Goulds, September 2, 1949, ASMSJ.

the sisters moved in without any fuss or fanfare. They arrived on September 2, 1949, and quietly took up residence in what was now the Sacred Heart Convent. There was no official welcome, but that same evening, the sisters attended benediction in the parish church. As they entered St. Kevin's Church, M. Madeline Trahey made her way to the choir loft and took her place at the organ, and for many years thereafter, the sisters directed the music at all parish functions. The Annals noted that there were no special seating arrangements for the sisters in the church—they occupied any available pew.[30] This, too, was a departure, for usually the sisters sat together in the pew assigned them by the pastor. It is unclear whether the parish priest, Rev. J. J. Lacey expressed a preference in the matter. It is more likely, however, that the superior, M. deSales Ahearn, decided that it was time to do away with this kind of nonsense. This may not seem a very important matter, but it was a sign that the Sisters of Mercy were uncomfortable with the practice of being singled out for special attention whenever they appeared in public.

When the sisters took over St. Kevin's School in Goulds, there were five classrooms, one for each sister. Five years later, in 1954, there was not enough room to accommodate all the students. A large garage at the rear of the convent was quickly fitted with a new ceiling, floor, windows, and a chimney, and within a few weeks, it was ready for use as an extra classroom. The sisters at Goulds, who were a very devout group of women, decided to dedicate the garage to St. Thérèse, which was known henceforth as St. Thérèse's Classroom. The following year, 1955, three additional classrooms were added, but that was just a beginning. So quickly did the population of Goulds increase that by the end of the century St. Kevin's School accommodated over 1,500 students. However, back in the 1950s, Goulds was a quiet, sleepy little place where, when the sisters went for a walk on the main road in the evenings, invariably they met a farmer leading his cows home for milking.

Soon after their arrival, the sisters began the ministry of visitation of the sick. As the years passed, the sisters were a familiar sight as they walked through the streets and the lanes to visit the sick in the four nursing homes that

---

30. Ibid.

were located in Goulds. M. Monica Matthews was particularly devoted to the sick and shut-ins. M. Monica's main task was caring for the convent and preparing the meals. Thus she was not tied to the school schedule and was free to visit a family or one of the nursing homes during the early afternoon hours. The people of Goulds anticipated M. Monica's visits with delight—visits that she continued faithfully until ill health forced her to retire.

In common with sisters all over Newfoundland, the sisters in Goulds responded with enthusiasm when word came from the superior general, M. Imelda Smith, that in future sister-teachers should attend meetings of the Newfoundland Teachers' Association (NTA). The first meeting of the NTA in Goulds was held on April 29, 1954.[31]

Early in 1954, the sisters began the practice of offering an annual three-day retreat for the boys and girls of the school. On Thursday, November 18, over forty senior boys began the retreat under the direction of Rev. Edward Lawlor. Rev. Cyril Eagan directed the girls' retreat. The annalist itemized the retreat schedule that began at eleven o'clock Thursday morning and concluded with ten o'clock mass on Sunday morning when thirty-eight boys were received into the Holy Name Society. There was considerably more fuss over the girls. At four o'clock that afternoon, Archbishop P. J. Skinner and his entourage arrived to receive a large number of young ladies into the Sodality of the Children of Mary, and he admitted an equally large number as aspirants—a preparatory step to becoming a Child of Mary. The annalist was careful to note the manner in which activities associated with religious practice were carried out. Page after page of the Annals contains lists of hymns that were sung by the children for various celebrations. The matter of religious vocations was not neglected. For instance, on June 5, 1957, two Presentation Sisters came and spoke to the girls on religious life. However, no one could accuse the Mercy Sisters of favouritism, for on the following day, two Sisters of Service came for the same purpose. There is no mention of anybody visiting the school to encourage vocations to the Sisters of Mercy, but one may suspect

---

31. Annals, Sacred Heart Convent, Goulds, April 29, 1954, ASMSJ.

that the sisters in St. Kevin's School insisted, day in and day out, that the Mercy congregation, too, welcomed more vocations.

In 1956, the school population of St. Kevin's increased dramatically when it was decided by the school board that, in future, high-school students from Petty Harbour should attend classes in Goulds. During that same school year, the pupils of St. Kevin's, under the direction of Sr. Madeline Reid, made their first appearance at the Kiwanis Music Festival in St. John's. The Trinity College of Music examinations had been introduced in St. Kevin's School shortly after the arrival of the sisters, and the practice had been continued through the years. It was Sr. Madeline Reid, also, who introduced the children to instruments such as the accordion, the guitar, the banjo, and the bells, and registered them for small ensemble classes in the music festival. Evidently, the novelty of the instrumentation as well as the excellence of the performance caught the attention of the adjudicators, for St. Kevin's was awarded first place on a number of occasions. Of course, the children from St. Kevin's performed in many other categories and classes offered in the festival syllabus. Music examinations were not neglected, for Madeline Reid was particularly anxious for her students to follow the graded syllabus of Trinity College, and by 1961, seventeen young pianists from initial to senior were successful in the examinations.

The requirement that all teaching sisters attend university classes during the summer months interfered with the traditional time for the sisters' annual retreat, which had been held from July 7–16. Consequently, many sisters went to St. Catherine's Convent in St. John's for the retreat that took place during the Easter holidays. Unfortunately, for sisters who looked forward to the music festival, this retreat coincided with the dates of the festival. Although the retreat was of paramount importance, it was acknowledged reluctantly that the music festival could not take place without the musicians. Other arrangements for retreat would have to be made to accommodate these bothersome music teachers. In the smaller houses, it often happened that if the entire community went off for retreat, the music teacher would be alone—something simply unheard of in those days. M. Julien Giovannini, found herself in this predicament in 1963. The matter was represented to the superior general, who immediately found a way to solve M. Julien's dilemma. It was with more than a hint of anxiety that the annalist for Sacred Heart Convent wrote, "Sr. M. Julien was left home alone with three Juniors who came in from Mercy Convent to replace the Sisters who went in retreat."[32] Happily, M. Julien survived the three juniors from Mercy Convent and suffered no obvious ill effects as a result of her exposure to Mercy Convent's finest!

Religious instruction and sacramental preparation were part and parcel of the denominational system of education that was guaranteed to Newfoundland by the Terms of Union with Canada. Thus, no matter when the archbishop decided to come for confirmation, the children were ready, even if this should coincide with the beginning of the school year. However, by this time, confirmation at St. Kevin's Church in Goulds was no longer a matter taking a half-hour or so from the archbishop's busy schedule. At three o'clock on the afternoon of September 11, 1958, Archbishop Skinner arrived to confirm 229 children from St. Kevin's School.

As was the case in other schools near St. John's, the opening of Holy Heart of Mary Regional High School meant the departure of the high-school students from St. Kevin's School in Goulds. However, the exodus was an unmixed blessing, for the town itself was continuing to grow, with the consequent increase in school enrolment. The sisters were particularly thankful for the extra space when, during a bad storm, the chimney blew down and four classrooms had to be vacated for several months while the damage was being repaired.

And so the years passed. The number of sisters in the community of Sacred Heart Convent remained fairly consistent. Until 1990, there were five, six or seven sisters in the community, but in 1990, the number dropped to four. By 1996, there were only three sisters living at Sacred Heart Convent. Although six sisters were named as members of the community, one was caring for her sick mother at home and two were studying at universities outside of Newfoundland. The following year, another member of

32. Ibid., April 5, 1963, ASMSJ.

Sacred Heart Convent, Sr. Eileen Penney, accepted a position as staff nurse with the hospital in Happy Valley, Labrador. In June 1997, Sr. Dorothy Willcott retired—the last sister to hold a teaching position in St. Kevin's School.

Nevertheless, Sacred Heart Convent remained open, and in September 1999, there were three sisters in residence. Sr. Elizabeth O'Keefe volunteered her services in St. Bonaventure's College, a privately run Catholic school. She also worked part-time in the accounting department of the Sisters of Mercy generalate. Sr. Sylvia Doyle worked as pastoral assistant at Mary Queen of the World Parish in St. John's, and Sr. Margaret Mulcahy worked as a volunteer at McAuley Convent and at DayBreak Parent Child Care Centre.[33]

However, a new era was about to begin in the ministry of the Sisters of Mercy in Goulds. After Sacred Heart Convent closed for the summer in June 2000, it underwent some major renovations. When the building reopened in September, it was no longer the Sacred Heart Convent, but Creedon House—a Hospitality and Spirituality Centre for people who were looking for a place to spend time in quiet prayer and meditation or for those who simply needed a place to go for a rest. The spirituality centre came about in response to a proposal by two sisters, Madeline Byrne and Loretta Chafe. Sr. Madeline Byrne was named director of the centre. People from the neighbourhood gather for morning prayer, for special celebrations during Advent and Lent, and on other special days in the Church's calendar. There are opportunities to attend conferences and lectures presented at Creedon House, as well as retreats and spiritual direction. However, Creedon House is also a hospitality centre where tired people are welcomed and given the opportunity to relax in quiet, comfortable surroundings.

The house known as Creedon House has presented several faces to passersby on Goulds Road. It was built more than fifty years ago to serve as a presbytery for the parish priest of St. Kevin's. When the Congregation of the Sisters of Mercy agreed to take over the administration of St. Kevin's School,

---

33. See chapters twenty-six and twenty-seven.

the presbytery was purchased by the Mercy congregation and for many years it was known as Sacred Heart Convent. Now the house has taken on a new face and a new purpose. At a period in history when people are looking for meaning and a closer relationship with God, Creedon House offers a warm welcome and an atmosphere of quiet and peace.

CHAPTER EIGHTEEN

THE WEST COMES OF AGE

The quality of mercy is not strain'd,
It droppeth as the gentle rain from heaven
Upon the place beneath: it is twice blest;
It blesseth him that gives and him that takes.
Shakespeare, *The Merchant of Venice*, 4.1.184–87

en years before the foundation of the Holy Name of Mary Convent in Marystown, members of the Mercy congregation had established a presence in the Humber Valley. All through the years since the establishment of the convent of St. Mary's on the Humber, the sisters had their hands full with activities associated with the schools and the visitation of the sick. M. Liguori Wade, a member of the community from 1923 to 1945, wrote an account of the sisters' visitation ministry in Curling, which was a well-organized ministry in the parish.[1] After the priest had returned from a sick call, he gave the name and address of the sick person to the sisters. However, the sisters did not confine their visitation to members of the Roman Catholic faith. People of all denominations looked to them for support and comfort at times of illness and bereavement. M. Liguori commented, ". . . there was a lovely intercommunication with all the churches in the Bay of Islands at that

---

1. M. Liguori Wade, "A History of St. Mary's on the Humber, Curling," ASMSJ, RG 10/11/55.

time."[2] Bus and taxi services were unheard of in those days, but the priest had a horse and carriage, and whenever it was available, the sisters used it to visit more distant places. Occasionally, they travelled on the railway coach that provided transportation to places around the eastern rim of the Bay of Islands, but most of the time they walked.

According to M. Liguori, one sister who excelled in the visitation of the sick was M. Alphonsus McNamara, the superior of St. Mary's on the Humber from 1928–1934. When M. Alphonsus visited the homes of the poor she helped by washing the patient, changing the bed linens, and doing other necessary chores to make the sufferer more comfortable. M. Liguori was present on one occasion when, after the patient had died, M. Alphonsus washed the body, dressed it, and got it ready for burial. At the time of the Depression in the early 1930s, all the sisters in Curling, under the leadership and direction of M. Alphonsus, made clothing; knit socks, mittens, and sweaters; and gave as much relief as they could afford at the time. In order to purchase the materials and the wool to make clothing for the poor, the sisters made candy and sold it in school during the week. To provide additional funds for this purpose, they operated a small bookstore where books and religious articles were sold. Visitation was carried on after school hours and on weekends and holidays, for nothing was allowed to interfere with a sister's duty to her class.

In the schools, the yearly success of the students in public examinations, in Trinity College of Music examinations, and later in the music festival was a source of encouragement and an impetus to try new and innovative methods and ideas. Perhaps no idea was more innovative—and prophetic—than the decision to allow the Sunday mass for the children to be celebrated in English.[3] M. Liguori reported that for several years following 1923 there were two masses celebrated in the parish. During first mass, at nine o'clock in the morning, the children sang all the parts of the mass in English; the second mass was sung and recited in Latin, the music consisting of Gregorian Chant sung by the choir. Extracurricular activities were initiated and enthusiastically promoted

---

2. Ibid., ASMSJ, RG 10/11/56.
3. It should be noted that this took place forty years before the Second Vatican Council permitted the celebration of mass in the vernacular.

by the sisters. In 1934, the Catholic Cadet Corps was organized at Holy Cross School. The forty boys who made up the first unit were divided into two companies, each of whose commanding officers and lieutenants volunteered their services. Weekly meetings held at the school included physical training, games, singing, and occasional lectures. The success of the Cadet Corps prompted the sisters to establish a company of Girl Guides in 1935.

During the year 1936, an auditorium was added to Holy Cross School in Curling and, in the following year, four new classrooms. The school was an up-and-coming institution, noted for its innovative approach to education. The auditorium was used for all sorts of activities. Singing and dancing classes were held there regularly, and the new hall provided plenty of space for M. Winefride Greene's classes in drawing and painting, as well as M. Mechtilde Gillis's classes in basketry and carpentry. The boys favoured the latter activities and showed considerable skill in making coffee tables, hall stands, and other small items of furniture. When these tasks were completed, M. Winefride supervised the painting and polishing to get them ready for sale. During the spring the boys made decorations such as ducks, animals, and birds—all popular ornaments for the gardens of Curling. Tools and materials, including a fretsaw, were supplied, and students found it difficult to keep up with the demand for their work.

Religious studies were taken very seriously by teachers and students alike. One year the pupils in grades VII and VIII completed a special project on the mass. They made miniature vestments, about one-quarter the size of actual mass vestments, and explained the meaning and history of each vestment. For many years afterwards, teachers at Holy Cross used these vestments for instructional purposes. Another project undertaken by Holy Cross students, under the direction of the sisters, was the school paper, *The Beacon*. It was the result of the combined efforts of pupils from grades V to VIII, who contributed stories, poems, and feature articles. M. Liguori Wade's commercial class helped by doing all the typing. Not to be outshone by the elementary students, the senior pupils at Holy Cross created their own paper, *The Owl*.

Although the convent of St. Mary's on the Humber was established in 1917, it was not until 1935 that it received its first postulant. On October 16 of that year, M. Winefride Greene, the superior of St. Mary's on the Humber, accepted Kathleen Morrissey of Brigus as a postulant. Kathleen remained in Curling until May 1936, when she accompanied M. Francesca Turpin to St. John's. M. Francesca, a member of the community, had contracted tuberculosis and had been advised to enter the sanatorium in St. John's for treatment. Unfortunately, the disease had progressed to a stage where nothing could be done. M. Francesca died a year later on September 2, 1937. The postulant, Kathleen Morrissey, was received as a novice at Littledale and given the name, Mary Geraldine.

In 1939, M. Assumpta Veitch was appointed superior of the convent of St. Mary's on the Humber. There does not seem to be much doubt that this appointment was made on the recommendation of the outgoing superior, M. Winefride Greene. Although M. Assumpta had made her final profession only four years earlier, M. Winefride was quick to discern the potential of this young, enthusiastic sister who combined a love for music and drama with obvious leadership qualities. Also, M. Winefride observed that M. Assumpta was never afraid to try something new. It is said that M. Assumpta was not too happy on receiving the news of her appointment. However, being of a naturally optimistic disposition and reflecting, "what can't be cured, must be endured," she accepted the appointment with as much good grace as she could muster. Subsequent events demonstrated that the congregation's confidence was not misplaced. During the next six years, the Holy Cross School became known for a succession of excellent plays and dramas produced under the direction of the talented young superior. On the suggestion of the parish priest, Father Michael Brosnan, and under the guidance of M. Assumpta, the students researched and wrote the history of the parish.[4] These literary, dramatic, and historical projects earned for the sisters' schools in Curling a reputation for innovative planning and programming.

In 1942, the Sisters of Mercy in Newfoundland celebrated the centenary of the foundation of the congregation in Newfoundland. On June 10, M. Assumpta made the first long-distance phone call from a convent on the West

---

4. Sr. Edward Mary Roche, conversation with author, April 12, 2003.

Coast to Mercy Convent in St. John's to send good wishes to all the sisters on this special anniversary. The date was wrong, but nobody can doubt the sincerity of her intentions.[5] Finally, before the expiration of her term of office, M. Assumpta was determined that the convent would be enlarged to suit the needs of the eight sisters who now lived there. In 1944, a two-storey extension was added to the rear of the convent. It provided a new community room on the first floor, and three bedrooms and a bathroom upstairs.

Everything in Curling was looking bright and prosperous. The population of the town was increasing, and the schools were flourishing. The sisters were rewarded for the hardships and toil of the early years when they saw their former students assume positions of responsibility in Curling, Corner Brook, and other nearby communities. But toward the end of 1948, disaster struck. In the early morning of Christmas Eve, the beautiful parish church at Curling was destroyed by fire. About half past two, M. Fintan Downey, unable to sleep because of a broken hip, noticed a reflection of fire through the window of her bedroom. She called another sister to investigate. It was discovered that the interior of the Sacred Heart Church, only a few feet away, was a mass of flames. The sisters immediately sent out the alarm and notified the parish priest, Rev. Leo Drake. By the time help arrived, it was too late to save the church. People worked frantically to salvage the priest's house and the convent, located on either side of the burning church. Bystanders saved the presbytery by draping the entire side of the house with blankets saturated in water. All the contents of the convent were removed to a place of safety, and the men worked desperately to save the building, which caught on fire several times. Eventually, the fire was brought under control, but the church was gone and the convent had suffered severe smoke and water damage. M. Fintan was brought to the home of Dr. O'Connell in Curling and made comfortable there until arrangements could be made for her transfer to St. Clare's Mercy Hospital in St. John's. The rest of the sisters were invited to stay at the Presentation Convent in Corner Brook until St. Mary's on the Humber could be made safe for occupancy.

---

5. The first Sisters of Mercy arrived in Newfoundland on June 3, 1842. Due to an error in M. Austin Carroll's *Leaves*, for many years the anniversary of the arrival was thought to be June 10.

After the fire, the work of rebuilding began, and in a relatively short time, the beautiful new Sacred Heart Church was blessed and opened for regular services. The convent, too, was quickly cleaned and painted. Within a few months, the fire was just a bad memory. M. Fintan, whose hip had healed, resumed her duties as superior and principal of the school.

By the year 1954, it was clear that the old Holy Cross School, now almost forty years old, had seen the best of its days. The school population continued to increase by leaps and bounds, and the overcrowding of the classrooms was a constant source of worry and concern to the sisters. The problem of finding money to build a new school had to be faced. It was three years before plans were finalized. Fortunately, the people of Curling were all in agreement that the new school was a priority for the parish, and they agreed to make monthly contributions toward the cost of the construction. In the spring of 1960, the building was ready for occupancy, and teachers and students moved into the new Sacred Heart School. The formal opening of the school was celebrated on May 1, 1960, and the old Holy Cross School was demolished. Sacred Heart School served all grades from kindergarten to grade XI until 1968, when, with the opening of Cabrini High School, Sacred Heart was designated an elementary school, for kindergarten to grade VI. The new Cabrini High was an all-girls institution, the senior boys being accommodated in the schools of the Christian Brothers in Corner Brook.[6]

In 1975, Memorial University of Newfoundland established a junior college in Corner Brook, the Sir Wilfred Grenfell College. Initially, two Sisters of Mercy were on the faculty of the new college, M. Williamina Hogan (English) and Sr. Nellie Pomroy (Mathematics).[7] The following year, 1976, M. Georgina Quick joined the history department at the college. All three sisters were members of the community of St. Mary's on the Humber.

---

6. On January 1, 1956, Curling was incorporated into the town (later, city) of Corner Brook, although it continues to retain its distinct identity.

7. Subsequently, Sr. Nellie was appointed assistant principal of the college, a position she held until 1993, when she was elected as a member of the General Council of the Congregation of the Sisters of Mercy.

By this time, the old building that had served as the convent since 1917 was in very poor shape. Over the years, bits and pieces had been added to the original structure, so that, for the uninitiated, the house was a veritable maze. Also, according to some imaginative people who lived there, the old convent was haunted. Wonderful, hair-raising tales are told of sisters being seen walking along the corridor and then disappearing into thin air. There were, also, unexplained moans and groans heard from time to time, especially on dark, dreary nights in the fall of the year. Nobody was willing to admit the more probable explanation—that these noises emanated from the neighbour's bad-tempered cat, who constantly prowled the convent garden in search of food. Nevertheless, the sisters loved the old building, and it was with reluctance that they agreed to having it demolished and a new convent built very close to where the old one had stood. On June 11, 1976, they moved into the new convent, and the following week, the workmen began the task of demolishing the old one where the Sisters of Mercy had lived for fifty-nine years. As this new community of sisters watched the old convent being taken down piece by piece, they did not dream that in less than twenty years the Sisters of Mercy would leave Curling and the beautiful new convent would pass into other hands.

As the years passed and, one by one, sisters retired from the schools or took up other ministries, it became clear that it was no longer feasible to maintain a large convent that was home to only one or two sisters. Consequently, and with a great deal of reluctance, the General Council of the Sisters of Mercy made the decision to close the Convent of St. Mary's on the Humber. Sr. Michelle Gibbons, the only sister in Curling at the time, was working in youth ministry in the Cathedral Parish of Holy Redeemer in Corner Brook. It was her responsibility to oversee the closing of the convent that had been purchased by the Diocese of St. George's for the use of personnel working for the diocese. In August 1994, Sr. Michelle passed over the keys of the convent and moved to a rented house in the city of Corner Brook, where she remained until her transfer to Labrador some years later.

The development of the US Air Force Base at Stephenville, about twenty-five miles south of Curling, brought a degree of prosperity to the west coast of

Newfoundland and particularly to the whole area of the Port au Port Peninsula, an area about forty miles south of Curling. This economic boost was especially true for Stephenville Crossing, which became an important trans-shipment point for mail, supplies, and travellers.[8]

Stephenville Crossing is a small town located a few miles from St. George's, right at the bottom of St. George's Bay. The first settlers in the area were farmers, many of them from Mattis Point, an old Mi'kmaq village. Others came from the Port au Port Peninsula and from Sandy Point. During the time when the railway was being built in the 1890s, the area, known at that time as La Grange, was the site of a large camp for labourers working on the construction of the railway and for loggers cutting railway ties.[9] With the completion of the railway, La Grange, now called Stephenville Crossing, was established as the regional headquarters for employees of the Newfoundland Railway and the main depot for the town of Stephenville and the entire Port au Port Peninsula. In 1901, the population of Stephenville Crossing was slightly over one hundred, but by 1945, it had reached almost one thousand.

In 1938, Bishop Renouf of St. George's raised the canonical status of Stephenville Crossing, known locally as "the Crossing," to that of a parish and appointed Rev. Jeremiah C. Stoyles as the first parish priest. At that time the church property consisted of a partly finished church and a two-room school that doubled as a hall where various town functions were held. Within a year of his appointment, Fr. Stoyles had completed the interior of the church, repaired the exterior and built a presbytery. The problem of the school was the next item on the pastor's agenda. Work on a new school was begun in the summer of 1940. Within a relatively short time, a one-storey school with four classrooms and a full basement containing cloakrooms, washrooms, recreation room, and an assembly room had been completed. The school was named St. Michael's to honour the new bishop of St. George's, Michael O'Reilly.[10]

---

8. During World War II, the base at Stephenville was the largest US Air Force base outside the continental United States and a major refueling stop for aircraft en route to Europe.

9. *ENL*, s.v. "Stephenville Crossing."

10. ASMSJ, RG 10/18/23.

Stephenville Crossing was also the site of a health care centre for the Port au Port Peninsula, with an eight-bed cottage hospital. Thus, when Father Stoyles approached the Sisters of Mercy asking to have the sisters establish a convent in the town, he pointed out that they would have plenty of scope for their traditional ministries of teaching and visitation of the sick. The superior general at the time, M. Imelda Smith, agreed and promised to take the matter up with the General Council at the first opportunity.

This was not the first time that Father Stoyles had been in communication with the Sisters of Mercy. In 1924, his sister Mollie had been received as a novice at Littledale and admitted to temporary profession of vows in 1927. At the time, sisters made annual vows for three years prior to being admitted to final profession. During her second year of annual vows, Mollie Stoyles developed pulmonary tuberculosis. Her doctor and the superiors hoped that rest and medical treatment would effect a cure, but this did not happen, and on the expiration of her third year of annual vows, Mollie left the congregation and entered the sanatorium where she spent two years. M. Philippa Hanley, the superior general at the time, explained what happened after that. "Acting on the advice of her physician, who realized that her health, though improved, was not quite equal to the strain of convent life, Miss Stoyles voluntarily returned to her home when discharged from the Sanatorium, July 1932."[11] Evidently, Father Stoyles expected his sister to return to the convent after her discharge from the sanatorium and was under the mistaken impression that the congregation had refused to readmit her. In September 1932, he wrote to the apostolic delegate, "She is anxious to return to the Religious Life but the Sisters of Mercy say they cannot take her back owing to her condition of health. May they refuse her re-admission on that ground alone?"[12] The delegate immediately wrote to Archbishop Roche asking him to look into the matter. Apparently, Mollie's desire to return to religious life was news to both Mollie and the Mercy congregation. In her reply to the archbishop's query, M. Philippa explained that Miss Stoyles had not requested readmittance to the

11. M. Philippa Hanley to Archbishop E. P. Roche, October 26, 1932, AASJ, 107/10/9.
12. Rev. Jeremiah Stoyles to Most Rev. Andrew Cassulo, DD, apostolic delegate, AASJ, 107/10/11.

congregation, and as a matter of fact, M. Philippa had not heard anything from her since her discharge from the sanatorium.[13] It appears that Mollie's impetuous brother fired off his complaint to Church authorities without taking time to ascertain her wishes in the matter. In any case, the matter was resolved to everyone's satisfaction. Contrary to what might have been expected, the big-hearted Fr. Stoyles carried no grudges, and for the rest of their lives, both he and his sister Mollie were close and loyal friends of the Sisters of Mercy. Consequently, when he received his appointment to Stephenville Crossing, Father Stoyles was determined that someday he would have a convent of the Sisters of Mercy in the parish.

Eventually, in the closing months of the year 1949, Father Stoyles received word that the newly elected General Council of the Sisters of Mercy had approved the establishment of a convent in Stephenville Crossing.[14] Immediately on receiving this news, he began preparations for the arrival of the sisters and arranged for the construction of a beautiful new convent, complete in every detail. It had been agreed that the Sisters of Mercy would assume the management of St. Michael's School in the Crossing in September 1950. Unfortunately, the convent was not quite ready for occupancy, but this little problem was no cause for alarm. The sisters at St. Michael's Convent, St. George's, could always find room to squeeze in a few more people. Accordingly, on August 20, 1950, the sisters appointed to the new community packed their bags and boarded the train for the west, arriving in the Crossing the following afternoon. Fr. Stoyles and Mollie met them at the station and drove them to the site of the convent, which was still under construction. After they had been given a tour of the school, the sisters were escorted to St. Michael's Convent, St. George's, where they lived until their own convent was ready. The superior of the group was M. Fidelis Parsons. Other members of the community were M. de Lourdes Carroll, M. Zita Hyde,

---

13. M. Philippa Hanley to Archbishop E. P. Roche, AASJ, 107/10/12.

14. In August 1949, the general chapter elected a new council consisting of M. Imelda Smith (superior general), M. Stanislaus Parsons, M. Philomena Walker, M. Chrysostom McCarthy, and M. Dolorosa Kinney.

and M. Louise Power. A fifth member of the new community, Marie Michael Power, joined them three months later.

School opened that year on September 4, and from that time until mid-November, the sisters commuted daily from St. George's. Every morning a car from the Crossing picked them up, drove them to school and brought them back to St. George's in the evening. To ensure that the sisters received adequate nourishment, the ladies of Stephenville Crossing provided a hot dinner at noon. For their part, the sisters, unaccustomed to such lavish repasts in the middle of the day, soon began to eye their expanding waistlines with consider-able alarm. However, not wanting to hurt anyone's feelings, they cleaned their plates as a tribute to the culinary skills of the generous ladies of the Crossing—while their waistlines continued to expand!

At last, the building was ready for the sisters to move to their new home. The Convent of the Assumption was blessed and formally opened on November 20, 1950. M. Fidelis Parsons reported, "When we moved into the Convent we had all the things that were necessary except salt and pepper shak-ers."[15] To remedy this oversight, she phoned the presbytery and asked the housekeeper if she could spare a set of salt and pepper shakers until the sisters could purchase their own. Apparently, word spread through the town, and by the next day, the sisters had enough salt and pepper shakers to supply the whole Congregation of the Sisters of Mercy and possibly the Presentation Sisters as well.

According to the Annals of Assumption Convent, there was no shortage of visitors from the other convents on the West Coast, and even some from the east. In fact, a person reading the Annals may detect a certain weariness creeping into accounts of visitors who arrived on the doorstep at all hours and especially when the sisters were trying to relax on weekends. M. Zita Hyde, who looked after the cooking, was kept busy preparing meals for hungry guests who arrived by train to enjoy the hospitality of the new convent. On the other hand, the sisters from the Crossing availed of every excuse to visit

---

15. M. Fidelis Parsons, speaking at the golden anniversary of the Parish of Our Lady of the Assumption, Stephenville Crossing, December 8, 1987, ASMSJ, RG 10/18/4.

St. Michael's Convent in St. George's, which was only a short run by train. The mobility of the sisters of the 1950s contrasts sharply with the isolation experienced by the four lonely pioneers from Providence who arrived in Sandy Point sixty years earlier. Nevertheless, within two years of their arrival at the Crossing, the sisters faced some severe trials and one heartbreaking loss.

On December 17, 1951, the sisters of Assumption Convent were invited to attend the annual distribution of prizes at the sisters' schools in St. George's. Two sisters from the Crossing set off by car, intending to return home after the concert. However, while the concert was in progress the weather began to deteriorate, making it impossible for them to return home. The hospitality of St. Michael's Convent must have been severely tested, for the storm lasted three days. The sisters at St. George's had to find accommodation not only for the two visitors from the Crossing, but also for three sisters from St. Mary's on the Humber who were stranded because the storm had wrecked the roads and the railway tracks.

Meanwhile, back in Stephenville Crossing, school opened as usual on the morning of December 18, although there were only a few children in attendance because of the stormy weather. At three o'clock that afternoon, Father Stoyles rushed over to tell the teachers to discontinue classes. The school was needed to shelter families seeking refuge from the high winds and the heavy seas that threatened to engulf their homes. In less than an hour, the building was packed with frightened people. The sisters helped by keeping the children occupied and making the sick and elderly as comfortable as the limited resources would permit. Meanwhile, darkness had set in. Because the wires were down, there was neither heat nor light except for the feeble glow of a couple of candles borrowed from a classroom shrine to the Virgin Mary and an oil lamp that M. de Lourdes Carroll discovered in a storage room in the basement. The problem of food was the most difficult to solve, for the limited supply in the convent pantry was soon exhausted. A few men battled the storm to fetch some canned goods, and later, a truck arrived from the United States Air Force Base with a truckload of food. Fortunately, no lives were lost, although there was a great deal of property damage.[16] It was a frightening experience for the people of the Crossing and for the sisters, who were helpless in the face of what might have been a major disaster.

Early in the new year, 1952, M. de Lourdes Carroll, who had been suffering from what she thought was arthritis, was advised to go to St. John's to see a medical specialist. A week later, the sisters at Assumption Convent were shocked to receive the news that M. de Lourdes was suffering from terminal cancer. Although she was given the option of surgery, the doctors offered little hope that it would be successful. M. de Lourdes declined the operation, but her condition was such that she was forced to remain in St. Clare's Mercy Hospital. She told her community, "I am glad of the opportunity to take the long road Home, and to suffer something for God."[17] God took her at her word, for she endured five months of intense suffering before she died peacefully on July 7, 1952.

In March of the same year, two more teachers at St. Michael's School in the Crossing became ill and were forced to take a leave of absence. The music teacher, Sr. Marie Michael Power, was summoned to preside over one of the grades, but even with her assistance and a radical realignment of classes, the absence of three teachers was a serious blow to the school. As soon as the superior general, M. Imelda Smith, was informed of the situation, she boarded the train for Stephenville Crossing, taking with her an experienced teacher, M. Gregory Stapleton, who remained there for the rest of the school year.

On Sr. Marie Michael's initiative, the Trinity College of Music examinations in both piano and theory were held for the first time in Stephenville Crossing in May 1952. When the results were published, the students' efforts had resulted in one hundred percent success. This was the beginning of a very successful music program in Stephenville Crossing, for in September 1952, M. Genevieve Drake, one of the congregation's gifted music teachers, arrived to replace Sr. Marie Michael, who had been assigned to the Immaculate Conception Convent, Conception Harbour.

---

16. Annals, Convent of the Assumption, Stephenville Crossing, vol. 1, p. 33, ASMSJ.
17. Ibid, p. 36.

Approximately 300 boys and girls were registered when the sisters assumed responsibility for St. Michael's School in 1950, and by 1955, the number increased to more than 400. By that time there were twelve teachers on the staff of the school, seven of whom were sisters. Within a few years, further extensions were made to the building, but even these additions could not keep pace with the growing population. On September 19, 1963, the new Assumption High School was opened for students in grades VII to XI. Children from kindergarten to grade VI were accommodated in the former St. Michael's All-Grade School, now called St. Michael's Elementary. Although most of the sisters were transferred to Assumption High, the sisters retained the position of principal at St. Michael's until June 1974.[18]

The Annals of Assumption Convent were kept with meticulous attention to detail, although some of those responsible for writing the Annals approached the task with strange ideas of what might be of interest to future historians. One individual wrote, no doubt with tongue in cheek, "A visiting priest celebrated Mass in the Convent Chapel at 7:00 o'clock this morning. He preached a most enjoyable sermon on eternal damnation." Another sister, knowing that her Annals were destined to end up in St. John's, could not resist gloating over superior weather conditions on the West Coast, "The weather here is beautiful, though a terrific snowstorm has been raging for some days in St. John's." Other entries suggest that the writer was preoccupied with the origin of food served at the convent table, for instance, "Had moose from the East Coast for dinner." One scribe conscientiously reported the failings of the superior, "Sister Superior forgot to phone Port au Port to tell the Presentation Sisters that our Concert was called off, and consequently six Sisters arrived this afternoon." Still others clothed possibly mundane events with an aura of mystery: "Sister Superior went to bed with a board." It is left to the reader's imagination to decide whether this was an act of penance or if the superior had problems with her back.[19]

---

18. In 1976, the new St. Michael's Elementary School was constructed through the federal Department of Regional Economic Expansion, the provincial government, and the Roman Catholic School Board for Bay St. George.

19. Quotations are from Annals, Convent of the Assumption, Stephenville Crossing, ASMSJ.

In 1973, almost 700 primary and elementary pupils at St. Michael's School were housed in two separate buildings. By this time there was only one sister attached to St. Michael's Elementary School—Sr. Phyllis Corbett, the principal, worked with a staff of seventeen lay teachers.[20] Five of the sisters at Assumption Convent were attached to Assumption High School and a sixth was religious consultant with the school board, for by this time sisters were involved in educational ministries other than classroom teaching. The twenty-fifth anniversary of the establishment of Assumption Convent in Stephenville Crossing was observed on November 22, 1975. Only two members of the first community were present, M. Fidelis Parsons and Sr. Marie Michael Power, who attended in a dual capacity, as a member of the original group and as superior general of the congregation.[21]

By the year 1983, there were only four sisters living in Assumption Convent, only two of whom were teaching at Assumption High School. A third, Sr. Gladys Bozec, was coordinator of French programs for schools under the Bay St. George School Board. In addition to this duty, Sr. Gladys acted as music and art consultant. M. Thomasine McHugh, the fourth member of the community, spent her time visiting the sick and attending to the poor who came to the convent door looking for help. With only four people living in such a large convent, the sisters realized that it was only a matter of time before they would need to make alternate arrangements for housing.

On October 18, 1983, at a combined meeting of the sisters of Assumption Convent and St. Michael's Convent, St. George's, Sr. Nellie Pomroy, a member of the General Council of the congregation, proposed that the two communities be combined and one of the convents closed. She point-

---

20. Subsequently, Sr. Phyllis Corbett entered St. Clare's School of Nursing. A few years after her graduation as a registered nurse, Phyllis earned a master's degree in administration. She filled the position of director of nursing at St. Clare's for a number of years, and was on-site administrator of the hospital for a short time before she left to study clinical pastoral education. At the time of writing, Phyllis is administrator of St. Patrick's Mercy Home.

21. Of the other founding community, M. de Lourdes Carroll and M. Zita Hyde had died, and M. Louise Power received a dispensation from her religious vows and left the congregation.

ed out that both convents had been built for seven to ten sisters so that either one or the other could be used to accommodate members of both communities. Moreover, in recent years, the new road that linked St. George's and the Crossing made travel between the two towns a matter of about ten minutes. Thus, sister-teachers could easily commute to school from either convent. The sisters agreed that the cost of keeping both buildings open was an unnecessary expense. Given the historical importance of the convent in St. George's, it was no surprise when word arrived from the General Council that Assumption Convent would be closed in June 1984 and turned over to the Roman Catholic School Board. As a result of this decision, sisters assigned to Assumption High School in Stephenville Crossing were asked to move to St. Michael's Convent, St. George's, and commute daily to Stephenville Crossing.

The transfer from Assumption Convent to St. Michael's Convent was accompanied by a good deal of confusion, harried nerves, and sheer desperation, as the sisters tried to juggle the various challenges presented by the closing of a convent. First of all, the move coincided with the final examinations that were taking place in school. In addition to correcting examinations, writing report cards, completing school registers, and making sure that classrooms were left in immaculate order, the sisters were preparing to leave for summer school. This was the yearly hassle to which all sister-students had grown accustomed. Now, with one eye on the calendar, they were faced with the colossal task of packing everything in the convent as well as their personal belongings before the movers arrived at the beginning of July. Treasures that previously had been guarded jealously found their way to the garbage as each sister tried to fit the essentials into already bulging suitcases. Finally, everything was ready, and the exhausted sisters viewed with sadness the empty rooms that had been home for thirty-four years. The final entry in the Annals of Assumption Convent, Stephenville Crossing, reads as follows:

> July 2, 1984: Household Movers arrived today. The packing and moving has begun in earnest. . . . Sisters M. Thomasine [McHugh] and Maureen [O'Keefe] will be staying for a few more days to

polish and shine and then pass over the keys to the School
Board staff.[22]

Finally, on July 12, 1984, Sr. Maureen O'Keefe closed and locked the doors of
Assumption Convent, passed the keys over to the school board, and she and M.
Thomasine McHugh drove to St. Michael's Convent, St. George's.

The "takeover" of the community of Assumption Convent by St.
Michael's was accomplished without too much disruption in convent routine.
After all, every year saw changes in the personnel of the different religious
houses. In this case, it meant simply that the community of St. Michael's now
numbered eight instead of five. It was, to a certain extent, a return to the earlier days of the 1950s when there were eight or more sisters attached to the
convent in St. George's.

The annalist for St. Michael's Convent, St. George's, began her task in 1958 by
summarizing the events of the twenty years since the 1930s. She noted that in
comparison with the enrolment of the early years, the number of boarders had
doubled during 1930s and '40s.[23] In those days, boarders and day pupils were
taught in separate classrooms and by a different staff of sisters. However, that
practice was discontinued as the number of boarders decreased in early 1950s
when the convent and boarding school underwent major renovation. New
recreational facilities were installed for the convenience of the boarding students, such as a television and a movie projector and screen. Modern, comfortable furniture replaced the more austere seating arrangements of former
years. In the mid-1950s, the availability of government bursaries and scholarships resulted in far more applications for admission to the boarding school than
the sisters could accept. In 1958, there were forty-nine boarders at St.
Michael's, with nine sisters in the community. It was that same year that the
annalist noted, "This year, for the first time in the history of the school, we have
a sufficient number of Grade Elevens to occupy a separate classroom."[24] This

22. Annals, Assumption Convent, Stephenville Crossing, July 2, 1984, ASMSJ.
23. Annals, St. Michael's Convent, St. George's, ASMSJ.
24. Ibid.

was encouraging, for it was indicative of the fact that not only the boarders but also the children of St. George's were serious about completing their high-school education and qualifying for entrance to a university. St. Joseph's School, also under the direction of the Sisters of Mercy, had been renovated and enlarged to accommodate the children from nearby Shallop Cove. Consequently, the school population was growing by leaps and bounds.

All schools administered by the sisters laid special emphasis on the religious education of the children and on their participation in the parish liturgies. In 1960, changes in the liturgy of the Roman Catholic Church began to make a tentative appearance in Newfoundland. The adaptations were adopted enthusiastically by the sisters and recorded conscientiously by the annalist in every convent. In St. George's, the sisters made sure that the children were thoroughly prepared for the changes and understood what was happening. Thus, an initiative to encourage the participation of the children in the celebration of mass was duly noted in the Annals: "[We held] our first practice in the Church for the Dialogue Mass, which is to be inaugurated on Sunday at the Children's Mass."[25]

It was in 1960 that the decision was made to hold one of the congregation's annual eight-day retreats in St. George's for the benefit of sisters who were attending summer school. There were sound economic reasons for this decision. It saved the expense of bringing sisters from the West Coast to St. John's, while those who were returning to the East Coast could interrupt their flight at Stephenville Airport, drive to St. George's for the retreat and at its conclusion, continue their journey home.[26] However, these "stopovers" were not as uneventful as might be imagined. On one occasion, four weary travellers, having endured many delays and some severe bouncing around on the small aircraft of the time, arrived at Stephenville and, with considerable relief, boarded the taxi for St. George's. While they bumped along over the lonely,

---

25. Ibid., March 4, 1960. In the "Dialogue Mass," instead of responses being made by the altar servers alone, the congregation made these responses and also joined the priest in praying certain parts of the mass, such as the Creed.

26. In those days there was no extra charge for stopping off for a period of time at some airport along the route.

unpaved road that was dotted with potholes deep enough to engulf a smaller vehicle, they consoled themselves with visions of hot cups of tea awaiting them at St. George's. Just as they arrived at the top of a steep hill, the car gave a terrific lurch and came to a sudden halt. One sister looked out the window, in time to witness one of the car's rear wheels careening down a precipitous slope toward the river seventy feet below. The four passengers and the driver stood around in the pouring rain for an hour and a half before another car appeared on the scene to lend assistance. Meanwhile, St. Michael's Convent community, deciding that the travellers had missed their flight, locked the door, drank the tea, turned off the lights and went to bed. About midnight, the doorbell rang, and when one of the sisters went to investigate, she found four bedraggled individuals, their clothes dripping water from every seam, standing on the doorstep seeking admittance. It seemed ironic that having safely negotiated the subways and the traffic in downtown Chicago for six weeks, they should meet with near disaster in peaceful, secure Newfoundland.

When school opened in September 1963, it was obvious that the existing school buildings in St. George's could not accommodate the students without serious overcrowding. Every available room in the school and the convent was in use. Consequently, construction of a new elementary school began immediately, and in January 1964, Our Lady of Mercy Elementary School was ready for occupancy, and the former all-grade school became known as St. Joseph's High School. It was in 1964, also, that St. Michael's Convent began a new ministry when two sisters made weekly visits to Mattis Point to teach religion to the children and prepare them for reception of the sacraments. Similar visits were made to Sandy Point on a regular basis.

During the 1960s, the Department of Education adopted the practice of sending children from small outports to a larger centre to complete high school. In 1964, children from Seal Rocks, Flat Bay, and St. Theresa's who were in grades VII, VIII, and IX were accommodated at St. Joseph's Junior High School in St. George's. The junior grades up to Grade VI were taught in the local schools, called "feeder schools," which were under the direction of a supervising principal. The first sister in St. George's to fill this role was M. Eleanor Savage. She was responsible not only for the schools in St. George's but the feeder schools as well. This required her to make frequent visits to these outlying places—no easy task at any time of year, but especially in the winter months when travel by road was uncertain and hazardous.

Meanwhile, further changes were being introduced in the liturgy of the Roman Catholic Church. Early in January 1965, the sisters from Stephenville Crossing and St. George's went to Corner Brook to attend a conference on the use of English in parts of the mass that, prior to the renewal, were sung by the choir. The speakers were Msgr. William Sommerville and his brother, Fr. Stephen Sommerville, from Toronto. The two priests visited the larger parishes in the three dioceses in Newfoundland from Corner Brook to St. John's, armed with plenty of copies of "The Mass of the Good Shepherd," the music of which had been composed by Fr. Stephen Sommerville himself. This was the first musical setting of the English translation of the mass that had been actively promoted in Newfoundland since the Second Vatican Council. As a result of the efforts of the brothers Sommerville, most parishes in Newfoundland adopted this dreary musical setting of the mass as if it had come down from heaven. Consequently, for over twenty years, long-suffering Roman Catholics in Newfoundland were treated to a steady, unvarying diet of Sommerville's "Mass." Apparently, other Canadian musicians and composers were slow off the mark in producing musically acceptable versions of the mass in English.[27] In the case of the sisters from St. George's, M. Genevieve Drake came home from the Sommerville conference with an armload of music and a barrel full of good intentions. Without delay, she gathered her singers and introduced them to this new way of celebrating the mass in English.

The Annals of St. Michael's Convent record faithfully many scholarships won by the students in the public examinations and in the fields of music and sports. Under the direction of M. Genevieve Drake and her successors, instrumental soloists, choirs, and vocal ensembles participated every year in the music festival that was held in Corner Brook. Every year the annalist recorded a long list of prizes awarded to successful participants from the

---

27. The "sung" parts of the mass are the "Lord Have Mercy," "Glory to God," "Holy, Holy, Holy," and "Lamb of God."

schools in St. George's. The sisters' interest in St. Joseph's School hockey team is seen in the pride with which the annalist reported the team's victory over Stephenville, and later, their triumphs over teams in Nova Scotia. In 1977, the annalist noted with great pride that the volleyball team from St. Joseph's High School had won the all-Newfoundland championship. The Annals present a clear picture of the willingness of the sisters to devote after-school hours to coaching the sports teams, practicing with school and parish choirs, holding Bible classes and religious discussion groups for adults, and directing school dramas. Furthermore, most sisters gladly dedicated the few precious weeks of summer vacation to study. Each year at the end of June, St. Michael's Convent was closed and the sisters were on their way to attend classes in some university. During the year, as well, sisters participated in workshops and conferences sponsored by various educational organizations. The result of all this was that, as a group, the sisters of both the Mercy and Presentation congregations were among the best-educated women in Newfoundland.

By the year 1967, the handwriting was on the wall for St. Michael's Boarding School in St. George's. In September of that year, there were only twelve boarders registered. This sudden drop in enrolment was due to the opening of a new high school in the Codroy Valley. Consequently, at the end of the school year in June 1968, the boarding school was closed. When school opened in September, for the first time in almost seventy years, there were no boarding students at St. Michael's. On the other hand, both Our Lady of Mercy and St. Joseph's Schools suffered from overcrowding because of a decision of the school board to admit fifty pupils from the amalgamated school in St. George's. As a result of this, several rooms in the convent continued to be used as classrooms.

The year 1968 marked the seventy-fifth anniversary of the establishment of the convent at Sandy Point in 1893. The sisters of St. Michael's Convent were determined to mark the anniversary in an appropriate fashion. November 1, 1968, was the day chosen for the celebration. It was appropriate that the celebrant of the mass, Bishop O'Reilly, wore a set of vestments that had been designed and hand sewn by one of the pioneer sisters, M. Corsini Dempsey. The silver chalice used at mass contained a cross of jewels that had once belonged to Mrs. Henrietta Brownell, the American benefactor of the first convent at Sandy Point.

At the second session of the 1967 general chapter, which took place in 1968, each sister was given the option of using her baptismal name instead of the religious name she had been given when she was received into the novitiate.[28] Most sisters chose to do this, especially those who had been given a masculine name at reception. Because the sisters were required to attend professional functions, the use of masculine names occasionally led to awkward situations. For instance, M. Thomas Hawco registered for a conference at the University of Edmonton. She arrived at the university residence and was given the key to her room. When she entered the room carrying her suitcase, she was shocked to discover a very large gentleman stretched out on one of the beds with a glass in his hand that obviously did not contain Purity Syrup.[29] The occupant of the room was even more startled than M. Thomas who, at the time, was dressed in the traditional habit of the Sisters of Mercy. They compared notes, only to discover that they had been given the same room due to the fact that the sister's registration was given simply as "Thomas Hawco." Needless to say, the situation was rectified immediately by the management.

The sisters' education ministry on the West Coast was expanded in 1970 to include the elementary school in Flat Bay East, a small fishing and mining community about eighteen miles south of St. George's. The first two sisters appointed to teach at St. Anne's School in Flat Bay East were Sr. Alicia Linehan (principal) and Sr. Susan Dober. Both sisters commuted from St. Michael's Convent, St. George's. That same year, the Bay St. George School Board hired its first religious education consultant in the person of M. Perpetua Bown. Originally, M. Perpetua had been a music teacher, but because of her interest in all matters religious, she had decided to pursue advanced courses in religious studies. M. Perpetua lived at St. Michael's Convent in St. George's for a couple of years until she was transferred to Assumption Convent at Stephenville Crossing.

28. "Minutes of the Ninth General Chapter, August 26, 1968," ASMSJ.
29. Purity Syrup in a variety of flavours is a concoction produced in Newfoundland. At one time it was very popular, especially with children.

In spite of the new elementary school of Our Lady of Mercy and further extensions to St. Joseph's High School, it was necessary to use four rooms in St. Michael's Convent to accommodate the overflow from the schools. Fortunately, the rooms used previously by the boarding students were available. But then a new emergency arose.

On October 2, 1972, the parish priest, Fr. Kelly arrived at the convent with three children, all under four years of age, whom the Department of Child Welfare had taken from a disruptive home. The department, unable to find suitable accommodation for such small children, brought them to the Sisters of Mercy. Srs. Rona O'Gorman and Ann Normore looked after them. The two sisters stayed up all night with the children in case they might be frightened at being away from home in surroundings so foreign to them. The next morning, a social worker arrived to take the children to Corner Brook. This provoked another crisis, for the children did not want to leave the sisters. Finally, Sr. Ann Normore took a leave of absence from school and, along with M. Thomasina Pomroy, accompanied the children to their new home in Corner Brook. Two days later, four more children arrived looking for shelter. The children, two boys and two girls, had been left alone in a freezing house. The two boys spent the night in the presbytery, while the girls were given a room in the convent. During the day, all four children stayed in the convent and had their meals there until a suitable home was found for them. These were the first in a succession of abused and abandoned children that were brought to the convent at all hours of the day and night for temporary shelter until the Department of Child Welfare could find a home for them. Although the sisters were happy to accommodate these poor little ones, the consequent loss of sleep with the added burden of caring for toddlers resulted in many nights when the sisters had little or no rest. Nevertheless, they did their best. If they dozed off in school the next day it was due, not to boredom but to loss of rest—they had been up half the night consoling some hurt and lonely child.

By the year 1973, most of the changes mandated by the general chapter of 1967 had been adopted. One of these was that each sister had the freedom to choose the time, place, and style of her annual retreat. Not all agreed with such "laxity" however. "For the first time in history there was no annual retreat held at St. Michael's Convent. Personal choice of time and place now enters into the question of retreat," sniffed the St. Michael's Convent annalist, disapproval dripping from every stroke of her pen.[30]

By this time, the congregation was becoming concerned over the safety of the old building that had served as St. Michael's Convent and Boarding School for over seventy years. Furthermore, it was much too large for a community of six or seven sisters. In May 1973, the decision was made to erect a new residence on a piece of ground on the west side of the original building. Unfortunately, the decision to erect a new convent required the sacrifice of some of the beautiful old trees that had graced the convent grounds since the days of M. Antonio Egan. As in the case of Curling convent, the sisters had to sacrifice more than trees. The stories and legends associated with the old St. Michael's Convent would fill a fair-sized book. One of the more popular tales described a tall, slender figure dressed in the traditional habit of the Sisters of Mercy who was seen floating along the corridor at a time when every living member of the community, except M. Lucina Cowley, the observer of the phenomenon, was seated in the community room.[31] It was with a feeling of nostalgia, then, that the sisters moved into the new St. Michael's Convent on March 9, 1974.[32] Although they appreciated the conveniences offered by their new home, it was hard to leave the old one that held so many memories and had played such a significant role in the history of the Congregation of the Sisters of Mercy. During the months of July, August, and September, the old St. Michael's Convent was taken down. It was said by one of the men who worked on the building that the six-inch pine beams were as fresh and strong as when they had been first put there more than seventy years before.[33]

All through the 1970s, there were nine or ten sisters attached to St. Michael's Convent in St. George's. Most of them taught in the schools in St.

30. Annals, St. Michael's Convent, St. George's, April 18, 1973, ASMSJ.

31. The story was told to the author by M. Lucina Cowley. M. Lucina was convinced that she had seen this mysterious apparition one summer evening.

32. The new St. Michael's Convent was officially blessed by Most Reverend R. T. McGrath, bishop of St. George's, on May 18, 1974.

33. Mr. Charles Foote to the author, August 1989.

George's. Two sisters continued to commute to the school in Flat Bay, and M. Barbara Wade provided volunteer services in Our Lady of Mercy Elementary School. However, early in the 1980s, there was a significant drop in the number of sisters who could be spared to teach in St. George's. While some sisters viewed this situation with concern, the more optimistic among them pointed out that in former years, the lack of qualified teachers necessitated the presence of the sisters. Now, because of the efforts of these sisters, an educated group of young Newfoundlanders was prepared to fill the places left vacant by the departure of the religious.

Meanwhile, the sisters who taught at St. Anne's Elementary School in Flat Bay were reaching out to all the people in that tiny community. During Lent 1984, Sr. Geraldine Mason started a Bible class that was attended by nineteen adults. Because there was no music teacher attached to the school, Geraldine gathered a group of teenagers and taught them some hymns and the music of the mass. Then, with the assistance of a couple of young lads who played the guitar, she put in place a regular choir for the little church. However, Geraldine did not confine herself to promoting religious knowledge and practice. She encouraged the teachers and the Altar Society to sponsor social events for the people of the town and, in particular, for senior citizens.

When school opened in September 1984, the community of St. Michael's Convent was joined by Sr. Marie Crotty, principal of Assumption High School and, for that year, the only sister attached to the schools of Stephenville Crossing.[34] A great deal of excitement accompanied the opening of the school year, for early in September, Pope John Paul visited St. John's. All the sisters from St. Michael's Convent went to the city for the event. Sr. Geraldine Mason and three teachers from St. Anne's School brought nineteen boys and girls from Flat Bay to see the Pope and participate in the celebrations surrounding his visit. Another sister, Gladys Bozec, was invited to proclaim in French the first Scripture reading of the Papal Mass.

---

34. In September 1985, another sister, Margaret Taylor, joined Marie Crotty on the staff of Assumption High School.

It was in the fall of 1984 that the sisters of St. Michael's Convent resumed one of the traditional ministries of the Sisters of Mercy, visitation of those in prison. In October, two sisters, Marie Crotty and Sharon Basha, began regular visitation of the Women's Correctional Centre in Stephenville. It often happened that some of the prisoners were unable to read or write. In such cases, another sister would volunteer to teach these individuals the basic literary skills. Consequently, many young persons, on being released from custody, enrolled in adult education courses until they had completed requirements for high-school graduation.

Traditionally, the sisters filled different roles on parish committees, such as Parish Council, Liturgy Committee, and the RCIA team.[35] Even though there were only two sisters in the school at Stephenville Crossing, the sisters of St. Michael's Convent made an effort to participate in the liturgies and other functions that took place in Assumption Parish. Both Assumption Parish in the Crossing and St. Michael's Parish, St. George's, served several smaller missions. Flat Bay and St. Theresa's were two of the missions served by St. George's, and the sisters took an active interest in both. One parish organization that was dear to the hearts of the sisters was the St. Vincent de Paul Society that looked after the needs of the poor. For instance, in December 1985, the Society, under the direction of Sr. Marie Crotty, distributed over eighty Christmas hampers to the poor in Stephenville Crossing. Furthermore, Sr. Marie was responsible for obtaining a government grant of money to support the thrift shop operated by the St. Vincent de Paul Society.[36]

The visitation of the sick and the bereaved had always been an important ministry for Sisters of Mercy everywhere. At times of tragedy, the sisters were always there to provide comfort and support. However, the exodus from religious life that occurred during the 1970s was felt more keenly every year. It became more and more difficult to fill positions vacated by sisters who reached the age of retirement or chose to engage in ministries other than

---

35. The Rite of Christian Initiation of Adults (RCIA) is a process through which a person interested in embracing Roman Catholicism is introduced to the faith by a team composed of members of the parish community.
36. Annals, St. Michael's Convent, St. George's, December 23, 1985, ASMSJ.

teaching. On February 13, 1985, the General Council announced that the Sisters of Mercy would relinquish the position of principal of Our Lady of Mercy School in St. George's, leaving only one sister, Mary Kelly, on the staff of the elementary school. Nevertheless, St. Michael's Convent remained open. The sisters continued their teaching ministry in Assumption High School in Stephenville Crossing until 1994, when Sr. Patricia Maher retired as principal of the school. At the time, it seemed as if this marked the end of the ministry of the Sisters of Mercy in Stephenville Crossing. Although nobody realized it at the time, before many years had passed the Sisters of Mercy would return to live in the Crossing.

The year 1993 marked the centenary of the arrival of the Sisters of Mercy at Sandy Point. Former students of St. Joseph's High School and St. Michael's College marked the occasion by holding a reunion. Almost 700 men and women, all graduates of the sisters' schools in St. George's, came for the celebrations. It was a time for remembering, rejoicing, and giving thanks.

Even though the sisters' teaching ministry had come to an end, St. Michael's Convent remained open, and the sisters continued to serve the people of St. George's and Stephenville Crossing through a variety of ministries. However, they realized that it was only a matter of time before they would be forced to leave St. Michael's Convent. Built to accommodate ten sisters, it was far too spacious a building for four. Reluctantly, the congregation decided to put the building up for sale. On October 26, 1995, the congregation's treasurer, Sr. Patricia March, phoned to say that the General Council had accepted a bid for the sale of the convent. The sisters, who did not want to leave St. George's altogether, searched the local papers and phoned all the real estate agents in the neighbourhood to see if there was a suitable house available in the town. Meanwhile, the presbytery in Stephenville Crossing was vacant due to the sudden death of the pastor, Father William Ryan.[37] After consultation with Bishop Lahey, the bishop of the Diocese of St. George's, the

---

37. After Father Ryan's death, the pastor of St. Michael's Parish, St. George's, Rev. John Kelly was given the added responsibility of administering Assumption Parish, Stephenville Crossing.

decision was made to rent the presbytery at Stephenville Crossing as a residence for the sisters.

The month of November 1995 was a period of frantic activity for the
four sisters of St. Michael's Convent. The presbytery in Stephenville
Crossing needed serious renovations to transform it from a residence for
one priest to a convent for four or five sisters. While carpenters, electricians, painters, and plumbers were busy repairing and fixing up the presbytery, the sisters were busy stripping St. Michael's Convent of the thousand
and one articles accumulated through the years that had made it a home to
so many. Eventually, everything was ready. On November 30, 1995, Sr.
Marcella Grant performed the last act in the long history of St. Michael's
Convent, St. George's, when she passed the blueprints of the convent and
the keys to the new owners of the house, William and Ann Vincent of
Stephenville.

It was during the 1980s that the shortage of ordained priests forced the bishops of Newfoundland to turn to the Sisters of Mercy and the Presentation
Sisters for help. Both religious congregations had had the foresight to see that
the time would come when their sisters would be asked to provide pastoral
assistance in parishes throughout the province. Consequently, there were a
number of sisters prepared and available to help in parishes where there was
no resident pastor. For example, in 1986, Bishop Raymond Lahey requested
the Mercy congregation send sisters to serve as pastoral ministers for a two-
year period in the parish of Our Lady of Grace, Bird Cove, on the Great
Northern Peninsula. Bird Cove is a small fishing village with a population of
almost four hundred.[38]

On September 20, 1986, Srs. Theresa Ryan and Alice Mackey arrived
in Bird Cove and began their official duties as pastoral ministers in charge of
Our Lady of Grace Parish. The parish boundaries extended from Flowers

---

38. *ENL*, s.v. "Bird Cove." Since that time many outports on the coast of Newfoundland
have experienced the effects of out-migration because of the collapse of the cod stocks.
Consequently, the population has decreased in recent years.

Cove in the north to Castor River South and included the communities of New Ferolle, Bartlett's Harbour, Castor River North, and Bird Cove itself, which was the largest community in the area. The six scattered communities had a Catholic population of about 1,100. The economy of the region was— and is—based on various aspects of the fishery. As pastoral ministers, Srs. Theresa and Alice were responsible for all the pastoral activities of the parish. These included celebrations of liturgy of the word,[39] baptisms, marriages, and funerals, as well as administrative duties in the parish. Priests from St. Anthony and Port au Choix celebrated mass once a month in each settlement and were available in cases of emergency and for the sacrament of reconciliation.

The two sisters began their ministry by visiting families in all the communities in the area. This was a slow process because of the distances separating each community. The people were very friendly, and the sisters received a warm welcome wherever they went. Furthermore, the people were eager to participate actively in the various religious and educational activities proposed by the sisters, even when it came to a sister presiding at religious ceremonies that had formerly been the sole prerogative of an ordained priest. Shortly after their arrival, Theresa and Alice presided at a wedding ceremony. After it was over, the mother of the groom thanked them saying, "That was some nice. I always knew women could put more romance into the wedding ceremony than the men!"[40]

It was not long before the sisters had identified the most pressing needs of the parish. They wrote, "Perhaps the greatest [need] is that of Evangelization: Youth and Adult Education in the Faith."[41] At that time, Newfoundland supported a denominational system of education. However, there were no Catholic high schools in the communities that comprised the parish of Our Lady of Grace. Consequently, students were deprived of the religious education pro-

---

39. Liturgy of the word is often celebrated in the absence of an ordained priest. It consists of prayers, readings from Scripture, occasionally a reflection on the Scripture reading and the distribution of Communion.
40. "Mercy Memo," December 1986.
41. Ibid.

grams offered to students who attended Roman Catholic high schools in the rest of the province.[42] Furthermore, there was, at the time, a lack of lay leadership in the parish. But, within weeks of their arrival, the sisters discovered that Catholics in the area had a desire and a readiness to learn more about their faith and to become involved in the life of the parish and the religious education of the children. Encouraged by this attitude, the two sisters placed their major emphasis on adult education in the faith.

From the beginning, the people had been told that the sisters would be leaving in 1988, but when in March of that year, Sr. Alice Mackey reminded parishioners that in April she would be returning to her mission in Peru, the news was greeted with consternation. The news spread quickly through all the communities belonging to Our Lady of Grace Parish, and from that time until the day of her departure, April 19, invitations to the sisters to "drop in for a cup of tea" arrived by the hundreds.

After Sr. Alice's departure, Sr. Theresa Ryan continued to minister in the parish for the next few months until the diocesan appointments were announced in June. People were happy to hear that they would have a resident priest once more; at the same time, they were sorry to lose the sisters. However, Sr. Theresa's skills were needed elsewhere, and so the ministry of the Sisters of Mercy in Bird Cove ended on June 26, 1988, when Sr. Theresa Ryan returned to St. John's.

However, the departure of the sisters from Bird Cove was not the end of Mercy ministry on the northwest coast of Newfoundland. In August 1990, Sr. Margaret Mulcahy was appointed pastoral minister of Holy Spirit Parish at St. Paul's, a small fishing community on the Great Northern Peninsula about thirty miles south of Bird Cove. The parish was formed in 1987, with Sr. Marie Murphy, a Presentation Sister, as its first pastoral minister. Thus, the presence of sisters was not a novelty to members of the parish. Consequently, Sr.

---

42. After denominational education had been abolished in Newfoundland, the religious education of Roman Catholic children became the sole responsibility of the parents. With the help and encouragement of pastors and teachers, every parish established programs to assist parents in their task of educating their children in the faith.

Margaret was spared the task of introducing parishioners to what was known as "priestless Sundays."

Holy Spirit Parish extends from Parsons Pond to Woody Point, an area of approximately ninety miles. At the time of Sr. Margaret's arrival, the parish numbered 135 families. There were four churches where services (liturgies of the word) were held weekly and mass celebrated monthly by a priest from Deer Lake. St. Paul's, the centre of the parish, is located within Gros Morne National Park. The spectacular beauty of the surroundings, the towering mountains, and the ever-changing moods of the ocean at her doorstep helped alleviate any feelings of loneliness Sr. Margaret may have experienced, especially during the winter when she was completely snowbound in her little house. Shortly after her arrival, she wrote an account of her experiences in her new mission, "The entire area offers superb geography for creation-centred spirituality. Sacredness breathes in the waves, the winds, the northern skies, the mountains and the trees."[43]

Sr. Margaret's pastoral ministry at St. Paul's was very similar to ministries carried on by sisters in other parishes in Newfoundland. At times, Sr. Margaret was required to attend meetings in St. John's or in other parts of Canada. In these instances, she was fortunate in being able to call on other members of the Mercy congregation for assistance. For instance, during the summer months of 1991, Sr. Edward Mary Roche presided at the weekend services, and on other occasions, Srs. Esther Dalton, Alicia Linehan, and Theresa Ryan supplied for Margaret when she was absent from the parish.

Among the many duties of a pastoral assistant, one of the most important is that of sacramental preparation. Some schools in the area provided religious instruction to Catholic students, but many Catholic children received their religious education through a home study program sponsored by the Canadian Conference of Catholic Bishops and coordinated on the Northern Peninsula by a Presentation Sister, Patricia King. Sr. Margaret discovered very quickly that, although the program was placed in the homes, frequently it was not taught there. Parents felt inadequate, and often the mother, who took

43. Sr. Margaret Mulcahy, "Mercy Memo," December 1990, p. 5.

responsibility to teach the program to her children, was a member of the Anglican faith and was unfamiliar with the tenets of the Roman Catholic faith. Thus, one of Margaret's first tasks was to establish support teams to help the parents in their efforts to educate their children in the faith. Also, in schools where there was provision for religious instruction, Margaret worked closely with the teachers, especially in preparing children for the sacraments. These activities, together with the visitation of the sick in their own homes and in the senior citizens' home in Neddies Harbour kept Margaret on her toes every day and often well into the night.

Meanwhile, the need for a new church building in Norris Point was becoming more urgent every day. On December 5, 1991, Bishop Lahey met with Sr. Margaret and three men from the community to discuss plans for building a new church. The bishop encouraged the people to proceed with the construction, promising them he would do all in his power to obtain financial support from the Catholic Church Extension Society of Canada. The bishop's promise was enough for the people of Norris Point. Men from all denominations in the settlement cut, sawed, and planed all the lumber for the new church during the winter of 1992, and construction began on July 6, 1992. Workers sponsored by the Department of Social Services and dozens of volunteers worked through the rest of the summer. Ten weeks later, the exterior of the church was completed.

However, the members of the Leadership Team of the Sisters of Mercy were not too happy that a sister was living alone in such a remote and difficult mission. The problem was solved when Sr. Georgina Quick, who had recently retired as vice-principal of Holy Heart of Mary High School in St. John's,[44] expressed an interest in joining Sr. Margaret to help in the parish. Margaret welcomed the decision with relief and gratitude. Bishop Lahey, too, was delighted to have the help of another pastoral worker and approved funding for an extension to the tiny house that had been Margaret's home since her arrival in St. Paul's. Two men from the community were hired to begin work on the

---

44. Previous to her appointment as vice-principal of Holy Heart, Sr. Georgina Quick was a member of the faculty of the Sir Wilfred Grenfell College in Corner Brook, teaching in the History Department.

extension, and, once again, other men from the area were most generous in providing volunteer help.

Sr. Georgina Quick joined Sr. Margaret in St. Paul's on August 24, 1992, and immediately, she was put to work, not as pastoral assistant, but as painter, cleaner, and general handywoman. Ladies from the parish helped the two sisters with painting the interior of the house and making drapes and sheers for the windows. Soon, the house was as spic and span as any convent on the island of Newfoundland. With the house in order, the two sisters settled down to their assigned work. It did not take Sr. Georgina very long to identify some of the problems that needed to be addressed. For most of her life, she had been involved with youth. Blessed with an ability to relate to young people and their problems, she took responsibility for coordinating the confirmation program in the parish, and she joined the Youth Strategy Transition Team at the Cow Head school complex. During the year this team planned many activities for youth. For example drug/alcohol awareness days were organized with the assistance of the ADDC and the RCMP,[45] with evening sessions offered to parents. Both sisters were members of organizations formed to benefit children, such as the Gros Morne Child Protection Team. This organization was formed to raise awareness of child sexual abuse and child neglect. Hand in hand with all these activities, the regular devotional and liturgical life of the parish continued as usual. The sisters shared responsibility for leading the services while, at the same time, training members of the parish to assume responsibility for conducting the liturgy of the word.

In May 1993, the parish received news from Rev. Tim Coughlan, president of the Catholic Church Extension Society of Canada, that the loan of $60,000 that had been approved for the construction of the new church at Norris Point had been converted to a grant of $60,000. Immediately, the building committee hired a foreman and an assistant to complete the interior of the church building. The ladies of the parish, who had been working diligently for years to provide funds for the church, succeeded in raising $35,000.

---

45. Alcohol and Drug Addiction Commission (ADDC), Royal Canadian Mounted Police (RCMP).

This was used to offset the cost of construction. Eventually, the big day arrived. On September 19, 1993, Bishop Raymond Lahey officially opened and dedicated Holy Spirit Church in Norris Point. Father Tim Coughlan from the Church Extension Society attended the celebration and spent a few days in the parish. Priests and sisters from nearby communities were present to congratulate the people on the opening of this beautiful building that was truly the work of their own hands.

Once the excitement of the opening of the new church had died down and all the visitors had gone home, Srs. Margaret and Georgina began to implement the plans they had made for the year ahead. Georgina was kept busy attending regular meetings of the Crime Prevention Group and the Youth Strategy Transition Team, while Margaret attended Gros Morne Child Protection Team meetings and the Bonne Bay Hospital Pastoral Care meetings. Activities involving youth and parents were planned for Alcohol and Drug Dependency Week, relevant literature was distributed to each household, and films and videos were shown to the public in the Anglican Church basement.

And so the months of autumn passed in a whirlwind of activity. There were no idle moments for the two sisters on the Northern Peninsula, and they looked forward to a few days of rest during the Christmas season. The New Year was greeted by dire warnings from the weather office of snow, blowing snow, blizzards, and high winds. On January 18, 1994, the seemingly indestructible Sr. Georgina stepped out of the house and was swept off her feet by winds of sixty miles an hour. When she arrived in hospital in Bonne Bay, it was discovered that she had broken her ankle and her wrist. This required the lengthy period of rest and healing that was provided by Srs. Anita Best and Michelle Gibbons at the convent of St. Mary's on the Humber. By early March, Georgina was able to return to St. Paul's, where, in the short span of a few weeks, she resumed her regular routine. During the summer months, when Sr. Margaret was absent from the parish, Georgina assumed the pastoral responsibility with the help of Sr. Sylvia Doyle.

However, the sisters' ministry in that part of the province was coming to an end. In August 1995, Sr. Georgina Quick was reassigned to the staff of McAuley Convent, and for the following year, Sr. Margaret was alone, once more. However, the work was proving to be too much for one person, and so, in the summer of 1996, Margaret resigned as pastoral assistant at Holy Spirit Parish. She was replaced by two sisters of St. Martha from Antigonish, Nova Scotia.

One hundred and ten years have passed since four Sisters of Mercy established a Mercy Convent on the west coast of Newfoundland. Through all these years, hundreds of Mercy Sisters lived and worked in various places in this rugged, beautiful part of the island. By their work in education, in visitation and care of the sick, and in pastoral ministry they touched many lives from the southern tip of the island northward up the western shore and across to Conche on the eastern part of the Northern Peninsula. But the years have brought many changes. Now, in the year 2004, five Sisters of Mercy remain on the West Coast. Srs. Gladys Bozec, Rona O'Gorman, and Esther Dalton work in the St. George's/Stephenville area; Srs. Alicia Linehan and Margaret O'Gorman live and work in Corner Brook, the former in ministry to the poor and the latter in faith development and sacramental preparation, and in several programs sponsored by women's organizations. Faithfully, day after day, these sisters continue to minister to the people of St. George's, Stephenville Crossing, and Corner Brook in a variety of ways but principally through their presence with the people in times of joy and sorrow.

CHAPTER NINETEEN

TENDER HANDS, CARING HEARTS

We do pray for mercy,
And that same prayer doth teach us all to render
The deeds of mercy.
Shakespeare, *The Merchant of Venice*, 4.1.200–02

The summer of 1950 was a period of both anticipation and apprehension for Roman Catholics in the Archdiocese of St. John's. The life of the man who had dominated the Church in Newfoundland for over fifty years was drawing to a close. Archbishop Edward Patrick Roche was dying. He had been a towering figure in Newfoundland history during the second quarter of the twentieth century. His coadjutor, Bishop Patrick J. Skinner, was moving quietly through the Avalon and Burin Peninsulas, performing all the duties usually reserved for the head of a diocese. What would happen when this reserved, scholarly man became the metropolitan archbishop of the Ecclesiastical Province of Newfoundland and head of the Archdiocese of St. John's was anyone's guess.

The people did not have long to wait. Archbishop Roche died in September 1950, and almost immediately after his installation (June 1951), the new archbishop, Patrick J. Skinner, announced a range of social policies through which he proposed to address the need for improved facilities in health care and education. His plans included the expansion of St. Clare's Mercy Hospital and its School of Nursing and the construction of new schools and churches. However, there was one area that was of major and immediate concern to the archbishop, and that was the plight of a large number of frail, elderly persons who were in critical need of shelter and care. Even in St. John's, the capital city, there was only one designated shelter for the destitute, old, and infirm, a house in the west end of the city, known as the "Poor House." From its beginning, this government-run institution was operated almost as a prison, the inmates living behind locked doors and barred gates and forbidden to leave the premises without the permission of their "keeper."[1] A grand jury, convened in 1907 to examine the state of the Poor House, concluded that it was "the saddest place in Newfoundland."[2] The institution underwent a major renovation in 1929, and two years later it was renamed "Home for the Aged and Infirm." Nevertheless, while conditions improved over the years, overcrowding remained a serious problem. In 1949, the Department of Public Welfare transferred fifty residents of this home to boarding houses and limited the number of residents who could be admitted to the institution. But still it remained the last refuge of mentally handicapped or poverty-stricken persons who had no place else to go. The home continued to be "the saddest place in Newfoundland," a description heartily endorsed by the Sisters of Mercy from St. Michael's Convent, Belvedere, who visited the inmates every week.

This was the state of affairs when Archbishop Skinner announced his intention to build "an institution dedicated to succouring the poor, the infirm, and the aged."[3] The archbishop envisioned an institution that would be partially self-supporting and provide security and care to senior citizens in surroundings that would lend dignity and comfort to the final years of life. He explained, "The institution will provide a desired haven of quiet and care for aged and infirm persons . . . it will be open to all creeds and to all classes with or without sufficient means."[4]

1. *ENL*, s.v. "Poor Relief."
2. Ibid., p. 375.
3. The quotation is from a bronze tablet on the wall near one of the entrances to St. Patrick's Mercy Home.
4. Archbishop P. J. Skinner, quoted in *The Monitor*, October, 1954, p. 2.

This first plank in the archbishop's platform of social reform aroused the enthusiastic support of the Catholic people all over Newfoundland. On February 8, 1953, the archbishop invited the men of the archdiocese to a meeting and announced that he was launching a campaign for funds in aid of the "Archbishop Skinner Social Welfare Fund." Everyone present gasped when he mentioned that he hoped to raise $150,000—an enormous sum of money at that time. But, even though he had been archbishop for only a few years, P. J. Skinner knew his people. Less than two months later, $157,000 had been collected, and on April 12, the archbishop informed the Catholic faithful that he was prepared to act on his plan to build a senior citizens home.

With the money in the bank, the archbishop's next problem was to find someone to administer the proposed home. At first he considered inviting the religious congregation known as the Little Sisters of the Poor to come to St. John's and operate the institution.[5] However, after lengthy correspondence with this congregation, he changed his mind and decided that the Sisters of Mercy were in a better position to meet the expectations of the people of Newfoundland. On March 24, 1954, Archbishop Skinner announced that the Mercy congregation had agreed to assume responsibility for the new home. He said, "Our own Newfoundland Sisters, knowing our conditions . . . will, I feel sure, carry out this work of social welfare with the same blessings that have crowned their zeal at St. Michael's Orphanage, Belvedere, and at St. Clare's Mercy Hospital."[6]

On October 2 of that same year (1954), in the presence of more than three thousand spectators, the archbishop turned the first sod for the home. In a brief but impressive ritual, he dedicated the new building to the glory of God and placed it under the protection of the Virgin Mary and St. Patrick, naming it "St. Patrick's Mercy Home." A much more elaborate ceremony for the lay-

5. The Little Sisters of the Poor are members of an international congregation of women religious who have dedicated their lives to the service of the elderly in thirty countries of the world.
6. Archbishop P. J. Skinner, Address to the people of the archdiocese, given in the Cathedral of St. John the Baptist, March 21, 1954, ASMSJ, RG 10/19/3.

ing of the cornerstone took place a year later on October 3, 1955. The ceremony was broadcast throughout Newfoundland through the facilities of the Canadian Broadcasting Corporation, for the proceedings were of interest to all people of the archdiocese. The archbishop explained:

> The new Home is meant to benefit the people of the whole Archdiocese. Recently on my confirmation tour in certain parts of Placentia Bay, I was consoled to see the spirit of several who wished to make a contribution toward our social welfare projects. . . . In one place some children gave me an offering of ten cents. One little girl had it carefully in a handkerchief. Such incidents are truly touching and show that the interest in our projects is not restricted to St. John's, but reaches <u>outside</u>, even to the smallest settlements.[7]

Incidentally, the mason for the laying of the cornerstone was John Conway, who was assisted by his sons. Five generations of Conways had worked on important construction projects in St. John's, and examples of their work may be seen in some of the older buildings in St. John's. The architect chosen for the project was John Hoskins of St. John's, a fellow of the Royal Architectural Institute of Canada.[8]

Two years later, on September 8, 1957, an impressive ceremony took place with the official opening of St. Patrick's Mercy Home and Convent, although the home was not yet ready for occupancy. A procession, formed at St. Pius X Church, moved up the hill to the steps of the new home while the Mount Cashel Band played appropriate music. It was a colourful occasion. The procession was composed of about four hundred Mercy and Presentation Sisters wearing white church cloaks over their black religious habits, one hundred altar boys in red cassocks and white surplices, mon-

---

7. Archbishop P. J. Skinner, Address on the occasion of the laying of the cornerstone of St. Patrick's Mercy Home, October 3, 1955, ASMSJ, RG 10/19/5.

8. Mr. Hoskins was the first Newfoundlander to achieve the honour of being accepted as a fellow of the institute. He did not live to see St. Patrick's Mercy Home in operation. The construction was completed under his supervision and the equipment was being moved in when he was stricken with a heart attack in 1957.

signori in rochet and purple soutane, priests in black soutane and white surplice, and Boy Scouts and Girl Guides in uniform. The archbishop, attired in rochet and red *cappa magna* and attended by a guard of honour from the Knights of Columbus in full dress uniform, followed the procession to the steps of St. Patrick's Mercy Home, where he celebrated mass. Immediately below the altar, at the foot of the front steps, a large platform was erected to accommodate the guests. Among those present were the Lieutenant Governor Sir Leonard Outerbridge and Lady Outerbridge, accompanied by Commander Fabian O'Dea, honourary aide-de-camp. Also, members of the provincial government and the opposition attended the ceremony, the music for which was supplied by the choir of Our Lady of Mercy School, directed by M. Edward Hodge.[9]

  The site chosen for the home was one of the most scenic in St. John's. Located by the side of one of the city's principal rivers, Rennies River, St. Patrick's Mercy Home looks out over the town toward the harbour. At the rear of the building, there is a beautifully appointed garden where the residents enjoy the fresh air and sunshine on fine summer days.[10] The building itself was designed to address not only the physical comfort of the residents, but also their spiritual and psychological well-being. A large auditorium located in the basement of the building provides a venue for entertainments, parties, and games. The chapel is on the second floor, a large, bright and airy room with a special gallery for non-ambulatory guests. It is, perhaps, one of the most attractive features of the home. Elderly residents of all denominations gather there to spend time in quiet reflection or to attend religious services conducted by clergy of the different faiths. Roman Catholic guests have the option of attending mass, which is celebrated daily by the chaplain.

  At last, on January 6, 1958, the construction and furnishing of the home was finished. Carpenters, electricians, and plumbers moved out, and the sisters moved in to put the finishing touches on bedrooms, dining rooms,

---

9. Annals, St. Patrick's Mercy Home, St. John's, vol. 1, p.1, ASMSJ.

10. This garden, named "The Mercedes Marshall Memorial Garden," was the gift of Mercedes Marshall, a lady who spent the last years of her life at St. Patrick's Mercy Home.

and lounges. The new St. Patrick's Mercy Home was the first long-term health care institution of its kind in Newfoundland. The day began with mass celebrated by Archbishop Skinner. The music was supplied by Our Lady of Mercy Novitiate Choir under the direction of M. Celine Veitch. On the same day, the sisters assigned to the home took up residence in St. Patrick's convent, which occupies one wing of the building.

The beginnings of St. Patrick's Convent were unlike that of any other Mercy convent in Newfoundland. Most new foundations were made with fewer than six sisters, but the first community of St. Patrick's numbered nine professed sisters and eight postulants, a total of seventeen in community. M. Alexius St. George was appointed superior of the convent and first administrator of the home. There were three registered nurses in the community, M. St. Joan McDonnell, M. Leo Davis, and a postulant, Catherine Greene. Two of the other sisters, M. Gerard Kennedy and M. Christina (Jane) McGrath, graduated as nurses a few years later. The first chaplain appointed to St. Patrick's Mercy Home, Father John Power, arrived on January 6, and took up residence in the chaplain's suite. With the exception of a few years, St. Patrick's has had the privilege of always having a resident chaplain on staff. During the period when there was no resident chaplain, the Jesuit Fathers from St. Pius Tenth Parish were generous in providing services for the home.[11]

In the interim between January 6 and the arrival of the first residents, the sisters were busy making beds, arranging furniture, checking supplies, and hiring staff. This period of "setting up" was subject to frequent interruptions as a succession of visitors arrived daily to ask for a tour of the building. But eventually, everything was in place. On January 20, 1958, the sisters welcomed the first guest to the home in the person of Father Andrew Nolan who had been a patient at St. Clare's Mercy Hospital for several months. Since that time, many priests have been cared for at the home during their final years on earth. Among these were the two who were responsible for the

11. Some of the priests who served as chaplains at the home were Fathers G. Hogan, F. Coady, V. Murphy, CSsR, C. Eagan, C. Strang, J. Punnakunnel, D. Hourigan, SJ. The most recent chaplain, Monsignor Dermot L. O'Keefe, died suddenly in May 2004.

planning and construction of St. Patrick's Mercy Home, Archbishop Patrick Skinner and his vicar general, Monsignor Harold Summers.[12] The annalist was careful to record the date of arrival and the names of the first male and female guests. She wrote, "On February 2, 1958, St. Patrick's Mercy Home welcomed its first female guest in the person of Miss Teresa Antle of Burin; the first non-clerical male resident was Mr. J. Pearson from Paradise (not Eden)."[13] From that day onward, the number of residents increased dramatically, so much so that at the end of six months, 187 guests were living at the home.

Many of the residents of St. Patrick's Mercy Home were financially independent and able to pay for the accommodations and services provided. However, the archbishop and M. Imelda Smith, superior general of the Sisters of Mercy, realized that there were many elderly persons who were not in a position to contribute anything to the cost of the care they needed. Therefore, as early as November 1957, the vicar general of the archdiocese, Monsignor Harold Summers, made subsidization arrangements with the deputy minister of health for the accommodation of persons receiving social assistance from the provincial government. In the same memorandum, it was noted that when the National Health Insurance became effective, it would cover the cost for accommodating twenty residents who required total nursing care.[14] Subsequently, the third floor of St. Patrick's Mercy Home became known as "the hospital floor." Twenty of the fifty-eight beds on the third floor were designated for coverage under the Newfoundland Hospital Insurance Plan (NHIP). Residents in the designated twenty beds had their care fully covered by the NHIP; other residents paid privately or were subsidized by the Department of Social Services. Nonetheless, all persons accommodated in this section received total nursing care twenty-four hours a day under the supervi-

12. Archbishop Patrick James Skinner died at St. Patrick's Mercy Home on September 19, 1988. Monsignor Summers died at the home on December 5, 1993. Monsignor Summers had been seventy-one years an ordained priest.
13. Annals, St. Patrick's Mercy Home Convent, St. John's, vol. 1, ASMSJ.
14. Memorandum noting telephone conversation between Right Rev. Harold A. Summers and Dr. James McGrath, November 20, 1957. ASMSJ.

sion of a registered nurse. Subsequently, St. Patrick's opted out of this coverage because of the inequity of the arrangement whereby some people paid from their own resources while others were fully subsidized under the NHIP. After the extension/renovation of the home in 1983–85, all areas of St. Patrick's Mercy Home provided total nursing care, and the reference to the third floor as the "hospital floor" was dropped.[15]

The first year St. Patrick's Mercy Home was in operation was a period of adjustment, of adapting to new circumstances for everyone involved, for the sisters as well as for the guests. For instance, one evening while the sisters were at supper in the convent, they noticed the door of the refectory opening slowly, inch by inch. Not knowing what to expect, every eye was on that door until finally a little old lady entered. She was attired in nightgown, slippers, and a large green hat and was carrying a handbag. She seated herself on a vacant stool,[16] helped herself to a large piece of cake and took an active part in the conversation that followed her appearance. She thoroughly enjoyed her visit and so did the sisters for, up to that point, they had been taking their meal in silence, listening to a reading from the lives of the saints.[17] After the lady had consumed more cake and several cups of tea, she was escorted back to her own room. On another occasion, M. St. Joan McDonnell met one of the male guests, a former fisherman, wandering disconsolately around the building. For the first time in his long life, he had nothing to do, and he was not at all happy with this state of affairs. Sister asked him if she could help him in any way. His face lit up as he responded to her question, "Oh, yes, Ma'am. Get me a swish and a bucket, show me the galley and I'll swab her up for you."[18] Frequently, unexpected guests were a problem for the hospitable sisters at St. Patrick's Mercy Home. One day the superior was called away from the dinner table to

15. I am indebted to Sister Margaret Williams for this information.
16. Prior to 1967, stools were used in place of chairs in convent refectories. This was intended as a form of penance, or perhaps it was a way of ensuring that Sisters did not linger too long at the table—wasting precious time that could be used for study, prayer, or housework!
17. Except on special occasions, sisters took their meals in silence while one of them read from a book dealing with the spiritual life.
18. A swish is a mop, and the galley is, of course, the kitchen.

answer the phone. Just as the dessert had been passed around, she returned to announce that a priest from St. Patrick's Parish had just decided to bring forty men from the Holy Name Society to entertain the guests. Whereupon M. Germaine Finlay was heard to murmur to the sisters near her, "Pass back your cake."[19]

The General Council of the Sisters of Mercy took care that there was always a sufficient number of sisters on staff at St. Patrick's. Thus, newly professed sisters could be almost certain of spending a few weeks at the home before being assigned to some more permanent ministry. Not only did their presence provide an opportunity for the permanent staff to take a well-deserved vacation, but also it allowed junior members of the congregation to experience Mercy in action. As a rule, the young sisters enjoyed their few weeks at St. Patrick's, where they were flattered, praised, and completely spoiled by the attentions of the gentlemen guests—all of whom were well over eighty years of age. Unlike the teaching sisters, those on staff at the St. Patrick's (or at St. Clare's Mercy Hospital) could not look forward to the change of pace provided by Christmas, Easter, and summer holidays. However, teaching sisters filled in during the summer vacation to allow members of the community at St. Patrick's Mercy Home and Convent to enjoy a well-earned holiday.

Sometimes elderly persons who came to live at the home were under the impression that they would sit quietly in a chair, with nothing to do and no place to go. A few hours at "St. Pat's" were sufficient to rid them of this idea. Because Newfoundlanders are fond of playing cards, within hours of being admitted, the new resident was invited to join a bridge club, an auction club, or simply a card club. In addition to these small groups, card parties and bingo games were held in the auditorium where relatives and friends joined the guests for an evening's amusement. People from the community at large went out of their way to assure residents at the home that they were not forgotten. Service clubs in the city fre-

---

19. These stories can be found in Annals, St. Patrick's Mercy Home Convent, St. John's, vol. 1. They are recorded here to illustrate the atmosphere that prevailed throughout the home and what life was like for the sisters who lived there. M. Germaine Finlay gave more than thirty-five years of service to St. Patrick's Mercy Home before ill health forced her to retire to Mercy Convent, Military Road. Subsequently, M. Germaine moved to McAuley Convent.

quently brought along groups of musicians or other entertainers to perform for the residents at St. Patrick's Mercy Home. Schoolchildren, particularly those from the sisters' schools, were periodic visitors. Children loved to perform for the residents at the home where everybody was delighted to see them and nobody in the audience was upset by mistakes. Children from the United States Air Force Base at Fort Pepperrell came to decorate the auditorium for Christmas, and choirs from all over the city offered to perform Christmas concerts. Then, on Christmas Eve, Santa Claus made his rounds, bringing gifts to every resident. Another Christmas activity was provided by members of the Rotary Club, who volunteered to drive the residents around the city to see the lights. This was a real treat, especially to people from small, isolated outports who had never seen St. John's lighted up for Christmas. At other times of the year, different forms of entertainment were provided. For instance, students from St. Clare's School of Nursing held debates and "singalongs," and various dramatic clubs put on plays and skits in the auditorium. During the summer months, service clubs in the city organized outings for the residents. The only problem was to find time to host all these different events.[20]

Nevertheless, in spite of the plethora of outside talent, the residents of St. Pat's were not dependent on others to provide entertainment. The residents and members of the staff periodically put off their own "Talent Show." A typical program included singing, instrumental music (piano, violin, accordion, guitar, and mouth organ), recitations, skits, and dancing. For a few years, the competitive dancing was adjudicated by one of the residents, a former professional dancing instructor, Mrs. Belle Cleary. These activities worked wonders for the spirits and even the physical well-being of those who participated. The annalist wrote of one elderly person who, prior to coming to St. Patrick's, could not be persuaded to get out of bed. On one occasion, his sons came to the home to visit their father and were told that he was attending a concert. To their amazement, when they entered the auditorium, they saw the formerly bedridden old gentleman performing a step dance on the stage.[21]

---

20. Annals, St, Patrick's Mercy Home, St. John's, vol. 1, ASMSJ.
21. Ibid., p. 53.

A little over a year after the arrival of the first residents, on September 24, 1959, ownership of St. Patrick's Mercy Home was transferred to the Congregation of the Sisters of Mercy.[22] Since that time, the congregation has invested large amounts of money in upgrading equipment and improving facilities at the home.

Initially, a majority of the residents of St. Patrick's Mercy Home were more or less independent, but as time passed, those admitted were already very sick or suffering from some form of chronic disability. Usually, there were between seventeen and twenty sisters exercising some form of ministry at the home, and over the years, increasing numbers of nurses, orderlies, and other support staff were hired to assist in the care of the sick and the upkeep of the institution. Furthermore, a number of volunteers from nearby parishes spent time reading to the patients, writing letters for them, and entertaining them in various ways. In 1969, on the initiative of the administrator, M. Mark Hennebury, St. Patrick's Mercy Home Auxiliary was formed.[23] The first president of the auxiliary was Mary Veitch, RN, and for many years, under the guidance of Miss Veitch and her successors, the auxiliary provided valuable service to the staff and residents of the home.

Although St. Patrick's Mercy Home had many friends in the city of St. John's and, in fact, throughout the whole province of Newfoundland, Archbishop Skinner took a personal interest in the welfare of the residents and staff of the home. Therefore, when the Knights of Columbus presented him with a substantial monetary gift on the occasion of the silver jubilee of his ordination to the episcopacy, he devoted the entire sum to the purchase of a minibus for St. Patrick's Mercy Home. The minibus was painted yellow and decorated with green shamrocks, and on its side, the name of the home was emblazoned in large letters. For many years, the little bus was a familiar sight on the streets of the city as it carried residents of the home to the malls on a shopping trip, out for a drive in the country, or perhaps on a picnic.

---

22. ASMSJ, RG 10/19/8. Subsequently, in 1984, St. Patrick's Mercy Home was incorporated and since that time ownership rests with St. Patrick's Mercy Home Inc.

23. M. Mark Hennebury was a younger sister of M. Fabian Hennebury, long-time administrator of St. Clare's Mercy Hospital. See chapter fourteen.

Some of the sisters who went to St. Patrick's during the first two years of the foundation remained there for the rest of their lives. M. Alexius St. George, M. St. Joan McDonnell, M. Fintan Downey, and M. Paul Ryall all died at the home. M. Fintan was the first annalist. She was a gifted writer, and the Annals covering the first five years of the home are filled with interesting descriptions and anecdotes. M. Paul Ryall, who worked in the business office at the home, was known for her charity to the poor. When her day's work was over, she spent the rest of her waking hours visiting the guests at the home and helping persons from outside the institution who came to her for assistance. One evening in November 1976, she was found in her workroom where she had died while packing a box of clothing for a needy person. Hundreds of people of all creeds and faiths flocked to the chapel of St. Patrick's Mercy Home to pay their respects to the woman who was known for her warm smile and her tender concern for those in distress. Then, while the Congregation of the Sisters of Mercy was still reeling from the shock of M. Paul's death, the first administrator of the home, M. Alexius St. George, died suddenly while receiving dialysis at the General Hospital.

St Patrick's Mercy Home was governed by a board of directors whose members were nominated and the appointments confirmed by the archbishop of St. John's and the superior general of the Sisters of Mercy. For a number of years after the home opened, the position of administrator was filled by one of the sisters from the nursing staff of St. Clare's Mercy Hospital. But as time passed, it became clear that the management of a large chronic-care facility required something more than the training and experience of a registered nurse. Therefore, the superior general of the time, Marie Michael Power, decided to send one of the sisters to a university that offered a degree program in hospital administration. While there was no shortage of sisters capable of completing studies in this field, Sr. Margaret Williams, who was working in the business office at St. Clare's Mercy Hospital, expressed an interest in working with the elderly. Because at that time courses in gerontology were not offered in Canada, Sr. Margaret turned her attention to universities in the United States and found what she was looking for at North Texas State University. In September 1974, she packed her bags and set off for Texas to prepare for what became the greatest challenge of her life—serving as administrator of St. Patrick's Mercy Home. Having completed the prescribed courses, she spent her internship year at the Isabella Geriatric Centre in Manhattan, N.Y., graduating with a master's degree in gerontology with a minor in business administration. On August 1, 1976, she was named administrator of St. Patrick's Mercy Home, a position she held until August 1995.

During Sr. Margaret Williams' term as administrator, significant changes occurred at the home. Because persons admitted to St. Patrick's in the 1970s and 1980s were less mobile and required more nursing care than did residents of former years, it became clear that the building itself and the range of services provided were inadequate to meet the needs presented at the time. Consequently, in the early 1980s, it was decided to begin a project of renovation and expansion. With financial assistance from Canada Mortgage and Housing Corporation, a major extension was added to St. Patrick's Mercy Home, and the existing facility underwent major renovations. The sod-turning ceremony for the new wing took place on May 30, 1983. Just one year later, in May 1984, St. Patrick's achieved full accreditation for two years from the Canadian Council on Hospital Accreditation. In its report, the council commended the board of directors of the home, the Sisters of Mercy, and the administration on their progressive leadership. The report continued, "It is evident that the care is centred on the residents' spiritual, social, psychological and physical needs. . . . Independence and the right to self-determination is fostered."[24] At the time, the staff at St. Patrick's Mercy Home numbered 165 persons, including nurses, orderlies, administrative personnel, and support staff.[25]

Meanwhile, work on the new extension was proceeding rapidly. The plan was that as soon as the new wing was ready for occupancy, the residents would be moved out of the older part of the building so that renovations could take place. This posed a major headache for Sr. Margaret Williams, the

---

24. *The Evening Telegram*, July 21, 1984, p. 5.

25. In June 2004, a staff of over three hundred persons is required to operate St. Patrick's Mercy Home. The home is always filled to capacity and there are more than three hundred names on the waiting list to be admitted as residents.

administrator, and for her staff. Beginning on July 9, 1984, when the new wing was ready for occupancy, Margaret, the rest of the sisters, and the staff relocated almost 160 residents to their new quarters. When all the work was finished, St. Patrick's Mercy Home had been expanded to include 214 beds.

However, the newly enlarged St. Patrick's offers more than extra beds. In addition to medical, nursing, and social services, a regular program of physiotherapy is available as well as various recreational activities such as carpentry and woodworking, sewing, knitting and painting, and music of all kinds. An ongoing recreational program is offered, and under the direction of Sr. Patricia Marie Decker, the Red Rose Café has been set up near the main entrance of the home where the residents and their guests can enjoy "Afternoon Tea." Much to the satisfaction of the ladies who reside at the home, there is a fully-equipped beauty parlour on the first floor where the services of professional beauticians are available.

Among the most popular visitors to St. Patrick's Mercy Home are a number of tail-wagging, four-legged friends whose owners co-operate in a program sponsored by the St. John Ambulance Therapy Dog Unit. The program is based on evidence that suggests that regular contact with dogs reduces stress and anxiety. In an interview with a reporter from *The Evening Telegram*, Sr. Patricia Marie Decker said that when the dogs visited some patients suffering from Alzheimer's disease there were surprising results. She said, "Those who have lost their ability to communicate go straight for the dogs to touch them and pet them."[26] In June 2004, in recognition of her involvement with the therapy dog program for the elderly at St. Patrick's Mercy Home, the lieutenant governor of Newfoundland invested Sr. Patricia Marie into the Order of St. John.

Although all these programs are necessary and valuable, there is still another that has become critically important to the residents and their families. Gradually, over the years, a new form of organized ministry took shape at

---

26. Patricia Marie Decker, RSM, quoted by Deborah Smith, *The Evening Telegram*, March 10, 1996, p. 3.

St. Patrick's Mercy Home, one that has its origins in a prescribed ministry of the Congregation of the Sisters of Mercy—visitation of the sick and elderly. The hiring of a number of lay professional nurses left sisters free to spend more time with the residents. Eventually, this became a full-time ministry for many of the sisters who live at St. Patrick's Convent. The sisters visit, provide companionship, pray, and offer words of encouragement to elderly persons whose friends and relatives have preceded them into the next world. The sisters' ministry embraces, as well, the families of the residents. When a person becomes very ill, and especially during the last moments of life, the presence of a sister is a consolation to the patient and to family members. After the death of one of the residents, the sisters attend the wake and the funeral, and continue to support the family in their loss.

After a while, church and civil authorities began to recognize this form of ministry as an integral part of health care services. The General Council of the Sisters of Mercy initiated a policy of releasing interested sisters for special studies in the discipline of pastoral care. Consequently, a number of sisters chose pastoral care ministry as a second career after they retire from teaching or nursing. At the time of writing, Sister Monica Hickey is director of pastoral care at St. Patrick's Mercy Home. Monica's warm smile and her gentle, compassionate presence has been a special gift to residents and their families during her years of ministry at the home. At the time of writing Monica is assisted by Srs. Marie Alma O'Gorman, Margaret Rose, and Ann Normore and a number of other sisters who volunteer a certain number of hours a week to ministry at the home. A number of other sisters who have earned diplomas in clinical pastoral education help staff pastoral care departments in many Newfoundland hospitals and nursing homes, as well as in St. Patrick's Mercy Home.[27]

The year 1995 saw the first major change in the administration of St. Patrick's Mercy Home when Sr. Margaret Williams retired. Because there was

27. Sr. Monica Hickey held the position as director of pastoral care at the home for several years before she was appointed for a two-year term as accountant at Mercy International Centre in Dublin. After her return to St. John's, Monica worked in the Pastoral Care Department at St. Clare's Mercy Hospital until her reappointment to St. Patrick's in September 2003.

no sister available to replace her, Ms. Katherine Turner was named administrator of the home. Ms. Turner was a capable administrator, respected and loved by staff and residents alike. But more than this, she succeeded in maintaining and strengthening the special charism of hospitality and mercy that the sisters had brought to the home through the years since 1958. In July 2000, Kathy Turner took a leave of absence from St. Patrick's Mercy Home to take a position with the Department of Health. Ms. Gail Rogers was named administrator for the interim period, but subsequently Ms. Turner accepted a position as administrator of Chancellor Park, a privately owned facility for assisted living, thus leaving the position of administrator vacant once again. However, by this time a Sister of Mercy, Phyllis Corbett, was available and qualified to administer St. Patrick's Mercy Home.

Sister Phyllis was the logical choice for the position. In addition to her experience as a registered nurse on the staff of St. Clare's Mercy Hospital, Phyllis had earned a master's degree in health care administration and had been director of nursing at St. Clare's for several years. She had also filled the post of on-site administrator of St. Clare's Mercy Hospital for a year before she retired, still in her early fifties. However, retirement is not a word that one associates with Sr. Phyllis Corbett. An energetic, dedicated woman, Sr. Phyllis had no intention of sitting quietly at home in the convent learning to knit. She decided to study clinical pastoral education in the United States. When she had completed the program of studies and received her certificate, she returned to work in the Pastoral Care Department at St. Clare's until she was asked to assume the administration of St. Patrick's Mercy Home in July 2001.

Prior to the appointment of Sr. Phyllis, in January 1998, during the tenure of Ms. Kathy Turner, St. Patrick's Mercy Home introduced a new concept in resident and family care, the purpose of which was to provide a restful, quiet area for family members of very ill and dying patients. Appropriately, it was named and dedicated in honour of the foundress of the Sisters of Mercy, Catherine McAuley, whose spirit and mission are reflected in the philosophy and mission of St. Patrick's Mercy Home. The suggestion to provide such a facility came from members of the nursing staff who were concerned for grieving families of residents who were dying. The Board of Directors of St.

Patrick's Mercy Home enthusiastically embraced this concept—which was fully endorsed and financially supported by the Congregation of the Sisters of Mercy. Families and friends of residents of the home made generous donations, so that within a short time, the Catherine McAuley guest suite was fully operational.

Meanwhile, in the years between 1993 and 1998, the Newfoundland government was considering major changes in the delivery of long-term health care.[28] The government was determined to consolidate all six nursing homes in the St. John's area under one board and one chief executive officer.[29] The first step toward the realization of this goal was taken in November of 1996, when the minister of health appointed a regional board, now known as the St. John's Nursing Home Board (SJNHB), with a mandate to implement the government's plan of consolidation. Sister Nellie Pomroy and Mr. Andrew Grant were representatives of St. Patrick's Mercy Home on this regional board.

In April 1997, the SJNHB engaged an executive director and established a transfer team with the mandate to work out an agreement with each of the nursing homes whereby governance would be assumed by the SJNHB, but the denominations would continue to own the property. For the next eight months the Congregation of the Sisters of Mercy and the Board of Directors of St. Patrick's Mercy Home bargained with the SJNHB in the hope of reaching an agreement that would allow the congregation to continue its mission at St. Patrick's. After many meetings, it became obvious that the proposed new arrangement would seriously diminish the influence of the Sisters of Mercy in key areas of the life of St. Patrick's and would not be compatible with the congregation's continuing ministry to the elderly. The draft agreement of December 1997 left no doubt that the Sisters of Mercy would have little or no

28. The information that follows, outlining the establishment of the St. John's Nursing Home Board and the negotiations that took place concerning the future of St. Patrick's Mercy Home, is taken from the Accountability Report presented to the Congregation of the Sisters of Mercy by the congregational Leadership Team at the general chapter that was held in July 2001.

29. The five denominationally operated homes are St. Patrick's Mercy Home (the Sisters of Mercy), Glenbrook Lodge (the Salvation Army), St. Luke's Home (the Anglican Church), Agnes Pratt Home (The United Church), Masonic Park (the Masons). Hoyles/Escasoni is owned by the government and was not directly involved with the negotiations.

authority regarding St. Patrick's Mercy Home but would continue to have all the responsibilities of ownership.

At that point the superior general of the Sisters of Mercy, Sr. Charlotte Fitzpatrick, initiated a series of discussions regarding these developments with the Board of Directors of St. Patrick's Mercy Home. She consulted also with representatives from the ownership bodies of other St. John's nursing homes and with professional consultants. After reflecting on the advice received, the Congregation of the Sisters of Mercy made a decision to continue the governance and management at St. Patrick's and to explore the option of sharing certain services with other nursing homes in the pursuit of efficiencies in the system. This decision was supported unanimously by the Board of Directors of St. Patrick's Mercy Home.

The next step in this long, difficult, and complicated process occurred in February 1998, when representatives of the Sisters of Mercy and St. Patrick's Board of Directors met with the minister of health to discuss the shared services option. This option was presented in a formal document that articulated very clearly the position taken by the Congregation of the Sisters of Mercy and the Board of Directors of St. Patrick's Mercy Home. The document outlined the reasons for the position and a four-phase process that would ensure that the objectives of cost savings and maintenance of quality care could be achieved through the shared services arrangement. As a result of this meeting, the board of St. Patrick's and the SJNHB worked out a "Memorandum of Understanding" that was signed by both bodies on September 16, 1999. The agreement outlined accountabilities and responsibilities specific to ownership issues, operational and fiscal requirements, and policy governance. St. Patrick's retained its own board of directors as well as the right to maintain and appoint an executive director. It acknowledged the jurisdiction of the SJNHB in the allocation of funds and in the establishment of region-wide policies for the nursing homes. Inherent in the agreement was St. Patrick's willingness to grow in collaboration with the SJNHB and to amalgamate certain support functions with the other nursing homes in the region. Subsequently, this "Memorandum of Understanding" was strengthened when the six nursing homes and the SJNHB engaged in a strategic planning exercise. The result was the collaborative development of "Shared Vision, Mission and Values Statements" and a set of strategic directions. The mission statement recognized a partnership arrangement of each nursing home with the SJNHB and with each other. Through the planning process, all partners gained new insights into the operational role of site-specific boards[30] and the evolving role of the SJNHB in setting region-wide long-term care policy directions, facility planning, education and research initiatives, human resource planning, and budget allocations.

Although this arrangement with the government and the SJNHB ensured that Christian principles, ethical decision making, and respect for life would continue to guide all the activities at St. Patrick's, the Leadership Team of the Sisters of Mercy and the Board of Directors of St. Parick's Mercy Home decided that they needed another group to support their efforts for the elderly. Therefore, in November 1998, the St. Patrick's Mercy Home Foundation was established and, subsequently, a foundation board was formed. The responsibilities of the foundation include fundraising, advocacy, and ethical decision making in the allocation and investment of funds. The foundation supports the mission, vision, and values of St. Patrick's Mercy Home and its ongoing efforts to ensure a comfortable and homelike atmosphere for the residents.

At the beginning of the year 1999, Sr. Madonna Gatherall initiated a year-long process at St. Patrick's for the development of a "Statement of Core Values" and for the revision of the "Statement of Philosophy" and the "Mission Statement." This involved participation on all levels at St. Patrick's Mercy Home. The mission statement referred to ethics as an integral part of the life and mission of St. Patrick's. The mandate of the Ethics Committee was to strengthen this dimension of the home and to foster an ethical culture. A subcommittee, formed to carry out initiatives in this regard, began with sessions for all the staff on the topic, "Dignity of the Human Person."

Right from the beginning, the sisters were sensitive to the opinions of the residents and their families. For this reason a Residents' Council had been established to provide a forum for residents to offer suggestions and express

---

30. For example, St. Patrick's Mercy Home Board.

opinions. By the late 1980s, this council had become inactive because of the increased age and frailty of many of the residents. Therefore, St. Patrick's Mercy Home Board decided to replace the Residents' Council with a Family Council that would meet regularly to voice concerns and offer suggestions.

At the time of writing, 214 residents are being cared for at St. Patrick's Mercy Home by a staff of over three hundred persons. These include the administrative staff, chaplains, pastoral care workers, physicians, registered nurses, licensed practical nurses, social workers, recreation therapists, dieticians, cooks, kitchen staff, and housekeeping and laundry staff. Furthermore, a number of faithful volunteers dedicate many hours a week to visiting the residents, bringing them to the chapel, to the garden, or to the many activities that are available at St. Patrick's Mercy Home.

Sadly, in recent years the number of sisters on staff has decreased from eighteen or twenty to five or six. But what is lacking in quantity is more than compensated by the dedication and devotion of those sisters who spend their time caring for the elderly and the sick. Moreover, the human and material resources that the Congregation of the Sisters of Mercy makes available to St. Patrick's Mercy Home have had a major impact on the life and vitality of St. Patrick's over the years. Through these efforts the Sisters of Mercy try to ensure that all the activities at the home are rooted in the same spirit of mercy and compassion that inspired Archbishop Skinner and Sr. M. Imelda Smith to undertake this ministry in the first place.

The years encompassing the episcopate of Most Rev. P. J. Skinner were marked by numerous foundations of the Sisters of Mercy throughout Newfoundland and beyond. Having persuaded the Mercy congregation to take over the administration (and eventually the ownership) of St. Patrick's Mercy Home, Archbishop Skinner—like Oliver Twist—decided to ask for more. Consequently, the next foundation that came about in response to a request of the archbishop was St. John Eudes Convent at Beaconsfield on Topsail Road in St. John's.

Originally, the estate known as Beaconsfield was the property of Sir Hugh Hoyles who was prime minister of Newfoundland from 1861–1865. Later, it became the property of another prime minister, Sir Edward Morris

(1909–1917). It was Morris who named the estate after Benjamin Disraeli, Lord Beaconsfield. In those days, that part of Topsail Road where Beaconsfield was located was outside the city limits and surrounded by farms and forest. In 1919, the Cathedral Palace, home of the archbishop of St. John's, was destroyed by fire. While the new palace was being built, Archbishop Edward P. Roche took up residence at St. Bride's, Littledale, where a special suite had been reserved for his use. It was while he was staying at Littledale, that the archbishop—who "enjoyed" poor health—decided that the country air was essential to his physical well-being. Subsequently, the Archdiocese of St. John's purchased the Beaconsfield estate and it became the official residence of the archbishop of St. John's.[31]

Therefore, when Patrick J. Skinner succeeded Roche as archbishop of St. John's, he took up residence at Beaconsfield. The secluded location and the quiet, peaceful surroundings were very attractive to this reserved and sensitive man. Archbishop Skinner had spent most of his life teaching in a seminary in Quebec. He was a gifted musician and spent whatever free time he had playing the piano, listening to music, or reading. There was only one hitch in his idyllic living situation. It was difficult to get a housekeeper to look after his meals and attend to the many chores required in a large house that was quite a distance from the centre of the city. Furthermore, the archbishop of St. John's was obliged to receive and entertain visiting bishops, priests, and other dignitaries. At a time when employment was at an all-time high, not too many qualified housekeepers were willing to undertake such a demanding job. In desperation, Archbishop Skinner turned to the Sisters of Mercy and asked for a few sisters to take care of his residence for a short time until he could find a suitable housekeeper.[32]

It was an unusual request, and one that did not conform to the traditional ministries of the Sisters of Mercy. However, mindful of the spirit of the congregation, "Mercy is called to respond wherever there is need," the superior

31. Beaconsfield was used as the episcopal residence for Archbishop Roche's successors until 1998, when the house was sold. A few years previously, the extensive property surrounding Beaconsfield house had been sold for a housing development.
32. ASMSJ, RG 10/20/1.

general, M. Imelda Smith, took pity on the archbishop's plight and agreed to
his request. Consequently, on February 2, 1953, three sisters from St. Bride's
Convent, Littledale, took up duties at the episcopal residence at Beaconsfield.
At that time, there was no mention of building a convent because the arrangement was intended to be of short duration.

On February 2, 1953, M. Rosalita Power, M. Dominica Flynn, and M.
Monica Matthews moved into a section of the archbishop's house at
Beaconsfield. M. Rosalita continued to teach at St. Augustine's School,
Littledale, while M. Dominica and M. Monica looked after the housekeeping
and the cooking at the archbishop's residence. This state of affairs continued
until 1959, although there were yearly changes in personnel. However,
because the living quarters provided for the sisters were small and cramped, a
small convent attached to Beaconsfield was built. The new convent was dedicated in honour of St. John Eudes, founder of the Congregation of Jesus and
Mary, of which Archbishop Skinner was a member. St. John Eudes Convent
was blessed and officially opened on September 3, 1959. The members of the
first community of St. John Eudes Convent were M. Lucina Cowley (superi-
or), Marie Michael Power, M. Lucia Walsh, and M. Cyril Spencer. Two sisters,
Marie Michael and M. Cyril, commuted to Holy Heart of Mary Regional High
School, while M. Lucina and M. Lucia looked after the housekeeping at
Beaconsfield. This arrangement continued, and for the next twenty years,
there were four sisters in the community at St. John Eudes Convent, two
looked after the housekeeping and two teaching sisters commuted back and
forth to school or university.

Apparently, Archbishop Skinner was not hard to please in matters of
diet. He ate what was put in front of him and was always gentle and considerate in his dealings with the sisters. He respected their privacy but accepted joyously the occasional invitation to have dinner with the sisters at the convent.

The sisters at St. John Eudes led a relatively sheltered existence in comparison with members of other convents. Out of respect for the archbishop's
privacy, sisters of the Mercy congregation were not encouraged to make
informal visits to St. John Eudes Convent. One never knew when the archbishop might be entertaining the premier, the apostolic delegate, or some

other exalted personage. In any case, when the archbishop had visitors, the sisters at St. John Eudes were up to their eyes in work and had no time for chatting with friends. There was, however, one resident of St. John Eudes Convent whose only purpose in life was to entertain the members of the community and any occasional visitors who might drop by. Early in the 1960s, the sisters acquired a parakeet. Although the bird's conversational abilities were limited, there were occasions when the unwary guest would be admonished, "Go, say your prayers!"

And so the years passed. The "short time" envisioned in 1953 came to a close twenty-six years later when Archbishop Skinner retired in June 1979. At that time his successor, Archbishop Alphonsus L. Penney, was informed that the sisters could no longer continue their ministry at Beaconsfield and, by mutual agreement between Archbishop Penney and the superior general, Marie Michael Power, St. John Eudes Convent closed on November 2, 1979.

Following the completion of St. Patrick's Mercy Home and St. John Eudes Convent, the superior general of the Sisters of Mercy, M. Imelda Smith, and her council decided to turn their attention to the overcrowding experienced by the sisters at St. Bride's Convent, Littledale. The period of the 1950s saw a notable increase in the number of young women who wanted to devote their lives to God as Sisters of Mercy. Littledale had been designated as the novitiate house. Hence the overcrowding experienced by the local community.

Throughout the preceding chapters of this book, reference has been made to the initial period of religious life known as "the novitiate." Any young person who wished to become a member of a religious congregation passed though several stages of formation before being admitted to profession of vows.[33] In the case of the Sisters of Mercy, when a young woman was accepted as a candidate, she began a six- to nine-month period of initiation called the "postulancy." As a rule, during this time the postulant attended classes to prepare her for a career in teaching or nursing. If she had already completed university training, she was assigned duties in school or hospital. Meanwhile, she

33. This is true up to the present day for all religious congregations.

lived in a convent, which may have been some house other than the novitiate house, and followed the same routine of prayer, work, study, and recreation as other members of the community. This provided the postulant with the experience of living in a religious community and allowed the community to decide if she had the qualities necessary for religious life. If the postulancy experience was mutually agreeable, the candidate was admitted to the novitiate. If not, she returned home.

In the past, the ceremony of reception into the novitiate was perhaps, the most spectacular event in the life of a religious. Following the homily of the Mass of the Holy Spirit, the postulant, dressed in a long white dress and veil, presented herself to the archbishop, the superior general, and her assistant. The archbishop questioned her, "My child, what do you demand?" To which the postulant responded, "The mercy of God and the holy habit of Religion." The next question determined the young woman's freedom of choice, "Is it of your own free will that you request the holy habit of Religion?" After the postulant had answered in the affirmative, the archbishop interrogated the superior general on the young person's suitability for religious life.[34] After this, the postulant left the chapel and retired to the convent where she put aside her beautiful white dress, and donned the religious habit and white veil of a novice. Part of the procedure involved having her hair cut to an appropriate length. This operation was performed in haste and in what can be described as a "chop-snip-chop" fashion, but fortunately, a tightly fitting coif concealed the less-than-flattering results. The former postulant, now a novice, reappeared in the chapel with a new name and garbed in the habit of a Sister of Mercy. For the novice, this was the beginning of a two-year period of prayer, study, and formation in the ways of religious life.

In the years prior to the amalgamation of the convents, there was no general novitiate. Young women who wished to enter religious life applied to the convent of their choice. Once having been admitted, they received their training from one of the sisters of the community. One of the most cogent rea-

---

34. Although these questions might seem to have been a mere formality, they were necessary to ensure that the young person understood and was freely choosing to assume the obligations involved in living as a religious.

sons for effecting the amalgamation in 1916 was to ensure the adequate training of novices, and the first act of the new General Administration was to
establish a general novitiate at Littledale. From 1916 onward, the sisters spent
at least one year of the prescribed two-year novitiate at Littledale.[35] There was
a distinct advantage in having the novitiate in the same building that housed the
student teachers at St. Bride's College. It provided an opportunity for postulants and novices to attend education courses on campus and allowed the
novice mistress to draw on the staff of the college when tutors were required
to coach any of her young charges who needed additional help. Moreover, it
presented a daily reminder to the college students that religious life offered a
viable and attractive option to a young woman trying to decide what to do with
her life. Also, the presence of the novitiate within the boarding school supplied
plenty of evidence that a young girl who was toying with the idea of a religious
vocation would have plenty of time to experience the life and make up her
mind before making a final commitment. This was clear from the number of
young women who gave religious life an honest trial and decided that it was
not for them. During the period from 1916 to 1925 the Sisters of Mercy
received fifty-eight young women as novices. Of these, twelve left the congregation before final profession, but forty-six stayed.

The decision to establish St. Bride's, Littledale, as the novitiate house,
required that a portion of the building be designated for this purpose. Over the
years, the location of the novitiate changed frequently as additional space was
required to accommodate more novices and also the students at St. Bride's
College. Eventually, with the opening of St. Augustine's Hall in 1943, the novitiate was relocated to the first floor of the west wing of St. Bride's College. A
partition was built separating the boarding school from the rooms that comprised the novitiate. The entrance to the novitiate was through St. Michael's
Corridor—so called because of a life-sized statue of the Archangel St. Michael
and the Devil that stood there, the most interesting feature of which was the
large spear held by the archangel and embedded in the Devil's ear. It was the

35. Members of the first group of novices to occupy the general novitiate were Margaret
Mary Collins, M. Paul Ryall, and M. Patricia Hogan. The first general novice mistress was
M. Benedicta Fitzgibbon.

duty of some unfortunate novice to clean the various crevices in St. Michael's wings as well as to remove more obvious dust that had collected in the Devil's brown ear. Some sisters of that generation still experience occasional twinges of earache due, no doubt, to the memory of frequent and lengthy meditation on the Devil's encounter with St. Michael's spear.

The move from the former novitiate quarters to the new novitiate in 1943 required many days of scrubbing and cleaning before the novice mistress, M. Camillus Dunphy, was convinced that the place was sufficiently sanitized to house her fourteen novices and four postulants. Then, to ensure that the novitiate would be sparkling with cleanliness, she purchased a few of tins of varnish and sent two supposedly intelligent young novices with paint brushes to varnish the floor of what was to be their community room. The two youngsters set to work with a will. They painted for several hours, and when they failed to appear for recreation, M. Camillus went down to see if they had encountered any problems. She discovered her two geniuses sitting on the floor in the far corner of the room where they were prepared to stay for the next twenty-four hours, waiting for the varnish to dry.

One year of the two-year novitiate (usually the first year) was known as the canonical year. During this period the novices were obliged to live in the novitiate house. They were not permitted to engage in any professional work, such as teaching or nursing, and their studies were limited to courses in various branches of religious knowledge. In the second year, the novice was permitted minimal involvement in professional activities such as participating in courses at the university or teaching in the classroom for a couple of hours a day. Occasionally, second-year novices lived in some convent other than the novitiate if there was a serious need of their services in that community. Nevertheless, they were still novices, and the scope of their activities was limited.

For many reasons, the presence of the novices was an asset to the overworked sisters of St. Bride's Convent. In spite of a tendency to break every dish that came within reach, the novices saved the professed sisters many hours of precious time by performing all the tasks of housekeeping and cleaning. The novices (and the professed sisters) rose at six o'clock and spent the next hour and a half in prayer. Mass and breakfast followed. While the professed sisters hurried off to prepare for school, the novices donned checkered aprons and began their "charges"—housecleaning duties that occupied them until ten o'clock, when they were expected to be back at their desks in the novitiate for a two-hour study period.

Initially, the subjects studied depended on the needs of each novice. One volume was compulsory, *The Catechism of the Vows*, a depressing little book that left the reader with the conviction that everything that was not actually painful was almost certainly an "occasion of sin." Another old standby was a three-volume treatise, *The Practice of Christian and Religious Perfection*, by V. F. Alphonsus Rodriguez, a sixteenth-century Jesuit. These volumes were very popular with novices of former years, not so much because of their elevated subject matter, but for the examples contained in the last section of each chapter. By means of these examples, Rodriguez attempted to depict, in gruesome detail, the fate that awaited the unfaithful religious. Regrettably, some novices regarded these stories, not as grounds for edification, but rather as sources of amusement. However, the novices were not permitted to spend all their time reading—and embellishing—examples from Rodriguez. The study of Scripture, various treatises on religious life, and the "Rule and Constitutions" of the Sisters of Mercy as explained in the *Guide* comprised the core of the novices' program of studies. This program, however, underwent considerable revision during the 1950s and '60s, especially after the Second Vatican Council. Mercifully, the *Catechism of the Vows* was replaced by courses on the theology of the vows. The canonical novices pursued studies in variety of subjects such as Church history, Scripture, theology, ethics, and—after the Council—the documents of Vatican II. Courses in speech and music lessons for the musically inclined, were provided during the second year of the novitiate.

The novices' day alternated periods of manual work, study, prayer, and recreation. Night prayers were recited in community in the chapel, and everyone was expected to be in bed with lights out by ten o'clock. In those days, there did not seem to be the frantic attempt to catch up with one's self, always more to do than can possibly be accomplished. There was a time and a place for everything. Apparently, this timetable suffered no appreciable change during the 1950s and '60s.

Having successfully negotiated the discipline of the novitiate for two years, the young novice presented herself to the General Council of the congregation and asked to be admitted to profession. This was an anxious time for the novices. Some "made the grade," others did not and arrangements were made for their return home. The decision to admit a person to profession was based on the recommendations of the novice mistress, the superior of the convent, and any sisters who worked with the novices as instructors. These recommendations were not an assessment of the person's character but rather a determination of whether or not she was being called by God to religious life as a Sister of Mercy. There is no doubt that occasional errors of judgment were made since neither the novice mistress nor the General Councils claimed infallibility.

In the period immediately following World War II, there was a veritable explosion of vocations to religious life. The top dormitory of St. Bride's Boarding School at Littledale was made into sleeping quarters for the novices and the novitiate dormitory was turned into a postulate. Up to this time, postulants and novices had shared the same community room and dormitories, and the novice mistress was responsible for both groups. This was becoming a task too onerous for one person, and so another professed sister was appointed "Mistress of Postulants." During all this time, the novice mistress of the time, M. Placide Conway, and her novices were storming heaven for a new novitiate building to provide more space for their varied activities. Eventually, in February 1957, the glad tidings were announced that permission to build had been granted. A month later the first sod was turned and construction of Our Lady of Mercy Novitiate was begun. The new building was located on the east side of the Littledale campus adjoining the section known as the Talbot Wing, the upper storey of which contained St. Bride's Convent Chapel.[36] In the course of constructing the new novitiate, the outer wall of the chapel was removed to make the novices' chapel an extension of the convent chapel and to provide access to Our Lady of Mercy Novitiate from St. Bride's Convent.

---

36. See chapter eight.

On July 5, 1958, the Archbishop P. J. Skinner celebrated the first mass in the chapel and blessed the new building. Less than two weeks later, on July 16, the archbishop returned to celebrate the ceremony of reception and profession. Twenty-four postulants received the white veil; seventeen novices made their first profession of vows for one year; and seven sisters made final profession.[37] When recording the events of that day, the novitiate annalist reported, ". . . there are now 41 novices."[38] There was still quite a lot of work to be done before the new novitiate building was completely finished. The sisters worked hard all summer, and by September 1958, everything was ready to receive the fourteen new postulants who took the place of those admitted to the novitiate in July.

By this time, too, the general councillors had come to recognize the importance of keeping a record of important events in the life of the congregation. Accordingly, word went out to every convent that some member of the community was to be given the task of writing the Annals. The directive was taken seriously by the novices and the novitiate annalist was meticulous in recording for posterity the daily events in the life of the novices. For example, "Nov. 19: The novices have their first Ethics assignments completed today. Sr. M. Williamena started the "Dagger Scene" from Macbeth in speech class this morning. Lovely program tonight for Sr. M. Elizabeth's feast day."[39] References to "a lovely program" crop up very frequently in the Annals of the novitiate. Evidently, it was the custom to have a short concert on the evening of a sister's feast day—to the acute discomfort of the sister so honoured. Apparently,

---

37. Up until 1916, the time of the amalgamation, the Sisters of Mercy made perpetual profession of vows when they had completed the two-year novitiate period. After the amalgamation, sisters made temporary vows for a three-year period before being admitted to perpetual (or final) profession. At the general chapter of 1955, the practice of making a three-year profession of vows was changed, and sisters made annual vows for three successive years before final profession. When the new Constitutions were adopted in 1983, the duration of the phase of first profession, or temporary vows, extended normally for a period of three to six years, during which time the sister renewed her vows annually before making final profession although the superior general could extend the period for a maximum of three years, "Constitutions of the Sisters of Mercy of Newfoundland," p. 23, article 67.

38. Annals, Our Lady of Mercy Novitiate, St. John's, 1958, ASMSJ.

39. Instead of celebrating birthdays, sisters celebrated the feast of her patron saint.

nobody enjoyed these concerts except the novice mistress, M. Placide Conway, who encouraged the performances as an educational tool to develop the imagination, initiative, and musical ability of her novices. Another reason for encouraging these activities was to advance good habits of voice projection and correct speech in the future teachers of the congregation.

During the period of the 1950s and '60s, every room in the novitiate building was occupied, but at the end of the decade, the number of applicants had dropped dramatically. This decrease in the number of young women entering religious life occurred at a time when the new St. Bride's College required additional sleeping accommodations for students. Therefore, in 1970, the sisters of St. Bride's Convent moved to empty rooms in the novitiate, and the former St. Bride's Convent, now an extension of the college, was renamed O'Connor Hall. The novices continued to occupy the second floor of Our Lady of Mercy Novitiate until July 1984, when the formation house was removed from the Littledale campus to St. Joseph's Convent on Signal Hill Road. The last novice to spend her canonical year in Our Lady of Mercy Novitiate was Sr. Eileen Penney.[40] Subsequently, the novitiate building was taken over by the professed sisters and renamed St. Bride's Convent.

40. Eileen Penney, RSM, was professed on August 6, 1985.

CHAPTER TWENTY

MOVING INTO A NEW AGE

See, I am making all things new.
Revelations 21:5

hen Archbishop Skinner introduced his program of social and educational reform, one of the major initiatives he proposed was the creation of regional high schools in St. John's. At the time there were a number of Catholic schools in St. John's and neighbouring communities. The archbishop saw that by providing central high schools it would be possible to provide the latest educational facilities and equipment at less cost. He announced his plan in the Basilica of St. John the Baptist on November 21, 1954.[1] The archbishop noted the overcrowded conditions of the schools that, he felt, would be relieved by the construction of two regional high schools in St. John's, one for girls and one for boys. However, construction of the first regional high school did not begin until October 1956. Built at a cost of over two million dollars, when it was finished it was one of the largest structures in the city of St. John's. On September 18, 1958, the formal opening took place when Paul Émile Cardinal Léger, archbishop of Montreal, blessed the school and dedicated it to the Holy Heart of Mary.

---

1. *The Monitor*, December, 1954, p. 1.

Nevertheless, it was November 17, 1958, before the building was ready for occupancy. On that day, nine hundred students from thirteen parishes, twenty-four schools in all, began classes at nine o'clock.[2] Originally, the new regional high school had fifty-two classrooms and could accommodate 1,100 students. There was also a gymnasium, cafeteria, laboratories, audiovisual room, and a number of specially equipped rooms for instruction in commercial subjects and home economics. A large section of the school was set aside as a music department. This consisted of a spacious orchestra room, an even larger choral room capable of seating a choir of two hundred singers, and several smaller rooms intended for practice and private instruction. In 1962, the school auditorium was added, and five years later, the original plan for the school was completed with the opening of an additional two-storey wing. This section contained the school library, the chapel, and additional classrooms. Over all, the new Holy Heart of Mary Regional High School for Girls was a "state-of-the-art" facility. However, there was one problem—the name of the school! Within a very short time, the students, finding the name too cumbersome, abbreviated it to "Holy Heart," or simply, "Heart." Nevertheless, the official title remained for many years.

The school was operated jointly by the Presentation and Mercy Sisters. The offices of principal and vice-principal were three-year terms, filled alternately by Presentation and Mercy Sisters. The first principal of Holy Heart was M. James Dinn, a Presentation Sister. The vice-principal was M. Assumpta Veitch from Mercy Convent. Every three years, the roles were reversed. A Mercy Sister assumed the office of principal, and a Presentation Sister became vice-principal. Initially, the staff consisted of thirty-nine sisters from the Presentation and Mercy congregations whose salaries were used to pay off the debt on the building, which had been built on land owned by the Congregation of the Sisters of Mercy. There was one lay teacher, who taught physical education. The students came from feeder schools located in St. John's and Roman Catholic parishes outside the city. Students from outside St. John's were bussed to school, but some stayed at St. Bride's College, Littledale.

---

2. Hogan, *Pathways*, p. 205.

From the beginning, it was clear that accommodations would have to be arranged for out-of-town students who wished to attend Holy Heart. The Sisters of Mercy agreed to add a student residence attached to the convent that was to be built for sisters teaching at Holy Heart. The new complex was named for the foundress of the Sisters of Mercy, Catherine McAuley. The convent was called St. Catherine's Convent, the student residence, McAuley Hall. On September 1, 1960, the Sisters of Mercy who were teaching at Holy Heart moved into the new St. Catherine's Convent.[3] The formal opening and blessing took place ten days later, on September 10. M. Hildegarde Dunphy, the first superior of St. Catherine's, and twenty-nine sisters made up the community. McAuley Hall was ready to accept its first student residents on September 8, a week after the convent opened.

It is interesting to note that students occupied McAuley Hall, not only during the academic year (September–June), but also during vacations. A note, dated July 2, 1961, provided information that during the summer months McAuley Hall was used as a residence for teachers who were attending classes at Memorial University of Newfoundland (MUN) and for sisters who were on the marking board for the provincial high-school examinations. This made good economic sense, for it ensured that the residence was occupied at all times and provided badly needed funds to help pay the debt on the buildings. When McAuley Hall opened to accept students in September 1961, there were eighty-five girls in residence. Since the building was capable of accommodating 135, the vacant rooms were occupied by young women who were studying at St. Bride's College, Littledale, and at Memorial University, as well as by sister-students.[4]

The Annals of St. Catherine's Convent covering the first year or two after its establishment are full of fascinating details for sisters who might want to take a stroll down memory lane, but are of little interest to someone who did not live at St. Catherine's during those years. The annalist was conscientious in recording the comings and goings of the sisters in the community, con-

3. Until St. Catherine's Convent opened, Mercy Sisters teaching at Holy Heart were accommodated at Littledale, Mercy Convent, and St. Michael's Convent, Belvedere.
4. Annals, St. Catherine's Convent, St. John's, p. 17.

certs and outings they attended, illnesses that required hospital attention, and other similar events. Every year the Annals listed the names of sisters in the community who had graduated from university with degrees ranging from B.A. or B.Sc. to Ph.D. Overall, the Annals present a picture of a group of women who constantly searched for deeper knowledge, who were tireless in their pursuit of higher learning, and who prayed for the wisdom and skill to interpret and pass on what they learned.

Furthermore, during the 1960s and '70s, the Annals of St. Catherine's Convent, and, in fact, those of other convents as well, provide important information on the changes that occurred in religious life and in the Roman Catholic Church during and after the Second Vatican Council. What is just as important, the Annals present a picture of how these changes affected the sisters who lived through these exciting times. On January 21, 1963, the annalist noted sadly, "Sister M. St. John Norris had applied for and received a dispensation from her vows, and went away this morning by train."[5] The entry sounded an ominous note in an account that, by and large, spoke of a dedicated, hard-working, self-less group of women who were content with little and who found joy in simple things. It was the first of similar entries that appeared with distressing and accelerating frequency in the years that followed, even though, at the time, the Congregation of the Sisters of Mercy was experiencing unprecedented growth. For instance, in the report sent to Rome for the years 1955–1961, the superior general wrote that in the five-year period, one hundred and seven novices had been admitted to profession. In 1961, the congregation numbered two hundred and sixty-five professed sisters, forty-nine of whom had temporary vows.[6] In 1963, McAuley Hall was not large enough to accommodate all the sisters who wished to avail of the retreat offered during the Easter break. Several of the retreatants commuted from nearby convents.

Through the years since it opened, sisters attending Memorial University lived at McAuley Hall not only during the summer, but also during the academic year. For instance, in 1972, twenty sisters who were studying full-time

---

5. Ibid., p. 27. Subsequently, Annie Norris (Sr. M. St. John) continued her career in nursing in Montreal until her death in 2001.

6. ASMSJ, RG 9/106/14.

at the university were accommodated at the residence. At the conclusion of the spring semester, these sisters were sent off to remote outports, where there was no convent, to spend the summer months providing catechetical instruction and tutoring students in various academic subjects such as mathematics. The former activity was particularly important during the first ten years after the Second Vatican Council. The liturgical changes mandated by the Vatican Council took time, patience, and a great deal of explanation before they were fully implemented everywhere in Newfoundland.

Meanwhile, M. Nolasco Mulcahy, a member of the community of St. Catherine's Convent, had been appointed principal of Holy Heart. M. Nolasco was a brilliant woman who, throughout her life, exerted significant influence in educational circles, not only in Newfoundland, but also throughout Canada, particularly in Ontario. On August 7, 1963, she was invited to represent Canada at a mathematics conference in Athens, Greece. Sadly, M. Nolasco had to decline the invitation because there was nobody available to accompany her, and according to the rules of that time, she was not permitted to travel alone. This incident pointed to the need for the reform of outdated regulations that had served women religious well in the past, but were no longer practical, helpful, or healthy in the second half of the twentieth century. Happily, change was just around the corner.

In 1961, a general chapter was held in St. John's. A new General Council was elected, and M. Assumpta Veitch replaced M. Imelda Smith as superior general. However, the chapter did more than elect a new administration. The delegates had serious reservations about the method used in the congregation to elect delegates to the general chapter. It was decided that the sisters in the congregation should be given a wider choice in the selection of sisters to serve as members of chapter. Therefore, the chapter directed the new council to investigate methods used by other Mercy congregations, a mandate that the new superior general, M. Assumpta Veitch, embraced with a great deal of energy and enthusiasm.

In the early days of the 1950s, the Sisters of Mercy all over North America were taking a hard look at the outdated theology and regulations that governed the living of religious sisters. In response to a growing desire for collaboration among religious congregations in Canada, the Canadian Religious

Conference was formed in 1954. Since that time, the Sisters of Mercy of Newfoundland have been active members in this organization. In the same year, 1954, the Mother McAuley Conference was established by congregations of the Sisters of Mercy in the United States.

Within a short time of her election in 1961, M. Assumpta Veitch decided to establish closer ties with Sisters of Mercy in other parts of the world. Accordingly, she welcomed opportunities offered by the Mother McAuley Conference to participate in discussions on matters of mutual concern and to share ideas with the Sisters of Mercy in the United States. Hints of change were already in the air, although at first it came slowly and in areas that were non-threatening to those who valued tradition above all else. Shortly after M. Assumpta's return from one of the meetings of the Mother McAuley Conference, word came from the generalate of changes in the manner of praying the Little Office of the Blessed Virgin Mary.[7] The sisters had been required to recite this office together in Latin at specified times during the day. For some strange reason, vespers and compline (the evening and night prayers of the Church) had been prayed at noon, while the morning prayers of matins and lauds were recited in the chapel at five o'clock in the afternoon. This arrangement made little sense. The new directives attempted to make the content of the prayer coincide with the hour of the day. This change, however, did not satisfy many sisters who wished to substitute the English translation of the Divine Office (eventually renamed, "Liturgy of the Hours") for the Little Office. M. Assumpta put the matter to a vote of the congregation, and on March 19, 1964, she announced that a majority had voted in favour of the change. However, because the recitation of the Little Office was mandated in the Constitutions of the Sisters of Mercy, permission from Rome was required to make the substitution. Rome sanctioned the

---

7. The term "Office" signifies a duty accomplished for God. The prescribed prayer of the Church, the Divine Office, consists of prayers that are recited at fixed hours of the day or night by priests, religious, clerics, and, in general, by all those obliged by their vocation to fulfil this duty. It consists of Psalms, readings from Scripture and the Fathers of the Church, and prayers. The Little Office of the Blessed Virgin Mary is a liturgical devotion patterned on the Divine Office. After the Second Vatican Council the term "Office" was changed to "Liturgy of the Hours" and the arrangement of Psalms and Readings was revised.

change, and on December 8, 1965, the liturgy of the hours, lauds, vespers, and compline became the daily community prayer of the Sisters of Mercy in Newfoundland.

The first translations of the psalms from Latin to English caused a great deal of distraction at prayer. For example, a passage from one of the psalms recited during lauds (morning prayer), ". . . and the darling grew fat and frisky,"[8] invariably brought the prayer to an abrupt halt while sisters struggled to regain the spirit of recollection appropriate to the occasion. On one memorable occasion a young sister, whose turn it was to introduce a psalm by proclaiming the first three words of the antiphon, stood in her place and announced to all and sundry, "I am expecting . . ." It was not until the startled community glanced ahead to the remainder of the antiphon that the statement became clear, "I am expecting good things from the Lord." This was the first of many translations of the psalms used in morning and evening prayer, and it signalled the beginning of more radical changes in the form and style of prayer prescribed for the Sisters of Mercy.

In 1965, inspired by the Second Vatican Council's call to renewal, the sisters present at the meeting of the Mother McAuley Conference in New Hampshire resolved to form a Federation of the Sisters of Mercy of the Americas. On her return from this meeting, M. Assumpta consulted the sisters in all the local communities and the decision was made that the Newfoundland Congregation of the Sisters of Mercy should join the federation.[9] The initial function of the federation was to serve as a channel of communication to all member communities. It was a vehicle through which major superiors would be kept up-to-date on proposed changes to the discipline of religious life in accordance with the teaching of the Church as expressed by the Second Vatican Council. A further goal of the federation was to emphasize the virtues of charity, zeal, and justice within all convents of Sisters of Mercy according to the teaching and spirit of Catherine

8. *Lauds, Vespers and Compline in English* (Collegeville, Minn.: Liturgical Press, 1965), p. 495.

9. ASMSJ, RG 10/5/3.

Mcauley.[10] M. Assumpta attended all the meetings of the federation and shared with the members of the congregation at home new information and fresh insights she had acquired as a result of these discussions.

Some of the deliberations that took place at meetings of the federation introduced the possibility of modifying the religious habit worn by Sisters of Mercy. As well, other less controversial matters, such as a revision of the numerous prayers and devotions prescribed by the *Guide* were debated.[11] Gradually, the freedom to adopt the method and style of one's prayer was introduced and had a profound effect on the life of individuals and of the community at large. New forms of communal prayer, such as Bible vigils, communal reflection, dialogue homilies, and twilight retreats engaged people in sharing their faith. The requirement that each sister make an annual retreat remained, but this had never been seen as an obligation to be fulfilled but rather as a privilege to be enjoyed. However, under the new order, each sister was free to choose the place and style of her retreat. There were guided retreats, directed retreats, preached retreats, thirty-day retreats, and many other forms of renewal available to the sisters, most of whom were delighted to grasp every opportunity offered. In addition, internationally acclaimed theologians and scholars were (and are) invited to speak to the sisters on a variety of subjects dealing with the renewal of religious life, liturgy, scripture, theology, and a variety of other topics.

Meanwhile, discussions on the changing of the religious habit had been ongoing. On October 6, 1963, M. Assumpta Veitch arrived home from Pittsburgh with pictures of a modified Mercy habit proposed by an Irish designer, Sybil Connolly. The sisters took one look at the pictures and agreed unanimously that they would not be found dead in such an outfit. They had been anticipating something more attractive and definitely more modern! The patient M. Assumpta took her pictures back and held more consultations with the federation. Eventually, on October 9, 1965, the sisters in St. John's and nearby communities were summoned to Mercy

---

10. On May 11, 1968, the Holy See issued a decree canonically approving and establishing the Federation of the Sisters of Mercy of the Americas.

11. See chapter seven.

Convent auditorium where M. Assumpta appeared on the stage attired in another habit, one proposed by the Sisters of Mercy of Bethesda, Maryland. There were a few moments of stunned silence, for not only was the superior general's hair attractively arranged in front of a short veil, but also her legs were exposed halfway up to her knees. The whole assembly took a deep breath and then broke into spontaneous applause. This was more like it!

M. Assumpta did not want any hasty decisions on such an important matter. She advised the sisters to go home and talk it over. However, most of the sisters had decided already. On October 20, 1964, the majority of the congregation agreed to adopt the model of the religious dress presented to them by M. Assumpta, but no change could be made without approval from the Sacred Congregation for Religious in Rome. M. Assumpta and the General Council acted quickly. Permission to adopt the new habit arrived from Rome on January 20, 1966. Almost immediately, the General Council made plans to implement the decision before July 16, 1966, when the new novices were due to receive the religious habit.[12] Each convent was notified that the change of habit would come into effect on July 2, 1966. Two of the sisters, however, had registered for summer school in the United States where classes began during the last week of June. Therefore, these sisters were given permission to change into the new habit on June 20, the day they were to leave for summer school— almost two weeks before the change in habit was due to come into effect. To friends and relatives accustomed to seeing the sisters clad in long black habits and flowing veils, the sudden change to a short veil (with hair showing), mid-calf dress, black silk stockings, and black pumps came as a shock. One of two sisters leaving for Chicago on June 20 had asked her brother to drive her to the airport. He arrived at the convent door promptly at seven thirty in the morning, and seeing her attired for the first time in her new outfit, he took one look at her and exclaimed, "Holy mackerel, girl, you'll never come back!"

The year 1966 saw more revisions in the traditional "Rule and Constitutions" of the Sisters of Mercy. In a previous section of this book it was mentioned that sisters were free to relinquish the religious name given them at

---

12. The change from the traditional habit of the Sisters of Mercy to the new, modified habit was ratified by the general chapter of 1967.

reception and revert to the name given at baptism. However, a more significant reform was the introduction of a new method of voting for delegates to the general chapter. Since the general chapter of 1961, members of the General Council had been studying various election methods used by Sisters of Mercy in the United States, and from several different systems, they selected two or three. The different methods that seemed to suit conditions in Newfoundland were presented to the whole congregation for study and comment. Eventually, the congregation decided to elect twenty-seven delegates from the total membership of the congregation with the superior general and general councillors as ex-officio members of the chapter.[13] Junior professed sisters were permitted to vote but were not eligible to be delegates themselves.[14]

On December 21, 1966, a remarkable innovation occurred in the daily routine and was recorded for posterity by the annalist of St. Catherine's Convent, "Reverend Mother (M. Assumpta Veitch) gave a television set to St. Catherine's Convent." Although, prior to the installation of this television set, the sisters at St. Catherine's might have been deprived of access to the latest media technology, they were provided with more than their share of spiritual resources. In October 1964, Rev. Cyril Eagan, a priest of the Archdiocese of St. John's, was appointed resident chaplain to St. Catherine's Convent/McAuley Hall. As soon as the announcement was made, a section of McAuley Hall that had been reserved for use as an infirmary was made into a suite of rooms for Father Eagan. He remained at McAuley Hall for five years until ill health forced him to retire. In the intervening years, he was available to the students and sisters for spiritual advice and counselling as well as for daily mass and regular celebration of the sacraments.

Meanwhile, interesting developments had been taking place on the campus of St. Bride's College, Littledale. Prior to the 1940s, St. Bride's housed an aver-

---

13. In the years following the amalgamation of 1916 until 1967, in the larger convents, the superior and one sister elected by the community were delegates; smaller convents were grouped together and sisters from those communities elected one of the superiors and one other sister as delegates to the chapter. The members of the General Council and superior general were ex-officio delegates to the chapter.

14. This system of electing delegates to the chapter was continued until 1993, when a new method of self-nomination, with no limit on the number of delegates, was introduced.

age of fifty-five to sixty boarders a year.[15] These included teachers-in-training and high-school students for the most part. In addition, a number of day students attended classes at Littledale. Grades from kindergarten to senior matriculation (grade XII) were taught. However, the number taking senior matriculation examinations in Newfoundland was never very large, and these examinations were discontinued for a while after 1930 because the material covered was equivalent to the first year program at Memorial University.[16] However, in 1938, St. Bride's instituted a new program entitled, "Professional Grade XII." This extra year of high school, with emphasis on religious, professional, and cultural subjects, was intended to prepare the students for further post-secondary education. In its first three years, the program produced eighty graduates.[17]

In 1942–43, an affiliation took place between the Memorial University College and St. Bride's College for the training of female teachers. M. Basil McCormack explained:

> This arrangement worked so well that, when the University College became the Memorial University of Newfoundland, St. Bride's was invited under date of May 26, 1950, to send a representative to the Senate meetings. As of July 1st, 1952, formal affiliation of St. Bride's College, Littledale with the Memorial University of Newfoundland came into effect.[18]

Between 1950 and 1960, there was a steady increase in the number of student teachers at Littledale. Every available space was occupied in the old buildings, but still the number of applicants grew. After lengthy and frequent consultation with Archbishop P. J. Skinner, Monsignor Summers, the vicar general, and with officials at Memorial University, the General Council of the

---

15. In 1920, however, M. Teresa O'Halleran wrote that there were eighty boarders and twenty sisters in residence at Littledale. See chapter eight, n. 72.

16. McCormack, "Educational Work", p. 76. Many years later, in the 1980s, grade XII became a regular part of the high-school program.

17. *ENL*, s.v. "St. Bride's College."

18. McCormack, "Educational Work," p. 80.

Sisters of Mercy came to a decision. In March 1964, M. Assumpta Veitch, the superior general, announced that plans were being drawn up for the erection of a junior college on the Littledale campus. Construction of the new St. Bride's College was begun in June 1965, on land immediately west of the existing buildings. When the buildings were completed, the old St. Bride's was converted into housing for sisters with temporary vows (juniors).

The new college consisted of a two-storey academic wing, with lecture rooms, a modern audiovisual room, a large music room, library, and administrative offices. A separate wing containing a large, multi-purpose gymnasium and swimming pool separated the administration offices from the chapel. The chapel, located in a separate building, was constructed and furnished according to the latest liturgical norms and was capable of seating a congregation of 350 students. There were two modern residences, Creedon and Coolock.[19] A large, state-of-the-art kitchen, with modern refrigeration and storage space serviced two cafeterias. In addition, there was a separate large dining room intended originally for the novices. Subsequently, this room was used as a conference room or a temporary chapel as circumstances dictated. Attached to the cafeteria wing was a large, two-bedroom apartment intended to accommodate a resident chaplain. A system of underground tunnels connected all the buildings on campus with one another and with the old St. Bride's. Modern electrical rooms, furnace rooms, and mechanical rooms were under the supervision of qualified personnel.

A separate wing of the new Littledale complex contained the residence and offices of the superior general and members of the General Council (later renamed, the Leadership Team). This was, indeed, a break from tradition. For 125 years, the centre of government of the congregation had been located at the mother house—Mercy Convent on Military Road. However, as M. Williamina Hogan pointed out, the expansion of the

---

19. Creedon Residence was named in honour of the foundress of the Sisters of Mercy in Newfoundland, M. Francis Creedon. Coolock Residence was named for the estate on which Catherine McAuley lived for many years when she was a ward of the Callaghan family.

congregation over the years called for "proportionate expansion in administrative facilities."[20]

A little more than a year after construction began, the generalate wing was ready for occupancy. On September 24, 1966, the Feast of Our Lady of Mercy, the members of the General Council moved from the mother house on Military Road to the new generalate of the Sisters of Mercy on the Littledale campus. A short time later, on October 3, 1966, classes began in the new St. Bride's College. However, because work on the buildings had not been completed, the formal opening of the new college was deferred until April 12, 1967. On that day, mass was celebrated in the new college chapel by Archbishop Skinner, after which the archbishop blessed the whole complex. At the conclusion of the religious ceremonies, the college entertained over 250 guests at a banquet held in the cafeteria. Guests included the archbishop of St. John's; the bishops of Harbour Grace and St. George's; other clergy; the premier, the Honourable Joseph Smallwood; assorted cabinet ministers; the lieutenant governor of Newfoundland; officials from Memorial University; and representatives of educational organizations. The superior general, M. Assumpta Veitch, and the principal of St. Bride's College, M. Nolasco Mulcahy, were on hand to welcome the guests as they arrived. The story is told that the premier arrived accompanied by one of his cabinet ministers rather than by his wife, who was a very retiring lady and rarely accompanied her husband to public functions. However, this time, the premier—and everyone else—had miscalculated. A few minutes after the premier's limousine arrived, a taxi bearing Mrs. Clara Smallwood drove up to the entrance of the college. As M. Nolasco welcomed her, Mrs. Smallwood explained, "This is one function I'm not going to miss. Joey is going to get the shock of his life when he sees me, and it will serve him right!"[21]

The construction of the new college was accompanied by a certain degree of heartache as sisters watched the demolition of many old landmarks that had been associated with Littledale for as long as anybody could remember.

---

20. Hogan, *Pathways*, p. 235.
21. This story was told to the author by M. Nolasco Mulcahy.

For instance, the farmhouse that had been the home of the caretaker and his family, the buildings associated with the farm, and even the farm itself were sacrificed in the interests of higher education. Some of the older sisters recalled that the produce of the farm had supported Littledale, the sisters, and the boarders during the time of the Depression. M. Williamina Hogan wrote, "Of greater importance were the people who had looked after the farm and those who provided janitorial services at St. Bride's."[22] It was a time when stories of Mr. Ned Dunne and Mr. Dick Murphy were told and retold, and their kindness to former boarding students and young, inexperienced novices was recalled with affection and gratitude.

The new college began its work with a spirit of hope and optimism. It was fortunate in having a highly qualified faculty and the most up-to-date resources and equipment. Courses in arts and first and second year education were taught. The curriculum included courses in English, French, Latin, history, mathematics, geography, music, education, speech, and religious studies. M. Nolasco Mulcahy, the first principal, was a highly competent individual and respected throughout Canada for her contributions to education. M. Nolasco remained as principal until 1970, when she was given a leave of absence to accept a position in the graduate division of the Faculty of Education at the University of Ottawa. Later, M. Nolasco was appointed head of the Division of Graduate Studies at the same university. M. Hildegarde Dunphy replaced M. Nolasco as principal of St. Bride's College. When M. Hildegarde retired in 1973, Sister Nellie Pomroy was appointed to succeed her.

The construction of the new St. Bride's College came at a time when the Mercy congregation was looking for more space in which to hold conventions and retreats that could be attended by a majority of sisters. The new college provided an ideal location for such gatherings. And so, in June 1967, delegates to the general chapter packed their bags and headed for Littledale to attend the most significant general chapter since the amalgamation took place in 1916.

---

22. Ibid., p. 236.

The special mandate of this chapter was to inaugurate a period of experimentation that would initiate the reforms and recommendations contained in the documents of Vatican II pertaining to religious life. The chapter delegates began an exhaustive study of the *Guide to the Rule and Constitutions of the Sisters of Mercy* with a view to making the changes suitable to conditions in the second half of the twentieth century. Although minor changes in the customs and practices of daily living had occurred prior to Vatican II, and especially during the 1960s, the sisters of 1966–67 followed the same daily schedule and many of the minutiae of the *Guide* as did their predecessors in 1866–67. Furthermore, over the years superiors had introduced practices that might have been necessary in particular situations but which no longer had any relevance to contemporary life. In three separate sessions of the chapter, the delegates sifted through mountains of material, discarding one antiquated custom after another. Among many decisions affecting the daily lives of the sisters, one important trend was set in motion—the gradual move toward a collegial style of government that led to a new understanding of authority within the congregation.

Most of the decisions of the 1967 chapter were greeted with enthusiastic relief by the congregation at large. One decision, however, stood apart from all the rest because it affected the lives of children who had been entrusted to the care of the Sisters of Mercy. At a special session of this chapter held from December 27 to 30, 1968, the delegates made the heart-rending decision to close St. Michael's Orphanage, Belvedere.[23] Social theories at that time encouraged the move away from placing homeless or neglected children in large institutions. It was felt that a small, family setting was more conducive to the emotional and social well-being of children than an orphanage where large numbers of children lived together. The chapter delegates bowed to the opinions of experts in child care whose advice had been sought in the matter and, reluctantly, voted in favour of closing the orphanage. The superior of St. Michael's Convent, M. Constance Travers, wrote to the director of

---

23. "Minutes of the Third Session of the Ninth General Chapter of the Sisters of Mercy of Newfoundland, December 30, 1968," ASMSJ.

the Department of Child Welfare and Correction and informed him of the decision. She requested that he make arrangements for the children who lived at Belvedere to be placed in foster homes at the end of the school year of 1969. And so, with the closing of the orphanage, the Sisters of Mercy concluded 115 years (1854–1969) of caring for the abandoned children of Newfoundland.

At the end of the third session of the ninth general chapter, the delegates decided that deliberations had gone on long enough. Certainly, the chapter had been a significant—even earth-shaking—event in the history of the Congregation of the Sisters of Mercy. Life for the Sisters of Mercy in Newfoundland would never again be quite the same! Many of the customs and practices that had been part of daily life since 1842 had been swept away. A new spirit of freedom and responsibility, born of the Second Vatican Council, had been embraced. New ways of thinking, praying, acting, and interacting had been initiated. Now it was time to let these changes take root.

In response to the move to a more collegial style of government initiated by the 1967 general chapter, the sisters of the congregation elected an advisory committee to the General Council in 1970. The purpose of this committee was to bring local issues to the attention of the council and to provide greater representation from the different regions of the province. It was an attempt to provide wider consultation among members of the congregation and a new understanding of how authority should be exercised in the light of the teachings of Vatican II. Sisters were permitted and encouraged to voice their opinions and concerns, to suggest changes, and to promote new ministries. It was the age of committees. Almost every sister in the congregation belonged to a committee on something or other. There were committees on community life, on ministry, on prayer, on option for the poor, on simple lifestyle, and on authority and governance. The amount of paper required to record the deliberations of all these committees ensured that the paper mills of Newfoundland were kept working to full capacity.

Consultation was the "in" word. The former practice of assigning sisters to different convents, and even to different ministries, without prior discussion between the superior general and the sister involved was abandoned. In future, every sister had an opportunity to review her living arrangements and her ministry with the superior general. Also, in place of the yearly list of assignments that used to appear on every convent bulletin board on August 15, sisters who were reassigned received a personal letter from the superior general informing her of her new posting. Some sisters were being encouraged to embrace ministries other than education and health care that, up to this time, had been the traditional works of the Sisters of Mercy. For instance, Sisters Helen Caule and Diane Smyth resigned from their teaching positions and reentered university to obtain degrees in social work. Subsequently, Sr. Helen was employed by the Department of Health in the area of child welfare while Sr. Diane worked in the Social Work Department of St. Clare's Mercy Hospital.[24] Another sister, Lorraine Power, was accepted at Memorial University Medical School, graduated and began practicing medicine in a remote section of Labrador.[25] Sr. Sheila O'Dea graduated with a master's degree in liturgy. She was employed as director of liturgy by the Archdiocese of St. John's and, subsequently, as a member of the faculty of Regis College in Toronto. Still later, Sr. Sheila was appointed associate director of the North American Forum on the Catchumenate in Washington, D.C.[26]

With the new emphasis placed by the 1967 chapter on individual freedom, many restrictive practices of the past were abolished. One of the first of these to be abandoned was the rule that required that a sister have a companion whenever she was outside the convent. Under the new dispensation, a sister might go shopping, visit the doctor, and attend meetings without having some other sister accompany her. However, the problem of transportation remained. Sisters were quick to take advantage of the new freedom, but most of the desired destinations were at quite a distance from the convent, and somehow, the expense of taking taxis had been overlooked in the revision of the old rules. M.

---

24. Several years later, Sr. Diane Smyth earned a certificate in clinical pastoral education and is a divisional manager in the Pastoral Care Department of the Health Care Corporation of St. John's. In this position she is manager of pastoral care at St. Clare's Mercy Hospital and of the Palliative Care Unit at the Miller Centre.

25. See chapter twenty-four.

26. At the time of writing, Sr. Sheila O'Dea is director of liturgy for All Hallows College.

Assumpta soon found a way out of this dilemma. On May 9, 1971, the annalist wrote, "St. Catherine's purchased a car—cheaper because purchased as one of a fleet."[27] Then, in line with the new emphasis on personal accountability, on September 1, 1971, each sister was given a personal allowance of fifteen dollars a month. This money was intended to cover her personal needs such as stamps, writing paper, small items of clothing, dry cleaning, and toilet articles.

Other radical changes took place between 1967 and 1973 that transformed the daily lives of the Sisters of Mercy. Most obvious to society at large—and most controversial—was, of course, the new style of religious dress. But for the sisters, a whole new way of living religious life was gradually supplanting the quasi-monastic structures that had governed convent life up to that time. Gone were the days of silence at meals, silence on the stairs and corridors, and "class days," when speaking was permitted at lunch or dinner, but rarely at breakfast.[28] It was no longer necessary to request permission from the superior to write a letter or make a phone call. All the trivia that had cluttered the lives of women religious had been swept away, and a new sense of maturity and freedom emerged.

Some of the directives of the 1967 chapter (and succeeding chapters) impacted on the governance structures of the congregation. Beginning in 1971, there were important changes in the method by which local superiors were chosen. Each convent was given the option of retaining the custom of having a local superior appointed by the General Council or of electing a member of the community to serve in that capacity. However, the chapters were nudging the sisters in the direction of more democratic government by insisting that

27. Annals, St. Catherine's Convent, St. John's, vol. 1, p. 126, ASMSJ.

28. Except for two daily periods of recreation (four o'clock to five o'clock in the afternoon and eight o'clock to nine o'clock in the evening), silence was observed throughout the convent. Special recreation days were organized according to the importance of the day in the Church's calendar. Solemn days, such as Christmas, Easter, Pentecost, December 12 (Foundation Day), and September 24 (Feast of Our Lady of Mercy) were first class days, when sisters could talk anywhere in the convent from after mass until night prayer. On second class days, talk was permitted from after the morning meal until after the evening meal. Third class days were those when conversation was allowed between ten o'clock in the morning and three o'clock in the afternoon and at the evening meal. On fourth class days, conversation was permitted at the evening meal but not during the day, except at the scheduled recreation periods.

local councillors must be elected.[29] Wisely, successive General Councils introduced these changes gradually, realizing that some sisters might be uncomfortable with the proposals. It was not until June 6, 1971, that the first elections
took place in local convents. The annalist at St. Catherine's wrote, "A meeting
of the Sisters [was held] . . . to decide if we are to elect our superior as the
Mother General and Council had directed, or to have the superior appointed."[30] The result of the vote showed thirteen out of twenty-eight favoured an
appointment, eleven wanted an election, and four sisters abstained. Other
communities, too, chose to stay with the old way of having an appointed superior. It is not hard to understand why some women were hesitant to accept the
challenge of exercising freedom of choice. After a lifetime of accepting the
decisions of others as "the will of God," many sisters lacked the self-confidence
to make up their own minds when dealing with matters related to community
living. Yet, many of these same women were successful and confident teachers
and administrators in other areas of their life and ministry.

Ongoing study of the documents of Vatican II changed the way in which
authority was understood and exercised. Discussions held during the 1967
chapter, but more particularly, briefs presented to and accepted by the 1973,
1977, and 1981 chapters, stressed the principles of subsidiarity, co-responsi-
bility, and accountability. Within the congregation at large, as well as within
local communities, these values were experienced in the change from the
dominance of the superior to participation of the group. The basic principle
underlying the vow of obedience remained unchanged—all legitimate authority comes from God and therefore obedience to this authority is a sacred duty.
The vow of obedience had—and has—for its object the union of the religious
with the will of God. By the vow, the religious commits herself without
reserve to seeking the will of God in all circumstances and to following it to
the best of her ability within the context of her religious community. In the
post-Vatican II era, the concept of "blind obedience" to the dictates of the supe-

29. The "Rule and Constitutions of the Sisters of Mercy" provided that the local superior in
each convent should be assisted by one or two councillors, depending on the number of
sisters in the community.
30. Ibid., p. 128.

rior gave way to an understanding of authority as exercised by the community. Decisions were made through processes of prayerful discernment.
Successive chapters encouraged participative government within the
Congregation of the Sisters of Mercy of Newfoundland. No longer were decisions to be handed down from "on high" without prior consultation with the
community or congregation.

Gradually over the years, titles indicative of rank, such as "mother superior" and "reverend mother" were abolished. Everyone was called "sister," and
eventually even that title disappeared within the congregation, and sisters
called one another by her baptismal (or religious) name.

In 1971, M. Chrysostom McCarthy was appointed as the first official
archivist of the congregation, a position she held for fourteen years.[31] M.
Chrysostom was well-suited to the position. One of the leading classical scholars
of the congregation, she had spent her life in education, and now in her retirement, she was looking for a new challenge. However, before she could begin collecting important documents and artifacts, M. Chrysostom had to find a suitable
place in which to store her treasures. A room on the first floor of the new generalate building at Littledale was designated for this purpose. Immediately upon
her appointment, M. Chrysostom set to work collecting letters and documents
that had been preserved from the early years of the congregation in
Newfoundland. Every morning, rain or shine, sleet or snow, she walked from St.
Catherine's Convent to the basilica, where she took the bus for Littledale to begin
her day's work in the archives. She corresponded with dozens of Mercy archivists
all over the world, hoping that letters from the early days of the Newfoundland
foundation might have been discovered. M. Chrysostom attended archivists' conferences in many parts of Canada and the United States to learn correct archival
practices and new techniques of cataloguing and preserving documents of historical interest. The Sisters of Mercy of Newfoundland owe her a debt of gratitude for finding and preserving most of the knowledge we have on the early days
of our congregation. In her task of gathering information, M. Chrysostom was

---

31. M. Chrysostom McCarthy held the position of archivist until 1985, when she resigned
for reasons of ill health. At that time, Sr. Marie Michael Power was appointed to succeed
M. Chrysostom.

fortunate in having at hand the results of M. Basil McCormack's research into the history of the Sisters of Mercy in Newfoundland. In collecting material for her thesis, M. Basil interviewed many sisters whose memories went back to the early part of the twentieth century and who knew people like M. Bernard Clune and M. Perpetua O'Callaghan. She examined newspaper reports from the nineteenth and twentieth centuries, and, by investigating the events surrounding early Newfoundland foundations, M. Basil made a major contribution to the knowledge we have of the history of the congregation.

In 1973, the six-year term of the General Council had been completed and delegates were elected for the general chapter that was held during the summer. M. Assumpta Veitch, having held the office of superior general for two six-year terms, was not eligible for re-election. In her place, the chapter elected Sr. Marie Michael Power, a quiet reserved woman whose style of leadership was in direct contrast to the more assertive stance of her predecessor. Marie Michael had been treasurer general of the congregation during the years 1967 to 1973 and had worked closely with M. Assumpta in managing the financial affairs of the congregation. Furthermore, strong ties of friendship and respect existed between the two women. Thus, Marie Michael was ideally suited to carry on the policies of her predecessor as well as to implement new initiatives mandated by the general chapter of 1973.

The chapter decided that the six-year term of the superior general and councillors should be reduced to a four-year term with the possibility of re-election for another four years. The term of local superiors was reduced to one year, with the possibility of serving a second year in the same convent. Although the 1967 chapter had ratified the 1965 decision of the General Council that replaced the traditional habit of the Sisters of Mercy with what was called, "the modified habit," by this time sisters were questioning the obligation to wear the habit, and especially, the veil. There were heated debates on this thorny issue, with input from sisters who attended the chapter as observers.[32] Eventually, the

---

32. At the general chapter of 1973, for the first time in the history of the congregation, sisters, other than elected delegates, were permitted to attend chapter sessions, and periods of time were set aside to allow sister-observers to have input into the discussions of the delegates.

definition of "habit" was broadened to include a navy blue suit or guimp with white blouse, or a simple navy dress with white collar. Nevertheless, the chapter voted that the veil was to remain part of the religious dress. However, during vacation time, on picnics, or on other similar recreational outings, sisters were free to wear contemporary dress. In the subsequent chapters of 1977, 1981, and 1985, the style of clothing worn by the sisters receded into the background in light of more important challenges facing the congregation, until finally, the wearing of distinctive clothing became optional. Chapters from 1981 to the present deal largely with the responsibilities of the congregation to the society in which we are called to minister. Issues of social justice, women's issues, protection of the environment—these topics are the focus of present-day chapters of the Sisters of Mercy.

Meanwhile, a number of regional high schools had been built in many of the larger outports in Newfoundland. Consequently, in the 1970s, the role of McAuley Hall changed from a boarding school for girls attending Holy Heart of Mary High School to a residence for female students attending Memorial University or the College of Trades and Technology. However, while there were numerous changes in personnel at St. Catherine's Convent over the years, the number of sisters in community varied only slightly, numbering between twenty-eight and thirty.

As time went on, St. Catherine's annalist began to list the occupations of some sisters in the community, but unfortunately these annotations were far from complete. Even in the case of individual sisters, many of their important achievements were overlooked, while minor accomplishments were given undue emphasis. Many sisters in St. Catherine's community were especially attentive to the visitation of the sick, the poor, and to persons experiencing difficulties or coping with grief. For example, M. Angela Fowler was noted for her involvement with the Home Economics Association of Memorial University, and after her retirement from teaching, she became actively involved in the Retired Teachers' Association and in the activities of various senior citizens' groups in the city, such as the Silver Chord Singers. Also, M.

Angela provided pastoral visitation to residents of some of the nursing homes in the city.

The sisters in St. Catherine's community were among the best and most qualified teachers in the congregation—and in the province of Newfoundland. The academic and musical successes of students of Holy Heart gave ample evidence of the ability of these women to challenge their students to strive for excellence. As in all areas of instruction at Holy Heart, Presentation and Mercy sisters staffed the music department. In addition to courses in music appreciation, students could avail of private instruction in piano, voice, and all the instruments of the orchestra. The spacious orchestra room could accommodate fifty or more instrumentalists.

From the beginning, the Holy Heart of Mary Orchestra played an important role in the life of the school. During the early years, the orchestra started off with a solid core of experienced young players from Our Lady of Mercy String Orchestra. These students were joined by girls who had attended schools administered by the Presentation and Mercy sisters, in each of which a vibrant music program had been in place for years. The Holy Heart of Mary Orchestra consisted of full choirs of woodwinds and brasses in addition to the string and percussion sections that moved up from Our Lady of Mercy School. In later years, under the direction of M. Celine Veitch, the Holy Heart Orchestra won awards for the "Most Outstanding Group Instrumental Performance" in successive music festivals. No concert, operetta, or musical was complete without the participation of the orchestra. However, what was more important, many of the young musicians who played in the Holy Heart Orchestra continued their interest in music. Some former members of the orchestra have become professional musicians and teachers. Thus, the musical traditions they learned at Holy Heart are being passed on to the successive generations of students.[33]

---

33. Among many former members of the orchestra who entered music as a profession are Mary Carol Nugent (viola), Pamela Walsh (cello), Susan Murphy-Quinn (violin and choral music), Gretchen Schoenberg-Foley (piano), Mary Jane Maloney (cello), Susan Mercer-O'Brien (voice and choral music), Sonia Abbott (clarinet), and Marina Picininni who is an internationally acclaimed flautist. Dr. Andrea Rose, a violinist, teaches in the Music Department of Memorial University.

Holy Heart students excelled, as well, in the field of choral music. The students who came to Holy Heart from schools operated by the Presentation and Mercy sisters had been involved in grade-choirs since kindergarten. The sisters from both congregations directed the choirs, and from the beginning, the Holy Heart choirs were acclaimed for their high standards of performance and interpretation, which seemed to improve year by year. Holy Heart choirs competed in the St. John's Music Festival where, year after year, they won the "Outstanding Award" in the choral music category. In 1980, thirty girls from the Holy Heart choir travelled to Toronto to compete in the International Choral Festival where they won first place overall, as well as first place in the musicianship category, and the Sister of Mercy who directed the choir received the trophy for Best Choral Director. Many of the Holy Heart singers graduated from the Music School at Memorial University and established a reputation for the excellence of their teaching. Several of these Holy Heart graduates have won national and international acclaim through competitions in music festivals in several countries. For example, the Holy Heart Quintessential Choir under the direction of Susan (Murphy) Quinn won the World Choral Trophy in Vienna, Austria, some years ago and, more recently, first place in the International Choral Competition in Wales.[34]

Of course, it was not only in the musical world that Holy Heart students made their mark. The general, overall excellence of the academic programs of the school was demonstrated by scholarships won by Holy Heart students in public examinations and national competitions. For instance, in 1963, students at Holy Heart entered the National Competitive Latin Examinations sponsored by the Association for the Promotion of the Study of Latin, New Jersey. Fifty-one thousand students from the United States, Canada, Mexico, Bermuda, and South America wrote the examinations. The students were remarkably successful. One student was awarded a gold medal, four won silver medals, and one hundred and twenty-one received achievement certificates. The school itself

---

34. The Newfoundland Symphony Youth Choir, directed by Susan Dyer-Knight has performed in Europe and in many parts of Canada. Jacinta Mackey-Graham, Susan Mercer-O'Brien, Noreen Greene-Fraize, and many, many other former music students of Holy Heart continue to build on the work begun by the sisters many years ago.

was awarded a trophy. In the field of sports, Holy Heart was fortunate in having a succession of capable and dedicated instructors. Basketball and volleyball were two sports in which teams from Holy Heart competed at intercollegiate, municipal, provincial, and national levels. Later on, in 1985, when the school became coeducational, the Holy Heart hockey team inspired great enthusiasm in teachers and students of the school and awe in the hearts of all opponents.

The two congregations of Presentation and Mercy Sisters worked together through the years. The practice of alternating the positions of principal and vice-principal was effected smoothly and without any major changes in policy or style of administration. For the convenience of their sisters who were teaching at Holy Heart, the Presentation congregation built Assumption Convent on the northern end of the school. St. Catherine's Convent was located on the opposite side. There were, therefore, opportunities for the sisters of both communities to spend time together in a relaxed, social atmosphere. Visits were exchanged especially at times of celebration, such as Christmas and provincial and national holidays.

However, as the 1980s approached, changes were in store for St. Catherine's Convent/McAuley Hall. As more and more sisters reached the age of retirement, many of them took up voluntary work. Some spent the whole day in remedial work with children in the school; others became involved in some form of pastoral ministry in a parish. Still others obtained certificates in pastoral care and worked in hospitals or nursing homes. Musicians continued to provide private instruction in the various disciplines of their art and were available to provide music for parish liturgies. In fact, few sisters actually retired—they worked as hard as ever, but without a salary. If the convent was attached to the school, retired sisters were welcome visitors. The sisters enjoyed chatting with the children during recreation periods, and the students loved to hear stories of former days, especially if these involved accounts of the escapades of a student's parent.

As time passed, the health of many of these sisters began to fail. Some became very frail and required constant nursing care; others needed only minimal care. However, in a convent where everyone else was rushing off to school or hospital, the care of the sick or elderly members of the community became a serious problem. Consequently, in 1982, the General Council of the Sisters of Mercy, under the leadership of Sr. Patricia Maher, made a decision to turn the top floor of McAuley Hall into a nursing unit for sick and elderly members of the congregation. An announcement was made that in September 1983, only the second floor of McAuley Hall would be available as a residence for young women attending the university or trades college. At the end of June, students who were living on the third floor of McAuley Hall moved out and carpenters, plumbers, and electricians moved in to begin the work of changing a residence for young women into a nursing unit for elderly and infirm sisters. The work of renovation took six months to complete, but by Christmas 1982, everything was ready for the first member of the new community of St. Catherine's Nursing Unit. Four sisters were appointed to work in the nursing unit, among them M. Callista Ryan, a certified nursing assistant, with M. Alverna Harnett as administrator. In addition, the congregation hired a staff of seven caregivers. On January 8, 1983, St. Catherine's Nursing Unit received its first resident, M. Stanislaus Parsons. M. Stanislaus, a former superior general and one of the congregation's first registered nurses, had been living in St. Patrick's Mercy Home Convent. She worked in pastoral care at St. Patrick's Mercy Home for several years until ill health and advancing age forced her to retire. For some time prior to coming to St. Catherine's, M. Stanislaus had been completely bedridden. Although the sisters at St. Patrick's were reluctant to see her leave, they realized that, because of their duties to the residents in the home, they could no longer provide the constant attention that she needed. Upon her arrival at St. Catherine's, M. Stanislaus was fussed over, petted, and pampered in a fashion she probably had not experienced since infancy. Consequently, although she could not speak, she was always smiling.

The second sister to be received into St. Catherine's Nursing Unit was Sr. Mary Baker, a young sister who was suffering from multiple sclerosis. A few days later, M. Ursula McNamara and M. Benignus Mullowney from Mercy Convent were welcomed. Both sisters were fairly active, although a trifle absent-minded. M. Ursula's constant fear was that she might miss mass. On the way back to the unit from attending morning mass, invariably M. Ursula would question, "And when is mass, dear?" The next sister to arrive at the unit was M.

Magdalen Baker from St. Clare's. For many years M. Magdalen had reigned supreme in the X-ray Department at the hospital. After her retirement, she spent her time visiting patients and producing exquisite needlework that was sold to support the hospital. One by one, the rooms in the nursing unit were filled. It was a new life for many of these elderly sisters. Before coming to St. Catherine's, they had spent many lonely hours in their convents while other members of the community were engaged in professional duties. Because the nursing unit was a part of St. Catherine's Convent, the sisters of the community spent much of their free time in the unit offering love and companionship to those women who had given their lives to God, to the people, and to the congregation.

In 1987, it became clear that St. Catherine's Convent/McAuley Hall was in need of major repairs. Educational and residential demands had changed since the building was opened in 1960. McAuley Hall had outlived its usefulness as a residence, and most of the sisters who were living at St. Catherine's Convent had either retired from teaching or were nearing retirement age. Furthermore, it was felt that the nursing unit was no longer large enough to accommodate the needs of the sisters. Consequently, the decision was made to build another nursing unit on Littledale property and dispose of the St. Catherine's/McAuley Hall buildings.

On June 3, 1991, the sisters who had lived in the nursing unit at St. Catherine's Convent and those who cared for them moved into the new McAuley Convent on the west side of the beautiful Littledale campus. Members of St. Catherine's Convent community who were engaged in ministries of teaching or pastoral work went to live in other convents in the city.

At the time McAuley Convent was under construction, St. Bride's Convent, on the east side of the Littledale campus, was in urgent need of renovation and repair. Originally intended as a novitiate house, the rooms in St. Bride's were small and ill-suited to professional women who needed space to prepare work for school or parish duties. Renovations had been delayed because of the problem of finding accommodations for the more than twenty sisters who lived at St. Bride's. However, on June 15, 1991, a little more than a week after McAuley Convent opened, the sisters of St. Bride's Convent moved to St. Catherine's to allow the renovations to take place. They remained there until December 7, 1991, when they returned to St. Bride's, Littledale. On the same day St. Catherine's Convent/McAuley Hall closed. It had been in operation just thirty-one years.

After the sisters had vacated the buildings, the Archdiocese of St. John's expressed an interest in obtaining the St. Catherine's Convent/McAuley Hall property in order to amalgamate all the archdiocesan offices on one site. On July 7, 1992, the archdiocese purchased the complex, and it was renamed the Archdiocesan Pastoral Centre. The centre had a short lifespan for, after a few years, it was found to be too large for the needs of the archdiocese. In 2002, the property was sold and the land on which St. Catherine's Convent/McAuley Hall once stood is now a parking lot for a supermarket.

Meanwhile, some years previous to the demise of St. Catherine's/McAuley Hall, the beautiful new St. Bride's College was facing unanticipated problems. In 1966, when the college opened, one hundred and fifty resident students and ten non-resident students registered for classes. During the next five years, the enrolment increased steadily, reaching its maximum number of 261 in the first term of 1970–71. However, the following two years saw a decline in the number of students applying for admission to St. Bride's. This was due, partly, to a surplus of teachers in Newfoundland. Therefore, it was inevitable that there were fewer students choosing teaching as a career. Because St. Bride's was concerned mainly with providing first- and second-year education courses, this had a direct effect on the enrolment at the college. Other factors played a part. The very year that the new St. Bride's opened its doors, 1966, a senate committee of Memorial University recommended that the university establish as many as five junior colleges throughout Newfoundland.[35] The first of these colleges, the Sir Wilfred Grenfell College in Corner Brook, opened in 1975. At the time, Grenfell College offered a program of studies very similar to that offered by St. Bride's.[36] Consequently, the opening of this college in Corner Brook had a

35. *ENL*, s.v. "Memorial University of Newfoundland and Labrador, Sir Wilfred Grenfell College."
36. Since that time, Sir Wilfred Grenfell College has expanded the number of programs available, including a bachelor of fine arts degree.

dramatic effect on St. Bride's, for it provided west coast students with an opportunity to attend classes nearer home. M. Williamina Hogan, who taught at St. Bride's College during this time, had this explanation for the decrease in numbers at St. Bride's:

> The reasons for this marked decline in the number of students seeking admission to St. Bride's College are varied and difficult to identify. At the time there was a move away from dormitory living and a decrease in teacher demand. Also, the new Memorial University campus had become the focus of student activity in St. John's and few college students wanted to be isolated from the constant bustle. Whatever the cause, the decline in the enrolment at St. Bride's College continued. The number registered for the first semester of 1973–74 was 134. This was further reduced to 102 in the second semester, January–April, 1974.[37]

It was clear that St. Bride's College was no longer a viable operation. When the plan to build the new college was first conceived in the early 1960s, nobody could have foreseen that within a few years junior colleges would be springing up in other parts of the province thus filling a need that had been met at Littledale since 1884. Consequently, in May 1974, Sr. Nellie Pomroy, the principal of St. Bride's College, requested that the university suspend St. Bride's affiliation with it as a junior college.

However, the buildings were not destined to remain empty. The Roman Catholic School Board for St. John's was quick to avail of the splendid facilities offered at St. Bride's. The board leased most of the college classrooms for use by St. Augustine's School. Other rooms in the academic building were set aside for private music lessons provided by two sisters from St. Bride's Convent, M. Genevieve Drake and M. Ita Hennessey. Furthermore, the college residences provided an ideal site for spiritual retreats, renewal programs, conferences, and meetings. From the time the college closed until recent years, they were in use from time to time, but not often enough to warrant the upkeep of the buildings.

---

37. Hogan, *Pathways*, p. 238.

In 1980, the students at St. Clare's School of Nursing moved into one of the residences on the Littledale campus. Subsequently, in 1990, the School of Nursing itself moved into the academic building of the former college. Eventually, in 1996 the schools of nursing in St. John's were combined into the "Centre for Nursing Studies" and for three years this centre was located at Littledale. However, because the provincial government had a number of empty buildings on its hands, in 1999 the Centre for Nursing Studies moved to a newly renovated building on the site of the old General Hospital on Forest Road. This move left the former college without any regular occupancy other than occasional conferences, retreats, and functions sponsored by the Mercy congregation.

Still, the congregation struggled on, trying to maintain the large complex. Many avenues were explored in an attempt to find an appropriate use for the buildings. Eventually, it was decided that the only solution was to sell the former college, retaining only the buildings that had comprised the "old Littledale," that is, the west wing, the centre block, the Talbot wing, and the former novitiate building, which had become St. Bride's Convent.[38] The older buildings underwent extensive renovation to provide offices for the general administration, the congregational archives and heritage room, meeting rooms, and apartment units for sisters who might choose this style of living. At the present time, St. Bride's Convent, located in the 1958 novitiate building, is home to a number of sisters who serve in a variety of ministries.

A review of the history of Littledale brings to mind the fact that 120 years ago, a young woman had a dream. With astonishing courage and unlimited trust in Providence, she set to work to realize her vision of reaching out to children in every little cove and inlet in Newfoundland. She planned to do this by establishing a boarding school that would provide the finest education possible to young women who would then go out and bring the benefits of learning, skill, and knowledge to people in all parts of this island. In spite of strong

38. At the time of writing, attempts to find a suitable purchaser for St. Bride's College complex have not been successful, and the property still remains in the possession of the Sisters of Mercy.

opposition, lack of money, ill health, and a host of other difficulties, she succeeded in establishing St. Bride's Boarding School and Convent, Littledale. For over one hundred years, Littledale was known throughout this land as a place of learning and culture. Thousands of young women passed through its doors and went out to hand on to their own children and to others the thirst for knowledge that they had acquired at Littledale. Some of these young women, inspired by the example of their teachers at Littledale, vowed their lives to God in service to the poor, to the sick, and in the cause of education. Truly, M. Bernard Clune's dream was realized in ways she may not have envisioned.

CHAPTER TWENTY-ONE

A TAPESTRY OF MERCY

They blossom for a time, then die—but their fragrance lingers on.

Kathrine E. Bellamy, RSM

With the establishment of St. Patrick's Mercy Home, Holy Heart of Mary Regional High School, and the new St. Bride's College, the period of the 1950s and '60s witnessed an expanding role for the Sisters of Mercy in education and health care in St. John's. Yet at the same time, the congregation was reaching out to other areas of the province as well. On September 3, 1961, a new convent was opened in Baie Verte, a town in the northern section of the Baie Verte Peninsula on the northeast coast of Newfoundland.

The history of Baie Verte goes back to the time when France controlled the fishing all around what was known as the French Shore. Although the French Shore problem was not settled until 1904, as early as the 1870s Newfoundland families were fishing and farming in the area.[1] However, in the latter part of the nineteenth century, mineral deposits were discovered on the Baie Verte Peninsula, and a copper mine was established not far from Baie Verte itself. Nevertheless, the rich forest resources of the peninsula remained the chief source of employment for the growing population of the settlement.

---

1. *ENL*, s.v. "Baie Verte."

In 1939, Mrs. Ella Whalen opened the first post and telegraph office in Baie Verte, and in the following year, for the first time, planes were used instead of dog teams to deliver the mail during the winter. During the summer, as soon as the ice moved out in May or June, boats delivered mail and passengers to the Baie Verte Peninsula. In 1957, the Bank of Nova Scotia opened a branch in Baie Verte, and the town was incorporated the following year.[2]

In 1961, there were almost one thousand people living in Baie Verte and with the discovery of a sizeable asbestos deposit nearby, its future expansion was assured. The parish priest, Rev. Leonard Kelly, anticipating an influx of young families to Baie Verte, wrote to M. Imelda Smith, who was superior general of the Sisters of Mercy at the time. It was clear that Baie Verte was an ideal location for the Sisters of Mercy to exercise their ministries of teaching and caring for the sick, and the decision was made to establish a convent in the town.

Accordingly, on Sunday, September 3, 1961, two men from Baie Verte, Michael Drover and Stephen Furey, drove to the convent of St. Mary's on the Humber in Curling to escort the founding sisters to their new home. Accompanying them were M. Francis Hickey and the newly elected superior general, M. Assumpta Veitch. For more than a mile from the entrance to the settlement, the road was lined with men and women, boys and girls. Whistles, horns, and bugles announced the arrival of the sisters, while a procession of cars, decorated and bearing welcome posters, accompanied them as they drove toward their new convent. Upon their arrival, the sisters, their new black habits covered with dust from their journey over almost one hundred miles of unpaved, dusty road, discovered to their dismay that a lady who had a movie camera was recording their progress for posterity. However, recalling the old saying, "What cannot be cured, must be endured," they made the best of it, and with what dignity they could muster, the sisters mounted the steps to their new convent. When they entered, they found that the house was completely finished, furnished, and ready for occupancy. Furthermore, the ladies of the parish had dinner prepared for them in the convent refectory. After dinner, they attended benediction in the parish church where Father Kelly, the pastor,

2. Ibid.

formally welcomed them. By coincidence they had arrived on the feast of St. Pius X, the patron of both the parish and the convent.

The first community of St. Pius X Convent consisted of six sisters, the superior, M. Justine (Loretta) Dower; M. Pauline Foster; M. Adrienne Keough; M. Gemma (Colette) Nagle; M. Stephanie Curran; and M. Lenora Molloy. However, the sisters did not have too much time to roam around and become familiar with the layout of the town because the school year began just two days after their arrival. St. Pius X was an all-grade school with an enrolment of 234 students: 140 boys and 94 girls. There were seven teachers in the school: the six sisters and one brave male teacher, Mr. Lawrence Walsh, who taught the grade III class.

The people of Baie Verte were overjoyed to have a convent in their town, and the sisters were showered with all sorts of goodies, such as homemade bread and rolls, and jams made from a variety of native berries. During the month of September, the sisters themselves took to the hills on Saturdays to pick blueberries, partridge berries, and cranberries that they made into jams and jellies.[3] After one such expedition the annalist noted with pride, "We arrived home with four gallons of berries."[4]

The parish of Baie Verte includes several smaller settlements. Shortly after their arrival, the sisters went to each of these places in turn, meeting the people and visiting the schools. Before long, they were taking an active part in the liturgies celebrated in the different missions of the parish such as Coachman's Cove and Fleur de Lys as well as in Baie Verte itself. Also, they began a regular schedule of visitation of the sick and elderly who were confined to their homes. Before long, the needs of parishioners in the scattered missions of St. Pius X Parish occupied almost all of the sisters' free time. Furthermore, in spite of the relative isolation of the town, visitors made their way to the convent with amazing frequency. When the bishop visited to

---

3. The making and bottling of jams and jellies is a Newfoundland tradition. Every Newfoundland family picked gallons of berries during the late summer. These were bottled and put away for the winter months when it was difficult to obtain fresh fruit, especially in the outports.

4. Annals, St. Pius X Convent, Baie Verte, vol. 1, p. 4, ASMSJ.

celebrate confirmation he brought along his vicar general and several priests who ministered in other parishes on the Baie Verte Peninsula. The sisters from Curling and from Corner Brook decided to visit before the snow came, and several relatives of the sisters had the same idea. Even the premier, Joseph R. Smallwood, with four members of his cabinet, decided to pay a visit.

Meanwhile, the music teacher, M. Lenora (Brenda) Molloy, was busy preparing for the school concert that took place in November. This was the first in a succession of musical productions directed by M. Lenora and other sisters who taught music at St. Pius X School. In response to popular demand, the Christmas play, *The Donkey and the Star*, was repeated three times, and the parish hall was packed for each performance. It was not long before the Canadian Broadcasting Corporation heard about the talented children of Baie Verte and sent along technicians to record the school choir and parts of their Christmas play to be aired during the annual "CBC Christmas Broadcast."

Following all the excitement and successes of their first few months in the new mission, the sisters in Baie Verte came down to earth with a disconcerting thump early in the following term. This seemed to be the lot of Mercy foundations. In most cases, the first year after the arrival of the sisters was marked by minor calamities of one kind or another. In the case of Baie Verte, it was illness and floods. In February 1962, the superior, M. Justine (Loretta) Dower, became ill and was advised to go to St. John's for rest and treatment. Under the rules of the time, another sister had to accompany her. Then, to add to the confusion, M. Gemma (Colette) Nagle was forced to stay in bed because of illness. This meant that three classrooms were without a teacher. M. Adrienne Keough, always ready for a challenge, cheerfully and competently managed and taught all the classes from grades V to XI until conditions returned to normal. But this was not the end of the sisters' woes. On March 2, 1962, an unusually heavy storm of wind and rain caused severe flooding in the convent. The sisters used buckets, tins, shovels, dustpans, and everything capable of holding liquid in an attempt to bail out the water that was pouring into the basement at the rate of sixty gallons an hour.[5] With the assistance of the senior boys from the school and some men who lived nearby, they worked in shifts all night and during the following day until the storm abated and the water slowed to a trickle. But there was still more trouble to come. The next morning, the transformer that supplied electricity to all the church buildings exploded, and church, school, and convent were without heat and light. Once more the people of Baie Verte came to the aid of the sisters, bringing along oil burners, kerosene lamps, and even an ancient Aladdin lamp. All of this goes to show that people who live in convents are not immune to the misfortunes that afflict other households.

As the school year drew to a close, the sisters had reason to feel satisfied with the results of their first year's work in Baie Verte. Schoolchildren were happy, parents were satisfied, the parish priest was delighted with the participation of the children in the parish liturgies, the sick and elderly had been visited, and the bereaved consoled. Then, when they returned to Baie Verte after attending summer school at various universities, the sisters found good news waiting for them. Twenty-nine students out of a class of thirty-three had been successful in the public examinations and one of the girls from the grade XI class, Sheila Sullivan, was to be admitted as a postulant at Littledale in September 1962. The following year one of the students from St. Pius X High School in Baie Verte won the Electoral Scholarship for the district of White Bay South.

In 1963, Baie Verte experienced a big economic boost when Advocate Mines began open-pit mining and the milling of large chrysolite deposits that had been discovered some years earlier. Up to 550 people were employed in the operation.[6] One year later, another company, Consolidated Rambler Mines, began operation and the town prospered. Within a few years, Baie Verte became the centre of secondary education and health services for the whole district.

However, St. Pius X School was not the only school in Baie Verte. Not too far away, children who belonged to other religious denominations

5. Annals, St. Pius X Convent, Baie Verte, vol. 1, p. 36, ASMSJ.
6. *ENL*, s.v. "Baie Verte."

attended the Amalgamated School. A spirit of warm co-operation existed between teachers and administrators of the two schools. The friendly rivalry exhibited by the two student bodies found expression in various sports activities and public speaking contests. These public speaking contests were regional in nature. The winner in each division went to Grand Falls to participate in the semifinals of the Provincial Public Speaking Contest. According to the Annals, year after year students from St. Pius X represented Baie Verte in the semifinal competition.[7] The friendship that existed between the two schools was more firmly cemented when the Amalgamated School was destroyed by fire in April 1963. The Roman Catholic pastor, Father Kelly, offered the use of the parish hall without charge as a substitute school for the remainder of the academic year. The sisters did their part, too, by providing books and other teaching materials to replace what had been lost. Teachers and students from each school supported concerts and social events put on by the neighbouring student body. In addition to fostering a spirit of co-operation among the young people of the town, preparing for these functions provided plenty of after-school activities for the youth.

In response to a request from Father Ronald Bromley, the parish priest of La Scie, the sisters of St. Pius X Convent agreed that two of them would spend the weekends visiting his parish and its missions. On Friday, November 13, 1965, M. Justine Dower and M. Eulalia Woolridge began their missionary activities in the parish of La Scie, visiting Brent's Cove and Harbour Round on Saturday and spending Sunday in La Scie and Tilt Cove. In all of these places they taught religion and singing to the boys and girls in the schools. On their return home they reported, "There is much to be done!" Their activities, however, lasted for only one year, for in September 1966, the Presentation Sisters established a convent in Brent's Cove.

A glance through the Annals of St. Pius X Convent indicates that the sisters were very attentive to the sick of the parish, especially after the new $2,000,000 hospital was opened on October 6, 1964. However, they continued to visit the sick at home and, in particular, sick children. "Included in regular

---

7. Annals, St. Pius X Convent, Baie Verte, vol. 1, ASMSJ.

visitation was visitation of four sick children whom the sisters prepared for First Communion."[8] On other occasions, the sisters went to the homes of sick and handicapped children to prepare them for confirmation.

> Visitation of Sick [was] carried out extensively this year—to the hospital as well as to the homes of the sick. Daily visits made to a patient dying of cancer—and especially Sr. M. Alexia [Eleanor Caul]—was very kind to the dying man—bringing specially pre-pared food for him. After his death, his widow expressed heartfelt thanks for the assistance provided by the Sisters. Sisters visited the elderly who looked forward to such visits. Sisters visited also the parents of the school children to discuss educational prob-lems and solutions.[9]

At the beginning of the school year, 1966–67, the population of St. Pius X School had increased to 430 students and 14 teachers. There was great rejoicing in the school when it was announced that one of the grade XI girls had won the Lions Club International Peace Essay Contest. The celebrations continued when the school junior basketball team won the regional tourna-ment and brought home the trophy. The whole town participated in even more rejoicing in March 1968, when St. Pius X basketball team won first place in the All-Newfoundland Tournament that was held in St. John's.

By the end of the decade, the school population had grown to the point where a new building was needed. In 1969, the new St. Pius X High School was opened and the former all-grade school became St. Pius X Elementary. The new high school, when completed, provided an auditorium, library, and science laboratory, as well as offices and six additional classrooms to accom-modate the quickly growing school population. When the sisters returned to Baie Verte after summer school in 1969, they discovered that the building was

---

8. Ibid.
9. Ibid., After her retirement from teaching, Sr. Eleanor Caul spent several years working in pastoral care at the Miller Centre in St. John's, a hospital for the chronically ill. Her gen-tle, quiet presence brought joy into the lives of men and women who had been confined to bed for lengthy periods of time. At the present time, Sr. Eleanor provides pastoral care at the Burin Health Services Centre.

not completely finished. However, because school was due to open on September 3, it was decided to use as much of the new building as possible. As a result, for the first few weeks of the academic year, teachers and students worked to the rhythm of hammers, saws, and the tramping of assorted carpenters, electricians, plumbers, and painters. When the building was completely finished, furnished, and equipped, parents, teachers, and students agreed that the temporary inconveniences were a small price to pay for this large, airy, and bright new school.

In 1971, the Sisters of Mercy agreed to take over the administration of St. Teresa's School in Fleur de Lys, commuting daily from Baie Verte. Sr. Alice Wilson was appointed principal, and Sr. Sheila Pumphrey was assigned as one of the teachers.[10] Two years later, both sisters were reassigned, and Srs. Anne Dobbin (principal) and Lydia Kelly replaced them. However, in this northern part of the province, winter arrives early in October and stays until the middle of May. Although Fleur de Lys is only fifteen miles from Baie Verte, for most of the school year, the buildup of snow and ice on the road made driving hazardous and often impossible, and so, at the end of 1974 the sisters withdrew from the Fleur de Lys school.

It was during this decade of the 1970s that, at the suggestion of the 1973 general chapter, a director of education for the congregation was appointed. It was almost inevitable that M. Teresita Dobbin would be selected for the position. M. Teresita had earned a Ph.D. from the Catholic University of America in Washington, D.C. She had taught in schools in many parts of Newfoundland and was aware of the difficulties encountered by teachers in remote areas of the province. During her tenure as director of education, M. Teresita travelled to all the schools administered by the Sisters of Mercy throughout Newfoundland, giving workshops in primary teaching methods and reading. According to the Annals, the sisters in Baie Verte looked forward to M. Teresita's visits, and not only for their educational value. In her travels, M. Teresita managed to pick up the latest news from the many convents she had visited—something very much appreciated by the sisters in this remote area of

---

10. Sr. Alice Wilson died a couple of years later, May 2, 1975.

the province, especially during winter months when travel between convents was limited.

Up to this time, all the children in Coachman's Cove had attended school in Baie Verte. In October 1977, a new primary school was opened in Coachman's Cove, and as a result, only thirteen children registered for kindergarten at St. Pius X Elementary. However, people continued to flock to Baie Verte looking for work in the asbestos mine, and in the year 1981, the population of the town had increased to 2,692.[11] During this same period, Advocate Mines began to experience trouble. Operations were suspended for three weeks in 1981, and in the following year, the mine was closed for three months. In 1982, a new company, Baie Verte Mines, reopened the mine, but the steady employment of the 1960s and '70s was a thing of the past. For the next few years, the mine suffered several shutdowns. Eventually, Terra Nova Mining Company obtained possession of the mine.

As the years passed, St. Pius X Convent was affected by the diminishing number of sisters available to fill teaching positions in the school. By 1990, there were only three sisters left in Baie Verte, Elsie Lahey (pastoral ministry), Maureen O'Keefe, and Sheila Grant.[12] By coincidence, all three had grown up in another mining town, Bell Island. Hence, they were particularly sensitive to the concerns of the people when ominous rumours of trouble in the mines began to circulate throughout the town. From a work force of over five hundred in 1963, the number of employees at the mine dropped to between seventy and eighty workers until finally, in 1995, the Baie Verte mines closed permanently. The future looked bleak. Some found employment in fishery and forestry, but more and more families were forced to move to mainland Canada to find work. In an attempt to boost the economy of the town, the mayor and council, with the support of the businessmen of the town, decided to build a ski slope, hoping to attract tourists to the area, and in 1995 the Copper Creek Ski Resort was

---

11. *ENL*, s.v. "Baie Verte."

12. In June 1989, the Sisters of Mercy relinquished the position of principal in St. Pius X Elementary School. The sisters continued to teach in the school until 1996. In June 1990, the sisters relinquished position of principal of St. Pius X High School although Sr. Maureen O'Keefe continued to teach there until 1994.

opened in Baie Verte. Unfortunately, the success of the venture depended large-ly on the weather, and the enterprise was only moderately successful.

Prior to all of this, and because of a drop in school enrolment, the num-ber of sisters assigned to Baie Verte in 1984–85 decreased from eight to six, and of these, only four were employed in the school. M. Lucia Walsh super-vised the kitchen and visited the sick and elderly in their homes and in the hos-pital. Sr. Brenda Phelan was employed by the parish as pastoral administrator, a role she filled from October to December 1984, when a priest was assigned to St. Pius X parish. At that point, Sr. Brenda became pastoral assistant. Sr. Brenda Phelan was well-prepared for her ministries as parish administrator and pastoral assistant, having served in both capacities prior to her appointment to Baie Verte. For four years (1978–82) she served as pastoral assistant in the parish of Topsail. Subsequently, she was named pastoral administrator in the newly created parish of the Holy Family in Paradise, Conception Bay.[13]

Sr. Brenda Phelan was a pioneer in pastoral ministry—a ministry that was to become more and more important to the local Church in Newfoundland and Labrador. For a number of years, she was the only Sister of Mercy engaged full-time as pastoral assistant in a parish.[14] In the recent past, however, a number of sisters, having acquired the necessary education and training, work as pastoral assistants and parish administrators in many areas of Newfoundland and Labrador. Some work in lonely missions in co-operation with a priest who vis-its occasionally to celebrate mass and the sacraments. Others have more spe-cialized roles, such as director of liturgy, of sacramental preparation, or of adult education. Parish and diocesan ministries provide an opportunity for sisters—and other non-ordained Catholics—to exercise their baptismal commitment to evangelization. It allows women to share in the priesthood of Christ, a right that is theirs in virtue of their baptism. On the practical level, in these days of short-age of ordained priests, it is to the advantage of Church authorities to have a

13. Paradise is a rapidly growing town not far from St. John's. During her years as pastoral assistant in Paradise, Sr. Brenda Phelan lived at St. Catherine's Convent in St. John's.

14. At that time, one or two sisters were working full-time in parishes, but usually as organ-ists and choir directors, or in parish outreach programs to the poor. These sisters were not involved in parish administration or sacramental preparation and their tasks did not fit the title, "pastoral assistant."

group of educated, skilled, and experienced persons to carry on the mission of the Church in places that otherwise would be without the services of trained personnel.

Sr. Brenda remained in Baie Verte as pastoral minister for four years. In June 1988, she was assigned to the parish of Burin, and Sr. Elsie Lahey was named pastoral assistant for Baie Verte and its missions. In fact, in September 1988, only Sr. Marie Crotty, the principal of St. Pius X High School, remained of the previous community. In addition to Sr. Elsie Lahey, there were three newcomers to Baie Verte. Sr. Maureen Lawlor had the unenviable task of teaching music in four schools, a duty that required her to drive to Fleur de Lys and Brent's Cove. Sr. Maureen O'Keefe, a French language specialist, was assigned to St. Pius X High School, and Sr. Patricia Gallant taught in the elementary school.

In June 1993, Sr. Elsie Lahey resigned her position as pastoral assistant with St. Pius X Parish in order to devote more time to visiting the sick and the elderly and to helping people with problems of one kind or another. Meanwhile, the three sisters rattled around in a large convent that had been built for eight. It was time to consider alternative housing arrangements. After consultation with the superior general, Sr. Marion Collins, the decision was made to return the convent building to the Diocese of Grand Falls. On June 1, 1994, the sisters moved to a rented house at 29 Water Street in Baie Verte.[15] The former St. Pius X Convent became "Our Lady of Perpetual Help Renewal Centre." Sr. Elsie Lahey was named director of the centre, and later, in September 1994, Sr. Maureen O'Keefe was assigned to assist her. Sr. Sheila Grant was the only sister teaching in the school. Incidentally, Sr. Sheila was not only an excellent classroom teacher, but also she had received a thorough musical education from the sisters at St. Edward's Convent, Bell Island. Because many young musicians who had been trained by the sisters had moved away from the Baie Verte area, Sr. Sheila served as organist in both Coachman's Cove and Fleur de Lys and substituted for the regular organist in

---

15. Subsequently, the Congregation of the Sisters of Mercy purchased the house at 29 Water Street.

Baie Verte. However, Sr. Sheila realized that it was important to train others to take her place should she be assigned to another convent. She discussed this with the parishioners. As a result, several women in Baie Verte, Fleur de Lys and Coachman's Cove expressed interest in learning how to provide and plan music for the liturgy. And so, in addition to teaching full-time in the classroom every day, Sheila drove off to Fleur de Lys after school and on Saturdays to teach music. All through the year, rain or shine, snow or sleet, the music lessons continued, and within a relatively short time, Sheila's pupils were ready to take her place at the organ for the Sunday morning masses.

On September 11, 1994, the bishop of Grand Falls, Faber Macdonald, arrived to bless and dedicate the first renewal centre in the northern part of the diocese.[16] Parishioners came from Fleur de Lys, Coachman's Cove, Brent's Cove, and all over Baie Verte to celebrate the occasion. After mass, the bishop installed the first board of directors for the centre. The board was made up of representatives from Baie Verte, Fleur de Lys, and Coachman's Cove, as well as members of the Knights of Columbus, the Catholic Women's League, and the Youth Committee. Programs at the centre began on October 3. Initially, there were lectures held once a week, followed by discussion on various topics of interest to parishioners. Other activities such as video presentations and sessions on prayer were held regularly and were well-attended. Groups such as the Catholic Women's League met regularly at the renewal centre, and all the activities associated with sacramental preparation for baptism, First Communion, confirmation, and marriage classes were held there.

At the beginning of this school year, 1994–95, the threat of losing the denominational system of education became very real. The provincial government of the day was determined to abolish the role of the churches in education and to establish a completely secular, government-run system. Parents were aware that this might be the last year when they would be able to send their children to a school of their own choosing. Finally, at the end of

---

16. The first spiritual renewal centre for the Diocese of Grand Falls was established in Conception Harbour in 1982 under the direction of Sr. Edward Mary Roche.

the school year, in June 1995, the government announced that a referendum would be held on September 5, 1995, asking people to vote on changing Term 17 of the Constitution of Canada that had guaranteed the system of denominational education in Newfoundland and Labrador. Officials of both the Roman Catholic and Pentecostal Churches were vehemently opposed to the proposal. The timing of both the announcement and the holding of the referendum was crucial to the government's plan, for during the summer months things related to school were put on the back burner by most people. Many people left home at the end of June, spending the few short weeks of the Newfoundland summer in the parks or by the seashore. Also, the government had promised that neighbourhood schools would be put in place to eliminate long bus rides to school for the children. This proposal was very attractive to parents who were forced to see small children leave home at an early hour in the morning to travel to school by bus and return in the late afternoon. The fact that this might continue under the new system proposed by the government was not mentioned in official information bulletins. Sadly, the apathy of many Catholics who did not bother to vote in the referendum meant that the government's proposal received a majority of votes cast. The Roman Catholic dioceses in Newfoundland and the Pentecostal Churches attempted to overturn the decision. They appealed to the Newfoundland Supreme Court, and eventually the matter went to the Supreme Court of Canada. Both courts ruled against the Churches' position. The denominational system of Newfoundland was gone forever.

With the introduction of the new secular system of education, the responsibility of instructing the children in their faith belonged to parents, some of whom were ill-equipped for the task. Consequently, parishes all over Newfoundland took up the task of educating parents in the latest techniques for imparting knowledge of the teachings of the Church and preparing children for the sacraments. In Baie Verte, as in every other parish where they worked, the sisters became deeply involved in this area of adult education and also in sponsoring programs for young people. St. Pius X Parish in Baie Verte was fortunate in having a very active youth group. Accompanied by their moderator, Sr. Maureen O'Keefe, young people from Baie Verte travelled to Grand

Falls and other towns to participate in leadership conferences and similar programs sponsored by the diocese. In this way, young people kept in touch with their parish and initiated and took responsibility for many activities in the parish. However, the sisters realized that if young people were to continue their interest in the parish community, it would be necessary to involve children in some kind of organization similar to the youth group. Therefore, they began the Young Christopher Program with members of the grade IX class. The main purpose of this program was to identify and develop the leadership qualities of the students.

Every year, Roman Catholic parishes offer the RCIA (Rite for the Christian Initiation of Adults). The RCIA is a process through which persons who are interested in learning about the Roman Catholic faith or who wish to become members of the Catholic community are introduced to the teachings and practice of the faith. The RCIA process is introduced in a series of carefully planned stages, marked by liturgical rites celebrated in the presence of the whole community, in which interested persons join in a continuing and deepening conversion into faith and discipleship. The needs of mature, practicing Christians from other faith traditions are considered on an individual basis. In Baie Verte, the sisters were leaders in the RCIA team of parishioners who accompany persons who have begun the journey toward baptism or reception into the Roman Catholic Church.

In 1996, the sisters in Baie Verte invited some parishioners of St. Pius X Parish to join the Sisters of Mercy Associate Partnership. This association was an initiative of the 1993 general chapter and is defined in the "Handbook for Mercy Associates":

> The charism of Mercy is compassion . . . taking form in health care, education, social services, pastoral work and other ministries that respond to social injustices . . . The Mercy Association seeks to embody this spirit in collaboration with the Community of the Sisters of Mercy in Newfoundland. The Association is composed of men and women who feel a unique response to the call of Mercy in the modern world. Through their daily lives, Associates bring varied gifts and perspectives to the works of Mercy as they

individually and collectively touch the lives of others in love, justice and mercy.[17]

In May 1996, the first coordinator of the associate program, Sr.
Adrienne Keough, went to Baie Verte to explain the association to the sisters
and to persons who expressed interest in becoming associates. Since that time,
twelve ladies of St. Pius X Parish have made their commitment as Mercy
Associates.

With the decline of the mining industry and the unfortunate out-migra-
tion of many trained miners and their families, in 1996, the population of Baie
Verte had fallen to just over 1,700 people. The Mercy community, too, was further reduced when Sr. Sheila Grant was assigned to the school in St. Lawrence.
Even though there were no sisters teaching in the schools, Srs. Elsie and
Maureen kept in close contact with the students by maintaining regular visits to
each school and through faith development programs offered at Our Lady of
Perpetual Help Renewal Centre. However, in 1997, Sr. Maureen O'Keefe was
elected as a member of the Leadership Team of the Congregation of the Sisters
of Mercy. In her place, Sr. Eileen Osbourne joined Sr. Elsie Lahey in Baie Verte.

Since the arrival of the sisters in Baie Verte, special attention had been
given to the visitation of the sick and the poor. This continued, even when
there were only two sisters left. The Annals contain numerous accounts of visits to the homes of the sick, the bereaved, and the needy. When going on visitation, the sisters rarely went empty-handed. Sometimes they made soup, or
cookies, or jams. When they visited homes that were practically unfurnished,
they collected articles of furniture and found material to make curtains for the
windows.[18] They made regular visits to the hospital and senior citizens' homes,
celebrating the liturgy of the word with the patients and bringing Communion
to the sick.

In the year 2002, Sr. Eileen Osbourne, who had suffered from ill health
for a number of years, became very ill. For months at a time, Sr. Elsie Lahey

17. *Mercy Associates: Members Handbook* (Newfoundland: Sisters of Mercy, 2000), p. 2.
18. Annals, St. Pius X Convent, Baie Verte, ASMSJ.

carried on alone, with the help of the Mercy Associates. Although she returned to Baie Verte as soon as her health permitted, Sr. Eileen required medical treatment that was available only in St. John's. Furthermore, the heavy workload, coupled with the difficulty of driving over the slippery roads in the winter were beginning to take their toll on Sr. Elsie. At the end of the year 2002–03, they decided that the time had come for them to leave Baie Verte. In July 2003, Sisters Elsie and Eileen were assigned to Bell Island.

For a few months the sisters' residence at 29 Water Street was vacant until, in January 2004, Sr. Josette Hutchings volunteered to minister in Baie Verte, and in September of the same year, Sr. Ruth Beresford joined her. Meanwhile, on the departure of Srs. Elsie and Eileen, Our Lady of Perpetual Help Renewal Centre was taken over by the Mercy Associates who offer days of retreat and other activities directed toward enriching the lives of parishioners. As well, the associates co-operate with Srs. Josette and Ruth in visiting the hospital and senior citizens' homes. Thus, the ministry of the Sisters of Mercy will continue in Baie Verte for the foreseeable future.

As noted previously, during the decade of the 1960s, the Congregation of the Sisters of Mercy was busy planning new foundations, paying for new buildings, and repairing older convents. About a year before the foundation at Baie Verte, the superior general, M. Imelda Smith, received a letter from Rev. Joseph Hogan, the pastor of All Hallows Parish, North River, Conception Bay, applying for four sisters to come to the parish to teach in a four-room coeducational school. In his letter, Father Hogan wrote that, should his request be granted, he intended to build a small house for himself near the church to leave the presbytery free to be used as a convent for the sisters.[19]

North River was traditionally a fishing and farming community. It is a quiet little community, nestled in the valley along the northwest bank of the river from which it derives its name. One of the most picturesque spots in Conception Bay, this is a town with no industries. Most of the residents work in Bay Roberts or other commercial centres scattered around the bay. In the

19. Rev. Joseph Hogan to Sr. M. Imelda Smith, August 5, 1960, ASMSJ.

late eighteenth and early nineteenth centuries, a few families from the fishing community of Port de Grave moved inland to North River in the summer months for the sake of the rich agricultural land that surrounds the river. In 1840, there were enough people living in North River to justify the establishment of a Roman Catholic school. By the year 1874, a Catholic Church had been built in the community, and All Hallows Parish was formally established there in 1906. Up to that time, North River had been a mission of St. Joseph's Parish, Brigus. The boundaries of the parish have remained unchanged since it was established and encompass a number of settlements. The large, bustling town of Bay Roberts, with proportionately few Catholic families, is a mission of All Hallows Parish.[20] Also, the parish includes the settlements of Shearstown, Butlerville, Hallstown, Clarke's Beach, South River, and Mackinsons.

Evidently, Father Hogan was a patient man, for it was not until January 23, 1961, that he received a reply from M. Imelda. She informed him that the General Council had agreed to send four sisters to North River, but that the councillors had expressed concern about the distance of the school from the proposed convent. She pointed out that sisters would be engaged in concert preparation, social events for the students, and a host of extracurricular activities. Convent rules at the time made it difficult for a sister—usually the music teacher—to be responsible for these functions if the convent was at a distance from the school. Although not stated in the correspondence, it is possible that past experience of sending sisters to live in former presbyteries had made the General Council wary of accepting Father Hogan's suggestion. In any case, M. Imelda added that the Sisters of Mercy were not in a position to build a new convent because of the expenses associated with paying for the new Holy Heart of Mary High School and St. Catherine's Convent/McAuley Hall complex.

Nevertheless, Father Hogan was determined to have the sisters in his parish. If the sisters could not live in the presbytery, the parish would build a convent, and he proceeded to do just that! However, nothing more has been discovered in the archives of the Sisters of Mercy about the proposed foundation

20. In the 1960s, Bay Roberts had a population of over 4,000 people—a large town in comparison with other outports.

in North River until August 24, 1962, when, according to the Annals, the Sisters of Mercy took up residence in the convent of Our Lady of Lourdes in North River.[21] The official opening of the convent took place on the following Sunday. A large number of sisters arrived from St. John's, Brigus, and Conception Harbour to take part in the celebrations. At half past three, a long line of sisters wearing white church cloaks over their long, black habits went in procession from the convent to the parish church. The streets were lined with people, not only those from the parish, but also members of other denominations who had never seen such a sight before. The church was crowded while mass was celebrated by the bishop of Harbour Grace/Grand Falls, who formally welcomed the sisters. It had been over one hundred years since the Sisters of Mercy had established the first convent outside St. John's in nearby Brigus. Incidentally, a special sisters' choir from St. John's provided the music for the occasion. After the church services had concluded, the celebrations moved to the convent. With altar servers leading the way and clergy walking behind the sisters, the procession slowly made its way back to the convent. One elderly gentleman was heard to remark, "My son, 'tis a sight for sore eyes!" The bishop blessed the building, and then parishioners were shown through the house and given an opportunity to meet the sisters who would be working with them.

The school year began the following week. Prior to the arrival of the sisters, the schools in North River had been singularly blessed in having a succession of excellent teachers. Year after year, the superintendent of education for the district submitted glowing reports of the school. It was not weakness in the education provided to the children of the parish that prompted the parish priest to go to the Congregation of the Sisters of Mercy looking for sisters. Rather, he was concerned for the faith development of a large number of Catholic families in the more remote missions of his parish. Furthermore, in addition to some pockets of poverty in these missions, there were sick and elderly parishioners who needed pastoral care and attention. Thus, the pastor saw the establishment of a community of the Sisters of Mercy as a means of addressing some of these needs. As for North River itself, almost the entire

---

21. Annals, Our Lady of Lourdes Convent, North River, August 25, 1962, ASMSJ.

population belonged to the Roman Catholic faith, and the coming of the sisters was seen as completing the structure of their parish community.

As was the custom in those days, the superior of the convent, M. Gonzaga Henley, was appointed principal of All Hallows High School. She worked closely with the former principal, Mr. Douglas Power, who taught the grade XI class. Mr. Power's co-operation and advice contributed greatly to the success of the teaching efforts of the sisters in North River. M. Annette Hawco was named principal of All Hallows Elementary School. Four other sisters completed the community, M. Rosalita Power, M. Cornelia (Monica) Maddox, M. Jacinta (Elizabeth) Maloney, and M. Odelia (Mary) Dunphy. There were, in addition, several teachers who had taught in the school in previous years.

True to the tradition established in Mercy schools, music became an important part of the school program. A school choir was formed, and soon the children were providing music for the liturgies in the parish church. Ten students—all girls, for the boys still were reluctant to engage in such a "sissy" occupation—entered the Trinity College examinations for piano and received marks ranging from seventy-nine to ninety-one percent. In June, twenty-eight children sat for different levels of theory of music examinations, again from Trinity College, and earned marks ranging from seventy-one to one hundred percent. By this time, two young lads were brave enough to ignore the taunts of their companions and register for the examinations. Their example and success persuaded more and more young men that music was not for girls only. In June 1963, the music pupils held a recital for parents and friends, thus providing an opportunity for the adults to hear and appreciate what had been accomplished in just one short year. Furthermore, the academic successes enjoyed by students in All Hallows in previous years continued after the sisters assumed the administration of the school. A total of forty-three students wrote the CHE examinations for grades IX, X, and XI, and one of the grade XI girls won the Knights of Columbus Scholarship for the district.

Successes, particularly in music, continued. In 1964, twenty-two students registered for piano examinations. The fact that seventeen of them earned marks between eight-five and ninety-four percent is evidence of unusual talent as well as superb teaching. From the beginning, the children in North

River were encouraged to participate in school plays and operettas. The elementary school principal, M. Annette Hawco, initiated a program that required every grade in the school to prepare some type of stage production. M. Annette had a special talent for "getting up concerts." In addition to preparing the children to participate, she spared no effort to see that the stage was suitably decorated for each production. She and M. Rosalita Power, who was nothing short of a genius in designing and making costumes for all sorts of characters, worked at the sewing machines late into the night, making curtains, costumes, and stage props for school pageants, plays, and musical recitals.

The sisters encouraged the children to engage in all sorts of activities such as public speaking, sewing, cooking, carpentry, and the collection of the many varieties of insects that inhabit the banks of the river. Annually, at the end of the school year, the whole town was invited to the parish hall to see what the children had accomplished.

Although every year saw a change in the personnel of the community, the traditions established by the first community of sisters in North River were continued by their successors. Visitation of the sick and elderly was carried on after school hours and on Saturdays and Sundays. The hospitality shown by the people was heartwarming, but occasionally embarrassing to the sisters. One hot summer's day, a sister from St. John's, who was on vacation in North River, accompanied M. Annette Hawco on her regular visitation. The two sisters arrived at the house of an elderly couple, and after a few minutes of conversation, they were asked if they would like a cup or tea or "a drink of something cold." M. Annette asked for tea, but her companion said that she would prefer "a cold drink." A few minutes later, the hostess arrived with a tray containing a cup of steaming hot tea for M. Annette with a plate of biscuits and a large glass of whiskey for her companion! The discomfited sister, who abhorred every brand of alcohol, toyed with the glass of whiskey for ten minutes while M. Annette entertained the hostess with the latest news of the parish. Seizing a moment when the attention of the hostess was centred on M. Annette, the visiting sister swiftly deposited the entire contents of the glass of whiskey in a pot containing a large, luxuriant fern that was the owner's pride and joy. A few minutes later the sisters took their leave. The following month, M. Annette visited the couple once again. She noticed that the furniture of the parlour had been rearranged and remarked this to her hostess. "Well, Sister," the lady replied, "you may remember the large, beautiful fern I had in the corner by the window. It was a healthy plant that I had for years and years. But shortly after you were here last, the fern turned yellow and died." It should be mentioned, however, that this episode was unique in the history of the visitation.

The sisters in North River did their best to reach out to people throughout the scattered area of the parish. However, the distances involved made it virtually impossible to reach some places, such as Butlerville—one of the smaller missions of the parish—more than once or twice a year. However, in 1978, two sisters of the North River community were assigned the sole ministry of visiting the sick in Butlerville and working with the children of the settlement. Because of its distance from the more populated areas, it was difficult for the people of Butlerville to attend mass or receive the sacraments. Also, the religious education of the children had been neglected for many years. M. Gregory Stapleton and M. Beatrice Courish travelled back and forth from Our Lady of Lourdes Convent in North River to the little school in Butlerville several times a week to provide religious instruction and to prepare the children for the reception of the sacraments. The two sisters, however, did not confine their efforts to Butlerville. Catholics were a tiny minority in many small villages within the parish boundaries, and there were many calls to M. Gregory and M. Beatrice for assistance. They found time to visit these places, and in some cases, they discovered that the children had not been inside a church since they were baptized. For instance, the Annals of Our Lady of Lourdes Convent for 1979 mentioned that a whole family of four children, whom M. Gregory had prepared, made their First Communion on May 22.[22]

The sister-principal of All Hallows School, North River, was the supervising principal for the school in Bay Roberts, and it was part of her duty to visit these schools every week. This lasted from 1962 until 1967, when the Bay Roberts school was closed and the pupils were transported by bus to the

---

22. Ibid., May 22, 1979, p. 83, ASMSJ.

schools in North River. After ten years in North River, the sisters were pleased to note that eight of their graduates had earned degrees at various universities and fourteen more had been accepted at university.

It was with a feeling of pride that the parishioners of North River Parish gathered on May 9, 1982, for the opening of the new $1,200,000 All Hallows Elementary School. The parish itself had raised ten percent of the capital cost of the building—a serious commitment for a parish of 1,000 people. The new school replaced two older buildings and accommodated 287 students from kindergarten to grade VIII. At the time, there were three sisters teaching in the school, Srs. Marcella Grant (principal), Mary Kelly, and Sheila Grant along with thirteen other teachers. More than ninety percent of the students were bussed to school from communities outside North River itself.[23] The new school contained thirteen classrooms, including remedial reading and hearing-impaired classes, a library, science laboratory, music room, cafeteria, and gymnasium.

In the fall of 1983, the sisters in the Conception Bay area were asked by the General Council of the Sisters of Mercy to discuss the possibility of closing one or more of the convents while, at the same time, continuing to minister in the towns where the convents were located. The sisters of St. Joseph's Convent, Brigus; Immaculate Conception Convent, Conception Harbour; and Our Lady of Lourdes, North River, met on October 24, 1983 to consider the council's suggestions. The sisters agreed that Immaculate Conception Convent should remain open because of winter driving conditions that would pose a hazard should the sisters have to commute to school. However, the communities could not agree on which of the other two convents, St. Joseph's (Brigus) or Our Lady of Lourdes (North River), would remain open. The sisters in North River put up a strong argument for keeping Our Lady of Lourdes, citing the increase in school enrolment, the possibility of industrial growth in Bay Roberts because of offshore oil development, and the large geographical area included in the parish. They pointed out that, although the congregation did not own the convent, it was the newest of the three buildings. Furthermore,

---

23. *The Compass*, May 12, 1982, p. 4.

the sisters had been in Brigus and Conception for well over one hundred years and perhaps it was time to move on. The sisters from St. Joseph's Convent, Brigus, for their part, pointed out the historical importance of Brigus as the first foundation outside St. John's. They mentioned that Brigus Parish, too, covered a wide geographical area, and that the very absence of industrial growth was sufficient reason for the sisters to stay around and contribute to the viability of the settlement. Finally, the three communities agreed to submit separate reports to the General Council.

The superior general, Patricia Maher, and the General Council had some difficult choices to make in the period of the 1980s, and this was just one of them. They pondered over the reports from the three Conception Bay communities, and on December 23, 1983, they decided that Our Lady of Lourdes Convent would close in June 1984, and that the sisters named to serve in North River would reside at St. Joseph's Convent, Brigus. The decision was greeted with enthusiasm by the sisters in Brigus, who were relieved that they did not have to abandon their historic old convent. For the next six years, two sisters continued to teach in North River, commuting daily from St. Joseph's Convent, Brigus. Moreover, they continued their ministry to the people of North River Parish and its missions by assisting at the liturgies and continuing their visitation of the sick and elderly. They had a twenty-minute drive to work every day, but by that time in Newfoundland, the Department of Highways saw that the road was kept free of snow and ice during the winter—at least, most of the time. However, in 1990, the Sisters of Mercy withdrew altogether from the schools in North River.[24]

The move from North River to the historic St. Joseph's Convent, Brigus, occurred at one of the busiest times of the year for the sisters of both communities. They had to attend to all the business associated with the closing of the school year—final examinations, correction of papers, writing of report cards for each student, and getting ready for summer school. At Our Lady of Lourdes Convent, all the furniture and household appliances belonging to the

---

24. After the closure of St. Joseph's Convent, Brigus, the sisters from Immaculate Conception Convent, Conception Harbour, continue to visit the sick of All Hallows Parish in North River.

Congregation of the Sisters of Mercy had to be packed and sent to the generalate in St. John's or given to the poor. In Brigus, the sisters had to store the boxes of books and clothing that arrived almost daily from North River and prepare extra rooms to receive the new members of St. Joseph's community. In spite of the dire prediction, "It will take us the rest of the year to clear up this mess," the sisters in North River completed preparations to move before mid-July. The house was cleaned and polished from attic to basement, and on July 11, 1984, Marcella Grant, the local superior, handed over the keys of the convent to the pastor, Father Fred Terry, and Our Lady of Lourdes Convent became part of history.

From the time of the sisters' arrival in Brigus, their schools were well-known around Conception Bay for sound teaching and for offering additional courses that were considered an important part of a girl's education, such as music, needlework, and foreign languages. Prior to 1900, the enrolment was relatively small, but during the twentieth century, the number of children attending the sisters' schools continued to increase. For instance, in 1923, one hundred and ten were registered in St. Joseph's School, twenty-eight of whom were in the high-school division. There were four classrooms and four teachers, and in addition, there was a full-time music teacher. In June 1916, Mr. Stephen James retired. When he started teaching in 1900, he taught the boys who attended St. Patrick's School, while the sisters, for the first time since their arrival in Brigus, taught only girls. Mr. James was replaced by M. Francis Holden, who had been reassigned from St. George's at the time of the amalgamation of the convents.[25] From that time, the sisters of St. Joseph's Convent were responsible for the teaching and administration of the boy's school until 1944 when both schools became coeducational.[26]

---

25. Ronald Kennedy, "Report of the Superintendent of Education, Diocese of Harbour Grace, for the Year Ended December 31, 1917," p. 24, ASMSJ.

26. From 1937–1944, there was some combination of classes of boys and girls, especially in the senior grades, ASMSJ, RG 10/3/21.

During the First World War, the boys and girls who attended Newfoundland schools were constantly reminded of their duty to support the soldiers of the Newfoundland Regiment who were fighting overseas. The sisters' schools in Brigus were no exception. A fund was set up to provide cots and beds for soldiers from the Newfoundland Regiment who had been wounded in battle. The report of the superintendent of education for the Harbour Grace diocese contains a list of contributors to the Hospital Cot Fund. The amount of donations from each person ranged from $1 to $3. The name of M. Teresa Slattery appears on the list, credited with the amount of $2, representing the number of pennies collected from the children attending St. Joseph's and St. Patrick's Schools in Brigus.[27] In 1917, the old St. Patrick's Hall was replaced by a splendid new building that enabled M. Francis Holden and her class of boys to enjoy the luxury of a bright, new school and the latest equipment available. This new St. Patrick's Hall, situated directly opposite the convent, consisted of two large classrooms and a coal pound.[28]

In 1916, M. Philomena Walker, a native of Brigus, was appointed superior of St. Joseph's Convent, a position she held until 1922. During M. Philomena's term of office a two-storey extension was added to the old 1861 convent. The first floor contained two large classrooms and a smaller room that was used to teach typing and shorthand. The chapel and sacristy occupied the entire length of the second storey of the extension. In both schools, grades VII to XI were taught in the senior classroom and grades I to VI in the junior room. This section of the convent was torn down in the 1960s and replaced by another extension to the convent that contained a smaller chapel and a couple of bedrooms on the second floor and on the first floor, the dining room and an office. However, at the time of the demolition of the 1916 extension, human remains were found. Presuming that the grave of one of the founding sisters had been discovered, the Congregation of the Sisters of Mercy had the remains removed and buried in the sisters' plot near the parish church. Subsequently,

27. Ronald Kennedy, "Report of the Superintendent of Education, Diocese of Harbour Grace, for the Year Ended December 31, 1915," p. ix.

28 M. Aquinas Hicks, "Notes on Brigus Schools," ASMSJ, RG 10/3/19.

a small monument containing the names of all the sisters buried in Brigus was erected near St. Joseph's Church.[29]

Life in the convent did not change much in the years prior to 1967. The sisters' days were ordered by the *Horarium*. They rose at six o'clock in the morning and went to the chapel for prayers at twenty after six, where they spent the next hour in prayer. After that they attended mass, had breakfast, swept and dusted the house and were in the classroom shortly after half past eight. School began at nine o'clock with an hour's break for lunch at noon. Classes were dismissed at half past three, and the sisters returned to the convent where recreation began at four o'clock. Usually they went for a walk, visited the sick, or the bereaved, or delivered food to the poor of the area. In bad weather, they stayed indoors and occupied the time doing needlework while they chatted around the community room table. Prayers were from quarter to five until six o'clock, then supper, class preparation until eight o'clock when there was an hour set aside for recreation, followed by night prayer, which in those days consisted of a private examination of conscience followed by the Litany of the Saints. Every sister was expected to be in bed and all lights out at ten o'clock. This was the *Horarium* followed in every Mercy convent from 1842 until after the 1967 chapter, when the whole approach to convent living underwent a radical change.[30]

Disaster struck in Brigus in 1935 when, on a beautiful summer afternoon, the lovely old parish church was burned to the ground. The convent, which was about five hundred yards from the church, was spared. The people of Brigus rallied around their parish priest, and before another year had passed, a new St. Joseph's Church had been completed. There was one problem, however. The sisters' cemetery had been located near the side of the old church. After the new building had been completed, it was discovered that several of these graves had disappeared under the new church. Consequently,

29. The name of those buried in the sisters' cemetery are Mary of the Angels Banks, M. Gonzaga Coady, M. Ultan Mullowney, and M. Veronica Crawley.

30. There were a few exceptions to this *Horarium*. For example, the demands of hospital duties often required some adjustments to be made at St. Clare's Convent. Similarly, St. Michael's Convent, Belvedere, and St. Patrick's Mercy Home found it necessary to adjust the hours for convent duties.

when Sr. M. Berchmans Meehan died in 1937, a new sisters' cemetery had to be opened. It is located on Bally Mona, a hill just behind the church, and here M. Berchmans rests, far away from her native Ireland and even from the sisters with whom she lived and worked.[31]

On September 16, 1961, St. Joseph's Convent celebrated its one hundredth anniversary. Mass was celebrated in the parish church by the bishop of the diocese. In his address, Bishop John M. O'Neill referred to the large number of religious brothers and sisters and priests who had been educated by the Sisters of Mercy in Brigus, which he attributed to the teachings and example of the sisters of St. Joseph's Convent.

The 1960s saw the beginning of two new schools in Brigus. The new St. Edward's Elementary School was ready to admit students in January 1966. For the next twenty-five years the Sisters of Mercy administered the school until June 1991, when Sr. Ann Normore, who had been principal since 1985, took a two-year leave of absence from teaching.[32] After 1991, the sisters assigned to St. Edward's Elementary taught under the administration of a lay principal. In 1964, St. Edward's High School was opened with M. Fidelis Parsons as its first principal. She was succeeded in 1967 by Sr. Ruth Beresford, who remained as principal until 1969 when the sisters relinquished the principalship of the high school. Nevertheless, Sisters of Mercy continued to teach at St. Edward's High School until 1973 when the new Bishop O'Neill Collegiate became the Roman Catholic high school for the Brigus area. The last two sisters to teach at St. Edward's High School were M. Evangelista Bulger and M. Carmel Peters. However, the Sisters of Mercy continued to teach at Bishop O'Neill Collegiate until the mid-1980s.

As the number of sisters teaching in Brigus was reduced to two or three, the Mercy congregation was forced to come to a decision about maintaining the two large convents in Brigus and Conception Harbour. With the departure

---

31. A few years later, Rev. James Walker died. He was buried in the Bally Mona cemetery, next to Sr. M. Berchmans. Father Walker was the brother of M. Philomena Walker. These are the only two graves in this cemetery.

32. Subsequently, Sr. Ann Normore taught in Marystown and Bay Bulls until she retired in 1998.

of Sr. Ann Normore, Sr. Eileen Osbourne was the only sister remaining on the teaching staff of St. Edward's Elementary School in Brigus.

Once more, the General Council had to make the painful decision on the future of one of the two remaining convents in Conception Bay. On January 31, 1991, Marion Collins, the superior general, sent a circular letter to the sisters announcing that at the end of the school year, St. Joseph's Convent in Brigus would close. Sr. Eileen Osbourne was assigned to the Immaculate Conception Convent, Conception Harbour. For the next few years, Sr. Eileen drove from Conception to Brigus to continue teaching the children at St. Edward's School.[33]

The decision to close the historically important Brigus convent was greeted with some consternation by the people of the town, for the Sisters of Mercy had been part of the small, closely knit community since 1861. The decision was particularly painful to the sisters who had grown up in Brigus and attended St. Joseph's School and also for those who had taught there. Nevertheless, the time had come for the sisters to leave. The property was put up for sale.

Eventually a buyer came forward with a proposal for the future use of the convent that was agreeable to the congregation. On March 1, 1994, Sr. Eileen Osbourne passed the keys of St. Joseph's Convent to Mr. Herbert Martin, who had purchased it for use as a boarding home for seniors. However, the building changed hands several times before it came into the possession of the present owner, Joseph Smallwood.[34] At the time of writing, the house is undergoing extensive repairs and renovations.

In June 1996, the Sisters of Mercy withdrew altogether from the schools in Brigus, thus bringing to a close 135 years of teaching ministry in that town. At the time of writing, Sr. Callista Ryan from the Immaculate Conception Convent, Conception Harbour, drives to Brigus every day, visiting the sick and

---

33. Sr. Eileen Osbourne retired from a salaried teaching position in June 1993 but continued to give voluntary service in St. Edward's Elementary School in Brigus until June 1996.

34. Joseph Smallwood is the grandson of the first premier of the province of Newfoundland, Joseph R. Smallwood, the person who played a major role in bringing Newfoundland into Confederation with Canada.

elderly of the parish. Thus the ministry of the Sisters of Mercy continues in Brigus even though the convent where the sisters lived, prayed and worked for 135 years will serve a different purpose in the future.

Through the years, the number of sisters living at the Immaculate Conception Convent in Conception Harbour remained fairly consistent. After the amalgamation there were, as a rule, five sisters living at the Immaculate Conception Convent. The first superior appointed by the new General Council in 1916 was M. Teresa Slattery. The young M. deSales Ahearn, who had taught in the school in Conception Harbour before asking to be admitted there as a postulant, made her novitiate with the Immaculate Conception community and was professed in the parish church at Conception Harbour in 1913. After her profession, she remained there until 1921. According to the annual reports of the superintendent of education for Roman Catholic schools in the Harbour Grace diocese, in the first decade of the twentieth century, music received much attention, and the superintendent's reports usually contained some reference to singing and music as an integral part of the curriculum. However, according to the sisters who taught at Conception Harbour, a play in which there was no singing or dancing had little appeal for the people or for the students. Hence, performances took the form of operettas. Instrumental music, chiefly piano and violin, was taught at the convent, but choral music was carefully cultivated in the schools.[35] The annual Christmas play or pageant was the highlight of the Advent season, and people came from neighbouring settlements to attend these performances presented by pupils of the convent school.

There seems to have been a very close bond between the sisters and their pupils at Conception Harbour. Older residents tell stories of how they vied with one another to bring messages from the school to the convent. This task involved walking through the long, long corridor that connected the old 1869 convent with the three-room school. On arriving at the kitchen door, the small messenger was sure of receiving a reward in the form of a cookie or a

---

35. ASMSJ, MG 2/1/220.

slice of freshly baked bread with molasses.[36] In this connection, the name of
M. Rosarii Wiseman was mentioned by one of the older residents of
Conception Harbour.[37]

As a small child, M. Rosarii had lost both parents. She was sent to
Belvedere and brought up by the Sisters of Mercy in St. Michael's Orphanage.
Later on, she asked to be admitted to the Congregation of the Sisters of Mercy
as a lay sister, and after her profession in 1911, she was assigned to Conception
Harbour. Apparently, she spent the rest of her life in the convent of the
Immaculate Conception. M. Rosarii's task was to look after the day-to-day running of the convent. In addition, she was in charge of the cow—for the sisters,
like most other outport households, kept a cow, some hens, and a vegetable garden. According to Mrs. Mary Dalton, a resident of the town, M. Rosarii had a
somewhat irreverent sense of humour—she called one of her hens "Mother
Francis" in honour of the superior, M. Francis Hickey. Evidently, M. Rosarii saw
a similarity between the way in which the hen, "Mother Francis," gathered her
chickens about her and M. Francis Hickey's manner of shepherding the sisters
across the meadow from the convent to the church for mass. It goes without
saying that M. Francis Hickey was kept in blissful ignorance of the hen's name.
Incidentally, when attending mass in the parish church, the sisters occupied a
pew behind the altar—evidence of the quasi-monastic lifestyle imposed upon
women religious in the days before the Second Vatican Council.

The children truly loved M. Rosarii Wiseman—and not only for her
cooking skills. While the other sisters in the convent were liked and respected,
they represented authority. Thus they were eyed with awe, and even with a certain degree of trepidation by less-than-diligent young scholars. M. Rosarii, on
the other hand, could be relied on not to report misdemeanours and was always
ready to make excuses for a child who dallied too long in the convent kitchen
consuming generous portions of the "Queen of All Puddings."[38] Mrs. Mary
Dalton remembered that M. Rosarii had a special fondness for the convent cat.

---

36. Catherine Kenny, RSM, a native of Conception Harbour, is the source of this story.
37. Mrs. Mary Dalton, conversation with author, May 5, 2004.
38. "Queen of All Puddings" was rice pudding with layers of strawberry jam, topped by
fresh cream and strawberries—when they were in season.

When Mary was eight years old, M. Rosarii gave her a kitten, Sammy, on condition that Mary would bring Sammy once a week to the convent for a visit. Whenever the convent cat produced a litter of kittens—something that happened with predictable and distressing frequency—M. Rosarii would have been happy to keep them all. Unfortunately, the superior did not like cats and permitted only one feline on the premises as a necessary protection against mice. However, M. Rosarii's popularity with the children of Conception Harbour ensured that all the convent kittens found good Catholic homes throughout the settlement. It is possible that the roaming felines that continue to stalk the convent garden through the years to the present day are merely returning to their roots. There was universal sadness throughout the juvenile population of Conception Harbour when news spread that M. Rosarii Wiseman was not feeling well and had to go to St. John's for treatment. After a few months' illness, she died on November 19, 1934.

M. Rosarii Wiseman was one of the "hidden" Sisters of Mercy. Some sisters may notice her name on the obituary list for November that hangs in every convent chapel and offer a prayer for this almost-forgotten member of their congregation. M. Rosarii Wiseman was not an administrator, or principal of a school, or superior of a convent; she was not a dynamic classroom teacher or mathematician; she was not a choir director or writer of books. But seventy years after her death, she is spoken of with affection and gratitude by a ninety-six-year-old lady who never forgot the woman who won the hearts of the children of Conception Harbour through simple human kindness and generosity.

Special efforts made by the sisters of the Immaculate Conception Convent to reach out to the sick and elderly further cemented the close ties between convent and town. During the Depression years, the sisters struggled to alleviate some of the more critical cases of poverty and sickness. On one occasion they visited a home where they discovered a teenage girl lying on a sack on the floor, for her parents could not supply her with a bed. The sisters, who had very few resources in those days, returned to the convent, collected blankets and whatever other materials they could find to make a mattress. When they were satisfied that their homemade mattress could provide a cosy resting place for the patient, they brought it to her home on a "truckley-muck"[39] and waited until the child was comfortably settled in her new "bed."

By the year 1929, the Immaculate Conception Convent, which was built in 1869, was urgently in need of repair. This convent was a replica of St. Joseph's Convent in Brigus, but for some reason, it did not seem to withstand the wear and tear of the years as well as its twin to the north. The superior, M. Agnes Doyle, discussed the matter with M. Philippa Hanley, the mother general at that time. M. Philippa visited the convent and was shocked at the condition of the house. Building inspectors were called in and, after a thorough investigation, condemned the building as being beyond repair.

It was the time of the Great Depression. The teachers' salaries were reduced to $20 a term (three months). Obviously, the sisters could not afford the cost of building a new convent until their financial situation improved. However, unless a new convent could be provided, the sisters would have to leave the parish at the close of the school year, June 1930. At the same time, the pastor, Monsignor Donnelly, had just retired, and Rev. John Scully had been appointed parish priest of St. Anne's Parish, Conception Harbour. Immediately on his arrival in the parish, Fr. Scully was briefed on the serious situation facing the convent and school. The new pastor, a man of action, summoned the men of the parish and obtained volunteers to give a certain number of days of free labour. Fr. Scully, who had private means, offered to make a loan of $10,000.[40] The problem was solved. The fathers worked, the mothers prayed, the sisters kept on teaching, and the new convent was built. M. Borromeo McNeil was one of the last sisters to live in the old convent, as well as one of the first to move into the new one. M. Borromeo wrote nostalgically of the old convent, "with its beautiful grounds of flowers and shrubs and shady trees, painted benches, and a small but restful summer house."[41]

---

39. A "truckley-muck" was a homemade cart consisting of a long strip of board that had been fitted with wheels. I am indebted to Mrs. Mary Dalton for this story.

40. M. Francis Hickey, *Mercy Communico*, June 1968, p. 2. M. Francis succeeded M. Ursula McNamara as superior of the Immaculate Conception Convent. M. Francis was not sure if the amount of money advanced by Fr. Scully was $7,000 or $10,000.

41. M. Borromeo McNeil, "Mercy Memo," June 1968, p. 2, ASMSJ.

Father Scully's prompt action had solved the problem of providing a new convent. The next thing facing the sisters was to find a place to live during the period of construction. Many years later, M. Francis Hickey, the editor of *Mercy Communico* asked M. Borromeo McNeil to write an account of this period in the history of Conception Harbour:

> In September (1930) we took up residence in a very small house opposite the old hall, belonging to Miss Maude Kennedy, who donated it to the Sisters for the time being. This house contained few conveniences. One room served for the community room and refectory; opposite this room was another little room which we made into a chapel, then another, a kitchen. There was a little room upstairs, but we managed and were quite happy. We felt sad to see the old convent being demolished. Every evening we visited the scene.[42]

The demolition of the old convent disrupted the lives, not only of the sisters, but of almost the entire population of Conception Harbour. Since 1867, the girls' school had been attached to the convent. Now that the sisters were living in Miss Maude Kennedy's house, Father Scully decided that the distance to the school was too great to allow the sisters to walk back and forth. Evidently, Father saw a difference between permitting the sisters to walk to school and having them trot halfway around Conception Harbour to visit the sick! In any case, he decided that, until the new convent was completed, the boys and their teachers should move to the former St. Anne's School, while the girls and the sisters moved into the boys' academy, know as the "Old Hall."[43]

The new Immaculate Conception Convent was built in the same field as the first convent, but further down toward the ocean. As a precautionary measure, it was built at a greater distance from the church in case one or other of the buildings caught fire. The last sisters to live in the old convent were the superior, M. Agnes Doyle, M. Gertrude Kennedy, M. Ursula McNamara, M.

---

42. Ibid.

43. I am indebted to Sr. Geraldine Mason for this story. Sr. Geraldine heard it from Helen Keating, whose father taught the boys in the "Old Hall."

Teresa Williams, M. Rosarii Wiseman, and M. Borromeo McNeil. Sadly, M. Agnes Doyle, who had been experiencing problems with her sight for several years, became completely blind in 1929. When she had completed her second term of office as superior she was reassigned to Mercy Convent. Subsequently, she went to live at St. Michael's Convent, Belvedere, where she spent the rest of her life.

When the sisters moved into the new Immaculate Conception Convent on August 15, 1931, M. Ursula McNamara had been appointed to replace M. Agnes Doyle as the superior. By this time, the General Council had released the assignments for the school year 1931–32. Both M. Teresa Williams and M. Borromeo McNeil had been transferred, and in their places, M. Fintan Downey and M. Carmela O'Brien were assigned to Conception Harbour with the distinction of being members of the first community to live in the brand new convent.[44]

Although the sisters in Conception Harbour were delighted with their new convent, there was something missing—a chapel. True, they set aside one of the larger rooms and decorated it with pictures, a statue or two, and designated it as a chapel. However, when they went to Brigus and visited the beautiful little chapel in St. Joseph's Convent, they returned home to Conception Harbour with a decidedly greenish tinge to their complexions! This state of affairs could not be permitted to continue. The sisters stormed heaven, and their prayers were answered. Before the end of 1934, a beautiful new chapel had been added to the east side of the convent.[45]

As the years carried on, the little town remained very much as it had been through the years after the arrival of the sisters. In addition to regular

---

44. The first five sisters to live in the new Immaculate Conception Convent were M. Ursula McNamara, M. Gertrude Kennedy, M. Fintan Downey, M. Rosarii Wiseman, M. Carmela O'Brien.

45. According to Mrs. Mary Dalton, a ninety-six-year-old resident of Conception Harbour, the convent was built under the supervision of Matthew Nugent, the father of M. Emmanuel Nugent. M. Emmanuel entered the Congregation of the Sisters of Mercy and taught for many years in schools administered by the Sisters of Mercy in many parts of Newfoundland. The exact date of the opening of the new convent chapel is unknown. However, John and Catherine Keating were married in the convent chapel on January 2, 1935. This information was provided by their daughter, Helen Keating.

classroom teaching, the sisters continued to teach instrumental, vocal, and choral music. Until 1949, the boys of Conception Harbour had been taught by "Masters" in the Old Hall. However, at the end of the school year 1948–49, the boys' school was closed and St. Anne's School, the "convent school," became coeducational from grades I–XI. To accommodate the boys, an extension was added to the school. At that time, St. Anne's was staffed entirely by sisters, a practice that was continued until the high-school students were transferred to the central high school in Avondale.[46] Far from distracting the girls (or the boys) from their studies, there seemed to have been a healthy rivalry between the sexes that resulted in several important scholarships coming to the school. For instance, in 1950, the province-wide competition for civics was won by a grade X student of St. Anne's School, as well as prizes for English and Latin, the Knights of Columbus Scholarship of $300, and the Grade X scholarship of $100. The following year, pupils of St. Anne's won the Grade X Maritime Scholarship of $1,500 and the King George V Jubilee Scholarship of $600. In the years that followed, the names of students of St. Anne's School, Conception Harbour, appeared regularly on lists of scholarship winners in the yearly CHE examinations.

In 1960, a new school was built that accommodated children in grades I–VI; students in grades VII to XI remained in the older part of St. Anne's School. Two years later, the old school was demolished and all students moved into the new St. Anne's School. An extension was added to the school in 1965 to accommodate children from nearby settlements of Kitchuses and Healey's Pond.

Meanwhile, the parish priest of Holyrood had made several visits to the superior general, M. Assumpta Veitch, requesting her to send a couple of sisters to teach in the school in Holyrood. M. Assumpta, who had spent her childhood years in Holyrood, listened with considerable sympathy to the pastor's tale of woe. After all, the schools in nearby towns of Harbour Main, Avondale, and Conception Harbour were staffed by either the Presentation or Mercy Sisters, while Holyrood—a much more important town in the pastor's eyes—

---

46. M. Jerome Walker, "Notes on Conception Harbour Schools," ASMSJ, RG 10/5/2.

was being overlooked by both congregations! M. Assumpta agreed to do whatever she could to respond to the priest's request. Accordingly, in 1968, two sisters from the Immaculate Conception Convent in Conception Harbour were
assigned to Holy Cross Central High School in Holyrood. Although it is probable that M. Assumpta intended that the sisters' presence in Holy Cross High
School would continue for years into the future, circumstances dictated otherwise. The sisters withdrew from the school in June 1971. Presumably, their
services were required more urgently elsewhere. Was "elsewhere" the neighbouring town of Avondale?

It was a time when the Government of Newfoundland was bitten by the
bug, "bigger is better." Consequently, large central high schools were being
built all over the province, one of them in Avondale, a settlement about five
miles south of Conception Harbour. In 1970, Roncalli Central High School
was opened under the direction of the Christian Brothers. During its first
year of operation, Roncalli was a single-sex school for boys. However, this
policy changed a year later. All high-school students from surrounding settlements, including Conception Harbour, were bussed to Avondale to attend
Roncalli High School. In September 1971, two sisters from the Immaculate
Conception Convent community were appointed to the faculty of the new
high school, Srs. Loretta Chafe and Diane Smyth. In September 1972, Sr.
Loretta was replaced by Sr. Patricia March, who remained at the school for
two years until June 1974, when the sisters withdrew from teaching positions
at Roncalli.

Nevertheless, in spite of the "goings and comings" of the high-school
teachers, the rest of the sisters at Immaculate Conception Convent soldiered
on faithfully, day in and day out, teaching small boys and girls in the primary
and elementary grades. By this time the teaching staff at St. Anne's School
included a number of lay teachers. There were only two sisters on staff, the
principal and a classroom teacher. When the two high-school teachers were
withdrawn from Roncalli High School, the General Council of the Sisters of
Mercy decided that the time had come to close the convent in Conception
Harbour.

The announcement of the closure of the Immaculate Conception Convent was greeted with almost universal consternation and disapproval. The parishioners in Conception Harbour were hurt and disappointed; the Sisters of Mercy who had grown up in the town and had been taught by the sisters were simply outraged! "After all," they said, "the sisters mean much more to us than simply persons who teach school all day! The Sisters of Mercy have been with our people all through the difficult years. They are part of Conception Harbour. It won't be the same town without them!" And so the battle raged for a year. Two sisters drove back and forth daily from St. Joseph's Convent, Brigus, and St. Anne's School continued as usual. Occasionally, winter snowstorms forced the sisters to stay overnight in the lonely old convent. This was not a pleasant experience, for in the absence of the sisters, several families of mice had taken over the building. The mice were not at all happy with their uninvited guests, and Sr. Phyllis Corbett has vivid recollections of getting up in the morning to discover a couple of mice resting comfortably in her shoes.

Eventually, two retired sisters, M. Clarissa Reddy and Sr. Kathleen Buck agreed to move to Conception Harbour and form a community with the two sisters who were teaching at St. Anne's School. The Immaculate Conception Convent was reopened in September 1975. The sisters were back; the mice were banished; everybody was happy; and life went on very much as it had since 1867.

In 1982, the sisters in Conception Harbour initiated a new venture, the establishment of a house of prayer and a spiritual renewal centre in the parish. This came about because of a shortage of priests in the Grand Falls diocese.[47] The bishop had decided that the parish priest from Avondale could look after the spiritual needs of the residents of Conception Harbour, Colliers, and the smaller settlements in the area. Consequently, the presbytery, where the parish

---

47. The Diocese of Harbour Grace was established in 1856, with Rev. John Dalton appointed its first bishop. Because of a population shift that occurred during the twentieth century, the administration of the diocese was moved to Grand Falls and on February 22, 1958, the diocese was renamed, "GrandFalls/Harbour Grace Diocese." Six years later, October 30, 1964, "Harbour Grace" was dropped from the title of the diocese, which became known as the Diocese of Grand Falls.

priest of St. Anne's Parish had resided for a number of years was vacant. Rather than let the house fall into disrepair, Bishop Faber MacDonald invited Sr. Edward Mary Roche to initiate a program of spiritual renewal in St. Anne's Parish. The old presbytery was designated as the renewal centre for the Grand Falls diocese.

For the first few months after her appointment to this new ministry, Sr. Edward Mary was, more or less, at sea. She met with the priests and representatives of the Conception Bay parishes and solicited ideas and suggestions that helped her in formulating programs that would meets the needs of parishioners in the area. But she did not stop there. She made all sorts of contacts with people, meeting them on the street and exchanging greetings, chatting in the stores and post office, and visiting the elderly and sick in their homes. Through these contacts, she gathered a number of ideas that propelled her into her new ministry. In January 1983, she was ready to start. Although renovations to the old presbytery were not completed, she offered opportunities for people to gather for prayer and reflection. At the end of the year, more than thirty groups from nearby parishes had gathered at the renewal centre for prayer and reflection on Scripture and for the celebration of mass and the sacrament of reconciliation. During the seasons of Advent and Lent, the renewal centre was in constant use. Ten years later, the following letter appeared in the local press:

> The Renewal Centre is a blessing to our area: is reaching out and positively touching the lives of many people . . . I write this article to bring to light a very important part of the Renewal Centre—its beginning, and in some small way to pay a long overdue tribute to its foundress, Sister Edward Mary Roche.
>
> When the house was designated as a House of Prayer . . . Much work was needed to convert the priest's house to a prayer house, to set up spiritual programs and get people involved. Through Sister's faith, prayers, courage, and guidance, this great task was accomplished . . .
>
> While setting up and furnishing the Centre, Sister Edward Mary formed an auxiliary group. This group . . . was open to anyone who wished to join . . . In her gentle way, Sister Edward Mary led

this auxiliary group onto paths of spiritual renewal. Many of these
same people are taking an active role in parish life today.[48]

Sr. Edward Mary Roche remained in Conception Harbour as director of the
renewal centre until September 1989, when she decided to take a sabbatical
year.[49] After her departure, the centre was under the direction of the
Presentation Sisters for a number of years.

Meanwhile, St. Anne's School was benefiting from the new government
regulations that required teachers to retire at the age of sixty years. As more and
more sisters retired from salaried positions in teaching, they volunteered their
time by providing a number of services in the schools, principally by tutoring
students in mathematics, reading, English, or science. A number of sisters who
had degrees in library science set up school libraries and served as librarians in
schools that did not have sufficient enrolment to warrant a salaried librarian.
This was the case at St. Anne's School in Conception Harbour, where M. Loyola
Power gave free service for eight years before ill health forced her into retirement. In addition to Sr. Loyola, a number of sisters provided volunteer service
to the children in St. Anne's School and elsewhere. For instance, when Sr.
Geraldine Mason retired as principal of St. Anne's, she was asked by the Western
Avalon School Board to work with four-year-old children. In response to this
request, Geraldine set aside an afternoon for "storytime." In addition to her
work with these children, she taught the grade VI religion program at St. Anne's
School, and in case she might have some free time on her hands she was asked
to teach a remedial reading program to students in grades I and III in the
Immaculate Conception School in Colliers. In her spare time (!) Geraldine took
the responsibility for the church choir in Conception Harbour and Colliers.
Although one of the parishioners was a competent organist, she had other commitments that sometimes interfered with liturgical functions being held in the
church. On these occasions, Sr. Geraldine filled in as organist.

48. Margaret Dalton, *The Compass*, May 27, 1992, p. 4.
49. At the end of her sabbatical year, Sr. Edward Mary was appointed to St. Mary's on the
Humber and then to St. Michael's Convent, Belvedere. At the time of her death, on October
16, 2004, she was a member of the community at St. Bride's Convent, Littledale.

In the mid-1990s, Sr. Geraldine's days in the classroom, even as a volunteer, were coming to an end. She was asked to provide pastoral visitation to several of the nursing homes in Holyrood and Harbour Main. However, because of the number of these homes, it was impossible for Sr. Geraldine to give the attention that each elderly person required. Consequently, Sr. Georgina Quick joined Sr. Geraldine in 1997 to assist in providing pastoral care in the nursing homes of the area.

By this time, there were only two sisters living in the Immaculate Conception Convent. Nevertheless, it was a beehive of activity, for Conception Harbour was a popular place for sisters to visit for a few hours to catch up on all the latest convent news. During the summer months, particularly, accommodation at the convent was in great demand, as sisters who were tired of the noise and bustle of the city went to Conception Harbour to spend a couple of weeks in the beautiful old convent of the Immaculate Conception. In this context, many of the senior members of the congregation like to tell of days long ago, when picnics were held over on Bally Hack, a little cove on the side of the harbour opposite the convent. During the summer vacation, on the appointed day, Paddy Wade, the brother of M. Liguori, M. Anthony, and M. Barbara Wade, brought his boat to the little jetty across the road from the convent. The sisters climbed on board, and Paddy rowed them across the harbour to the sheltered little cove where they spent the day swimming in the ocean, looking for wild berries, or just reading in the shade of a spruce or fir tree. The days of picnics on Bally Hack are long gone, but the memory lingers.[50]

At the time this account is being written, three sisters live in the convent at Conception Harbour, Srs. Geraldine Mason, Alverna Harnett, and Callista Ryan form the community of the Immaculate Conception Convent. Sr. Alverna calls herself, "the minister of hospitality." Persons on a diet should not visit the Immaculate Conception Convent, for most people who spend any length of time there return home very much increased in girth. In addition to her work in the convent, Sr. Alverna visits the sick in Conception Harbour and

---

50. The three Wade sisters died several years ago. Their brother, the generous and kindly Mr. Paddy Wade, died early in the year 2005.

accompanies Sr. Geraldine when she visits the nursing homes in Holyrood. Sr. Callista Ryan provides pastoral care to the sick in Brigus and North River, for while the sisters no longer live in these towns, they continue to feel a responsibility to the people with whom the Sisters of Mercy lived and worked for so many years.

Sr. Geraldine Mason continues her work of pastoral visitation but, in addition, the bishop of Grand Falls, Bishop Martin Currie, asked her to assume the direction of the renewal centre. She is assisted in this ministry by Miss Helen Keating. The centre is a hive of activity, for people seem to be searching for deeper spiritual meaning in their lives and closer union with God. For example, it is not unusual for Sr. Geraldine and Helen to have as many as thirty couples registered for marriage preparation courses.

The Immaculate Conception Convent is one of two Mercy convents remaining in Conception Bay. However, as long as the sisters remain on Bell Island and in Conception Harbour, they will continue to weave the tapestry of Mercy that reminds people of the constant and abiding mercy and love of God.

CHAPTER TWENTY-TWO

PERU

How beautiful are the feet of those who bring the gospel of peace!

Romans 10:15

In 1959, Pope John XXIII published a document expressing concern over the plight of the Church in Latin America.[1] Archbishop P. J. Skinner of St. John's responded by agreeing to release a diocesan priest for ministry in a Peruvian town, Monsefú, a parish that had been without the services of a priest for over four years. The archbishop's choice as pastor for the new mission was a young priest, Father Charles O'Neill Conroy, who left St. John's in November 1960 to establish the new mission. Seven months later, Father John Maddigan, also from the Archdiocese of St. John's, joined him. The priests took up residence in the little *pueblo* (town) that was to hold a special place forever in the hearts of the Sisters of Mercy of Newfoundland.

Monsefú is a small town with an area of about one square mile located about four hundred and fifty miles north of Lima. In the 1960s, it had a population of about 14,000 people. Another 5,000 people lived in the surrounding countryside that was also part of the parish of Monsefú. The inhabitants are pure-blooded Indians, the majority of whom are engaged in agriculture. Each

---

1. Charles O'Neill Conroy, *Peruvian Journal: Letters of a Gringo Priest* (Montreal: Palm Publishers, 1966), p. xiv.

family owns a small piece of land for the purpose of growing its own vegetables and selling the small surplus in a common marketplace. There are a host
of small industries, but due to lack of modern machinery, these provide very
little in the way of earning a livelihood. Most of the dwelling houses are made
of *adobe*—a type of mud that was to become all too familiar to the sisters as
they walked the streets of Monsefú in their long, white habits.

In early 1960, shortly after the announcement of Father Conroy's
appointment to Monsefú, rumours of an impending Mercy foundation in
South America made their way through the convent grapevine. This rumour
was given considerable weight when it was announced that Mr. Muzychka
from Memorial University would be coming to Mercy Convent twice a week
to teach Spanish, and sisters were encouraged to enroll in his class. About
twenty sisters from around the St. John's area enthusiastically accepted the
offer.

Although deliberations of the General Council are strictly confidential,
sisters at Mercy Convent, Military Road, were in an ideal position to witness
the frequent trips across the Basilica Hill made by the superior general, M.
Imelda Smith, and her assistant to confer with the archbishop. These visits were
the source of endless speculation among the sisters in community. Finally, the
announcement was made. The Sisters of Mercy would be sending a group of
sisters to Peru to establish a school and undertake the traditional Mercy ministry, visitation of the poor and the sick. A short time later, a message came
from the General Council inviting applications from sisters who were interested in offering themselves for the mission. Sisters of all ages responded
including, it is reported, a few who were well over eighty years of age!

Early in 1961, M. Dorothy Carroll was appointed superior of the new
mission. The following sisters were named to accompany her: M. Immacula
O'Leary (assistant), Marion Collins,[2] Helen Best, Maura Mason, and Bernetta
Walsh. When some imprudent soul let fall the statement that the General

---

2. After the chapter of 1973, any sister who wished to do so, might resume her baptismal
name. To avoid confusion, any sister who availed of this option and who is mentioned in
later chapters is referred to by her baptismal name.

Council had chosen "only the best" for Monsefú, there was, naturally, some reaction among the non-chosen!

The sisters appointed to the new mission—all qualified, experienced teachers—immediately began an intense preparation by enrolling in courses in Spanish, first aid, and Peruvian history, while cheerfully ignoring the considerable teasing of their companions about the superior status accorded them as being "the best." Soon the light-hearted ribbing stopped, as the rest of the community acknowledged that the foundation in Peru was going to demand a wrenching sacrifice on the part of each sister assigned to the mission. As the time drew near for the departure, every sister in the congregation was affected. Some were facing separation from family—a blood sister or cousin; others were experiencing the impending loss of close friends and companions from novitiate days.

On the evening of October 22, a departure ceremony was held in the Basilica-Cathedral of St. John the Baptist in St. John's. The vast cathedral was filled with relatives and friends of the departing missionaries. A special sisters' choir provided the music. As the six sisters knelt for the archbishop's blessing, all those present realized that a new chapter in the history of the archdiocese, and in particular of the Sisters of Mercy, was about to begin. Early in the morning of November 1, 1961, the six sisters and Father Charlie Conroy boarded the plane en route to Peru. This was the first foundation of the Newfoundland Congregation of the Sisters of Mercy outside the island of Newfoundland. On their arrival in Lima the next morning, they were greeted by Sister M. Jogues of the Marist Sisters and Mother M. Trinita of the Sisters of the Immaculate Heart of Mary. It marked the beginnings of the long and close friendship of the Mercy Sisters and the IHM's,[3] a friendship that was cemented several years later by the tragedy that claimed the lives of two Sisters of Mercy and saw two more severely injured.[4]

---

3. IHM is an abbreviation used to identify members of the Sisters of the Immaculate Heart of Mary.

4. Most of the information that follows, up to 1985, is taken from the Annals, Convent of Mercy, Monsefú, ASMSJ.

Having cleared Customs and Immigration, the Newfoundlanders were driven to the convent of the IHM sisters, Villa Maria, for a few hours rest before attending a dinner given in their honour by the apostolic nuncio, Monsignor Romolo Carboni, who officially welcomed them to Peru. After the speeches were over, the Newfoundlanders were glad enough to return to the simplicity and hospitality of Villa Maria. The next few days in Lima were filled with activity. Their hostess, Mother M. Trinita, made sure they had an opportunity to visit the various points of interest in Lima, as well as the *barriada* (quarters) that housed the poor. Here, for the first time, the sisters saw the conditions in which the vast majority of the poor were forced to live. They were deeply moved by the experience, and it had a far-reaching effect on the future of the Newfoundland mission in Peru.

Soon it was time for them to leave the security of Villa Maria, the warmth and friendship of the IHM sisters and branch out on their own. On November 5, they went by plane to Chiclayo, where they would stay while they were attending Spanish lessons. On their arrival, they were brought to a small, three-room apartment in a *hacienda* (property) owned by Señor de la Piedra, president of the Chiclayo School Association. In order to make the best possible use of the limited space, they put three beds in each of the two small bedrooms. The quarters were so cramped that they took turns getting in and out of bed! The inevitable collisions were the cause of much mirth—so much so that by the end of three weeks in the apartment, the rule of the "Great Silence" was in shambles. The third room served every purpose—chapel, community room, dining room, parlour, and laundry. Despite the inconvenience and strangeness of it all, the sisters managed quite well. Right from the beginning they showed an extraordinary ability for "making things do." A big problem, however, was what to do with the laundry when it was lifted, dripping wet, from the pan. The solution came with a box of rhythm band instruments shipped to them by the thoughtful Mother Trinita. After they unpacked the parcel, they used the twine as a clothesline. While this served the purpose quite well, it had its drawbacks. When a sister in a hurry was going from one room to another it was not unusual to receive a damp smack in the face from some garment that was hanging up to dry. Even the rhythm band instruments were called into service by the resourceful Sr. Maura Mason, who took great delight in banging vigorously on a cymbal to call the others to community duties and especially to prayer at six o'clock in the morning. The de la Piedra family provided meals and transportation for the sisters—a circumstance that was to cause much embarrassment to the sisters in the future.

On Monday, November 7, they made their first visit to Monsefú. As they drove through the streets, they had a feeling of unreality, of watching an episode from a movie—the rice and cane fields along the way, the mud huts, the dirty streets, and children clad in mud-stained, dusty clothing. As they moved slowly along, women stood silently in the door of their huts, children clinging to their skirts, some hiding behind their mothers and peeping out at these strange, white-clad foreigners. The poverty and deprivation that unfolded before the sisters evoked an instant response of concern and compassion for those who were—and are—victims of such injustice. In spite of all their good intentions, energy, and desire to be of service, the sisters asked themselves the question, "Where do we start?"

That same evening, M. Dorothy Carroll met the Chiclayo School Committee for the first time. The original plan was that four of the Mercy sisters would open a school in Chiclayo for the children of the more affluent citizens. The fees paid by these students would support a school for the poor children in Monsefú that would be staffed by the other two sisters. This was very much in the tradition of Catherine McAuley herself, who sanctioned the practice of establishing such pension schools to provide the financial basis for the work of the sisters in providing education for the children of the poor.[5]

Within the week, the sisters began Spanish lessons with a member of the congregation of *Madres de la Reparadores*, a community of religious who had been driven from Cuba in the early days of the Castro regime. The Newfoundland sisters made frequent visits to Monsefú, especially on Sundays, and were saddened by the small number of people at mass and by the lack of attention on the part of those who were there. They began to realize that their real work would be one of evangelization. Through these initial

---

5. Sullivan, *Catherine McAuley*, p. 228. See also Savage, *McAuley*, p. 220.

visits, the people of Monsfú became accustomed to having the sisters among them, and it was not long before they were being greeted warmly as they passed through the dusty streets of the *pueblo*. The sisters were especially moved by the affection shown them by the children who ran along behind them calling, "Madrecita! Madrecita!" Like Henri Nouwen they felt "embraced by a warmly loving people in a way [they] had not known before."[6] But there was still the promised school for Chiclayo.

On November 21, another meeting was held with the members of the Chiclayo School Committee, who were anxious to make preparations for the new school year, to begin in March 1962. This posed a real dilemma. The sisters were becoming increasingly aware of the gulf separating the rich landowners of Peru and the poor, exploited people. The de la Piedra family and others who had befriended them were among these wealthy landowners. At the meeting, it was clearly stated that the Sisters of Mercy were expected to open a school for children of the wealthy families of Chiclayo. The original plan was to accept students in an English school up to the fifth grade. However, much to their surprise, the sisters learned that the committee planned to add a grade each year that would, in a short time, see the school extend through the completion of high school.

After this second meeting, the sisters began to question seriously their role in establishing a school along the lines proposed by the committee. Their experiences in Monsefú had opened their eyes to many injustices that seemed to be taken for granted in Peruvian society. Up to this time, no sister had discussed her misgivings with the others. Now they began to ask themselves openly if they were not co-operating in the evils of social injustice by having a separate school for the rich and another for the poor. Although they had not signed a contract with the committee, the Mercy congregation had promised a school to the people of Chiclayo. Furthermore, the de la Piedras and other leading families had been extraordinarily kind in providing them with a place to stay and supplying them with food and transportation. The sisters prayed, deliberated among themselves, sought advice

---

6. Henri J. Nouwen, *!Gracias! A Latin America Journal* (New York: Orbis Books, 1993), p. 3.

from the Newfoundland priests and other teaching missionaries, and prayed some more. From all these sources the advice they received was unanimous: "Avoid separate schools. Don't be allied with the rich. The poor need you urgently." They decided to get in touch with M. Assumpta Veitch, the recently elected superior general, and lay the problem before her. M. Dorothy met with Señor de la Piedra and asked him to postpone any further plans for the school until final word was received from the General Council in St. John's. Señor was most gracious, never dreaming that all his plans for the Chiclayo school were at stake.

Needless to say, the sisters were in a very awkward position, dependent as they were on the hospitality of the de la Piedra family. They decided to move to an apartment house on one of the main streets of Chiclayo. This was just one in a series of housing arrangements before they finally settled in their own convent in Monsefú. As evening approached on their first day in the new apartment they discovered, to their consternation, that there were no lights! They managed with a candle stuck on to the top of a milk can. The next morning on their return from mass at seven o'clock, they discovered the apartment was flooded. What else could go wrong? They were to discover the answer very shortly.

Early in December, a column in a Peruvian newspaper announced that the Sisters of Mercy were about to open a school in Chiclayo. Much to the discomfort of the sisters, dozens of people started knocking on the door of their apartment to register children for school. Because they had not yet received from St. John's the approval of their plan to work for the poor in Monsefú, they were not able to give a satisfactory answer. The problem was exacerbated by their limited ability to communicate in Spanish. One of them came up with the bright idea of writing their response to the questions and reading it out. Soon they had it memorized, and the Spanish phrases tripped off their lips as if they had been speaking the language from birth.

Finally, on December 4, a letter arrived from the General Council of the Sisters of Mercy in St. John's approving the decision to decline the offer of a school in Chiclayo in order to establish one for the poor children in Monsefú. The significance of this decision should not be overlooked. A spirit of loving service to the poor and the marginalized and the refusal to co-operate with a tradition that dehumanizes people marked the Mercy mission in Monsefú long before the term "option for the poor" had come into daily parlance. The Sisters of Mercy in Newfoundland fully realized that the costs involved in operating the school in Monsefú would rest entirely with their congregation, for very little could come from the families of the children who would attend. In addition, the sisters themselves would be completely dependent on support from home, since they would earn no salary. In giving approval to the change of plan, the General Council stated that any sisters sent from Newfoundland to Peru in the future would be assigned to the Monsefú mission. This stipulation was a major obstacle to the plan proposed by the Chiclayo School Committee. It was a difficult and delicate situation. M. Dorothy Carroll and M. Immacula O'Leary, accompanied by Father Conroy, who had advised against the Chiclayo plan from the beginning, visited the bishop of Chiclayo to present the new proposal, namely, that the Sisters of Mercy would concentrate their efforts in the parish of Monsefú. Although disappointed, the bishop gave his wholehearted approval. The following day, Srs. M. Dorothy and Marion Collins went to inform Señor de la Piedra of the latest developments. The good gentleman was thoroughly shocked, but in spite of his disappointment, he offered to help the sisters in every way possible and assured them of his continued friendship and support. The next step was to meet with the school committee and inform them of the decision. Opposition from the *hacienda* owners in the Chiclayo area was strong against the sisters in their decision to serve the people of Monsefú. The committee members found it difficult to understand why poor Indians were given preference over them. Members of the de la Piedra family, however, continued to befriend the sisters and were unfailingly kind and gracious in all subsequent dealings with them.

Time was flying, and Christmas was just around the corner. It was all so different from home. Instead of biting winds, frost, and white, white, snow, they were enjoying beautiful, hot, sunny days. Still, plans had to be made for the celebration. Christmas began with a visit by Fathers Conroy and Maddigan who managed to procure a Christmas tree—of sorts! It was a little shabby, to be sure, but after some readjustments and the grafting of branches from one part of the tree to another, it began to take shape. Decorations posed no problem to the ingenuity of Newfoundlanders. Shining instruments from the rhythm band, some artistically crafted paper ornaments, and a few lights served to brighten up the tree. Finally it was finished, and they all agreed that there was no finer tree to be found anywhere in the world—outside of Newfoundland. Midnight Mass was celebrated in their little chapel, and it was with mixed feelings of joy and loneliness they sang the parts of the mass and the carols.

The first step in the sisters' mission work began on January 6, when they went with the priests to different parts of the parish for mass. Two days later, catechism classes began in Monsefú and Santa Rosa, a fishing village a few miles distant. It was holiday time and schools were closed, but the sisters, nothing daunted, gathered the children from the highways and byways for instruction. At this time, another change in their living arrangements was made when the Dominican Sisters of Lambayeque invited them to stay at their convent. The actual moving, on January 25, 1962, caused quite a stir in the neighbourhood, and a large crowd gathered to watch the six sisters, skirts tucked up in their cinctures,[7] loading the jeep with buckets, pans, and the precious carton of rhythm band instruments. Their new residence consisted of a large dormitory that served them as community room and sleeping quarters; the adjoining lavatory became their kitchen and dining room. There, surrounded by wash basins, they cooked and ate their meals for the next two months.

By this time the sisters were becoming more fluent in Spanish, especially Maura Mason, who made a practice of memorizing a page of Spanish words from her dictionary every night before going to bed. Because of their frequent visits to Monsefú, the sisters were now on a first-name basis with many of the people there. They had the opportunity, too, of meeting members of other religious congregations who were working in the country, and this period saw the beginnings of friendships that have endured to the present day. Invitations to visit different areas of Peru gave them the chance to become more familiar with the country as a whole. On one such occasion, the sisters had the opportunity

---

7. A leather belt that was worn as part of the original Mercy habit.

to go on horseback to the mountains. That same evening, they were invited to a dinner given by the bishop of Chiclayo in honour of some visiting dignitaries from Canada. One of our brave missionaries was anxious to show her proficiency in Spanish after so short a time. She announced to the bishop and the visiting Canadians that she had just returned from an enjoyable ride "a pollo."[8] The assembled guests greeted the statement with polite incredulity, while the rest of the Newfoundlanders nobly resisted the impulse to "unseemly mirth."[9]

Meantime, plans for their teaching activities in Monsefú were formulated. The sisters agreed with Father Conroy that they should aim to establish a parish school, even though it would be, more or less, a makeshift arrangement for a year or two. Parish schools, at the time, were not common in Peru, for schools were owned either by the state or by private individuals. Monsefú had a vast school population, with ten public schools that used all available space to house children who were lucky enough to receive an education. In the mud-hut schools, where partitions consisted of a curtain or portable blackboard, conditions were by no means conducive to study. In consultation with the priests and a committee of parishioners, it was decided that four sisters would teach full-time in the parish school, leaving the other two free for catechetical work in the public schools of the area. Later on that year, the sisters started evening classes five days a week to teach the elements of reading and writing to the several hundred *empleaditas*—youngsters from eight to twelve years of age who worked in the fields or in private homes and were unable to attend regular school.

The first step in the opening of school was the registration of children, boys and girls, from ages five to eight years for *transicion* (transition) and *primer año* (first year). Certificates of baptism and marriage certificates of the parents were required of all. This posed an immediate difficulty. Most parents had gone through a civil ceremony with the intention of having their mar-

---

8. Literally, "on chicken-back." She intended to say "a caballo"—on horseback.

9. An expression used by V. F. Alphonsus Rodriquez. See Rodriquez, *The Practice of Christian and Religious Perfection*, 3 vols. (Dublin and London: James Duffy, 1870). The more memorable sections of his books describe the awful fate awaiting the unfaithful religious. These examples were memorized by the more mischievous novices and used on appropriate occasions to frighten the wits out of their more pious companions. One weakness that Rodriguez frequently warned against was that of "unseemly mirth."

riages blessed by the Church *mañana*.[10] Consequently, the priests were kept busy celebrating the sacrament of marriage for the dozens who came belatedly for the ceremony. The sisters, on the other hand, sat in the little office for days on end waiting to register students for school, not realizing the *mañana* mindset that caused more than two hundred smiling parents to show up with their offspring on the last day of registration.

Toward the end of March, the sisters moved to Monsefú, to the house of Dr. Miguel Custodio. The good doctor and his family moved out of their home to put it at the disposal of the sisters for as long as they needed it. On their arrival, they found people crowded in every door and window along the street to watch the arrival of the *madres* (mothers). There were, also, plenty of little helpers willing and able to assist them unload the jeep and carry their belongings into the house. The house was very small, but it had three bedrooms. One of these they reserved for a chapel and arranged the other two as sleeping quarters. One room held four beds so closely packed together that the only way into bed was by climbing in over the foot of the bed! The other bedroom was quite tiny and held the other two beds. There was no ventilation in either room. Because there was no running water, the sisters bought barrels of water from the men who sold it daily in the streets. On the first night in their new apartment, they were roused from their sleep by the sound of voices and heavy pounding on the door. Sr. Maura called out, "¿Que quiere?" To which came the anxious reply, "El doctor, Señora." This knocking continued regularly for several nights until the news spread that the *madres* were living in the doctor's house.

From the start, the sisters loved Monsefú and its people. The people, for their part, were fascinated with these strange *madres* who spoke broken Spanish with an Irish accent and taught the children to sing Newfoundland folk songs. The children, especially, fell in love with their *madres* and in return were loved dearly by those same *madres*, who thought there were no children half so precious as those brown-eyed, Peruvian darlings.

Late in March, a group of Ursuline Sisters from Canada visited the Newfoundland sisters in Monsefú. Much to the relief of the Newfoundlanders,

---

10. The sisters were to learn that *mañana* (tomorrow) was a common expression in Monsefú.

the Ursulines decided to take over the school in Chiclayo that had been originally intended for the Mercy Sisters. At the same time, the Mercy Sisters were making immediate preparations for the opening of their school. Since there was no parish school building, three provisional classrooms were set up with three plywood partitions—but no doors—in the Señor Cautino Chapel adjoining the church. Later on during the year, full partitions were supplied, but still, no doors!

At last the big day arrived. At nine o'clock in the morning, April 2, 1962, the school opened to receive the first pupils. One hundred and fifteen children took their places in classrooms with brightly decorated walls. The sisters conducted their classes in both Spanish and English. As the months passed, enthusiasm for the school and catechetical programs remained at a high level, even though, in the latter area, the sisters laboured under some difficulty. Ever since their arrival, Sr. Maura Mason had been deploring the lack of suitable catechetical texts. With the resourcefulness for which she is well noted, Maura wrote Loyola University Press in Chicago and presented the need of the Monsefú Mission. On May 1, 1962, a large carton arrived containing one hundred copies of the approved catechism, *Jesu y yo (Jesus and I)*.

An interesting feature of this mission endeavour is the enthusiastic support the sisters in Monsefú received from the Sisters of Mercy at home, for example, the work of Sr. M. Benignus Mullowney. Through the collection, preparation, and sale of used stamps, M. Benignus financed the education of a Peruvian boy who graduated in 1972 from the sisters' school and went on the receive a degree in engineering. A young girl from Monsefú was helped through school in the same way and went on to have a successful career as a secretary. The objective of the sisters in Peru was to educate the people to educate themselves so that they might improve their society and pass on to their children their own culture.

After the opening of the school, the next project for the sisters was the building of the convent. On May 14, a cheque from the General Council in St. John's arrived to provide the first payment on the convent. By the same mail, they received a donation of $200 from the children of Our Lady of Mercy Glee Club, an award won by the choir at the recent Kiwanis Music

Festival.[11] The property on which the convent was to be constructed was called Los Animas. It belonged to the Church and had been donated by the bishop. It was just outside the town and, notes the annalist, ". . . at the end of one of the dirtiest streets of the *pueblo*."[12] One would suspect that the meticulously clean M. Dorothy was resolved, in short order, to effect changes to the condition of that street.

From the first, the sisters participated in all the local parish activities. They assumed the care of the sacristy and altar in the church, the Legion of Mary, and they accompanied the priests to the mission churches on Sundays. They experienced their first Peruvian religious procession and found the celebration to be quite different in style from the solemn, sedate manner in which these processions were carried out at home in Newfoundland. At the appointed time everyone gathered at the church. As they knelt in the church trying to pray, the sisters were distracted by a succession of hoots and toots as the local band tuned up. Finally, everything was ready for the procession to start. The acolytes, cross bearer, and clergy wended their way slowly through the narrow, dusty streets, followed by the band. The entire population of Monsefú turned out for the event, including assorted dogs, cats, and a couple of curious donkeys. Everyone was welcome. The children ran back and forth, admiring alternately the *madres* and the band.[13] For their part, the *madres* were amused to see that each band member had a sheet of music attached by a clothes pin to the back of his shirt so that the player behind him could read the music. At every street corner, the procession stopped and the sisters sang the hymns for benediction. After several hours, the procession arrived back at the parish church for the conclusion of the ceremony. A good time was had by all. The sisters went home and collapsed!

As the months passed, the sisters took on more and more duties. In Puerto Eten, they agreed to train as catechists a group of about twenty young

---

11. The award and the consequent donation to Monsefú became an annual gift for the next several years. Our Lady of Mercy Glee Club was a choir composed of one hundred and thirty students from grades I to VIII at Our Lady of Mercy School, Military Road, in St. John's.

12. Annals, Convent of Mercy, Monsefú, ASMSJ.

13. In Monsefú, the Sisters of Mercy were called the *madres*.

women from the Legion of Mary, an activity that was to become central to their ministry. In June, First Communion was celebrated by groups of children from the fiscal and private schools. The sisters made every effort to make this a memorable occasion by serving breakfast to the children and their parents. Now, with First Communion classes completed, the sisters initiated programs of religious instruction and sacramental preparation in several neighbouring towns. In July, there was great excitement in the parish with the arrival of Father Jim Doody, another Newfoundlander, who had been assigned to Monsefú in April. With his enthusiasm, sense of humour, and deep spirituality, he was a valuable addition to the mission. Later on, he was to stand by the sisters in the tragedy that afflicted the mission and, in fact, the whole Congregation of the Sisters of Mercy of Newfoundland.

The Annals from that period recount successive celebrations of the sacraments of initiation, with increasing numbers of children enrolled in the sisters' program and growing co-operation from the townspeople wherever the sisters ministered. One of the red-letter days was November 5 when a celebration of First Communion was held for the first time in the history of Valle Hermosa, a small town not far from Monsefú. Mass was to be celebrated in the one-room school that needed a great deal of "fixing up" in order to meet the requirements for such a celebration. With the help of the boys and the teacher, the room was prepared. The boys went in every direction and borrowed straw mats to cover the mud floor near the altar. On their own initiative, the boys built an altar rail with *adobe* bricks and covered it with white cloths, to set off the little sanctuary. No cathedral could equal the beauty of this little room in the eyes of the Mercy sisters as they inspected the work of so many loving hands. The sisters brought white dresses and veils for the girls and white arm ribbons for the boys—thirty children altogether, ranging in age from eight to sixteen years. The whole population of the village turned out to see the children in their dresses and suits going in procession to the school for the occasion. By the time mass began, the little room was crowded; those who could not find room knelt outside the door. Mass was celebrated by the pastor, Father Charlie Conroy, with the children forming the choir and singing Spanish hymns that had been taught them by the sisters. The celebration concluded in the usual Peruvian fashion with *globos* (globes) and firecrackers. The Annals record that in spite of their poverty, the generosity of these people was extraordinary. Whenever the sisters visited, they were presented with flowers and homegrown vegetables and, on one occasion, with a live and very vocal hen. In fact, whatever the people had they shared with the *madres*.

The impending visit of M. Imelda Smith and M. Assumpta Veitch raised the question of accommodations. Because Dr. Custodio's house was inadequate, even for the six sisters who were in Monsefú, it was clearly impossible to find room there for two more. Father Conroy urged them to move into the priests' newly finished and comfortable residence to receive their visitors from St. John's and also to stay there until the convent was finished. The sisters accepted this generous offer and the priests returned to the old *adobe* school where they had lived for the past ten months. Thus, on December 13, 1962, the sisters moved for the fifth time. Sleeping two in a room, with running water available was a luxury they had not known for over a year. In Dr. Custodio's house, they had to wash in the nearest available room with the prize possession of a plastic pan, a jug, or a bucket containing a few cups of hot water heated on the stove. They discovered that the Spanish language has no word for "privacy," and even if it had, they could not have availed of it during those early days in Peru. Nevertheless, they kept clean, healthy, and happy. With more modern conveniences at hand, they forgot the hardships of the past and prepared to enjoy showers and baths in profusion—or at least, for as long as the water supply remained stable.

After the arrival of the visitors from St. John's, the big event for the town of Monsefú was the official school closing. The program consisted of choral singing and dancing by the children, the year-end report, and the distribution of prizes. The little hall was full to overflowing with the successful students and their proud parents, grandparents, and other assorted relatives. The appearance of a stray donkey or two had no effect on the serious atmosphere that prevailed for the occasion. The public, totally unaccustomed to seeing such order and discipline among the children, went away marvelling at their conduct and at the beautiful decorations that had appeared as if by magic. Another aspect of this event that astonished the native Peruvians was the fact that the performance began on time. The children, who by now were used to the strange ways of the *madres*, were in their places at the appointed hour. Three quarters of the townspeople, however, arrived after the concert had ended, which was a good thing because there was only standing room in the little hall. The *padres de la familia* (parents of the family) were so enthusiastic about the performance that they arranged to present it to wider audiences outside of Monsefú through television. So successful was this first television performance that the children were asked to appear again on a Christmas Eve broadcast. On December 24, the first television set in Monsefú arrived in time to be set up on the roof of the parish house. Crowds gathered from far and near, sitting in semicircles on the ground, to watch with justifiable pride as their talented children performed with considerable charm and grace for the television audience in the city of Chiclayo. After the program was over and the crowds had dispersed, the sisters went home to prepare for Midnight Mass. This was their second Christmas away from home, and as they sang the familiar, well-loved carols, their hearts were filled with gratitude. After the frantic pace of the past few months, they looked forward to a period of prayer and quiet during the annual three-day retreat that took place between Christmas Day and New Year's Day. The summer holidays that followed provided the sisters with a few days' rest and relaxation before facing the task of moving into the new convent.

By the middle of February 1963, the convent was just about completed, and the sisters prepared to move from the priests' house. Once again they had lots of help, in fact, the sisters' ingenuity was put to the test trying to invent chores for willing little helpers—just to get them out from underfoot. The priests looked after most of the heavier items, loading them on a borrowed truck. In true masculine fashion, they gathered up everything in sight—big and small—and, in a letter home, one of the sisters described what happened when Father Conroy dropped someone's sewing box on the floor of the truck. The vision of the tall, lanky pastor on hands and knees searching for buttons, needles, pins, and yards of tape reduced some of the sisters to a state of helpless mirth, while the rest stood by offering directions to the exasperated cleric. Finally, when most of the paraphernalia had been retrieved, the offending box was shoved into its owner's hands with the admonition, "For goodness sake, in future will you put an elastic band around this unholy mess!"

The blessing of the Our Lady of Mercy Convent took place on February 25, 1963. According to Peruvian custom, at a blessing there must also be a christening with *padrinos* (godfathers) and *madrinos* (godmothers) present for the occasion. Following the adage, "When in Rome, etc." Father Conroy and the *padres de familia* selected twelve sets of "godparents," one set for each room in the house. Now the sisters' plan was to invite religious from nearby towns, priests, and a few special guests in the morning and serve them a simple lunch. In the afternoon there would be an "open house" for the people of Monsefú, but the people had other ideas. By nine o'clock in the morning, almost the whole population of Monsefú had turned up. Little noses were pressed against every window, and as far as the eye could see, people were lined up waiting to enter the *madres'* house. All were delighted with the new convent; the children were fascinated at the sight of running water coming from the taps and flowing down into the basin. In fact, a major flood was narrowly averted when one enterprising young lad decided to climb into the laundry sink and let the water flow over him. He was rescued, dripping wet, by one of the sisters who, fortunately, heard his squeals of delight and decided to investigate. That night, for the first time in sixteen months, each sister slept in her own room. But the celebrations were not over. On the following day a group of natives from the *selva* (jungle), men and women all dressed alike—except for the chief who wore feathers on his head and pencils in his ears—and speaking their own dialect, called *en masse* to see the "Great House." They were most enthusiastic about everything, but they were especially excited to see a reflection of themselves in a mirror. This seemed like magic. They danced with delight and returned again and again to the scene of such wonder to have another look and to admire the delightful visions in the mirror before they waved their farewell.[14]

In March, the sisters were joined by four Sisters of St. Joseph, who were to stay in Monsefú until their own convent was built. During the weeks

---

14. *The Monitor*, April 1963.

that followed, the Sisters of St. Joseph and the Sisters of Mercy forged a close bond that lasted through the years and benefited members of both congregations. The Newfoundland priests, however, could not let the opportunity pass to have some fun at the expense of the sisters. They composed a set of "Rules" and presented them to the members of each community for approval. For instance, Rule #4: "Among the duties of the superior there must rank high the need of comforting the feeble-minded, rebuking the unquiet, and exercising patience with the priest"; Rule #10: "The exclamation 'Joseph!' should no longer be employed as a curse word by the Sisters of Mercy; neither shall the St. Joseph Sisters express frustration by exclaiming, 'Mercy me!'"; and Rule #11: "Care shall be taken that if leftovers go into a second meal and are left over again, they should not *always* be given to the priests." No doubt some form of retaliation was planned, but unfortunately, evidence as to the nature of the sisters' revenge has not survived. Documents like this, while not of great historical importance, show the friendly, relaxed relationship that existed among the Sisters of St. Joseph, the Sisters of Mercy, and the Newfoundland priests.

April and May that year brought all sorts of excitement and surprises. Toward the end of the month, preparations were in high gear for the arrival of Archbishop P. J. Skinner of St. John's and the vicar general of the archdiocese, Monsignor Harold Summers. On their arrival in Monsefú, they were met by representatives of every organization in the town and were escorted from their car to the back of a truck that had been decorated with flowers. One may well imagine the feelings of the neat little archbishop as he was pelted with rice and almost buried in flower petals by enthusiastic people lining the route. Later that day, the visitors attended a concert at the school and Archbishop Skinner, a highly trained and talented musician, expressed his amazement at the high standard of performance achieved by the children in so short a time. Before his departure, the archbishop laid the cornerstone for a new school and presented Father Conroy with a cheque for $15,000 to help defray the cost of the building. The sisters were presented with a Volkswagen, a gift from the Mercy Sisters at home.

Toward the end of May month, M. Immacula O'Leary suffered a heart attack. This was a serious blow, not only to the work of the mission, but to life in the community. "Mac," with her sense of humour and her eye for the ridiculous, had been a real source of strength for each one of them. There was no situation so desperate that Mac would not be able to see something to smile about. One result of the sister's illness was the hiring of the first lay teacher, Señorita Clara Carmona, who looked after the office work and taught a Spanish subject in each class. On July 13, M. Immacula left for Newfoundland and thus, sadly, the first chapter of the Monsefú mission was concluded.

After M. Immacula's departure, the regular routine was resumed. The Annals record numerous successes of the schoolchildren in their studies and also in the various forms of entertainment. Under the direction of the sisters, and especially of Sr. Helen Best, the children were taught many different styles of dancing for which they showed a special aptitude. The boys excelled not only in dancing but also in performing intricate exercises in marching and drill. The sisters received frequent requests from nearby towns and from the local television stations for the children to perform. This presented a constant challenge to provide new and more sophisticated material. Thus gradually, month by month, the standard of these performances improved. More important, from the sisters' perspective, increasing numbers of children and adults became actively involved in parish life.

December 16 marked the close of the sisters' second successful school year in Monsefú. This year, the presentation of prizes and diplomas concluded with the singing of their very own school song, "Our Lady of Mercy," the words and music of which had been composed by one of the sisters at home in St. John's. The final concert of the year was, again, taped for television. While Srs. Helen Best, Marion Collins, and Bernetta Walsh went with the children to the studio for the taping, Srs. M. Dorothy and Maura Mason distributed Christmas gifts to two hundred children of the Sunday catechism classes. The gifts had been obtained from various sources—business firms in Chiclayo and gifts from the children in schools operated by the Mercy and Presentation Sisters in Newfoundland.

Up to this point, the Vatican Council, currently in session in Rome, had not released the Decree on the Renewal of Religious Life. The Sisters of Mercy in Peru, however, were several steps ahead of the learned bishops and theologians in deciding that some modification of the traditional religious dress was necessary. Several designs were invented by the more imaginative among them, and wild and wonderful approximations of the original head-dress were produced. All of these underwent prolonged and not always gentle criticism—some did not want their hair showing, others wanted to make sure their naturally curly tresses received due recognition. A couple of the sisters who were sporting permanently red noses because of prolonged exposure to the sun, demanded that the new headdress be designed to shield this sensitive area. Finally, one of the sisters at home agreed to work on a "modified habit." After several attempts, a final decision was made on the shape and style of the new habit, and approval to adopt it was readily given by the General Council in St. John's. While the sisters in Monsefú were delighted with their new look, comments in Newfoundland were anything but complimentary. These comments, as far as is known, were not passed on to the missionary sisters, who remained blissfully ignorant of the unflattering remarks that were making the rounds at home. And so, the Monsefú sisters dutifully sent home numerous pictures of themselves for the admiration of their northern colleagues.

Never satisfied with their command of Spanish, the sisters availed of every opportunity to acquire even greater fluency. Vacations were spent in Lima, attending courses in the language of their adopted homeland. By this time, they had formed close associations with members of other religious teaching orders and had become members of the various professional organizations. Thus, from the very beginnings of their work in Peru, the Newfoundland sisters participated in all events and activities designed to deepen and strengthen the unity that was developing among the different religious congregations ministering to the people of Latin America.

Soon all their meetings and Spanish classes were over and the sisters hastened back home to Monsefú to prepare for the opening of school. Classes began on April 6 in the new school, called Nuestra Señora de la

Misericordia.[15] The school had twelve large, bright, and airy classrooms, quite a change from the cramped quarters of the little chapel. The children were overjoyed when they entered this new building for the first time. There was no doubt that, at last, there would be plenty of room for all the activities that had become so important to them and, indeed, to the town as a whole.

In May 1964, there was great rejoicing at the arrival of Sr. Mary Ennis from home,[16] and a few weeks later, news arrived that two additional sisters had been appointed to the mission, Srs. M. Carmelita Power and M. Aquin English.[17] The latest message contained another piece of exciting news— arrangements had been made for the five pioneers to spend the Christmas vacation in Newfoundland. Finally, the big day arrived. The five sisters of the original band left Monsefú on December 18 for the trip to Newfoundland. The weather forecast promised snow, and in their eyes nothing could have provided a more fitting welcome! Needless to say, their dear ones at home did not share these sentiments.

Meanwhile, Srs. Mary Ennis, M. Carmelita, and M. Aquin spent most of the Christmas vacation at language school. Thus, when the five returned from home, they found the new recruits fairly proficient in Spanish. Even with the three extra sisters, there was more than enough to keep them busy from dawn to dark. The many hours devoted to the training of catechists were beginning to bear fruit beyond what the sisters and priests had dared hope. In letters home, Father Conroy wrote:

> Some of our Legion of Mary girls have become real apostles. Towards the end of the summer—winter to you up north—they concentrated on preparing for First Holy Communion more than one hundred children ...
> ... a word about Sister Mary Dorothy ... How she, in spite of ill health, continues in the circuit of the government schools, catechising all day long, hour after hour, is beyond my understanding. She and Sister Mary Aquin have the hardest of all the jobs, struggling

---

15. Our Lady of Mercy.
16. Sr. Mary Ennis's religious name was M. Wilma.
17. M. Carmelita and M. Aquin arrived in Peru in January 1965.

to keep the attention of about two thousand children in the course of a week. They go from one poky little classroom to another, helping teachers whose own knowledge of the faith is little better than that of their pupils. The work is hard, but is just as necessary as the more specialized efforts of the parish school …

The work of the Sisters is the most important factor in all the parish developments. Most of the time is given to the parish school, but through the young people they are reaching into every home in one way or another. Other schools are imitating their methods. The people of our thriving big-neighbour town, Chiclayo, look enviously at what is being done for the cholos or mixed-blood country children who, they feel, will walk away with all the prizes.[18]

However, life for the sisters was not "all work and no play." There were opportunities for an occasional picnic by the seashore or a trip to the mountains. They found ways to relax and enjoy themselves. The evening recreations were filled with storytelling and laughter, as they relived their experiences of the day. Late in December, a new member joined the Mercy community—a dog to serve as watchman. Patriotic to the core, the sisters named him "Newfy." The priests complained that he got away with murder and considered him "a scandal in the community because of his appearance—white and fluffy from frequent bathing, and perfumed with talcum powder as no respectable canine should be."[19]

Before they knew it, another year had flown, and on January 10, 1966, the summer program began in areas of the parish that the sisters could not reach during the regular school year. There they found children from ten to fifteen years of age who had never gone to school. The sisters spent three hours every day teaching religion, arithmetic, and reading. On Saturday afternoons, after the sisters had completed sacramental instructions with the children, the Newfoundland priests celebrated an open-air mass in each place. On one such occasion, as Father Maddigan moved back to genuflect he stepped on a cat. The indignant feline emitted a series of piercing shrieks that could be heard

18. Conroy, *Peruvian Journal*, pp. 160, 168, 172.
19. Ibid., p.180.

throughout the village. The priest was visibly shaken while the sisters showed a regrettable lack of sympathy both for the offending cleric and the affronted animal! The cat was last seen heading for the highest peak of the Andes, out of range of Father's sturdy boots.

Toward the end of February, two sisters of the congregation of the Holy Family of Nazareth visited the Newfoundland sisters in Monsefú. Everybody was in a holiday mood, and in this spirit, it was decided to take the guests to visit the famous ruins in Trujillo. The trip was planned for Monday, March 1. Promptly at half past nine in the morning, Father Conroy drove up in the jeep, and the visiting sisters, M. Charlotte and de Chantal, along with M. Dorothy Carroll, Marion Collins, M. Carmelita Power, and M. Aquin English started off on the fateful journey. That same day, Srs. Maura Mason and Helen Best left by plane for Lima to join Srs. Mary Ennis and Bernetta Walsh at Villa Maria. In their dormitory at Villa Maria, the four Newfoundland sisters, delighted to be together again, talked well into the wee hours of the morning. They had just dropped off to sleep at half past three, when one of the IHM sisters awakened them with news that the sisters in Monsefú had been involved in a serious motor accident. The annalist wrote, "It seemed as if the walls of the building came crashing in on them."[20] The four of them returned immediately to Chiclayo and were met at the airport by Father Jim Doody who told them that the accident happened at about half past seven in the evening. It was thought that the victims were lying on the road for some time before anyone came along. On being notified of the accident, he went to the hospital and was shocked to find Father Conroy already dead. M. Aquin English died as they were lifting her into the ambulance. Sr. Maura and her companions went immediately to the hospital where they were horrified to see the extent of the sisters' injuries. The Annals give a vivid description of what they found.[21] It is not easy reading, and one can only imagine the suffering endured so bravely by the survivors. M. Dorothy Carroll was critically injured and hovered between

20. Annals, Our Lady of Mercy Convent, Monsefú, ASMSJ.
21. Ibid, p. 88 ff.

life and death for almost two weeks. She died on March 14 without regaining consciousness.

The sisters of other religious congregations offered immediate help. The Ursuline Sisters were on the scene right after the accident, and it was their difficult task to identify the victims even before they had received any medical treatment. At seven o'clock mass in Monsefú, the news was released of the death of Father Conroy and of M. Aquin. The parish was in an uproar. The news spread instantly, radios were turned off, and twenty-four hours' mourning was declared. Men, women, and children wept openly in the streets.

After visiting the injured, the remaining Sisters of Mercy went to the morgue. Throngs of people from Monsefú were lined up at the door, keeping vigil. Sr. M. Magdalena, superior of the Dominican Sisters of the Holy Rosary, a Peruvian, went to the morgue at seven o'clock in the morning and washed the body of Sr. M. Aquin prior to the embalming. Srs. Maura Mason and Mary Ennis dressed her in the habit of the Sisters of Mercy and watched as she was laid gently in the casket and brought to the chapel to be waked. At three o'clock, the coffins of Father Conroy and M. Aquin were taken in solemn procession by motorcade to Monsefú. Thousands of people lined the streets to see the funeral go by. At the entrance to the town, the coffins were taken from the hearse and carried to the church on the shoulders of the men of the parish. Other men joined hands to keep the crowds away from the sisters and the coffin so that they would not be crushed by the masses of people who came to embrace them. The whole scene might have become unmanageable except for the quick thinking of Sr. Maura. Surrounded by throngs of sobbing parishioners, she began the rosary. This seemed to bring a sense of calm to the crowd, and all prayed while the procession very slowly approached the church. On entering, the coffins were placed one on each side of the sanctuary. The doors were opened, and the people passed through the sanctuary to pray for the dead and to look for the last time on the faces of the priest and the Sister of Mercy who had served them with such love and dedication. Thousands had congregated. Those who could not find a place to stand in the church stood outside in total silence while the bishop of Chiclayo celebrated mass. The annalist described the events of the evening: "At 7:30 Sister's body was carried

to the convent on the shoulders of the men and all the people, carrying lighted candles, formed a procession through the streets weeping and praying as
they walked. Such a sad but beautiful procession! Sister was waked in the
community room in her beautiful white coffin and practically all night people
came to the wake."22

Meanwhile, M. Dorothy Carroll was unconscious and in critical condition. The other injured sisters, Marion Collins and M. Carmelita Power and
the two sisters of the Holy Family, M. de Chantal and Charlotte, were in considerable pain and in shock. Two Sisters of Charity, both registered nurses, had
arrived at the hospital earlier that afternoon to care for the victims who, up to
that time, had not even had their habits removed.

As news of the accident reached other religious communities in the
area, sisters from Villa Maria in Lima, Talara, Chiclayo, and Cayalti hastened to
Monsefú to offer their support. They looked after the convent, bought gro-
ceries, prepared meals, and provided consolation to the sisters and to the
grief-stricken people of the town. On March 3, the funeral mass for M. Aquin
was celebrated by Father Doody on the school patio, after which her coffin
was carried on the shoulders of the girls of the Legion of Mary to the convent
grounds for burial. That same morning, Father Conroy's body was brought in
procession to the cathedral in Chiclayo so that the thousands of grieving
parishioners and friends could pay their last respects to the man who had
given himself so generously in service and in love. Later that evening, Father
Conroy's remains were brought to Lima and from thence back to
Newfoundland for burial.23

Home in Newfoundland the sisters, unaware of the accident, rose as
usual at six o'clock on March 2. At Mercy Convent, it was quite obvious that
something very serious had occurred, for when the *angelus* was recited at
twenty after six, not one of the general councillors was at her place in
chapel. A few minutes, later M. Assumpta Veitch entered and, her voice
choked by grief, announced that there had been a serious accident in Peru.

22. Ibid., p. 91.
23. Father Charles O'Neill Conroy is buried in the priests' plot in Belvedere Cemetery in St. John's.

Although information was scrappy, it was reported that Father Conroy and one of the sisters had been killed, five others injured, but at that time no further details were available. The news was communicated immediately to all the Mercy communities. For the next few weeks, the convents were strangely hushed and quiet. Sisters went about their usual duties in a daze— Peru was so far away. Everyone felt helpless and lost. All they could do was wait and pray.

M. Assumpta made plans to fly to Peru immediately, taking with her M. Immacula O'Leary who was now fully recovered from her heart attack. On their arrival, they went directly to the hospital. While they were shocked to see the extent of the injuries suffered by Srs. Marion Collins and M. Carmelita Power, they had not fully realized the gravity of M. Dorothy's condition. With the co-operation of the medical authorities, the superiors of other religious communities, and of their faithful friend, Augusto de la Piedra, arrangements were made for the injured sisters to be flown to Lima, where five ambulances were waiting to transport them to *Clinica Americana* (the American clinic). Nursing sisters from religious communities in Peru came to care for the injured day and night. The medical doctors, experts in their fields, offered their services without charge. This outpouring of concern was a source of strength to the Mercy congregation and an authentic witness to God's abiding love in the midst of so much grief and darkness.

The days dragged on. In spite of the pain and suffering caused by broken bones, cuts, and abrasions, the condition of the injured sisters showed some improvement—all except M. Dorothy. For days the sisters watched, hoping against hope that she might, at least, regain consciousness. Despite the best medical care, her condition continued to deteriorate. On March 14 at ten o'clock in the morning, with the sisters of her community around her bed, Sr. M. Dorothy Carroll entered quietly into eternal life.

Arrangements were made for Sister's body to be taken back to Monsefú for burial, and on March 15, another sad procession took place. The men bearing the casket on their shoulders marched slowly through the streets to the church where mass was celebrated by Fathers Doody and Maddigan. Immediately after mass, M. Dorothy was laid to rest next to M. Aquin in the convent garden.[24] In a final acknowledgement of sister's life of fidelity, M. Assumpta, a close friend and a member of M. Dorothy's profession group, placed a copy of her vows on the top of the casket as it was lowered gently into the ground. The sisters stood around with tear-filled eyes as they saw the last of the woman whose courage and determination had carried them through the difficult early days of the mission.

The death of M. Dorothy, however, was not the end of the sorrows to beset the stricken community. During the afternoon of March 14—the day of M. Dorothy's death—another victim of the accident, M. de Chantal of the Sisters of the Holy Family, died suddenly. This death was completely unexpected, for Sister was very much better and was well enough that day to sit up for the first time.

These were, indeed, very difficult days for the infant mission in Monsefú. But in the midst of the darkness, the light of faith, hope, and love continued to shine brightly. In spite of the grief they felt over the death of two of their sisters, they rejoiced in the knowledge that Marion and M. Carmelita were making a slow but steady recovery. M. Carmelita's disc went back in place overnight—almost miraculously, it seemed. Her broken nose, however, was not noticed until she felt well enough to look in a mirror. She took one look, and then in aggrieved tones, she complained, "That's not MY nose!" Sure enough, when the doctor investigated further he found that it was fractured, and so she was whisked off to the operating room to have the offending proboscis straightened out. Finally, on St. Patrick's Day, March 17, she was discharged from the hospital and joined Marion Collins at Villa Maria, the convent of the Sisters of IHM, where both sisters stayed until they were strong enough to rejoin the community in Monsefú.

The aftermath of the accident brought expressions of sympathy from all parts of Canada, the United States, and Peru. Archbishop Skinner and Monsignor Dermot O'Keefe arrived from St. John's. Their arrival, along with that of M. Assumpta and M. Immacula, was greeted at first with some

---

24. When the decision was made to vacate the convent in Monsefú, the remains of M. Dorothy and Aquin were transferred from the convent garden to the general cemetery in Monsefú on March 2, 1988.

trepidation—the people of Monsefú feared lest they had come to take the sisters back to Newfoundland. Their fears were soon put at rest when they were assured that M. Immacula would remain in Monsefú and other sisters would arrive in the near future so that the work of the mission could continue. A further cause for rejoicing was an announcement that the Archdiocese of St. John's would fund the building of a high school in Monsefú in memory of Father Conroy.

Shortly after the departure of the visitors from Newfoundland, the school year began. The enrolment in the parish school continued to increase. M. Carmelita and Marion were still recovering from their injuries, and apart from the personal loss felt by sisters and students, it was very difficult to carry out the same programs with four fewer sisters on staff. They did their best, each one adding a few extra duties to an already strenuous workload. Sr. Helen Best, who had been taking lessons in Spanish dancing from a teacher in Chiclayo, was working very successfully with the children in the fields of music and dancing. Although the work was hard, the sisters were cheered by the presence of M. Immacula, who managed to create an atmosphere of fun and relaxation in spite of hectic schedules. By the time M. Carmelita and Marion had returned to resume their duties, things were just about back to normal. But the disappointments were not over.

The seemingly indestructible and irrepressible Sr. Maura Mason developed a serious ear infection. In spite of the best medical treatment available in Chiclayo and Lima, the condition persisted. Maura's illness was a source of great concern at home in St. John's, for nobody quite understood what was causing the problem. It was decided that the best and safest course was for her to return to St. John's. This left only three members of the original six. The presence of M. Carmelita and Mary Ennis and the promise that other sisters were to join them soon made the parting with Maura a little less painful, but they would miss her wit and humour and her hearty, infectious laugh. As for Maura herself, no one knows what it cost to leave her beloved Monsefú, for she kept it to herself. In her usual matter-of-fact manner, she accepted the decision and prepared to leave for home.

The new school year began on April 3, 1967, with an enrolment of 452 pupils, 22 of whom formed the first year *media*—the first class to register for the Carlos O'Neill Conroy Memorial High School, which opened that year with M. Carmelita Power as principal. Added to the teaching staff of Nuestra Señora de la Misericordia were Srs. Betty Morrissey and Rosemary Ryan from Newfoundland and three lay teachers. The lay teachers received government salaries—an arrangement negotiated by the minister of education, Dr. Tola, who had visited the school in February and was impressed by the curriculum content, the set-up, and the qualifications of the staff.[25] Srs. Marion Collins and Mary Ennis replaced Sr. Maura in the catechetical work and conducted classes in the fiscal and particular schools of the parish, thus providing instruction to over two thousand children. In addition, they provided in-service training for teachers. A new area of ministry began when one of the women asked Sr. Mary Ennis to teach her how to cook. This initiative was later expanded to include sewing classes, basic health care conferences, and the organization of a mothers' club to provide a forum for discussion and advice on family living. Education of the adults was also a priority for the sisters. Special groups formed of priests, religious, and lay people provided catechetical instruction for adults. The teaching was done informally in homes on a selected block in town. For this reason the groups were called "street groups." By mixing religion with social visiting and entertainment, the street groups made successful contact with the people and thus achieved their main objective of teaching the basic principles of the Catholic faith. And so the work continued, day after day of teaching, visiting the sick, being with the poor as one with them—living, loving, and praying, all in the name and spirit of mercy.

The faithful annalist has left a comprehensive record of the activities of the Sisters of Mercy in Monsefú. The failures and the successes are carefully documented, although the latter far outweigh the occasional disappointments. Throughout it all, it is impossible not to be touched by their practical courage, faith, self-forgetfulness, and commitment to one another and to those they

---

25. The sisters received no salaries; all their expenses were paid by the Mercy congregation in Newfoundland.

served so generously. As the months and years unfolded, the teaching and influence of the sisters reached deeper and deeper into the hearts and lives of the people of Monsefú. The annalist continued to record the successes of the children, but none with such a air of triumph as the following entry from 1967, "Misericordia came through with their first football victory in the series when they won over San Pedro 1–0."[26]

The years passed quickly and brought more changes in personnel. Two members of the original six, Srs. Helen Best and Bernetta Walsh, returned to Newfoundland. Each one had made a difference to the people of Monsefú— Helen with her gift of music and dancing and Bernetta by her extraordinary ability to instill a love of learning in the youngest children. Each of these young women felt that God was calling her to a different state of life. After much soul-searching, reluctantly and sadly, Helen and Bernetta asked for and received a dispensation from their religious vows. Both are now happily married, but they have not severed their ties of friendship and affection with the sisters who were and are so much a part of their lives. It is not true to say that other sisters replaced them, for each one is unique and irreplaceable, but other sisters went to Monsefú and continued the ministry that had been exercised so faithfully and well. These sisters brought new and different gifts, and the mission continued to flourish.

Over the years, the sisters drew closer and closer to the people of Monsefú and the surrounding area. The manner in which the sisters were invited to enter into the joys and sorrows of the people is clearly delineated in little anecdotes that appear from time to time in the Annals. For instance, there is the story of Manuela, an old lady who was paralyzed and practically abandoned. Her only possession was a straw mat in the corner of an old house where she sat and slept day in and day out. When asked how she was, invariably Manuela responded, "Bien, el único que no anda."[27] The sisters had received a donation of $30 from one of the schools in Newfoundland. They used the money to buy a bed for Manuela. They went over and gave her a

---

26. Annals, Convent of Our Lady of Mercy, Monsefú, ASMSJ.
27. "Fine, only I can't walk!"

bath, probably the first one she ever had, and then fixed her up in her new bed.

The periodic arrival of additional sisters from Newfoundland gave new life to the community and was reassurance to the people that the Sisters of Mercy were there to stay. By April 1968, the enrolment had increased to 550 students, with 470 in primary and 80 in first and second year of *secundaria* (secondary). School concerts continued, and invitations from the television studios presented a constant challenge to the students and teachers. However, the challenges were not all artistic in nature. On one occasion, about five minutes before leaving for the TV studio in Chiclayo, Sr. Betty Morrissey had to find a pair of shoes for one little fellow who turned up barefoot.

The sisters found ways to alleviate problems of inadequate clothing without offending the pride of the people. Faithfulness to the Sunday catechism classes was rewarded by prizes—dresses or shoes for the girls and trousers, shirts, or shoes for the boys. But while these prizes brought joy to the parents, the sisters did not forget to include a small toy to delight the hearts of the children. A concert and the awarding of prizes and diplomas marked the closing of each school year. As the little children from kindergarten went home, proud possessors of a lovely diploma, the annalist for 1965 noted sadly, ". . . the first and last for many of them." The deplorable economic situation of Monsefú at the time put further schooling out of reach for many children who had to work in the fields to help support the family. Nevertheless, the work of education went on, and the sisters were encouraged by the steady increase in enrolment each successive year. For the next few years, the priests and sisters worked as a team with the people in the parish. Monsefú soon elected its first parish pastoral council and liturgy and finance committees, in all of which the people played an active role.

When the school year began in April 1970, everything looked bright. The educational thrust of the mission in Monsefú had been strengthened by the arrival of the Christian Brothers of the Western Province of the United States who took over the administration of the high school. M. Carmelita Power became principal of Our Lady of Mercy School. Enrolment in both schools was at record levels, and everyone looked forward to another successful academic year.

On May 31, 1970, the sisters were holding a garden party on the patio outside the convent when Peru was hit with a disastrous earthquake. When the first tremor was felt, none of the eight hundred people gathered paid much attention. As the tremors became more frequent and more severe, people began to take notice. "There was a sound of drumming in the ground. People fell to their knees, crying and praying, girls and women fainted. Others tried to run for their homes to rescue the little ones and elderly parents. They made it as far as the narrow streets where buildings crumbled in clouds of dust."[28] Children were screaming and clinging to the skirts of the *madres*. After the tremors subsided, the sisters walked through the town to offer any help they could. Hundreds of the little mud huts that people called home had collapsed in ruins on the street. Some of the houses were still standing, but people were afraid to enter them.[29] While the terrible shaking of the earth had ceased, there was still the danger of an aftershock. Fortunately Monsefú, with its population of 14,000, suffered no loss of life, although there was considerable property damage. Other towns were not as fortunate. "Some mountain villages were entirely eliminated by rolling mud flowing down the mountains, which in some cases entirely obliterated the villages."[30]

The earthquake was a devastating setback to a country that had been struggling to achieve a degree of economic stability. In the face of such a catastrophe, the Sisters of Mercy did what they could to alleviate the sufferings of the people. Under the direction of the mayor, commissions were set up. Father Maddigan and Srs. Marion Collins and Rosemary Ryan were members of the commissions. Sr. Mary Ennis took charge of donations of clothing. With the help of fifteen girls, six boys, and the sisters, they washed, ironed, sewed, and packed clothes for three full days. In Monsefú, the poorest of the poor gave what they could. If they could not give money or clothes, they came with vegetables, fruit,

28. Annals, Convent of Our Lady of Mercy, Monsefú, ASMSJ.
29. Sr. Rosemary Ryan quoted in "News Scene," *The Daily News*, June 16, 1970, p. 3.
30. Ibid.

or whatever they had. Friends in Chiclayo gave food, clothing, and money to help the victims of the earthquake. The sisters packed all these provisions in their little van and drove back and forth over 300 miles to bring relief to Chimbote, a city heavily populated by refugees from the stricken areas. After the first few days of shock and disbelief, the natural resilience of the people asserted itself. People started rebuilding. The great generosity of the people of Monsefú was never more evident as neighbour helped neighbour restore houses and farmland. The sisters pitched in to help wherever they could. In a few days, school reopened, and gradually life returned to normal.

The following year, another disaster hit the little town. A vicious rainstorm occurred during the night of March 17–18, 1971. The sisters awoke to see water and mud flowing like a river through the streets. They dressed quickly and went to help the people dig trenches around their homes to keep them from being washed away. Once more the scene was one of utter devastation. Men stood by helplessly in silence as they watched their small farms being washed away by the waters of the big Reque River. Again, the sisters marvelled at the resilience of the people, as with courage and hope, they started once more to rebuild what was left of their homes and farms.

Just as things settled down after the floods, a new problem faced the mission. The government of Peru had adopted an aggressive policy of nationalization. The sisters learned that plans for educational "reform" were being initiated, and word spread among the lay teachers that by continuing to teach in the particular schools, they would lose all the rights of the state, such as salary and pension rights. The next few months were filled with uncertainty. In November 1971, a letter arrived from the minister of education asking the sisters to collaborate by using the parish school as a centre for the new education system. After meeting with parishioners, the sisters agreed to the proposal.

By the time school was ready to open in April 1972, it was obvious that things would have to change. With no support from the state, the parish had to assume responsibility for all costs. Beginning in October of that year, a series of meetings was held to discuss with the teachers and parents the nationalization of the school and the passing over of the administration to lay principals. In December 1972, Brother Bernardo and M. Carmelita Power resigned from the office of principal of their respective schools. When school opened in April 1973, the administration was, for the first time, in the hands of Peruvians. Although the *primaria* (primary) continued as a parish school until 1974, the high school functioned as a national school. Sr. Mildred Brennan, who had arrived from Newfoundland in 1967, continued teaching in the high school. The annalist remarked, "Now she is getting paid—the grand sum of 400 soles a month—about $9.00."

In April 1974, two Peruvian priests took up residence with the Newfoundland priests. The parish itself was expanded to include the neighbouring towns of Santa Rosa, Eten, Puerto Eten, and Reque. This expansion called forth a new commitment on the part of the sisters. Three of them were working in catechetics. Sr. Anita Best set up a workshop where she held classes in sewing, cooking, nutrition, and hygiene for single girls and young married women. Subsequently, Sr. Anita became involved in the formation of a weaving shop, an enterprise that turned out to be quite successful. For her part, Sr. Rosemary Ryan spent most of her time working with the Peruvian coordinator of catechetics. Only one sister, Alice Mackey, remained in the school, but her time was limited, for in the following year the Peruvian government assumed the right to appoint all teachers. The withdrawal of the Newfoundland priest in June 1974 marked the end of an era for the Monsefú mission. In his place, Peruvian priests were appointed pastors. By October 1975, the General Council of the Sisters of Mercy in St. John's was debating the wisdom of closing the mission and recalling the sisters to Newfoundland. Discussion continued between the sisters in Monsefú and the administration in St. John's.

Storm clouds continued to gather. The government policy of replacing "gringo" priests and teaching sisters by native Peruvians was accelerating rapidly. At the national level, the communist wing continued to mount an aggressive campaign against the Catholic Church and Church projects, especially those directed and maintained by foreigners. In one section of the country, a parish-run co-operative came under attack. In Chimbote, the target was a health clinic run by the parish; in Trujillo, the Irish sisters were forced to close their maternity clinic; and in Monsefú, the target was the parish school, Nuestra Señora de la Misericordia, now renamed, Number 10064.

Since their arrival in 1961, the sisters had been accepted, supported, and appreciated by the people of Monsefú and the surrounding areas. Now, in some quarters, they were looked upon with suspicion and were the objects of open criticism and outright antagonism—all of this in a very short time. These attitudes were being manifested not so much in personal attacks but by an organized communistic movement against the Church. Also, there was a very strong anti-capitalistic, anti-imperialistic, "anti-Yankee" mentality being carefully nurtured in the country, and some people looked upon the sisters as being part of a system that had oppressed them for centuries.

In a report to the general chapter of 1977, the Monsefú sisters presented the situation, describing with great clarity and openness the conditions in Peru. Then they questioned:

> Is our presence a sign or an anti-sign of the Kingdom? The Gospel clearly tells us that we cannot always expect to live in the light of success and appreciation. Are such words coming to life in our midst? . . . We do know that the most convenient and appealing solution many times is to pack our bags and buy our plane tickets, but to do that we feel that we would be failing in our commitment to Christ and showing a lack of courage in the face of difficulties. Our presence here provides one of the biggest obstacles to the communists. . . . We also must think of those people who have been so true to us over the years, and much more so now in our time of difficulties. They need our help and support to stand firm in their convictions as much as we need theirs.[31]

M. Carmelita pointed out in a letter to St. John's that even though the people supported the idea of having Peruvians administer the schools, this did not mean they wanted the sisters to leave the *pueblo*. She identified areas where the sisters were needed—to work with native teachers and with youth groups and to prepare leaders in the community.[32] There was so much uncertainty at the time in Peru that it was difficult for the sisters at home to understand just what was happening.

---

31. ASMSJ, MG 37/2/261.
32. ASMSJ, MG 37/2/259.

The General Council reached a decision in 1977—the mission in Peru would close at the end of the year. Three of the sisters, Alice Mackey, Marion Collins, and Mildred Brennan were called home for consultation. The whole congregation prayed for the guidance of the Holy Spirit. The matter was discussed at the general chapter, but the delegates pointed out that the opening and closing of convents was the prerogative of the General Council in consultation with the sisters of that specific community. Consequently, the matter was promptly tossed back into the collective lap of the superior general and council. Eventually, the decision was reversed, the sister delegates returned to Peru, and additional sisters were appointed to the mission.

By this time the mission had taken a completely new direction. After the schools were nationalized in 1974, they were staffed entirely by native Peruvians. The sisters continued to work in catechetics and to assist poor women. As in earlier years, their ministry was not confined to Monsefú but also to neighbouring towns and villages, notably Reque, Eten, and Puerto Eten. Following the initiative of Srs. Mary Ennis and Anita Best, the sisters offered workshops in basic life skills, cooking, nutrition, hygiene, sewing, and embroidery. The traditional Mercy ministry of visiting the sick poor and preparing the dying for the last anointing occupied a great deal of their time. Just as in the early days, the sisters observed with sadness the circumstances in which many of the people lived. As they visited homes to bring Communion to the sick, in some cases, the hens and chickens were jumping around the mud floor while the prayers were being said. Life settled into a fairly regular routine, although the sisters had learned by this time that nothing in Peru can be taken for granted.

With the departure of the Newfoundland priests, new and serious difficulties arose. Some of the Peruvian clergy appointed to the parish had been very much influenced by the *Opus Dei* movement within the Roman Catholic Church.[33] The conservative stance adopted by these priests relative to the laity,

---

33. *Opus Dei* is a conservative religious organization that operates in a Roman Catholic environment. Founded in 1928 in Spain by Josemaria Escriva, *Opus Dei* has been controversial among Catholics because of its secretive nature, its emphasis on discipline, and its conservatism and wealth.

and especially to the role of women as collaborators in ministry, made the work of the sisters very difficult, and in some cases, impossible. Nevertheless, for the sake of the people who depended on them, they did what they could within the boundaries that were permitted them.

The year 1979 was significant in the history of the mission of the Sisters of Mercy in Peru, for it was in 1979 that Lily Ferrero, the first Peruvian to enter the Congregation of the Sisters of Mercy of Newfoundland, left for St. John's. After living as an "associate" for a short period, she requested acceptance into the novitiate. Lily was born in Lima in 1942. In 1960, she became a member of the Sisters of the Immaculate Heart of Mary, a 2,500-member congregation based in Pennsylvania, USA, but she left that congregation in 1971 to devote her life more fully to the poor and oppressed in the slums of Lima. She joined a group of four other women, two of whom worked as teachers to support the group financially, while the other three worked with rural immigrants. After a few years, the group disintegrated. Because most of them had come from well-to-do families, it was a shattering experience for them to be so deeply immersed in the lives of the very poor. Lily continued on alone. To support herself she taught part-time at the Catholic university in Lima. Even before she left the IHMs, Lily had been impressed with the work of the Sisters of Mercy among the poor in Monsefú and its environs. After prayerful reflection, Lily realized that she could accomplish much more for the poor of her beloved Peru by joining a group of other women whose goals and objectives were similar to hers. Having made up her mind, Lily acted quickly. She resigned her position at the University of Lima and flew to St. John's to enter the novitiate of the Sisters of Mercy.

In 1984, members of a club called *Dama de Lambayeque* approached the mayor of Monsefú with an offer to establish a place where poor children could have breakfast. At the request of the mayor, M. Carmelita Power agreed to set up a dining room in Jésus Nazareno Cautivo, a poor section of Monsefú. A sympathetic lady of the town offered three rooms in her house, and the ladies of *Lambayeque* supplied tables, benches, cutlery, plates, and food. With the help of neighbours, the place was cleaned and the *adobe* walls whitewashed. Everything was ready now for the plan to be put into action. The sisters met with groups of women who agreed to take turns cooking and serving breakfast at seven o'clock in the morning, before the children left for school. Initially, about two hundred children were served. Brother Richard Glatz, CFC, who was working in Monsefú at the time, procured help from the USA to purchase food.

Still, the space was very inadequate. When José Mario Capuñay, an engineer from Monsefú, saw they were operating in such cramped quarters, he donated land for the construction of a dining room and an *artesanal*.[34] The cornerstone for the building was laid in 1987. All materials used in the construction were donated by friends of the project. Some of the men in Jésus Nazareno offered free labour. Señor Capuñay agreed to be responsible for the construction and appointed his brother Juan to oversee the work. Later in the year, Sr. Patricia Maher, superior general of the Sisters of Mercy, visited the site. Work had stopped because all donated material had been used. As she walked through the unfinished building, she resolved that somehow she would see that it was completed. Shortly after this visit, the sum of $5,000 was left to the Sisters of Mercy.[35] It was like an answer to prayer. Immediately Patricia forwarded the money to the sisters in Monsefú. Work on the dining room resumed, and when it was completed, a plaque was placed on the wall in memory of John Smith whose generosity had contributed so much to the work. However, there was still more to be done.

In the original gift of the land, José Capuñay had designated it for an *artesanal* centre as well as a dining room. The sisters began to look around for assistance so that his intentions could be realized. The person in charge of American aid projects at the time was Veronica Díaz, the wife of Sr. Lily Ferrero's cousin, Eduardo Ferrero. Veronica was quick to see the value of establishing such a community centre and managed to procure the necessary help to complete the second storey of the building. The new section of the centre was blessed in 1989. Since that time, the building is in constant use for

---

34. A centre for crafts.

35. The money was left to the Sisters of Mercy by John Smith, brother-in-law of M. Alphonsus Noonan. M. Alphonsus, a dedicated teacher, had been a generous supporter of Monsefú, engaging her pupils in all sorts of little projects to raise money for the mission. After M. Alphonsus' death in 1983, her sister, Mrs. Rose Smith, continued to send money in her memory. This money was always used to support the mission.

classes on health promotion and literacy. Retreats and scriptural reflection sessions take place regularly at the centre. Groups of women meet to work at different activities, producing beautiful articles of needlework to sell. Some of these women work on a farm and cultivate vegetables, some of which they take home to feed their families, the rest are used in the dining room of the community centre, Jésus Nazareno Cautivo.

The decade of the 1980s was to witness further changes for the sisters in Peru. There were changes in personnel—sisters who had served for years were recalled home, and other sisters came and brought different gifts and fresh ideas. Sr. Marion Collins, the last of the pioneer group, was elected as a delegate to the 1981 chapter, later to the office of vicar general of the congregation and eventually to the office of superior general. This required her presence in Newfoundland. Sr. Marion had seen the mission grow, and much of its success was due to her courage, energy, and foresight. She had been a source of strength to the sisters during the difficult early days. With her easygoing ways and unfailing good humour, she carried them through many dark and lonely hours. By her encouragement and strong sense of purpose, she stood with the people in their efforts to rebuild their lives after the losses caused by the earthquake and the flood. As the people came by the hundreds to say goodbye, the only consolation she could offer them was that someday she would return.[36]

On August 18, 1985, in the presence of her mother, three of her sisters, and practically every member of the Congregation of the Sisters of Mercy in Newfoundland, Lily Ferrero promised to devote the rest of her life to the service of the poor, the sick, and the uneducated as a Sister of Mercy. Shortly after her profession, Lily left to join the other Sisters of Mercy in Monsefú. Her arrival in Peru marked the beginning of yet another chapter in the unfolding story of the mission. Already the locus of the Mercy ministry had changed. This called for a re-examination of the style of community living.

---

36. After completing two terms as superior general of the Sisters of Mercy, Sr. Marion Collins returned to Peru in September 1999, where she ministers in the parish of Ichocan. The parish is very extensive, consisting of about forty *pueblos*.

The sisters perceived a contradiction between their ministry and their living accommodations. Over the years they began to feel more and more uncomfortable as they returned every evening to their beautifully equipped convent after having spent the day in the homes of the poorest of the poor. They felt that they could no longer continue to live in surroundings so different from those of the people with whom they worked. This was not a criticism of those who had provided what was considered appropriate accommodations for a group of teaching sisters. In fact, the convent in Monsefú was a very modest structure according to North American standards—it was simple but adequate. Furthermore, the convent was always at the service of the people; the sisters shared whatever they had—time, food, and space. But the building was a palace in comparison with the *adobe* huts in which most of the people lived. Thus, during a visit by Sr. Patricia Maher in 1986, the sisters suggested to her that their living accommodations should be on a smaller and simpler scale. They mentioned moving from the convent in Monsefú to a smaller house in another parish of the area in which they worked. Later on, in November of the same year, they talked over their plan with Sr. Marion Collins. Sr. Marion agreed and urged them to look for a suitable house. Eventually they found one in Puerto Eten and began immediate plans to move.

Before such a move could be effected, the sisters were very conscious that the remains of Srs. M. Dorothy Carroll and M. Aquin English were resting in the convent garden. They felt that it would be wise to transfer them to the general cemetery. To this end, they wrote the president of the *Beneficiencia* requesting space in the cemetery for two plots. In early March 1987, Srs. Lily Ferrero, Mildred Brennan, and M. Carmelita Power met early in the morning in the convent garden with representatives of the *Beneficiencia*. M. Carmelita describes the scene:

> It was very quiet and the lack of spectators created an atmosphere of reverence and awe for what we were about to do. It was a solemn moment when the coffins were removed from the vaults. The form of the bodies was still intact, clothed in their long white habits. . . . As the transferal to the new coffins was made there was a feeling of reverence around us—a moment of deep

> reflection and prayer on the meaning of mission. I was moved pro-
> foundly—thinking of Marion and myself and the mystery of why
> we were saved. It was a moment of gratitude, too, to be part of
> the contribution of our congregation to the life of the Church in
> Peru.[37]

The new site of the graves is marked by a simple design—the Mercy cross in the background and the names of the deceased sisters with their date of death written on the granite top. The removal of the remains of M. Dorothy and M. Aquin from the convent garden to the town cemetery further cemented the bond that exists between the Sisters of Mercy and the people of Monsefú. Many people continue to visit the graves and leave flowers—convincing evidence of the love the people had for the sisters and the respect in which they are held.

With the transferal of the bodies of the deceased, the way was clear for the sisters to vacate the convent in Monsefú and take up residence in their new home in Puerto Eten, a few miles distant. As its name implies, Puerto Eten is a seaport town, once a thriving sugar cane export centre and holiday resort. With the decline in exports, employment in the town was greatly reduced, and as a result, most of the people live in poverty. The neighbouring community of Eten, on the other hand, is larger and relatively more prosperous. The Sisters of Mercy were well-known in both places, for they had been working among the people there for many years. And so, on March 17, 1988, the Convento de la Misericordia in Monsefú closed, and Srs. Lily Ferrero, Carmelita Power, Alice Mackey, and Mildred Brennan moved into a modest little house situated among the simple houses of the poor in the village of Puerto Eten. Even though the house is much, much smaller than the convent, they have the advantage of a roof patio that looks over the rolling Pacific Ocean and an expansive sandy beach. The sound of the ocean at their back door is like old, familiar music to the ears of the Newfoundlanders. Not so musical, however, are the nightly choruses of a variety of animals who occupy the ground spaces

---

37. ASMSJ, RG 10/23/111.

surrounding the sisters' house and the roosters who proclaim loudly every morning that they have just caused the sun to rise.

Shortly after the sisters moved to Puerto Eten, a young woman Rosa Silva Cumpa, who was interested in discerning a vocation to religious life, joined them. After completing the postulancy program, Rosa was admitted to the novitiate in Lima. The Mercy novitiate in Lima is a collaborative venture by four Mercy congregations: three from the United States and the Newfoundland congregation. By establishing a central novitiate, the congregations hoped to provide novices with the opportunity to share experiences, to study the history of the Sisters of Mercy and the life and teaching of Catherine McAuley, and to avail of good programs in scripture and theology. In 1996, Sr. Mildred Brennan who had completed studies in formation was named director of formation for the Sisters of Mercy in Peru for a period of four years.

Meantime, work in Puerto Eten continued. The desperate health situation in Peru prompted the planning of a health clinic during 1989. The official blessing and opening of the clinic, Nuestra Señora de la Misericordia,[38] took place on December 3, 1989. The clinic, located in Eten, is funded by the Newfoundland Congregation of the Sisters of Mercy and coordinated by the sisters in Puerto Eten. The coordinating doctor for the project is Dr. César Castellanos, a native of Puerto Eten, who donates his services to the clinic. In addition to Dr. Castellanos, there are three other medical doctors, one nurse, and three nursing assistants. Among the doctors who worked in the clinic with Dr. Castellanos were two former pupils of the sisters' school in Monsefú, Lorenzo Arce and Jacinto Custodio. Three times a week, a pediatrician from the clinic visits the town of Reque to look after the needs of sick children. These visits are funded also by the Sisters of Mercy.

Nevertheless, while such financial support is crucial to the work of the mission, the main focus for the sisters is to enable people to direct their own lives, to facilitate the efforts of the people in developing their own abilities, and to become leaders in matters that directly affect them. To do this, they

---

38. Our Lady of Mercy.

work with Peruvian priests in four parishes with about 60,000 people. They meet each week to read the word of God and, in light of what the Gospel says, to talk about the problems of their community and attempt to arrive at concrete solutions. This gentle, reflective, co-operative stance requires great patience, as well as healthy doses of faith, hope, and love on the part of all those involved in the struggle for peace and justice. Often it is a case of two steps forward and one step back—but at least some progress is realized.

Then, in 1991, Peru was ravaged by an epidemic of cholera. The towns where the sisters worked, Monsefú, Puerto Eten, Eten, and Reque were not spared. It was very fortunate that the clinic, Nuestra Señora de la Misericordia, was in place and fully operational. The presence of such a facility, as well as the organization of volunteer medical personnel, proved to be a great blessing in this critical situation. The clinic, however, although it was utilized to its fullest capacity, could not accommodate the large numbers who needed hospitalization. The parish rooms in Eten were converted into temporary hospital wards. Some patients were lucky enough to have beds, but the majority had to lie on mattresses or straw mats on the floor. Makeshift stands were quickly set up to hold intravenous solutions. Doctors, nurses, nursing aides, and the sisters worked around the clock to care for the cholera victims and to try to bring the epidemic under control. Once again, the people at home in Newfoundland responded to the crisis. Prayers for the sisters and for the cholera victims were offered in every Mercy community. Schools, parishes, church groups, and many individuals sent monetary donations to provide antibiotics and other medical supplies needed to treat the victims of the disease and to respond to the needs of all who came to the clinic. Nearly one thousand people were treated in the clinic in the space of a few weeks. As they returned each evening to their little home in Puerto Eten, the sisters recalled the story of Srs. Francis Creedon and Joseph Nugent who faced a similar situation in St. John's in 1847. Once the epidemic was brought under control, the sisters could relax, and within a short time, they were able to resume their usual activities.

The following year was one of great significance. Not only did it mark the one hundred and fiftieth anniversary of the arrival of the Sisters of Mercy in Newfoundland, but also in a striking coincidence, on March 29, 1992, the first Sister of Mercy of the Newfoundland congregation to be professed in Peru made her vows. In the little parish church of Puerto Eten, Sr. Rosa Mercedes Silva Cumpa pronounced the simple vows of chastity, poverty, and obedience and promised to devote her life as a Sister of Mercy to the service of the poor, the sick, and the uneducated. The ceremony, patterned on the traditional rite of profession, incorporated elements that spoke strongly of Rosa's heritage. Before the presentation of gifts, two *gestos* (gestures), or symbolic actions, took place. First, a large vessel of sand from the beach at Puerto Eten was presented. This was a symbol of the coast of Peru where Rosa was born. It symbolized, too, Rosa's homeland, so loved by its people, a land that all too often has been exploited, pillaged, and ravaged by violence, oppression, poverty, and death. Then, a large crucifix and a copy of the Mercy "Rule and Constitutions" were presented so that the sisters—and all those present—would recall the words of Catherine McAuley, "Ours is a Congregation founded on Calvary, there to serve a Crucified Redeemer."[39] In the midst of celebration, this was a stern reminder that religious life is not for the faint-hearted.

The addition of Rosa to the community at Puerto Eten opened the way for Sr. Alice Mackey to join the pastoral team in Nasca, a town about 265 miles south of Lima. Living and working with an Irish Sister of Mercy, Evelyn Horan, Alice quickly became involved in an evangelization program with families, specifically *Catequesis Familiar* and Marriage Encounter. *Catequesis Familiar* is an adult evangelization program, the drawing card being the First Communion of the child. The long-range goal of the project was to form basic christian communities. Teenagers acted as "animators" for groups of children, and thus all age levels were involved—a model that might be imitated by parishes at home! Although it was a long, slow process, Alice described it as "the church alive, vibrant, active, and committed."[40] The sisters lived in a district of Nasca, named Vista Alegre, literally, "Happy Sight," a relatively new *pueblo* that was created in 1952. The population of 12,000 was made up mostly of *campesinos*

---

39. Constitutions of the Sisters of Mercy.
40. ASMSJ, RG10/23/187.

(farmers) who came down from the mountains looking for better working conditions and more educational opportunities for their children.

After the general chapter of 1989, the community in Peru—Srs. Carmelita, Mildred, Alice, Lily, and Rosa (a postulant at the time)—received approval to open a new mission. The bishop of the Diocese of Cajamarca, Bishop José Dammert Bellido, had invited them on numerous occasions to establish a mission in his diocese. In 1991, after a lengthy period of discernment, they accepted the invitation and decided on Ichocan, a *pueblo* in a very large rural area of the diocese where there had been no resident priest for many years. As an added encouragement, word was received from St. John's that two more sisters, Brenda Phelan and Verna Aucoin, would be joining the mission. However, just at that time a group of terrorists called "The Shining Path" began to gain strength in Peru. For several years, they held the country in a grip of fear because of the frequency and violence of their attacks. Thus, the opening of the new mission had to be deferred until the situation had improved. On May 3, 1993, Srs. Lily Ferrero, Verna Aucoin, and Rosa Silva Cumpa left Puerto Eten to open the new mission in Ichocan, Cajamarca.

Ichocan is perched on top of a mountain about 10,600 feet above sea level with a breathtaking view. Huge mountains tower over the village in every direction. In the rainy season, the terraced slopes of the valley and mountains are a shade of deep, rich green. Ploughing on the mountainsides is still done with oxen because the slopes and ravines are too steep to allow the use of more modern equipment. The parish of Ichocan is quite extensive with a population of about 16,000 scattered among four districts with over forty *caserios* (little villages) hidden in every ravine. Some of these villages are accessible by truck, others by donkey or mule, while some can be reached only by walking for several hours over very rough terrain. The lengthy rainy season in this mountainous area makes travel difficult and often hazardous. The people live off the land and are very conscious of their dependence on nature and on the God who provides the rain, sun, and fruits for the harvest. Their lifestyle is extremely simple, and the sisters learned quickly to step back into history in order to appreciate where the people are coming from and to understand their rich culture and traditions.

Immediately after their arrival in Ichocan, the sisters began the task of visiting as many *caserios* as possible. In September, Monsignor Simón of the Diocese of Cajamarca offered them the position of coordinator of religious education in the schools of their zone. This was a welcome appointment, for it provided the opportunity for the sisters to meet the children, the teachers, and the parents in dozens of different places, some of which are reached only by riding on the back of a mule. After their first experience of this form of transportation, the sisters came home stiff and sore, and on being invited to sit down for a cup of tea, they politely refused—not the tea, but the chair!

The problem of communicating with people in the more remote areas seemed almost insurmountable. Finally, the sisters decided to send messages by the local radio stations to invite representatives from each *caserio* to come to a meeting in Ichocan in November. On the morning of the appointed day, they waited anxiously, not knowing how many had heard the broadcast and praying that at least ten people would show up. They were surprised and delighted when three times that number appeared in time for the meeting. Some came from the furthest corners of the parish, walking five hours to reach Ichocan; others came on horseback, riding for three or four hours. The sisters were overwhelmed and inspired by the simplicity, interest, and commitment of these people. There had been no resident priest in the area since 1985, and people were overjoyed to know that someone was interested in their *pueblos* and offering to work with them to reactivate the life of the parish. This first meeting was an unqualified success. At its conclusion, the sisters served the participants a dinner using the produce of their own vegetable garden. The cooking was done with wood over an open fire in clay pots. In their enthusiasm, the sisters experimented making bread in an ancient clay oven. Unfortunately, they miscalculated somewhat and turned out over four hundred pieces of bread instead of the one hundred and fifty they actually needed. Nevertheless, the participants returned home well-fed, full of enthusiasm, and ready to implement the suggestions presented at the meeting. As a bonus, each one brought home a large package of bread! Within a short time, training sessions for catechists had been scheduled, a parish council elected, and plans made to visit the more remote areas of the five districts. Before they knew where they were, the sisters were swept up in preparations for the celebration of Christmas.

Christmas Eve in Ichocan is marked by special celebrations. All the people participate. There is a nativity scene, different people taking the parts of Mary and Joseph, with Magi, shepherds, and occasionally a real live infant, all accompanied by singing, dancing, and lively, syncopated carols. On Christmas Day, the young people with their musical instruments accompany the sisters to neighbouring *pueblos* where the liturgy of the day is celebrated. The climax comes on the Feast of the Epiphany when the Magi, mounted on donkeys, arrive to adore the Christ Child.

As their first year in Ichocan drew to a close, the annalist recorded, "We thank God that everywhere we've been the people have welcomed us more than warmly and have expressed their desire that we accompany them in learning more about their faith and how to celebrate it even more fully."[41] During the next few years, the sisters established a warm relationship with the people in all the districts of the parish. They soon discovered that the standard of education is very low. Schools lack even the bare necessities and provide little incentive for children or teachers. The teachers are poorly paid and many of them work in isolated areas where they have to walk for hours to reach their villages. The smaller villages have no high schools and most of the children, especially the girls, rarely progress beyond grades V or VI. After leaving school, they help at home, work in the fields, or pasture the animals. To provide an alternative for some of those young people, the sisters made an agreement with the Department of Education to set up an Occupational Education Centre that offers courses in sewing, carpentry, food services, and computer science. These programs employ eleven people, five of whom are paid by the government. From the initiation of these programs, the young people responded with great enthusiasm. Some of them walk two or three hours every day to attend classes. The centre provides them with an opportunity for socialization, personal development, and formation on different levels.

41. Ibid., ASMSJ, RG10/23/179.

The work of evangelization continues to this day and people are encouraged to take the responsibility for faith development and worship in each local community. A retired priest visits the parish to help out at Christmas and Easter. For the rest of the year, the sisters, together with catechists, provide pastoral care in the different villages that make up the parish. The parish itself embraces four districts, and each of these is composed of about ten villages. The catechists are chosen by the people of their respective villages and approved by the parish. They are responsible for gathering the people each week for paraliturgical celebrations. About thirty of them, men and women, meet the sisters every month to study Scripture and prepare the liturgical celebrations for their communities. The continuing formation of these lay leaders is one of the main preoccupations of the sisters in Peru. They are engaged, also, in works of human development such as mothers' clubs and health education and in assisting the people in various projects to improve living conditions within the community. The sight of a sister standing on top of a ladder wielding a hammer with great expertise is no strange sight in the parish of Ichocan. More important than anything is the sisters' presence among the people to be with them in their struggle for justice and peace in a country where poverty and violence still hold sway.

In 1998, the sisters in Ichocan were joined by a Sister of Mercy from New Zealand, Anne Campbell, and a year later the sisters welcomed Sr. Marion Collins to the community. In addition to the two extra, they were joined by a young lady who lives with the sisters and volunteers her time to work in the parish, and there is plenty of work to keep every one of them busy. In a letter dated March 30, 2000, we read:

> Our house and parish is gradually getting smaller and smaller as we expand with more courses and workshops for the people of the area. Our sewing classes are growing each day, and now we have a former primary teacher (also excellent tailor) taking over more classes while his wife and another Señora teach every afternoon. In the meantime, there is a mixture of young kids, one older man and a teacher all involved in carpentry. We have two full-time teachers working through a project we received from a NGO from Spain. Besides teaching they do all kinds of repairs around

> the parish and house and church, and also various jobs for the
> pueblo. ... It gets quite wild at times as the groups are coming and
> going all day from early morning, and especially when the instruc-
> tors decide they all need materials at once ..."We need WOOD
> NOW!!!" Or they inform us that the wood and poles they
> brought up last week will take six months to dry before they can
> begin to use it.[42]

This account draws a picture of a place that is humming with activity all day. But the sisters are also constantly on the move, travelling to far distant villages in their district, especially during the days and weeks preceding the big litur- gical feasts of the year. For instance, during Holy Week 2000, between them they managed thirty-three celebrations in nineteen villages, arriving at each one by truck, leg muscle, or police car. Sr. Marion Collins wrote home:

> The universe was probably vibrating with richness of song and
> prayer that bounded around and off our planet during those days.
> Among the cacophony God heard our simple prayers, "Keep the
> truck on the road; Don't let my legs seize up!" The truck came in
> to the finish line on Easter Sunday night after two flat tires, a bro-
> ken spring, shock absorbers that absorbed none of the bumps on
> the road, need I say, ready for repairs. Our legs having clocked up
> to eight hours walking and climbing also arrived a little stiff but
> operational.[43]

Frequently, the young people of Ichocan accompany the sisters on their journeys to distant parts of the parish. Their songs and laughter fill the back of the truck and echo across the valleys as they bump their way to the mountains of Shirac or down to La Grama valley.

Life in Peru presents the Sisters of Mercy with a great deal of satisfac- tion and more than a fair share of heartaches and disappointments. The natural disasters experienced all too frequently by the Peruvian people constantly challenge the sisters to exercise the ministry of love and compassion that is at

---

42. Letter from Sr. Verna Aucoin, March 30, 2000, ASMSJ, RG 10/23/182.
43. Sr. Marion Collins to Leadership Team, May 3, 2000, ASMSJ, RG 10/23/177.

the heart of the Mercy vocation. One such event was the El Niño phenomenon of 1997–98. It was first manifested in early May 1997, when the temper-
ature of the atmosphere and the Pacific Ocean rose, sparking extensive damage in the fishery and agriculture. An intense and almost continuous rainfall
was concentrated in the northern coastal regions and caused extensive flooding and devastating landslides bringing death and destruction to the northern
and central parts of the country. Many regions were isolated as roads and
bridges were destroyed, making it difficult and, at times, impossible for relief
agencies to provide help to the thousands in distress.

Dealing with the effects of natural disasters was nothing new to the sisters in Peru. As was the case during the other catastrophic events, they were
with the people, working with them, praying with them, and experiencing
their distress. The Sisters of Mercy in Newfoundland shared their concern and
were eager to do everything they could to help. There was constant communication between St. John's and Puerto Eten, except when floodwaters short-
circuited the telephone jack. On March 2, 1998, Sr. Brenda Phelan succeeded
in sending a fax to the General Council. She wrote:

> The state of things here in Puerto Eten, Reque, Monsefú is terri-
> ble. Yesterday morning . . . the bridge over Reque River went
> down . . . So now we are truly isolated from Chiclayo. In Eten,
> Puerto & Monsefú hundreds of homes are destroyed. People are
> in refuge shelters . . . with Gov't supplying food, but now with
> transport cut we don't know what will happen. Cholera is ram-
> pant both here and in Eten. The Porta Medicos are only attend-
> ing the cholera cases, nothing else—24-hour service. But now
> with our roads cut off there is worry about lack of medical sup-
> plies . . . everyone looks to the church for help. Centro Medico is
> now without doctors but attention and medicine are free. They
> are attending "other than Cholera" as the Porta's treat only
> cholera.[44]

A few days later, Srs. M. Carmelita Power and Alice Mackey returned to
Puerto Eten to find the street almost impassable. They immediately went off

---

44. Sr. Brenda Phelan to Leadership Team, March 2, 1998, ASMSJ, MAN 10/23/2.

to interview the mayor who promised to bring in heavy equipment to repair the damage. The people who had lost their homes were given shelter in the parish centre, the church, the social club, and one of the schools. The government supplied breakfast and dinner for the 250 people who were housed there. Throughout the following months, the sisters worked desperately to provide what relief they could to the stricken families. The Mercy congregation in Newfoundland sent money to purchase thousands of mattresses, blankets, clothing, shoes, and food. In Eten, Srs. M. Carmelita Power, Brenda Phelan, Father Emigdio, and some of the lay people in the parish worked as a team to visit the poorest families in the area to assess their needs and secure whatever help was available.

The effects of El Niño continued well into the year 1999. In a letter of February 18, 1999, Sr. Brenda Phelan reported that the sisters were successful in getting good prices for rice, sugar, beans, and oil and that all the blankets, mattresses, and two-thirds of the school shoes had been distributed. The floodwaters receded, and the process of rebuilding began once more. Although the people have so little in the way of material goods, God has blessed them with gifts of patience, superb courage, and joy in living. It is no wonder that the Sisters of Mercy find constant strength and inspiration from living and working in the midst of such people.

The Sisters of Mercy are very conscious of the fact that many of the people who live in the villages and more remote parts of Peru suffer from lack of ordinary medical care that most of us take for granted. In June 2003, the Sisters of Mercy, Newfoundland and Labrador, working in Ichocan, Cajamarca, organized an ophthalmological campaign, in collaboration with a group of specialists and volunteers from British Columbia, Canada (Third World Eye Care Society, TWECS). In a period of two weeks, the team of sixteen Canadian surgeons, optometrists, and volunteers attended almost four thousand people from the Ichocan Parish and surrounding areas. Three surgeons performed cataract operations and minor surgeries for others in the hospital in Cajamarca.

One of the biggest challenges was working with the Ministry of Health and Customs in Lima to make the necessary arrangements for the team's entry into Peru, especially in light of the fact that they carried with them their own equipment and medicine. The bureaucracy was incredible, but due to the sisters' efforts, everything was in place for the team's arrival. The Sisters of Mercy were responsible for setting up the eye clinic in the parish centre, providing accommodations to those travelling from afar, as well as preparing meals and providing translation. Local town councils and health clinics were involved in arranging registration and transportation for people travelling from the distant villages. It was a heartwarming experience for all those involved to witness the gratitude of the people of Ichocan for the service provided by the Canadian team who so freely and generously shared their resources and skill. For our part, the Congregation of Sisters of Mercy of Newfoundland were happy to have been part of this venture, collaborating closely with others in the region and above all providing a Mercy presence to people who came seeking help in their time of need.

More than forty years have passed since the Newfoundland Sisters of Mercy first set foot in Peru. They arrived, a group of teachers, dressed in the traditional long habit and veil. Their duties were clear; times of rising and retiring, of prayer and recreation were fixed; and their lives were ordered by the clock—even in distant Monsefú. But soon it became evident that the seeds of change were being planted. Within one short decade, religious life within the Roman Catholic Church was changed forever. The restlessness that swept through the Church was felt most strongly, perhaps, in the convents of women religious throughout the world. The political events that changed the focus of ministry for the Sisters of Mercy in Peru merely anticipated the desire of the sisters themselves to move out of the relative enclosure of convent walls to be present to the people they served. The documents of the Second Vatican Council were examined and discussed by the sisters, and the call for renewal was embraced with enthusiasm. The implications of "Liberation Theology" with emphasis on option for the poor and the call for justice for the disenfranchised and oppressed found a ready response in the hearts of the Sisters of Mercy in Monsefú. The closing of the convent was more than just a change of residence—it signified the throwing off of a more secluded, privileged lifestyle to live more simply in an ordinary house, on an ordinary street. Instead of the regular routine of classes that marked the early days of the mission, the sisters are available at all hours to respond to the needs of the people. It might be a simple request by a little boy to teach him the Ten Commandments before he has to face the teacher the next day, or it might be a wake-up call at six o'clock in the morning to take someone to the hospital. Every day brings new surprises and challenges. Certainly, life is not boring or static for the Newfoundland Sisters of Mercy in Peru. As for the future, who knows? The only thing certain is that all of the future is in God's hands, and where better could it be!

CHAPTER TWENTY-THREE

NEW FOUNDATIONS, WEST AND SOUTH

Yon wild mossy mountains sae lofty and wide,
That nurse in their bosom the youth o' the Clyde,
Where the grouse lead their coveys thro' the heather to feed,
And the shepherd tends his flock as he pipes on his reed.[1]

Robert Burns

Beginning with M. Francis Creedon, who hoarded her pennies to buy new boots, those elected to the General Council of the Sisters of Mercy were frugal, competent women who managed financial affairs with an eye to promoting the teaching and nursing ministries of the congregation. In the 1950s and '60s, the challenges presented by the fiscal demands of constructing new convents and maintaining the old, with the cost of university education for all sisters, demanded more than a little penny-pinching. But there was more to come. Early in the 1960s, the decision was made to build a new college on the Littledale campus.[2] This was a momentous decision and required an enormous monetary commitment by the congregation, but the Sisters of Mercy were never afraid to accept challenges. Then, in

---

1. Robert Burns, "Yon Wild, Mossy Mountain," in *Collected Works* (Dumfries, Scotland: Creedon Publications, 1966), p. 428.
2. See chapter twenty-four for a discussion of St. Bride's College.

the midst of the flurry associated with the opening of the new college, came a request from Father Roderick White for a foundation in Upper Ferry, a small town in the Codroy Valley on the west coast of Newfoundland.

The whole area of the Codroy Valley is one of spectacular beauty. The Grand Codroy River runs serenely through lush green fields, while on the eastern side of the Codroy Valley, the Long Range Mountains fold in one behind the other, little streams of water cascading down the slopes. Therefore, when word filtered down through the ranks that the Sisters of Mercy were going to open a convent in "The Valley," many fervent prayers were directed heavenwards by sisters longing to be sent to this section of Newfoundland called Upper Ferry.

Upper Ferry is a farming community located on the banks of the Grand Codroy River. The river flows out into the Gulf of St. Lawrence at a point originally called "The Gut," but renamed Searston in honour of Rev. Thomas Sears. The first settlers, mostly Nova Scotians of Scottish descent and some Acadians, arrived in the late 1700s. They built their homes and farms on a site near the mouth of the river on the southern shore of The Gut (Searston). Later on, more settlers arrived, mainly from Nova Scotia. The newcomers established large farms about five miles upstream at a place where the river narrows. Over the years, this point of crossing became known as Upper Ferry.[3]

On August 15, 1967, the names of the four sisters selected for the new foundation in the Codroy Valley were posted in community rooms of every Mercy convent on the island. Like Catherine McAuley before her, the superior general of the time, M. Assumpta Veitch, had great confidence in youth. The sisters selected to go to Upper Ferry were all under thirty years of age, the superior, Charlotte Fitzpatrick, age twenty-six years, had made her perpetual profession of vows two years previously, in 1965. Bridget Patterson, who was a year older, was named assistant. The other two members of the community, Frances Gibbons and Sheila Sullivan, were juniors who had not yet been admitted to perpetual profession. Both were in their early twenties. Prior to the departure, Sr.

---

3. Many years ago, two ferries provided transportation across the river, one near the mouth of the river at Searston and the other one at a point further up the river, thus, "Upper Ferry."

Charlotte was given twenty dollars to cover their expenses. Thus equipped, the four young sisters destined for Upper Ferry boarded the train at St. John's at half past eleven on the evening of August 30, 1967, for the twenty-two hour journey across the island of Newfoundland. M. Assumpta, who was visiting the convents on the West Coast, joined them at Stephenville Crossing, and all five arrived at Doyle's Station in the Valley at eight o'clock the following evening.

The parish priest, Father Roderick White, was at the station to meet them and escort them to the presbytery, where they were to spend the next few months until the convent was ready for occupancy.[4] The following morning, as they approached the church to attend mass, they received an energetic and vociferous greeting from Father White's large dog who, conscious of his duty to protect parish property, was immediately suspicious of these strangely garbed intruders. The four young sisters were reluctant to proceed any further, but M. Assumpta, who allowed no obstacle to stand in the way of duty, silenced the dog with a glance and sailed serenely past the cowed animal, followed closely by four hesitant young sisters.

The official welcome was held the following Sunday. At half past eight in the evening, the sisters proceeded to the parish hall, where they were greeted at the door by the pastor and escorted into the hall to the accompaniment of bagpipes. Only the awesome presence of M. Assumpta—who admitted later that she was dreading the reaction of her four embarrassed companions— ensured their composure. It was an evening of speeches, but also a reminder to the sisters that they had a reputation to maintain. Many of the adults present in the hall were graduates of St. Michael's Boarding School in St. George's and held firm opinions on the manner in which Sisters of Mercy should conduct themselves.

The schools opened two days later. Sr. Sheila Sullivan had been appointed principal of Searston Elementary School, which was not too far from the presbytery. Sr. Sheila walked into a well-equipped school that had been in operation for a number of years. Thus, she was spared the fate that awaited the

---

4. During the months the sisters lived in the presbytery, Father White stayed with the assistant pastor, Father Patrick Cooney, in Great Codroy.

rest of her community. The other three sisters, Charlotte, Bridget, and Frances, left by bus at nine o'clock in the morning for the new central high school in Upper Ferry. The school was coeducational with an enrolment of slightly over 200 students from grades VII to XI. There were four teachers in addition to the three sisters. On their arrival, they found that the school had four classrooms, earthen floors, no electricity, no blackboards, no desks, no books, and 200 youngsters eagerly waiting to see "the nuns." Consequently, after meeting the teachers and enrolling the students, Sr. Charlotte sent the children home with orders to return the following week.

The first week of September was one of exploration and discovery for the newcomers. They visited the schools in South Branch and Port aux Basques and spoke to the students and teachers. The desks for the school in Upper Ferry arrived a few days later, although not enough for all the classrooms. Only the grade XI and grade VII classes had regular desks; everyone else put up with whatever was available. The sisters, however, were no strangers to improvisation. They found enough tables and chairs for the grade VIII classroom; students in grades IX and X had to be satisfied with benches. Because the new blackboards had not arrived, they used blackboards from the old school. These were propped up on chairs until more professional materials arrived. And so, school began a week late on Monday, September 11.

The newly opened Belanger Memorial High School was intended to accommodate students from several different settlements in Codroy Valley. Consequently, many of the students were strangers to one another; furthermore, they had no intention of associating with people from any place other than their own. As a result, lunch and recess periods were very quiet. Students from St. Andrew's pulled their chairs in one corner of the room, while Great Codroy students huddled in the opposite corner; South Branch students congregated in a third corner; and Searston children occupied the fourth—members of each group with their backs to other occupants of the room! Sr. Charlotte observed this state of affairs and promptly went into action. Among other initiatives, she persuaded the students to form sports teams and a school band. Through these shared experiences, barriers were torn down so that before long a common school spirit began to emerge.

Meanwhile, for more than three months, the sisters lived in the presbytery. At that time, the pastor's sister Margaret White was the housekeeper. Her kindness to the four young sisters is part of the story of the foundation in Upper Ferry. But, in spite of the hospitality shown them, the sisters were looking forward to having a home of their own. Instead of going to the expense of erecting a new building, Father White had decided to buy two houses, move them from their original site on Radio Range to a piece of land near the high school, then join them together to form one house. On September 6, the houses were placed on floats and moved as far as the church in Searston, where they rested overnight. The following day, the two floats started off once more, heading toward the site of the future convent. As the houses were unloaded on a piece of land near the school, crowds of people gathered around while Mr. Allan McArthur played a medley of lively tunes on the bagpipes. An army of small boys risked life and limb as they darted in and out among the men who were trying to ease the houses from the floats to their designated resting place. Finally, about half past six in the evening, both houses were resting securely in their new location. But it was almost the end of October before cement was poured to complete the substructure of each house. A big step forward was made on November 2, when the first house was moved onto its foundation and again a week later when the second house was in place. At last the sisters were able to examine the rooms and make some decisions on how to make one convent out of two separate houses. As they were rummaging through the attic of one of the houses, they discovered a Mercy cross. Nobody knows how such an object, unique to the Sisters of Mercy, found its way to that place. By mid-December the first house was ready for occupancy, but it was to be another two years before both houses were joined.

On December 16, the sisters packed up their belongings, tidied the rooms they had occupied since September, thanked Father White and his sister Margaret for their kindness, said goodbye to Father's large dog, borrowed a kettle and took their departure. The following day, they celebrated the opening of Holy Trinity Convent by cooking a special dinner. In spite of the inexperience of the cooks—and the fact that they had forgotten to buy flour—the meal was a success. Nobody complained about the absence of gravy. There were plenty of complaints, however, about the new washing machine that vibrated so much they were forced to take turns sitting on it while it was in operation.

According to the Annals of Holy Trinity Convent, as the new foundation was called, the sisters led very busy lives. Shortly after their arrival they began weekly religious instructions at Port aux Basques for Roman Catholic students attending St. James' Anglican School.[5] Also, they visited the sick, the elderly, and families who had suffered bereavement in the various settlements in Codroy Valley, not only those in Upper Ferry. In some of the more isolated places, they found children who had been baptized but who had not seen the inside of a church since that time. For example, the annalist described an occasion when the assistant priest, Father Cooney, brought them to visit a Catholic family in one of these smaller places. There they discovered that the children had received no religious instruction. The sisters provided what instruction they could, and the next day, on their way to Port aux Basques, they picked up the children and brought them to Sunday mass. It was the first time these children had attended mass.[6]

The start of the second year of the sisters' tenure in Upper Ferry was marked by a great deal of fuss and flurry in preparation for the arrival of the bishop of the diocese who was coming to bless the new high school. The ceremony took place on September 2, 1968, and the building was named Belanger Memorial High School in memory of the first priest to work on the west coast of Newfoundland, Father Alexis Belanger. School opened the following day, and things returned to normal in Upper Ferry.

The sisters entered very much into the lives of the people and especially of the students who were quite at home in the convent. One of the sisters remembered that on Saturday nights the convent was crowded with students. She wrote:

Eli's Dance Hall always attracted a crowd, and the Convent just across the way was usually the first stop. Every Saturday night

---

5. The Catholic school in Port aux Basques had been forced to close because of an insufficient number of pupils.

6. Annals, Holy Trinity Convent, Upper Ferry, ASMSJ.

around eight the doorbell would start ringing and pretty soon
our living room would be filled with the sounds of guitars and
singing.[7]

But the sisters' interest extended far beyond the activities of the schoolchildren. They attended wedding anniversary celebrations, attended ball games and
continued to provide religious instruction to Roman Catholic children in outlying villages. In 1969, two extra sisters were added to the teaching staff,
Elizabeth Davis and Carmel Doyle. Finally, in September 1969, two years after
the sisters arrived in the Valley, work began on joining the two buildings that
comprised Holy Trinity Convent.[8] For almost three months, the sisters patiently endured the parade of carpenters, painters, electricians, and plumbers as
they began to make one home out of what had been two separate dwellings. By
December, all the work had been finished and the sisters held an open house on
two occasions, one for the adults of the parish and the other for the students.

In 1969, Sr. Sheila Sullivan, a member of the founding group, was reappointed to Brigus and named principal of St. Joseph's School. The people of
Searston greeted the news with consternation. In the short two years since her
arrival, Sr. Sheila had earned the respect and gratitude of the parents whose
children attended Searston Elementary School. The children admired and
respected their talented young principal who knew how to help them over
rough places on the road to learning, but who also could teach them new and
exciting ways to acquire knowledge. Three years later, Sr. Charlotte Fitzpatrick
was transferred to St. Bride's Convent, Littledale, and with her departure, the
first chapter in the history of Holy Trinity Convent came to an end. Sr.
Charlotte had made a lasting impression on the staff and students of Belanger
Memorial High School. It was she who inspired the students to design the first
crest and motto for the school. She urged the establishment of the first Student
Council and the first yearbook. Sr. Charlotte encouraged extracurricular

---

7. Sr. Charlotte Fitzpatrick, Address on the occasion of the 25th anniversary of Belanger
High School, ASMSJ, RG 10/25/72.

8. During the school year, 1968–69, the sisters continued to occupy only one of the houses. The second house was rented to a married couple, teachers in the school.

activities such as participation in Reach for the Top, a province-wide television program sponsored by the Canadian Broadcasting Corporation in which students competed by answering questions on a variety of topics. Neither did she neglect the whole area of sports, particularly hockey and basketball.

The sisters in Upper Ferry continued to assist the pastor by planning liturgies and providing religious instructions to children in the outlying missions of the parish. Occasionally the drive back and forth to the missions presented problems, especially in the winter. For instance, one Christmas Day, three of the sisters from Holy Trinity Convent went to Port aux Basques with the priest to assist at the noon mass. As they were on their way home, a sudden, blinding snowstorm swept down from the mountains stranding them on the side of the road. Fortunately, a young man, David Bragg, from a nearby settlement came along and brought them to his own home where they found twenty-five people celebrating Christmas. The addition of four more to the party was no strain on the hospitality of Mr. and Mrs. Nathan Bragg. The newcomers joined the group and enjoyed the fun and games until nine o'clock when the storm abated sufficiently to allow them to return home to their two lonely companions who had spent Christmas Day wondering what had become of the travellers.

And so the years unfolded. No earth-shaking event disturbed the even tenor of life in the Valley. The personnel of the convent changed from time to time, and each sister made her own contribution to the education of the children of the Valley. Time seemed to fly, and before anybody realized it, the sisters had been almost ten years in Upper Ferry. However, in that tenth year (1977), tragedy struck the Congregation of the Sisters of Mercy and, in particular, the community of Holy Trinity Convent. Shortly before three o'clock on February 10, Srs. Brenda Peddigrew, Monica Hickey, and Marie Costello left to drive to Deer Lake where Sr. Brenda planned to spend the night at the Presentation Convent before boarding a flight to New Jersey to attend a workshop. Srs. Marie and Monica were expected back in Upper Ferry around quarter after eleven. The superior, M. Josepha Young, was home alone. She had the kettle on the stove and bread in the toaster when, at eleven o'clock, the local doctor, Dr. Ring, phoned to say that the sisters had been involved in an accident and he was leaving immediately to attend to them. He told her that the parish priest, Father Kevin Ryan, was already at the scene of the accident. At midnight, Father Ryan phoned to report that the sisters had been brought to the hospital in Port aux Basques where he had anointed them. Sometime later, Fr. Ryan phoned to say that Sr. Marie's condition was critical. The doctors suspected that she had sustained internal injuries and were requesting permission to operate immediately. The devoted priest stayed all night in the hospital and kept in constant touch with M. Josepha, who sat by the phone until morning. The only interruption to her lonely vigil happened when the convent car, which had been almost completely demolished, was towed into the school playground. At seven thirty in the morning, Father Ryan returned to Upper Ferry and went immediately to the convent, where he arranged that the car should be towed away before the children arrived for school.

Meanwhile, M. Josepha had notified the superior general, Sr. Marie Michael Power, of the accident. After classes had begun in the school, one of the teachers drove M. Josepha to the hospital in Port aux Basques, where she was joined by Sr. Theresa Ryan and the priest from St. Fintan's. They found Sr. Marie unconscious and Sr. Monica in great pain and with a cast on her broken ankle. Later on that day, Sr. Marie Michael arrived from St. John's with Sr. Lucy Power from St. Clare's Mercy Hospital. They went immediately to the hospital in Port aux Basques, while Sr. Theresa Ryan went back to the convent to answer phone calls and prepare some hot soup for the sisters on their return late that night. The following morning they returned to the hospital and were at Sr. Marie's side when she died at three thirty on Saturday, February 12.

Arrangements were made to transfer Sr. Marie's remains to St. John's for burial in the sisters' plot at Belvedere Cemetery. On Sunday afternoon, all the sisters on the West Coast were at Stephenville Airport to meet the sad little procession from Upper Ferry and to bid farewell to one of their own. When the plane arrived in St. John's, the airport was filled with sisters who had come to meet Sr. Marie Michael and those who accompanied her. Sr. Marie's body was brought to St. Bride's Convent, Littledale, where two days later Archbishop P. J. Skinner celebrated the funeral mass in St. Bride's College Chapel. The bishops of Grand Falls and Corner Brook concelebrated with more than twenty-seven priests. Another dozen or more priests were present in the congregation. The chapel was filled to overflowing with Sr. Marie's family and friends. The school boards had given permission for the teaching sisters to be absent from classes so that they could attend the mass. Father Kevin Ryan, who had been such a staunch and faithful friend to the sisters, read the prayers at the graveside.

Before Sr. Marie Michael left Upper Ferry, she made arrangements for Sr. Monica Hickey to be transferred to St. Clare's Mercy Hospital so that she would not be alone after the sisters had left to go to St. John's for the funeral. There was one happy note to conclude this tragic episode. Sr. Monica recovered fully from her injuries, returned to the Valley and later resumed her duties as principal of St. Anne's Elementary School.[9] Sr. Frances Gibbons was assigned to Upper Ferry to take Sr. Marie's place in the school, and M. Assumpta Veitch returned with the community of Holy Trinity Convent and stayed with the sisters for several weeks to provide encouragement and support at that difficult time. Strangely, and by a sad coincidence, M. Josepha Young, who wrote an account of the accident in the Annals of Holy Trinity Convent, was killed in a motor accident seven months later.[10] Subsequently, the Sisters of Mercy established a scholarship for the elementary school in memory of Sr. Marie Costello and a high-school scholarship in memory of Sr. M. Josepha Young.

By the end of the school year 1979–80, the Congregation of the Sisters of Mercy was beginning to suffer from a shortage of teachers. Accordingly, the General Council decided reluctantly that some convents would have to close. On May 4, 1980, the sisters posted a notice in the parish bulletin announcing that the sisters would be withdrawing from Upper Ferry. The announcement met with a flurry of protest. Nobody wanted to see the sisters leave, and for a while, the people had their way. Nevertheless, when school opened in September, for the first time since 1967 there was no sister-principal in Belanger Memorial High School. The writing was on the wall. Eventually, the decision could not be postponed any longer, and the announcement was made that the sisters would

---

9. At the time of writing, Sr. Monica Hickey is director of pastoral care at St. Patrick's Mercy Home.

10. M. Josepha Young died while returning to St. John's from the funeral of a relative on September 13, 1977. The car in which she was a passenger missed a turnoff to the Trans-Canada Highway and slammed into a ditch. M. Josepha was killed on impact. The driver, a friend of hers, was unhurt.

leave the Valley at the end of the school year. On awards night, June 18, 1981, the people of Codroy Valley presented a plaque to hang permanently in the corridor of Belanger Memorial High School: "Presented to the Sisters of Mercy by Belanger Memorial High School in recognition of their contribution to life in the Codroy Valley. 1967–81." The name of every sister who worked in the Valley was inscribed on the plaque—twenty-three sisters in all.

On June 21, 1981, the following note appeared in the parish bulletin:

> On behalf of all the Sisters of Mercy who have taught and worked in Codroy Valley since 1967, we wish to offer appreciation and gratitude to all the people of the Valley.
>
> The circumstances that have made it necessary for the Sisters to leave the Valley have been received with regret and disappointment.
>
> We feel sure we are speaking for all the Sisters, when we say that it has been a pleasure working with you. We have been enriched as individuals and as a Congregation by our interaction with you. For your strongly evident support we are grateful.
>
> We leave you now with a promise of prayer and a request for yours. With every blessing and good wish for the future,
>
> Yours sincerely,
> Sister Frances Gibbons, Sister Eileen Flynn,
> Sister Sheila O'Dea. [11]

The closure of Holy Trinity Convent left three convents remaining on the West Coast. In 1968, a year after the establishment of the convent in Upper Ferry, another priest, Father Hugh Cassidy from St. Fintan's on the West Coast, was knocking on the door of the mother house in St. John's looking for sisters to teach in the parish schools in St. Fintan's—a tiny settlement located beside Crabbes River on the west coast of the island of Newfoundland. It was known originally as Crabbes Station when an employee of the Newfoundland Railway made his home there. Later, some farmers moved into the area, and together with a few telegraph operators and land surveyors, they built a small community. When the sisters arrived in 1968, the economy was poor, the people finding

---

11. Annals, Holy Trinity Convent, Upper Ferry, ASMSJ.

only seasonal employment in fishing and cutting pulpwood for the paper mill at Corner Brook.[12]

Many of the first settlers of Crabbes Station were Roman Catholics. and in 1931, the parish of Sts. Teresa and Columcille was established and the settlement renamed St. Fintan's in honour of Bishop Michael Fintan Power, the former bishop of St. George's diocese. The new parish included Heatherton and Highlands, with St. Fintan's as the parish centre. There was, at first, no resident pastor, and until 1945, there were no roads or bridges. A priest from St. George's visited the parish periodically, travelling by dog team, horse, or train, and stopping off at various missions along the way to care for the spiritual needs of the people. The first resident priest in St. Fintan's was Rev. Leo Drake, who was appointed to the parish in 1945. When Fr. Drake arrived in St. Fintan's, he found that a church and school had been built some years before. However, because there was no parish house, his first task was to build a two-storey presbytery. In the next ten years, St. Fintan's was served by a succession of priests. A new and larger church was built in 1954. The first church was moved some distance from its original location and adapted to serve as a residence for teachers. Still later, in the early 1960s, a new central high school was built in St. Fintan's. Then, in 1966, Father Hugh Cassidy was appointed parish priest. A year later, Father Cassidy arrived at Mercy Convent with his request for the Sisters of Mercy and received a favourable response. When he was on his way home from St. John's, the small car that he was driving hit a moose and the young priest was killed instantly.

In spite of this tragedy, plans for the new foundation were confirmed by Father Cassidy's successor, Rev. P. J. Cooney, and M. Assumpta Veitch agreed to send four sisters to St. Fintan's in September 1968.[13] Father Cooney leased the presbytery to the Sisters of Mercy for use as a convent and began construction on a smaller house for himself. The former presbytery was named St. Hugh Convent in memory of Father Cassidy.

On August 28, 1968, the four founding sisters, Elsie Lahey (superior), Marcella Grant, Diane Smyth, and Mona Rumboldt, arrived at St. Fintan's.

---

12. ASMSJ, RG 10/26/9.
13. Father Cooney died four years later in June 1972.

When the sisters arrived in St. Fintan's, there were two schools in operation with a total enrolment of 225. The population of St. Fintan's itself was, at the time, about two hundred. However, children came from nearby settlements to attend the parish schools. The children from grades III to XI were taught in St. Jude Central High School; grades I and II attended classes in a smaller two-room building. In addition to the four sisters, there were six lay teachers. The schools were coeducational and, to a certain degree, inter-denominational, as children from other religious denominations attended the school.

A year after the sisters arrived in St. Fintan's, on October 15, 1969, classes were held for the first time in the new Cassidy Memorial Elementary School. The new school initially contained six classrooms and housed children from grades I to VI. However, it was not until October 28, 1970, that the new bishop of the St. George's diocese, Richard T. McGrath, arrived to bless the school. In honour of the occasion, over one hundred guests were present for dinner at the Canadian Legion Club in nearby settlement of Jeffrey's. Among those present was Mrs. Mary Cassidy, mother of Father Hugh Cassidy, the late pastor of St. Fintan's. Mrs. Cassidy had come from Ireland to be present for the dedication of the new school named in memory of her son.

In addition to the regular curriculum, music was introduced in both schools. Almost as soon as she arrived, Sr. Mona Rumboldt gathered groups of children together, and within weeks, there were several small choirs making music in the school. Another member of the community, Sr. Diane Smyth, supplied the piano accompaniments for school concerts. By the end of the year, the elementary schoolchildren were performing three-part arrangements of choruses for treble voices. After school hours, Sr. Diane provided piano instruction for several students who were interested in music. After their arrival in St. Fintan's, the sisters organized a choir for the parish church of Sts. Teresa and Columcille. In the mission parishes of the Highlands and Heatherton, they played the harmonium and led the singing at all the liturgical services.

Unfortunately, it was not always possible for the Mercy congregation to supply a music teacher in every school administered by the sisters. Nevertheless, the want of a music teacher did not deter the sisters from encouraging the children to develop poise and self-confidence. Therefore, when there was no music teacher in the school, they trained the children in choral speech. This proved to be a successful program, so much so that in 1970, Cassidy Elementary School registered its first entrants in the Kiwanis Music Festival in Corner Brook. Twenty pupils from grades IV and V competed successfully in the choral speech division.

In the years after the sisters came to St. Fintan's, there was a rather dramatic increase in the number of children attending the Roman Catholic schools. This came about when the Anglican school had closed because of a small enrolment and the inability to obtain qualified teachers. Consequently, Anglican children from grades V to XI attended the sisters' schools. Also, a few Anglican families with children in the lower grades decided to send their children to the Roman Catholic school for kindergarten to grade IV as well. In light of this, Cassidy Elementary School was enlarged to include an additional classroom and a resource centre (library and audiovisual materials).

Besides teaching in the schools, the sisters carried out the usual duties of visitation of the sick and elderly in their homes. They made a special effort to visit the homes of the schoolchildren, especially of those who were having problems in school. Then, to occupy their "spare" time, the sisters looked after the church building in all three parish centres, Heatherton, Highlands, and St. Fintan's.[14]

The period 1980 to 1994 was one of constant and rapid change. Declining economic opportunities forced a majority of the young people in the area of St. Fintan's to move to mainland Canada. This out-migration coupled with a low birth rate had a drastic effect on the number of children in the Bay St. George South region—the area that constituted the parish of Sts. Teresa and Columcille. Within the district the Integrated and Roman Catholic school boards each operated a primary-elementary school and a high school, with a total enrolment of approximately 450 children. Originally, the distances involved in travelling from one place to another made this duplication

---

14. The duties of sacristan included preparing the altar for mass, caring for altar linens and other items needed in the celebration of the sacraments, and seeing that the church premises were kept neat and clean.

of services a matter of necessity. However, the construction of a bridge over Crabbes River in the 1980s reduced driving time between the two school systems to ten or twelve minutes, and almost immediately, the possibility of shared, inter-denominational services among neighbouring settlements became a matter of discussion and debate.

On April 29, 1989, representatives of the Denominational Education Committee (DEC) met with local school board members, superintendents of education, and local representatives to explore the possibility of shared services in the area.[15] A few weeks later, the Bay St. George Roman Catholic School Board agreed to a system that would provide a kindergarten to grade VI school in St. Fintan's and a school for grades VII to XII in McKay's. However, at that time the Integrated board could not come to a similar agreement. Representatives from McKay's insisted that there should be one kindergarten to grade XII school in that community to serve the whole area. Obviously, representatives from other settlements would not accept this proposal and the RC board rejected it. Negotiations on shared services had reached a deadlock.[16]

For the next few months, meetings were held throughout all the settlements involved in the dispute over the location of the schools. Concerned parents, local school committees, joint committees, school boards, and representatives of the DEC vied with one another for meeting time and space. In some quarters, the issue was portrayed as a conflict of religion, Roman Catholic versus Protestant. Sr. Theresa Ryan, a member of the RC board, did not agree with this interpretation of the issue. She wrote, "Although there may have been nominal aspects of religious bigotry, the main bone of contention was community identity."[17] Small settlements did not want to lose their school, and the main concern, improved educational opportunities for children, was lost in the fray.

Meanwhile, the old high school in St. Fintan's was no longer fit for use and a tender had been awarded for a new one to be built. The contractor began

---

15. Sr. Theresa Ryan, "Shared Services, A New Beginning," ASMSJ, RG 20/27/29.
16. Ibid.
17. Ibid.

construction not knowing if the school eventually would be used by high-school or primary/elementary students. As well, the sight of ongoing construction in St. Fintan's added fuel to the fire of those who opposed the idea of shared services. In the spring of 1990, the DEC appointed a mediation team made up of representatives of the school boards, the parents, and educators. The team met in St. Fintan's parish house and received oral and written briefs from individuals and groups before preparing a final report which recommended shared services in a manner to be implemented by a joint decision of the Integrated and Roman Catholic school boards of the district.

After months of heated arguments, defeated motions, disrupted meetings, and shelved agendas, in June 1990, the Integrated board decided to accept shared services with a kindergarten to grade VI school in St. Fintan's and a grades VII to XII school in McKay's. This left very little time for the principals and teachers to prepare for the new system in September. Meanwhile, during all the time these discussions were taking place, the new school in St. Fintan's was taking shape!

The school year 1990–91 opened in a state of chaos in the Bay St. George South district. The new school in St. Fintan's, Cassidy Elementary, was not ready to accept students until late September. During that month, the sisters and the lay teachers spent their days organizing for students and curriculum, decorating classrooms and exploring the equipment of the new, modern facility. On the other side of Crabbe River, the walls of E. A. Butler High School (under the jurisdiction of the Integrated board) were bulging at the seams with an enrolment that had doubled since the students had left for summer holidays in June. Here, too, the opening of school had to be postponed for two weeks to allow the staff to decide on student placement and iron out some wrinkles in the curriculum. Srs. Esther Dalton and Dorothy Willcott, who were assigned to E. A. Butler High School, were the first Sisters of Mercy to hold a permanent teaching position in a school under the jurisdiction of the Integrated Board of Education. It was a period of constant adjustment and continual change. Sr. Dorothy described the frustration experienced by all the teachers in attempting to attend to 220 students in a school built to accommodate less than half that number. During the first year of shared services, an even more serious problem arose from the duplication of subject teachers and academic courses. Nevertheless, there was a conscious effort on the part of teachers, students, and parents to emphasize the long-term benefits of the educational system that was being initiated. In March, the school held a very successful "Spirit Week," an event that further cemented new friendships formed among the students from different settlements.

Meanwhile, on the other side of Crabbes River in St. Fintan's, Sr. Ann Willcott was dealing with problems at the new Cassidy Elementary School. The original building specifications had been for a building to accommodate Roman Catholic children. With the beginning of shared services, the school had to accommodate children from the former integrated school as well. Sr. Ann provided remedial teaching to children who were experiencing difficulties in reading, but the lack of space prevented her from giving the individual attention that many of the students needed. The fourth sister in the community of St. Hugh Convent was Theresa Ryan. In her role as pastoral assistant in the parish of Sts. Teresa and Columcille and member of the RC School Board for Bay St. George South, Theresa was an active participant in the educational debates. She fully supported the implementation of shared services, recognizing that it was the best educational and social system for the children of the area. Theresa argued that in addition to educational advantages, such a system would be a means of breaking down the barriers that existed among the communities. Unfortunately, her stand on shared services placed her in opposition to a small number of Roman Catholic parishioners who were reluctant to see their teenage sons and daughters attend the integrated school in McKay's. The whole story of the implementation of shared services between schools of different denominations was a sign of things to come, for a few years after these events, the provincial government abolished denominational education in Newfoundland.

The sisters continued to teach in both Cassidy Elementary and E. A. Butler High School, although as time passed, the Mercy congregation could provide only one sister for each school. Nevertheless, the sisters were instrumental in forming 4-H Clubs and Allied Youth Associations. Both organizations engage young people in after-school projects and activities and help build self-confidence, a sense of values, and a community spirit. In 1992, Sr. Alicia Linehan was appointed principal of Cassidy Elementary. She set to work immediately to encourage the involvement of teachers in developing goals and a mission statement for the school, and she reached out to the parents of the children, encouraging them to become active partners in their children's education. She did this through meetings, newsletters, and in-school participation. Hence, it was no surprise to anybody in the district of Bay St. George South when Sr. Alicia was nominated for the Fortis Educational Leadership Award. The citation read in part:

> The uniqueness of our shared services school brought with it many challenges and frustrations, many of which have been addressed since Sr. Alicia has been with us. Through her creative and understanding qualities she has brought teachers, parents, district office personnel and board officials together in a closer working relationship where all are considered equal partners. A true spirit of ecumenism is evident as the community shares in school religious celebrations, and the spiritual needs of teachers are met through liturgies at staff meetings.[18]

Sr. Alicia was not a principal who operated from behind a desk in her office. She was a participant—and usually the leader—in all the activities of the school. She was often seen playing the guitar for a group of children, cooking hamburgers, or out on the school grounds playing "Farmer in the Dell" with children in grade I. She took her turn doing "corridor duty," and she spent many hours counselling teachers and students. Furthermore, Sr. Alicia provided opportunities for the teachers to avail of personal and professional development programs. For example, she invited another Sister of Mercy, Irene Neville, to direct a workshop on the Myers-Briggs Personality Indicator as part of a program of staff development.

Throughout the years, an outstanding feature of the schools in St. Fintan's was the level of parental involvement. Parents were involved with the

---

18. Citation written on the occasion of Sister Alicia's nomination for the Fortis Educational Leadership Award by the Parent-Teachers Association of Cassidy Elementary School, St. Fintan's, ASMSJ, RG 10/27/34.

school lunch program, in classroom support for reading, in supervision of field trips and students' parties and dances, and with lamination and preparation of teaching aids. Each Christmas, some of the parents cooked a complete Christmas dinner for the students and staff of the school. For its part, the school provided several adult programs for parents. For example, Sr. Esther Dalton and school guidance counsellor, David Warren, offered Parent Effectiveness Workshops. A similar program was offered to parents of pre-schoolers. Pre-school sessions were offered twice a week from February to June to children who would be attending kindergarten in September. During the school year 1993–94, Sr. Alicia initiated what was called "The Fish Friends Program." The program involved conservation activities, a fish incubation unit, and a thorough study of the salmon through the stages of its life cycle. Children from the grade IV class placed the eggs in an incubator and later transplanted them in the original brook from which they came.

It came as something of a shock to the children, the teachers, and the whole population of St. Fintan's when Sr. Alicia announced that she was retiring from the teaching profession. Her retirement was precipitated by cutbacks in the field of education. This, coupled with a threat from government to cut benefits caused a large number of teachers to retire in protest before the conclusion of the school year. Nevertheless, although she retired officially in February 28, 1994, Sr. Alicia continued to work in the school until the end of the year, assisting the new lay principal, the teachers, and the children.

The departure of Sr. Alicia Linehan left only one Sister of Mercy in St. Fintan's, Esther Dalton. Rather than have Sr. Esther live alone in St. Fintan's, the congregation decided to close St. Hugh Convent in July 1994. Sr. Esther continued to teach in Cassidy Elementary School, commuting from her residence in Stephenville. In 1996, she was asked to share in prison ministry at the correctional centre in Stephenville, and with her departure, the ministry of the Sisters of Mercy to the people of St. Fintan's came to an end.

Three years after the establishment of the convent in St. Fintan's in 1968, the Sisters of Mercy agreed to another foundation, this time in Rushoon on the Burin Peninsula. Rushoon is a small fishing village located in a valley along the east side of Rushoon River and on both sides of a deep harbour where the river runs into Placentia Bay.[19] The village is about twenty miles north of Marystown, the largest town on the Burin Peninsula.

When the sisters arrived on August 27, 1971, the population of Rushoon was a little more than four hundred. The majority of the residents were Roman Catholics. Because work had not been completed on the house that was to be their home, the parish priest, Fr. Joseph Barbour, invited the sisters to stay at the presbytery, while he found accommodation elsewhere. Accordingly, for the first month, the sisters shared the priest's house with Mrs. Wylie, the housekeeper, and Father's two cats.

The four sisters who were assigned to the new mission were all under thirty-five years of age. Srs. Regina Cahill (superior) and Sheila O'Dea were attached to St. Paul's High School, where Sr. Regina had been appointed principal. Srs. Sylvia Doyle (principal) and Carmelita McDonald taught at St. Teresa's Elementary. At the time of the sisters' arrival, the high school had an enrolment of one hundred and five, while eighty-seven children attended the elementary school. Both schools were coeducational.

The first big celebration after the sisters' arrival took place on September 24, the feast of Our Lady of Mercy. In the presence of the entire village, the sisters renewed their vows at mass in the parish church. Three days later, they moved into what was called the sisters' residence. The house was owned by Christ the King Parish in Rushoon and leased by the Congregation of the Sisters of Mercy. As they entered their new home and looked around, their first impression was one of emptiness for the furniture had not arrived from St. John's. Furthermore, the waterline had not been connected, so for the first week, the sisters and some of the boys from the school carried water from the presbytery in buckets, pots, and pans.

Not long after they were comfortably settled in their new home, the sisters received news that Father Barbour was being transferred to Mount Carmel, Salmonier. The people and the sisters were deeply disappointed at the prospect of losing this young priest who had all sorts of practical ideas for the

---

19. *ENL*, s.v. "Rushoon."

development of the parish and who possessed the energy and dedication to see his plans come to fruition. Nevertheless, when the new pastor Father Hubert (Bert) Whelan arrived, he received a warm welcome, and within a few weeks, with his warm, friendly manner and down-to-earth approach to parish matters, he won the affection and confidence of all the people of the parish. Father Whelan welcomed the assistance of the sisters and especially their attention to the sick and shut-ins. The neighbouring village of Parker's Cove, located about five miles from Rushoon, was one of the missions of Christ the King Parish. As a rule, the sisters accompanied the priest on his visits to Parker's Cove to celebrate mass. This custom was the reason their first Christmas in Rushoon was unlike any other they had experienced as religious. Since the day when they had been accepted as postulants at Littledale, the sisters had spent Christmas Day quietly in the convent, receiving visits from members of their families for an hour or so in the afternoon. On Christmas Day, 1971, they attended mass in Rushoon at nine o'clock in the morning and then went to Parker's Cove to assist at a second mass, celebrated at ten o'clock. After that they were invited to a five-course lunch by an immigrant family from the Philippines who lived in Parker's Cove. They finished the day by joining Father Whelan for dinner at the presbytery. Apparently, quiet Christmases at home in the convent were to be a thing of the past.

The New Year of 1972 brought its share of hardship to the four young foundresses in Rushoon. Early in January, a fierce winter blizzard caused a break in the power lines that serviced that area of the Burin Peninsula. The sisters depended on electricity to heat the house. The power outage meant that they had no heat at all and no means of obtaining hot food or water. As they shivered in the cold, one of their neighbours came to the rescue. He brought them to his own home, served them hot breakfast and invited them to spend the day around his blazing wood fire. Later on that evening, when the sisters returned to their cold residence, they were warmed not only by hot cocoa and a thermos of boiling water but by the kindness and concern shown by Mr. Norman and his family. When they discovered that it would be another day before the power lines could be repaired, the sisters decided to pack up and go to the convent in Marystown until the electricity was restored in Rushoon. But their troubles were not over. A few days later, they attended a meeting of the school board to plan for a new high school and a new elementary school in the area. During their absence from the residence, the pipes froze so that when they returned home, they discovered that there was no water. The resourceful four gathered a few pots and pans and collected some of the clean white snow near the river. With the melted snow they washed some potatoes and put them on to boil for dinner. About ten minutes later, the lights went out and they were left with half-cooked potatoes and some bread and cheese for their evening meal. And the troubles continued! During the month of January, the sisters had to bring water from the presbytery for drinking and from the river for washing. When the river was frozen—which was most of the time—they cut a hole through the ice with an axe. The plumbers worked on the pipes for a week in an attempt to clear them but were unsuccessful. Early in February, Father Whelan connected an overground pipe to his well. To the delight of the sisters, water started to flow freely into the residence—for all of five minutes! Then the power was cut off once again. Schools were closed the next day because of a heavy storm with high winds and drifting snow. The sisters waded through snow that was up to their waists in order to fetch water from the presbytery. During the next two months until the end of March, episodes of frozen pipes, no water, no light, and no heat occurred with distressing frequency. To add to their discomfort, the sisters were visited by an unwelcome guest whom they named Jasper. A large river rat, Jasper made his first appearance toward the end of February. For a week, the sisters put all sorts of temptation in his way in an attempt to coax him into the large trap placed strategically behind the pantry door. Finally, on February 27, 1972, the annalist reported, "Jasper the rat—deceased."

The sisters in Rushoon greeted the coming of spring with a collective sigh of relief. Although they continued to experience occasional power outages, they did not have to deal with frozen pipes. Furthermore, they were busy preparing for the elementary school concert. Prior to the coming of the sisters, it had been the custom in Rushoon for the whole family to attend the school concerts. Since, for the people of Rushoon, "family" included just about everyone in the community, including infants, the concerts suffered from frequent and noisy interruptions. To avoid such competition with the performers on the night of the concert, the sisters decided to have a matinee and invite all small children, especially infants, to attend. As a result, the matinee ended up as a wailing contest, and although no prizes were awarded to the infant who howled loudest and longest, everyone enjoyed what they could hear of the concert.

Early in January 1974, Father Whelan became very ill, and the parish of Christ the King was left without a priest for several months. At the end of February, Archbishop Skinner commissioned Sr. Regina Cahill to be "Extraordinary Minister of the Eucharist" for the parish.[20] This was a break with tradition and a matter of wonder and congratulation in the parish, for the practice of designating "Extraordinary Ministers of Communion" was still a novelty in the Roman Catholic Church. During that same month, Sr. Regina was appointed to "Project Overseas" to work on the team chosen to go to Ethiopia. The project was sponsored by the Canadian Teachers' Association in conjunction with the Newfoundland Teachers' Association. Sr. Regina was the first sister from Newfoundland to be chosen for such a project.

In May 1974, the archbishop's office announced that Father Bert Whelan was to be replaced by Rev. Gerard Whitty. Although people were sorry to see Father Whelan leave the peninsula, they realized that his health was not strong enough to allow him to continue his ministry to many of the more remote parts of the parish that were accessible only by boat. Thus, news that a younger priest had been appointed was greeted with a good deal of excitement. The new pastor, Fr. Whitty, took a personal interest in all the schools in his far-flung parish. He persuaded Sr. Regina Cahill to go with him to visit the schools in South East Bight and Petit Fort to prepare the students for the sacrament of confirmation. Sr. Regina, who grew up on Bell Island and was no stranger to the discomforts of travel by boat, was the best equipped among the little community to accompany Father on these excursions.

---

20. The title, "Extraordinary Minister of the Eucharist" was applied to a person other than a cleric in Holy Orders who had been appointed by the bishop of a diocese to distribute Holy Communion and bring Holy Viaticum to the dying. The practice of permitting lay Catholics to distribute Communion is quite common today, but in the 1970s only in cases of emergency, when no priest was available, did the bishops issue such permission.

However, the little community of sisters in Rushoon had just settled down to work for the school year 1974–75, when Sr. Alice Wilson became ill. Early in November, she was admitted to St. Clare's Mercy Hospital for surgery. A week later, the sisters were informed that her condition was serious. All through the winter, Alice's health deteriorated, and she died on May 2, 1975 at the age of thirty-one. Furthermore, on March 17, 1975, Sr. Regina Cahill was admitted to St. Clare's Mercy Hospital with malaria that she contracted during the previous summer while working in Ethopia. Sr. Regina spent five weeks in the hospital before returning to Rushoon to complete the school year. The two remaining sisters in Rushoon, Frances Flynn and Barbara Kenny, carried on their work in the elementary school and the parish. Their duties often required that one or the other had to stay alone in the convent, especially during the winter months when snowstorms marooned one or the other in Marystown or St. John's. The superior general, Marie Michael Power, was aware of the difficulties that were being experienced by the sisters in Rushoon. She was concerned, too, for Sr. Regina's health, and for that reason, Sr. Regina was replaced by Sr. Esther Dalton for the new school year beginning in September 1975. Sr. Irene Kennedy was the second sister assigned to St. Paul's High School, while the staff of St. Teresa's Elementary remained unchanged.

Meanwhile, Sr. Frances Flynn, the principal of the elementary school, had big plans for the children. She decided that in place of the usual school concerts that consisted of a few songs and recitations, the children would take part in operettas. Operettas had the advantage of combining signing, dancing, acting, and speech—all necessary accomplishments—and in addition, provided plenty of challenge for participants, teachers, and the parents who were expected to do their part inventing appropriate costumes. Happily, the operettas were a great success and set a new standard of performance for the schoolchildren of Rushoon.

By this time, the trend toward centralization and shared services had reached the Burin Peninsula. St. Paul's High School and St. Teresa's Elementary in Rushoon and also St. Jude's Elementary in Parker's Cove were all vacated, and the children came together with students from Baine Harbour Integrated

High School in a new building at Baine Harbour Junction. The new school, Christ the King All-Grade School, was opened September 6, 1977, with an enrolment of 315 children. The increased number of students made it possible for the first time for several new subjects to be introduced into the curriculum on a regular basis: physical education, music, home economics, and industrial arts. The staff consisted of fifteen teachers.

The year 1980 brought a new adventure for the children of Rushoon, for on May 16, 1980, Srs. Juanita Broderick and Veronica Lidster left with a group of students for a five-day tour of Quebec. This was the first time the school had sponsored an inter-provincial tour. Then, two years later, the same two sisters travelled with twenty students for a week-long tour of the same province. In September 1981, Sr. Margaret Pittman was named principal of Christ the King All-Grade School. She held this position until June 1988, when she was granted a year's leave of absence for reasons of health. Sr. Margaret returned to Rushoon the following year but not to the schools, for she had decided to take an early retirement from teaching. By that time, the congregation had no sister to replace her in administration and for this reason, the Sisters of Mercy relinquished the position of principal of Christ the King All-Grade School in June 1989. Thus, Sr. Margaret Pittman was the last sister-principal in Rushoon.

However, the sisters remained in the school as classroom teachers. The former principal of St. Teresa's Elementary School in Rushoon, Sr. Frances Flynn, was reassigned to the community in Rushoon and taught in the school from 1990 to 1995.[21] When Frances was transferred in 1995, to all appearances, it seemed that the teaching ministry of the Sisters of Mercy in Rushoon had come to an end. Sr. Cecilia Lambe, who retired from teaching in June 1992, was appointed pastoral assistant in the parish of Christ the King, and for a few years, Cecilia lived alone in the sisters' residence in Rushoon. In September 1997, Sr. Margaret Taylor, who had been teaching in Labrador, was forced to take a period of sick leave from teaching. She was invited to go to Rushoon for a period of rest and relaxation and to provide company for Sr. Cecilia. In 1997, her health restored, Sr. Margaret was assigned to Christ the

---

21. Sr. Frances Flynn was principal of St. Teresa's Elementary School in Rushoon from 1972–77.

King All-Grade School where she worked as a classroom teacher until she retired in June 2001. She was the last sister to teach in the school in Rushoon.

Since September 2001, and until her unexpected death in May 2004, Sr. Cecilia Lambe had been living alone in Rushoon. However, after the sisters had retired from teaching, the school board for the district decided to sell the house that the Congregation of the Sisters of Mercy had rented since 1971. Sr. Cecilia began immediately to look around for a place to live. She was fortunate in finding a small bungalow in Rushoon that the owner was eager to rent.

For a number of years, Rushoon has not had a resident priest. At the time of writing, the pastor of Christ the King Parish lives in St. John's and drives to Rushoon to celebrate weekend masses and any funeral services that may be required. For the rest, the people depended on Sr. Cecilia to provide liturgy of the word, Holy Communion, sacramental preparation, and visitation of the sick and the dying. Sr. Cecilia's duties brought her to outlying places such as Parker's Cove, South East Bight, and Petit Fort. Fortunately, a road to Petit Fort was built in the 1990s, and although the road is not paved, the journey by car was infinitely preferable to travelling by means of a small boat on the often stormy waters of Placentia Bay. Although Sr. Cecilia lived alone for most of the year, she was happy and satisfied with her lot. She knew that she had an important role to play in the life of the people of Christ the King Parish and its missions, not only through her active ministry, but simply by her quiet, gentle presence among the people. Early in May 2004, Sr. Cecilia was admitted to the Burin Health Care Centre for surgery. As a result of complications, she was transferred to the Health Sciences Centre in St. John's where she died a few days later. The outpouring of grief when the news reached Rushoon was witness to the affection and esteem in which Sr. Cecilia Lambe was held by the people of the parish.

For a short time the parish of Christ the King was left without the services of a pastoral assistant. However, in September 2004, Sr. Barbara Kenny volunteered for ministry in Rushoon. For the first few months, Sr. Barbara lived with the community at Holy Name of Mary Convent in Marystown, but at the time of writing she is living in a rented house in Rushoon, where she carries on the ministry so generously and selflessly provided by Sr. Cecilia Lambe.

Still, the work goes on. Over the course of the years, the spiritual needs of people in isolated parishes like Rushoon became a matter of concern, especially in light of a shortage of ordained priests. The Sisters of Mercy responded, and this response saw the beginning of ministries that require a sister to move to a settlement where she lives and works without the companionship of other members of the congregation. For instance, on December 1, 2001, Sr. Maureen Lawlor, who had been pastoral assistant in the Basilica Parish, was appointed pastoral minister of St. Joseph's Parish, Lamaline.

A small outport at the foot of the Burin Peninsula, Lamaline is about twenty miles west of St. Lawrence.[22] The fishery was the main source of employment until the decline of the cod stocks in the mid-1980s forced people to seek work in neighbouring communities.

Sr. Maureen works closely with the pastor of St. Thomas Aquinas Parish in St. Lawrence, Father Francis Puddister, who is the canonical administrator of St. Joseph's Parish, Lamaline. The priest is available to celebrate mass and the sacrament of reconciliation on weekends. Except when mass is celebrated, Maureen conducts all other liturgical celebrations in the parish, including weddings and funeral rites. Preparation for the reception of the sacraments by children and adults forms a major part of her work, but she spends many hours visiting the homes of the sick and elderly. In times of anxiety or bereavement, Sr. Maureen's presence provides a measure of comfort and consolation for families. Although she lives alone in what was once the local presbytery, Sr. Maureen's days are too full to allow her to experience loneliness. Furthermore, the sisters in Marystown are within easy driving distance, and Sr. Lucia Walsh in St. Lawrence claims that her kettle is always at boiling point to provide the "good cup of tea" recommended by Catherine McAuley.

Another Sister of Mercy who enjoys the cup of tea and assorted goodies supplied by Sr. Lucia in St. Lawrence is Sr. Nellie Pomroy, who works as pastoral minister in Terrenceville, a small settlement on the western shore of the

---

22. The name may be a corruption of the French, *La Maligne*, a term that may refer to the dangerous shoals and small islands at the entrance to the harbour. See *ENL*, s.v. "Lamaline."

Burin Peninsula. This is a relatively new ministry for Sr. Nellie, who spent most of her life in education as classroom teacher, university professor, and administrator. Elected to the Leadership Team of the Sisters of Mercy, she was a member of three different administrations. When her term of office had expired, Sr. Nellie offered to serve in one of the more remote parishes of the Archdiocese of St. John's.

Since she moved to Terrenceville in 2002, Sr. Nellie has become involved with every facet of parish life, including liturgical music. Her musical activities are worthy of mention, for as every Sister of Mercy in Newfoundland knows, Nellie recognizes the sound of the national anthem only when the people around her rise to their feet. Characteristically, this handicap proved to be an incentive rather than an obstacle to Sr. Nellie. She was determined to form a choir to provide music for all the liturgies celebrated in the parish. Sr. Rosemary Ryan agreed to arrange a liturgical music workshop for Terrenceville's future music ministers.

On the appointed day, Sr. Nellie and her aspiring musicians arrived at McAuley Convent in St. John's to attend the workshop that had been planned by three sisters from the community. Sr. Sheila Grant led a discussion on the selection of appropriate music for various liturgical functions and seasons. Sr. Rosemary Ryan instructed on correct methods of providing guitar accompaniment to the music of the mass and other liturgical celebrations. Finally, Sr. Georgina Quick directed a session on the topic of "deportment." Sr. Georgina's lecture came as something of a shock to the teenagers from Terrenceville. Sr. Georgina began with the basics. They were told that once mass began there was to be no talking, no giggling, no chewing gum. "You cannot sing and chew gum at the same time," announced Sr. Georgina—a statement received by her audience with polite incredulity. However, when the session concluded, everyone agreed that it had been a valuable learning experience. The group returned to Terrenceville, determined to put into practice all they had learned in St. John's.

Back in Terrenceville, Sr. Nellie encouraged some adults to join the music ministry. Eventually, natural talent, along with Sr. Rosemary Ryan's help and Nellie's encouragement produced results beyond anyone's expectations.

Consequently, liturgies celebrated in the little Catholic church in Terrenceville are alive with the sound of vibrant young voices. All of which goes to show that one does not need a degree in music to form a parish choir.

The formation of the choir is but one of the many ways in which Sr. Nellie Pomroy has brought new life to Terrenceville. Her enthusiasm is contagious. As she carries out the duties of a pastoral minister, the people respond to her efforts with co-operation and appreciation.

And so, day after day, in many outports of Newfoundland and Labrador a Sister of Mercy may be found bringing God's message of love and compassion to people in a tiny area of an isolated province in the large expanse of Canada.

CHAPTER TWENTY-FOUR

MERCY MOVES NORTH

Have you entered the storehouse of the snow?

Job 38:22

During the general chapter of 1973, the plight of Roman Catholics in Labrador received some discussion, but no action was taken at that time. However, at the request of the Extension Department of Memorial University, in 1980, M. Williamina Hogan went to Goose Bay, Labrador, where she conducted classes in second and third year English during the winter semester. In 1981, Sr. Edward Mary Roche went to Goose Bay to teach university courses in religious education during the spring semester.[1]

Meanwhile, Bishop Peter Sutton, OMI, bishop of Labrador City-Schefferville, and the Roman Catholic School Board for Labrador were eager to ensure some stability in the teaching personnel of the school in Black Tickle, a rocky little island off the southeast coast of Labrador. This remote fishing village is about a 180 miles southeast of Goose Bay and is home to about 200 people. The rock is black and barren, and except for a few months during the summer, the island is surrounded by ice. In 1967, a

---

1. Hogan, *Pathways*, p. 408.

806

new centennial school replaced a little one-room schoolhouse.[2] The largest building for miles around, the new school, operated by the Labrador Roman Catholic School Board, measured sixty feet by forty feet. After its completion, the school became the cultural centre, recreation facility, dance hall, chapel, and residence for any priest who happened to pay a visit to the island.

For a number of years, it had been difficult to induce teachers to remain in Black Tickle, not only because of its isolation, but also in view of the harsh living conditions experienced on the rocky little island where, at the time of the sisters' arrival, running water meant, "Get a bucket and run for it!" Bishop Peter Sutton urged the superior general of the Sisters of Mercy, Sr. Patricia Maher, to consider sending sisters to this lonely little outpost where the people were in such great need of education and faith development. Sr. Patricia listened sympathetically to Bishop Sutton's woes and promised to do her best to address the problems he had presented to her. In January 1984, Sr. Patricia and Sr. Marion Collins visited the towns and coastal communities in Labrador to assess the needs of the area. On their return, they presented their findings to the entire General Council, and the decision was made to send two sisters to Black Tickle. Consequently, in August 1984, Srs. Charlotte Fitzpatrick and Verna Aucoin were appointed to the mission.

On August 26, 1984, Srs. Charlotte and Verna left St. John's airport for the first permanent mission of the Sisters of Mercy in Labrador. They spent three days in Happy Valley-Goose Bay, where Bishop Sutton met with the priests, religious brothers, and sisters who were working on the Labrador coast. On August 29, they boarded a small plane, accompanied by Sheila Sullivan who was assigned to Black Tickle by the RC board.[3] An Oblate priest,

---

2. The year 1967 marked the centenary of the Canadian Confederation. Newfoundland, however, did not become part of this Confederation until 1949 when, by a very narrow margin, Newfoundlanders voted to become a province of Canada.

3. Sheila Sullivan had been a member of the first group of sisters to be assigned to Upper Ferry. Subsequently, she left the Congregation of the Sisters of Mercy and since that time she has been working in various parts of Labrador.

Fr. Oliver Rich, went along to introduce the sisters to the people of Black Tickle. As they approached the island, they could see a small group of people gathered on the rocks near the floating dock. One of the two trucks on the island brought the newcomers and their luggage to the Mission House, which was to be the home of the Sisters of Mercy in Black Tickle for almost twenty years.

Because the Mission House had been vacant for some time, the first task of the two sisters was to roll up their sleeves, find a couple of scrubbing brushes and get to work. As they scrubbed, they may have reflected on a passage in Lewis Carroll's *Through the Looking Glass*:

> "If seven maids with seven mops
> Swept it for half a year,
> Do you suppose," the Walrus said,
> "That they could get it clear?"
> "I doubt it," said the Carpenter,
> And shed a bitter tear.[4]

Water was scarce at the best of times, but that summer, very little rain had fallen in the area so the sisters had to be content with the contents of only one small bucket. However, with the assistance of a full bottle of Mr. Clean and the expenditure of plenty of kinetic energy, in a couple of hours their new home, if not up to usual convent standards, was passable. The following Sunday, they presented themselves in church, their rubber boots—standard footwear in Black Tickle—an incongruous accessory to the religious habit.

The school year began with mass celebrated in the church. Before the service began, Sr. Verna gathered the children for a short practice of the music that was to be sung during the liturgy. It was the beginning of regular classes in singing held in the school. Initially, the repertoire consisted of "If You're Happy and You Know It," "Jack Was Every Inch a Sailor," and other

---

4. Lewis Carroll, "The Walrus and the Carpenter," in chap. 4 in *Through the Looking Glass* (Berkley: First Publications, 1990).

Newfoundland folk songs. However, in between spirited renditions of "We'll Rant and We'll Roar Like True Newfoundlanders," Verna managed to prepare a few hymns for the Sunday's liturgy. Even though the school enrolment was small, totalling sixty students from grades I to grade IX, the teachers worked hard. The sisters soon discovered that the children of Black Tickle were, for the most part, intelligent and keen to learn. However, prior to the arrival of the sisters, for a variety of reasons, the teachers assigned to Black Tickle were unable to complete the school year. Thus, through no fault of their own, a majority of the children needed individual help to complete the requirements of their respective grades. In addition to the two Sisters of Mercy there were three lay teachers—two of whom were teaching for the first time. Because the classes were small, two grades were taught in every room up to grade VI. Grades VII, VIII and IX were accommodated in one room. This was a difficult task because, even within each grade, students were at different levels of learning.

Strangely enough, in spite of the isolation of Black Tickle, the sisters had a number of visitors during their first few months in the north. It seemed that people were constantly coming and going from the mainland to the island. These included government officials, school-board personnel, social workers, and the Royal Canadian Mounted Police. Brother Norman, an Oblate from Montreal, and Ray Bernatchez, a carpenter hired by the Oblates, were working on the church, and they, with the pastor, Father Ollie Rich, OMI, joined the sisters for meals every day. At the same time, the men were building an extension to the sisters' house to provide an extra bedroom, a chapel, and some storage space.

The shortage of water was a situation that required very careful and strategic planning. For instance, two weeks after the arrival of the sisters, a company that was building an airstrip on the island drilled a well for the use of its employees. The company offered the sisters the use of the laundry and showers. In a letter home, Sr. Charlotte described their first visit to the construction site:

> It was a cold, rainy day as we took off around the harbour, drag-
> ging garbage bags full of laundry, since practically everything we
> owned needed to be washed. While our clothes were washing,
> we took showers. Facilities were somewhat rudimentary and
> conditions weren't exactly convent-clean, since it was a men's
> construction camp. To avoid stepping on the muddy floor, we had
> to step gingerly from the shower into our rubber boots which
> we had placed strategically nearby. To relieve the tedium
> between wash cycles, we went to the cookhouse where Bill, the
> cook, treated us to tea and raisin buns. It was a most interesting
> and rewarding day, for even though our water supply was bog
> water, it was wet and hot, and our bodies and spirits were
> refreshed.[5]

A few weeks later, a milestone was reached when Brother Norman pumped water from a nearby well into a holding tank in the basement of the sisters' house. The sisters were fortunate in having the support of an old friend and colleague, Sheila Sullivan. Sheila's presence was invaluable to Sr. Charlotte and Verna while they were becoming accustomed to life in the north and, indeed, for the duration of their ministry in Labrador.

There were many challenges facing the sisters during that first year in Black Tickle, not the least of which was the poverty they witnessed. Sr. Madonna Gatherall, a member of the General Council of the Sisters of Mercy, visited the mission in December and wrote of her experiences:

> You will be happy to know, though, that our Sisters visit the fam-
> ilies in the village as often as possible, assist them and are pres-
> ent to them in many ways. I could not help but notice their com-
> passionate concern for these people . . .
> Our mission in Black Tickle in not easy. One must cope
> with isolation, severe cold (combined with strong wind), lack of
> water, not to mention the expected frustrations of teaching stu-
> dents about two grades behind the normal level.[6]

---

5. Sr. Charlotte Fitzpatrick to Sr. Patricia Maher and sisters, September 18, 1984, ASMSJ, RG 10/28/23.

6. Sr. Madonna Gatherall, "Visit to Black Tickle, Labrador," in "Mercy Memo," December 1985. ASMSJ, RG 10/28/19.

During the sisters' second year in Black Tickle, they were joined by one
of the novices, Eileen Penney. Eileen had been assigned to the mission for the
six-week ministry experience that had become part of the formation program
in the congregation. Eileen was a nursing student, and the posting to Black
Tickle provided her with the opportunity to work with the two nurses who
were stationed in Black Tickle.

Meanwhile, the bishop of Labrador City-Schefferville, Bishop Peter
Sutton, had been actively lobbying various levels of government on behalf of
this neglected little island off the coast of Labrador. As a result of the bishop's
efforts, the government began to take action to improve living conditions in
Black Tickle. In April 1987, Sr. Charlotte reported in "Mercy Memo":

> The Mercy Mission in Black Tickle is now in its third year.... Quite
> a lot of changes have occurred ... as Black Tickle gradually mod-
> ernizes. Since our arrival in August, 1984, Black Tickle can boast of
> an airstrip, three street lights, a weekly garbage collection, a new
> Grenfell clinic, two privately owned TV dishes, and a new store
> (with ten second-hand shopping carts—would you believe!).
> Gone are the days of the floating dock and scrambling up flakes
> and stages. Gone are the days of burning your own garbage in the
> landwash and singeing your eyebrows in the bargain.[7]

At a more personal level, the sisters now had the advantage of a fairly
secure supply of water. Their first attempt at obtaining a supply of this necessary commodity was to set up a system for collecting rainwater. This served
fairly well except when there was no rain for several consecutive days. But all
the time, Brother Norman Peladeau, OMI, who worked on the house extension, insisted that the abandoned artesian well near the house should be able to
produce enough water for their use. After two attempts to dynamite the well,
which was 204 feet deep, the water broke free in October 1985. Little did the
sisters realize at the time that they would have to drain the well every day for
twelve months before the water was fit for use.

---

7. Sr. Charlotte Fitzpatrick, "Mercy Memo," April 1984, p. 3, ASMSJ, RG 10/ 28/16.

School life in Black Tickle presented a constant challenge. Although the sisters found the children very friendly, it was difficult to hold their interest in scholastic matters. This is not to suggest that there were no academic achievements in Black Tickle. For example, in 1986, the students participated in a provincial "readathon" and won an Atari computer for the best overall average of books read and money collected. Through the sponsorship of the International Grenfell Association, the sisters arranged a trip to St. John's for the students of grades VIII and IX. For most of these children, it was the first time they had been on the island of Newfoundland, and they marvelled at the sights and sounds of St. John's. The experiences of riding the escalators in the shopping malls and the sight of so much merchandise on display in the shops were occasions of wonder and amazement. For their part, the children were uniformly friendly and polite—a credit to their parents and to the school.

However, not all the children in Black Tickle were models of good behaviour. One morning, Sr. Charlotte went to open the school and discovered that there had been a break-in during the night. She called the RCMP detachment in Cartwright. The Mounties arrived by boat the following day and began their investigation. It was not long before they had identified the culprit and handed him over to Sr. Charlotte. This was punishment, indeed, for since her arrival in Black Tickle, the children had idolized this gentle but firm young sister and worked hard to win her approval. In a few well-chosen words, Charlotte pointed out to the young man the seriousness of the offence and the inconvenience and expense resulting from his actions and then pronounced "sentence." The unfortunate youth was to spend the next few weeks cleaning up the mess and repairing the damage he had caused. Obviously, Charlotte believed in making the punishment fit the crime! Happily, he learned from his experience and developed into a model student.

There was a change of personnel in Black Tickle in June 1988. Sr. Verna Aucoin left for a year's study in Toronto and was replaced by Sr. Margaret (Margie) Taylor.[8] Then, during the general chapter of 1989, Sr. Charlotte

8. Subsequently, in 1991, Sr. Verna Aucoin was assigned to the mission in Peru. See chapter twenty-two.

Fitzpatrick was elected to the General Council of the Sisters of Mercy. Reluctantly, Sr. Charlotte said goodbye to the people of Black Tickle and returned to St. John's in June 1989. Sr. Ellen Marie Sullivan replaced Sr. Charlotte as principal of St. Peter's School.

In 1989, during Sr. Ellen Marie Sullivan's tenure as principal of St. Peter's, the provincial Department of Environment and Lands, in conjunction with the Newfoundland and Labrador Women's Institutes, established an annual Environmental Awards Program. A selection committee made up of specialists in the environmental field chose the winners in the five designated categories. In the youth category, members of the Challenge '89 Youth Group of Black Tickle were selected for work in promoting a clean and healthy environment in their community. Two grade X and two grade XI students, with Sr. Margie Taylor, accepted the award. This, and similar achievements by the students of St. Peter's School, demonstrated to educational authorities the ability of these children to participate on an equal footing with pupils anywhere in Newfoundland. All that was needed was the provision of dedicated teachers and adequate school facilities and equipment. Consequently, the school board for Labrador decided to build an extension to the existing school.

In June 1989, Sr. Ellen Marie, having completed her assignment as principal of St. Peter's School, decided to take a year's sabbatical leave. Sr. Margie Taylor was appointed to replace her as principal, and Sr. Barbara Kenny was asked to move to Black Tickle and take over Sr. Margie's position as classroom teacher in St. Peter's School. Meanwhile, the blessing of the new extension to the school was scheduled to coincide with the first high-school graduation to be held in the remote little island community. This took place on May 17 and 18, 1990. Sr. Rosemary Ryan represented the General Council of the Sisters of Mercy at the celebrations. Later she wrote of her visit:

> My six-day visit began on the morning of May 16 with a ninety-minute flight on Labrador Air from Goose Bay to Black Tickle followed by a twelve-minute skidoo ride from the airstrip over the barrens of the island ... and into Black Tickle. Sr. Margie Taylor, my driver, gave orders to hold on tightly and lean in the direction she leaned, and I followed orders obediently. In some places we drove

over ten feet of snow but we scraped over rocks and splashed
through bog and mud in others. Despite it all, I arrived safely and
in one piece.[9]

The next day, five invited guests arrived by skidoo. Each visitor represented a unit in the educational structure of the province. In addition to these
guests, three intruders from the north arrived to investigate the unusual events
in Black Tickle. Apparently the three, a family of polar bears, merely wanted
to keep an eye on things, for they contented themselves with prowling around
on a point of land near the sea and posed no threat to anybody attending the
festivities.

Meanwhile, during the late 1980s, the Canadian government had established a new program, "Stay in School." Sr. Margie Taylor greeted this news
with enthusiastic relief. She saw that participation in such a project would help
to address some of the educational problems of Black Tickle. Under Margie's
leadership, the staff of St. Peter's School studied ways of participating in the
project. As a result of many meetings and much discussion, the school drafted
a proposal that outlined a comprehensive program of intervention to reduce
the incidence of school dropouts and increase the number of high-school graduates. Subsequently, with the support of the local service district of Black
Tickle and the Roman Catholic School Board, St. Peter's School submitted this
proposal to the federal government. In September 1991, Sr. Margie received
word that the proposal had been accepted. Subsequently, the school received a
grant of $35,000 that was used for tutoring services and adult education pro-
grams offered in the school.[10]

In spite of the improvements that had taken place since the arrival of the
sisters in Black Tickle, they found it wise to prepare for the unexpected. As the
year 1992 began, Black Tickle experienced some of the coldest temperatures
on record for that region, with average temperatures of minus twenty-five or
thirty degrees celsius. The water supply to the school was frozen solid, and
water had to be hauled by skidoo, an uncomfortable and time-consuming

9. Sr. Rosemary Ryan, *The Monitor*, June 1990, p. 34.
10. ASMSJ, RG 10/28/48.

occupation. Furthermore, the main well on the island showed signs of failing, and as a result, water was in short supply. Due to the poor water conditions, various epidemics of sickness broke out on the island, and during their few precious free moments after school, the sisters visited the sick and did what they could to alleviate the distress experienced in many homes on the island.

Nevertheless, despite weather, water, and winter, the school community maintained a lively and spirited atmosphere. In addition to regular classes, the children were offered a number of extracurricular activities such as guitar lessons, tap dancing, computer studies, arts and crafts, and various sports activities. Adult education classes, youth group activities, and choir practices were available also to those interested, and there was no shortage of participants in these activities.

In February 1992, everyone in the little community took part in the Grenfell Centennial Celebrations, an event held to commemorate the achievements of Dr. Wilfred Grenfell. For many years in the early part of the twentieth century, Grenfell had worked for the people of northern Newfoundland and Labrador, establishing hospitals to serve the medical needs of people in these remote areas. Black Tickle was the site where Dr. Grenfell dropped anchor when his ship arrived in Labrador.[11] Consequently, the celebrations held special significance for the people of the island. The opening ceremonies included a parade of flags, prayers, and greetings from various organizations. Sr. Barbara Kenny's poem in honour of Dr. Grenfell was read, the ribbon was cut by the ninety-two year old Alex Turnbull, and the festivities began. The day consisted of games, including soccer—a sport introduced by Dr. Grenfell—dogsled races, and other types of winter sports. In the evening, the staff of the medical clinic prepared a potluck supper for the community. This was followed by a movie on the life of Dr. Grenfell, a short skit performed by the staff of the clinic, and the presentation of awards during which Sr. Barbara received a medal for first place in the poetry contest! None of this would be very important from the point of view of the historian except that it illustrated the close

---

11. Srs. Barbara Kenny and Margaret Taylor, "Bits and Bytes from Black Tickle," ASMSJ, RG 10/28/46.

ties the sisters had formed with the people they served in Black Tickle. This was true, not only of Black Tickle, but also of all the places where the Sisters of Mercy lived and worked.

A few days after the celebrations, winter struck Black Tickle with a fury that the sisters had not experienced since their arrival. The wind, at eighty-five miles an hour, shifted a plane that had been anchored down with two drums of oil. Early on Sunday morning, the electricity was cut off, and for three days, the sisters depended on a small kerosene heater. Each day they donned new layers of clothing, and each day new layers of soot from the kerosene heater were added to their already grimy countenances. Fortunately, the telephone lines were able to withstand the storm. The people in the community were very concerned and kept calling to see how the sisters were managing. Numerous offers of shelter were offered, for the people of the community had wood-burning stoves, but the blizzard was so severe that it would have been impossible for the sisters to leave their house. One man offered to come and bring them to his home, but he warned them that there was standing room only, because all his relatives had sought shelter in his tiny house. The storm, which began on a Saturday, eventually blew itself out, and by Tuesday, a helicopter was able to land at the hydro plant. Within hours, electrical power was restored. As soon as they could, the sisters set out to assess the damage in the school. Before they had gone more than a few feet, they were met by a group of men who warned them of the presence of a polar bear near the community. To their dismay, the sisters discovered that the storm had caused extensive damage to the school. The only solution was to arrange to hold classes in various places throughout the community. And this was not the end of their troubles. A few weeks later, Sr. Margie Taylor was riding home on a skidoo driven by one of the students when there was an accident, and Sr. Margie found herself being taken by helicopter to the hospital in St. Anthony and later to St. Clare's Mercy Hospital in St. John's. As it happened, her injuries were not serious, and she was able to return to Black Tickle after a few weeks rest. In March, Sr. Barbara took advantage of the mid-term break to travel to St. John's. During her absence, Black Tickle was visited by another storm, and when she returned after her holiday, Barbara found the house resting serenely in the midst of what appeared to be a sizeable pond. Once more, the damage was fairly extensive, but repairs were made quickly and efficiently.

In May 1992, Srs. Margie and Barbara were able to rejoice with four young women who were graduating from high school. High-school gradua-tions were becoming an annual event in Black Tickle. This was indicative of the co-operation that had been established between the home and the school, for prior to the arrival of the sisters, such achievements were unknown in Black Tickle. Furthermore, a small boy from the grade IV class won second prize in a province-wide colouring contest sponsored by the Knights of Columbus in St. John's. A high-school student from St. Peter's was selected to attend a conference in Grand Falls on "Women in Science and Engineering." But there was more to follow. The school had just settled down after the excitement of these announcements, when Sr. Margie received word that seven students from St. Peter's School had been chosen to travel to Cambridge, Ontario, as part of an exchange trip for "Voyager 125."[12] And there was further rejoicing throughout the community when it was announced that St. Peter's School had won $4,000 in the Grenfell Centennial Contest. The money was used to sponsor a summer camp for the students. Srs. Margie and Barbara coordinated the camp with four student assistants. The programs offered during the summer camp included sports, arts and crafts, computer studies, hikes, picnics, and library activities.

It was at this period, in the early 1990s, that the people of Newfoundland realized that the northern cod stocks were diminishing at an alarming rate. For 500 years, the fishery had been the main staple of the Newfoundland economy. On July 2, 1992, the federal minister of fisheries announced a moratorium on fishing for the northern cod in the waters sur-rounding Newfoundland. Almost 20,000 fishermen and fish-plant workers were directly affected. For places like Black Tickle, where the fishery was the only means of employment, the effects of the moratorium brought unimag-inable hardship. Not only were the people of this little settlement prevented

---

12. Voyager 125 was a federally sponsored project to celebrate the 125th anniversary of Confederation.

from fishing for cod, but also, because their traditional fishing boats did not meet the required specifications, they were not eligible to apply for licences to harvest other species such as crab, shrimp, scallops, and turbot.[13] The Canadian government put in place a program to assist those who had lost their means of livelihood, and everyone hoped and prayed that the cod would return after a few years. The school played a role in the implementation of the government-funded unemployment insurance program, referred to as "The 10–42."[14] In a letter published in Mercy Memo Srs. Margie and Barbara wrote:

> We survived the "10–42 make-work projects." The school hired ten people in an effort to place one hundred and fifty people who needed stamps [i.e. unemployment insurance stamps]. Where does one find work for that many people on this small island? This was the first time that fisherpeople can ever remember being involved in these projects. . . . The projects were completed on December 27, 1991. . . . Much of our work this year has been rallying government through the various media for immediate help for the people. Many times we have remembered a quote from Catherine McAuley, "When I do mercy, I please people. When I do justice, I irritate people."[15]

As the year 1992 drew to a close, lack of work and the humiliation of having to depend on government assistance had a serious effect on the morale of the people of Black Tickle. When they were not engaged in school or parish work, Srs. Margie and Barbara spent much of their free time visiting families in distress. The two were called upon in all sorts of emergencies. For example, one evening they were summoned to the medical clinic to assist in the delivery of a baby who had decided to arrive several weeks ahead of time. The school continued to play its part in the lives of the people by offering

---

13. *The Evening Telegram*, December 7, 1997, p. 3.

14. Since there was no regular work available, the government paid people to dig ditches, build wharves, repair cemeteries, etc. These jobs were called "make work projects." A person who was employed for ten weeks was entitled to forty-two weeks of insurance coverage.

15. Srs. Margaret Taylor and Barbara Kenny, "Mercy Memo." February 1992, ASMSJ.

upgrading programs to allow adults who had left school at an early age to earn a high-school diploma. The fact that many of their parents were attending classes was an added inducement to young people to stay in school.

Through all the years of the Mercy mission in Black Tickle, the members of the General Council took care to keep in touch with the sisters who worked in this lonely outpost. Every year, a member of the team visited the little island off the coast of Labrador to attend graduation exercises at St. Peter's School. However, in spite of good intentions on the part of the leadership of the congregation, the weather or other unforeseeable difficulties sometimes intervened to disrupt even the most carefully laid plans. In 1993, the graduation was scheduled for Friday, May 7. With that date in mind, Sr. Rosemary Ryan made reservations to arrive in Black Tickle a day ahead of time to help Sr. Barbara Kenny make dessert for the graduation dinner. The sudden death of thirty-four-year-old Maynard Howell put the whole community of Black Tickle in mourning, and even the graduation ceremony, the highlight of the year, was postponed out of respect for the grieving families. The funeral service was to take place in the Anglican Church on Sunday, May 9, but on Sunday morning the people awoke to a raging blizzard. Everyone in Black Tickle was "snowed in" and the funeral had to be deferred until the following day. To complicate matters still more, in mid-morning, the phone rang in the sisters' house with the news, "Sister Margie, Uncle Alonzo Dyson died during the night, and his funeral will be Wednesday morning, weather permitting!"[16] Uncle Alonzo's death meant that the graduation had to be delayed again. By five o'clock in the evening, the weather had cleared sufficiently to allow the priest to celebrate Sunday mass. After mass, the three sisters, Margie, Barbara, and Rosemary Ryan headed into the snow and wind to make their way to the Dyson house to pay their respects to Uncle Alonzo. When they arrived, they found the old gentleman laid out in an improvised coffin. The family explained that they hoped to have a suitable casket brought in from Goose Bay as soon as the weather cleared. On Monday morning, Srs. Margie and Rosemary went by skidoo to

---

16. In Newfoundland outports, the title "Uncle" or "Aunt" does not imply any blood relationship. It is, rather, a mark of respect for a person who manages to survive for sixty years or more.

Domino, a place a few miles distant, to attend Maynard Howell's funeral, leaving Sr. Barbara to take care of the school. Sr. Rosemary described the scene that met their eyes:

> It truly was a unique sight to see about one hundred people gathered in the wind, snow and bitter cold outside Howell's house as the front door was taken off the hinges and the coffin passed out over the "bridge" and onto the shoulders of six pall-bearers who carried the remains to the newly constructed Anglican Church. An Honour Guard of six Wildlife officers walked before the coffin, rifles on their shoulders and grief on their faces as they prepared to say farewell to their friend and co-worker by means of a gun salute in the cemetery. The little church was filled beyond capacity . . . while many stood on the steps and on the grounds outside . . . After the service the coffin was placed on a "coachy box" and pulled by skidoo to Spotted Island where the cemetery is located.[17]

Although Sr. Rosemary Ryan did not achieve the purpose of her visit—to represent the General Council at the graduation—she returned to St. John's feeling very much enriched by her experience of life in Black Tickle. She wrote, "I experienced a community in love and support of one another in their mourning, and I can testify to the way MERCY is being witnessed and shared by Margie and Barbara on the Labrador coast."[18]

As time passed and the cod moratorium dragged on, the economic outlook for Black Tickle looked very bleak. Nevertheless, the school was an enduring beacon of hope for the future for parents and children. The parish continued to grow under the leadership of its full-time pastor, Fr. Jack Davis, OMI, who was keenly interested in promoting a faith-development program for adults. Srs. Margie and Barbara entered enthusiastically into Father's plans, and with the co-operation of the people, the program was a success. Furthermore, the parish established groups of Brownies and Cubs for the younger children and a 4-H program for older students. Early in

---

17. Sr. Rosemary Ryan, "Black Tickle Adventure," ASMSJ, RG 10/28/14.
18. Ibid.

1994, St. Peter's School received funding from the provincial government for an exchange trip with St. Mary's School in St. John's. The St. Mary's students visited Black Tickle for a week in February, while students from Black Tickle spent the first week of March visiting the St. Mary's students in the city.

However, in October 1994, the dynamic school principal, Sr. Margie Taylor, became ill and was forced to go to St. John's for treatment. Sr. Margie returned to Black Tickle in January 1995 and remained until May, when illness once again forced her to return to St. John's. It was clear that Margie's health was not strong enough to withstand the hardships of life in Black Tickle. Since there was no sister available to replace Sr. Margie, Sheila Sullivan agreed to take over the position as principal of St. Peter's School. Sr. Barbara Kenny remained in Black Tickle as the only sister on the staff of the school, and for two years, she carried on alone. These were difficult years. The enormity of the problems facing the fishery and the possibility that the stocks might not recover haunted every waking hour of those who depended on the sea for their livelihood.

For seven years, the people of Black Tickle pleaded for quotas to fish species other than cod, but the federal Department of Fisheries ignored all requests.[19] By 1997, eighty percent of this hard-working and hitherto independent community depended on social assistance to survive. The Newfoundland government provided a school breakfast and lunch program for the children in St. Peter's School. A front-page story in the *Toronto Globe and Mail* prompted the St. John's press to describe Black Tickle as Canada's "charity case."[20] The Community Food Sharing Association, a charitable organization based in St. John's, responded by having emergency food supplies airlifted to Black Tickle.[21] Following reports from Black Tickle that included a story of a child having to burn clothes to stay warm, the people of Newfoundland responded with gifts of clothing, food, and toys for the children for Christmas. The government minister responsible for Labrador commented, "The problems in our economy over the past decade, compounded by the cod moratorium,

---

19. *The Evening Telegram*, November 25, 1997, p. 3.
20. Ibid.
21. Ibid, December 7, 1997.

have affected every community in this province but none to the extent of Black Tickle."[22]

Finally, the provincial government decided to act. The premier, Brian Tobin, established a special committee of Cabinet to respond to the crisis. Tobin, himself, with the minister of fisheries and aquaculture, went to Black Tickle to report directly to the people on the work of this committee. On December 15, 1997, Ernie McLean, minister responsible for Labrador, read a statement in the House of Assembly in which he announced the establishment of a job creation program for Black Tickle. The sum of sixty-five thousand dollars was provided to employ twenty-three people to upgrade the fish plant. Other initiatives included funding for a Literacy Outreach Program to employ thirteen people to train workers for an ongoing community learning project. Funds were provided to employ another twenty-three people to upgrade the local community centre.[23] Although these measures could not address the real problems of Black Tickle, the people appreciated the fact that the government was aware of the situation and was taking steps to find solutions to the problems that had devastated this once prosperous little community.

When the school year ended in 1997, the situation in Black Tickle appeared grim indeed. Sr. Barbara Kenny packed her suitcase at the end of June and left for summer school, promising to return in August to get ready for another year in Black Tickle. But this was not to happen. During the summer, Sr. Barbara became ill and was rushed to hospital where she underwent serious surgery. She remained in the Intensive Care Unit in the hospital in St. John's for several months, and although she recovered, she had a very long and difficult convalescence. Consequently, for the first time since 1984 there was no Mercy presence in Black Tickle.

Nevertheless, the Sisters of Mercy were not about to abandon the people at this time of need. In November 1997, Srs. Charlotte Fitzpatrick and Maureen O'Keefe left St. John's to spend a weekend with the people in Black

---

22. Hon. Ernie McLean, minister responsible for Labrador, December 15, 1997, http://www.gov.nf.ca/releases/1997/labrador/1215n09.htm.

23. Ibid.

Tickle. No sooner had they landed, than the weather "came down" and the weekend stretched into six full days. Sr. Maureen wrote of their trip in the *Mercy Memo* and remarked that not even "the Queen in her wide-brimmed hat and white gloves" would have been more enthusiastically welcomed than was Sr. Charlotte. The people were delighted that the Sisters of Mercy had not forgotten them, and they looked forward to the day when some member of the congregation would live among them once more.

By the end of the school year, in June 1998, it became clear that Sr. Barbara Kenny's health would not allow her to return to the mission and there was no sister to take her position in St. Peter's School. In September 1998, Srs. Alverna Harnett and Betty Morrissey flew to the island to spend some time with the people and collect Sr. Barbara's clothes and books. Meanwhile, Sr. Mona Rumboldt, who was working as pastoral assistant in one of the parishes in St. John's, generously volunteered to go to Black Tickle as soon as her current assignment was completed in September 1998.

On October 14, 1998, Sr. Mona arrived in Black Tickle to begin her ministry, not as a teacher in the school, but as a parish worker. Sr. Mona was well-suited for this position. Before leaving the teaching profession, Sr. Mona had looked ahead and prepared for her "second career," for it is a well-known maxim among the Sisters of Mercy that a sister does not "retire," rather, she is "recycled"! Throughout her career as a teacher, Sr. Mona had taken a special interest in parish activities. Gifted musically, she established parish choirs where no choir had existed, she started singing classes in schools where there was no assigned music teacher, and she was keenly interested in sacramental preparation for the children. In Black Tickle, she found plenty of scope to exercise her musical talent and further her interest in faith development.

Within a short time, Sr. Mona had made friends with the people of Black Tickle. In the absence of a priest to celebrate mass, Sr. Mona celebrated the liturgy of the word in the church on Sundays and feast days. At first, the congregation was small. Only six people showed up for the service, but Mona persevered, and within a month, the congregation had increased to twenty-two. At the same time, she began preparations to celebrate the baptism of five children, and to her delight, thirty families enrolled in sacramental preparations for confirmation and First Eucharist. It was a start! However, Sr. Mona soon found out that she was to be "all things to all people." For one who liked to organize her time, she found that scheduling her day was wasted effort. She never knew from one minute to the next what might be required. Instead of retiring at her usual hour of ten o'clock, she frequently found herself at midnight sitting at a bedside in the clinic with a person waiting to be airlifted to hospital in Goose Bay. The poverty and discouragement she witnessed during her visits to the sick and elderly of the community saddened her. She wrote:

> The struggle to live is great here, with no income for many families this year. There are stories of no food, furnaces broken and no money for parts, which means living in the cold. I've seen stoves with holes in the sides, canvas worn to the boards, and floors with no canvas at all.[24]

However, the bishop of the diocese established a special Black Tickle fund to help, and throughout the diocese, people co-operated to provide each needy family with a good Christmas dinner. On the island of Newfoundland, groups collected clothing and gifts for the children. Consequently, Sr. Mona was able to report that every family in Black Tickle was able to celebrate Christmas.

By the summer of 2000, things were looking up for the people of Black Tickle. The renovated fish plant had gone through a $2,000,000, privately funded conversion from a pre-moratorium groundfish processing plant to a modern shellfish operation.[25] The opening of the plant in August 2000 provided work for more than forty people. It was a start. Those who were not successful in obtaining work at that time were promised that over time the plant would be capable of employing up to ninety people. With the prospect of a brighter future, the community of Black Tickle started to rebuild itself with new energy and determination.

24. Mona Rumboldt, "Love on the Rocks," 1998, ASMSJ, RG 10/28/91.
25. *The Telegram*, August 24, 2000, p. 3.

Sr. Mona Rumboldt spent four years in Black Tickle ministering to the people through various parish programs. She encouraged the establishment of Alcoholics Anonymous and organized the young people to participate in programs for development and peace. However, Sr. Mona realized that she could not stay in Black Tickle forever and that, with shortage of personnel, the congregation would find it hard to replace her with another sister. Furthermore, since the arrival of the sisters in 1984, they had worked with the people so that eventually individuals within the community were prepared to assume leadership within the parish. By the year 2002, Sr. Mona's health was beginning to suffer. Furthermore, she felt that her work in Black Tickle was finished. It was time to move on. Earlier that same year, 2002, Sr. Helen Harding, the congregational leader of the Sisters of Mercy, received a letter from Bishop Crosby inviting sisters to minister in various parts of his diocese in Labrador. In response to this request, Sr. Mona Rumboldt was assigned to Labrador City and subsequently appointed director of liturgy for the diocese, a position she held for two years before accepting an assignment to minister in Gambo on the island of Newfoundland.

Three years after the foundation in Black Tickle, a new Mercy ministry was begun in the "Big Land" of Labrador. On July 1, 1987, Sr. Lorraine Power, M.D., arrived at Forteau to begin her work as a medical doctor at the Grenfell Regional Health Station. Sr. Lorraine was the first Sister of Mercy in Newfoundland to practice as a physician, and her first posting after graduation was to Labrador. Sr. Lorraine had been attracted to the northern part of the province of Newfoundland since 1970–71, when she had served as supervising principal in a school in Port au Choix, a settlement on the northwest coast of Newfoundland. During the course of her medical studies, as a clinical clerk she chose the hospital in St. Anthony to gain the required cottage hospital experience.[26] While she was there, she visited Forteau in Labrador to assist the resident doctor. Sr. Lorraine's visit occurred during a particularly stormy week

---

26. St. Anthony is the major service centre for the Great Northern Peninsula. It is best known as the headquarters of the International Grenfell Association.

in January when she had to be transported to the clinic by skidoo because the storms were too violent to venture out on foot, even for residents who were used to severe weather. It was while she was in Forteau that Lorraine became aware of the great need of the people for stable medical services. She learned that the problem of securing doctors for this remote area had been addressed by hiring foreign graduates. In most cases, the primary concern of these physicians was to fulfill the residency requirement to allow them to move to other parts of Canada. A more important consideration for Sr. Lorraine was the lack of religious services and spiritual support for Catholics in the area. She was determined to try to address this problem. Consequently, after her graduation from medical school, Sr. Lorraine applied for a two-year posting as resident physician in the medical clinic in Forteau.

On her arrival in Forteau, Sr. Lorraine took up residence in the house provided for the doctor who served the area—a large geographical area that included settlements up to fifty miles from the clinic in Forteau. Shortly after her arrival, Sr. Lorraine was joined by Sr. M. Eugenio Carroll, who volunteered to go to Forteau to provide pastoral service to the Catholics in the area. Sadly, Sr. Eugenio's ministry in Forteau was of relatively short duration, for after fourteen months, she was forced to return to St. John's for reasons of health. After Sr. Eugenio's departure, Sr. Lorraine was alone.

When she began her practice in Forteau, Sr. Lorraine was the sole practitioner of medicine in the area, responsible for the health care of 2,600 people living along the southern shore of Labrador. She worked with six nurse practitioners in a regional health centre equipped with basic laboratory, X-ray, and four holding beds. However, there was no time to indulge in loneliness. She was soon caught up in the never-ending work at the health centre and she was on twenty-four hour call.

It was not long after her arrival in Forteau that Sr. Lorraine realized the influence of a religious sect that had managed to recruit many followers in the area. Members of the sect entertained and encouraged a hostile attitude toward all of the mainline religious denominations in the region—Anglican, Roman Catholic, and United Church. They were particularly vehement in their denunciation of Catholicism. At the same time, they respected Sr.

Lorraine for her medical skills, her compassion, and her dedication to the sick of all faiths. Nevertheless, their active and aggressive proselytizing of the very ill or of those experiencing tragedies of various kinds was a source of concern to Lorraine, who urged respect for all people, irrespective of religious belief or lack of it.

During her tenure in Forteau, Sr. Lorraine did not confine herself to the practice of medicine. Sr. Lorraine devoted the hours when she was free from duties at the health centre to the spiritual and emotional needs of Catholics in the area. With the permission of the bishop, she brought Communion to Catholic patients. As well, she held prayer services and Eucharistic celebrations for Catholic families in the neighbourhood and for Catholic nurses on shift work at the health centre. However, in spite of such a tightly packed schedule, Sr. Lorraine was wise enough to spend one day a week completely removed from her work. On these days, she drove to a little parish house in Quebec to spend a day in quiet prayer. There were opportunities, also, for her to visit the sisters in other parts of Labrador.

In 1989, Sr. Lorraine Power was offered a post in the Notre Dame de Lourdes Hospital in Blanc Sablon in Quebec. Blanc Sablon is a small village on the Quebec side of the border between that province and Newfoundland and Labrador. The hospital was built by the diocese and had been run by the Sisters of the Holy Family until it was passed over to the Government of Quebec. In June 1989, Sr. Lorraine met with Dr. Roy, the chief of staff of Notre Dame Hospital. He pointed out the advantage of a lighter workload and offered more favourable working conditions that those available in Forteau. Moreover, she would enjoy greater religious freedom for herself and the opportunity to respond more fully to the spiritual and religious needs of her patients. This, in fact, was her principal reason for moving from Forteau to Quebec.

However, there were other factors involved in Sr. Lorraine's decision to move to Quebec. Dr. Elizabeth Fowler, the only female physician at Notre Dame Hospital in Quebec, was leaving to pursue postgraduate work. Dr. Fowler, a close friend and colleague of Sr. Lorraine, pointed out that after her departure, the population of about 10,000 would be left without the services of a female physician. As an added incentive, Sr. Lorraine was aware of the need for a physician with a special interest in the elderly to assume primary care duties at the eighteen-bed chronic care facility at Notre Dame Hospital. After consulting with the General Council of the Sisters of Mercy in St. John's, Lorraine decided to accept the offer. In November 1989, Lorraine drove the relatively short distance from Forteau, across the Quebec border to Lourdes de Blanc Sablon to a better equipped, fifty-bed hospital. In every way, the move was a good one for the overworked doctor. At the same time, she has not lost touch with her former patients in Labrador, who are quite happy to travel the eighteen miles to consult their trusted physician.[27]

The ministry of the Sisters of Mercy to the people of Labrador continues to expand. In the spring of 1999, Srs. Patricia Maher and Eileen Penney accepted an invitation to move to the community of Happy Valley-Goose Bay. On April 23, they boarded a plane for Happy Valley to look for housing and to meet Bishop Doug Crosby, OMI, of the Diocese of Labrador City-Schefferville and the pastor, Fr. Jack Davis, OMI. Sr. Patricia was appointed pastoral assistant at Our Lady Queen of Peace Parish in Happy Valley. Sr. Eileen, who is a registered nurse, was offered a position in the local hospital. The two sisters spent the summer months finalizing plans for the new mission and purchasing items for their work, furnishings for the house, and a car. It was decided that Sr. Eileen would travel by boat with the car and larger items needed for the house, while Sr. Patricia would make the journey by plane. Finally, on Saturday, August 28, 1999, after a tearful goodbye to family and friends, Sr. Eileen boarded the *Sir Robert Bond* for the thirty-four hour journey to Happy Valley. In a letter home, Sr. Eileen described the voyage, "The crossing was perfect. . . . I had an opportunity to sit on the ship's deck and take in all the beauty of the Labrador coastline that soon would be my new home. The whales were numerous and playful and some of the icebergs were massive in size."[28] Early Monday morning, after an idyllic voyage, Sr. Eileen landed in Goose Bay with forty-five minutes to

---

27. In the early 1990s, Notre Dame de Lourdes Hospital underwent extensive renovations and an expansion of the facilities. Subsequently, the name of the hospital was changed to "Centre Santé de la Basse Côté."

28. Sr. Eileen Penney, "Mercy Memo," October 1999, ASMSJ.

spare before she was due to meet Sr. Patricia at the airport and drive to 8 Campbell Street, the location of their new home.

The sisters spent the first few days of their venture with their sleeves rolled up as they set their house in order. Their first visitors were Fr. Jack Davis, the acting pastor, and the ever-faithful Sheila Sullivan, who had been such a good friend to the Sisters of Mercy in Black Tickle. That evening they attended their first mass as members of Our Lady Queen of Peace Parish and were given a warm welcome by the parishioners. A few days later, Bishop Doug Crosby, who was delighted to have the Sisters of Mercy established in Happy Valley-Goose Bay, came to welcome them to Labrador.

The arrival of Srs. Patricia and Eileen in Happy Valley-Goose Bay was like a gift from heaven for Sr. Mona Rumboldt in Black Tickle. The knowledge that two Sisters of Mercy were only a couple of hours away helped to alleviate some of the isolation she experienced on the east coast of Labrador. Accordingly, on September 23, Sr. Mona arrived, bag and baggage, at the door of 8 Campbell Street just in time to spend the weekend and celebrate the feast of Our Lady of Mercy on September 24. The next day, Saturday, Sr. Eileen decided that it was a good time to pick some of the partridge berries that grow in abundance in the woods. In spite of her eloquent pleading, threats, and the offer of bribes, neither of her companions agreed to go along, and so she enlisted a friend from the nursing staff of the hospital. She started off on her mission amidst dire warnings to watch out for the bears that frequent the woods around Happy Valley—and often appear in the town. In spite of all the doom and gloom accompanying her forage into the woods, Eileen set off armed with eight large tin cans. She returned five hours later, laden down with the cans filled to the top with berries and gloating that her two fearful friends had missed a beautiful day in the woods, and she said, "Nary a bear to be seen."[29]

Sr. Patricia's ministry began almost immediately. Initially, her ministry was in the area of pastoral outreach to families; to the sick and elderly in their homes, in the hospital, and nursing homes; and to the prisoners at the correctional centre. In this way, she grew to know the people, and very quickly, she

29. Annals, Sisters' Residence, Happy Valley-Goose Bay, September 25, 1999, ASMSJ.

became aware of the special needs of this northern community. In her efforts to meet the challenges presented by her new ministry, Sr. Patricia had plenty of support from the parish team. In addition to Sr. Patricia, the team consisted of the pastor, Fr. Oliver Rich, OMI; Fr. Jack Davis, OMI, who served the coastal communities; Br. Joseph Lasowske, the financial administrator; Sheila Sullivan, diocesan catechetical coordinator; and Suzanne Mealey, the secretary.

Within two weeks of their arrival, Srs. Patricia and Eileen were off to Sheshatshiu, an Innu village, to attend mass. During the liturgy, three children celebrated First Eucharist with family and friends present. The small reception after mass provided the sisters with an opportunity to meet the native people of the village.

However, Sr. Patricia also had commitments in St. John's where she served as member of the Board of Trustees of the Health Care Corporation of St. John's and on the Responsible Sharing Committee of the Congregation of the Sisters of Mercy. These latter responsibilities required her to travel to St. John's every month for meetings. Although these visits provided an opportunity for Patricia to visit her family and keep up-to-date with the latest convent news, the meetings themselves required many hours of preparation, especially at a time when the entire health care system of the province was being restructured.

For her part, after her arrival in Happy Valley, Sr. Eileen had a few days to rest and enjoy the experience of being in a new place, among new people, before she began her orientation at the Melville Hospital on September 20. The areas assigned to her ranged from general nursing duties on the maternity unit, emergency department, surgical and medical wards, as well as ICU and CCU. Because this hospital provides medical services to the coastal communities from Nain to Black Tickle,[30] a member of the nursing staff is required to go by plane or helicopter to these areas and accompany patients back to Melville Hospital for treatment. When an individual's condition requires treatment not available at the hospital, the patient is flown to St. John's. The process is known as "medivac," and within a short time of beginning work at the hospital, Sr.

---

30. Nain is the most northerly settlement in the Province of Newfoundland and Labrador.

Eileen began training for the program. It proved to be one of the most exciting and challenging aspects of her nursing experience. She wrote:

> Medivac Nursing takes me above and beyond this "Big Land" . . .
> Health Labrador performs between four and five hundred medi-
> vacs a year. What many do not know is that medivacs are . . . on
> an individual, voluntary basis only. There are about ten nurses with
> whom I work doing medivacs and serve the thirty thousand peo-
> ple . . . in the communities of Black Tickle, Makkovik, Davis Inlet,
> Rigolet, Churchill Falls, Cartwright, Hopedale, Postville, Nain,
> Northwest River and Sheshatshit [sic] . . .
>
> Most people cannot understand how we can get up in the
> middle of the night, get into a small plane or helicopter and fly to
> a remote area without knowing what we will face once we get
> there. Many times the condition of the patient changes while en
> route. The satisfaction comes when you see the look of relief on
> the faces of the coastal nurses and the patient's family because
> you have arrived to accompany them back to the hospital. Just
> before Christmas I brought a little Innu boy, who had been in hos-
> pital, home to Makkovik. When we were approaching his commu-
> nity I could hardly keep him in his seat because he was so excit-
> ed that Santa would not have to make an extra trip to Happy
> Valley to find him on Christmas Eve.[31]

However, Sr. Eileen did not confine her interests to the hospital. She became
involved at the parish level as a member of the Baptismal Preparation Team. As
well, Sr. Eileen took an active role in the children's liturgy celebrated every
Sunday in the parish.

Very soon, both sisters were caught up in the demands of their ministries, and the year passed quickly. In addition to attending various meetings
in St. John's, in Quebec, and in other parts of Labrador, Srs. Patricia and Eileen
had a number of visitors, principally sisters from the island of Newfoundland
who were eager to see how this new mission in Labrador was working.

Meanwhile, Sr. Eileen was becoming accustomed to nursing in the
north. Melville Hospital was nearing the end of its usefulness as a medical

---

31. Sr. Eileen Penney, "Mercy Memo," February 2001, ASMSJ.

facility. Consequently, within a year the new Labrador Health Care Centre in Happy Valley-Goose Bay opened its doors. The new hospital, opened September 8, 2000, has twenty-eight beds including two labour/delivery rooms, three ICU/CCU beds, and one palliative care bed.[32] The hospital boasts two operating rooms with a day surgery room and a very busy emergency room. The hospital offers child, youth, and family services; public health; home care; addiction services; and mental health care. Through the generosity of the local Ministerial Association, the patients and staff have access to a beautiful chapel that was furnished by funds raised through a community telethon. As well, the atrium and corridors of the new facility have a display of art depicting the natural scenery of Labrador.[33]

As the years passed, Sr. Patricia has become more and more involved in the day-to-day affairs of the parish, especially when the pastor is absent from the community. In addition to making regular visits to the homes and health-care institutions, Sr. Patricia is a member of the parish council and responsible for preparing and leading the Catholic service held monthly in the correctional centre. One of her duties is to work with the liturgy committee in planning the regular Sunday liturgies, but also, Sr. Patricia plays an important part in organizing other events of importance that occur in the parish. These events range from seeing that the annual garden party goes off without a hitch, to leading orientation and formation sessions for people interested in exercising a liturgical ministry in the parish, to participating in Bible study and faith sharing sessions, to preparing for ordinations.

At the same time that Srs. Patricia Maher and Eileen Penney were making plans to begin their mission on the east coast of Labrador, another Sister of Mercy, Michelle Gibbons, was preparing to begin a new ministry in Labrador City. Labrador City is a mining town located not far from the Quebec border in western Labrador. The major source of employment is a large iron ore mine

---

32. The official opening of the Labrador Health Care Centre took place on November 3, 2000.

33. Sr. Patricia Maher, "Carillon," December 2000, ASMSJ.

operated by the Iron Ore Company of Canada. From a small company town, Labrador City has grown to become the largest community in Labrador.

Sr. Michelle arrived in Labrador City on September 21, 1999. Early in October, Sr. Michelle began her work as pastoral assistant at the Cathedral Parish of Our Lady of Perpetual Help in Labrador City and at the Church of Our Lady of the Assumption in Wabush, a smaller mining town about three miles from Labrador City. Her first task was to form a Liturgy Committee in the parish in Wabush and to assume the position as spiritual director of the Wabush Catholic Women's League (CWL). To her dismay, at the very first meeting of the CWL, Sr. Michelle was informed that not only was the league preparing to celebrate the thirtieth anniversary of its establishment, but had been asked to host the annual CWL Convention in June 2000. These two events required a great deal of planning and preparation. As she drove home from the meeting, Michelle reflected that, indeed, this was to be her "baptism by fire." However, she was caught up very quickly in a whole range of parish activities ranging from COR weekends (Christ in Others Renewal) for the youth of both parishes, to weekends for couples preparing for marriage, to sponsoring a national RCIA Institute. Furthermore, shortly after her arrival, Bishop Douglas Crosby asked her to attend a conference on pastoral formation at St. Francis Xavier University in Nova Scotia. Subsequently, Michelle agreed to pilot a diploma in ministry program, also from St. Francis Xavier University.

As a member of the pastoral team for the Cathedral Parish of Our Lady of Perpetual Help and its mission in Wabush, Sr. Michelle has responsibilities in the areas of adult faith development and liturgy. Nevertheless, she does not confine herself to these activities, but is involved also in ministry to youth, a ministry for which she has a special talent.

In September 2000, a fifth Sister of Mercy accepted the invitation to minister to the people of Labrador. Sr. Marie Crotty had some previous experience of the "Big Land." Her first visit to this northern part of the province was in 1979 when she visited the sisters in Black Tickle. Three years later, she returned to Labrador to accompany a group of students who planned to visit the little island as part of a school project. Unfortunately, when they arrived in Goose Bay the weather "came down" and Sr. Marie was forced to remain in a barracks for four days—with eight teenagers! It may have been because of this latter experience that Sr. Marie received the invitation to minister in Labrador with a regrettable lack of enthusiasm. However, after prayer and reflection, Sr. Marie recognized the invitation as what she described as "a gospel call."[34] She arrived in Labrador City on September 21, 2000, and was welcomed by Sr. Michelle Gibbons, who would be her nearest neighbour. A few days later, Marie set out from Labrador City to drive to Churchill Falls, which was to be the scene of her future ministry. It was a long, lonely, difficult route, about two hundred miles of unpaved road. Four hours later, she arrived in Churchill Falls and took up residence in the parish house. The thoughtful parishioners had prepared for her arrival. Every room was sparkling, the beds were made, and the refrigerator and cupboards were stocked with food.

The town of Churchill Falls was built to accommodate the families of employees of the huge hydroelectric power station that is located near the town. It is approximately halfway between Happy Valley-Goose Bay on the east and Labrador City on the west.

The population is approximately 1,500, and within a short time, Sr. Marie knew most of them by name. But first, on September 25, 2000, she was officially installed as pastoral animator during mass celebrated by Bishop Douglas Crosby, OMI. Sr. Marie brought considerable experience and training to her new ministry. She had graduated from Regis College in Toronto with a master's degree in ministry and spirituality. Furthermore, she has diplomas in spiritual direction and clinical pastoral education. With this imposing array of qualifications, Sr. Marie began her ministry in Churchill Falls. At the suggestion of the parishioners of St. Peter's Parish, she began her ministry by visiting the homes and sharing family meals. She discovered immediately that she had come to a warm and friendly town and that St. Peter's parishioners are a very welcoming and receptive group of people.

---

34. Sr. Marie Crotty, "Churchill Falls Calls," December 2000, ASMSJ.

Sr. Marie has had many opportunities to exercise her learning, her skill, and her compassion. In addition to parish activities, she is often called on for help in other areas. For instance, when a small boy died unexpectedly, she spent many hours in the school counselling the children, especially those who were in his grade III classroom. She is invited frequently to deliver the homily at school and parish liturgies, and she makes a point of attending recitals and concerts held in the town, for Sr. Marie throws herself enthusiastically into whatever activity is taking place around her. This may be the secret of her success with people.

That same year, during the summer of 2000, the Sisters of Mercy were once more called upon to provide pastoral assistance in a northern community, this time on the island of Newfoundland. On September 4, 2000, Srs. Ellen Marie Sullivan and Rona O'Gorman offered to move to Conche on the eastern part of the Great Northern Peninsula to bring the spirit and charism of Mercy to the people of the region. At the time, there was no ordained priest in the area, and for this reason, the sisters decided to concentrate their efforts in the parish of Conche and its missions. These included Croque, Roddickton, Englee, and Main Brook, all of them small fishing villages in the area.

On their arrival in Conche, the sisters took up residence in the parish house. Rev. Edward Terry, the parish priest of Port au Choix,[35] arrived a few days later to welcome the Sisters of Mercy to the parish. Before his departure, the sisters accompanied him to Croque[36] for the celebration of mass. This provided an opportunity for the sisters to meet the people with whom they would be working.

---

35. Port au Choix is a fishing community of the west coast of the Great Northern Peninsula. It has significant historical interest. Long before Newfoundland was discovered by Europeans, Port au Choix was home to prehistoric peoples. Researchers from Memorial University have discovered numerous Palaeo-Indian burial sites. The culture represented is known to archaeologists as Maritime Archaic and has been dated between 3,900 and 3,200 years ago. Furthermore, remains of a Dorset (Palaeo-Eskimo) village have been discovered in the area. Both sites are included within Port au Choix National Historic Park. See *ENL*, s.v. "Port au Choix."

36. Croque is about two-and-a-half hours by road from Conche.

The arrival of the sisters coincided with the opening of school. However, because denominational education had been abolished in the schools of Newfoundland, the sisters did not anticipate that they would be invited to participate in any activities in the school. Therefore, they were delighted to receive a call from one of the teachers asking if they would prepare a celebration in the church to ask God's blessing on the teachers and children at the beginning of the school year. A few days later, the pupils from grades I to VI were invited to visit the sisters' house for an ice-cream party. In the following weeks, the sisters hosted a similar party for students from the intermediate and senior grades. This was the beginning of a close relationship between the sisters and the school, a relationship that grew very close as the year progressed. So much so, that it was unthinkable that the Srs. Rona and Ellen Marie would not be present and involved in all the school activities. Furthermore, the sisters were careful to involve the young people in celebrations of liturgies of the word and other functions held to enrich the spiritual and religious life of the people. Throughout the year, ladies of the parish met regularly with the sisters for Scripture study and various forms of prayer and reflection. As for the two sisters, their work was not confined to Conche. When there was no priest available to celebrate mass, the two sisters travelled to Roddickton and other villages of the mission to celebrate liturgy of the word for the people. Also, from the beginning, the sisters established a close rapport with the teachers in the school. Hence they were pleased and delighted when invited to help in the sacramental preparation program.

However, as Sisters of Mercy, Rona and Ellen Marie were devoted to the ministry of visitation. They set aside three days a week to visit the sick, the elderly, and the bereaved. However, they were always available in case of an emergency or if a person had a special need of counselling and support.

And so the months passed. In May 2001, the bishop of the diocese visited Conche to celebrate the sacrament of confirmation. During his visit, he informed the sisters that in September a priest would be available to take up residence in Conche. The sisters and the people greeted his news with consternation. Although the people were happy to have the services of an ordained priest, they would miss the friendship and the ministry of the two sisters who had become so much a part of their lives. The sisters realized that, although they might stay in the area and continue to minister to the people, there were many other places where their services were needed more urgently. And so, reluctantly, they made their preparations to leave these people who had welcomed them so warmly and given so generously of their friendship. A little over a year after their arrival, on September 26, 2001, Srs. Rona O'Gorman and Ellen Marie Sullivan packed their belongings and left Conche to take up new duties in other parts of the province. Sr. Rona O'Gorman took up duties at the correctional centre in Stephenville Crossing; Sr. Ellen Marie Sullivan was appointed to McAuley Convent in St. John's.

But still the call of the north continued to echo in the convents of the Sisters of Mercy throughout Newfoundland. In September 2003, at the invitation of Bishop Crosby, OMI, Sr. Ellen Marie Sullivan took up residence in West St. Modeste, a small fishing village on the Labrador side of the Strait of Belle Isle, where she began a pastoral ministry to the people of the area.

And so, quietly, without fanfare, six Sisters of Mercy continue their ministry in Labrador and Quebec. No newsworthy or earth-shaking events interrupt the even tenor of their days. They are just six women who, faithfully, day after day, do their best to bring the message of God's healing love and mercy to the people of the north.

CHAPTER TWENTY-FIVE

THE CONTINUING MINISTRY OF MERCY

For everything there is a season,
and a time for every matter under heaven.

Ecclesiastes 3:1

t various points throughout this story, attention has shifted back to Mercy Convent on Military Road. This is as it should be because, until the opening of the new generalate on the Littledale campus on September 24, 1966, major decisions relating to the Sisters of Mercy in Newfoundland had been made at Mercy Convent. With the exception of St. Michael's Convent, St. George's, the sisters who went out to staff new convents, for the most part, came from the mother house. Furthermore, Our Lady of Mercy School was always a leader in educational and artistic achievement in Newfoundland.

In 1931, Sisters of Mercy throughout the world celebrated the centenary of the establishment of the Congregation of the Sisters of Mercy by Catherine McAuley in Dublin. In light of the fact that people everywhere, sisters included, were suffering from the effects of the Great Depression, it was decided to have a celebration of a completely spiritual nature. With the support and co-operation of Archbishop Roche, a *triduum*[1] in honour of Our Lady of Mercy was held in the

---

1. A *triduum* consisted of religious devotions celebrated on three consecutive days.

Cathedral of St. John the Baptist on December 9, 10, and 11 at half past seven in the evening. The archbishop celebrated solemn High Mass in the cathedral at half past ten in the morning on December 12. The organist for the occasion was Charles Hutton, one of the leading musicians of Newfoundland, a former student of M. Xaverius Dowsley of Mercy Convent and a lifelong friend of the Sisters of Mercy. A large group of former pupils of Our Lady of Mercy School formed the special choir for the occasion. However, the sisters felt that it was important to have some tangible reminder of this significant anniversary and managed to find a suitable way to mark the occasion. Visitors to the Sacred Heart Oratory at Mercy Convent and to the chapel of St. Bride's Convent, Littledale, will notice in both chapels three beautiful stained glass windows that were erected by each of these communities to commemorate one hundred years of Mercy history.

During that same year, 1931, the superior general, M. Philippa Hanley, decided that something should be done for sisters who were in very frail health, particularly those who lived at Mercy Convent. She felt that they would be better off away from the hustle and the bustle of a busy convent where their rest was continually disturbed by the ringing of bells. At that time, each sister in the community was assigned a certain number of tolls on the bell; the more junior the sister, the greater number of tolls assigned to her. Particularly during after school and evening hours, bells were almost constantly ringing as sisters were called to the door or the phone to respond to some matter, usually related to school business. The question—what to do? The outport convents had no space to accommodate extra sisters and to transfer them to another convent in the city would be to send them "out of the frying pan into the fire!" Prior to the 1930s, a separate annex had been built behind the Balsam Hotel that was situated on land adjacent to Mercy Convent. In 1931, the Mercy congregation decided to lease the annex from the hotel and set it up as a rest home for sick sisters. In May 1931, M. Bernard Dooley, M. Gerard Biggs, and a postulant, Rita Young (later M. Josepha), were appointed to the Balsam Annex to care for three sick sisters.[2] The three

---

2. "Historical Notes, Convent of Our Lady of Mercy and Our Lady of Mercy School, Military Road," unsigned manuscript, ASMSJ, RG 10/1/94.

invalids were M. Gerard O'Reilly, M. Xaverius Armstrong who died on March 16, 1932, and M. Agnes Doyle who had recently lost her sight.[3] For some reason the experiment lasted for a few months only, and the rest home closed in November of that same year. Perhaps the three invalids preferred to live at Mercy Convent with the rest of the community in spite of the bells!

Meanwhile, Our Lady of Mercy Academy was making news in the world of scholarly achievement. In 1925, the Senior Jubilee Scholarship, worth $1,500—a princely sum in those days—was won by Helena McGrath, a pupil of OLM.[4] Again in 1931 and in 1940, the Jubilee Scholarship was won by students of OLM. In recognition of the number and excellence of the programs available at the school, in 1940, it was named as a member of the Roman Catholic Colleges for Females and known henceforth as the College of Our Lady of Mercy.[5] In 1950, a system of electoral scholarships was inaugurated by the Newfoundland government for grades X and XI. Other Scholarships that were established were the Calvert C. Pratt Scholarships, awarded in grades IX, X, and XI for children of those who fought in World Wars One and Two, and the Sabbath Scholarship for the students having the highest average in grade X. All these scholarships were based on a student's success in the public examinations. Every year, when the results of the public examinations were announced, the names of students of the College of Our Lady of Mercy appeared as winners of one or more of these scholarships.[6] In 1950, a graduating student of Our Lady of Mercy won the Governor

3. M. Gerard O'Reilly lived as an invalid at Mercy Convent until her death in 1944. M. Agnes Doyle who lost her sight completely mastered the study of Braille and taught it to others who had suffered a similar affliction. She was assigned to St. Michael's Convent, Belvedere, where she lived for many years until her death in 1955.

4. Helena McGrath continued her education at Memorial University College and was the first student to graduate from the college. Helena continued her studies with distinction at the University of Toronto where she earned a master's degree in English and Latin, graduating with *summa cum laude*. Subsequently, she married Dr. G. Alain Frecker. They are the parents of Mrs. Shannie Duff, also a graduate of the College of Our Lady of Mercy, and former mayor of the City of St. John's.

5. ASMSJ, RG 10/1/95.

6. Records of the College of Our Lady of Mercy, ASMJ..

General's Medal, the first time that this medal was awarded.[7] However, not all the students of Our Lady of Mercy were budding geniuses. One of the sisters who taught grade VII made a note of some definitions submitted by members of her English class. What was lacking in accuracy was more than offset by imaginative invention. For instance, "Moratorium: something to do with a dead man; Gargoyle: something you take for sore throats; Post-mortem: means you shouldn't have died yet; Elocution: how they kill people in some countries."[8]

The year 1940 marked the twenty-fifth anniversary of Archbishop Roche's episcopal ordination. Clearly, this important event required fitting and enduring recognition. M. Bridget O'Connor, who had been elected as superior general in 1937,[9] was determined that if a memorial were to be erected, it should be something that would benefit the students at Our Lady of Mercy. One of M. Bridget's most cherished dreams for OLM was an extension to provide an auditorium and a gymnasium. The construction of such a facility would, so to speak, kill two birds with the one stone—it would be a magnificent monument to the archbishop's twenty-fifth anniversary and supply two urgently needed additions to Our Lady of Mercy Academy. The General Council agreed, and the archbishop granted permission to proceed. To obtain the necessary space on Military Road, the congregation purchased land on the east side of Mercy Convent, and construction of the new extension began in April 1941.[10] So rapidly did the work progress that, less than a year later, on February 16, 1942, the formal opening and blessing of the new facility took place. Archbishop Roche was delighted. His crest was placed over the main entrance to the new building where it remains as a reminder of this archbishop's remarkable contributions to the Church and to education in Newfoundland.

---

7. Ibid.

8. *Inter Nos*, June 1944, p. 32.

9. M. Bridget O'Connor held the office of superior general from 1916 to 1925, when she completed her second term of office. She could not be elected for a third consecutive term and was succeeded by M. Philippa Hanley. When M. Philippa had completed two six-year terms in 1937, M. Bridget O'Connor was elected for another six-year term as superior general.

10. Annals, Convent of Our Lady of Mercy, St. John's, April 1941, ASMSJ.

It was a happy coincidence that the opening of the new auditorium/gym-
nasium occurred in 1942, the year of the centenary of the arrival of the first
Sisters of Mercy in St. John's. The establishment of the first Mercy Convent in
the New World was celebrated in June of that year. In addition to the religious
observances of the anniversary, which took place in the cathedral, an impressive pageant was staged in the new auditorium of the school. The pageant consisted of eight episodes in which the history of the Sisters of Mercy in
Newfoundland was presented in prose, poetry, song, and dance by the students
of the College of Our Lady of Mercy. M. Basil McCormack was the author of
the prose section of the text; M. Mercedes Agnes Slattery composed the poetry that accompanied every episode. The musical part of the program was under
the direction of M. Edward Hodge and M. Celine Veitch, the latter providing
the piano accompaniments for all the musical selections. The string orchestra
consisted of nineteen violins and three cellos. Altogether, over two hundred
children from the school took part in the pageant, from the senior girls in grade
XI to the smallest children in kindergarten—four of whom played the part of
cherubs in the final tableau. Subsequently, the editor of *The Monitor* had this to
say of the pageant:

> The pageant portrayed the principal events leading up to the
> coming of the Sisters to Newfoundland. . . . To show the results
> of their efforts in this country . . . the various events selected
> for portrayal most effectively gave a correct sketch of the his-
> tory of the Order in Newfoundland, indicated the courage
> required to face life in a new and backward country, and
> stressed the piety and charity which took root and thrived so
> luxuriantly in our soil.
>   Episode followed episode in such a manner that the final
> tableau was a climax of magnificent beauty. The performance was
> the most artistic, arousing varied emotions of laughter and tears,
> but especially it filled the hearts and minds of all beholders with
> love and admiration for the remarkable, outstanding achieve-
> ments of the Order of Mercy Nuns in our country.[11]

11. *The Monitor*, July—August 1942, p. 13.

Preparations for the pageant began early in the school year, for this was to be one of the most elaborate productions in the history of the school. In later years, the sisters involved in directing different parts of the performance recalled amusing incidents that occurred during the long and tiresome rehearsals. For instance, on the afternoon of the first dress rehearsal, a group of performers was sent out to the playground while the choir practiced a difficult passage in the music. The choir was interrupted in mid-phrase when one of the children rushed in with the news, "Sister, you'd better come quickly because 'Bishop Fleming' is chasing 'Mother McAuley' around the garden, threatening to kill her if she doesn't give back her new hair band." When M. Edward Hodge went to investigate she discovered "Bishop Fleming" garbed in colourful episcopal robes, in hot pursuit of "Mother McAuley" who, dressed in full religious habit, was having some difficulty in keeping ahead of the enraged "prelate." The whole incident was being witnessed by a group of interested spectators who happened to be passing by on Military Road. However, when M. Edward appeared on the scene the combatants stopped in full flight, the hair band was returned promptly to its owner, and the rehearsal continued without further interruption.

September 1948 marked a new chapter in the story of Our Lady of Mercy School. For the first time, lack of space forced the sisters to discontinue accepting boys for kindergarten. However, this decision did little to solve the problem of accommodation. On October 17, 1951, the College of Our Lady of Mercy purchased a neighbouring house and property on Barnes Road that had belonged to a lawyer by the name of Richard Cramm.[12] Immediately, carpenters, plumbers, painters, and electricians moved in to adapt the rooms of this large, elegant home into classrooms. When the renovations were completed, business education students from the College of Our Lady of Mercy moved to the first floor of the house while high-school classes occupied the second storey. For some reason, this new addition to the school was not given an official title, or if the sisters did give it a name, that name has been lost in

---

12. Annals, Convent of Our Lady of Mercy, St. John's, October 1951, ASMSJ.

the mists of time! The students, however, continued to call this new extension, "Cramm's House."[13]

Meanwhile, within the wider community, Newfoundland's future as an independent country hung in the balance. Since 1934, the country had been ruled by a commission of government consisting of three British and three Newfoundland commissioners, "all appointed by and answerable solely to the British Government."[14] Responsible government that had begun in 1855 was suspended. This commission of government came about because of the financial difficulties and political turmoil that Newfoundland experienced in the late 1920s and early '30s. However, according to the agreement signed in 1934 that established commission of government, "as soon as the island's difficulties are overcome and Newfoundland is again self-supporting, responsible government, on the request of the people of Newfoundland, would be restored."[15]

With the onset of the Second World War, Americans and Canadians recognized Newfoundland's strategic position relative to the rest of North America. The United States constructed military bases of all types in Newfoundland, thus providing plenty of work for Newfoundlanders. American soldiers, sailors, and airmen were sent to defend the bases and brought millions of dollars to boost the Newfoundland economy. Newfoundland's financial troubles seemed to be over. In August 1941, the Atlantic Charter was signed by Winston Churchill and Franklin Delano Roosevelt in Placentia Bay. Ironically, as John E. FitzGerald pointed out:

> The Charter's third article affirmed the right of all peoples to self-government, and the existence of Commission of Government in Newfoundland stood as an egregious exception to the principles

---

13. "Cramm's House" was used as an extension of Our Lady of Mercy School until 1975 when enrolment at Our Lady of Mercy School began to decrease. Subsequently, it was leased, for nominal rent, to the "Teach-a-Tot" organization that offers educational and housekeeping skills for low-income mothers and small children. Later, the name of the group was changed to "DayBreak Parent Child Centre."

14. *ENL*, s.v. "Government."

15. *Newfoundland Royal Commission 1933 Report* (London: His Majesty's Stationery Office, 1933), p. 197.

for which the war was being fought and the Charter stood. But removed from their poverty, Newfoundlanders were distracted by the war . . . and for many, constitutional determination and the political future of their country was the furthest thought from their minds.[16]

All through the war years Canadian and British politicians were in touch with a group of Newfoundlanders who favoured Confederation with Canada:[17]

> The referenda of June and July 1948, in which Newfoundlanders chose Canada, were the culmination of a long and extensive process of constitutional determination and policy-making by the governments of Newfoundland, the United Kingdom, and Canada. Because Newfoundland was not self-governing, policy on Newfoundland's future was quietly arranged by civil servants away from the glare of public scrutiny. Even before Newfoundland politicians became publicly involved, it had been decided that union with Canada was Newfoundland's ultimate destiny, and political plans and structures were put in place to facilitate the union.[18]

On December 11, 1945, the British prime minister, Clement Atlee, announced the establishment of a National Convention in Newfoundland. Forty-five members representing thirty-eight districts in Newfoundland were elected as delegates to the National Convention on June 21, 1946.[19] The convention forwarded recommendations to the British government on possible forms of future government to be chosen by the people in a national referendum. The battles between the "confederates" and those who wanted a return to responsible government raged hot and heavy. It was no secret that Archbishop Roche favoured a return to responsible government, and his

---

16. John Edward FitzGerald, "The Confederation of Newfoundland with Canada, 1946–1949," (master's thesis, Memorial University of Newfoundland, July 1992), p.11.

17. For a thorough and brilliant analysis of the events leading to Newfoundland's Confederation with Canada, see FitzGerald, "Confederation."

18. FitzGerald, "Confederation," p. 1.

19. Although the events that led up to Confederation are of critical importance in the history of Newfoundland, a discussion of these events is outside the scope of this book.

position was supported by a majority of Catholics in St. John's. At this critical time in Newfoundland's history, Archbishop Roche encouraged all religious, sisters, and Christian Brothers, to exercise their right to vote in the referendum. He anticipated, no doubt, that every sister would support his stand and cast her vote for responsible government. However, statements that lay religious had been "released from their vows" by the archbishop in order to cast a vote are not correct.[20] It is true that, prior to 1948, women religious did not exercise their right to vote, but that was more a matter of custom and had nothing to do with the religious vows. In community rooms of Mercy convents across Newfoundland, issues facing the country were studied and debated. When the time came, each sister was expected to vote according to her conscience. Apparently, most of the sisters at Mercy Convent—but not all—agreed with the archbishop that the future of Newfoundland should be decided only after responsible government had been restored to the people.[21]

Eventually, a referendum was held on June 3, 1948. There were three choices on the ballot, a return to responsible government, commission of government, and Confederation with Canada. The sisters from Mercy Convent and Belvedere, the sisters from Presentation Convent, Christian Brothers, and priests in the area voted at polling stations in the gymnasium of the College of Our Lady of Mercy. The story is told that one elderly sister, a strong Newfoundland nationalist, entered the voting booth with the remark, "Well, here's one vote for responsible government." When she emerged from the booth she was beaming with satisfaction, "I marked a big, black X in the second box." The sister to whom she spoke said, "But, Mother Bernard, that means you voted for commission of government!" Poor Mother Bernard begged and pleaded to be given two more chances to vote, one to negate her previous vote, and the other to express her real choice, remarking, "Who—in her right mind—would vote for commission of government!" It took all the eloquence of the returning officer and the persuasion of the sisters who were

---

20. FitzGerald, quoting Harold Horwood in "Confederation," p. 205.
21. M. Basil McCormack, conversation with author, September 8, 1999.

present to convince her that to allow a second vote would be against the law. As she stomped back to the convent, she was heard to remark, "Too bad that we are all such law-abiding citizens!"

Finally, when the results were tabulated, 69,400 (44.55%) Newfoundlanders chose responsible government, 64,066 (41.13%) chose Confederation with Canada, and 22,311 voters (14.32%) wanted a continuation of commission of government.[22] Because the results were considered to be inconclusive, another campaign began almost immediately, leading up to a second referendum. This time commission of government was dropped from the ballot and Newfoundlanders were left with two choices, responsible government or Confederation with Canada. On July 22, 1948, Newfoundlanders went to the polls once more to decide on the fate of their country. When the votes were tabulated, Confederation with Canada won by a slim majority, receiving 78,323 votes to 71,334 for responsible government.[23] On March 31, 1949, the Terms of Union were signed in Ottawa. The following day, April 1, Newfoundlanders woke up to the fact that they were now Canadians. The significance of the day, "April Fools' Day," was not lost on the population, and for the next few weeks, the section, "Letters to the Editor," in the daily newspapers dripped with satire—but also with heartbreak for lost nationhood.

In the years following these events, the bitter hostility between opposing factions that marked the period leading up to March 31, 1949, gradually disappeared. Nevertheless, some Newfoundlanders are convinced that their forebears were railroaded into Confederation with Canada. Newfoundland may have been the only country to voluntarily give up its sovereignty and the control of its own natural resources to become a "have-not" province in a large and very diverse nation. Nevertheless, from a purely material standpoint, the first few years of confederation brought many worthwhile changes to Newfoundland. The post-war years saw a distinct improvement in living conditions and the introduction of Family Allowance, known locally as "the baby bonus," and an increase in Old Age Pensions brought added income to many

---

22. FitzGerald, "Confederation," p.198.
23. Ibid., p. 258.

families. Money was available for roads, education, and improved health serv-ices, and most regions of the new province enjoyed an unprecedented degree of prosperity.

One of the military bases established by the United States government in Newfoundland was Fort Pepperrell in St. John's. Several hundred American servicemen and their families moved into the houses that were constructed on the base. In the autumn of 1952, the US chaplain visited Mercy Convent to ask for the sisters' assistance in providing religious instruction to the children who lived on the base. Beginning in January 1953, three sisters went to Fort Pepperrell every Sunday where, after mass, they prepared the children for the sacraments and held regular religion classes. The first three sisters assigned to this duty were M. Hildegarde Dunphy, M. Pauline Foster, and M. Aquin English. Sisters from Mercy Convent continued to provide this service for a number of years until the Americans withdrew from the base in May 1960.[24]

Two years before the ministry to Fort Pepperrell began, the superior general, M. Imelda Smith,[25] had decided to establish a "Principals' Association of Sisters of Mercy." M. Imelda hoped that through regular meetings and informed discussion, younger sisters appointed to administer schools would learn from more experienced principals. Furthermore, it provided a forum to which younger principals could bring problems and seek solutions. M. Basil McCormack was elected president of the associa-tion, with M. Hildegarde Dunphy as vice-president and M. Teresina Bruce as secretary. The association lasted from January 1952 until January 1966 when it was disbanded.

By the mid-1950s, the school population in St. John's was increasing by leaps and bounds. In an attempt to meet the demand for more school accom-modation, Archbishop Skinner decided to build a new school and chapel in the area known as Smithville on the north side of Elizabeth Avenue, near

---

24. Annals, Convent of Our Lady of Mercy, St. John's, ASMSJ.

25. M. Imelda Smith was elected to the office of superior general on August 15, 1949, and reelected to the same office in 1955. After completing her second term of office in 1961, she was not eligible for reelection and was succeeded by M. Assumpta Veitch.

Rennies River.[26] On September 19, 1955, the new school, named in honour of St. Pius X, was opened. It was placed under the direction of the Sisters of Mercy, with M. Benignus Mullowney as its first principal. The first two sisters to be assigned to St. Pius X School as classroom teachers were M. Georgina Quick and Paula Marie Myers. *The Monitor* announced that the ground floor of the two-storey structure, "intended to provide a future auditorium and parish hall, will be used in the interim as a parish church."[27] The second storey of the building contained five classrooms to accommodate children from kindergarten to grade IV. In addition, there were boys' and girls' rest rooms, a teachers' rest room, the principal's office, and a health clinic. Eventually, St. Pius X included the grades from kindergarten to grade VIII.

Gradually, over the years, more sisters from Mercy Convent were added to the staff of St. Pius X. Initially, most of these sisters were juniors. Every morning, Cyril Bambrick's taxi arrived at Mercy Convent door at twenty after eight to bring M. Benignus and the sisters to school. M. Benignus's practice was to recite the Litany of the Blessed Virgin Mary aloud as the taxi proceeded toward St. Pius X. However, although she was a very prayerful woman, she was also very observant, noticing and commenting on everything including the signs on the buses. And so, the litany would proceed something like this: "Holy Mary," to which the young sisters would respond, "Pray for us." "Holy Mother of God." "Pray for us." "Pay as you enter." To which the answer would follow—with due solemnity—"Pray for us." By the time the taxi drew up at the school door the litany would be completed and the prayer, with all its additions and distractions, offered humbly to God.

Eventually, there were seven sisters on the staff at St. Pius X School. M. Benignus Mullowney held the office of principal at St. Pius X for seven years. She may have had her little eccentricities, but she was a wise, kind, and capable

---

26. St. Pius X Chapel was dedicated by Archbishop P. J. Skinner on January 15, 1956. At first it was a mission of the Basilica Parish of St. John the Baptist, but in 1962 the parish of St. Pius X was created, and members of the Society of Jesus (Jesuits) were invited to assume responsibility for the new parish. Some years later, a new, modern church was built next to St. Pius X School and dedicated to St. Pius X on December 1, 1976.

27. *The Monitor*, September 1955, p.1.

administrator, and under her direction, the school became a first-class institution. From the beginning, M. Benignus was determined that the students from St. Pius X would be part of all the cultural activities offered in the city. Consequently, participation in the Kiwanis Music Festival was an important objective. Every year in September, M. Benignus lined up her small group of young sisters and appointed each as director of some activity to be entered in competition at the festival. Categories included choral speech and classroom choirs. Every class participated, as did the St. Pius X School Choir that was made up of students selected from each classroom in the school. Even the children in kindergarten were not overlooked, for M. Benignus decided that, while their singing was not quite "up to scratch," they would be capable of performing in a rhythm band. The music teacher was charged with imparting musical knowledge and skills, but since a director was necessary, some non-musician was appointed to this task. On one occasion, the young sister appointed to direct the rhythm band objected, "But Mother Benignus, I don't know how to play the drums." This, to M. Benignus was a very lame excuse, "Dear child, you don't have to play the drums. All you have to do is count to four and wave your arms around."[28]

St. Pius X School was blessed with a succession of well-qualified and very capable principals. M. Benignus Mullowney was replaced as principal by a young sister, M. Eulalia (Jean) Woolridge, who remained at St. Pius X for just one year. In September 1964, M. Gonzaga Henley assumed the duties of principal for the next four years, and she was succeeded by Sr. Margaret Pittman. The pressure of new foundations in the 1970s involved taking sisters from the city schools and assigning them to schools in the outports. Thus, when Sr. Colette Nagle became principal at St. Pius X there was only one other sister on the staff. By that time, the school had an enrolment of about six hundred students and a staff of twenty teachers. In 1978, the Congregation of the Sisters of Mercy made a decision to withdraw the sisters from St. Pius X School. One reason for this decision was that some of the smaller schools in the outports had a more urgent need for qualified teachers than did schools in

---

28. I am indebted to Srs. Rosemary Ryan and Madeline Byrne for these stories.

the city. The last sisters to teach at St. Pius X School were Sr. Helen Harding, the principal, and Sr. Patricia Gallant.

Five years after the opening of St. Pius X School and Chapel, a similar facility was opened at Nagle's Hill in the northern section of St. John's on September 2, 1960. This building was dedicated to Our Lady of Lourdes. Once more, the Sisters of Mercy were asked to administer and provide staff for the new school. M. Paschal Dwyer was named as the first principal, and several of the junior sisters at Mercy Convent were appointed as classroom teachers. Subsequently, every morning, two taxis arrived at the door of Mercy Convent at twenty after eight, one to drive the sisters to St. Pius X and the other to take a second group to Our Lady of Lourdes, Nagle's Hill. However, it appears that M. Paschal was not distracted from her prayers by passing buses for there are no stories of non-prayerful asides as the litany was recited on the way to Nagle's Hill. Almost six years later, on January 9, 1966, Our Lady of Lourdes School and Chapel were destroyed by fire. While the new school was being built on the same site, the sisters and students were accommodated in the Canadian Legion Rooms at Fort Pepperrell.[29] Since construction of the new school had proceeded without a hitch, the new building was ready for occupancy in October of that same year. The sisters continued to teach at Our Lady of Lourdes until 1974. A few years later, the school closed.

The year 1955 was a significant milestone in the history of the Roman Catholic Church in Newfoundland, for that year marked the centenary of the consecration of the Cathedral of St. John the Baptist in St. John's. Week-long celebrations were planned to mark the occasion. In 1953, a program of reconstruction and redecoration involving the entire fabric of the cathedral was begun. At the completion of the work in 1954, a new Casavant pipe organ was installed. It is an instrument of sixty-six stops and over 4,000 pipes. While the work was going on, parish masses were celebrated in the auditorium of the College of Our Lady of Mercy, causing it to be referred to by the students as "the co-cathedral." Word would be passed around the school, "Practice for the concert at 3:30 in the 'co-cathedral'!"

---

29. Annals, Convent of Our Lady of Mercy, St. John's, 1966, ASMSJ.

On March 30, 1955, the cathedral was raised to the rank of minor basilica.[30] Celebrations to mark the occasion began on the feast of St. John the Baptist, June 24, with the arrival of Cardinal McGuigan of Toronto. On the following day, the apostolic delegate to Canada, Archbishop Giovanni Panico was officially welcomed to the archdiocese by a liturgical reception in the Basilica-Cathedral. A number of archbishops, bishops, clergy, and religious were present for the Solemn Mass of Thanksgiving that was offered on Sunday, June 27.[31] Crowds of people packed the large cathedral, and many more, who could not be accommodated in the building, stood outside on the grounds.

In addition to the liturgical commemoration, a committee under the chairmanship of Monsignor John Murray was established to plan for a special pageant-drama that was to be the focus of the week-long celebrations. Members of this committee were Dick O'Brien, the producer and director of the pageant; M. Williamina Hogan, the coordinator of the events; and John Holmes, stage manager. The script of the pageant, entitled, *The Triumph of Sacrifice*, had been prepared by two Sisters of Mercy, M. Williamina Hogan and M. Perpetua Bown. It depicted events in the history of the Cathedral of St. John the Baptist and was staged in St. Patrick's Hall Auditorium by Dick O'Brien with local amateur and professional actors.[32] The musical part of the program consisted of an orchestra composed of sixty-one young musicians from the College of Our Lady of Mercy; St. Bride's College, Littledale; and St. Bonaventure's College. The choir consisted of over two hundred voices from the Catholic high schools in the city and another two-hundred-voice boys' choir. The choirs were directed by one of Newfoundland's leading musicians, Ignatius Rumboldt. The orchestra was under the direction of Brother Draney from St. Bonaventure's College.[33] Prior to the presentation of the pageant, the Sisters of Mercy and the Presentation Sisters were kept busy preparing the students to take part in the choirs and the orchestra, for although they did not direct the public performances, they taught the music to the participants. When

---

30. *The Evening Telegram*, March 31, 1955, p. 3.
31. Kennedy, *Centenary*, p. 59.
32. Hogan, *Pathways*, p. 71.
33. Kennedy, *Centenary*, pp. 96–97.

all the celebrations were over and the visitors had returned home, everyone involved breathed a sigh of relief for tasks well done. The centenary was, indeed, a memorable event in the history of the Roman Catholic Church in Newfoundland.

The opening of St. Pius X School in 1955 provided accommodation for some students who otherwise would have attended Our Lady of Mercy. Consequently, it was feared that enrolment at the historic old school might decline. Nevertheless, in 1956, more classroom space was needed at the College of Our Lady of Mercy. Arrangements were made to use some of the rooms in the building that housed the Catholic Youth Club on Harvey Road. At the beginning of the school year 1956–57, two classes of grade I pupils moved over to their new quarters in what became known as "Little Mercy."[34] Subsequently, "Little Mercy" accommodated several primary grades, including kindergarten. At one time Our Lady of Mercy School on Military Road was so overcrowded that the three grade V classes had to be accommodated at "Little Mercy." This division of the school closed in 1973 when the classes returned to the main building on Military Road. But during the thirteen years that "Little Mercy" was in existence, the children participated in the activities that were carried on in the rest of the school, particularly in the area of music. Three times a week, one of the music teachers from "Big Mercy" came to the school to ensure that music was included in the daily curriculum. Beginning with kindergarten, the children participated in rhythm bands and in choral singing classes.

Over at "Big Mercy," the students had the option of belonging to the school choir or joining the orchestra, which during the 1960s was under the direction of M. Edwardine Furlong. The departure of the senior students in grades X and XI was a serious blow to the orchestra. Nevertheless, the loss of the more experienced players was a challenge to the younger students to work hard so that they could measure up to the expectations of their director.

---

34. Annals, Convent of Our Lady of Mercy, St. John's, September 1956, ASMSJ.

By the year 1962, enrolment at Our Lady of Mercy School had increased to over a thousand students.[35] However, at the end of the school year, in June 1963, the school board decided that students entering grade IX in September should attend Holy Heart High School. But in spite of the loss of the grade IX's, the enrolment at Our Lady of Mercy in September 1963, was just thirteen short of one thousand students. The Mercy Convent annalist noted, "Despite the exodus of Grade IX to HHM and more than seventy of our girls to the new St. Raphael's, enrolment is 987."[36] That same year, two music students of Mercy Convent, Patricia Connolly and Rosalie Lake, won first place in Canada in their respective grades in piano performance in the Trinity College of Music examinations. This was by no means the first time that music pupils at Our Lady of Mercy had won such honours. Periodically, since Newfoundland students first entered the Trinity College of Music examinations, students of Our Lady of Mercy distinguished themselves in these examinations.

Choral music always played a big part in the life of Mercy students, and children at every level participated in singing. However, prior to 1960, the official school choir was made up of students from the senior grades. But, in 1958, with the opening of Holy Heart of Mary High School, Our Lady of Mercy, like the other Catholic schools in the St. John's area, lost all its senior students to the high school. In 1960, Our Lady of Mercy Glee Club was formed consisting of 130 students from grades I to grade IX.[37]

The only requirement for admission to the group was the ability to sing in tune and a commitment to after-school and Saturday morning rehearsals. After a few months, the choir became so popular that just about every girl in the school wanted to become a member. This meant that another condition for admission had to be added—the choir could not accept more than 130 girls because the stage was too small to accommodate any more!

---

35. Annals, Convent of Our Lady of Mercy, St. John's, September 9, 1962, ASMSJ. The annalist noted that the enrolment was 1,038 students. There were twenty-six teachers on staff.

36. Ibid., September 3, 1963, ASMSJ.

37. In 1962, the grade IX students were required to go to Holy Heart, and from that time until 1967, the glee club accepted students from grade I to grade VIII.

From the beginning, the glee club was popular with the students. The first major performance for this choir was the Christmas concert. The concert was such a success that the local station of the Canadian Broadcasting Corporation asked permission to record the choir for an hour-long Christmas program that was broadcast throughout the province. The reaction of the public was very positive. Congratulations poured in from all over Newfoundland. But this was just the beginning. The next major challenge for the choir was the Kiwanis Music Festival that took place in the spring of 1961. Once more, the Mercy girls were successful, and students from Our Lady of Mercy carried off first place in almost every category in which they competed. Also, Our Lady of Mercy Glee Club was awarded the plaque for the "Most Outstanding Performance" and the Silver Cup that had been won a few years previously by the Immaculate Conception Choir, Bell Island.[38] Year after year, the choir improved as new and more difficult challenges were presented, and year after year, it won the award for the "Most Outstanding Performance" of the festival.[39]

Furthermore, every child at Our Lady of Mercy participated in her own classroom choir. In addition, students competed in solo instrumental and vocal classes; in duets, trios, and triple trios; and in various choral groupings. In 1964, Our Lady of Mercy Glee Club received the highest mark ever awarded in the festival up to that time. Every year, at the conclusion of the festival, the Mercy students presented a concert at Holy Heart auditorium so that their parents would have an opportunity to hear some of the music performed during the competition. The Mercy Convent annalist noted that 960 children took part in the concert held in Holy Heart auditorium on April 6, 1964.[40]

In 1964, Our Lady of Mercy Glee Club, consisting of girls from the age of six to fourteen years, won the George S. Mathieson Trophy for most outstand-

---

38. Since the inauguration of the music festival there had been enthusiastic competition among many schools for the Silver Cup, awarded each year to the choir that obtained the highest mark in choral competition. Any choir that was successful in winning the cup for three successive years was awarded final possession of the trophy. Eventually, in 1962, Our Lady of Mercy Glee Club was awarded possession of the Silver Cup.

39. The "Most Outstanding Performance" award consisted not only of a plaque, but also of a cash award of $200 that Our Lady of Mercy Glee Club donated every year to the Mercy mission in Peru.

40. Annals, Convent of Our Lady of Mercy, St. John's, August 1964, ASMSJ.

ing junior choir (nineteen years and under) in all of Canada. The trophy was awarded on the recommendation of British adjudicators for performance at festivals affiliated with the Federation of Canadian Music Festivals. Winning choirs from all over the country submitted taped performances, and the winner of the trophy was selected from hundreds of these competing choirs. Each choir performed two compositions. Our Lady of Mercy Glee Club sang, "In Monte Oliveti" by G. B. Martini and a Gregorian Chant, "Esto Mihi." In awarding the Mathieson Trophy to Our Lady of Mercy Glee Club, the adjudicators noted that the choir's performance was "outstanding on account of the unanimity and blending of tone, awareness of pitch in the plain chant excerpt, which was sustained for a period of over five minutes."[41] Another commentator remarked, "It is clear that the girls of Our Lady of Mercy Glee Club have a deep love for and appreciation of music, and the sincerity and sensitiveness of the approach which they bring to their songs is something very unique and truly their own."[42]

After the announcement that the choir had been awarded the Mathieson Trophy, the next thing was to arrange for the presentation of the trophy to the choir. For this reason, a concert was held on September 14, 1964. At the conclusion, Mrs. Peg O'Dea, wife of the lieutenant governor of Newfoundland, presented the trophy to the choir director. The editor of *The Evening Telegram*, whose daughter was a member of the Glee Club, published an editorial on the choir. Among other things, he wrote of his daughter and the choir:

> She's only one of 130 singers between 6 and 14 years, so her contribution is relatively small. But it is the synthesis, the sum total of these small contributions that produced a sound of music which this year received national acclaim and brought credit to school, city and province.[43]

This was not the end of music-making by Our Lady of Mercy Glee Club. In 1966, the choir received an invitation from the mayor of Montreal, Jean

---

41. Adjudication of Our Lady of Mercy Glee Club, St. John's, Newfoundland, given in Calgary, Alberta, July 2, 1964, ASMSJ.
42. Quoted in the souvenir program published on the occasion of the presentation of the Mathieson Trophy to Our Lady of Mercy Glee Club, September 14, 1964, ASMSJ.
43. Michael Harrington, *The Evening Telegram*, July 24, 1964, p. 4.

Drapeau, to perform six concerts at Expo '67. Before making any decision, the sisters invited the parents of the choir members to meet in the Mercy auditorium to discuss the invitation. Without any hesitation, the parents agreed unanimously that this was a wonderful opportunity for their children and an honour to be invited to participate in such an event. A parents' committee was formed, and plans were made to raise money to send the children to Montreal. For the next year, the parents held card parties, bake sales, and craft fairs. The choir members, too, did their part to raise money for the trip to Montreal. Early in 1967, nine girls from the Mercy Glee Club formed a group called The Emcees and entered a CBC television competition. The Emcees—Ann Darcy, Shelley Keough, Terry Mitchell, Karen Oakley, Anita Power, Doreen Power, Margo Power, Kathy Wall, and Patsy White—took first place, and the prize money was donated to help cover the costs of sending the glee club to Expo '67. Meanwhile, the children set to work to prepare enough material to fill six hour-long concert programs. This involved learning eighty different compositions.

Finally, everything was in place. On August 25, 1967, one hundred and thirty girls from the ages of six to fourteen years descended on St. John's airport ready to board the Air Canada flight to Montreal.[44] Two sisters from St. Clare's, both registered nurses, accompanied the choir, M. Kieran Hartery and M. St. Clare Maddigan. The children were organized in groups of ten, each group under the care of a Sister of Mercy. Altogether, with the choir director and the accompanist, M. Celine Veitch, seventeen Sisters of Mercy accompanied the choir to Montreal.

While in Montreal, the choir was housed in a boys' boarding school that was vacant during the summer months. One hundred and thirty cots were set up in a huge dormitory. Consequently, the biggest challenge for the sisters was to make sure that the older girls, the thirteen and fourteen year-olds, did not stay up all night talking. Inevitably, there were a few unanticipated problems. For instance, there was the night that the sister on duty was awakened by the sound of hastily muted squeaks and squeals. When she investigated, she discovered that four or five of the older students had decided to pierce one another's

---

44. *The Evening Telegram*, August 26, 1967, p. 22.

ears. Fortunately, the attempt stopped short when the first volunteer uttered the howl that awakened the sister in charge. Another choir member fell madly in love with a young lad who had been hired to help the school janitor. She could not speak a word of French, and the object of her affections suffered from a similar handicap with reference to English. Then there were the scraped knees, cut fingers, and upset stomachs that are the inevitable lot of small children. The most serious event occurred when one child had to be brought to the hospital with an attack of appendicitis. Fortunately, the pain subsided after a few hours, and she was able to take part in all but one of the concerts at Expo.

The experience of performing at Expo '67 was something that the participants would remember, probably for the rest of their lives. The six concerts they performed at different international pavilions were very well-attended, and the comments and congratulations they received on the quality of their singing was a source of encouragement and an incentive for each child to continue to make music an important part of her life.

Finally, it was over, and the choir returned home on September 1 to an enthusiastic welcome in St. John's. Three days later, on September 4, Our Lady of Mercy Glee Club performed one final concert for parents and friends in St. John's. The Canon Sterling Auditorium was packed for the occasion, for this was a farewell concert. When school began the next day, the choir was reorganized, and a new chapter began in the history of music at Our Lady of Mercy School.

Before leaving the story of Our Lady of Mercy Glee Club, it must be acknowledged and recognized that much of the success of this choir was due to the sensitive and brilliant piano accompaniments of M. Celine Veitch. But M. Celine brought more than her splendid musicianship to Our Lady of Mercy Glee Club. In all the years that this outstanding choir was in existence, through her quiet presence and encouragement, her suggestions and constructive criticism, Sister M. Celine contributed more than anyone else to the unique beauty of tone and expressiveness that characterized this choir and made it something very special. M. Celine's musicianship, her outstanding ability as a pianist, and her lifelong devotion to music and to the students she taught was acknowledged when, on June 2, 2004, she was inducted into the Hall of Honour of the Music Festival Association.

Through all the years when new Mercy convents were opening in various parts of Newfoundland, flourishing for a time, and then closing, the sisters' schools on Bell Island soldiered on through good times and bad. Apparently, almost from the beginning, the Immaculate Conception School was filled to overflowing, and the numbers kept increasing:

> On September 29, 1938, the Archbishop visited the Convent School and seeing that the accommodations were very inadequate, he made arrangements for the building of three classrooms, the basement serving as separate dressing halls for boys and girls. (There were seven Sisters on the staff this year).[45]

The extension was completed on January 17, 1938. Grades IX, X, and XI occupied one of the new classrooms, grades VI, VII, and VIII the other. The third room was used for singing, drill, and other activities, and a second music room was provided. It was in 1938 that students of the Immaculate Conception School wore uniforms for the first time.

However, in spite of the extra classrooms provided there was not enough space to accommodate the number of students. From July to November, 1944, the school was once more under reconstruction and repair with a major extension attached to the existing building. This time a whole new storey was added that consisted of four extra classrooms, an assembly hall, library, commercial room, science room, and two music rooms. The new extension also included a special room fitted out as a domestic science room. During the construction period, classes for the senior grades were held in St. James Hall.[46]

The convent, as well, proved to be too small to accommodate the number of sisters required for the school, and in 1933, an extension was added to the convent. It was the time of the Depression, and money was very scarce. The sisters purchased the necessary materials, and because the mines were

---

45. The entry is from the logbook in the office of the principal of the Immaculate Conception School. The information was compiled by M. Assumpta Veitch and sent to M. Basil McCormack. The logbook was destroyed by fire in 1969. ASMSJ, RG 10/15/26.
46. Ibid.

working only two days a week at the time, the men of the parish contributed free labour. In 1938, a new chapel was added to the convent and the old chapel converted into bedrooms. Then, in 1946, a fourth floor was added to the convent to provide the extra space needed for twelve sisters.

Still the school enrolment continued to climb. Sr. Adrienne Keough recalled that in 1944, she was assigned to Immaculate Conception School to teach grade III. For a few weeks, until work on the extension was completed, there were twenty-four desks in her classroom with three children in a desk. All unnecessary furniture, such as extra bookcases and large statues, were removed from all the classrooms to make more room. Sr. Adrienne remembered that one day a four-foot statue of St. Joseph was placed outside the grade II classroom. The principal, M. Benignus Mullowney—who was nearsighted—noticed the little figure standing forlornly on the corridor and rushed off to fetch a chair from her office so that "the poor child might have a place to sit"![47] But, in spite of crowded classrooms and nearsighted principals, the Immaculate Conception Academy was a progressive school. It had a reputation for academic scholarship, musical achievements, and dramatic ability. The educational authorities recognized this, and on December 8, 1944, the school was granted the status of an academy.[48]

In the meantime, World War II broke out. Ore from Bell Island was in great demand by the allied countries. Consequently, the island was a target for enemy action—in fact, Bell Island was the only place in North America to have seen such action in this war. The pier where eighty thousand tons of iron ore was stored for shipping was torpedoed by German U-boats in 1942. At low tide, the relics of the four ships that were sunk during the attack can still be seen under the waters of Conception Bay. Many years later, a memorial was built on the shore to commemorate the sixty-nine men who lost their lives in this attack.

---

47. Adrienne Keough, "The Way We Were," Address given at reunion of the staff and students of Immaculate Conception Academy and St. Kevin's School, July 22, 1995, ASMSJ, RG 10/15/12.

48. Copied from the Annals, Immaculate Conception Convent, Bell Island, by M. Assumpta Veitch. The Annals were destroyed by fire in 1969. ASMSJ, RG 10/15/53.

In September 1951, work was begun on the basement of the new extension to the school. This provided six additional classrooms as well as a spacious basement.[49] In September of the same year, M. Assumpta Veitch was named principal of the Immaculate Conception Academy. At the time, M. Finbar (Kathleen) Buck was one of the music teachers at the school. The two sisters co-operated in producing a series of very fine musical and dramatic performances that demonstrated the ability of the students and were a source of first-class entertainment for the public—and extra income for the school!

For a number of years, there was no commercial room in the Immaculate Conception School, but this omission did not prevent the sisters from teaching commercial subjects. Apparently, M. Catherine Greene, the first sister to teach business courses at Immaculate Conception, taught her classes in the convent parlour. After M. Catherine was assigned to another convent, M. Kevin Kennedy continued to use the parlour until the school was able to provide two extra classrooms. One of these rooms was equipped with typewriters and the other reserved for additional commercial subjects such as bookkeeping, shorthand, business English, and accounting. In 1953, M. Kevin was assigned to St. Joseph's Convent in St. John's, and M. Thérèse (Irene) Kennedy took over the direction of the commercial studies at the Immaculate Conception Academy. These subjects were in great demand by the young people of Bell Island, for in the 1940s and '50s, jobs were plentiful. Consequently, young men and women of all religious denominations came to the Immaculate Conception Academy to enroll in business education courses offered by the school.

Music, too, played a very important role in activities at the school. Most of the Bell Island children were very musical and loved to be involved in musical activities. Beginning in 1945, and for the next five years, M. Edwardine Furlong entered a class of about twenty girls in the singing examinations of Trinity College of Music. The choir did so well the first year that they continued through the grades up to higher local in 1950. In 1950, a student of M. Finbar (Kathleen) Buck from the Immaculate Conception Academy, Agnes Fleming,

49. Logbook, Immaculate Conception School, Bell Island, copied by M. Assumpta Veitch.

received first place in Newfoundland in the intermediate examination from Trinity College, receiving ninety-four percent in pianoforte performance.

In the period from 1955 to 1960, music continued to play a major role in the life of the Immaculate Conception Academy. The students not only continued to produce plays and operettas—with costumes imported from Montreal—but also availed of the opportunity to perform for St. John's audiences at the Kiwanis Music Festival. Every class in the school, grade I to grade XI, entered the music festival. The lower classes up to grade VI entered the classroom choir category appropriate to the grade. The students from grades VII to XI entered several categories such as folk song choirs, sacred music choirs, girls' choirs fourteen years and under, and girls' choirs eighteen years and under. Furthermore, the children participated in solo instrumental and vocal classes, duets, and vocal ensembles. This meant that even when the Christmas concert was over, the sounds of singing continued to ring through the halls of the Immaculate Conception Academy from early morning until half past four in the afternoon when the choir director had to be back in the convent for prayers.

In those days, boys from that section of the parish attended the Immaculate Conception Academy until they had completed grade IV.[50] The boys, too, participated in the music festival in various solo vocal and instrumental categories, as well as in choral singing classes and rhythm bands. One of the major headaches for the music teacher responsible for these classes was the problem of transporting large groups of children back and forth across the Tickle in all kinds of weather and arranging for buses to bring them from Portugal Cove to St. John's and back again. There was the occasion when a rumour spread like wildfire throughout the island—all the rats had left the *Elmer Jones*, the ferry that was on the regular run across the Tickle. This was an infallible sign that the boat was going to sink on its next attempt to put to sea. Fortunately, someone spotted a large rodent sauntering up the gangplank of the *Elmer Jones* an hour before the young singers were due to leave the island. It was judged safe to proceed to St. John's!

---

50. After completing grade IV, the boys moved to St. Kevin's Boys' School.

The responsibility of bringing the children back and forth across the Tickle in the years between 1955 and 1960 was shared by most of the twelve sisters living at Immaculate Conception Convent, each one of whom was willing to lend a hand. As well, since each classroom teacher travelled with the members of her class, the children were thoroughly supervised. The boys, however, frequently managed to escape the watchful eye of the music teacher and avail of the opportunity to visit the store on the "Beach" to purchase and devour large quantities of chips and candy before boarding the boat—with disastrous results. During the week of the festival, the unfortunate music teacher often made as many as six trips a day across the Tickle, accompanying different groups back and forth to St. John's. On one occasion, the entire sixty-member senior girls' choir was stranded in St. John's because a sudden storm prevented the boat from sailing back to the island. However, the sisters in St. John's came to the rescue. Beds were found at Littledale and at Belvedere for the marooned Bell Islanders, and the worrisome event turned into a happy adventure. This occurred on the last day of the festival when the Immaculate Conception Choir from Bell Island won the highest mark awarded in the festival, coming ahead of all the more prestigious St. John's choirs. The Immaculate Conception Choir returned three days later to perform at the "Stars of the Festival" concert. At that time, they were awarded a prize of $200 for the most outstanding performance and the coveted Silver Cup that was presented annually by the Music Festival Association to the group that achieved the highest mark. It was the first time that either of these prizes had been won by a school from outside the capital city.

While the students of the Immaculate Conception Academy were very involved in music and drama, these activities were not permitted to detract from the time spent in more academic pursuits. Many graduates of the school entered the teaching profession and, through the years, made a significant contribution in the field of education in Newfoundland and elsewhere. Others entered the field of business and carved out successful careers in that area. A number of graduates entered St. Clare's Mercy Hospital School of

Nursing to devote their lives to the care of the sick, and some entered the Congregation of the Sisters of Mercy.

The 1950s was a period of great prosperity for Bell Island. The abundance of work brought about a growth in population, so that in 1961, there were 12,281 people living on the island. But already in the late 1950s, a dark cloud was beginning to gather that affected the lives of the majority of the population. Rumours began to circulate of competition from other sources where new methods of production produced a better quality ore at less cost. On April 19, 1966, an announcement was made that the Bell Island mines would close. Although, for several years, ominous rumours had been circulating on the future of the mines, most people were shocked by the news. The closure of the mines led to a huge exodus from Bell Island. Because hundreds of families were forced to pack up and move to other parts of Canada to look for employment, there was a decrease in enrolment in all the schools on Bell Island.

For the next few years, the school situation on Bell Island was in a state of continual reorganization as the school board tried to come to grips with the rapidly decreasing school population. In 1967, the Immaculate Conception Academy opened with a total of six hundred students and twenty-three teachers. On the other hand, St. Edward's School at the Front had only fifty-six girls registered in the high-school grades. Because of this, it was decided that the high-school students from St. Edward's should attend classes at the Immaculate Conception Academy during the school year 1967–68. The following year, in 1968, the students found themselves shuttled off once more to a different school. Girls up to and including grade VI and boys up to Grade III attended the Immaculate Conception Elementary School. St. Edward's became a central high school for girls from grades VII to XI. All boys from grades IV to XI continued to attend St. Kevin's. But this was not the end of the school reorganization. In 1969, the Immaculate Conception was designated as a kindergarten to grade VI elementary school. St. Edward's became a coeducational regional high school, accommodating boys and girls from grades IX to grade XI. Apparently the reason for the change was not completely grasped by some of the male students. When asked to define "coeducation" one lad wrote,

"Coed is joining together of boys and girls in a common classroom for the sake of banishing all foolishness from the school."[51]

The school situation on Bell Island was a matter of serious concern to the General Council of the Sisters of Mercy in St. John's. This was the time when new foundations were being requested in other parts of Newfoundland, but as usual, there were not enough sisters to fill all these demands. It was clear that it was no longer necessary to maintain two large convents on Bell Island, for either of the two was able to accommodate the number of sisters teaching on the island. Reluctantly, the General Council decided to close the Immaculate Conception Convent at the end of June 1968. The sisters of that community were assigned to St. Edward's Convent. Nevertheless, they continued to teach at the Immaculate Conception School, leaving St. Edward's in the morning and returning in the evening. They continued to use the Immaculate Conception Convent for lunch breaks and for after-school duties such as the correction and preparation of work. Consequently, there did not seem to be any urgency for removing documents and records from the convent at that time.

Things continued as usual for another year, until the night of December 12–13, 1969. The sisters at St. Edward's celebrated Foundation Day, December 12, in fine style with a special dinner in the evening and an extended recreation period after dinner. Because it was Friday evening, nobody had to rush off to correct papers or prepare lessons for the next day. Everyone was in bed and sound asleep when the phone woke them. Mrs. Nellie O'Neill had phoned to tell Sr. Colette Ryan, the superior, that the Immaculate Conception Church and School were on fire and that her husband, Cyril, was on his way to drive the sisters to the convent so that they could remove anything of value. By this time, most of the sisters had heard the phone and were getting ready to leave. Cyril O'Neill was at the door within minutes, but by the time they arrived at the scene of the fire, the convent was already in flames. It was a heartbreaking experience for the people of the parish and for the sisters to listen to the roar of the fire as it consumed the interior of the beautiful

---

51. Annals, St. Edward's Convent, Bell Island, ASMSJ.

Immaculate Conception Church and to watch the great sheets of flame thrusting through the roof and windows. About fifteen minutes after the sisters arrived on the scene a loud crash was heard as the floor of the choir gallery collapsed and the large Hammond organ fell two stories to the basement of the building. All three buildings, church, school, and convent, were engulfed in flames, and there was no hope of saving anything. All the school records, the Immaculate Conception Convent Annals, and other important documents were lost. In addition, the house next door to the convent, which was the home of the Kolonel family, was destroyed.

The fire, an act of arson, started sometime after midnight. At quarter to three, Mrs. Vincent Barry heard three loud explosions, one after another.[52] She looked out the window and saw the side of the Immaculate Conception Church in flames. Her husband, Vincent, the principal of St. Kevin's Boys' School, sounded the alarm. Within minutes the eight members of the Volunteer Fire Brigade were at the scene. People gathered quickly, and more than thirty additional volunteers joined in a futile attempt to halt the progress of the fire.[53] When it became obvious that the church buildings and the Kolonel home could not be saved, the firemen and all the volunteers worked desperately and successfully to prevent the fire from spreading to other homes and businesses in the vicinity.

By five o'clock in the morning, there was nothing left of the large complex—church, school, convent—except part of the concrete structure of the church and heaps of smoldering rubble that marked the place where the large school and convent had stood. Cyril O'Neill drove the sisters back to St. Edward's Convent in silence—nobody had the heart for conversation. Since 1966, Bell Island had endured many hard knocks with the closure of the mines and the exodus of hundreds of families. Now with the loss of the Immaculate Conception Church, School, and Convent it was almost as if the heart and soul had been taken out of that section of Bell Island known as the

---

52. Sr. Colette Ryan, conversation with author, June 3, 2000. The three explosions heard by Mrs. Barry were caused by the shattering of the stained glass windows in the church.

53. ASMSJ, RG 10/15/103.

Mines.[54] Everyone realized that these buildings would never be replaced. Certainly, in time, a church and a school would have to be built, but the community could never afford to restore what had been lost.[55]

The following week, representatives from the Roman Catholic School Board came to Bell Island and worked with M. Brian Carroll, the principal of the Immaculate Conception School, and the principals of other Catholic schools to work out a means of accommodating students displaced by the fire. It was decided that the majority could move to St. Cecilia's School in the West Mines and the rest to St. Kevin's Boys' School, using a shift system until such time as a new elementary school would be built.

Construction of the new school was begun in 1970. Sr. Marilyn Doyle was designated principal of St. Kevin's School, a position she held until 1972, when the new Immaculate Conception Elementary School was opened and Sr. Marilyn was named its first principal. The sisters continued to administer the Immaculate Conception School until 1993 when Sr. Madeline Byrne retired. Sr. Madeline was the last sister-principal of the Immaculate Conception School. After that, the sisters continued to teach there under the administration of a lay principal.

During all the years that the Immaculate Conception Convent and School were developing and expanding, St. Edward's School at the Front was experiencing similar growth. When, in 1928, the new six-room St. Edward's School was built opposite St. Michael's Church, a small commercial school was included. The former school, St. Joseph's Hall, served as a boys' school until it was replaced by St. Michael's Boys' School in 1941.

Naturally, there was a healthy rivalry between the students of St. Edward's and the Immaculate Conception. But when it came to supporting the Bell Island hockey team, there was no question of divided loyalties. During the years between 1940 and 1960, this team was one of the finest on the Avalon

---

54. The official name for that section of Bell Island is Wabana, but at that time, most people referred to it as "The Mines."

55. The new Immaculate Conception Church was opened in 1972. It was constructed on the same site as the original St. James basement church and the upstairs church that was dedicated to the Immaculate Conception. The new church was a much smaller, one-storey building.

Peninsula. Among the team's most ardent supporters were the sisters in the two convents on the island. There is a legend that every year Monsignor George Bartlett, the parish priest,[56] brought all the hockey uniforms to the convents where the sisters sewed medals into the hems of the sweaters. This was to ensure the success of the team in fiercely contested games against Bell Island's archrival, the mighty St. Bonaventure's team in St. John's.

By the year 1952, it became clear that St. Edward's School was far too small for the number of students living in that section of Bell Island. Subsequently, a major extension (completed in 1953) provided eleven classrooms, two music rooms, large well-equipped general science and home economics laboratories, a library and reading room, a teachers' conference room, and a principal's office. A social room, tiered at one end, was capable of being converted to a large choral room.

Since the time of M. Aloysius Rawlins, one of the founding sisters, music played an important part in the curriculum at St. Edward's. Every year during the 1950s, the music students went to the Kiwanis Music Festival in St. John's to take part in various categories. However, in the spring of the year the Tickle is often packed with ice. This happened two years in succession, in 1960 and '61. The children of Bell Island, who had worked so hard to perfect their performances, were unable to compete because of the ice in the Tickle. Consequently, in 1962, the people of Bell Island decided to have their own local music festival on the island. At the time, the music teacher at St. Edward's was M. Ita Hennessey. She prepared over three hundred of the pupils to take part in singing, choral speech, and vocal and piano solos. Several awards were won by the school, including prizes of twenty dollars each to Marian Kennedy and Sheila Grant. Subsequently Sheila became a Sister of Mercy. Up to the present time, she refuses to reveal what she did with the twenty dollars!

During the 1970s, the sisters continued their work in St. Edward's and Immaculate Conception. Except for the continuing depletion of the school population, things continued very much as they had been since the closure of

---

56. Rev. George Bartlett was ordained to the priesthood in 1924 and assigned as curate to Rev. J. McGrath on Bell Island. Fr. Bartlett spent his entire priestly life on Bell Island, succeeding Fr. McGrath in 1936.

the mines. During the school year 1981–82, there were seven sisters living in St. Edward's Convent. Two sisters were on the teaching staff at the high school, and a third volunteered her services in the school. Three sisters taught at the Immaculate Conception Elementary, and Sr. Theresa Ryan worked in St. Michael's Parish as pastoral assistant.[57] Sr. Rosaline Hynes spent most of her spare time after school in encouraging parents to become involved in activities for teenagers. She held meetings and information sessions with several groups to enlist good advocates for the purpose of forming a youth organization. The results of all this work were realized the following year when the Youth Ministry Organization was formed. An adult executive body and a youth executive group directed the organization. A number of young people between the ages of sixteen and twenty-one years joined the organization and found constructive ways to spend time. At the beginning of the school year in September 1983, the leaders of the Youth Ministry group visited the convent in despair. Sr. Rosaline Hynes had been reassigned to St. Mary's on the Humber, and the group was looking for a sister to "take charge"! Sr. Alicia Linehan, who admitted that she was frightened to death of teenagers and post-teens, agreed—with much trepidation—to undertake this ministry. She led the group for the next four years with a great deal of success, providing leadership to both parents and youth. Activities included basketball twice a week, triathlons during good weather, ball games, social activities, and charitable activities, such as fundraising for the Boys and Girls Clubs, the hospital, and the school. The group planned and sponsored evenings for seniors and educational activities such as speech nights and debates. Under Sr. Alicia's direction, retreats were held every year, and guest speakers were invited to address the group on a variety of subjects. In addition, the young people were encouraged to participate in the church liturgies as readers, Eucharistic ministers, and altar servers. The Youth Ministry Organization was responsible for initiating candy stripers at the hospital, and members of the group visited the sick on a regular basis.[58]

---

57. The sisters on the staff of St. Edward's were: Sr. Colette Nagle (principal), Sr. Ruth Beresford, and Sr. Paula Penney (volunteer); at Immaculate Conception: Sr. Monica Hickey (principal), Sr. Maureen Lawlor (music), and Sr. Rosaline Hynes.

58. Annals, St. Edward's Convent, Bell Island, 1983–84.

In the mid-1980s, the original St. Michael's Church was torn down because of structural weakness. The Immaculate Conception Church at The Mines was renamed St. Michael's and became the titular parish church. At the same time, St. Edward's High School was beginning to show the wear and tear of years. The Roman Catholic School Board decided that, rather than attempt to repair the ravages of time, it would be less costly to abandon the old school and build a new, modern high school. The new school was built on the land where the former parish church had stood. Thus, it was appropriate that when it was completed, it was named St. Michael's High School. Shortly before Christmas, on December 20, 1985, the students moved into their new school. Subsequently, the old St. Edward's School was demolished.

By the year 1986, the number of sisters at St. Edward's was reduced to five. Thus, when the ice moved into the Tickle, the convent was able to accommodate some of the teachers and nurses who found themselves marooned on the island.[59] Each year, the number of sisters diminished. For instance in 1988–89, only four sisters remained in the convent, then three, and eventually two sisters were left. In June 1990, the Sisters of Mercy relinquished the principalship of St. Michael's High School. The last sister to hold this position was Sr. Michelle Gibbons.

November 21, 1990, marked the centenary of the establishment of the Newfoundland Teachers' Association. In honour of the occasion, the Bell Island Branch of the NTA celebrated an ecumenical service at St. Cyprian's Anglican Church. M. Paula Penney, who had taught on Bell Island for a number of years, was guest speaker for the occasion. Some months later, on February 15, 1991, a banquet was held to commemorate the anniversary of the founding of the NTA on Bell Island. The annalist noted, "M. Paula Penney attended the banquet because the hockey game was cancelled."[60] There was no mistaking M. Paula's priorities!

By the end of the year 1990, it became clear that the days of St. Edward's Convent were numbered. It all began in September 1989, when one evening

---

59. Ibid., March 21, 1987.
60. Ibid., February 15, 1991.

during supper Sr. Madeline Byrne mentioned to the other three sisters that the board of directors for the daycare program was looking for a larger space for their operation. Sr. Madeline pointed out that the convent would make an ideal place for such an activity since there were four large rooms on the first floor and eight or nine rooms upstairs that could be used. As the meal continued, Sr. Madeline mused, "the daycare program could be extended to include adult education, parent groups, etc." Then she added, "I think we should sell the convent!" Srs. Michelle Gibbons and Elizabeth O'Keefe thought it was a brilliant idea. M. Paula Penney, on the other hand, declared it was "simply outrageous!" Later on, the matter was broached once more at a community meeting, and all four agreed to present the proposal to the treasurer general, Sr. Patricia March. For her part, Sr. Patricia was somewhat taken aback by the suggestion, but knowing Sr. Madeline and her habit of dreaming the "impossible dream," Patricia was not altogether surprised. She agreed to bring the matter to the next meeting of the General Council. Within two weeks (October 1989), Sr. Patricia informed St. Edward's community that they could go ahead with the idea of selling the convent to the daycare board if the organization was interested. This was good news for the sisters. The upkeep of the convent was proving to be quite costly. The roof and most of the windows had to be replaced, and the whole building needed to be painted. Furthermore, the convent, intended to house twelve sisters, was much too large for the four who remained.

Within the next few weeks, the house was appraised and the land surveyed. Meanwhile, meetings were held with members of the board of the daycare centre who were most anxious to purchase the property if the necessary funding could be procured from Newfoundland and Labrador Housing Corporation. After dozens of meetings and even more petitions, the funding was not forthcoming. However, two ladies from Bell Island heard of the proposed sale of the convent. Marilyn Windsor and Maude Newton Chancey arrived one evening and were given a tour of the convent. Both ladies were very impressed by the architecture, the cleanliness, the spacious rooms, and the number of bedrooms. They told the sisters that they were interested in purchasing the house for a bed and breakfast facility if they could secure the necessary funding and permission from various levels of government. This request and many subsequent offers to purchase the convent for various enterprises were duly submitted to the General Council. Eventually, two years after the original proposal had been made, the convent was sold to Maude Newton Chancey on August 10, 1991.[61]

Meanwhile, the sisters decided to look for a place to live, just in case they might have to move out of the convent with little or no advance warning. Srs. Madeline Byrne, Theresa March, and Theresa Boland, the three sisters remaining on Bell Island in 1990, looked at a number of houses. Some were too big, some were too small, some were too expensive, others seemed just right but needed major repairs. One of the vacant houses that seemed suitable was on Snob Hill.[62] The house, which belonged to the hospital, needed extensive repairs and renovations. Sr. Patricia March arranged with the hospital to rent the house, and renovations began immediately. However, when the convent was sold in August 1991, the renovations were far from being completed. The three sisters were like the fabled O'Brien of the Southern Shore, who had "no place to go!" Fortunately, the parish priest, Fr. David Butler came to the rescue and invited them to stay at the presbytery until the house on Snob Hill was ready for occupancy. Fr. Butler, arranged also for the sisters' furniture to be stored in the club room of the parish hall.

Sr. Theresa March, one of the three remaining sisters on Bell Island, left an account of the closing of the convent. She wrote:

> August 19th (1991) was a sad yet hope-filled day for St. Edward's community—sad, because the convent was officially given over to new owners; hopeful, because we felt that the building would be put to good use and the spirit of Mercy hospitality would

---

61. Mrs. Chancey Newton renamed the convent "Wabana Inn" and operated it as a bed and breakfast facility for a couple of years. The business was not a success and the property passed into other hands. Most recently it was used to house a group of teenage boys from Labrador who had been sent to Bell Island for rehabilitation.

62. When the mines were in operation, the managers and other such exalted personages built their homes on this street, Dosco Hill. The local people renamed it "Snob Hill" and, for better or worse, the street is still unofficially referred to as Snob Hill.

continue in a bed-and-breakfast facility to serve the people of
Bell Island.[63]

The sisters had their hands full with the task of packing everything that had
been accumulated over the past seventy-four years since the convent was
established. Nevertheless, they proceeded with great foresight. Before dis-
turbing anything or removing any of the furniture, they arranged for a pho-
tographer to record on video tape every room in the convent. Furthermore,
they invited all sisters who had worked on Bell Island, as well as those who had
been born on the island, to visit the convent for the last time. As usual, they
could depend on the traditional generosity of other sisters to help them in the
task of packing. Sure enough, that same evening Sr. Alicia Linehan arrived by
the seven o'clock boat, and the three set to work to prepare the table for the
visitors who were invited for the following day. On Sunday, August 11, thirty-
five sisters arrived for lunch. It was a sad, yet happy day for sisters who had
spent several years at St. Edward's. M. Placide Conway, a native Bell Islander,
remembered the sisters who had been on the foundation. The Annals from the
foundation days were displayed and the framed text of the first house blessing,
dated 1919, was presented to Sr. Marion Collins for the archives. By six
o'clock, all the visitors had departed, leaving only Srs. Alicia Linehan, Loretta
Chafe, and Esther Dalton to help with the packing. Immediately, they set to
work. Dishes were washed, carefully wrapped, and packed; blankets, pillows,
sheets, and towels were stored in boxes and marked; pots, pans, and boilers
soon disappeared into boxes. Predictably, arguments broke out about what was
good enough to give to the poor, what to keep, what to throw away, and what
should go to the archives. No agreement was reached, so everyone decided to
go to bed. The next day, they started in again. Sr. Madeline Byrne, with the
help of two boys, tackled the wood room and the coal room. Srs. Patricia
March and Sr. Marion Collins arrived from St. John's to make a final decision
on the furniture and the more valuable items that had been donated to the convent many years before. During the week, three more sisters arrived to help

63. Theresa March, "Closing of St. Edward's Convent, Bell Island, August 19–28, 1991,"
ASMSJ, RG 10/10/30.

with the dismantling of St. Edward's Convent: Srs. Maureen Lawlor, Michelle Gibbons, and Agnes Brennan. As each box was packed, it was given a num- ber—the last and highest number was fifty-five. The two large statues in the chapel were donated to Fr. Robert Ryan for Roncalli parish in St. John's.

On Saturday, August 17, a huge transport truck arrived at the door at quarter to eight in the morning. Sr. Patricia March was not far behind. Then the loading began according to the destination of the goods. The altar proved to be a problem. It had been given by Archbishop Roche when the convent was opened in 1917, and the sisters wanted to preserve it intact. With a great deal of effort, the men, hampered by unwelcome advice and numerous admoni- tions from the sisters, removed the altar from the chapel and loaded it on the truck. It was to be stored in St. Catherine's Convent until a home was found for it in some needy parish church. By Monday, August 19, everything was fin- ished. The rooms were mopped and dusted, cupboards washed, odds and ends disposed of, and the convent that had been home to the Sisters of Mercy was bare and empty. As the keys were passed over to the new owner, the sisters said goodbye to seventy-four years of history. Suitcases in hand, they walked up the hill to the presbytery where they were to live for the next few months until the house on Snob Hill was ready for occupancy.

At the end of October 1991, the sisters were told that repairs of the house on Snob Hill had been completed, and they were free to move. On November 2, the truck arrived at the door of the presbytery and drove the sis- ters, bag and baggage, to their new residence.[64] The work involved in moving into a new house was in addition to the sisters' regular ministries. Sr. Madeline Byrne was principal of the Immaculate Conception School; Sr. Theresa March was liaison person between home and school; and Sr. Theresa Boland taught grade I. In addition to their school duties, the sisters took a good deal of responsibility for parish ministries. For instance, when the pastor, Fr. David Butler, was on holidays, the sisters took turns presiding at the celebration of liturgy of the word in the parish church.

---

64. The official blessing of the new residence took place on December 8, 1991.

In June 1993, both Srs. Madeline Byrne and Theresa Boland retired from teaching and assumed new ministries in other parts of the province. In August 1993, Sr. Margaret Pittman joined Sr. Theresa March on Bell Island. Sr. Theresa continued to act as liaison between home and school. Also, she was involved in a number of parish ministries, such as the Family Aid Committee, Child Protection Team, chairperson of the Liturgy Committee, and when the priest was absent, she presided at celebrations of the liturgy of the word. Sr. Margaret Pittman was involved in pastoral care to the sick. Most of her time was taken up with visitation to the hospital and to the sick in their homes. She took responsibility, also, for the pre-baptismal program for the parish. In 1994, Sr. Margaret Pittman was assigned to pastoral ministry in Marystown, leaving Sr. Theresa March as the only sister on Bell Island. This situation lasted for only one year, for in 1995–96, there were three sisters assigned to Bell Island. In addition to Sr. Theresa March, Sr. Josephine Ryan was appointed pastoral minister for the parish with special responsibility for visitation of the sick. Sr. Mary Tee was assigned as grade VI teacher at the Immaculate Conception School, where she remained for the next few years. Sr. Theresa March was released for a sabbatical year. Sr. Mary Tee was joined on Bell Island by Sr. Eleanor Savage and then by Sr. Dorothy Willcott, each of whom worked in pastoral ministry in the parish. After Sr. Mary's retirement from teaching in 2000, Sr. Dorothy remained alone on Bell Island until September 2003, when she was appointed director of catechetics at Corpus Christi Parish in St. John's.

For a few weeks after the departure of Sr. Dorothy Willcott from Bell Island, it looked as if the ministry of the Sisters of Mercy on the island had come to an end. Therefore, the news that Srs. Elsie Lahey and Eileen Osbourne had been appointed to Bell Island was greeted with a sigh of relief by the parish priest of Bell Island, Fr. Wayne Dohey, and by the people of the parish. Sr. Elsie Lahey had been born on Bell Island, and throughout her religious life, she kept in close touch with relatives and friends on the island. Thus, she understood all the changes that occurred through the years since the closure of the mines. She was aware, too, of the valiant efforts made by the people of the town to sustain their way of life on Bell Island.

Since their arrival in September 2003, Srs. Elsie and Eileen have become involved in a variety of parish projects, in visiting the sick, and in being available when people are in trouble and need assistance. They are very conscious of being limited in what they can do, but the words of Catherine McAuley, "It began with two . . ." encourage them in their efforts to continue the Mercy ministry that had was initiated by the four pioneer sisters in 1917.

CHAPTER TWENTY-SIX

MULTICOLOURED THREADS

In the morning sow your seed and at evening do not let your hand be idle;
for you do not know which will prosper—or whether both alike will be good.

Ecclesiastes 11:6

Although life for the Sisters of Mercy in Newfoundland might seem to have been a classic case of "all work and no play," this is not a true picture of convent life. In addition to working hard, most sisters knew how to relax—although it must be confessed that the Mercy congregation has always had its share of "workaholics." Prior to the 1967 general chapter, a two-week summer vacation was a matter of obligation for every sister. These vacations were spent in some convent belonging to the congregation, or in rare cases and under special circumstances, in a sister's family home. After the 1970s, there was no stipulated period of time set aside for vacation. The matter was left to the discretion of each individual, but most people took from three weeks to a month during the summer. However, as more and more outport convents were closed, the choice of places to spend one's vacation became limited. One place, however, was in great demand during the summer months—a little cottage in Witless Bay named Kilcash.

The first owner of the property was Thomas O'Connor of Kilcash, Ireland, who immigrated to Newfoundland in the early 1800s. After clearing the land, for the forest grew to the edge of the cliff overlooking Gallows Cove,

Thomas built his house and married a young girl from the settlement named Mary Carew. They called their home and property "Kilcash" as a reminder of Thomas' birthplace.[1] After the death of Thomas and Mary O'Connor, the property came into the possession of their son, Patrick. Patrick O'Connor and his wife, Mary (Vickers), had several children, three of whom survived to adulthood. The eldest, Bridget, entered the Congregation of the Sisters of Mercy and was known as M. Augustine, a sister who spent her life in the service of the students at Littledale. Another daughter, Marcella, chose a career in nursing and played a significant role in both nursing and administration at St. Clare's Mercy Hospital until her death in 1965. The youngest, Kathleen, became a teacher and taught at St. Joseph's School, Littledale, until her retirement in 1960. After M. Augustine's early death in 1942, both Kathleen and Marcella O'Connor remained closely associated with the Sisters of Mercy. For their part, the sisters looked upon the two O'Connor sisters as "part of the family." After Marcella's death, Kathleen, the only surviving member of the family, passed over the entire homestead to the Sisters of Mercy in the hope that it would benefit them as a summer residence. This generous gift provides the sisters with an opportunity to enjoy the fresh air and the ocean in quiet, secluded surroundings.

From the beginning, the sisters from St. Clare's Convent took a great interest in Kilcash. Under the energetic direction of M. Brenda Lacey, the old house was painted, cleaned, and renovated. Sr. Catherine Kenny[2] was conscientious in keeping a record of the history of Kilcash after it came into the possession of the Sisters of Mercy on June 8, 1965. She wrote:

> At 12:30 p.m., June 23, 1965, thirty-eight Sisters including the former Mother General, (M. Imelda Smith) . . . left by bus for the newly acquired summer resort, gift of the O'Connor family . . . A very simple but very lovely little ceremony marked the opening. Before entering the home, all stood and . . . offered a prayer for

---

1. ASMSJ, RG 10/31/1.

2. Sr. Catherine Kenny had been given the name, Mary Xaverius, at her reception into the novitiate. After the 1973 chapter, she preferred to be called by her baptismal name.

the deceased members of the O'Connor family and a prayer for the donor.[3]

A few days later, six sisters from St. Clare's began their annual vacation in the newly acquired summer residence. They found plenty to occupy them. Annually in late June or early July, the caplin arrived, and the sisters went to the beach daily to "dip" some caplin, bring them home, and fry them for dinner.[4] In July 1971, the swimming pool at Kilcash was ready for use. M. Brenda Lacey was the prime mover in having the pool started and brought to completion. Funds for the erection of the pool were raised through M. Brenda's initiative and consisted of donations from the various convents, handmade gifts for lottery, and support from the General Council of the congregation. Subsequently, any hardy soul who was not afraid of bone-chilling water had a nice, safe place to swim.

By the end of 1974, a metal storehouse had been assembled and erected, a floor was built and the entire house set up and completed by M. Brenda and M. Vincent McDonald. Gradually, over a period of years, substantial improvements were made to the little house in Kilcash. The sisters did much of the work themselves, again under the direction of M. Brenda Lacey, who could wield a hammer as well as any male carpenter. Nevertheless, some of the more technical work required certified electricians and plumbers, but by the summer of 1979, the sisters in Kilcash enjoyed the luxury of running water and electricity. A year later the General Administration decided to provide Kiilcash with a new refrigerator to replace the small one that had served them up to that time. The new fridge arrived on July 22, 1980. There was only one hitch. The doors of the old house were too small to admit the new, modern refrigerator. This was no problem to M. Brenda. Without batting an eyelid, she declared, "We'll remove the doors." And so it was done and the shining, new refrigerator installed.

---

3. Catherine Kenny, "History of Kilcash, Sisters of Mercy Summer Residence," ASMSJ, RG 10/31/2.

4. "Dipping" caplin refers to the method of using buckets or pails to catch these small fish as they come in to the beaches to spawn.

The sisters in Kilcash were never short of visitors. From the beginning, it was more or less understood by the whole congregation that the month of July was reserved for the St. Clare's sisters because they had done most of the work in adapting the old O'Connor home for use as a summer residence. However, for the remainder of the year, the house was available on a "first come, first served" basis, and there was no shortage of requests. However, sisters use Kilcash for more than recreation. It is not unusual for a couple of sisters to take time off to go to Kilcash for a week of quiet and prayer.

Meantime, during the general chapter of 1981, there was a great deal of discussion regarding plight of young girls who were experiencing minor emotional, behavioral, or social problems and were unable to function in their own homes or in foster homes. As a result of these discussions, in 1984, the superior general, Sr. Patricia Maher, and her council made a decision to open a special foster home for the care of needy teenage girls. In the course of the next few months, a house adjoining the Littledale property was purchased by the congregation and then enlarged and renovated to make it suitable to serve the needs of prospective residents. The new facility was named Mercy Residence.

On June 12, 1986, the minister of Social Services, Mr. Charles Brett, and Sr. Patricia Maher, superior general of the Sisters of Mercy, signed an agreement that marked the official beginning of Mercy Residence.[5] The agreement outlined the terms of reference under which the special foster home would operate. The ministry at Mercy Residence was directed toward providing care, shelter, and guidance for girls. According to the agreement, the girls admitted to Mercy Residence were to remain under the guardianship of the director of Child Welfare and would be referred to Mercy Residence by social workers from that department.[6] An Admission Committee was put in place to determine if a person might benefit from accommodation at Mercy Residence and if she could fit in with the group already in residence.

5. Diane Smyth, "Mercy Memo," December 1986, p. 4, ASMSJ.
6. RG 10/19/1, ASMSJ.

The criteria was based on an age limit of from twelve to sixteen years and a history of presenting problems of minor social, emotional, or behavioral nature. Mercy Residence was governed by a board of directors appointed by and directly responsible to the superior general of the Sisters of Mercy.[7] All finances for the operation of Mercy Residence and for the needs of the residents were provided by the Department of Social Services.

Sr. Diane Smyth was appointed the first administrator; Sr. Helen Caule was named assistant and assumed responsibility for the residence when Diane was absent. Both sisters were qualified social workers. In addition to the sisters, the staff consisted of four women, two of whom worked full-time (forty hours a week) and two were hired for part-time duty.[8]

On June 15, 1986, the new staff of Mercy Residence began a two-week orientation program. Professionals from the Department of Health, the Adolescent Counselling Centre, and the Department of Child Welfare provided input in the areas of adolescent development and psychology, behaviour management, and social services for teenagers. There were lengthy meetings to plan the program for the residents, as well as to determine house rules and specific procedures.

At last everything was ready. Srs. Diane and Helen moved into the residence on June 22, 1986, although both remained members of the community of St. Joseph's, Signal Hill. The first resident, a fifteen-year-old girl, was admitted to Mercy Residence on July 7 as an "emergency" placement, and by July 20, five girls between the ages of twelve and fifteen years had been accepted. However, things were difficult during these first few months, as the girls were unused to structure or consistency in their lives. Consequently, it became obvious that Mercy Residence was not the best placement for some of these girls, and so, alternate arrangements were made for their care.

In order to provide as much consistency as possible, the girls at Mercy Residence remained in their own schools, unless it was determined that this arrangement would not be in their best interests. During the first two years

---

7. Mercy Residence was incorporated on April 28, 1988.

8. The number of persons on the staff of Mercy Residence varied over the years. In March 1989, there were three full-time workers in addition to the administrator.

after the facility opened, the average length of time that a girl remained in residence was 134 days.

The home-like atmosphere, the disciplined and supervised structure, and the various activities of Mercy Residence provided the main segment of the program. Definite steps were taken to provide a program that best suited the needs of each individual. A regular period of study was set aside each day, and tutorial services were provided. Each girl received an allowance twice a week and residents were free to invite school friends to visit them at home in Mercy Residence. To promote a sense of independence and responsibility, the girls were encouraged to move independently around the city and to use their leisure time constructively. The goal was to help prepare each resident to return to her own home or to another, long-term living situation.

In most cases, a plan for each resident was discussed with her social worker, especially in reference to home visits, school, and special needs.[9] During the summer holidays, the residents were invited to spend some vacation time together, away from the city. One of the favourite vacation places was Eastport on the Bonavista Peninsula, where the girls and one or two staff members either went camping or rented a cabin in the area. The Burin Peninsula and St. Pierre were other popular vacation venues. One of the highlights for the residents was a ten-day trip to Prince Edward Island. On their own initiative, a couple of the older residents obtained summer jobs through community development programs sponsored by the government.[10] The girls were given the opportunity to participate in skating, cross-country skiing, swimming, aerobics, tennis, dancing, movies, and other recreational events as these became available throughout the year. Sometimes people from the community came to Mercy Residence to share their experiences and/or conduct short courses with the girls. Among those who offered this kind of service was Dick Reeves, formerly of a local radio station, VOCM. Mr. Reeves came on a regular basis to conduct courses on self-esteem. Also, a representative of Mary Kay Cosmetics showed the girls how to apply makeup. Representatives from

---

9. The social worker for each girl was appointed by the Department of Social Services.

10. Diane Smyth, "Report submitted to the Board of Directors of Mercy Residence," March 13, 1989, ASMSJ.

arts and crafts organizations came to Mercy Residence to teach various crafts to the girls who were interested in such activities. Sometimes one or other of the instructors invited the girls to their homes—experiences for which the girls were deeply grateful. Birthdays were always occasions for great celebration at Mercy Residence, and family members were always invited to share the birthday meal. Moreover, Mercy Residence had the opportunity to celebrate several high-school graduations, and these were occasions of great excitement and joy for the girls, their families, and friends, and especially for the staff of Mercy Residence.

In 1988, there was a change in the administration of Mercy Residence when Srs. Diane Smyth and Helen Caule moved to other positions. Sr. Sharon Basha, by profession a teacher with a recent degree in guidance counselling, was named the new administrator. Sr. Sharon's experience in high school and her insight into the needs of teenagers fitted her admirably for her new ministry. She had the wisdom to know when to be lenient and when to "put her foot down." Although one of Sr. Sharon's main concerns was to ensure that the girls attended school, participated in school activities, and completed assignments, she constantly encouraged the girls to be their best, whatever that best might be.

Although Mercy Residence was established to provide short-term care until a girl was ready to return to her own home or to a foster home, some of the girls remained for several years. One girl remained at Mercy Residence for almost six years. With the help and encouragement of Sr. Sharon and the staff, she graduated from high school, spent a year at Memorial University, completed a program at one of the technical colleges in St. John's, and secured permanent employment.

Subsequently, she married and went to live on the mainland of Canada, continuing to keep in touch with Sr. Sharon through frequent phone calls. Most of the former residents keep in touch—some more than others. Very seldom does a week pass without a phone call or email from one or other of these young women. Sometimes this is a cry for help, but more often it is simply making contact with "home."

By the year 1998, Mercy Residence had been operating for twelve years, with review and evaluation taking place on an ongoing basis. In spite of the dedication of Sr. Sharon and her staff, a constant turnover of social workers from the Department of Human Resources led to a degree of instability and lack of continuity. Furthermore, the mandate of Mercy Residence suggested that those accepted would range from twelve to sixteen years. However, in the period of 1996–98, most of the girls referred to the residence were over fifteen years of age. This left little opportunity of helping the young people make any long-lasting changes in their lives. While acknowledging the value of the service provided by Mercy Residence for twelve years, the Congregation of the Sisters of Mercy decided that the time had come to relinquish this ministry. The Department of Social Services was informed of the congregation's decision, and on June 28, 1998, Mercy Residence was closed.

Some months prior to the closing of Mercy Residence, Sr. Sharon Basha proposed to the Leadership Team that the building be used as a place where women who needed short-term relief from their daily environment and whose situation offered them no alternatives, could come to enjoy a safe, homelike, and nurturing atmosphere. Because Mercy Residence was already set up according to the required safety and security codes, it was an ideal site for such a ministry. The Leadership Team agreed that Sr. Sharon's suggestion was consistent with the Mercy spirit and tradition and with recent chapter directives. Hence, the congregation accepted the proposal and named Sr. Sharon Basha to this ministry. On Saturday, October 24, 1998, the sisters of the congregation were invited to an open house. A prayer of blessing took place at two o'clock, followed by the customary cup of tea and a tour of the house. Mercy Residence was ready to begin a new ministry.

Since its formal beginning in 1998, the ministry at Mercy Residence has unfolded in a multitude of ways, and as needs become known, it continues to evolve. It remains as a short-term respite for women who need to avail of such a place. It provides opportunities for women to come together to share their stories and to build a community of trust and support. A core group of women meet regularly at Mercy Residence, sometimes to pray and reflect, sometimes to watch a movie or share a meal, at other times to strategize around advocacy issues. Programs are offered according to expressed needs and many women have availed of sessions such as Enneagram, Myers Briggs, Healing Touch, Reflexology, Reiki, Resumé Writing, Job Search Skills, Budgeting, and Cooking. Evening retreats and prayer services for special events are also part of the ministry of Mercy Residence. Furthermore, Mercy Residence has become involved in the collection and distribution of clothing, household items, children's toys, and occasionally, food hampers. Many of the women who availed of the services provided by the sisters at Mercy Residence found that this ministry has enabled them to reach out to other women and their families in mutual support and in advocacy for change in the systems that continue to oppress women.

The period of the late 1980s and '90s saw a number of sisters retiring from teaching in the schools. Some left because they had completed the number of years required to receive a pension; others left because they saw more pressing needs in areas other than education and health care. For instance, three sisters were employed by the Archdiocese of St. John's for a few years in the fields of Liturgy, Adult Faith Development, and Social Justice.[11] Most of the sisters who retired were still in the early or mid-fifties and could look forward to many years of active ministry. This led to sisters accepting invitations to minister in small outports where no convent had been established and where there was no resident priest to care for the spiritual and religious needs of the people.[12] For example, in 1989, the archbishop of St. John's, Most Rev. Alphonsus Penney, approached the Sisters of Mercy requesting a couple of sisters for pastoral duties in St. Joseph's, Salmonier.[13] Srs. Anita Best and Margaret O'Gorman

---

11. The three were Sr. Sheila O'Dea (Liturgy), Sr. Brenda Peddigrew (Faith Development), and Sr. Lorraine Michael (Social Justice).

12. Earlier chapters of this book dealt with the ministries in Bird Cove, St. Paul's, Conche, Black Tickle, and other isolated places in the Province of Newfoundland and Labrador.

13. Salmonier consists of a number of small settlements scattered along the Salmonier Arm, which is one of four long inlets that branch into St. Mary's Bay on the southern part of the Avalon Peninsula. Locally, this area is known as Salmonier, although each settlement retains its distinct identity.

offered their services and took up residence in the parish house in St. Joseph's in September 1989.[14]

St. Joseph's is a fishing community on the eastern shore of the Salmonier Arm. At the time of the sisters' arrival, the population numbered about two hundred. The parish centre was in Mount Carmel, on the western side of the Arm, but the parish itself included five or six settlements. The parish priest, Fr. Kenneth Walsh, celebrated a weekend mass in one or other of the mission churches, while the sisters presided at the liturgy of the word and distributed Communion in the other churches belonging to the parish. The visitation of the sick and elderly, sacramental preparation, and the planning of and attendance at numerous parish functions left the sisters with little time for rest or recreation. Furthermore, at the time of Sr. Anita Best's appointment as pastoral minister, Archbishop Penney gave her permission to witness the sacrament of marriage and to celebrate baptisms when the priest was not available. Sr. Anita Best spent four years in St. Joseph's, Salmonier, (1989–1993) before she returned to St. John's to take up duties at "The Gathering Place."[15] In 1990, Sr. Margaret O'Gorman was reassigned, and Sr. Denise Costello joined Sr. Anita in Salmonier. Sr. Denise stayed for two years in Salmonier until she was replaced by Sr. Josette Hutchings in 1992. After Sr. Anita's departure, M. Josephine Ryan joined Sr. Josette (1993–95), and the two sisters continued to offer pastoral ministry in St. Joseph's and nearby settlements until September 5, 1995, when both sisters were assigned to other missions.

In 1997, two years after the departure of the sisters from St. Joseph's, Salmonier, plans were made to convert the parish house in St. Joseph's into a house of prayer and hospitality. The Congregation of the Sisters of Mercy arranged to lease the house from the parish for this purpose, and on February 5, 1998, Srs. Madeline Byrne and Theresa March took up residence and renamed the house "Sabbath House" to reflect the purpose for which it was to be used.

---

14. Sr. Margaret O'Gorman ministered in St. Joseph's for one year, 1989–90 when she was replaced by Sr. Denise Costello, who remained for two years, 1990-92.

15. The Gathering Place is a social centre where people who are in need can meet to enjoy a hot meal and receive companionship and support. See chapter twenty-seven.

Sabbath House was intended to provide a place of retreat for individuals and groups who were interested in spending some time in prayer and reflection. The sisters were patient, hoping that the idea would provide a number of local people with the opportunity to enrich and deepen their relationship with God. After a year, the Annals noted:

> [There are] not as many people coming as we had expected. [We] had expected more people in St. Joseph's to come for prayer, but . . . they have their own form and style of prayer and are not looking for something different. Maybe we need to launch out and try something new. . . . Since few people are taking advantage of Sabbath House, [we] are branching out more into community and Parish work. However, [we] always make time for people when they are at the house. The mission is not developing . . . as originally planned—but "God's ways are not our ways."[16]

Eventually, the sisters decided to accept the invitation of the new pastor, Fr. Patrick Power, to assist in the various programs sponsored by the parish and to continue regular visitation to the senior citizens home and to the sick and elderly. Nevertheless, they did not lose sight of the original purpose for establishing Sabbath House. The Annals mention the occasional visitor who came to spend some time in prayer and reflection away from the hustle and bustle of the city. From time to time, organizations such as the Catholic Women's League and volunteers from The Gathering Place drove to Salmonier to spend a day in prayer at Sabbath House. But, for the most part, the sisters were involved in coordinating parish programs and activities. In June 1999, Sr. Theresa March was assigned to Holy Name of Mary Convent in Marystown and Sr. Bridget Patterson took her place in Salmonier. At that point it seemed that the ministry of the Sisters of Mercy in Salmonier would continue for the foreseeable future. But on October 13, 1999, Rev. Jerome Hann, the parish priest at the time, visited the sisters to inform them that he planned to change his residence from Mount Carmel to St. Joseph's and that their lease, which was due to expire in January 2001, would not be renewed. Furthermore, he

---

16. Annals, Sabbath House, St. Joseph's, Salmonier, February 7, 1999.

intimated that he was anxious to move into the house as soon as possible. Under these circumstances, the sisters decided that no useful purpose could be served by remaining in the area, and so in March 2000, Sabbath House closed.

The people of the whole parish were upset and disappointed to see the sisters leave. There were many visits and letters from the persons who expressed appreciation for the work that had been accomplished by the sisters since the arrival of Sr. Anita Best in 1989. One person wrote:

> I am so sorry to see you go. It has been such a joy to have had you and the Sisters here for these past years. I was hoping we would have you forever. Thank you for all your kindness and help in the parish. I know you will touch lives wherever you are. May God continue to bless you.[17]

However, six months later, in September 2000, Sr. Madeline Byrne's dream of providing a hospitality and spirituality centre for people who were looking for a place to spend time in quiet prayer and meditation was realized when the former Sacred Heart Convent, Goulds, became Creedon House.[18]

Prison ministry is another area that some sisters chose as a "second career" after they retired from teaching. This, of course, is not a new ministry, for from the early days of the foundation, the Sisters of Mercy visited the penitentiary every week. This visitation was part of the Sunday morning routine at Mercy Convent. A list was posted in the back of the chapel with the names of those appointed to visit the General Hospital and the penitentiary. Promptly at ten o'clock in the morning, two sisters left Mercy Convent and walked to the penitentiary on Forest Road. On their arrival, they were escorted to a large room where the male inmates had assembled for prayer and a brief religious instruction. After that, there was an opportunity for the sisters to meet and converse with the men before leaving to go to the

---

17. Mary Dobbin to Sr. Madeline Byrne, March 4, 2000, ASMSJ.
18. See chapter seventeen.

women's section of the penitentiary. An unsigned paper in the archives of the Sisters of Mercy reports the following:

> The good old Irish Sisters of those early days had many incidents to relate, some humorous, others not at all humorous; e.g., a Sister who came to the country in 1858 and who used often visit the institution told me (1912) that she and her Sister companion were present the morning the first man to be executed in the country was being led to the gallows, July 8, 1889, according to the records of the penitentiary. Passing through the jail, on his way, he asked the warder to free his hands 'till I say good-bye to the nuns.[19]

Most sisters welcomed the opportunity to visit the prison, for it was clear that their visits were appreciated by inmates as well as by the staff. However, the work of M. Francis Hickey on behalf of prisoners merits specific mention in the story of Mercy ministry in Newfoundland.

M. Francis, who had a special sympathy for persons who were in trouble with the law, was convinced that if offenders were treated with kindness and respect, this would do more to rehabilitate them than long prison terms. She was a woman who practiced what she preached. She visited the penitentiary several times a week, bringing not only the wisdom she had acquired over the years but also treats, reading material, and movies to brighten up the lives of the prisoners. She encouraged education for them, procuring the help of other sisters to help them in their studies, to teach them handicrafts, and to help them understand and participate in the mass. She managed to brighten their lives by occasional movies and gifts of cigarettes and candy.

However, M. Francis did not confine herself to the penitentiary in St. John's, but also made regular visits to the Men's Correctional Centre in Salmonier. At Christmas, she persuaded the authorities to allow her to bring

---

19. ASMSJ, RG 10/1/36. This certainly was not the first execution to take place in the penitentiary. According to Paul O'Neill (*A Seaport Legacy*, p. 590), the person executed on July 8, 1889 was William Parnell, convicted of murdering his employer. O'Neill mentions several occasions on which the Sisters of Mercy were present in the penitentiary immediately prior to an execution, and the oral tradition at Mercy Convent (*circa* 1944) supports his statement.

extra treats to her beloved prisoners. During the four weeks of Advent, she had the junior sisters at Mercy Convent busily engaged in rolling cigarettes and packaging candy and cookies as gifts from Santa Claus for prisoners who were not permitted to go home for Christmas.

When M. Francis Hickey died on October 20, 1973, the crowds of people who attended her wake and funeral were a tribute to her work for the poor and unfortunate of society. Many who came to Belvedere for her wake remembered M. Francis's words of advice and encouragement during the most difficult time of their lives. A number of officers from the penitentiary formed an Honour Guard for her funeral, and representatives of the Royal Newfoundland Constabulary—in full dress uniform—attended the mass, celebrated by Archbishop P. J. Skinner in the basilica. Conspicuous in the large congregation were uniformed guards from the penitentiary and dozens of recipients of M. Francis's understanding and compassion.

However, the ministry of the Sisters of Mercy to prisoners did not come to an end with the death of M. Francis Hickey. On April 2, 1985, the superior general, Sr. Patricia Maher, sent the following memo to the members of the Mercy congregation:

> To mark the 200th Anniversary Year of the Church in Newfoundland, we decided to address more fully our commitment to prison ministry—a ministry which has been special in our Congregation since its foundation. We set up a Prison Ministry Fund and we committed ourselves to have a sister full-time in this ministry.[20]

In a further memo, Sr. Patricia informed the sisters that the congregation had set up a Prison Ministry Fund of $200,000, the interest from which would be used for prison ministry as the needs and the direction in which the Church planned to move were established. Meantime, a circular was sent out inviting any sister who felt an interest in this ministry to apply.

---

20. Memo to the sisters from Sr. Patricia Maher, April 2, 1985, ASMSJ, RG 1/12/134a. The decision was confirmed in July 1989.

In February 1985, Sr. Esther Dalton accepted the invitation to leave her teaching position and minister full-time in the Newfoundland prison system. Shortly afterwards, she was hired as associate chaplain in the Ontario federal prison system and began her ministry in Kingston's Prison for Men in September 1985. Essential elements of her employment were a daily exposure to the details of life in prison for incarcerated persons as well as clinical pastoral education units that were credited courses at Queen's University.

At the conclusion of her nine-month training period, Sr. Esther was appointed chaplain at Her Majesty's Penitentiary in St. John's and at the Salmonier Correctional Institute. For the next five years, Sr. Esther ministered as the only full-time member of an inter-denominational pastoral care team. One of her objectives was to help develop a Pastoral Care Department based on the mission statement of Corrections Canada. This statement encouraged a restorative model of justice rather than the punitive one that was deeply rooted in tradition.

Sr. Esther's duties as chaplain to the prisoners involved individual counselling of both staff and prisoners, crisis intervention, mediation sessions, conflict resolution, helping prisoners and their families grieve losses and deaths, and leading worship services and other activities that were designed to help those to whom she ministered. Her work required her to be in constant touch with Prison Administration, Parole Services, Probation Services, Temporary Absence Boards, and other agencies. All of this Esther accomplished with respect and compassion for those who found themselves in difficult situations, separated from their families and friends and—all too often—treated with suspicion and even dislike.

After five years in a ministry that required her to be on call twenty-four hours a day, seven days a week, Sr. Esther felt that it was time for a change. In a letter to the superior general of the time, Sr. Marion Collins, Esther wrote:

So now the time has come to move on. There are many factors involved besides the fact that it is the amount of time I committed myself to. I could stay on as many of my confreres do. But after five years one tends to settle in and not be shocked at the injustices

> and violence any more. That is the first sign that it is better to pass
> on the torch. . . . It won't be easy to leave, but it is over.[21]

After leaving prison ministry, Sr. Esther Dalton returned to her first love, teaching. After her retirement from the classroom, she volunteered her time at the Correctional Centre in Stephenville. More recently, she devotes many hours a week as a volunteer at the Metro Chaplaincy Centre in St. John's.

Nevertheless, it was the memory of M. Francis Hickey's service to the prisoners that inspired another sister, Sr. Margaret Rose, to embrace the same ministry when she volunteered for the Women's Correctional Centre in Stephenville. Although the sisters in St. George's had been visiting the Women's Correctional Centre in Stephenville on a regular basis, this was in addition to their other duties in the school. At that time (1993), there was no person on staff at the correctional centre to help the residents complete their education. In September 1993, Sr. Margaret Rose began an education ministry in the prison. Her duties included preparing some women to complete the requirements for a high-school diploma, teaching interested persons how to use a typewriter, and introducing them to the computer skills of word processing and graphics programs. Through Sr. Margaret's efforts, the computer programs, in particular, proved to be a huge success and led, eventually, to full employment for some of these women. Relative to this aspect of Sr. Margaret's work, the literary coordinator of the John Howard Society wrote, "While computers are powerful teaching tools, most of the credit for the program's success belongs to a Sister of Mercy [Margaret Rose] and the volunteers providing the direct services."[22]

Within weeks of her taking up duties in the correctional centre, Sr. Margaret's role was expanded to include pastoral ministry to the inmates. This involved many hours of listening as individuals spoke to her in private of the problems and difficulties that had led them into trouble with the law. At times of trouble and sorrow, for instance on hearing of the illness or death of a family member, these women turned instinctively to Sr. Margaret for comfort and

---

21. Sr. Esther Dalton to Sr. Marion Collins, December 31, 1989, ASMSJ, RG 1/13/134a.
22. Darlene George, *The Western Star*, June 22, 1995, ASMSJ, MG 13/1/15.

advice. As the staff began to realize that Sr. Margaret's vocabulary did not include the word "no," she was asked to take on even more responsibilities. The planning and preparation of special inter-denominational religious services and helping coordinate parties and treats for the inmates to mark special occasions soon became part of Sr. Margaret's routine.

However, in 1996, the government decided to move the Women's Correctional Centre from Stephenville to Clarenville on the east coast of the island of Newfoundland. The buildings formerly occupied by the women in Stephenville were converted into a correctional centre for men. When the news of the move was announced, the Leadership Team of the Sisters of Mercy agreed with Sr. Margaret's proposal that she move to Clarenville and continue her ministry at the new site. Subsequently, Sr. Margaret rented an apartment in Clarenville, and after the new correctional centre opened in 1997, she was ready to resume her ministry.

Three years after Sr. Margaret Rose moved to Clarenville, Sr. Bridget Patterson joined her.[23] Initially, Sr. Bridget's ministry was to hearing-impaired persons in the area. Subsequently, Sr. Bridget was appointed pastoral minister in Our Lady of Fatima Parish in Clarenville. In June 2001, Sr. Margaret Rose resigned from her "second career" at the correctional centre and began her "third career" as a volunteer in the Pastoral Care Department at St. Patrick's Mercy Home in St. John's. She had spent seven years in prison ministry, and now it was time for a change of pace. Sr. Margaret (Margie) Taylor volunteered to replace Sr. Margaret Rose at the Correctional Centre for Women, and in September 2001, she moved into the sisters' little house on Birchy Drive in Clarenville.

Srs. Margie and Bridget have a very heavy schedule. In addition to parish duties,[24] Sr. Bridget is a member of the Hospital Auxiliary and of the Alternative Measures Program—a program that attempts to resolve minor criminal offences by young persons through mediation or diversion without going

---

23. Sr. Bridget Patterson began her ministry in Clarenville in March 2000.

24. The duties of sisters engaged in pastoral ministry include celebrating liturgy of the word in the absence of a priest; visiting hospitals, nursing homes, and the homes of parishioners who are sick, elderly, or in need of counselling and help; sacramental preparation; religious instruction of children and adults; membership in various parish organizations; and a host of related duties.

through the judicial system. Sr. Margie Taylor is chairperson of the Pastoral Care Committee at the correctional centre and a member of the Victim Services Advisory Committee in Clarenville. Moreover, as part of her ministry at the correctional centre, she coordinates programs on anger management, victimization, stress, and grief.[25]

Meanwhile, a new and very different ministry was initiated in 1998 when Sr. Rosaline Hynes moved into a rented house in Harbour Grace to work with persons living with HIV[26] and their families in the Conception Bay North area. Sr. Rosaline had become familiar with the effects of this disease when her nephew, a hemophiliac, was infected with HIV from tainted blood products. Sr. Rosaline spent many hours with him and witnessed first-hand the sufferings of her nephew and his family during the months before his death in 1991. Since 1991, Sr. Rosaline had been a member of the Newfoundland and Labrador AIDS[27] Committee and was well aware of the need that existed for persons trained in counselling to work with the persons living with HIV and with their families.

In 1995, Sr. Rosaline had been appointed liaison person between Health and Community Services Department and the junior high schools to educate children on the dangers of contracting HIV. After she retired from teaching in 1995, she took two years' sabbatical leave to decide on her ministry for the future. However, Sr. Rosaline could not forget the sufferings caused by HIV and AIDS that she had witnessed over the past few years. The superior general of the time, Sr. Marion Collins, suggested that she study for a degree in pastoral counselling. Sr. Rosaline followed this advice and completed studies for a master's degree at Loyola University in Chicago.

Meanwhile, in 1997, Gerard Yetman, the executive director of the Newfoundland and Labrador AIDS Committee, asked Sr. Rosaline to establish a resource centre for the Conception Bay North region. At the time, Rosaline

---

25. At the time of writing, Srs. Bridget Patterson and Margaret Taylor continue their ministry in Clarenville.

26. Human Immunodeficiency Virus.

27. Acquired Immune Deficiency Syndrome.

was studying in the United States, but with the encouragement and support of the Leadership Team of the Sisters of Mercy, she agreed to the request. During the summer of 1998, Rosaline moved into an apartment in Harbour Grace,[28] and in September, of that year she began her work as HIV counsellor and home support worker. Her work takes her to several communities of Conception Bay North. As part of her ministry, she resumed her role as a liaison between Health and Community Services (HCS) and the schools. Sr. Rosaline is in constant demand to speak at various functions and in many venues on the topic of HIV. In particular, she has been invited by the United Church to speak in a number of churches in Conception Bay on behalf of the "Beads of Hope" campaign. This is an effort to raise funds to support women and orphans in Africa who are living with HIV and AIDS.

In consequence of Sr. Rosaline's efforts, some of the stigma surrounding HIV and AIDS has been lessened, although not entirely removed. Nevertheless, the work is never-ending. One of Sr. Rosaline's major accomplishments since she started work in this field was the coordination of a project to prepare and publish a self-care manual for people living with HIV/AIDS. It was developed with the co-operation of other professionals and volunteers in the field and published with the help of a government grant. Since then, this manual has been distributed and used by organizations and groups across Canada and in the United States. The manual presents discussions of treatments available to persons living with HIV and AIDS, how to obtain help, and how to find information on proper nutrition and diet. It also contains articles of particular interest to women and advises how to protect children and present the facts in a format and language that children can understand. One of the most important sections of the book contains a number of stories written by persons living with HIV. These accounts are very moving and put a human face on the suffering of these people and their families. There is also a section on spirituality. The self-care manual is an example of what a small community can do to support similar organizations dedicated to the treatment and care of persons living with HIV and of their families.

---

28. Subsequently, this arrangement proved to be unsatisfactory, and Sr. Rosaline moved into a rented house.

Sr. Rosaline Hynes spent much of her life in the classroom. Her "second career" as HIV counsellor and home support worker for people living with HIV and their families is even more demanding on her time and energy. But, like many "retired" sisters, her work is characterized by the same spirit of dedication and enthusiasm that she brought to her profession as a teacher for more than twenty-five years. In 2003, Sr. Rosaline's efforts to bring hope and healing to suffering people was given international recognition when she was awarded the Queen's Golden Jubilee Medal for her outstanding service to persons living with HIV/AIDS and their families.

And so, the works of Mercy continue to be carried out through a variety of ministries and through many hidden and unrecognized acts of charity and compassion. Perhaps one of the ministries closest to the spirit of the foundress of the Sisters of Mercy is the care of sick and elderly members of the congregation itself. This ministry is carried on at McAuley Convent.

When McAuley Convent opened in 1991, Sr. Marie Alma O'Gorman was appointed the first administrator of the new facility. Mrs. Marie Chafe, a registered nurse and graduate of St. Clare's Nursing School, was hired as director of Nursing Care. A staff of seven sisters and ten caregivers provide twenty-four hour care for sick and elderly sisters. Also, members of the congregation discharged from hospital after surgery or suffering from some illness are cared for at McAuley Convent during a period of recuperation.

There have been many changes since the new nursing unit opened in 1991. Although some members of the original staff have retired, their replacements continue to provide the same gentle and compassionate care. Nevertheless, at least half of the original housekeeping staff still work at McAuley Convent. Mrs. Marie Chafe remains as director of Nursing Care, and M. Annette Hawco, who worked in St. Catherine's Nursing Unit, continues to care for the sick at McAuley Convent. Another sister who moved with the original staff from St. Catherine's is M. Fabian Hennebury. Retired now from nursing duties, M. Fabian offers her services in the reception office at McAuley Convent. In addition to M. Annette and M. Fabian, five sisters provide full-time care to the sick at McAuley Convent:

Srs. M. Georgina Quick, Maureen O'Keefe, Barbara Kenny, Sheila Grant, and the administrator, Sr. Rosemary Ryan.

When McAuley Convent opened in 1991, thirty elderly and infirm sisters moved into the nursing unit. Gradually, one by one, each of these sisters was called to her eternal reward. Altogether, fifty-one sisters have died since McAuley Convent opened. A number of sisters from the city convents take turns helping out at the switchboard, sitting with the sisters, and helping in other capacities. Since the nursing unit opened, M. Thaddeus Mullowney volunteered her services as accountant, a demanding position, since there are twenty-six paid employees working at McAuley Convent.[29]

At the time of writing (2005), twenty-two sisters are being cared for at McAuley Convent. Three of these sisters moved in with the original group. M. Aquinas Hicks and M. Agnes Camilla Heffernan moved from St. Catherine's Convent; at the same time, M. Teresina Bruce transferred to McAuley Convent from St. Bride's Convent, Littledale.

M. Teresina celebrated her one hundred and second birthday in December of 2004. During her professional career, M. Teresina was acknowledged as a brilliant scholar and educator. In recognition of her contribution to education, the Memorial University of Newfoundland awarded her with the degree of doctor of laws, *honoris causa*, on May 29, 1982. In his citation, Mr. Shane O'Dea, public orator, stated that in honouring M. Teresina, the university was recognizing both her personal contributions to education in our province as well as the contribution of the Sisters of Mercy. He continued:

> While the years have seen at St. Bride's (College) many highly qualified and dedicated teachers, we like to remember that Sister M. Teresina was among those who helped guide the destinies of Littledale in the days when funds were low, equipment meagre, and the problem of maintaining high standards an ever present and urgent demand.
>
> Sister M. Teresina's contribution to education in Newfoundland however, is not confined merely to the classroom

---

29. M. Thaddeus retired from her position as accountant at McAuley Convent in 2004.

but is recognized also by her scholarly research done in preparation for her master's and her doctoral degrees, both of which
she received from the University of Ottawa.[30]

M. Teresina was closely associated throughout her life with St. Bride's College. Hundreds of women and teachers throughout Newfoundland were influenced by her love of learning and her thirst for knowledge. Even at an advanced age, M. Teresina's mental faculties and her sense of humour are as keen as ever.

M. Aquinas Hicks is another Sister of Mercy whose influence is widespread throughout Newfoundland. A kind-hearted, outgoing person, she has friends in every corner of the province. Up until a few years ago, M. Aquinas kept in touch with dozens of her former students and colleagues who remember her with affection and respect.

The sisters who live at McAuley Convent are there for a number of reasons. When a sister decides that she can no longer look after her own needs, she may request a transfer to McAuley Convent. Other sisters are assigned to the nursing unit if their physical condition is such that they require the special facilities available at McAuley Convent.

Nestled into the side of a hill, McAuley Convent overlooks the Waterford Valley. The setting is one of peace and tranquillity. Surrounded by the love and attention of a grateful congregation, the sisters at McAuley Convent continue to devote themselves to the works of Mercy, not through active involvement in ministry, but through prayer. In fact, the ministry of prayer is given first place in the list of congregational responsibilities. It is a ministry that the sisters at McAuley Convent have made particularly their own. Requests for prayers come in from all parts of Newfoundland, and those who make such requests can feel confident that their intentions are presented to God fervently and continuously through the ministry of prayer at McAuley Convent.

30, Shane O'Dea, Citation delivered at the Convocation at Memorial University of Newfoundland, May 29, 1982. Copy in ASMSJ, MG 39/1/16.

CHAPTER TWENTY-SEVEN

GATHERING UP THE THREADS

O God, you are my God, I seek you . . .
Your steadfast love is better than life . . .
So I will bless you as long as I live.

Psalm 63:1, 3, 4

I n the process of weaving a tapestry, the weaver has at hand a multitude of coloured threads. Some of these threads are woven partway through the material and left hanging, while new, different colours intertwine in a continuous pattern. Then, finally, the weaver takes up the threads left from different sections of the tapestry and continues to follow the design until the pattern is complete. The storyteller has a similar task. At the beginning there are only a few characters in a central location. Then the story expands to include more people and many different places. Sometimes events succeed one another in an orderly fashion, but then the pace quickens—everything seems to happen at once and it is difficult to maintain an orderly, chronological account. But sooner or later, loose ends have to be gathered and events brought up to date until the work is complete. And so it is with the story of the Sisters of Mercy in Newfoundland. Two threads left hanging from earlier parts of the tapestry trace the stories of the first two convents in Newfoundland, the Convent of our Lady of Mercy on Military Road, the mother house of the Congregation of the Sisters of Mercy of Newfoundland, and St. Michael's Convent and Orphanage at Belvedere.

Of all the ministries of the Mercy congregation, perhaps none benefited more from the 1916 amalgamation than St. Michael's Convent. Although there had been occasional changes in community membership prior to 1916, for the most part the care of the orphans was a lifetime commitment for sisters assigned to Belvedere. For instance, M. Alexius Tobin, born in Tipperary, came to St. John's in 1861 to join the Sisters of Mercy at Mercy Convent. Shortly after her profession in 1864, she was transferred to St. Michael's Orphanage where she remained for sixty-eight years until her death in 1932. Shortly after her appointment to Belvedere, M. Alexius was assigned to the House of Mercy that had been established in association with the orphanage.[1] However, her love for the poor and her deeds of charity were not confined to the House of Mercy or the orphanage. She was a familiar figure in the lanes and alleyways of St. John's as she made her rounds, visiting the sick and the poor and bringing comfort and relief wherever she went.[2] An article dealing with the life of Brother Alexis O'Regan that was published in *The Christian Brothers Educational Record* (1952) told of a curious incident involving M. Alexius Tobin:

> When Thomas was two years old, he was so severely burned about the chest and arms that his life was despaired of. His pious mother, when she realized that medical aid was of no avail, took the child to her great friend, Sister M. Alexius, of the Sisters of Mercy at Belvedere Orphanage. The good Sister seeing the distress of the fond mother and the serious condition of the boy, was moved to pity. . . . She offered fervent prayers that all might be well. . . . In a few days the child was pronounced out of danger. . . . In gratitude, Thomas, on his reception into the Order of the Christian Brothers, selected St. Alexis as his patron.[3]

Thirteen years after her death, *The Monitor* published an account of the life of M. Alexius entitled "A Social Worker for More Than Sixty Years." The

---

1. Hogan, *Pathways*, p. 97. See also chapter five.
2. "A Social Worker for More Than Sixty Years," *The Monitor*, December 1945, p. 8.
3. *The Christian Brothers Educational Record* (Dublin: Bray Printing, 1952), p. 384.

writer recalled that she was "at home" every Sunday afternoon to welcome the relatives and friends of children who lived in the orphanage. He wrote:

> Nothing was too much trouble: to see over the house, the schools ... to answer endless questions about the children's health and happiness. Then the parting at the door: "God bless you now until we see you again; 'tis now five o'clock and we must be off to our prayers."[4]

Another sister who made a lasting impression on the children who came under her care was M. Ignatius Guinane. M. Ignatius, who came from Limerick, followed her older sister, Bridget (M. Joseph Guinane) to become a Sister of Mercy in Newfoundland. She spent more than forty years of her life at Belvedere. After her death, the sisters at St. Michael's Convent received letters from former residents of the orphanage paying tribute to M. Ignatius. The affection in which she was held by her students is reflected in the following excerpt taken from a letter written to M. Genevieve O'Mara:

> I would like very much to give to the Orphanage Chapel, a Chalice or crucifix in memory of my most esteemed friend and mother, if it would be acceptable, if you would kindly reply as soon as you can, as I would like to get which ever you think would be most acceptable, so it could be blessed and used on Easter morning. ... It would be a source of great happiness to me to give something in her memory as I would like to have both the children as well as the community to always keep her in memory.[5]

M. Clare Lawless was another whose name was closely associated with the care of the orphans at Belvedere. A Newfoundlander by birth, Sr. Clare entered the community at Belvedere where she was professed in 1918. This was only two years after the amalgamation—a time when many of the younger sisters were being transferred from the convent where they had been professed to

---

4. *The Monitor*, December 1945, p. 8.
5. Marion Burke, a former resident of Belvedere, to M. Genevieve O'Mara, January 13, 1910, ASMSJ, RG 10/2/30.

some other community. M. Clare was one of the few who was not asked to change residence. As M. Williamina Hogan remarked, "Perhaps those in authority realized how essential Sister Clare was to the lives and the happiness of the children at Belvedere." M. Clare gave more than fifty years of service to the smallest children in the orphanage. She was in charge of "the babies," and sisters who did summer duty at the orphanage remember that if a child cried during the night, Sr. Clare was at her bedside in an instant, remaining there until the little one drifted back to sleep.

It is beyond the scope of this book to mention the hundreds of sisters who carried on an apostolate of service within the walls of Belvedere. Most of them were gifted women who were equally at home in the classroom or out on the fields "making" the hay for the cows that supplied fresh milk and cream to the orphanage. The land on which McPherson Academy and Holy Heart of Mary High School stand today was once used to grow fresh vegetables for Belvedere. The sisters and the older children spent hours after school and during the summer months helping to weed the gardens, "make" the hay, and in the fall of the year, collect the vegetables for the winter. This was very much in the tradition of outport Newfoundland, where many of the sisters and the children were born. Far from being looked on as an onerous burden, these sessions were more in the nature of "outings." The children took a break from the work by munching on a sandwich or—on rare occasions—a chocolate bar. However, no such treat was provided for the sisters who, in those days, were forbidden to eat in public. At a time when money was scarce, the produce from the farm ensured that the children were supplied with fresh, wholesome food. In addition, Belvedere had its own bakery. The aroma of freshly baked bread and rolls wafting through the corridors provided a warm, homelike atmosphere to what was, after all, an institution.[6] In later years, the construction of schools on what had been Belvedere property brought an end to these halcyon days in the fields. Instead, on the fine, warm days of summer, the children spent their free time

---

6. I am indebted to M. Annette Hawco for this information. M. Annette spent many years caring for the orphans in Belvedere. After she was transferred from the orphanage, she worked as teacher and principal in schools all over Newfoundland. Since her retirement from teaching, she has devoted her life to caring for the sick and elderly sisters at McAuley Convent.

in an open-air swimming pool that was built in 1955 just outside the recreation hall. Incidentally, the sisters, too, made use of the pool when the children were otherwise engaged.[7]

Prior to 1949, the superior of the convent was also in charge of the orphanage and of the children's education. At the time of the amalgamation in 1916, M. de Chantal O'Keefe was superior of St. Michael's Convent, Belvedere. It was not in M. de Chantal's character to overlook any opportunities that might benefit those under her care. When she reflected on the success of the commercial class at Our Lady of Mercy Academy, she wanted no less for the girls at Belvedere. Accordingly, she arranged for interested students from the senior grades at the orphanage to enroll in the commercial classes conducted by M. Joseph Fox at Mercy Convent. Then, to make sure that her girls had sufficient practice, M. de Chantal purchased several typewriters and appointed one of the young sisters on the staff of the orphanage, M. Francis Hickey, to provide additional instruction at home.[8] The superintendent of education reported that in 1918, eight students in the orphanage were given special training in typing, shorthand, and bookkeeping.[9] In time, there was an increase in the number of Belvedere students studying these commercial subjects in preparation for a career in the business world. The 1929–30 report of the Bureau of Education described the school at Belvedere:

> The orphans not only receive a useful education, but their subsequent welfare is provided for. Those who display particular aptitudes are trained along these lines. There are classes in music, cooking, needlework, and stenography. The Belvedere girls are

---

7. The swimming pool was the gift of a former pupil of the Sisters of Mercy at Mercy Convent and Littledale, Madame Gomez-Quato (Mary McCarthy), Havana, Cuba. Additional support came from donations of money and from bequests made to the orphanage.

8. I am indebted to Loretta Chafe, RSM, for this information. Loretta's mother was brought up at Belvedere and was one of the first Belvedere students to enroll in the commercial classes at Our Lady of Mercy Academy. Mrs. Chafe said that she was M. Francis Hickey's first student.

9. "Report of the Superintendent of Education for Roman Catholic Schools for the Year Ended December 31, 1918," AASJ.

prepared for life's work as well as those of any institution in the country. [10]

Through the years since the beginning in 1859, the girls who lived at Belvedere were taught in classrooms in the orphanage. After the establishment of the CHE examinations, Belvedere's high-school students attended classes and wrote the examinations at Our Lady of Mercy Academy.[11] This practice continued until 1938. After that time until 1957, all the classes, including grade XI, were taught at Belvedere. In addition, Belvedere had its own examination centre until the opening of Holy Heart of Mary Regional High School (HHM) in 1958. Subsequently, high-school girls from the orphanage attended HHM. However, Belvedere's elementary children received their education in the orphanage until 1967. After that date, they attended Our Lady of Mercy School. This did not apply to the smaller children, however. Through all the years, kindergarten and primary children were taught at Belvedere. Once a girl reached the age of eighteen years, as a rule, she was encouraged to leave the shelter of the orphanage and make her own way in the world. Of course, there were exceptions, depending on the needs of the individual. Over the years, some of Belvedere graduates chose to become Sisters of Mercy, but most went to work and eventually married.

There was always plenty to occupy the time of the children at St. Michael's Orphanage, Belvedere. From the beginning, music, dancing, drawing, and sewing were assiduously cultivated. Even the smallest children were involved in these activities, and when the music festival was established in 1954 there were no keener contestants than the students from St. Michael's, Belvedere. Belvedere girls participated in choirs, piano and vocal solos, and in speech—usually with remarkable success. For instance, in 1955, the Belvedere Choral Speech groups received special commendation from the adjudicator who awarded first place to each of the three groups from the school.

---

10. Annual Report of the Bureau of Education, 1930, p. 83.
11. McCormack, "Educational Work," p. 117.

Another cultural activity in which students were encouraged to participate was that of drama. In 1958, the girls from Belvedere entered the
Provincial Drama Festival. At the conclusion of this event, the six young
actresses, selected from grades VIII to grade X, were awarded the second highest mark in the festival for their presentation of *When Shakespeare's Ladies Meet*.
The girls practiced for this event at the College of Our Lady of Mercy, where
M. Williamina Hogan coached them after regular school hours.

Meanwhile, big changes were in the offing for Belvedere. Although the
orphanage had developed high standards of care and education over almost 110
years, by 1967, it was obvious that the varieties of social service required to
meet the needs of children who were coming to Belvedere could not be
accommodated in an institutional setting. Rather, it was felt that children who
needed care would be better off in smaller, homelike surroundings where they
would experience a more normal family life. In keeping with current social
trends, the ninth general chapter of the Sisters of Mercy, which took place in
1967, reluctantly concluded that it was time to consider the phasing out of St.
Michael's Orphanage, Belvedere.[12] At a special session of the ninth general
chapter, held from December 27–30, 1968, the final decision was made to
close the orphanage. The superior of St. Michael's Convent, M. Constance
Travers, wrote the director of Child Welfare and Corrections informing him of
the decision and requesting that the children be placed in foster homes as early
as possible after the school year of 1969.[13]

After the last child in the orphanage had been placed in foster care in the
summer of 1969, two young women remained. Always named together as
"Mary and Margie," these two sisters had been placed in St. Michael's
Orphanage when they were quite young. Long after the age when other young
women left to find work, to marry, or to enter religious life, Mary and Margie
stayed on as wards of the sisters. Belvedere was their home, and it was unthinkable that they would be sent away to fend for themselves. They were given their
own living quarters in the convent and were encouraged to help around the

---

12. See chapter twenty.
13. ASMSJ, RG 10/2/206.

house to the extent of their ability. A number of sisters continued to live at St. Michael's Convent and taught in the classrooms of the former orphanage that had been converted to a junior high school for girls. Eventually, in 1975, the junior high school was phased-out, and the entire orphanage building was converted into offices for the Roman Catholic School Board.

But still, a number of sisters continued to live in St. Michael's Convent, each sister involved in a different ministry somewhere in the city of St. John's. Then, in 1999, when the government abolished denominational education, the Roman Catholic School Board, which had been located in St. Michael's Orphanage, ceased to exist. The newly established Avalon East School Board rented space in an office building in another part of the city, leaving the former orphanage vacant. For two years, St. Michael's Convent existed side by side with the empty orphanage buildings. These were uneasy times for the sisters who lived in the convent. Situated at the end of a long avenue and at quite a distance from their nearest neighbours, the Presentation Sisters at Assumption Convent, St. Michael's Convent and the former orphanage were targeted by vandals. Even though the windows of the vacant buildings were boarded, there was always the danger of vandals breaking into the empty orphanage and destroying the building by fire. It was time for the sisters to leave Belvedere.[14] In May 1999, St. Michael's Convent, Belvedere was closed. The Sisters of Mercy had lived there for 140 years.

There were many obstacles in the way of selling the property. Not only was it in a heavily populated school zone, but both St. Michael's Convent and Orphanage had great historical interest and value. After lengthy discussions with St. John's City Council, permission was obtained to put the property up for sale. Eventually it was purchased, and the buildings converted into offices.

The total amount of money realized from the sale of the property was placed in a trust fund under the direction of a volunteer board of directors. The intent of the fund was to make available a number of grants for which former

---

14. On the evening of November 5, 2001, the house occupied by the caretaker in former years, which was located a short distance from the convent, was set on fire and only the quick action of the St. John's Central Fire Department prevented what could have been a major disaster.

residents and their children might apply. In the years since the property was sold, the total amount has been distributed according to the guidelines established when the trust fund was established. This money provided financial assistance and support to former residents of the orphanage and their children to enhance and improve their quality of life and their self-reliance.

Several volumes would be required to tell the story of Belvedere. The Sisters of Mercy who lived at St. Michael's Convent through the years recall the older sisters with love and affection. Their hospitality was legendary. M. Rosalita Power recalled a bitterly cold day when M. Patrick Flynn, seeing some men working on the road near the convent, put a pot of soup on the stove to heat and sent M. Rosalita to invite the men to come in and have some hot soup to keep them warm. There were many such incidents—examples of small, unseen, and unacknowledged acts of kindness. They are hardly worth recounting except to highlight the fact that these Sisters of Mercy were loving, compassionate women whose chief delight was in bringing joy and comfort to other people. The sisters at Belvedere always provided a hot lunch for their workers and for the hungry people who came to the door. No one was ever turned away without a kind word and something to help them in their distress.

But it was not only the poor who came to their door who were the recipients of the sisters' concern. Every Sunday, the sisters from Belvedere visited the "Poor House" on Sudbury Street. This was an institution that housed the destitute and the elderly who had no one to care for them. Largely forgotten by the general population, these men and women looked forward eagerly to the weekly visits of the sisters who brought small treats consisting of candy and cookies, reading material, and best of all, the latest news of the town. Even in those days, few people knew about these—and many other—small acts of kindness, for the Sisters of Mercy were not interested in trumpeting their good works. They were concerned only that poor, lonely people were visited and comforted.

Throughout its long history, St. Michael's Orphanage, Belvedere, was one of the most treasured ministries of the Sisters of Mercy in Newfoundland. Even for those sisters who never had the opportunity to work in the orphanage, Belvedere held a special place in their hearts and in their prayers. Thus, when allegations of abuse surfaced in 1989, the congregation was shocked and bewildered. The initial period of confusion and disbelief was succeeded by a deep feeling of shame, coupled with concern and pity for those who felt they had been ill-treated during their time at Belvedere.

When the matter first came to the attention of the congregation, the superior general, Marion Collins, and the General Council attempted to reach out in mercy and compassion to individuals who had made complaints of physical and/or emotional abuse. On behalf of the congregation, Sr. Marion expressed regret for the suffering of these women and their families and offered professional help to anyone who felt that her pain was a result of time spent at Belvedere. Consequently, in 1989, four women requested therapy and the Congregation of the Sisters of Mercy arranged that all four received from four to six years of treatment from a highly qualified professional therapist.

But it was not until 1997 that the cloud hanging over Belvedere broke in all its fury. Several women came forward with stories of harsh treatment they claimed to have received while they lived at the orphanage. These stories were picked up by the media and aired in a highly sensational television program. In every community room in Newfoundland, sisters watched the unfolding of the program in bewildered silence. Drama, of its nature, works by isolating and heightening selected episodes. The brief program that dramatized events alleged to have taken place in Belvedere made no attempt to present impartial testimony from other women who lived in the orphanage at the time of these purported activities.

The universal reaction of the congregation to the program was one of deep distress and concern for the sisters who had worked so hard and devoted the best years of their lives to caring for the children in Belvedere. But also there was sympathy for the alleged victims, who in addition to the pain of separation from parents, may have suffered from a discipline considered appropriate in the 1950s and '60s but frowned upon in the 1990s. Fifty years ago, the adage "spare the rod and spoil the child" was more or less taken for granted, and there are few adults today who did not receive the occasional slap on the hand—or on another portion of the anatomy—for some misdemeanour. In a press release, the superior general, Sr. Marion Collins stated:

> Disciplinary methods used at Belvedere Orphanage in the 1950s were the same as those that would have been common in schools and homes of that time.... I can state categorically that Belvedere did not have a concentration camp environment. There was no barbed wire and no guard dogs.[15]

In the same press release, Sr. Marion invited anyone who felt that she had been abused or treated badly at the hands of the Sisters of Mercy to come forward and discuss it with representatives of the congregation. In outlining the congregation's policy with regard to alleged physical abuse, she said, "As soon as a complaint is made, the congregation will act immediately to investigate and take whatever action is necessary. At the same time, the sisters will attempt to respond to the needs of the person making the complaint."[16] She stated further, "It is the policy of the Sisters of Mercy to inform the appropriate authorities and co-operate fully with any investigation that may result. Any sister named in a complaint will be removed from a position of trust involving children and provided with whatever help and assistance she may need."[17]

The allegations of abuse against Belvedere were followed by an intense and comprehensive police investigation that stretched over several years. In the course of the inquiry, officers of the Royal Newfoundland Constabulary interviewed hundreds of witnesses in many parts of Newfoundland, other parts of Canada, and the United States. Subsequently, the officer in charge of the inquiry stated that after an exhaustive investigation, no grounds for charges had been discovered.[18] On February 11, 1999, the Royal Newfoundland Constabulary issued the following news release:

---

15. *The Telegram*, November 6, 1999, p. 3. The reference to "barbed wire" and "guard dogs" was in response to an article that appeared in *The Telegram* a few days prior to the press release.

16. Ibid.

17. Ibid.

18. *The Telegram*, February 10, 1999, p. 3.

As stated in an earlier press release [February 9, 1999], the Royal Newfoundland Constabulary has concluded its investigation into allegations of abuse that occurred at Belvedere Orphanage in the 1950s and 1960s. As indicated in the earlier release, all complaints were concluded without charges being laid. The reason(s) behind such dispositions were for one or more of the following reasons:

1.   The alleged offender is deceased.
2.   The inability to identify the alleged offender or potential witnesses.
3.   The lack of supportive evidence or information.
4.   Details surrounding the alleged offence were vague or inaccurate.
5.   The information provided by one complainant was not supported by other alleged witnesses.[19]

The investigation was terminated, but the stigma remains.

There are many sides to the story of Belvedere. In the recent past, only one side of the story made the headlines in the public press. It is only just and right that the major part of Belvedere's story be remembered and acknowledged. The truth is that for over 110 years, the Sisters of Mercy at Belvedere provided a home to many disturbed and neglected youngsters who had suffered various forms of deprivation. For the most part, these children received the best care that could be provided at the time. Some people understand and relate well to children, while others do not. Most adults remember teachers who were loved and respected and others who were disliked and feared. No doubt, women who grew up in Belvedere share similar memories. If some children were treated harshly at St. Michael's Orphanage, it could have left painful memories for individuals who may have been the recipients of such treatment. It is particularly distressing for the Sisters of Mercy because it throws a deep shadow on an otherwise exemplary, courageous, and unselfish record.

For those who love and revere the memory of Belvedere and all that it stood for, it is consoling to remember that the last thirty years in the life of the

---

19. Royal Newfoundland Constabulary, News Release, February 11, 1999, ASMSJ.

orphanage were graced by the presence of one of the most-loved figures in the history of the Mercy congregation in Newfoundland, M. Bernard Gladney. After her return from St. Lawrence in 1940, M. Bernard went to Belvedere, where she spent the rest of her life caring for the needs of the children. M. Williamina Hogan wrote of her: "This charming, gracious woman's distinguishing feature was courtesy and respect for the individual, young or old. Her service in every human affliction was marked by a gentle compassion and kindness."[20] Sr. Bernard's "surgery" was the refuge for lost, lonely children, who often faked some sort of ailment as an excuse to visit the kindly sister who knew how to soothe every ache or pain, both physical and emotional. Her parting words to each, "God bless you, my pet," accompanied by a gentle pat on the cheek, sent the child away knowing that here was someone who understood her, cared about her pain, and loved her. Although past allegations cast a shadow over the orphanage and its history, it must be remembered and acknowledged that the compassionate presence of Sr. M. Bernard Gladney and others like her brought comfort, love, and healing over the years to thousands of children who had nowhere else to turn.

In the 110 years that St. Michael's Orphanage existed, it offered shelter and hope for the future to more than four thousand children. Most of these remember Belvedere as a busy, disciplined but humanly compassionate place. It provided thousands of girls with an education that was equal—and sometimes superior—to that offered in any other school in the city. It gave them a start in life and, more often than not, a helping hand at difficult points along the way. But most of all, Belvedere provided a home, the best that the sisters could manage, to thousands of needy, orphaned, abused, and abandoned children. It is a source of great sadness to the Sisters of Mercy that some of them felt pain and subsequent bitterness. But when sisters were faced with the onerous task of parenting simultaneously over two hundred little girls, it was inevitable that ultimately some would feel they had not received enough attention.

---

20. Hogan, *Pathways*, p. 101.

Nevertheless, the record shows that Belvedere made a positive contribution to the reform of child care in Newfoundland. Furthermore, the
Congregation of the Sisters of Mercy addressed itself—and at considerable
personal sacrifice to the sisters—to the constant improvement of its facilities
for the children at St. Michael's Orphanage. At a time when Newfoundland's
provision for needy children moved from the non-existent to the grudging and
inadequate, when nobody else was willing or able to give shelter to destitute
or neglected children, the Sisters of Mercy shared the little they had—and all
of their lives—with the orphans and rejected children of Newfoundland. It is
unfair to blame the sisters if what they did was less than perfect. Many in the
wider community did nothing at all.

The teaching ministry entrusted to the Sisters of Mercy was initiated at Mercy
Convent on Military Road. However, that ministry, too, was gradually drawing to a conclusion. Beginning in the early 1970s, the enrolment at Our Lady
of Mercy School began to decline. When registration for the school year
1973–74 was completed, it became obvious that there was no longer a need
to maintain the school on Harvey Road. Consequently, "Little Mercy" was
closed in June 1973, and the pupils in grades I and II were transferred to
"Cramm's House" on Barnes Road. Sr. Cecilia Lambe was the last sister to
teach at "Little Mercy." Three years later, the classrooms in "Cramm's House"
were no longer needed, and that building, too, was closed.

The reasons for the decline in enrolment at Our Lady of Mercy can be
explained by the fact many people were moving away from the centre of the
city into more residential areas. Both St. Pius X School on Elizabeth Avenue
and Mary Queen of Peace School on Torbay Road were in these residential
areas, and their enrolment was increasing at the expense of the older, inner-
city schools. Many homes in the Military Road area had been converted into
offices, and the centre city was in danger of being vacated in favour of business
establishments.

Nevertheless, Mercy School continued to accept students through the
1970s and '80s. However, there were fewer and fewer sisters teaching in the
school. For instance, in September 1974, there were twenty-three teachers at

Our Lady of Mercy School, but only five of them were sisters. The enrolment that year was six hundred and fourteen.[21] Ten years before, in 1964, the enrolment had been over one thousand students. Nevertheless, there were twenty-six sisters living in the community at Mercy Convent. Some of these were students at Memorial University and others had retired from teaching and were engaged in a variety of ministries. In 1976, the sisters were asked to visit the Pleasantville Reform School for Girls and Boys. Many of these children were Roman Catholics who had received minimal religious instruction. Three sisters from Mercy Convent agreed to visit the institution and prepare the children to receive the sacraments. When the sisters arrived at the reform school, they found a group of hurt and confused children who responded instantly to the interest and kindness shown them by the sisters. Very soon, the sisters were planning little treats for the boys and girls at Pleasantville, even to the extent of obtaining permission from the authorities to hold a Christmas party for them at Mercy Convent.[22]

As one year succeeded another, the enrolment at the four schools surrounding the basilica-cathedral continued to decline.[23] In December 1986, the Roman Catholic School Board for St. John's decided that the school system within the district would become coeducational, except for St. Bonaventure's and Our Lady of Mercy. The board was determined to maintain these two schools as single-sex schools for grades kindergarten to grade VIII to serve the entire school system administered by the board.[24] The General Council of the Sisters of Mercy greeted this announcement with concern. It was feared that the designation of Our Lady of Mercy as the only all-girls school in the system would attract only the daughters of the wealthier class, and the Sisters of Mercy were not interested in operating a school that might be perceived as "elitist." The only way out of the dilemma was to with-

---

21. Annals, Convent of Our Lady of Mercy, St. John's, September 1974, ASMSJ.
22. Ibid., October, 1976.
23. The four schools were the Presentation School, Our Lady of Mercy, St. Bonaventure's Boys' School, and St. Patrick's Hall Boys' Schools. Each of these schools was a single-sex school.
24. *The Evening Telegram*, December 17, 1986, p. 3.

draw the sisters from Our Lady of Mercy School. Because of the historical importance of Our Lady of Mercy School, the high academic standards maintained at the school, its reputation for achievement in music, and the place it held in the affection and loyalty of hundreds of citizens, this was a very serious course of action.

The superior general, Sr. Patricia Maher, and her council consulted the congregation. Many sisters agreed with the stance of the administration, but just as many were opposed to the withdrawal of the sisters from the school. Finally, on February 21, 1987, the Congregation of the Sisters of Mercy announced that it would withdraw its services from Our Lady of Mercy School in June 1988, after 145 years of teaching there.[25] In making the announcement, Sr. Patricia Maher said, "The sisters support the change to a coeducational system in St. John's. They also respect the right of the school boards to provide a single-sex option in the coeducational system. The choice of the congregation, however, is not to administer and/or teach in a school which will become an exclusive district school."[26]

Reaction to this announcement was swift and vehement. Letter after letter appeared in the papers denouncing the decision of the Sisters of Mercy to withdraw from the school. A few letters appeared supporting what was called the sisters' "courageous" action, but by and large, feeling was running strong against it. Nevertheless, the difficult decision had been made in the sincere conviction that it was right for the time, and the congregation remained firm. Ironically, at the time this decision was made, Our Lady of Mercy was anything but a school for the children of the wealthy. The majority of the students came from the inner city of St. John's, where poverty and need were rampant. Sisters who worked with the poor in that part of the city were on the constant lookout for clothing, shoes, and especially winter boots, for many little children at Mercy were poorly clad.[27] On June 24, 1988, the Sisters of Mercy withdrew from the school that they had opened in 1843. It was the end of an

25. Ibid., February 21, 1987, p. 3.
26. Ibid.
27. Records of the Basilica Family Care Centre, Basilica Parish of St. John the Baptist, St. John's, AASJ.

era and foreshadowed the final chapter in the long story of Our Lady of Mercy School.

After the sisters had left, the school continued under the administration of a lay principal. The tradition of music at the school continued under the direction of Mrs. Korona Brophy, a former student of M. Edwardine Furlong at Our Lady of Mercy. Mrs. Brophy's small string orchestra worked hard to keep up the reputation of the school's music program. Little by little, enrolment declined until in 1991–92, only two hundred girls were registered at Our Lady of Mercy. On June 14, 1992, *The Evening Telegram* carried a headline "Only all-girl school closes Friday." In view of the low enrolment, the Roman Catholic School Board for St. John's had decided that the time had come to close the school. As a consequence, the single-sex option at St. Bonaventure's was eliminated, and the former students of Our Lady of Mercy were accommodated at St. Bonaventure's—the first time that hitherto all-male establishment housed little girls within its hallowed walls!

The last principal of Our Lady of Mercy School was Ms. Catherine Green. Although she had been at the school for only one year, when interviewed by *The Evening Telegram* staff writer she said, "Working here is a teacher's dream. The students are so motivated, achievement-oriented and disciplined—we find it a real pleasure."[28] Ms. Green remarked that in light of the educational excellence and long tradition of Our Lady of Mercy, the board had made a very difficult decision in announcing that the school would close. June 19, 1992, was the last official day of school at Our Lady of Mercy and the end of single-sex education in St. John's.

It was a strange yet poignant coincidence that the closure of Our Lady of Mercy School occurred just as the Sisters of Mercy were celebrating the one hundred and fiftieth anniversary of the arrival of the first Sisters of Mercy in Newfoundland. Consequently, a tinge of sadness permeated a summer of celebrations, at least for the sisters and former students of Our Lady of Mercy School. However, there was much to celebrate, and preparations began on September 29, 1991, when over 150 former students of Our Lady

---

28. Catherine Green, quoted in *The Evening Telegram*, June 14, 1992, p. 3.

of Mercy School, representing four decades of collective achievement and academic excellence met in the choral room at Holy Heart High School. This marked the beginning of an alumnae association. Various organizing committees were established to plan for the festivities that would take place in August 1992. One of the proposals that was received enthusiastically by those at the meeting was the re-establishment of Our Lady of Mercy Glee Club, for 1992 was also the twenty-fifth anniversary of the choir's participation at Expo '67. The first practice took place on October 13 at Holy Heart Choral Room when approximately eighty former students of Our Lady of Mercy gathered for the first rehearsal. Many of the singers had been members of the Expo '67 choir. When word spread of the reunion that was being planned for August 1992, former Mercy students in other parts of Canada and the United States requested copies of the music so that they could participate in the concert that was to be held as part of the celebrations. The proposed choir concert was but one of the activities that was planned for the week of August 3, 1992.

Although Our Lady of Mercy School was officially closed, the sisters agreed to make the building available to former students who wished to visit their school and renew old friendships. There was great excitement as school friends who had been separated for years met once more in their old classrooms. The sisters at Mercy Convent and many of the alumnae had collected class pictures of long-ago years. These were posted on the walls of the classrooms. Photograph albums containing the pictorial record of school concerts, sports teams, choirs, and orchestras were placed on tables in the corridors and in the gymnasium. The afternoon of August 6, 1992 was a time of tears and laughter as women from many parts of the world spoke with affection and pride of their old school and of the sisters who taught them. The words "remember when" echoed and re-echoed throughout the afternoon. Dozens of class reunions were planned and took place during a week of celebrations. However, the main social function was a dinner that was held at Hotel Newfoundland and attended by over 700 graduates of Our Lady of Mercy School. The guest speaker for the occasion was the mayor of

St. John's, Mrs. Shannie (Frecker) Duff, a graduate of Our Lady of Mercy School.

Meanwhile, the Congregation of the Sisters of Mercy of Newfoundland was making its own plans to celebrate this anniversary. Each convent in Newfoundland arranged to have a special anniversary mass celebrated in the local parish church. In every case, a reception was held after mass to provide an opportunity for the sisters to thank the people for their friendship and support through 150 years. The principal liturgical celebration was held in the Basilica-Cathedral of St. John the Baptist, with mass celebrated by the archbishop of St. John's, James H. McDonald. Our Lady of Mercy Alumnae Choir provided the music for the mass. In addition to the Casavant pipe organ, the choir was accompanied by a small instrumental ensemble made up of former students of Our Lady of Mercy School.

The main events planned by the Congregation of the Sisters of Mercy for the anniversary took place at the Littledale Conference Centre, where over four hundred Sisters of Mercy, friends, and colleagues gathered for four days of celebration. One hundred and twelve Sisters of Mercy representing congregations from the United States, Central and South America, South Africa, Australia, the Philippines, England, and Ireland came to St. John's to celebrate one hundred and fifty years of Mercy presence in North America.[29] Well-known scholars, all of them Sisters of Mercy from different countries, presented a series of concurrent lectures on the theme of Mercy. There were opportunities for visiting sisters of other nationalities to enjoy Newfoundland hospitality, and all the guests were invited to the concert presented by Our Lady of Mercy Alumnae Choir at Holy Heart Auditorium on the evening of August 5. It was a poignant moment when, toward the end of the program, the last group of students to attend Our Lady of Mercy School joined Our Lady of Mercy Alumnae Choir in presenting the final public performance of the school song, "Blue and Silver Shall We Wear." Because music has been so much a part of the tradition of the Sisters of Mercy since the time of M.

---

29. I am indebted to Sr. Rosemary Ryan for this information. Sr. Rosemary was largely responsible for planning and supervising the events that took place during the anniversary celebrations.

Francis Creedon, M. Rose Lynch, M. Ursula Frayne, and M. Joseph Nugent, it was appropriate that the anniversary celebrations should conclude with a musical presentation by a choir from the school that these sisters established in 1843.

In the meantime, Mercy Convent itself was in urgent need of repair. In the first place, the bedrooms had been designed to conform to the quasi-monastic lifestyle led by the sisters in 1857. These rooms had remained unchanged since that time and were totally unsuitable for women of the 1990s. Furthermore, electrical and plumbing systems had deteriorated, and the interior of the building needed to be adapted to living conditions in the twenty-first century. Obviously, such major renovations required the convent to be vacated for several months. But what to do about the sisters who were living there?

The problem was solved when Monsignor John Wallis, pastor of the Basilica Parish, offered the use of the Basilica Residence. At that time, Monsignor Wallis was living in St. Joseph's Presbytery in the east end of the city, and the Basilica Residence was empty. The sisters were delighted with Monsignor's offer and accepted with alacrity. Nine members of the community agreed to move to the residence. Alternate accommodations were found in Littledale, St. Patrick's Mercy Home Convent, and St. Michael's Convent, Belvedere, for the other five. The annalist wrote, "On Friday, January 12, 1996, the Mercy Convent community vacated Mercy Convent for the first time in 150 years in order to make way for necessary renovations."[30]

That morning was one of frantic activity. The movers arrived at half past nine and while the men loaded the heavier pieces of furniture onto the truck, Sr. Maura Mason was busy directing traffic on the fourth floor. Sr. Maura had spent many years as a Sister of Mercy and was well aware of the uproar that would ensue should someone's belongings be mislaid, overlooked, or delivered to the wrong destination. Consequently, she ensured that every sister's trunk

---

30. Annals, Convent of Our Lady of Mercy, St. John's, January 12, 1996, ASMSJ. The mention of one hundred and fifty years is not quite accurate. The sisters moved into the present convent in October 1857. However, the Sisters of Mercy have lived on the present site since 1842, although the original convent was taken down in 1856.

was marked with her name and the location of the room she would occupy in the "Palace."[31] While Sr. Maura was busily engaged in the fourth floor, Sr. Colette Ryan was similarly occupied in the kitchen, helping the staff pack food into boxes and making sure there were no crumbs left around to attract any four-legged intruders. Before the end of the day, all the sisters were comfortably settled into their new quarters.

It was four months before the renovations at Mercy Convent were completed and the sisters could return home. The most noticeable changes to the interior of the building involved the bedrooms. The original tiny bedrooms had been combined so that two rooms were made into one, thus providing space for a writing desk and a bookcase. Furthermore, each room was equipped with a hand basin and hot and cold water—an undreamed of luxury!

However, more than physical appearance has changed at Mercy Convent. No longer do the sisters enjoy the luxury of having a chaplain provide daily mass in the beautiful little convent chapel. Instead, every day, they walk across the hill to the basilica to participate in the parish mass. In place of a community of women involved in teaching, every sister is engaged in a different ministry. But still, Mercy Convent stands tall and strong, a reminder of more than 160 years of faithful service to the people of St. John's and, indeed, to all of Newfoundland and Labrador.

It is true that the original ministry of teaching in the schools is no longer part of the life of the Sisters of Mercy. However, the Sisters of Mercy have always shown a special concern for the poor. People came to the convents at all hours of the day, and sometimes in the night, looking for assistance of one kind or another. The same was true of the Presentation convents and clergy residences. Furthermore, it was customary for parishes of every denomination to prepare Christmas hampers for needy persons in the area. Gradually, this service was extended throughout the year, at great expense to the individual parishes. It was at the instigation of a Sister of Mercy attached to the Basilica

---

31. Up until recent time, the Basilica Residence was known as the "Palace," a title that was used in former years when the house was the residence of the archbishop. After Vatican Council II such regal-sounding designations were dropped.

staff that, in 1992, two Anglican and two Roman Catholic parishes in the inner city agreed to establish an inter-church food bank to address the problem of hunger in the inner city of St. John's.[32] The Basilica Parish volunteered the use of several rooms adjoining the Basilica Residence, and on April 16, 1992, Emmaus House Food Bank was formed. In addition to working in the food bank, the coordinator, a Sister of Mercy, visited the homes of those in need, bringing food and clothing as required. It was through this activity that the Board of Directors of Emmaus House became aware of problems of families who lived in deplorable housing conditions and of many of the poor who lived in rooming houses. Many of these houses were overcrowded, rundown, and unheated. The Emmaus House board decided to investigate the possibility of providing some venue where these people could come to socialize in comfort, have a snack, watch a movie, listen to music, play games, or read a book. However the cost of running such an establishment and, at the same time, continuing to supply the food bank with sufficient quantities of food to meet the needs of families with children was beyond the means of the inner-city parishes.

By coincidence, at the same time that Emmaus house was working to establish a social centre, the Leadership Teams of both the Presentation and Mercy congregations were meeting to discuss the issue of poverty in the inner city of St. John's. Because the coordinator of Emmaus House was a Sister of Mercy, the Mercy congregation was aware that Emmaus House had identified the need for some type of community social centre for persons living in poverty. Eventually, the Mercy and Presentation congregations decided to establish an inner-city community centre in what used to be Our Lady of Mercy School on Military Road. They named the new centre, The Gathering Place. The Gathering Place is owned by the Sisters of Mercy and co-sponsored with the Presentation Sisters. It is financed by the Presentation and Mercy Sisters in collaboration with the Anglican and Roman Catholic inner-city parishes that make up the Emmaus House Food Bank.

---

32. The four parishes involved in this venture were the Basilica-Cathedral of St. John the Baptist, the Anglican Cathedral of St. John the Baptist, St. Thomas' (Anglican), and St. Patrick's (Roman Catholic). Subsequently, in 1999, St. Michael's and All Angels Anglican Parish became a member of Emmaus House.

On November 9, 1993, The Gathering Place was incorporated as an inner city drop-in centre.[33] It began by offering space to community service groups that work on behalf of the underprivileged and at-risk persons. The first areas of service to be established were service groups of the Boys and Girls Club, Listen, Peace Centre, and, more recently, the Mercy Centre for Ecology and Justice under the direction of Sr. Mary Tee. All of these groups rented space and moved into The Gathering Place. Meanwhile, the Presentation and Mercy Sisters invited representatives of the Emmaus House Food Bank to co-operate with them in planning the hospitality centre of The Gathering Place, that is, the kitchen, dining room, social, and reception areas.[34] A board of directors was established consisting of the Leadership Teams of the Presentation and Mercy congregations.[35] Two co-directors were appointed, Sr. Alicia Linehan from the Mercy congregation and Sr. Regina Vickers of the Presentation Sisters. A finance committee was put in place consisting of the treasurers-general of the two congregations and the two co-directors. In addition, a Directional Committee was established made up of the co-directors and a representative from each of the Emmaus House parishes. The purpose of the committee was to ensure the continued involvement of the parishes in giving moral support, monetary or food contributions, and a great ecumenical flavour to the venture.[36] Volunteer coordinators oversee the operation of the kitchen, the dining room, and the social areas. The "hands-on" work of the centre is carried out by over one hundred and twenty-five volunteers from around the city, but especially from the five parishes of the Emmaus House group. The permanent staff is made up of sisters from the Presentation and Mercy Congregations who volunteer for the duty.

Eventually, everything was ready and The Gathering Place received its first guests on October 26, 1994.[37] From the beginning, The Gathering Place

---

33. Annals, Convent of Our Lady of Mercy, St. John's, November 9, 1993, ASMSJ.

34. Madonna Gatherall, "Notes from an Orientation Session for New Board Members, The Gathering Place," October 23, 2001, p.1, ASMSJ, RG 10/37/50–55.

35. In 2001, there was a change in the board of directors, with fewer members of the Leadership Teams and the addition of Mrs. Eileen Young, Mr. Dennis O'Keefe, and Mr. Frank Fowler.

36. Gatherall, "Notes," p. 2, ASMSJ, RG 10/37/50–55.

37. Ibid.

has been open to adults who are lonely and seeking companionship and the support of friends. People living alone in bed-sitting rooms who have little, if any, housekeeping amenities are welcome to come to The Gathering Place. A hot meal is served three times a week at midday. On Tuesdays and Thursdays, a lunch, consisting of soup and sandwiches or pizza and a dessert is served. For several years, the principal cook at The Gathering Place was a volunteer, Vicente Carhuapoma. Vicente was a landed immigrant from Peru, who had come to Newfoundland in 1995. Shortly after his arrival in St. John's, Vicente was befriended by Sr. Maura Mason and introduced to The Gathering Place, where he offered his services as a volunteer in the kitchen. Every day, Vicente, clothed in a large white apron and cook's hat, helped in the kitchen. Sadly, Vicente became very ill and died in the palliative care at the Miller Centre in St. John's in the autumn of 2003. Hundreds of volunteers and guests from The Gathering Place attended his funeral mass at the Basilica-Cathedral of St. John the Baptist. Vicente's dedication and his generous service to The Gathering Place is remembered with gratitude by the Mercy and Presentation Sisters and by the people he befriended during the six years he spent in St. John's.

After the noon meal, guests at The Gathering Place are free to wander casually back and forth between the dining room and the three social rooms. Many sit and watch television or listen to music; others play darts, pool, or cards; some put together jigsaw puzzles; while others join the craft circle or learn painting from one of the talented volunteers. Furthermore, the facility offers regular adult literacy programs that promote competency in basic reading, writing, and numeric skills.

Guests who come to The Gathering Place include individuals in crisis because of economic circumstances, loneliness, depression, hunger, addictions, or mental illness. Since the early days of The Gathering Place, there is a core group of people who come and spend the day, but the vast majority of the guests come for the free hot meal or lunch. Early in 1995, it was agreed that there would be a membership requirement and a cover charge of two dollars per semester.[38]

---

38. The two dollar fee is collected at the beginning of September and during the first week of January.

This was seen as a way of allowing the guests to develop a sense of self-worth through the knowledge that they were making a contribution to the centre. However, The Gathering Place does not turn away any person who is hungry or in need of companionship. An average of eighty to eighty-five meals are served daily, although sometimes the number can go to more than one hundred. The kitchen is under the direction of a Sister of Mercy, Gertrude Bennett. Since her retirement from teaching, Sr. Gertrude made the amazing discovery that she possesses hitherto unsuspected talents in kitchen management, meal planning, and cooking. She has been kept busy! For instance, 9,971 meals were served at The Gathering Place in the year 2000. In the words of one of the guests, "Them's a lot of potatoes, Sister!"

The Gathering Place reaches out to the wider community in a variety of ways. For example, various institutions use it as field placement for students. The Memorial University School of Nursing and the Centre for Nursing Studies have sent students to facilitate workshops in providing nutrition, maintaining hope, guiding relaxation as a means to overcome stress, teaching first aid, and informing on other health issues. Students from the School of Social Work at Memorial University visit The Gathering Place to design programs, activities, or support groups that are deemed appropriate and necessary. Seminarians from Queen's College[39] have been placed at The Gathering Place to acquire pastoral experience. From time to time, high-school students from Holy Heart Work Experience Program and the Leadership Program of St. Bonaventure's College visit The Gathering Place to participate in some of the activities. In particular, Corrections Canada uses the centre to place offenders who have been ordered by the courts to do community service work.

In addition to the multitude of activities that take place in the hospitality section, The Gathering Place provides rented accommodations for a number of groups that operate within its mission and philosophy. For instance, the

---

39. Queen's College is affiliated with Memorial University. It is a training college for persons preparing for ordination to the Anglican priesthood. In addition, it offers programs that are of interest to persons of all faiths.

Pentecostal Church rents the former auditorium and gymnasium building and offers its programs of worship and youth activities.

Over the years since it began, The Gathering Place has experienced changes in personnel and organization, some of which came about as a result of the expansion in its ministry. One of the first co-directors, Sr. Alicia Linehan, was asked to take a position in Corner Brook. Another Mercy Sister, Maura Mason, replaced her at The Gathering Place. In a decision by the two congregations in 2003, the structure of administration at The Gathering Place was modified slightly. It was agreed that there would be one director. The position is for three years and is to be filled in turn by a sister from the Presentation congregation and then by a Mercy Sister. In June 2003, Helen Corrigan, PBVM, was appointed director of The Gathering Place.

Nevertheless, the Sisters of Mercy are still very active in the operation of the centre. Sr. Maura Mason, who lives at Mercy Convent, is responsible for the safety and security of the buildings; Sr. Gertrude Bennett continues to preside over the kitchen area; and a number of other Mercy Sisters volunteer many hours a week in the social, dining, and reception areas of the centre.

> The Gathering Place was born out of the charism of the Presentation and Mercy Congregations in their concern for the poor and according to its mission, it continues in that same spirit; that is the inspiration out of which it takes its life, its strength, its ability to continue to reach out, to gather, to touch hearts, to heal souls, to restore spirits, to nurture relationships, to bless the poor, to heal broken hearts and spirits, to carry sorrow, to slake thirst, to feed the hungry—all in the spirit of the Beatitudes.[40]

In the beginning, when Catherine McAuley opened the House of Mercy on September 24, 1827, her purpose was merciful service to the poor. But she also believed in calling others to join with her in the spiritual and corporal work of Mercy. Surely, the decision of the Sisters of Mercy to devote this historic building to the direct service of the poor is according to the spirit and

---

40. Gatherall, "Notes," p. 6, ASMSJ, RG 10/37/55.

example of their foundress. And, without any doubt, the Sisters of Mercy who lived and worked on this site through all the years since 1842 would agree.

And so, the building that once was a centre of learning, music, art, and drama is now a place where lonely, needy people come to find acceptance, friendship, and the comfort of knowing that they are loved and valued as children of a compassionate, merciful God. There is no doubt that M. Francis Creedon would approve!

CHAPTER TWENTY-EIGHT

AND WHAT OF THE FUTURE?

God is our refuge and our strength,
an ever-present help in distress.
Therefore we fear not, though the earth be shaken
and the mountains plunge into the depths of the sea;

Psalm 46:2–3

If the story of the Sisters of Mercy is seen only in the context of providing education and health care in a certain well-defined period of history, then it is clear that the story is coming quickly to its conclusion. In the year 2004, Sr. Patricia Gallant was the only Sister of Mercy still engaged in classroom teaching, Sr. Eileen Penney was the only active registered nurse, Sr. Lorraine Power continued to practice medicine in Quebec. Although Sisters of Mercy are involved in many forms of ministry, for most of them this is a "second career," entered upon with great generosity after many years spent in the teaching or nursing profession.

A glance at the Register of Sisters shows that during the fifteen years between 1954 and 1969, a total of 191 young women were professed as Sisters of Mercy. However, this interest in following a vocation to religious life seems to have been a temporary phenomenon, for of those who were professed at that time, 110 women requested a dispensation from their vows in order to pursue a different vocation. Consequently, within a few years the Sisters of

Mercy of Newfoundland experienced the same decline in numbers as congregations of women religious all over North America. Furthermore, beginning in the 1970s, there was a drastic decrease in the number of young women seeking admission to religious life. In fact, in the twenty-three years between 1969 and 1992, only sixteen women were professed as Sisters of Mercy, and of these, six left the congregation. Coupled with the lack of new members, the problem for the congregation was not only that people were leaving religious life, but also there were no new members coming to take their places and the rest of us—teachers and nurses—were approaching the mandatory retirement age. The question is, what has happened that religious life no longer seems to be option for young women?

One reason for the decline of vocations to religious life is the fact that society is changing. In comparison with earlier times, there are unlimited opportunities for young women to pursue careers in business, law, medicine, and the arts. Another explanation for the lack of interest in religious life is that, for the most part, members of religious congregations are no longer a vital, visible influence during the formative years of childhood. Years ago, the presence of religious in the classroom provided an opportunity for young girls to learn something of what religious life was all about. A third factor might be the absence of the visible, corporate presence and ministry of religious within the local parish. Now, alternative forms of community living provide opportunities for sisters to live alone or with another sister in an apartment. Thus, as many Catholics complain, "Sisters have become invisible."

At one time, the Sisters of Mercy in Newfoundland constituted a relatively cohesive group of teachers or nurses. Sisters were known, recognized, and appreciated for their influence on and contribution to education and health care. Today the Sisters of Mercy in Newfoundland and Labrador and Peru are found working in soup kitchens, food banks, and shelters for the homeless, and caring for persons living with HIV and AIDS. Sisters of Mercy continue to look after the elderly, care for the sick and the helpless in nursing homes, and provide pastoral care in hospitals and in spirituality centres. It is not unusual to find a Sister of Mercy deeply involved in parish ministry or serving as administrator of a parish. Sisters are no longer enclosed within convent walls, sheltered from the storms that buffet the rest of our society. We know that there are no limits to the challenges that face us.

When the Sisters of Mercy came to Newfoundland, they read the "signs of the times" and addressed contemporary needs—to educate the children, to shelter the orphan, to care for the sick and the dying. In contemporary society, government agencies with highly skilled professionals look after these needs.

For the past few years Sisters of Mercy have questioned, "Where are we going? What is our future?" Over and over again, general chapters have exhorted us in the words of Deuteronomy (30:19), "Choose life, that you and your descendents may live." Everything that we have learned assures us that the future will be born out of fidelity to the past and the present. The ravages of injustice, poverty, hunger, and disease are all around us still. The cry of the poor is still as urgent as it was in the time of Catherine McAuley and M. Francis Creedon. These women and their companions had the generosity, the creativity, and the self-forgetfulness to answer this cry.

The question is, do the Sisters of Mercy of today have the courage and energy, the spirit of self-sacrifice, the vision, and the same passion for justice that constantly urged our predecessors to press on to new ways of thinking and acting, so that we can continue to bring the message of God's love and mercy to all people?

BIBLIOGRAPHY

1. Archival Sources

Archives of the Archdiocese of St. John's

Archives of the City of St. John's

Archives of the Diocese of Providence, Rhode Island, United States of America

Archives of the Diocese of St. George's in Corner Brook

Archives of the Irish Sisters of Mercy, Dublin, Ireland

Archives of the Presentation Sisters, St. John's

Archives of the Presentation Sisters, Galway, Ireland

Archives of the Sisters of Mercy, Bermondsey, London, England

Archives of the Sisters of Mercy, Birmingham, England

Archives of the Sisters of Mercy, Dundalk, Ireland

Archives of the Sisters of Mercy, Galway, Ireland

Archives of the Sisters of Mercy, Geelong, Australia

Archives of the Sisters of Mercy, Mercy International Centre, Dublin, Ireland

Archives of the Sisters of Mercy, Providence, Rhode Island, United States of America

Archives of the Sisters of Mercy, St. John's

Dublin Diocesan Archives, Ireland

Library of Mount St. Francis Monastery, St. John's

Limerick County Archives, Limerick, Ireland

National Library of Ireland, Dublin, Ireland

2. Newspapers

The Compass

The Courier

929

The Daily Colonist
The Daily Courier
The Daily News
The Evening Telegram
The Globe and Mail
Halifax Chronicle
The Harbour Grace Standard
The Limerick Chronicle
The Monitor
The Newfoundland Indicator
The Newfoundlander
The Patriot
The Patriot and Catholic Herald
The Patriot and Terra Nova Herald
The Providence Visitor
The Public Ledger
The Reporter
The Sunday Telegram
The Telegram
The Waterford Mail
The Waterford Mirror
Weekly Orthodox Journal
The Western Star

3. Journals

Ave Maria
Inter Nos
Journal of the House of Assembly
Mercy Communico

4. Secondary Sources

Bolster, Sister M. Angela. *Catherine McAuley, 1778-1841*. N.p.: Irish Messenger Publications, 1978.

———. *My Song is of Mercy and Justice: The Spirituality of Catherine McAuley*. Cork: Tower Book, 1984.

———. "Report of the Historical Commission of the Cause of Catherine McAuley, Foundress of the Sister of Mercy." Privately printed.

———. *Catherine McAuley: Venerable for Mercy*. Cork: D. & A. O'Leary, 1998.

———. *The Correspondence of Catherine McAuley, 1872—1841*. Cork and Ross: Sisters of Mercy, 1989.

Bonnycastle, Sir Richard Henry. *Newfoundland in 1942*. 2 vols. London: Henry Colburn, 1842.

Brennan, Bonaventure. *"It Commenced with Two . . ." The Story of Mary Ann Doyle, First Companion of Catherine McAuley*. Northern Province, Ireland: Sisters of Mercy, 2001.

Brosnan, Very Reverend Michael. *Pioneer History of St. George's Diocese, Newfoundland*. Edited by The Catholic Teachers' Guild of St. George's Diocese. Toronto: Mission Press, 1948.

Bruce, Sister M. Teresina. "The First Forty Years of Educational Legislation in Newfoundland." Master's thesis, University of Ottawa, 1956.

Byrnes, John Maclay. *The Paths to Yesterday: Memories of Old St. John's, Newfoundland*. Boston: Meador Publishing, 1931.

Carroll, M. Austin. *Leaves from the Annals of the Sisters of Mercy*. Vol. 1, *Ireland*. New York: Catholic Publication Society, 1881.

———. *Leaves from the Annals of the Sisters of Mercy*. Vol. 2, *England, Crimea, Scotland, Australia, and New Zealand*. New York: Catholic Publication Society, 1883.

————. *Leaves from the Annals of the Sisters of Mercy*. Vol. 3, *Newfoundland and the United States*. New York: Catholic Publication Society, 1889.

————. *Leaves from the Annals of the Sisters of Mercy*. Vol. 4, *South America, Central America, and the United States*. New York: P. O'Shea, 1895.

Christian Brothers Educational Record, The. Dublin: Bray Printing, 1952.

Connolly, R. J. *A History of the Roman Catholic Church in Harbour Grace*. St. John's, NL: Creative Printers and Publishers, 1986.

Conroy, Charles O'Neil. *Peruvian Journal: Letters of a Gringo Priest*. Montreal: Palm Publishers, 1966.

Consedine, M. Raphael. *A Listening Journey*. Victoria, Australia: Congregation of the Presentation of the Blessed Virgin Mary, 1983.

Craig, Mary. *Pictorial History, Roman Catholic Schools, Bell Island, 1875–1983*. St. John's, NL: Memorial University of Newfoundland, 1983.

Darcy, Brother J. B. *Fire Upon the Earth: The Life and Times of Bishop Michael Fleming, O.S.F.*. St. John's, NL: Creative Book Publishing, 2003.

Degnan, M. Bertrand. *Mercy Unto Thousands: The Life of Mother Mary Catherine McAuley, Foundress of the Sisters of Mercy*. Westminster, Md.: Newman Press, 1957.

Downer, Don. *Turbulent Tides: A Social History of Sandy Point*. Portugal Cove, NL: ESP Press, 1997.

Encyclopedia of Newfoundland and Labrador. 5 vols. St. John's, NL: Newfoundland Book Publishers and Harry Cuff Publications, 1981–94.

Edwards, Ena Farrell, with R. E. Buehler. *Notes Toward a History of St. Lawrence*. St. John's, NL: Breakwater Books, 1983.

————. *Billy Spinney, the Umbrella Tree and Other Recollection of St. Lawrence*. St. John's, NL: Breakwater Books, 1990.

Evely, Louis. *That Man is You*. Translated by Edmond Bonin. New York: Paulist Press, 1963.

Fialka, John J. *Sisters, Catholic Nuns and the Making of America*. New York: St. Martin's Griffin, 2003.

FitzGerald, John Edward. "The Confederation of Newfoundland with Canada, 1946–1949." Master's thesis. Memorial University of Newfoundland, 1992.

———. "Conflict and Culture in Irish-Newfoundland Roman Catholicism, 1892–1850." Ph.D. diss., University of Ottawa, 1997.

Fleming, R. B. *The Christian Brothers Educational Record*. Cork: Our Lady's Mount, 1898.

Greene, John P. *Between Damnation and Starvation: Priests and Merchants in Newfoundland Politics, 1745–1855*. Montreal and Kingston: McGill-Queens University Press, 1999.

Guide for the Religious Called Sisters of Mercy. London: St. Anne's Press, 1888.

Gunn, Gertrude E. *The Political History of Newfoundland, 1832–1864*. Toronto: University of Toronto Press, 1966.

Heschel, Abraham Joshua. *I Asked for Wonder: A Spiritual Anthology*. Edited by Samual H. Dresner. New York: Crossroad Publishing, 1984.

Historical Highlights of St. Theresa's Parish (1930–1980). St. John's, NL: St. Theresa's Parish, n.d.

Howley, Very Reverend M. F. *Ecclesiastical History of Newfoundland*. Boston: Doyle and Whittle, 1888.

Hogan, Sister M. Williamina. *Pathways of Mercy: History of the Foundation of the Sisters of Mercy in Newfoundland, 1842–1984*. St. John's, NL: Harry Cuff Publications, 1986.

Kennedy, P. J., ed. *The Centenary of the Basilica Cathedral of St. John the Baptist*. St. John's, NL: Archdiocese of St. John's, 1955.

Killerby, Catherine Kovesu. *Ursula Frayne: A Biography*. Freemantle, Australia: The University of Notre Dame, 1996.

Lahey, Raymond J. "Michael Anthony Fleming." In *Dictionary of Canadian Biographies*. Vol. 7. Toronto: University of Toronto Press, n.d.

Lappetito, M. Michael. *Our Life Together in Mercy: Toward an Apostolic Spirituality*. Burlington, Vt.: Federation of the Sisters of Mercy of the Americas, Mercy Press, 1980.

Lauds, Vespers and Compline in English. Collegeville, Minn.: Liturgical Press, 1965.

Leamon, John. *Brigus: Past Glory, Present Splendour*. St. John's, NL: Harry Cuff Publications, 1998.

Lennon, Sister Mary Isidore, ed. *Mother Catherine McAuley: A Great Social Worker*. Privately printed: Sisters of Mercy of the Union, St. Louis Province, 1954.

Maloney, Queen. *Trail Wanderings: A Folk History of Bay Bulls, Newfoundland*. St. John's, NL: Creative Book Publishing, 1994.

Mannion, John J. *Irish Settlements in Eastern Canada: A Study of Cultural Transfer and Adaptation*. Toronto: University of Toronto Press, 1974.

Marshall, Frances. *The South Coast Pioneers: 150 Years in the Growth of St. Patrick's Parish Burin, Newfoundland, 1833–1983*. St. John's, NL: Creative Printers and Publishers, 1984.

McCann, Philip. *Schooling in a Fishing Society: Education and Economic Conditions in Newfoundland and Labrador, 1836–1986*. St. John's, NL: ISER Publications, Memorial University of Newfoundland, 1994.

McCormack, Sister M. Basil. "The Educational Work of the Sisters of Mercy in Newfoundland, 1842–1955. Master's thesis, Catholic University of America, 1955.

McLay, Anne. *Women Out of Their Sphere: A History of the Sisters of Mercy in Western Australia*. Northbridge, Australia: Vanguard Press, 1992.

Mosdell, H. M. *Newfoundland, A Country of Infinite Possibility and Manifold Attractions to the Capitalist, the Settler and the Tourist*. St. John's, NL: The Executive Government of Newfoundland, 1920.

Moyles, R.G. *Complaints Is Many and Various, But the Odd Divil Likes It: Nineteenth Century Views of Newfoundland*. Toronto: Peter Martin Associates, 1975.

Murphy, James. *A Century of Events in Newfoundland.* St. John's, NL: James Murphy, 1924.

———. *From the Colony of Newfoundland, England's Oldest Possession.* St. John's, NL: James Murphy, 1925.

Neumann, Sister M. Ignatia, ed. *Letters of Catherine McAuley.* Baltimore: Helicon Press, 1969.

Newfoundland Royal Commission 1933 Report. London: His Majesty's Stationery Office, 1933.

Nevitt, Joyce. *White Caps and Black Bands: Nursing in Newfoundland to 1934.* St. John's, NL: Jesperson Press, 1978.

Nouwen, Henri J. *!Gracias! A Latin America Journal.* New York: Orbis Books, 1993.

O'Connor, M. Loretta. *Tell Us About Catherine McAuley.* Manville, R.I.: Salve Reina Press, 1946.

O'Hara, Sister M. Nathy *Catherine McAuley: Mercy Foundress.* Dublin: Veritas Publications, 1929.

O'Neill, Paul. *The Oldest City: The Story of St. John's, Newfoundland.* Vol. 1. Erin, ON: Press Porcepic, 1975.

———. *A Seaport Legacy: The Story of St. John's, Newfoundland.* Vol. 2. Erin, ON: Press Porcepic, 1976.

———. *The Seat Imperial: Bay Bulls, Past and Present.* St. John's, NL: Harry Cuff Publications, 1983.

Power, M. Calasanctius. *The St. Clare's Mercy Hospital School of Nursing, 1939–1979.* Privately printed, 1982.

Prowse, Daniel Woodley. *A History of Newfoundland from the English, Colonial and Foreign Records.* Portugal Cove-St. Philip's, NL: Boulder Publications, 2002.

Regan, M. Joanna. *Tender Courage: A Brief Sketch of the First Sister of Mercy.* Gwynedd, Pa.: 1978

Rodriquez, V. F. Alphonsus. *The Practice of Christian and Religious Perfection.* 3 vols. Dublin and London: James Duffy, 1870.

Rothney, G. O. "Newfoundland: A History." Historical Booklet No. 10. Ottawa: The Canadian Historical Association, 1964.

Rowe, Fred W. *The Development of Education in Newfoundland*. Toronto: Ryerson Press, 1964.

———. *The History of Education in Newfoundland*. Toronto: Ryerson Press, 1952.

Savage, Roland Burke. *Catherine McAuley: The First Sister of Mercy*. Dublin: M. H. Gill and Son, 1949.

Schneiders, Sandra M. *Selling All: Commitment, Consecrated Celibacy, and Community in Catholic Religious Life*. New York: Paulist Press, 2001

Sears, Monsignor Thomas. "Report of the Missions, Prefecture Apostolic Western Newfoundland." 1877.

Sisters of Mercy, Bermondsey. *Catherine McAuley: The Mercy Ideal*. London: n.p., n.d.

Sisters of Mercy, Iowa. *Sketch of the Life of Mother M. Catherine McAuley*. Iowa: Monarch Printing, 1929.

Sullivan, Mary C. *Catherine McAuley and the Tradition of Mercy*. Dublin: Four Courts Press, 1995

———, ed. *Correspondence of Catherine McAuley, 1818–1841*. Baltimore: Catholic University of America Press, 2004.

Winter, Sir J. S., P. J. Scott, and A. B. Morine. *French Treaty Rights in Newfoundland: The Case for the Colony Stated by the People's Delegates*. London: P. S. King & Son, 1890.

INDEX

KATHRINE E. BELLAMY, RSM, was born in Bay Roberts and received her early education at St. Matthew's Anglican School. At the age of twelve, she boarded at St. Bride's College, Littledale, St. John's, where she completed high school and then went on to Mount Saint Vincent University in Halifax. When she was eighteen, she entered the Congregation of the Sisters of Mercy of Newfoundland. After her profession, she was assigned to Our Lady of Mercy School, Military Road, St. John's, where she began her career as a music teacher. Sister Kathrine is recognized mainly for her work with the school choirs at the Immaculate Conception Academy, Bell Island, and at Our Lady of Mercy School and Holy Heart of Mary High School, St. John's. Under her direction, Our Lady of Mercy Glee Club received many awards, and it was the first Newfoundland choir to win the Mathieson Trophy for the best junior choir in Canada. By coincidence, one of her former pupils, Margo Cranford, is the publisher of this book!

In addition to her work in the schools, Sister Kathrine was organist and choir director at the Basilica of St. John the Baptist, a position she held for twenty-four years. In 1984, Sister Kathrine directed an archdiocesan choir for the visit of Pope John Paul II to the basilica where, in addition to her duties as music director, she was deeply involved in the parish outreach to the poor.

Having completed this book, Sister Kathrine is fully occupied in researching the contribution of the Sisters of Mercy to the musical life of this province. At the same time, she keeps in touch with her former pupils, especially the "Mercy girls," and with her only nephew, the Very Reverend William J. Bellamy, former rector of the Anglican Cathedral and dean of the Anglican Diocese of Eastern Newfoundland and Labrador.

In May 2006, Sister Kathrine was awarded the degree of doctor of letters, *honoris causa*, by Memorial University, St. John's, Newfoundland and Labrador.